Ward 9–Precinct 1

City of Boston

List of residents; 20 Years of Age and Over

(Females Indicted by Dagger) As of April 1, 1926

Unknown

Alpha Editions

This edition published in 2020

ISBN : 9789354031236

Design and Setting By
Alpha Editions
email - alphaedis@gmail.com

Ward 9—Precinct 1

CITY OF BOSTON.

LIST OF RESIDENTS
20 YEARS OF AGE AND OVER

(FEMALES INDICATED BY DAGGER)

AS OF

APRIL 1, 1926

HERBERT A. WILSON, } *Listing*

JAMES F. EAGAN,   } *Board.*

CITY OF BOSTON—PRINTING DEPARTMENT

Canton Street Court

B	Murray John	2	laborer	54	here
C	Lecion Lawrence	3	"	30	Canada
D	Lecion Rena—†	3	houseworker	27	"

Canton Street Place

F	Kennedy James J	1	printer	59	here
G	McAllie Willian	1	retired	55	40 Emerald
H	Richardson Daniel	1	laborer	54	here

Draper's Lane

K	Cambell Alice—†	31	housewife	40	here
L	Day Woodbury	31	retired	83	"
M	Merton Hermina—†	31	housewife	21	21 E Canton
N	Gaede Henry	31	laborer	41	here
O	Serpert Mary—†	31	clerk	29	21 Bedford

Fabin Street

P	Clark Margaret—†	3	houseworker	51	here
R	Allston Sarah—†	3	housewife	66	"
S	Monahon Julia—†	3	"	38	"
T	Monahon Micheal G	3	laborer	32	"
U	Caffey Anna—†	4	clerk	23	58 W Dedham
V	Caffey Mary—†	4	houseworker	52	58 "
W	Dempsey Jermiah	4	laborer	35	here
X	Dolan Patrick	4	"	38	"
Y	Farrell Mary—†	4	housewife	60	"
Z	Mahoney Catharine—†	4	"	70	"
A	O'Neal Patrick	4	laborer	57	"
B	Steele Robert	4	"	45	"
D	Hon Lun	10	"	39	"
E	Wing Lee	10	"	22	"
G	Grom George	10	"	70	"
H	Grom Mary—†	10	housewife	60	"
K	Cox Abbie—†	12	"	34	17 Fabin

Page	Letter	FULL NAME.	Residence, April 1, 1926.	Occupation.	Supposed Age.	Reported Residence, April 1, 1925. Street and Number.

Fabin Street—Continued

	L	Cox Joseph L	12	laborer	34	17 Fabin
	N	Hill Louise—†	14	houseworker	26	20 Norwich
	O	Hill William	14	laborer	33	20 "
	P	Bonds Oscar	14	"	56	here
	R	Bonds Saddie—†	14	housewife	40	"
	T	Perry Carrie—†	16	houseworker	50	"
	Y	Mathews Albert	27	carpenter	70	"
	Z	Wilson Mary—†	27	houseworker	28	Cambridge
	C	Feair Addie—†	31	housewife	30	here
	D	Feair Thomas	31	laborer	50	"
	E	Sams Thomas	31	"	35	"
	F	Moore Mary—†	31	housewife	28	"
	G	Moore William	31	laborer	21	"
	H	Soms Elizabeth—†	31	housewife	28	"
	L	Crumpton Alberta—†	33	"	29	129 Lenox
	K	Crumpton Moses	33	laborer	31	129 "
	M	Krey Agnes—†	33	housewife	29	here
	N	Timberlake Fredrick	35	laborer	22	33 Fabin
	O	Timberlake Gome	35	"	57	33 "
	P	Timberlake Laurah—†	35	housewife	47	33 "
	R	Mates Augustas	36	laborer	31	Canton O
	S	Mates Bertha—†	36	houseworker	24	"
	T	Mouradion Florence—†	36	"	25	here
	U	Mouradion Sarkis	36	laborer	31	"
	V	Bryant George	37	"	65	"
	W	Bryant Kate—†	37	houseworker	47	"
	X	Brown Nathon	38	laborer	39	Medway
	Y	Brown Sarah—†	38	housewife	36	"
	Z	Garddion Sarkios	38	laborer	32	Cambridge
	A	Geary Peter J	43	"	60	here
	B	Pallock Evelyn—†	43	housewife	34	70 E Dedham
	C	Pallock George	43	chauffeur	36	70 "
	D	Carey Annie—†	43	housewife	28	here
	E	Carey Christopher	43	laborer	37	"

Ivanhoe Street

	K	Alker Charles	8	laborer	34	8 Noanet
	L	Alker Maria—†	8	housewife	35	8 "
	M	Saltmon Morris	8	laborer	28	here

3

Page	Letter	Full Name	Residence, April 1 1926	Occupation	Supposed Age	Reported Residence, April 1, 1925. Street and Number.

Ivanhoe Street—Continued

	N	Saltmon Rebeca—†	8	housewife	23	here
	O	Ryon Margaret M—†	12	"	67	"
	P	Ryon Thomas	12	laborer	74	"
	R	Fegerson Harry	12	"	45	"
	S	Dooly John	14	"	56	17 W Newton
	T	Steele Agusta	14	"	49	here
	U	Steele Catharine—†	14	houseworker	27	"
	V	McAvoy Edward	14	laborer	49	"
	X	Boynton Ernest	26	machinist	29	Ft Wayne Ind
	Y	Boynton Hazel—†	26	housewife	26	"
	Z	Morse Bertha A—†	28	"	55	Franklin N H
	A	Morse John W	28	carpenter	70	"
	B	Morse Marie—†	28	laundress	27	Salisbury N H
	C	Shaffener Annie—†	28	housewife	48	26 Ivanhoe
	D	Shaffener Edward	28	laborer	61	26 "
	E	Tobin Elsie—†	28	houseworker	21	26 "
	F	Bolan Arthur	30	laborer	22	48 Dundee
	G	Hicks Russell	30	"	30	48 "
	H	Hicks Sarah—†	30	housewife	38	48 "
	K	Jackson Joseph	32	laborer	63	484 Tremont
	L	McDougal Peter	32	plasterer	51	Lawrence
	M	McCarty Margaret—†	32	houseworker	54	222 Shawmut av
	N	Nelson Neal	32	carpenter	51	here
	O	Rose Ida—†	34	housewife	55	"

Newland Street

	P	Menard Sarah—†	4	houseworker	50	here
	R	Sullivan John	4	shipper	46	185 Warren av
	T	Boyd James	4	storekeeper	50	here
	U	Boyd Mary—†	4	housewife	45	"
	V	Hayden Albert J	4	laborer	33	"
	W	Hayden Iream—†	4	housewife	27	"
	X	Dunham Charlotte E—†	4	"	27	77 Warren av
	Y	Dunham Louis	4	salesman	29	77 "
	Z	Zartman Birdie—†	4	dressmaker	45	here
	A	Stevens Catherine—†	5	housewife	48	"
	B	Stevens Paul G	5	student	20	"

4

Page	Letter	Full Name	Residence, April 1, 1926	Occupation	Supposed Age	Reported Residence, April 1, 1925. Street and Number.

Newland Street—Continued

c	Stevens Raymond W	5	checker	22	New Hampshire
d	Stevens Willard C	5	packer	54	here
e	Engram Elizabeth S †	5	housewife	31	Canada
f	Engram John M	5	carpenter	32	here
g	Hendry Albert S	5	paper ruler	46	"
h	Hendry Evelyn †	5	housewife	41	"
k	Hendry George J	5	paper ruler	65	16 Charles
l	Salami Joseph	6	laborer	50	here
n	Saif Anna †	6	housewife	32	"
o	Saif Solomon	6	carpenter	38	"
r	Gollzi Joseph	7	baker	25	5 Newland
s	Blake Elizabeth †	8	laundress	42	345 Shawmut av
t	Cummings Catherine H †	8	operator	47	345 "
u	Graham Mary †	8	housewife	27	Brookline
v	Graham Maxwell, jr	8	laborer	27	"
w	Fitz Annie †	8	houseworker	43	here
x	Fitz Catherine †	8	stenographer	20	"
y	Senter Fred	8	sign painter	33	"
z	Losinski Christina †	8	housewife	41	"
a	Losinski Frank	8	seaman	38	"
b	Nicholson Normand	8	laborer	22	"
c	Hanaway Frederick	15	painter	41	Lexington
d	Hanaway Joseph G	15	cook	41	here
e	Cambell Regina †	15	retired	45	"
f	McMahon Mary †	15	laundress	62	"
g	Humphries John L	15	cook	48	"
h	Humphries Mary E †	15	nurse	56	"
k	Sorenson Christian	18	laborer	54	"
l	Timiny John C	18	real estate	40	"
m	Hearn Josephine †	18	laundress	46	"
n	King Mary †	19	none	45	"
o	Relly Mary †	19	cook	28	"
p	Jones Annie †	19	housewife	40	"
r	Jones Thomas	19	laborer	40	"
s	Jackson Annie †	20	dressmaker	48	"
t	Jackson Clarence J	20	laborer	52	"
v	Kasparian Charles	20	book seller	22	6 Dwight
w	McCarthy Margaret †	22	houseworker	38	264 Third
x	Leary John	22	laborer	33	Ireland
y	Murphy James	22	"	50	145 Arlington

Newland Street—Continued

z	Harrington Edger S	23	clerk	37	here
A	Harrington Gertrude †	23	housewife	41	"
B	Currin Catherine †	24	"	49	53 E Dedham
C	Payette Homer	24	blacksmith	62	Providence R I
D	Currin Dennis	24	laborer	61	53 E Dedham
E	Doherty Edward	24	"	50	here
F	Gilmore Frank	24	"	55	"
G	Cianciarulo Mary †	26	clerk	21	"
H	Cianciarulo Nicholos	26	musician	55	"
K	Cianciarulo Rose †	26	housewife	43	"
M	Moor Elmer E	29	laborer	30	"
N	Moor Margaret L †	29	housewife	27	"
O	Ransome Joseph	29	laborer	23	"
P	Venable Anna L †	29	housewife	32	10 Chesterton
R	Venable James W	29	laborer	35	762 Shawmut av
S	Williams Fannie E †	29	laundress	50	here
T	Brown Annie †	33	"	50	"
U	Franklin Ester †	33	maid	40	"
V	Lasiter Emma †	33	none	84	"
W	Blake Dennis F	37	awning maker	42	605 Harris'n av
X	Blake Sadie †	37	housewife	38	605 "
Y	Christie Richard	37	chauffeur	27	here
Z	Sturback Rose †	37	housewife	24	"
A	Sturback William H	37	rubberworker	25	"
B	Williams Hellen G †	37	candymaker	27	83 W Brookline
C	Williams John	37	laborer	50	New Bedford
D	Williams Mary A †	37	housewife	50	83 W Brookline
E	Buckingham Arthur	41	shipper	44	here
F	Clements Celena H †	41	housewife	53	"
G	Clements Chester H	41	locksmith	84	"
H	Sandberg Josephine A †	41	laundress	41	Framingham
K	Numes Joe	43	laborer	38	New Bedford
L	Numes Rose †	43	housewife	33	"
M	Houlihan Peter P	53	laborer	22	628 Mass av
N	Grater Frederick A	53	salesman	56	here
O	Poyhomen Alexandria †	53	furrier	40	"
P	Stedman Christina E †	53	shoemaker	53	"
R	Stedman Edward J	53	bellboy	24	"
S	McCance Alexander	55	brushmaker	55	1305 Wash'n
T	McCance Harriet S †	55	housewife	43	1305 "

Page.	Letter.	FULL NAME.	Residence, April 1, 1926.	Occupation.	Supposed Age.	Reported Residence, April 1, 1925. Street and Number.

Newland Street— Continued

	U	Spencer Edward	55	retired	79	18 Rutland
	V	Garlick Ellen E—†	55	housewife	63	here
	W	Garlick William F	55	salesman	64	"
	X	Barack Samuel	55	tailor	44	"
	Y	Slosberg Lena—†	55	housewife	42	"
	Z	Slosberg Richard	55	salesman	42	"

Pelham Street

	D	Ash Charles H	6	chef	48	here
	E	Bray Harold	6	clerk	20	"
	F	Bray Margaret—†	6	laundress	50	"
	G	Dennehy Frank	6	steamfitter	44	52 Dedham
	H	Dennis Cyril F	6	machinist	37	here
	K	Dennis Ethel—†	6	clerk	32	"
	L	Deschener Alfred	6	shoemaker	55	Lowell
	M	Hannigan Leo	6	roofer	26	New Jersey
	N	Joyce Lillian D—†	6	housewife	24	Lowell
	O	Joyce Thomas	6	steamfitter	25	"
	P	Murray William T	6	ironworker	55	here
	R	O'Connell Caroline—†	6	housekeeper	60	"
	S	O'Connell Charles	6	assembler	20	"
	T	O'Toole Julia T—†	6	housewife	48	"
	U	Ryder Mary—†	6	storeroom	47	229 Shawmut av
	V	Veecki Pellegrino	6	shoemaker	55	here
	W	Day Mary—†	8	maid	62	5 Ringgold
	X	Haggerty Margaret A—†	8	"	52	here
	Y	Kearns Hannah T—†	8	"	48	9 Milford
	Z	Kearns William J	8	cook	49	9 "
	A	Anderson Anna—†	10	housewife	53	here
	B	Anderson Carl	10	asbestos worker	45	"
	C	Anensen Amalius	10	laborer	44	"
	D	Benson Alfred	10	meatcutter	44	"
	E	Brand Theodore	10	storekeeper	65	229 Highland
	F	Hansworth Wallace	10	waiter	54	here
	G	Larkin Benjamin	10	teamster	35	147 Sixth
	H	Larsen Lena—†	10	housewife	50	47 Emerald
	K	Miller Henry	10	ironworker	48	29 Cedar

Pelham Street Continued

L	Norton Mary †	10	cook	50	here
M	Shean Michael	10	laborer	48	331 Shawmut av
N	Anderson Jennie †	14	housewife	45	here
O	Anderson Storrs	14	painter	50	"
P	Bogue Cornelius	14	salesman	65	"
R	Edmonson Albert	14	paperhanger	60	"
S	Magee James	14	repairman	60	"
T	Shea Daniel	14	laborer	71	"
U	Canney Daniel E	16	fireman	20	"
V	Canney John J	16	tel worker	24	"
W	Canney Mary †	16	housewife	49	"
X	Corcoran John	16	laborer	32	Haverhill
Y	Corcoran Josephine †	16	housewife	21	"
Z	McNerney Marion †	16	housekeeper	24	here
A	McNerney William	16	baker	26	"
B	Ross Frances †	16	supervisor	32	"
C	Dooley Helen M †	18	housewife	23	"
D	Dooley William B	18	policeman	30	"
E	Brown Anna †	20	housekeeper	54	"
F	Clarke Frank	20	carpenter	64	"
G	Halberg Andrew	20	laborer	54	Malden
H	O'Brien Ella †	20	retired	68	here
K	O'Brien Richard	20	fireman	57	"
L	Allan Alice †	22	clerk	25	44 Bennington
M	Devoy Isabelle †	22	housewife	45	here
N	Kenyon Edward	22	tea blender	40	Woburn
O	Kenyon Helen †	22	chambermaid	40	"
P	Slavin Mary E †	22	housewife	40	here
R	Carey Frank E	22	printer	59	"
S	Carey Sarah †	22	cook	39	"
T	Flemming Annie †	22	laundress	42	"
U	Flemming Catherine †	22	"	43	"
V	Moran Bridget †	22	housewife	42	"
W	Moran Michael	22	chef	52	"
X	Blacknick Mark	24	baker	50	5 Dwight
Y	Burns Bessie †	24	coat presser	43	58 W Newton
Z	Farron James	24	steamfitter	52	5 Dwight
A	Gildea Annie †	24	waitress	33	5 "
B	Green William H	24	painter	50	Somerville
C	Larsen Lawrence	24	cement finisher	65	5 Dwight
D	Malakian Mishan	24	laborer	30	20 W Dedham

8

Pelham Street—Continued

E	Marlow John	24	shipper	30	20 Upton
F	McConlogue Neil	24	longshoreman	43	42 Anderson
G	McConlogue Nora C—†	24	housewife	35	42 "
H	Morris John F	24	waiter	45	5 Dwight
K	Murray David	24	piano mover	67	13 Dover

Pembroke Court

L	Francis May M—†	1	laundryworker	44	here
M	Hester Muke	1	laborer	35	15 Greenwich pl
N	Webb Elizabeth—†	2	housemaid	75	here
O	Morris Martha—†	3	housewife	40	1 Pembroke ct
P	Henry Frances—†	4	housemaid	28	Providence R I
R	Nilesen Aage	4	laborer	21	New York City

Pembroke Street

C	Monahan Mary—†	9	housekeeper	68	here
A	Ryder Delia—†	9	"	74	"
B	Ryder Frank	9	retired	71	"
E	Knight George P	11	tester	25	1718 Com av
F	Allaire Agnes C—†	11	housewife	54	114 Westville
G	Allaire Alexander G	11	boxmaker	39	114 "
H	Allaire Louis	11	"	64	114 "
K	Gray Eliza A—†	11	retired	79	here
L	Kerkin Lucien J	11A	salesman	38	"
M	Kerkin William T	11A	"	29	"
N	Porter Sarah A—†	11A	housekeeper	65	"
O	Sandes Edward A	11A	salesman	40	"
P	Sandes Effie—†	11A	housewife	25	"
R	Larsen George H	11A	machinist	34	"
S	Larsen Margaret M—†	11A	housewife	33	"
T	Davis Ralph	11A	accountant	21	"
U	Macdonald Olga M—†	11A	housewife	33	"
V	Macdonald Walter L	11A	foreman	35	"
W	Campbell Harold J	15	plumber	22	"
X	Campbell John J	15	"	50	"
Y	LeBlanc Joseph P	15	electrician	28	122 Pembroke
Z	Libby Nancy C—†	15	housekeeper	55	here

Pembroke Street— Continued

	FULL NAME	Residence	Occupation	Age	Reported Residence
A	Hayden Harry V	15	molder	45	here
B	King George	15	laborer	23	Canada
C	Norton Della H—†	15	housewife	55	here
D	Norton Winfield C	15	laborer	31	"
E	Eilenberg Hans	15	electrician	74	"
F	Frayman Alvina—†	15	housewife	40	Pittsburgh Pa
G	Patenaud Henry	19	painter	28	here
H	Patenaud Joseph	19	chauffeur	27	465 Columbia rd
K	Simpson Burleigh E	19	brakeman	33	here
L	Simpson Maria B—†	19	housewife	29	"
M	Gleason James	21	cook	55	16 Parnell
N	Kramer Mary E—†	21	housekeeper	40	16 "
O	McLaughlin Thomas	21	cook	34	16 "
R	Bates Mary J—†	21	housekeeper	56	Vermont
T	Oliver George	21	porter	32	here
U	Porter Arthur H	21	janitor	25	"
V	Gallagher Mary—†	21	nurse	55	Lowell
W	Coggswell Maria—†	23	housewife	27	New Haven Ct
X	Selig Eugenia M—†	23	"	46	here
Y	Miller Doris—†	27	laundress	35	"
Z	Miller George	27	garageman	40	"
A	Harvey Florence—†	29	housekeeper	43	"
B	McGanell Edward	29	painter	44	"
C	Mullen John	29	clerk	51	"
D	Molholland Ralph	31	auto mechanic	25	Maine
E	Potter Georgia E—†	31	housewife	36	here
F	Potter Harry W	31	starter	37	"
G	Gaum Madeline—†	33	housekeeper	45	"
H	Goddard Percy	33	laborer	23	Maine
K	Perkins Arthur E	33	salesman	55	New York
L	Smith Barney	33	retired	90	here
M	Smith Frank	33	janitor	50	"
N	Wells George H	33	laborer	68	"
O	Waters Blanche—†	47	housemaid	47	1272 Tremont
P	Paraskos James	47	grocer	28	here
R	Paraskos Mary—†	47	housewife	27	"
S	Gray Susie—†	47	waitress	28	54 Rutland
T	Quinlan Frederick W	47	mariner	53	here
U	Quinlan Mabel L—†	47	housewife	44	"
V	Harmoosh Lattefy—†	47	"	42	"
W	Harmoosh Mitry R	47	factory worker	44	"

10

Pembroke Street— Continued

X	Guerno Joseph	49	barber	28	here
Y	Guerno Mildred— †	49	housewife	26	"
Z	Gerrish Louis	49	steamfitter	55	"
A	Gerrish Mary M— †	49	housewife	55	"
C	Batson Jones H	49	plumber	52	"
D	Batson Minnie E— †	49	housewife	43	"
E	Earle Alfred	49	printer	50	"
F	Earle Harriett A— †	49	housekeeper	80	"
G	Gouner Helen S— †	51	housewife	27	"
H	Gouner John	51	waiter	29	"
K	Arouchon John	51	barber	26	773 Tremont
L	Arouchon Rose— †	51	housewife	20	773 "
M	Arouchon Selma— †	51	"	55	here
N	Arouchon Sophie— †	51	clerk	29	"
O	DeCotes Gus	51	paperhanger	25	Providence R I
R	Platt Elliott	53	laborer	51	235 W Canton
S	Platt Minnie— †	53	housewife	43	235 "
T	Platt Ruth— †	53	factory worker	21	235 "
U	Platt Theresa— †	53	"	20	235 "
V	Morgan Annie— †	53	housemaid	35	here
W	Cowett Gladys— †	53	"	25	Cambridge
X	Adamson Robert	53	butler	32	"
Y	Adamson Winnefred— †	53	housewife	31	"
Z	Austin Chester J	57	porter	37	here
A	Austin Wilhelmina— †	57	elevatorwoman	25	"
B	Martin Anna L— †	57	housemaid	22	"
C	Whitehead Jane— †	57	"	34	"
D	Whitehead Louis L	57	porter	40	"
E	Henderson Anita— †	57	hairdresser	29	"
F	Tasco Eula J— †	57	housewife	35	"
G	Tasco Stillman A	57	shipper	35	"
M	Dupree Jackson	57	laborer	40	Cambridge
N	Taylor Mary J— †	57	dressmaker	35	New York
O	Barlou Francis	57	porter	29	here
P	Barlou Loretta— †	57	nurse	23	"
R	Webster Joseph H	57	tailor	34	"
S	Webster Mary— †	57	housewife	31	"
T	Ackles William	65	carpenter	35	"
U	Allen Minnie— †	65	stitcher	21	"
V	Powers Clark	65	retired	71	"
W	Powers Earnest T	65	auto mechanic	21	"

Pembroke Street—Continued

x	Powers Forest E	65	musician	23	here
y	Powers Ida—†	65	housekeeper	58	"
z	Morrison Evelyn M—†	65	housewife	38	"
a	Morrison William	65	baker	42	"
b	Papasotenion George	65	barber	46	"
c	Cameron Herbert	67	machinist	38	"
d	Gilchrist Stella—†	67	waitress	40	"
e	Hanson Alfred	67	expressman	42	"
f	Hanson Anthony	67	"	38	"
g	Strasser Emil	67	instruments	46	"
h	Osgood Roland F	67	plumber	20	"
k	Darling Charles	69	retired	69	"
l	Harbert Joseph	69	inspector	36	167 Warren av
m	McLean Fred	69	student	40	here
n	Sonnier Bliss	69	painter	70	"
o	Walker Emma J—†	69	housekeeper	45	"

Shawmut Avenue

a	Nader Charles	335	machinist	39	here
b	Nader Sylvia—†	335	housewife	32	"
d	Perry Mary—†	335	forewoman	31	"
e	Sandelind Alex	335	painter	48	"
f	McCarthy John J	335	motorman	36	"
g	McCarthy Michael J	335	shipper	30	"
h	O'Leary Catherine J—†	335	housewife	40	"
k	O'Leary Michael J	335	custodian	60	"
l	Erickson Ester—†	335	clerk	42	"
m	McNally Elizabeth J—†	335	housewife	50	"
n	McNally Joseph	335	watchman	69	"
o	Serafen Charles	335	waiter	25	Malden
p	Johnson Freeman	335	painter	39	Cambridge
r	Ward John J	335	reporter	67	580 Tremont
s	Ward Mary—†	335	housewife	67	580 "
t	Butter Edward	335	student	27	70 Waltham
u	Carr Jessie—†	335	housekeeper	60	218 Col av
v	Anognos William	335	waiter	21	here
v¹	Goudas Pauline—†	335	housewife	38	"
w	Goudas Thomas	335	barber	38	"
x	Fullerton Margaret—†	335	boxmaker	22	"

12

Shawmut Avenue—Continued

Y	Mahoney Lillian—†	335	housewife	28	here
Z	McRae James	335	laborer	45	"
A	McRae James B	335	chauffeur	25	"
B	McKinnon Daniel I	335	carpenter	27	Bangor Me
C	McKinnon Joseph N	335	"	32	"
D	McKinnon Lenore—†	335	housewife	35	"
E	Almond William	339	laborer	33	Canada
F	Blanchard Frank B	339	agent	58	here
G	Chay Frank	339	laborer	55	"
H	Demore Bessie—†	339	clerk	36	"
K	Lazey Charles	339	"	40	"
L	Lynch Bernard	339	repairer	35	"
M	McLean Herbert J	339	laborer	42	"
N	Murphy John	339	"	50	179 W Newton
O	Murray Mathew	339	fireman	39	here
P	Witham Arthur J	339	laborer	45	Bangor Me
R	Witham Eliza—†	339	housewife	54	"
S	Ahern John J	341	painter	43	here
T	Austin Marie E—†	341	housekeeper	61	"
U	Barry David	341	tailor	36	"
V	Cawley Patrick	341	machinist	55	Salem
W	Grobbet Charles	341	porter	61	here
X	Margosian Charles	341	"	39	"
Y	Margosian Sabina—†	341	housewife	28	"
Z	McDermott Michael	341	painter	54	"
A	Porteous Adam	341	gardener	47	"
C	Drew John B	345	machinist	54	"
D	Drew May—†	345	housewife	42	"
E	Salami Diab J	345	laborer	34	6 Newland
F	Young Louis	345	electrician	45	here
H	Allen Gertrude—†	345	housekeeper	45	"
K	Allen Harry	345	machinist	49	"
L	Cormier Arthur	345	carpenter	27	30 Ivanhoe
M	Cormier Emile	345	"	31	here
N	Cormier Mary E—†	345	housewife	23	30 Ivanhoe
O	Cearns Frank R	345	salesman	36	Revere
P	Cearns Sophie E—†	345	housewife	38	"
R	Field Samuel	345	painter	33	Melrose
S	Morris Lawrence	345	"	34	Norwood
V	Cyeddis John B	348	machinist	48	447 Shawmut av
W	Cyeddis Leon R	348	laborer	25	447 "

13

Shawmut Avenue—Continued

	U	Cyeddis Mae K—†	348	housekeeper	25	447 Shawmut av
	X	Field George E	348	"	50	3 Worcester pl
	Y	Karavcoyian John	348	janitor	57	here
	Z	Kelley Francis	348	retired	55	"
	A	Murray Philip	348	hotelman	30	New York City
	B	Perry Joseph	348	laborer	50	35 W Dedham
	C	Ryan Thomas	348	dishwasher	48	Cambridge
	D	Arakelian Garkis	350	laborer	76	here
	E	Clark Mary—†	350	housekeeper	65	"
	F	Clark Patrick	350	laborer	55	"
	G	Gekain Edward	350	"	28	"
	H	Gekain Martin	350	hotelman	40	"
	K	Hart George	350	machinist	58	"
	L	Karacoyian Martha—†	350	housewife	42	"
	M	McDonald John	350	laborer	27	1872 Wash'n
	N	McDonald Margaret—†	350	housekeeper	66	here
	O	Moore Harvey	350	laborer	59	"
	P	Moore William	350	"	62	"
	R	Mulligan Evelyn M—†	350	housekeeper	23	639 Tremont
	S	Murray George	350	machinist	57	here
	T	Oaks Frank E	350	real estate	55	"
	U	Scott John P	350	laborer	41	1453 Wash'n
	W	Caseley William A	352	painter	64	9 Laconia
	X	Ericson Carrol	352	buttonholes	30	Milton
	Y	Ketting Michael	352	choreman	55	190 E Brookline
	Z	Legere Peter	352	engineer	65	23 W Canton
	A	Murray Patrick	352	chef	45	30 Ivanhoe
	B	Poirier Barthelemy	352	carpenter	76	30 "
	C	Poirier Mary A—†	352	housekeeper	63	30 "
	D	Tittus Effie—†	352	baker	25	154 Falcon
	E	Eriksen Matilda †	353	housekeeper	67	54 W Canton
	F	Brown Annie G †	354	"	63	here
	G	Brown Thomas R	354	laborer	76	"
	H	Mereen Irving F	354	chauffeur	21	"
	M	Detry Harriet—†	357	housekeeper	60	"
	N	Detry Raymond	357	chauffeur	25	"
	O	Detry Walter	357	salesman	27	"
	R	Fallon Margaret †	359	housewife	47	"
	S	Fallon William P	359	teamster	45	"
	T	Gott Ella E—†	360	housekeeper	80	"
	U	Gott Ella G—†	360	bookkeeper	54	"

14

Shawmut Avenue—Continued

v	Mulick Margaret L —†	360	housewife	21	65 Green
w	McEchron Ernest	360	teamster	50	here
x	McEchron Lillian A —†	360	housewife	40	"
d	Correy Isaac	366	laborer	54	13 Hudson
e	Correy Sarah —†	366	housewife	50	13 "
f	Khonry Isaac	366	rubberworker	55	13 "
g	Khonry Sarah—†	366	housewife	50	13 "
h	Purland Cecil J	366	window cleaner	40	24 E Brookline
k	Purland Margie E —†	366	housewife	29	24 "
l	Moohan Alice E —†	366	housekeeper	39	34 Ryan
m	Moohan Margaret —†	366	laundress	34	34 "
n	Moohan Mary A —†	366	"	40	34 "
o	Carroll Frank	366	waiter	40	here
p	Carroll Marie —†	366	housewife	29	"
r	McGaffigan Edward	366	builder	30	62 W Dedham
s	McGaffigan Mary —†	366	housewife	27	62 "
t	Tattlebaum Jacob	367	shoemaker	67	here
u	Tattlebaum Lawrence	367	chauffeur	20	"
v	Tattlebaum Sarah—†	367	housewife	59	"
w	Tattlebaum William	367	laborer	26	"
x	DuPlain Bessie M—†	368	nurse	36	"
y	Smith Bessie M—†	368	housewife	41	"
z	Wilkins Elizabeth J—†	368	housekeeper	64	"
A	Wilkins Samuel F	368	clerk	79	"
B	Wrayton Marion E—†	368	nurse	39	"
c	King Adie—†	369	housewife	36	"
D	King James E	369	porter	46	"
E	Young Harry	369A	laundryman	61	"
F	DeGroot Bessie †	370	housewife	24	143 Ruggles
G	DeGroot Ralph	370	cigarmaker	28	143 "
H	Boucher Lucy—†	370	factory worker	43	24 Rutland
K	Haugek Arthur	370	ironworker	35	Cambridge
L	Dawley Jennie —†	370	seamstress	40	1524 Wash'n
M	Dawley William	370	machinist	33	1524 "
N	Mangelinck Hugo	370	cigarmaker	46	11 Cortes
o	Mangelinck Mary A —†	370	housewife	42	11 "
p	Burke Mary—†	371	housekeeper	77	here
R	Connelly Barbara A—†	371	"	62	"
s	McDonald Bertha—†	371	waitress	67	"
t	Flanagan Robert	372	laborer	34	"
u	Hough Ane—†	372	housekeeper	53	"

Page.	Letter.	FULL NAME.	Residence, April 1, 1926	Occupation	Supposed Age.	Reported Residence, April 1, 1925. Street and Number.

Shawmut Avenue—Continued

	V	Lappin Elizabeth —†	372	housekeeper	71	Cambridge
	W	Mulgrew Edward	372	retired	58	here
	X	Slack Henry	372	machinist	62	Salem N H
	Y	Anderson Mary—†	373	housekeeper	47	here
	Z	Foreman Henry	373	artist	55	"
	A	Gaffney Rose —†	373	housekeeper	49	"
	C	Gray James	373	laborer	32	Salem
	D	Johnson Nora —†	373	clerk	33	here
	B	Letour Clifford	373	laborer	51	Chelsea
	E	McGavigan John	373	"	53	here
	F	Riley John	373	machinist	48	123 W Concord
	G	Hallax John	374	cook	41	here
	H	Hallax Mary —†	374	housekeeper	36	"
	K	Jennings Mary—†	374	laundress	60	Cambridge
	L	Nichols Dimos	374	dishwasher	58	here
	M	Callahan Edward	375	laborer	50	"
	N	Dwyer Ellen—†	375	housekeeper	53	Hopkinton
	O	Dwyer Michael J	375	laborer	49	"
	P	Rogers Bernard	375	"	30	here
	R	Ryan William	375	plumber	49	"
	T	Bailey Nellie —†	376	shoeworker	45	"
	S	Conley Hellen —†	376	housemaid	60	"
	U	Ormsby Catherine—†	376	housewife	70	"
	V	Baranski John	377	farmer	40	Framingham
	W	Shuck Dominic	377	optician	42	Malden
	X	Brody Frank H	378	carpenter	60	395 Shawmut av
	Y	Eagle Mary—†	378	housewife	41	here
	Z	Eagle Samuel	378	laborer	44	"
	A	Finnin Agnes —†	378	housewife	43	"
	B	Keith George	378	broker	55	"
	C	McKee Frank	378	laborer	44	Brookline
	D	O'Donald Thomas	378	mason tender	50	here
	E	Phiney William B	378	shoemaker	62	105 Appleton
	F	Ray Samuel	378	laborer	58	105 W Dedham
	L	Dow Alice—†	385	housewife	39	here
	M	Dow Harry	385	chauffeur	22	"
	N	DiGiorgia Elizabeth—†	385	housewife	54	"
	O	DiGiorgia Joseph	385	barber	54	"
	R	Bower Evelynn —†	391	housewife	21	51 E Springfield
	S	Bower James	391	barber	49	51 "
	T	Bower Sarah —†	391	housewife	42	51 "

Shawmut Avenue—Continued

u	Pemberton Frank A	391	boilermaker	48	Everett
v	Pemberton Josephine—†	391	housewife	49	"
w	Tucker Joseph	392	storekeeper	35	here
x	Tucker Molly—†	392	housewife	29	"
y	Barber Edward L	392	window cleaner	33	395 Shawmut av
z	Sanders Virginia—†	392	housewife	29	395 "
a	Hinkley Annie—†	392	housekeeper	53	Cambridge
b	Lincoln Arthur H	392	pianoworker	53	"
c	Finkelstein Louis	392	cleanser	54	here
d	Finkelstein Maud—†	392	housewife	48	"
g	Herman Eva—†	394	housekeeper	40	"
h	Herman Jacob	394	tailor	43	"
k	Brant Bessie—†	394	housewife	35	New York City
l	Brant Harry	394	painter	40	"
m	Hoopers John	394	marketman	30	here
n	Hoopers Mary—†	394	housewife	35	"
o	Reynolds Mary—†	394	"	70	"
p	Reynolds William	394	plumber	30	"
r	Shargabain George	394A	storekeeper	27	395 Shawmut av
t	Carter George	395	painter	30	609 Mass av
u	Casey Thomas	395	mason	45	here
v	Church Letriccia—†	395	housekeeper	43	1038 Col av
w	McLeod Alice—†	395	housewife	22	5 Cunston
x	McLeod John	395	fishcutter	34	5 "
y	Shaffner Charles N	395	fireman	32	here
z	Shaffner Henreiatta—†	395	housewife	30	"
a	Sullivan John J	395	fireman	25	Providence R I
b	Vincent William	395	machinist	25	here
c	Wellman Benjamin O	395	janitor	63	30 Corning
e	Pashalian Diran	401	clerk	37	Providence R I
f	Bailey Anna—†	401	housekeeper	88	here
g	Bailey Jennie—†	401	clerk	50	"
h	Afarian Samuel	401	janitor	44	31 Sharon
k	Afarian Sarah—†	401	housewife	27	31 "
l	Bartavian Mary—†	401	dressmaker	55	Cambridge
m	John Philip	401	laborer	55	here
p	Edes Louis P	409	custodian	58	"
r	Boothby Asa S	411	caterer	70	"
s	Boothby Mary A—†	411	housewife	70	"
t	Bordman Max	411	gardener	50	"
u	Bragdon Frank A	411	salesman	70	"

Shawmut Avenue—Continued

v	Chronis Anita—†	411	clerk	30	Somerville
w	Coleman Daniel	411	baker	48	here
x	Hart Adeline—†	411	seamstress	40	"
y	Maguire Charles F	411	elevatorman	35	"
z	Page John	411	cook	40	12 Acton
a	Phinney Paul	411	clerk	35	1761 Wash'n
b	Sullivan Dennis J	411	retired	50	here
c	Cole Herbert	413	laborer	40	Somerville
d	Durgin Ida—†	413	housewife	55	"
e	Durgin Irving	413	laborer	60	"
f	Gillihan James	413	stableman	30	129 W Concord
g	Mathews Elizabeth—†	413	seamstress	70	here
h	Savill Emma—†	413	housekeeper	65	"
k	Strong Newton B	413	retired	70	"
l	Vagrinis Peter	413	cashier	30	"
m	Vagrinis Thomas	413	cook	35	"

Tremont Street

v	Addson Annie—†	592	seamstress	65	Salem
w	Connely John	592	real estate	45	Brockton
x	Ferguson George	592	machinist	35	Lowell
y	Fraser Frank	592	mechanic	40	here
z	Fraser Louise—†	592	housewife	48	"
a	Grant Justin F	592	physician	48	"
b	Larson Harry F	592	typist	38	Hull
c	Mills Ella H—†	592	housewife	60	Braintree
d	Pecce Charles	592	mechanic	30	Lynn
e	Pokraka Lawrence	592	broker	35	Lawrence
f	Staples Lucy K—†	592	nurse	53	Brookline
g	Williams Mary—†	592	housekeeper	26	Caribou Me
h	Casey Fred	594	painter	25	here
k	Joslin Norman	594	cook	25	"
l	Joslin Stanley	594	"	30	"
m	Knox Henry	594	laborer	35	"
n	Knox Maud—†	594	nurse	30	"
o	McKenny Josephine—†	594	houseworker	35	"
p	Mitchell Earl L	594	painter	26	"
r	Mulherin Robert E	594	"	40	41 Dartmouth
s	Mulherin Theresa M—†	594	clerk	21	41 "

18

Letter	FULL NAME.	Residence, April 1, 1926.	Occupation.	Supposed Age.	Reported Residence, April 1, 1925. Street and Number.

Tremont Street—Continued

T	Olson Axel	594	cook	35	here
U	Rogers John	594	painter	35	"
V	Wilcox Hilda—†	594	waitress	28	Portland Me
W	Wilcox Richard	594	driver	50	"
X	Williams Arthur	594	laborer	31	here
Y	Williams Ida—†	594	housekeeper	30	"
A	Callahan Edward	596	salesman	30	Brookline
B	Church Lucelle—†	596	waitress	27	here
C	Clapp Mary—†	596	operator	60	666 Tremont
D	Cooper John	596	electrician	40	here
E	Donovan John F	596	carpenter	54	"
F	Donovan Marion—†	596	housekeeper	50	"
G	Enstrom John	596	mechanic	35	Malden
H	Goodwin Isabelle—†	596	milliner	37	here
K	Hamm Elizabeth—†	596	clerk	45	Dover N H
L	Lafebbe Nathaniel	596	salesman	50	9 Hanson
M	Lowery Agnes—†	596	housekeeper	50	here
N	Magnet Charles	596	salesman	35	"
O	Mason Henry F	596	clerk	45	98 W Newton
P	Bogdasian Arshaw	598	waiter	28	here
R	Cox Ella J—†	598	clerk	38	"
S	Cox Leon G	598	baker	45	"
T	DeGarabedian Kegham	598	shoemaker	25	"
U	DeGarabedian Kreikor	598	"	30	"
V	Flynn Jennie L—†	598	housekeeper	54	"
W	Flynn William E	598	inspector	60	"
X	Freeman Herbert J	598	porter	40	28 Upton
Y	Harding Estelle—†	598	waitress	22	here
Z	Harding Grace—†	598	clerk	42	"
A	Kaove Joseph	598	machinist	22	Providence R I
D	McFarland Henry H	598	broker	50	"
B	Murphy Charles J	598	roofer	30	New York City
C	Murphy Gertrude—†	598	cashier	34	Brockton
E	Randby Frederick	598	machinist	46	here
F	Randby Lenor—†	598	maid	45	"
G	Randby Sigred	598	machinist	44	"
H	Sherman Sarah—†	598	housewife	50	"
K	Sherman Ulysses W	598	retired	61	"
L	Ahlberg Samuel	600	laborer	23	118 Chandler
M	Cole Esther—†	600	waitress	30	758 Tremont
N	Davis Eunice M—†	600	housekeeper	50	758 "

Tremont Street—Continued

	Letter	FULL NAME.	Residence	Occupation.	Age	Reported Residence
	o	Dolan Arthur	600	laborer	27	Lynn
	P	Douglas Daniel	600	"	50	330 Tremont
	R	Horne Mabel—†	600	housekeeper	38	758 "
	S	Hurley William	600	cook	40	here
	T	Robbins Grace —†	600	clerk	28	431 Mass av
	U	Robbins Harrald	600	painter	30	431 "
	V	Sall Samuel	600	laborer	30	496 Col av
	W	Sigren Albert	600	clerk	21	Chicago Ill
	X	Styffe Benjamin	600	laborer	23	114 Chandler
	Y	Travis Henry F	600	"	45	Natick
	Z	Travis Minnie —†	600	housekeeper	30	"
	A	Wilson Albert W	600	salesman	67	here
	B	Blenn Marion—†	602	cashier	50	"
	C	Bourden Anna— †	602	hairdresser	40	"
	D	Bourden Raoul	602	engineer	42	"
	E	Comeau Alphonsus	602	janitor	21	Salem
	F	Crawford Mabel—†	602	housekeeper	41	here
	G	Danilson Andrew	602	ironworker	50	"
	H	Johnston Daisy —†	602	real estate	35	"
	K	Johnston Isaac T	602	"	44	"
	L	Masterson Larry	602	painter	43	"
	M	McAlister Daniel	602	"	34	Salem
	N	Tucker George L	602	laborer	50	here
	o	Burroughs Alvin	604	meatcutter	21	"
	P	Burroughs Elizabeth—†	604	houseworker	47	"
	R	Burroughs Nora— †	604	housewife	21	"
	S	Chabot Norman	604	painter	28	"
	S¹	Faulkner Dorothy —†	604	stitcher	23	"
	T	Faulkner James	604	clerk	47	"
	U	Keller Catherine —†	604	housewife	32	"
	V	Keller Emil	604	counterman	35	"
	W	Marshall Georgia —†	604	housewife	48	"
	X	Marshall William W	604	conductor	70	"
	Y	Rideout Addie —†	604	stitcher	45	"
	Z	Smith Lais—†	604	housewife	39	"
	A	Wright Mary P †	604	stitcher	59	"
	B	Baxter Marian—†	606	housewife	26	New York City
	C	Baxter Robert	606	painter	27	"
	E	Falla Joseph M	606	clerk	58	623 Tremont
	D	Falla Kathryn—†	606	housewife	57	623 "
	F	Fisher Addie M— †	606	laundryworker	45	Nova Scotia

20

Tremont Street—Continued

Letter.	FULL NAME.	Residence, April 1, 1926.	Occupation.	Supposed Age.	Reported Residence, April 1, 1925. Street and Number.
G	Geary Edward R	606	clerk	38	42 Monument st
H	Geary Margaret E—†	606	waitress	35	42 "
K	Kelly Margaret—†	606	cook	50	10 Upton
L	LaPointe Joseph	606	laborer	46	604 Tremont
M	Libby Nellie—†	606	cook	58	Dover N H
N	Lutz Leo	606	shoeworker	25	14 Harold
O	Mahoney John	606	plumber	40	55 Dover
P	Marshall Robert F	606	paperhanger	72	here
R	McPherson Nellie—†	606	housewife	21	Somerville
S	McPherson Robert P	606	clerk	24	"
T	Merrill Frederick F	606	cashier	58	Hyannis
U	Ratnode Lillian V—†	606	waitress	37	Lynn
V	Roberts George L	606	glazier	57	480 E Fourth
W	Robertson Elizabeth—†	606	housewife	20	571 Col av
X	Robertson Thomas	606	clerk	23	here
Y	Sherman Harry E	606	painter	51	604 Tremont
B	Abbott Fred	612	cook	40	24 Dartmouth
C	Behbaum Otto	612	engineer	62	here
D	Bishop Francis H	612	salesman	36	"
E	Bishop Hellen G—†	612	housewife	23	"
F	Kelly Edward	612	painter	45	"
G	Kelly Mary—†	612	housewife	42	"
H	Manning William	612	cook	26	Lowell
K	McWilliams John I	612	expressman	50	here
L	Murdo Elizabeth A—†	612	housewife	42	"
M	Murdo Walter J	612	gilder	42	"
N	Newton Albert	612	retired	71	"
O	Newton Irvin L	612	fireman	47	"
P	Schneider Peter	612	janitor	62	177 Warren av
R	Taylor Gertrude—†	612	housewife	26	New York
S	Taylor William	612	helper	36	"
U	Betcher Charles W	616	bookkeeper	41	here
V	Betcher Florence E—†	616	nurse	35	"
W	Crosby Edwin E	616	machinist	28	"
X	Fleming Agnes—†	616	seamstress	40	"
Y	Greenough David H	616	latherer	60	"
Z	Kiley Margaret E—†	616	clerk	43	"
A	Knowles Ina J—†	616	housewife	49	"
B	MacDonald Jane—†	616	retired	74	"
C	MacLean Cassie—†	616	nurse	50	"
D	Naelin Loraine E—†	616	typist	26	"

Tremont Street—Continued

E	Rackstrom Agnes —†	616	stitcher	22	895 Martin
F	Sarr May—†	616	waitress	24	New York
G	Worthylake Regina †	616	bookkeeper	26	14 Worcester sq
H	Zaveen Joseph	616	shipper	26	Cambridge
K	Brodeur Augustine	618	salesman	33	Rochester N Y
L	Brodeur Jeanette—†	618	housekeeper	34	"
M	Given Winnifred †	618	clerk	25	Canton Me
N	Jackson Margaret—†	618	maid	25	Halifax N S
O	Jackson Roy A	618	ironworker	30	"
P	MacClery Oakley P	618	engineer	48	Nova Scotia
R	MacClery Ruth —†	618	housewife	40	"
S	MacFarlen Hazel—†	618	clerk	28	"
W	MacLean Charles G	618	"	26	Pictou N S
T	Magalis Emma —†	618	housewife	30	New York
U	Magalis Wiley	618	electrician	35	Rochester N Y
V	Maksoodian Christy	618	real estate	40	here
X	Sullivan Agnes—†	618	clerk	30	Providence R I
Y	Sullivan Margaret —†	618	housewife	45	Concord N H
Z	Sullivan Mary—†	618	saleswoman	35	Providence R I
A	Sullivan William	618	electrician	55	Concord N H
B	Bonacine Margaret —†	620	bookkeeper	26	here
C	Carpenter George	620	clerk	55	"
D	Eldredge Georgie †	620	retired	50	"
E	Grenier Eugenia †	620	housekeeper	65	"
F	Hughes Gertrude —†	620	clerk	35	"
G	Marsh Florence †	620	"	40	"
H	Patterson Claud	620	manager	35	"
K	Ruby George	620	printer	48	"
L	Snow William	620	clerk	45	"
M	Callender Austin	622	student	23	"
N	Callender Robert	622	engineer	54	"
O	Clifford Emma †	622	teacher	70	41 Child
P	Haynes Mary W —†	622	stenographer	35	here
R	Paine Isabella S †	622	housekeeper	68	"
S	Brink Jennie—†	624	housewife	37	775 Tremont
T	Brink Mitchell	624	coatmaker	40	775 "
U	Bruno Clara— †	624	tiemaker	40	626 "
V	Daley Eddie	624	truckman	35	Hingham
W	Griffin Emma †	624	housekeeper	60	626 Tremont
X	Grady Thomas	624	laborer	60	84 W Canton
Y	Gray Joseph	624	"	29	Brooklyn N Y

Tremont Street—Continued

z	Gray Mary—†	624	housewife	32	Brooklyn N Y
A	Hall Benjamin	624	salesman	35	656 Tremont
B	Hall Lillian—†	624	housewife	40	656 "
C	Phillips George	624	shoemaker	40	579 Columbia rd
D	Phillips Nellie—†	624	housewife	35	579 "
E	Rogers Wilbur	624	laborer	26	here
F	Ware Sumner	624	foreman	53	"
G	Webb Ethel—†	624	housewife	35	Fort Revere
H	Alberti William	626	tailor	30	here
K	Brown Charles	626	retired	75	Maine
L	Brown Martha—†	626	housewife	60	"
M	Curry John	626	salesman	50	44 E Newton
N	Hollis Clifton	626	painter	39	Somerville
O	Hanna Robert	626	"	40	"
P	McCabe Joseph	626	contractor	33	Wollaston
R	McKenzie John	626	cook	33	Connecticut
S	Miller Margaret—†	626	laundress	25	here
T	Morris Louis	626	chef	25	26 Union pk
U	Murphy Catherine—†	626	waitress	23	Newton
V	O'Neil Edith—†	626	housewife	36	Gloucester
W	Stokel Mark	626	clerk	50	here
X	Whipple Helen—†	626	waitress	22	"
Y	Whipple Henry	626	trainman	26	"
Z	White Charles	626	salesman	32	Somerville
A	Nerbonne Amedee	628	shoeworker	35	here
B	Nerbonne Elizabeth—†	628	hairdresser	39	"
D	Daniels Esther—†	634	housekeeper	54	370 Col av
E	Duffly Helen—†	634	nurse	34	49 Atherton
F	Kennelly Patrick	634	laborer	56	here
G	Shea Vincent	634	chauffeur	22	360 Col av
H	Sheeley Jerimiah	634	laborer	61	here
K	Travers Elizabeth—†	634	housewife	35	"
L	Adams Nellie—†	636	saleswoman	40	"
M	Bates Ella—†	636	stitcher	53	200 Warren av
N	Bates William	636	carpenter	56	200 "
O	Byrnes Elsie—†	636	marker	26	here
P	Byrnes Robert	636	laundryman	28	"
R	Campbell Fred	636	salesman	47	Wilmington
S	Keenan Florence—†	636	waitress	28	Revere
T	McVetty Florence—†	636	"	25	Canada
U	Melanson Lena—†	636	stenographer	28	here

	Letter.	FULL NAME.	Residence, April 1, 1926.	Occupation.	Supposed Age.	Reported Residence, April 1, 1925. Street and Number.

Tremont Street—Continued

	Letter.	FULL NAME.	Residence, April 1, 1926.	Occupation.	Supposed Age.	Reported Residence, April 1, 1925. Street and Number.
	v	Melanson Lindley	636	laborer	29	here
	w	Mooney James	636	packer	53	"
	x	Mooney Mary †	636	housekeeper	49	"
	y	Murray Frances †	636	"	36	"
	z	Murray William	636	machinist	40	
	A	Sturgeon Alfred	636	retired	48	New York City
	B	Swazdowick Elizabeth —†	636	housewife	27	10 Groton
	C	Swazdowick Michael	636	painter	34	10 "
	D	Bennett Iva P †	638	saleswoman	30	496 Mass av
	E	Bennett Louis A	638	chauffeur	29	496 "
	F	Bernier Marie A C —†	638	stitcher	26	here
	G	Crosman Cora E —†	638	houseworker	57	"
	H	Crosman Herbert E	638	carpenter	63	"
	K	Dempsey Agnes †	638	houseworker	22	"
	L	Dempsey George	638	waiter	26	"
	M	McAuliffe William	638	manager	47	"
	N	McGarrill Delia †	638	houseworker	65	"
	O	Osgood Mary †	638	candymaker	50	"
	P	Parker Harold	638	billposter	31	"
	R	Parker Mary —†	638	houseworker	27	"
	S	Purchase Harriett—†	638	cook	57	"
	T	Stuart Charles S	638	waiter	34	"
	U	Stuart Madeline—†	638	boxmaker	30	"
	W	Beard Anna— †	652	saleswoman	27	"
	X	Drapeau Benjamin	652	mechanic	22	6 Union Park
	Y	Gillis Allan	652	laborer	32	700 Tremont
	A	Hewitt Mary A †	652	clerk	27	here
	B	Hewitt Ozar	652	blacksmith	56	"
	C	Hewitt Robert P	652	salesman	36	"
	D	Howell Florence †	652	housewife	35	1 Ringgold
	E	Howell Joseph	652	laborer	36	1 "
	F	Pulo Andrew	652	barber	24	603 Tremont
	G	Rueter Anna †	652	housewife	62	Worcester
	H	Rueter Carrie M— †	652	"	45	here
	K	Rueter Herman	652	boxmaker	34	"
	L	Thorin Hector	652	ironworker	32	3 Worcester sq
	M	Thorin Margaret —†	652	housewife	32	3 "
	N	Wukusie Nicholas	652	pedler	45	here
	P	Case Anna M —†	654	retired	60	"
	R	Kennison Frederick M	654	physician	63	"
	S	Kennison Mary P—†	654	housewife	54	"

	Letter	FULL NAME.	Residence, April 1, 1926.	Occupation.	Supposed Age.	Reported Residence, April 1, 1925. Street and Number.

Tremont Street—Continued

	Letter	FULL NAME.	Residence	Occupation	Age	Reported Residence
	T	Kennison Ralph	654	engineer	27	here
	U	McPhaill Mabel—†	654	nurse	46	"
	V	Ready Lucy M—†	654	dressmaker	48	"
	W	LeGraw George	654	clerk	33	Somerville
	X	Simpson Jerold A	654	chauffeur	23	29 Chandler
	Y	Tenney George B	654	grocer	59	here
	Z	Tenney Mary F—†	654	housewife	55	"
	A	Thorsen Fredrick	654	clerk	64	620 Tremont
	B	Whalen Margaret—†	654	housewife	55	here
	C	Whalen Thomas F	654	laborer	65	"
	D	Chicoine Adolphe	656	pressman	33	Portland Me
	E	Chicoine Marion—†	656	housewife	28	"
	F	Cromwell Elizabeth—†	656	"	40	here
	G	Cromwell James	656	accountant	50	"
	H	Juno Josephine—†	656	checker	23	"
	K	Loveland Bessie—†	656	housewife	58	"
	L	Loveland Edward	656	real estate	60	"
	M	McKnight Robert J	656	clerk	40	"
	N	McKnight Robert P	656	shipper	60	"
	O	Petrin Katherine—†	656	housewife	40	"
	P	Riley George	656	chauffeur	25	Cambridge
	R	Riley Helen—†	656	housewife	25	"
	S	Wansburg Ture	656	machinist	25	Lynn
	T	Wansburg Viola—†	656	housewife	23	here
	U	Arsonal Elizabeth—†	658	"	24	618 Tremont
	V	Arsonal George	658	chauffeur	25	618 "
	W	Chamberland Walter	658	laborer	50	here
	X	Chase Charles T	658	messenger	65	Newport
	Y	Couch Nellie—†	658	housewife	50	here
	Z	Couch William R	658	painter	49	"
	A	Courtan Edward	658	janitor	42	337 Col av
	B	Jackman Norman N	658	waiter	26	89 Shawmut av
	C	Kelly Robert H	658	salesman	26	New York City
	D	McCall Julia—†	658	housewife	45	here
	E	Merland Alvin E	658	waiter	30	605 Tremont
	F	Murphy James S	658	laborer	60	here
	G	Murphy Mary S—†	658	housewife	55	"
	H	Raymond Marie—†	658	waitress	24	"
	K	Semich Charles	658	salesman	26	Medford
	L	Sleight Andrew	658	laborer	38	here
	M	Sleight Edith—†	658	housewife	37	"

Tremont Street— Continued

N	Vengestel John	658	cigarmaker	52	Salem
O	Vengestel Marie— †	658	housewife	54	"
P	Weber Robert S	658	chauffeur	26	89 Shawmut av
R	Boice Anna— †	660	cook	49	here
S	Cambell James B	660	engineer	30	"
T	Clark Gertrude H —†	660	waitress	44	"
U	Elliott James E	660	engineer	30	"
V	Fandes Nicholas C	660	cook	40	"
W	Goodman Benjimin F	660	salesman	52	"
X	Greenlaw Alice M—†	660	clerk	33	142 W Canton
Y	Haley Charles	660	steeplejack	65	665 Tremont
Z	Hunter Eletho †	660	housewife	42	here
A	Hunter Stewart A	660	engineer	40	"
B	Morash Allen R	660	clerk	30	658 Tremont
C	Morash Helen A —†	660	housewife	26	650 "
D	Munroe Jarius J	660	clerk	57	here
E	Rich George	660	waiter	42	"
F	Secolloc Emily—†	660	saleswoman	50	"
G	Willard Ira A	660	motorman	65	"
H	Acker Edgar	662	manager	46	"
K	Davis Bessie M—†	662	dressmaker	49	"
L	Fein Millie—†	662	bookbinder	37	"
M	Frye Susie—†	662	seamstress	60	"
N	Greenlaw Cora—†	662	nurse	36	"
O	Greenlaw Frank	662	laborer	45	"
P	Jackman Susie C—†	662	houseworker	33	42 Hanson
R	Kenney Susie—†	662	laundress	47	here
S	Malker Charles	662	shoecutter	50	"
T	McDonnell Mary A—†	662	nurse	45	"
U	Roberts John	662	laborer	66	"
V	Stacy Myrtle B—†	662	bookkeeper	35	496 Mass av

Trumbull Street

Z	Boudreau Edna—†	4	laundress	25	here
A	Boudreau Philip	4	carpenter	29	Canada
B	Garfield Eva—†	4	housewife	32	here
C	Garfield James	4	painter	35	"
D	Boivin Hannah—†	5	housewife	33	3 Glover ct
E	Boivin Romeo	5	shipper	38	3 "

Trumbull Street— Continued

F	Cruze Ernest	5	longshoreman	48	3 Glover et
G	Dixon Harold	5	clerk	48	226 Dover
M	Masse Bridget—†	10 & 12	housewife	39	here
N	Masse Chester	10 & 12	machinist	37	"
O	Patnode Charles	10 & 12	ironmolder	32	79 E Dedham
P	Patnode Lelina—†	10 & 12	housewife	31	79 "
T	Banks Jacob	16	cook	22	here
U	Banks Minnie—†	16	housewife	50	"
W	Tunsell Cecelia—†	18	"	62	"
X	Tunsell Mary L—†	18	dressmaker	29	"
B	Engram Elizabeth—†	34	housewife	38	"
C	Engram Jonas	34	carpenter	32	Newfoundland
D	Engram Thomas	34	"	39	here
F	Simms Elvina E—†	35	housewife	39	"
E	Simms John C	35	laborer	43	"
G	Stickland John W	37	"	38	"
H	Strickland Sarah—†	37	housewife	33	"

Upton Street

A	Berry John	10	waiter	27	here
B	Berry Mary B—†	10	waitress	38	"
C	Brooks Maude—†	10	housekeeper	39	"
D	Crotean Ammie	10	laborer	35	52 Joy
E	Digman William	10	"	38	162 Melrose
F	Farlie Edward	10	"	35	47 Warren av
G	Kezer Louis R	10	"	38	17 Hanson
H	Landstrong Victor	10	"	37	24 "
K	McCarthy Frank	10	teacher	50	here
L	Pappas George	10	waiter	38	Providence R I
M	Cullum Bessie—†	12	housewife	52	here
N	Cullum Dennis	12	laborer	54	"
O	Kahkyran Mazan	12	cook	37	"
P	Kiely Patrick	12	plumber	60	"
R	Lowe Harry W	12	laborer	39	110 Union Park
S	McNiff James	12	shoecutter	52	here
T	Thompson Edward	12	laborer	52	"
U	Thompson Ellen—†	12	housewife	52	"
V	Young Mary—†	12	retired	64	"
W	Bent Lois—†	14	housewife	38	234 Mass av

Age.	Letter.	FULL NAME.	Residence April 1, 1926.	Occupation.	Supposed Age.	Reported Residence, April 1, 1925. Street and Number.

Upton Street—Continued

	Letter	FULL NAME	Res.	Occupation	Age	Residence
	x	Norman Sylvester	14	fireman	54	here
	y	Stowe Harriet M—†	14	housewife	60	234 Mass av
	z	Toal Thomas	14	waiter	36	226 "
	A	Whitley Mary—†	14	housewife	24	234 "
	B	Whitley Ralph	14	leathercutter	28	234 "
	C	McKinnon Annie—†	14	retired	65	here
	D	Morrison Daniel	14	carpenter	38	"
	E	Morrison Sadie—†	14	waitress	23	"
	F	Morrison Sadie—†	14	housewife	38	"
	G	Dolan John	14	laborer	45	"
	H	McAskill Angus	14	"	37	Canada
	K	McLeod Dobena—†	14	clerk	30	here
	L	Morrison John	14	laborer	23	246 Cedar
	M	Crowley Catherine M—†	14	housewife	60	here
	N	Crowley Daniel	14	clerk	29	"
	O	Crowley Dennis J	14	laborer	60	"
	P	Crowley Thomas J	14	"	30	"
	R	Roach Mary—†	14	waitress	45	"
	S	Twoomey Daniel	14	laborer	65	"
	T	Allen Irene—†	16	waitress	24	Worcester
	U	Green Annie—†	16	houseworker	37	here
	V	Green Bessie—†	16	"	55	"
	W	MacDonald John	16	laborer	29	"
	X	MacQuinn Duncan	16	ironworker	60	Medford
	Y	Neal Eugene I.	16	retired	69	here
	Z	Neal Eugenia V—†	16	housewife	65	"
	A	O'Leary Timothy	16	fireman	28	143 Appleton
	B	Paulding George	16	machinist	32	here
	C	Reed Mabel—†	16	waitress	29	Worcester
	D	Reed Ralph	16	laborer	30	"
	E	Cronin Daniel	18	chauffeur	55	Lowell
	F	Dramer Nicholas	18	cook	31	43 Jefferson
	G	Ferries James	18	shoemaker	38	here
	H	Ferries Joseph	18	"	35	"
	K	Ferries Yemma—†	18	housekeeper	32	"
	L	Goldsmith Samuel	18	florist	48	25 Melrose
	M	Harfoush Joseph	18	laborer	35	15 Upton
	N	Kent Frank	18	cook	45	here
	O	Nicacos Sattiros	18	machinist	40	Lowell
	P	Noonan John	18	porter	24	32 Dwight
	R	Thomas Felthy—†	18	waitress	26	here

28

Upton Street—Continued

		FULL NAME.	Res.	Occupation.	Age	Reported Residence
s		Thomas Nettie—†	18	houseworker	33	here
t		Vrongalis Louis	18	shoemaker	35	348 Tremont
u		Brown Nathan	20	house cleaner	45	here
v		Brymer Elsie—†	20	dressmaker	50	"
w		Busbee Henry	20	retired	73	"
x		Capolas Louis	20	laborer	35	"
y		Chechames Charles	20	cook	38	"
z		Garrity George	20	laborer	25	"
a		Kelly Catherine—†	20	housewife	44	"
b		Kelly John J	20	engineer	45	"
c		McGee James	20	laborer	50	"
d		Mullens John	20	retired	40	"
e		O'Brien Margaret —†	20	housewife	74	"
f		Shashian Mishian	20	tailor	28	"
g		Shedigan Aran	20	laborer	35	"
h		Taylor Frank	20	retired	60	"
k		Trekrekas George	20	laborer	40	Lowell
l		Cole Howard	22	cook	26	"
m		Densmore William	22	carpenter	45	here
n		Hagstrom Rudolph	22	painter	40	"
o		Jackson Thomas	22	laborer	23	"
p		Kennedy James	22	"	37	"
r		Kostoria Philip	22	cook	35	"
s		Masa Joseph	22	"	25	Clinton
t		McLeod Alex	22	carpenter	28	128 Berkeley
u		McLeod Margaret—†	22	housekeeper	26	128 "
v		McGrogery Robert	22	machinist	38	27 Upton
w		Olson John F	22	cabinetmaker	60	here
x		Scott John	22	laborer	30	"
y		Thomas John J	22	printer	35	"
z		Thomas Rose—†	22	houseworker	32	"
a		Beauiel Anthony	24	painter	45	Fall River
b		Crommins Dennis	24	laborer	40	here
c		Delaney Florence J	24	painter	52	"
d		Delaney Juliah—†	24	housewife	43	"
e		Maloney Thomas	24	laborer	45	Cambridge
f		McCarthy Jeremiah	24	truck driver	30	2 St James
g		Morris Richard	24	shoeworker	50	Medford
h		Sheridan Annie—†	24	housewife	43	48 Putnam
k		Sheridan Thomas	24	clerk	48	48 "
l		Smith James	24	cook	50	111 W Brookline

Upton Street—Continued

M	Stevens Annie—†	24	housewife	47	Brockton
N	Sullivan Annie—†	24	"	70	12 Upton
O	Sullivan Jeremiah	24	waiter	50	210 Col av
P	Burnstein Morris D	26	tailor	35	here
R	Burse Nathan H	26	printer	58	"
S	Dupree Ida M—†	26	housewife	50	"
T	Grasher John	26	laborer	43	"
U	Jenkins Alfred J	26	cook	55	Vermont
V	Kalis Charles	26	retired	33	here
W	Kingston John J	26	laborer	42	"
Y	McElanson Harvey	26	printer	40	"
X	McGee Joseph A	26	brakeman	37	"
Z	Morressey William J	26	"	33	"
A	Newland Edward J	26	fireman	51	"
B	Walden William	26	laborer	50	"
C	Walsh Thomas P	26	inventor	55	"
D	Cadigan John	28	laborer	40	"
E	Conigan John	28	"	50	New Bedford
F	Evans Thomas	28	"	50	Detroit Mich
G	Green George	28	"	40	here
H	Hackey Joseph	28	"	24	"
K	Hunt Thomas	28	"	38	New Bedford
L	Manuel Catherine—†	28	housekeeper	42	here
M	Manuel Friedman	28	laborer	38	"
N	McShane Daniel	28	"	56	"
O	Webber Fredrick	28	seaman	25	New York
P	Gerbena John	30	laborer	56	Haverhill
R	Gray Harry	30	clerk	40	Dover N H
S	Gsalket John	30	cook	35	here
T	Hayden Augusta S—†	30	retired	50	Lowell
U	Lennard Patrick	30	laborer	50	here
V	Maloof Abraham	30	stitcher	22	"
W	Maloof Elsie H—†	30	houseworker	50	"
X	Maloof Joseph	30	cook	28	Manchester
Y	Manazin Salem	30	waiter	30	here
Z	Manazin Tawfik	30	carpenter	30	"
A	Ryan Frank	30	cook	45	"
B	Younis Joseph J	30	laborer	40	"
D	Younis Sarah—†	30	housekeeper	30	"
E	Colmentes Carl	32	painter	60	"
F	Coyne Juliah—†	32	housewife	65	"

Upton Street— Continued

	G	Curtin Daniel	32	laborer	70	19 Common
	H	Gerow Alfred F	32	shoeworker	40	here
	K	Jonas Albert	32	laborer	45	54 Waltham
	L	Lanon Michael	32	shoemaker	50	here
	M	Madden James B	32	laborer	35	"
	N	Porpagelies George	32	"	50	"
	O	Sahagian Ahron	32	merchant	65	Cambridge
	P	Sarndian Moses	32	barber	65	here
	R	Scanlon Harry J	32	marbleworker	45	84 Waltham
	S	Berman William	34	plumber	35	Maine
	T	Bithage Errick	34	cook	21	4031 Wash'n
	U	Coes Fred	34	laborer	56	Lowell
	V	Doherty Patrick	34	"	45	here
	W	Galvin Mary—†	34	housekeeper	54	66 W Rutland
	X	Hullinger Otto	34	painter	29	325 Medford
	Y	Kelly Alfred	34	laborer	29	682 Benningt'n
	Z	Kelly William	34	"	26	682 "
	A	Rabail Joseph	34	cook	21	5 Taylor
	B	West Forrest J	34	optician	50	Ashland
	C	Ahearn John	36	shoemaker	32	24 Taft
	D	Arthur Leon	36	laborer	45	567 Tremont
	E	Frangavis Peter	36	waiter	35	here
	F	Gazette Alfred	36	foreman	35	"
	G	Gazette Jean—†	36	housewife	33	"
	H	Groser Charles	36	laborer	42	86 Waltham
	K	Hesgesheimer Charles	36	seaman	35	New York
	L	Hughes Arthur A	36	laborer	30	29 Humboldt av
	M	Hughes James	36	plumber	38	535 Shawmut av
	N	Kane Mary—†	36	waitress	24	10 Union Park
	O	McCabe Bridget—†	36	laundress	40	here
	P	Owens Margaret—†	36	cashier	26	"
	R	Russell Marion—†	36	waitress	35	"
	S	Vall Charles	36	laborer	64	"
	T	Cullinan James	38	janitor	50	"
	U	Euck William	38	cigarmaker	45	525 Mass av
	V	Hickey Joseph	38	electrician	50	here
	W	Murrey John	38	laborer	35	Canada
	X	Sulkey Herbert	38	janitor	25	24 Upton
	Y	White Harry	38	waiter	35	Waltham
	Z	Whitford Elizabeth—†	38	houseworker	42	here
	A	Whitford William	38	cigarmaker	44	"

Upton Street—Continued

Letter	FULL NAME.	Residence, April 1, 1926.	Occupation.	Supposed Age.	Reported Residence, April 1, 1925. Street and Number.
B	Bourigaily Naheel —†	40	housewife	45	here
C	Bourigaily Nalil	40	laborer	50	"
D	Chmarach Frank	40	"	35	"
E	Chriv Michael	40	"	35	"
F	Duduch Michael	40	teamster	35	"
G	Handy Abraham	40	"	28	"
H	Lakage George	40	"	30	"
K	Lakage Richard	40	"	32	"
L	MacArthur Sarah —†	40	clerk	24	"
M	Melnyn Michael	40	laborer	33	"
N	Pane George	40	"	30	"
O	Stacinopolous Christopher	40	teamster	30	15 Upton
P	Talbach James	40	laborer	28	here
R	Thems Andres	40	"	35	"
S	White Arthur	40	teamster	35	"
T	Abovjaily John	42	laborer	45	"
U	Abovjaily Sadie —†	42	housekeeper	38	"
V	Archuck Nicholas	42	laborer	35	"
W	Barry David	42	"	50	"
X	Deeb Joseph	42	"	23	"
Y	Deeb Nichlas	42	"	39	"
Z	Gandener Samuel	42	"	30	"
A	Garbadian Stephen	42	"	30	13 Upton
B	Hart Patrick	42	"	30	here
C	Henlakis William	42	"	30	Lowell
D	Koch Blanche —†	42	waitress	38	here
E	Lambrides Antanias	42	carpenter	35	"
F	Martucci Vincent	42	laborer	57	"
G	Masano Joseph	42	"	38	"
H	Sacks John	42	"	50	Dedham
K	Susi Olindo	42	"	35	here
L	Varbekis Toney	42	"	30	"
M	Barton Frank A	44	electrician	45	"
N	Cocoran James	44	retired	80	"
O	Drinkwater Dorothy—†	44	houseworker	26	22 E Brookline
P	Drinkwater Ester—†	44	housewife	46	22 "
R	Drinkwater Ruth—†	44	houseworker	23	22 "
S	Dunbasa William	44	steamfitter	40	35 Brookline
T	Frost Hannah—†	44	houseworker	50	here
U	Frost Melven R	44	retired	65	"
V	Gagerty Bridget—†	44	houseworker	50	Weymouth

Upton Street—Continued

w	Marcus William	44	cigarmaker	35	here
x	Mehan Joseph	44	laborer	22	Lowell
y	O'Connor Edward	44	waiter	27	here
z	Raymond Lewis	44	merchant	35	"
a	Suttie Alfred	44	plumber	60	"
b	Walsh Rose—†	44	clerk	50	Malden
c	Adams Annie—†	46	waitress	25	Salem
d	Barton Blanch—†	46	housewife	50	here
e	Barton John	46	chef	65	"
f	Chulzinsky Alice—†	46	housewife	27	54 Howard
g	Chulzinsky Frank	46	packer	30	54 "
h	Collins Mary A—†	46	domestic	24	here
k	DeSisto Catherine—†	46	brushmaker	28	"
l	Howard Sam	46	cook	28	54 Howard
m	Killem Hannah—†	46	nurse	40	294 Col av
n	Kouzoupis Demosthemis	46	cook	38	here
o	Kouzoupis Hattie—†	46	housewife	30	"
p	Rostand Hilda—†	46	laundress	50	"
r	Tragnee Robert	46	laborer	28	"
s	Wayland William	46	painter	64	"

Washington Street

u	Dudley Agnes—†	1435	laundress	48	Cambridge
v	Graham Aida—†	1435	housekeeper	52	81 Dover
w	Hancharoff Mary—†	1435	"	32	20 Mora
x	Manning John	1435	upholsterer	52	Somerville
y	Peary Ethel—†	1435	usher	28	25 Vernon
z	Shamis John	1435	stockkeeper	42	385 Col av
a	Smith Arthur	1435	laborer	34	Carver
b	Smith Clara J—†	1435	housewife	34	"
c	Barnett Annie—†	1437	housekeeper	55	here
d	McDevitt John	1437	meatcutter	40	"
e	Page Katherine—†	1437	cook	40	Manchester N H
h	Burnside William	1443	rubbercutter	50	3 E Canton
k	Donohue Frances—†	1443	retired	70	56 E Springfield
l	McKeon Edith—†	1443	housewife	52	1623 Wash'n
m	McKeon Edward	1443	elevatorman	52	1623 "
n	Nichols Georgie—†	1443	housekeeper	48	1623 "
o	Sullivan Cornelius F	1443	retired	69	1623 "

Page.	Letter.	FULL NAME.	Residence, April 1, 1926.	Occupation.	Supposed Age.	Reported Residence, April 1, 1925. Street and Number.

Washington Street— Continued

	P	Sullivan George	1443	kitchenman	49	317 Col av
	R	Canney John	1445	plasterer	58	here
	S	O'Brien Catherine —†	1445	housekeeper	58	"
	T	Scannel Mary —†	1445	laundryworker	58	"
	U	Sheehan Mira—†	1445	domestic	60	"
	V	Sheehan Philip	1445	kitchenman	55	"
	W	Sullivan Mary —†	1445	waitress	62	"
	X	Whalen James	1445	teamster	55	"
	A	Brennan James J	1451	laborer	52	"
	B	Osgood Charles	1451	kitchenman	40	30 Canton
	C	Osgood Mary —†	1451	housewife	45	30 "
	D	Turner Mary —†	1451	kitchenworker	40	here
	E	Whynot Charles R	1451	chef	56	75 Albion
	F	Brown Mary —†	1453	housewife	35	here
	G	Brown William	1453	kitchenman	46	"
	H	Fisher Fannie E —†	1453	housewife	55	1581 Wash'n
	K	Fisher Freeman A	1453	laborer	56	1581 "
	L	Kirby Emma —†	1453	houseworker	40	74 Rutland
	M	Mayotte Carrie —†	1453	housekeeper	65	189 Harris'n av
	P	Kilroy Frances R —†	1463	"	37	here
	R	Kilroy James M	1463	retired	76	"
	S	Kilroy Katherine C —†	1463	bookkeeper	44	"
	T	Kilroy Mark T	1463	salesman	51	"
	V	Downey John	1463	stableman	45	Cambridge
	W	McMillan Alice †	1463	housekeeper	40	here
	Wt	Hadjian Rose—†	1463	housewife	24	"
	X	Hadjian Sarkis	1463	storekeeper	26	"
	B	Walsh Francis J	1469	taxi driver	38	"
	C	Walsh Jennie—†	1469	housewife	44	"
	D	Deuquette Andrew	1469	painter	57	26 W Dedham
	E	McCarthy Helen M—†	1469	housewife	51	here
	F	Bowers Irene—†	1469	waitress	30	"
	G	Forinier Amy M—†	1469	housekeeper	50	"
	H	Shaunessessy Martin	1469	boilermaker	63	"
	K	Wong Sun	1475	laundryman	49	"
	L	Cretto Charles	1475	cutter	24	"
	M	Crye Patrick	1475	laborer	22	"
	N	Fulton John	1475	"	54	"
	O	Goulette Ourelie —†	1475	weaver	38	"
	P	Jonah Cora—†	1475	housekeeper	47	Medford
	R	Keith Alfred J	1475	roofer	44	here

Page.	Letter.	FULL NAME.	Residence, April 1, 1926.	Occupation.	Supposed Age.	Reported Residence, April 1, 1925. Street and Number.

Washington Street—Continued

	s	Maschand Emma—†	1475	clerk	27	here
	T	Sablock Czamoer	1475	laborer	45	Maine
	U	Sullivan John J	1475	"	55	here
	V	Triggs Thomas A	1475	broker	59	"
	W	Webster Louise C—†	1475	housekeeper	49	"
	X	Winnard Thomas	1475	printer	48	"
	Y	Buckley Timothy J	1479	cook	65	49 Rutland
	Z	Burns John L	1479	laborer	39	90 Warrenton
	A	Burns Mary—†	1479	nurse	38	90 "
	B	Cleade Louise—†	1479	seamstress	60	1437 Wash'n
	C	Houghton Edna A—†	1479	housekeeper	32	Salem
	D	O'Donnell Edward	1479	carpenter	65	"
	E	Olsen Christ	1479	shipper	46	Somerville
	F	Shaughnessey Alice—†	1479	saleswoman	28	Lowell
	G	Wright Edward	1479	dishwasher	50	Lynn
	H	Wright Mary—†	1479	waitress	40	"
	K	Basmajian Charles	1483	salesman	24	here
	L	Basmajian Esther—†	1483	housewife	48	"
	M	Clark Gerald P	1483	salesman	26	"
	N	Clark Mary E—†	1483	seamstress	49	"
	O	Deraney Nellie—†	1483	housewife	43	Salem
	P	Deraney Samuel M	1483	mechanic	45	"
	T	Clark Mary A—†	1485	retired	62	Lynn
	U	Cook Helena S—†	1485	seamstress	36	56 E Dedham
	V	Cook Herbert P	1485	machinist	41	56 "
	W	Carson Charles R	1485	laborer	52	23 Worcester
	X	Carson Jemillia—†	1485	housewife	32	23 "
	Y	Cameron Daniel	1485	carpenter	58	98 W Dedham
	Z	Segarri Carrie—†	1485	clerk	43	98 "
	A	Bernard Joseph	1489	fireman	43	here
	B	Better George	1489	elevatorman	71	"
	C	Brooker John H	1489	chauffeur	49	"
	D	Brown James W	1489	retired	56	408 Tremont
	E	Capocelly Patrick	1489	laborer	37	here
	F	Cormicar Thomas	1489	horseshoer	49	"
	G	Hauser Henry	1489	laborer	59	"
	H	Johnson Axel	1489	machinist	57	"
	K	Kelley John F	1489	teamster	53	2 Medford ct
	L	Lomonte Joseph	1489	cook	36	54 Oak
	M	Martin George	1489	barber	30	here
	N	Michard Alfred	1489	carpenter	26	Lynn

Page.	Letter.	FULL NAME.	Residence, April 1, 1926.	Occupation.	Supposed Age.	Reported Residence, April 1, 1925. Street and Number.

Washington Street—Continued

	o	Motto William	1489	laborer	59	Bath Me
	p	Riley James	1489	"	27	here
	v	Brennan Catherine—†	1501	domestic	48	Bath Me
	w	Brennan Raymond	1501	laborer	50	"
	u	Gidney Robert	1501	"	30	New York
	x	Shamas Annie—†	1501	housewife	29	here
	y	Haddad James	1503	merchant	36	"
	z	Haddad Louis	1503	barber	30	"
	٨	Haddad Phileminia—†	1503	housewife	30	"
	B	Lampeses Augusta—†	1503	"	24	"
	c	Lampeses Dorothy—†	1503	none	58	"
	D	Lampeses Louis	1503	retired	68	"
	E	Lampeses Spiro	1503	shoemaker	25	"
	K	Anderson Charles	1507	carpenter	68	"
	L	Barry James F	1507	painter	78	
	M	Coffey Mathew J	1507	laborer	69	25 Thornley
	N	Fralus Edward J	1507	shipper	46	here
	o	Griffon Walter	1507	roofer	52	422 Harris'n av
	p	Joudry Zilla A—†	1507	housekeeper	48	85 Burrell
	R	Kelley Charles A	1507	mechanic	50	here
	s	Kenneally Edward F	1507	painter	40	"
	T	McDonald David	1507	retired	82	Salem
	u	Miller Bessie I—†	1507	domestic	25	here
	v	Nye William J	1507	chauffeur	40	15 Union pk
	w	Parker Charles J	1507	meatcutter	67	here
	x	Patrone Antonio	1507	laborer	32	"
	y	Touney John C	1507	tinsmith	83	Bath Me
	A	Horne Isabella K—†	1513	housewife	38	New York
	B	Jerohna Anthony	1513	tailor	31	Bath Me
	c	Daley Mary—†	1513	bookbinder	36	here
	D	Dunkerton Sarah—†	1513	laundress	65	"
	E	Hatch Mary—†	1513	seamstress	70	"
	F	Reynolds Susie E—†	1513	bookbinder	46	"
	G	Smith Andrew E	1513	conductor	49	Salem
	H	Karkavdsos Helen—†	1513	housewife	24	"
	K	Karkavadsos Nicholas	1513	merchant	35	"
	L	Ross Annie K—†	1513	housewife	49	here
	M	Ross Ethel R—†	1513	stenographer	28	"
	N	Ross William	1513	manager	50	"
	o	Dugas Michael	1513	laborer	50	Bath Me
	p	Hassett Bertha—†	1513	housewife	26	New York

Washington Street—Continued

R	Seaver Helen—†	1513	housekeeper	44	1105 Wash'n
T	Corrigan Catherine—†	1513	waitress	38	here
U	Corrigan Louise—†	1513	clerk	21	"
V	Riley Collena—†	1513	housekeeper	50	"
W	Riley Margaret G—†	1513	clerk	36	"
X	Riley Michel J	1513	retired	65	"
Y	Anderson Carl R	1513	watchman	57	1469 Wash'n
Z	Crowell Henry A	1513	engineer	62	here
A	Crowell Mary—†	1513	housewife	60	"
B	Fitzgerald Alice—†	1513	"	41	"
C	Fitzgerald William	1513	waiter	42	"
D	Clarodo Louisa—†	1513	housewife	28	New York
E	Clarodo Michael	1513	tailor	40	"
G	Fitzgerald John C	1521	laborer	66	here
H	Fitzgerald Julia T—†	1521	housewife	41	"
K	Foley Charles	1521	chauffeur	41	"
L	Maloney Joseph	1521	retired	70	"
M	O'Neil John J	1521	laborer	59	"
N	Stickney Samuel T	1521	chauffeur	66	"
O	Merrill Grace—†	1521	housekeeper	39	"
P	Price Lillian—†	1521	brushmaker	24	Salem
R	Rigg John T	1521	salesman	37	here
S	Rushwood Mary—†	1521	domestic	42	480 Shawmut av
T	Vayo William	1521	baker	62	here
U	Chapman Olanson	1521	engineer	31	Bath Me
V	French Arthur E	1521	physician	37	here
W	French Clara L—†	1521	housewife	36	"
X	Kalos George T	1521	cook	25	Bath Me
Y	Melvin Clarence L	1521	retired	77	here
Z	Melvin Gertrude H—†	1521	housewife	61	"
A	Smith Jessie A—†	1521	dressmaker	56	"
B	Young Caroline E—†	1521	seamstress	51	Bath Me
C	Gelford Morris	1521	clerk	30	here
D	Gelfond William	1521	chauffeur	21	"
E	Kacavas George	1521	merchant	34	"
F	Kacavas John	1521	"	36	"
G	Killam Catherine M—†	1521	housewife	58	"
H¹	Killam Hiram E	1521	machinist	60	"
K	Maloney Daniel C	1521	fireman	41	"
L	Donovan Francis J	1521	waiter	56	"
M	Marshall Beatrice—†	1521	housekeeper	52	"

Washington Street—Continued

N	Marshall Mary— †	1521	stenographer	24	here
O	Yoriges Angelo	1521	merchant	45	"
P	Donovan Helen— †	1521	housewife	35	"
R	Donovan Timothy	1521	roofer	37	"
S	Murphy Margaret— †	1521	bookbinder	35	"
T	Murphy Patrick	1521	shipper	48	"
U	Tibbetts Ellen F— †	1521	housewife	43	"
V	Tibbetts James	1521	mechanic	43	"
W	Bearse Carrie— †	1521	retired	72	"
X	Carr Edna— †	1521	laundress	30	Salem
Y	Libby Berthram W	1521	clerk	54	here
Z	Libby Ethel F— †	1521	"	47	"
A	Libby Victor F	1521	lineman	24	"
B	Manning William	1521	salesman	35	2 James
C	Poulis John	1521	chef	36	here
D	Brewer Robert	1521	nurse	42	Bath Me
E	Cobb George E	1521	chauffeur	30	"
F	Enos Edward	1521	salesman	29	here
G	Horne Margaret— †	1521	actress	25	Bath Me
H	Saunders Delia— †	1521	housewife	59	"
K	Fletcher Gertrude— †	1521	waitress	32	here
L	Karlis Nicholas	1521	chef	35	"
M	Marchand Bertha— †	1521	dressmaker	37	"
N	Robicheau Louis	1521	chauffeur	30	Salem
O	Robicheau Mildred— †	1521	housewife	21	"
P	Shea Alice— †	1521	housekeeper	38	here
R	Workman Clara— †	1521	housewife	65	"
S	Workman George	1521	meatcutter	63	"
T	Clauson Charles	1521	carpenter	50	"
U	Estella Florence— †	1521	housewife	34	"
V	Ricker George	1521	elevatorman	26	Bath Me
W	Shannon Herman	1521	real estate	38	here

West Brookline Street

Z	Ahern Mary— †	61	retired	45	here
A	Ashton Eliza A— †	61	"	90	"
B	Avery Mary E— †	61	"	59	"
C	Barry Mary E— †	61	"	64	43 E Brookline
D	Bartz Christina— †	61	clerk	41	here

Page.	Letter.	FULL NAME.	Residence, April 1, 1926.	Occupation.	Supposed Age.	Reported Residence, April 1, 1925. Street and Number.

West Brookline Street—Continued

E	Bergen Johanna M—†	61	retired	78	here
F	Bovard Mary—†	61	maid	22	"
G	Brennan Hannah—†	61	retired	70	"
H	Buckley Julia A—†	61	"	66	"
K	Coffey Mary—†	61	attendant	65	"
L	Connolly Delia—†	61	retired	75	"
M	Counihan William R	61	engineer	20	"
N	Crowley Mary C—†	61	retired	70	"
P	Daley Martha A—†	61	maid	35	"
O	Daly Mary—†	61	retired	65	"
R	Doyle Hannah M—†	61	"	56	"
S	Dwyer Mary—†	61	milliner	60	"
T	Dunn Agnes—†	61	maid	58	"
U	Dunn Elizabeth—†	61	retired	72	Lynn
V	Dunphy Johanna—†	61	"	67	here
W	Fee Mary—†	61	laundress	65	"
X	Ferris Catherine—†	61	retired	60	"
Y	Finigan Catherine—†	61	laundress	60	43 E Brookline
Z	Foley Jane—†	61	retired	80	here
A	Forsyth Mary—†	61	"	70	"
B	Giard Rosalia—†	61	"	66	"
C	Glennon Mary—†	61	tailoress	65	"
D	Gray Helen—†	61	tel operator	28	Quincy
E	Hasenfus Catherine—†	61	houseworker	65	here
F	Hayes Annie—†	61	retired	77	215 Warren
G	Hourihan Hannah—†	61	"	70	135 Main
H	Hubbard Elizabeth—†	61	"	70	here
K	Igo Mary—†	61	"	80	43 E Brookline
L	Keefe Nora—†	61	waitress	60	here
M	Lee Susan—†	61	retired	75	"
N	Mahoney Margaret—†	61	"	65	Manchester N H
O	Mahoney Margaret A—†	61	"	67	Waltham
R	Martin Mary S—†	61	superior	60	here
S	McCorl Annie—†	61	retired	62	"
T	McGrath Elizabeth—†	61	maid	60	"
U	McGrath Winifred—†	61	retired	75	"
V	Mullins Mary—†	61	"	75	43 E Brookline
W	Murphy Hannah—†	61	"	60	here
X	Neally Myrtle L—†	61	houseworker	40	Worcester
Y	Nelson Katherine—†	61	maid	22	here
Z	Nerille Nora—†	61	retired	44	"

West Brookline Street— Continued

A	O'Brien John J	61	fireman	33	Quincy
B	O'Brien Mary—†	61	retired	70	here
C¹	O'Malley Mary—†	61	"	68	"
D	Quinn Delia—†	61	houseworker	55	"
E	Regan Catherine D—†	61	retired	64	"
F	Roberts Mary—†	61	"	65	"
G	Shalley Catherine—†	61	"	70	615 Centre
H	Sheridan Minnie—†	61	laundress	45	43 E Brookline
K	Stevens Mary—†	61	retired	72	here
L	Storen Nora—†	61	"	72	Hyde Park
M	Sullivan Elizabeth—†	61	"	72	here
N	Sullivan Mary—†	61	"	73	"
O	Sullivan Mary A—†	61	"	65	"
P	Tiernan Teresa B—†	61	"	69	"
R	Walsh Margaret—†	61	"	85	"
S	Walsh Nora M—†	61	"	67	"
T	Cushing Catherine—†	73	housewife	42	146 Warren av
U	Cushing Walter H	73	garageman	46	146 "
V	Hovsepian Eliezar H	73	storekeeper	38	here
W	Panenondas George	73	baker	35	1 Waterford
X	Panenondas Helen—†	73	retired	41	1 "
Y	Panenondas John	73	waiter	58	1 "
Z	Panenondas Nick	73	counterman	30	1 "
B	Theodonus Zoe	73	housewife	23	1 "
A	Theodonus John	73	electrician	29	Brookline
C	Torosian John	73	storekeeper	33	36 Sharon
D	Torosian Nonvart—†	73	housewife	22	36 "
E	Burns Thomas	73	barber	54	here
F	Murphy John F	73	bookkeeper	53	"
G	Murphy Margaret T—†	73	housewife	39	"
K	Baldes Fredrick	75	auto washer	36	"
L	Baldes May—†	75	laundryworker	31	"
M	Glynn Patrick	75	janitor	41	"
N	Jean Frank	75	factory worker	40	"
O	McDonald John W	75	laundryworker	30	70 W Newton
P	McDonald Margaret—†	75	"	36	70 "
R	Regan Patrick	75	laborer	40	here
S	Sanborn Julia—†	75	housekeeper	56	"
T	Doherty Fred	77	teamster	46	16 Groton
U	Ingham Annie—†	77	housewife	33	16 "
V	Ingham John H	77	chauffeur	34	16 "

West Brookline Street—Continued

w	Mahoney Martin D	77	painter	70	2 Garland
x	Shea Thomas F	77	shoecutter	37	16 Groton
y	Skivirk John	77	waiter	38	Connecticut
z	Foley Martin	79	billposter	40	36 Harrison
A	McDermot Maranet— †	79	housekeeper	65	here
B	Mulcare Nora—†	79	houseworker	50	"
C	Shallon William	79	teamster	35	16 Upton
E	Conroy Hannah— †	82	saleswoman	35	48 Gray
F	Percy Mary A—†	82	housekeeper	73	48 "
G	Rich Grace—†	82	"	23	here
H	Rich William	82	chauffeur	40	"
K	Berry Arthur	82	tallyman	27	Haverhill
L	Berry Pauline—†	82	housekeeper	26	"
M	Green Fred	82	laborer	28	here
N	Palen Louise—†	82	waitress	30	"
O	Daley Thomas	82	laborer	41	"
P	Dargan Ellen— †	82	housekeeper	40	"
R	Sheedy John T	82	ironworker	39	6 Worcester pl
S	Sheedy Mary G—†	82	housekeeper	34	6 "
T	Bitofsky Eli	83	plumber	27	22 Genesee
U	Killion Clarence	83	gardener	23	here
V	McKinnon Florence—†	83	houseworker	25	"
W	Rubin Harry	83	student	22	121 W Newton
X	Rubin May—†	83	housewife	22	121 "
Y	Thornton Catherine—†	83	laundress	26	35 Upton
Z	Williams Beatrice — †	83	housekeeper	31	here
A	Williams Harry J	83	salesman	39	"
C	Bornstien Ada— †	84	housekeeper	58	"
D	Bernstien Louis	84	tailor	60	"
E	Brewster Alice—†	84	housekeeper	33	"
F	Brewster Edward	84	fireman	35	"
G	Morrow Margaret— †	84	stitcher	41	"
K	Wiley Laura J— †	85	housekeeper	49	"
L	Archibald Greta C—†	85	clerk	29	"
M	Burkhard May—†	85	saleswoman	30	"
N	Jayne Almer W	85	inspector	29	36 Milford
O	Jayne Nellie D— †	85	housekeeper	20	36 "
P	Livingston Mary—†	85	housewife	50	here
R	Livingston William W	85	policeman	51	"
T	Harrall George	87	radioman	35	10 Melrose
U	Krally Harry	87	cook	25	79 W Brookline

	Letter.	Full Name.	Residence, April 1, 1926.	Occupation.	Supposed Age.	Reported Residence, April 1, 1925. Street and Number.

West Brookline Street—Continued

	Letter.	Full Name.	Res.	Occupation.	Age	Reported Residence
	V	Mattimore John J	87	cook	48	Illinois
	W	Roy Arthur	87	"	40	8 Cumston
	X	Roberts Alice—†	88	bookkeeper	57	here
	Y	Roberts Eliza A—†	88	retired	78	"
	Z	Connors Minnie—†	89	"	40	"
	A	Dailey Mary E—†	89	housekeeper	40	"
	B	Hughes Mary A—†	89	retired	73	"
	C	Hurley Lawrence M	89	repairer	50	"
	D	Stuart Josephine—†	89	stitcher	21	"
	E	Van Akin Lawrence	89	painter	35	"
	G	Frany Axel	91	laborer	27	"
	H	Holm Henry	91	"	30	Idaho
	K	Lennan Betty—†	91	rubberworker	30	Springfield
	L	Lennan Harold	91	"	28	"
	M	Martin Robert	91	decorator	29	here
	N	Mattson Eric	91	factory worker	24	Sweden
	O	Mattson Oscar	91	"	30	Everett
	P	Olson Allan	91	painter	29	here
	R	Olson Karin—†	91	housewife	27	"
	S	Chase Emily A—†	93	houseworker	52	"
	T	Chase George S	93	auto washer	60	"
	U	Fratus Mary A—†	93	housewife	50	"
	V	Fratus William H	93	retired	53	"
	W	Fratus William L	93	engineer	30	"
	X	Olson Henry P	93	longshoreman	31	"
	Y	Olson Mary—†	93	housewife	26	"
	Z	Eastman Ethel—†	94	housekeeper	25	"
	A	Grimes Frances—†	94	housewife	33	"
	B	Grimes Robert	94	shipper	35	"
	C	Locke Susie—†	94	housewife	48	"
	D	Norman Sadie—†	94	housekeeper	46	"
	E	Norman William	94	laborer	50	"
	F	Stride Charles	94	janitor	50	"
	G	Stride Rose—†	94	housewife	48	"
	H	O'Connell Mary—†	94	"	35	"
	K	O'Connell William	94	plumber	28	"
	L	Franze Frank	95	machinist	43	"
	M	Franze Giorgiana—†	95	housewife	30	"
	N	Sullivan Julia—†	95	housekeeper	43	333 Shawmut av
	O	Lairde Frank	95	painter	34	13 W Dedham
	P	Lairde Mary—†	95	housewife	30	13 "

Page	Letter	Full Name.	Residence, April 1, 1926.	Occupation.	Supposed Age.	Reported Residence, April 1, 1925. Street and Number.

West Brookline Street— Continued

R	Young Effie—†	95	housewife	36	155 Warren av
S	Young Joseph	95	building work'r	43	155 "
U	Donegan Ann—†	97	housewife	54	614 Tremont
V	Donovan Ella—†	97	"	50	here
W	Donovan Frank	97	retired	70	"
X	Gardner Leroy	97	U S A	32	614 Tremont
Y	Gardner Mary—†	97	housewife	30	here
Z	Johnson Ruth—†	98	housekeeper	28	"
A	Johnson William	98	teamster	46	"
B	Cherry Edgar	98	painter	27	"
C	Cherry Marcia—†	98	housewife	30	"
D	Daley Joseph A	98	watchman	53	"
E	Tobin Arthur M	98	tel tester	25	"
F	Tobin Frederick J	98	draftsman	26	"
G	Tobin Margaret A—†	98	houseworker	44	"
H	Tobin Margaret E—†	98	tel operator	22	"
O	Dorsey Joseph F	103	manager	42	"
P	Dorsey Louise—†	103	operator	32	"
R	O'Hara Mary—†	103	retired	54	7 Pembroke
T	Steele Celia C—†	105	dressmaker	45	here
U	Wormell Kate—†	105	operator	75	"
V	Ames Frederick	105	stableman	62	"
X	Cambell Catherine—†	111	housewife	55	"
Y	Granbays Delia—†	111	housekeeper	52	70 E Dedham
Z	Hill George A	111	painter	67	1 Arlington ter
A	Hill Margaret—†	111	housekeeper	58	1 "
B	Martin John	111	laundry worker	60	here
F	Chubb Elmer	119	boilermaker	52	"
G	Woodward Lena—†	119	housewife	34	"
H	Woodward Percy J	119	boilermaker	36	"
K	Carmon Agnes—†	119	factory worker	28	"
L	Carmon Florence—†	119	student	20	"
M	Carmon Mary—†	119	bookkeeper	25	"
N	McNeil Catherine—†	119	housewife	33	"
O	McNeil James	119	machinist	35	"
P	Achilos Angelo	119	waiter	41	"
R	Bakalos Despenet—†	119	housekeeper	32	"
S	Bakalos Steven	119	waiter	34	"
T	Klitarn Antaca—†	119	dishwasher	60	"
U	McEvoy Annie—†	119	housekeeper	53	"
V	McEvoy James F	119	cementfinisher	20	"

West Brookline Street—Continued

w	McEvoy John J	119	cementfinisher	52	here
x	McEvoy Mary—†	119	bookkeeper	21	"
y	Mansell Charles J	121	chauffeur	28	"
z	Mansell Catherine—†	121	housekeeper	58	"
A	Mansell Helen—†	121	saleswoman	25	"
B	Mansell Samuel F	121	candymaker	29	"
c	Keenan Annie—†	121	housewife	42	1084 Saratoga
D	Keenan John J	121	printer	43	1084 "
H	Fallon John W	126A	janitor	73	here
L	McAskill Daniel J	128	carpenter	30	"
M	McLean Archibald	128	"	79	"
N	McLean Margaret—†	128	housewife	64	"
o	McRury Annie—†	128	dressmaker	38	20½ St James
P	Wilton Richard	128	electrician	23	here
R	Riley Lena C—†	128	housewife	35	"
s	Riley Peter A	128	carpenter	36	"
T	Morrison Dorothy W—†	128	housekeeper	51	"
U	Nutter Albert C	128	metalworker	33	17 Dartmouth
v	Nutter Alice E—†	128	laundress	25	17 "
w	Kennedy Archibald	128	clerk	20	102 Appleton
x	Kennedy Sadie C †	128	housewife	41	Nova Scotia
y	Kennedy William J	128	carpenter	53	102 Appleton
z	Balfour Annie—†	128	laundress	46	here
A	Balfour Elizabeth—†	128	housekeeper	72	"
B	Balfour Tays	128	tinsmith	40	"
c	Wilkins William	128	plumber	58	"
D	MacKinnon Abigail—†	128	secretary	29	"
E	MacKinnon Alexander	128	carpenter	62	"
F	MacKinnon Mary—†	128	housewife	69	"
N	Clifton Margaret—†	130	housekeeper	45	"
o	Mathson Florence—†	130	domestic	50	Nova Scotia
P	Arbean Robert	130	laborer	43	here
R	Carter Mathew	130	"	60	"
s	Johnson Anna M—†	130	housekeeper	39	"
T	Nassau Thomas	130	barber	40	"
U	Royal Marie—†	130	laundress	30	"
v	Ryan John J	130	teamster	35	"
w	Sullivan Charles E	130	clerk	37	"
x	Alderman Fred C	130	foreman	50	Cambridge
y	Arsnault Fidel	130	salesman	29	here
z	Cresswell Frances—†	130	domestic	60	"

West Brookline Street—Continued

A	Cunie Mary—†	130	retired	70	Malden
B	Macauley Rachel—†	130	housekeeper	58	here
C	Roy Donalda M—†	130	bookkeeper	24	"
D	Roy Ralph	130	machinist	27	"
E	Bradford John	130	carpenter	40	Brookline
F	Mackeigan Annie—†	130	housekeeper	38	15 Warren av
G	Mackeigan Donald	130	carpenter	53	15 "
M	Macvicar Effie—†	130	houseworker	53	39 Appleton
L	McMillan Mary—†	130	operator	21	Nova Scotia
H	McGuire Annie—†	130	houseworker	70	15 Warren av
K	McQuaig Clarence	130	laborer	20	Malden
N	McKay Norman	130	"	26	Norwood
O	Morrison Daniel	130	floorlayer	42	39 Appleton
P	Toomey Catherine—†	130	seamstress	67	39 "
R	Fleming Patrick	130	inspector	37	here
S	Nyhan Harold	130	clerk	23	"
T	Quin Alexander	130	chauffeur	23	"
U	Shea John	130	clerk	23	"
V	Shea Margaret—†	130	tel operator	22	"
W	Blake Frank	130	janitor	60	"
X	Duffy Malachi	130	chauffeur	27	Brookline
Y	Frizzell Mannie—†	130	housekeeper	56	here
Z	Harrington Evelyn—†	130	waitress	33	128 W Brookline
A	O'Brien Walter	130	manager	40	Malden
C	Smith Fred	131	baker	30	Revere
D	Smith Sarah—†	133	housewife	35	"

West Canton Street

C	Lamont Anna—†	5	inspector	24	here
D	Lamont Catherine—†	5	housewife	52	"
E	Lamont Helen—†	5	operator	23	"
F	Lamont Samuel	5	hostler	52	"
G	Lyons John	5	laborer	49	"
H	Gegas Josephine—†	5	housewife	42	Lowell
K	Isgur Emma—†	5	"	36	Billerica
L	Isgur Jacob	5	florist	38	"
M	Morrow Matilda—†	5	housewife	62	82 E Canton
N	Tupper Mildred—†	5	"	25	82 "
V	McClure Annie—†	29	"	33	27 Dover

Page.	Letter.	FULL NAME.	Residence, April 1, 1926.	Occupation.	Supposed Age.	Reported Residence, April 1, 1925. Street and Number.

West Canton Street— Continued

	W	McClure John	29	laborer	35	27 Dover
	X	Ducy Thomas	29	busboy	27	44 Sharon
	Y	Mossey Lillian—†	29	housewife	42	44 "
	C	Bowie Edgar	32	chauffeur	24	here
	D	Joy Harry B	32	laborer	35	"
	E	Nickerson Emma—†	32	housewife	39	"
	F	Nickerson Morton C	32	laborer	52	"
	G	Chamberlain Sanford	33	salesman	61	"
	H	Leonard Gaylord	33	laborer	65	77 Shawmut av
	K	Mason Frank	33	painter	45	Cambridge
	L	Powell Mary E—†	33	housewife	46	here
	M	Reardon Daniel	33	retired	70	"
	N	Sullivan Timothy	33	"	64	"
	O	Young George	33	builder	61	"
	T	Greene Frances R—†	46	dressmaker	24	"
	U	Greene Nellie E—†	46	hairdresser	47	"
	V	Greene William S	46	porter	54	"
	X	Tilton Mary E—†	48	laundress	38	"
	Y	Johnson Abraham W	48	barber	47	"
	Z	Johnson Alice—†	48	housewife	45	"
	A	Johnson James H	48	painter	21	"
	B	Payne James C	48	cook	22	"
	D	Henderson Alice—†	50	housewife	53	1 Northampton
	E	Henderson Gertrude—†	50	factory worker	30	1 "
	F	Henderson James H	50	clerk	29	1 "
	G	Henderson James H	50	porter	56	1 "
	G¹	Henderson Richard E	50	chauffeur	22	1 "
	P	Buchanan Beatrice R—†	59	housewife	48	here
	R	Buchanan James O	59	laborer	53	"
	S	Easterling Dorothy—†	59	elevatorwoman	25	"
	T	Snyder Helen R—†	59	housewife	24	Westerly R I
	U	Waldron Emma T—†	60	"	38	here
	V	Waldron Thomas J	60	engineer	48	"
	W	Quigley Michael J	60	clerk	50	"
	X	Murray James E	63	"	29	78 W Canton
	Y	Powers Margaret—†	63	housekeeper	74	here
	A	Daley Daniel J	64	chauffeur	36	"
	B	Daley Mary B—†	64	housewife	34	"
	C	Engle Theresa—†	65	laundress	37	"
	D	Bibby Annie—†	65	housekeeper	58	"
	E	Bibby Bartlett W	65	wireless op'r	22	"

West Canton Street—Continued

F	Serene Alexander		65	grocer	38	here
G	Serene Sadie—†		65	millworker	33	"
K	Freeley Austin		67	laborer	63	"
L	Kirby William		67	"	63	"
M	Tully James		67	"	41	"
N	Tully Winifred—†		67	housewife	41	"
O	Maloney Catherine †		71	"	29	43 Newland
P	Maloney John		71	fireman	33	43 "
R	Jones Mary—†		73	housekeeper	40	Hull
S	Douglas Anna—†		73	"	30	here
T	Douglas Samuel		73	laborer	32	"
X	Kelley Marie L †		78	housewife	55	"
Y	Kelley William J		78	ironworker	60	"
Z	Gordon Thomas J		78	painter	46	"
A	Maguire Francis		79	"	57	"
B	Maguire Jenneatte—†		79	housewife	45	"
C	MacDonald Anna L—†		79	housekeeper	50	"
D	MacDonald Ronald		79	carpenter	49	"
F	Betts Harold W		82	chauffeur	29	16 Upton
G	Betts Jennie C—†		82	housewife	40	16 "
H	Keenan Evangline—†		82	"	29	21 Pembroke
K	Keenan Frank S		82	painter	29	21 "
L	Runnals Alice M—†		82	housewife	30	7 Newland
M	Runnals Nelson S		82	garageman	33	7 "
O	De Ossie Paul		86	upholsterer	27	here
P	De Ossie Pearl M—†		86	housewife	24	"
R	De Ossie Robert F		86	machinist	20	"
S	Dern Hellen—†		86	housewife	24	"
T	Dern Louis		86	painter	28	"
V	Marceau August H	rear 88	tailor	61	"
W	Guigge Sophie—†	" 88	cook	50	"
X	Messick Miles	" 88	carpenter	73	"
Y	Volk Harriet—†	" 88	housekeeper	63	579 Tremont
Z	Kidd John	" 88	engineer	57	here
B	Reddington Thomas	" 88	machinist	50	"
C	Sullivan Catherine—†		90	maid	39	"
D	Sullivan Patrick J		90	bricklayer	39	"
E	Howe Lillian—†		90	cook	42	"
F	Buckley Helena—†		90	laundress	65	"
G	Ross Frank		90	cook	56	"
H	Cochran Frederick A		90	laborer	53	94 W Canton

47

Page	Letter	FULL NAME.	Residence, April 1, 1925.	Occupation.	Supposed Age.	Reported Residence, April 1, 1925. Street and Number.

West Canton Street—Continued

Letter	FULL NAME.	Residence	Occupation.	Age	Reported Residence
K	Cochran Isabella M —†	90	housewife	33	94 W Canton
L	Campbell Mary †	90	laundress	45	here
M	Perkins Annie E—†	90	pianist	60	638 Harris'n av
P	Jones Maud †	94	packer	35	here
R	Robideau Wilfred	94	silversmith	23	"
S	McKaskle Annie †	94	cook	55	"
T	Kirby William	94	driver	46	"
V	Sheehan Ella †	98	housekeeper	56	"
W	Sheehan John	98	chauffeur	20	"
X	O'Leary Helen †	98	housekeeper	24	"
Y	O'Leary Richard T	98	chauffeur	25	"
A	Downey Charles	100	"	30	104 W Canton
B	Downey Margaret—†	100	housewife	28	104 "
C	Cleary Edward F	100	mason	49	here
D	Cleary Ivy M—†	100	housekeeper	47	"
E	Taylor Howard	100	carpenter	30	"
F	Wagner Rita †	100	saleswoman	27	"
G	Slater Joseph	100	chauffeur	30	"
M	Redding Catherine —†	104	cook	48	"
N	Toms Margaret—†	104	housekeeper	47	"
P	Hagerty Beatrice —†	108	housewife	25	"
R	Hagerty Frederick T	108	spinner	36	"
S	McElroy Harold	108	laborer	27	"
T	White Bertha F—†	108	housekeeper	53	"
U	Dyer Catherine †	108	cook	60	Brookline
V	Daniels Eugene	108	"	45	here
W	Daniels Genevieve —†	108	housekeeper	27	"
X	Covey Alice L †	110	housewife	57	"
Y	Covey Frank E	110	painter	63	"
Z	Covey Leslie E	110	cook	33	"
A	Mariner Daisy —†	110	"	35	"
B	Stevens Edward N	110	student	26	"
C	Stevens Elleanor C—†	110	housekeeper	23	"
D	McGovern Mary—†	110	"	60	121 W Canton
E	Foley Mary—†	110	"	66	here
F	Gould Robert	110	cook	38	"
G	Hearle James	111	watchman	50	"
H	Hearle Josephine †	111	housewife	60	"
K	Tulty Mary—†	111	housekeeper	70	"
N	Bacon Catherine E—†	115–119	"	68	"

West Canton Street—Continued

O	Bacon William E	115–119	foreman	39	here
R	Olson Helen G—†	115–119	housekeeper	21	"
S	Olson James J	115–119	jam maker	22	"
T	Kirby David T	116	mechanic	46	"
U	Kirby Mary G—†	116	housekeeper	66	"
V	Curran Emma M—†	116	housewife	30	"
W	Curran William J	116	printer	32	"
X	Gilbert Alfred D	116	fisherman	47	"
Y	Gilbert Clara H—†	116	housewife	52	"
C	Allen Charles	122	salesman	23	"
D	Allen Dora—†	122	housekeeper	55	"
E	Allen Ralph	122	pressman	32	"
F	Allen Ruby—†	122	bookkeeper	29	"
K	Jones Anthony A	125	mason	54	"
L	Jones Catherine—†	125	housewife	54	"
M	Sam Lee	126	laundryman	52	"
O	McKenna Ella—†	128	housewife	53	"
P	McKenna Terence	128	ironmolder	62	"
S	MacGuire Frederick M	128	shipper	42	"
T	MacGuire Lavinia A—†	128	housewife	38	"
Z	Miller Elizabeth J—†	135	housekeeper	41	"
A	Miller Hedley J	135	chauffeur	43	Wellesley
B	Panos Constantinos	135	storekeeper	35	here
C	Panos Sophie—†	135	housekeeper	25	"
E	Doans Mary E—†	135	"	50	"
F	Rodman Michael	135	butcher	49	Stoughton
G	Lyman David	135	waiter	42	here
H	Lyman Lena—†	135	housewife	38	"
K	Ruckoffe Bernard	135	storekeeper	45	"
L	Tidd Ethel M—†	135	dressmaker	34	"
M	Thomas Minnie—†	135	housekeeper	62	"
N	Thomas Oscar W	135	packer	62	"
O	Fitzgerald Alice—†	135	saleswoman	36	"
P	Fitzgerald John J	135	inspector	39	"
R	Fitzgerald Mary—†	135	housewife	65	"
S	Fitzpatrick Patrick	135	watchman	64	"
T	Ellison Adelaide—†	135	housekeeper	65	

West Dedham Street

B	Hill Louise—†	rear 12	housewife	44	here
C	Hill Willis H	" 12	janitor	45	"
D	Reaves Luther	" 12	laborer	37	"
E	Smith Edward	14	painter	40	"
F	Wildes Mary G—†	14	housekeeper	74	"
G	Cunningham Bridget—†	14	"	53	"
H	Connors Annie—†	14	housewife	33	40 Dartmouth
K	Connors Patrick J	14	porter	35	40 "
L	Tingley Hattie—†	14	stitcher	30	here
M	Chandler William	15	shipper	21	Claremont N H
N	Grozinger Charles L	15	toolmaker	51	15 Newland
O	Hayes Mary—†	15	stitcher	56	here
P	Hill William	15	cook	55	"
R	Jones Dora—†	15	housewife	30	New Brunswick
S	Jones Walter	15	butcher	36	"
T	Landers Alice—†	15	instructor	29	here
U	Landers Hannah—†	15	housekeeper	64	"
V	Landers Margaret—†	15	"	33	"
W	Landers Michael	15	retired	64	"
X	Merintz Herman	15	mechanic	36	E Douglass
Y	Ross Catherine—†	15	housekeeper	40	Canada
Z	Ross Margaret—†	15	"	50	"
A¹	Caldwell Annie—†	17	"	70	here
B	Fautch Emma—†	17	clerk	27	Plymouth
C	Ford Dennis	17	retired	55	474 Shawmut av
D	Gillis John	17	engineer	46	here
E	Jackson Jennie—†	17	retired	70	"
F	McDonald John	17	engineer	62	"
G	McDonald John F	17	plumber	63	"
H	McDonald Mary E—†	17	housekeeper	43	"
K	McLean Peter	17	laborer	30	"
L	McLean Roxie—†	17	housewife	27	"
M	McSorley Roger	17	porter	62	"
N	Roche Oscar	17	cook	22	Malden
O	Shelos Peter	17	"	27	here
P	Swett Charles	17	shoemaker	23	Lynn
R	Thayer Mary—†	17	retired	72	23 E Concord
S	Freaney Alice M—†	18	chiropodist	41	here
T	Molloy Elizabeth M—†	18	housekeeper	56	"

Page.	Letter	FULL NAME.	Residence, April 1, 1926.	Occupation.	Supposed Age.	Reported Residence, April 1, 1925. Street and Number.

West Dedham Street— Continued

	U	Molloy Julia B—†	18	chiropodist	40	here
	V	Molloy Mary A—†	18	"	52	"
	W	Bosdanjoglon Aneta—†	19	missionary	33	613 Mass av
	X	Brubaker Henry G	19	student	27	Grantham Pa
	Y	Constantine George	19	baker	35	10 Cobb
	Z	Reed George	19	student	26	Somerville
	A	Robertson Mary—†	19	stitcher	40	613 Mass av
	B	Sarro Nicholas	19	ironworker	27	Chelsea
	C	Sarro Olive—†	19	housewife	24	"
	D	Yphantis Paul	19	student	27	10 Cobb
	E	Yphantis Santouh—†	19	housekeeper	55	10 "
	F	Coakley Ellen—†	20	"	70	here
	G	Higgins Richard	20	laborer	55	"
	H	Howard Elizabeth—†	20	dressmaker	45	"
	K	Pantagis John	20	cook	30	Cambridge
	L	Quinlan Thomas	20	laborer	45	10 Rutland
	M	Sweeney Anne—†	20	cook	70	here
	N	Sweeney Maria—†	20	at home	66	"
	O	Bannon Anna—†	21	housewife	37	Cambridge
	P	Bannon Thomas	21	chauffeur	40	"
	R	Costine Michael	21	laborer	35	14 E Canton
	S	Costine Peggy—†	21	clerk	30	14 "
	T	Cronin James	21	mechanic	45	18 "
	U	Dentrimont Marie—†	21	waitress	46	here
	V	Domit Joseph	21	retired	89	"
	W	Domit Sadie—†	21	housewife	50	"
	X	Mahoney Michael	21	laborer	50	35 W Dedham
	Y	Sumner Catherine—†	21	retired	75	378 Shawmut av
	Z	Xipidias Catherine—†	21	stitcher	28	here
	A	Zipidias George	21	cook	30	"
	B	Duffy Mabel—†	22	housekeeper	25	New Brunswick
	C	Eldridge Charles	22	attendant	22	13 Irving
	D	England Albert W	22	laborer	32	420 Mass av
	E	Lyman William	22	"	33	1402 Wash'n
	F	Monleson John P	22	cook	41	29 Lynde
	G	Scully Joseph	22	salesman	30	13 Irving
	H	Strout William	22	chef	53	Arlington
	K	Webb Catherine T—†	22	housewife	25	4 Vinton
	L	Webb Thomas	22	chauffeur	28	New York
	M	Averill Charles	23	painter	38	111 W Brookline
	N	Averill Mary—†	23	housewife	35	111 "

51

Page.	Letter.	FULL NAME.	Residence, April 1, 1926.	Occupation.	Supposed Age.	Reported Residence, April 1, 1925. Street and Number.

West Dedham Street—Continued

o	Grasso Carmelo	23	sailor	36	605 Tremont
o¹	Grasso Fannie —†	23	laundress	30	605 "
P	Jennings Edward J	23	laborer	40	23 Magazine
R	John Lettie —†	23	housewife	33	433 Shawmut av
s	Landsay Charles D	23	mechanic	35	21 W Dedham
T	Lindsay Nellie—†	23	housewife	29	21 "
U	Logan Margaret —†	23	"	38	50 Pembroke
V	Logan Michael	23	laborer	40	50 "
W	St Pierre Edward	23	cook	40	Peterboro N H
X	Welch Joseph	23	retired	56	here
Y	Winters John	23	laborer	50	Chelsea
Z	Young Dell	23	student	35	43 Rutland sq
B	Singleton Helen —†	24	housewife	34	here
C	Singleton Theodore	24	laborer	45	"
D	Noel Athlin —†	24	housewife	38	"
E	Noel Wellington D	24	carpenter	40	"
F	Baldwin Herbert	25	painter	55	"
G	Brewster Dorothy —†	25	cook	22	"
H	Curran Thomas	25	salesman	45	"
K	Fisher Joseph	25	roofer	48	"
L	Jennings John	25	mechanic	42	6 Union Park
M	Keefe John K	25	teamster	58	here
N	Kincaid Rita A —†	25	housekeeper	43	"
O	McDonald John	25	machinist	41	"
P	Noyes Mary E—†	25	saleswoman	45	"
R	Perry George V	25	laborer	48	"
S	Perry Mabel —†	25	housewife	46	"
T	Saunders William G	25	machinist	39	"
U	Taylor Elsie—†	25	saleswoman	36	23 W Dedham
V	Collins Daniel	26	freighthandler	37	28 Rollins
W	Donaghue Agnes —†	26	housekeeper	50	516 Shawmut av
X	Donaghue Henry	26	laborer	58	516 "
Y	Higgins Daniel	26	boilermaker	56	here
Z	Hill Emma —†	26	housekeeper	65	37 W Dedham
A	Long John	26	retired	56	here
B	McCarthy Helen —†	26	housekeeper	47	"
C	McCormack Sarah—†	26	"	47	"
D	Mooney Leo	26	laborer	43	"
E	Moran James	26	"	58	"
F	Moran Mary—†	26	housekeeper	49	"
G	Sullivan Daniel	26	plumber	49	5 Newland

West Dedham Street—Continued

H	Taft David	26	iceman	41	here
K	Taft Gertrude —†	26	housekeeper	45	"
L	Bunker Anna T—†	28	maid	42	"
M	Bunker George H	28	salesman	55	"
N	Baker Gertrude —†	28	housewife	37	"
O	Abbot Elizabeth —†	28	housekeeper	60	"
P	Goldberg Lena —†	28	housewife	30	4 Wilkes
R	Goldberg Morris	28	tailor	40	4 "
S	Lurie Mattes	28	salesman	55	Newton
T	Kutuchian Jacob	28	laborer	48	here
U	Kutuchian Mary—†	28	housekeeper	46	"
V	Graham Frank	29	engineer	22	"
W	Graham John	29	printer	28	"
X	Graham Marwell	29	mason	50	"
Y	Graham Mary—†	29	housewife	48	"
Z	Argeras Harry	30	shoemaker	30	"
A	Argeras Lena —†	30	housewife	25	"
B	Crehan Delia—†	30	housekeeper	35	46 E Dedham
C	Childs Bessie —†	30	milliner	48	here
D	Pickard Albert	30	janitor	46	"
G	Paraskeva Dimitro	33	roofer	50	19 W Dedham
H	Paraskeva Sophia—†	33	housewife	39	19 "
K	Mayo Cecilia—†	35	housekeeper	27	here
L	Mayo Frank	35	paperhanger	49	"
R	Rohan Francis	43	clerk	24	"
S	Rohan Isabella —†	43	housekeeper	55	"
T	Rohan John A	43	salesman	27	"
W	Obanion Mary—†	46	shoeworker	36	"
X	Smith James	46	laborer	75	31 Fabyan
Y	Taylor Ida—†	48	seamstress	43	here
Z	Taylor Richard	48	machinist	40	"
A	Patenaude Marie F—†	49	housewife	28	"
B	Patenaude Philip H	49	painter	34	"
C	Barrett Elizabeth L—†	49	housewife	42	"
D	Barrett Thomas J	49	clerk	40	"
E	Shaughnessy Anna—†	49	housekeeper	64	"
F	Shaughnessy John H	49	clerk	38	"
G	Wright Florence—†	49	"	40	"
H	Wright Henry S	49	"	45	"
K	Doyle Marie—†	49	operator	41	"
L	Burke Pearl—†	49	housewife	38	"

Page	Letter	FULL NAME	Residence April 1 1926.	Occupation.	Supposed Age.	Reported Residence, April 1, 1925. Street and Number.

West Dedham Street—Continued

	Letter	FULL NAME	Res.	Occupation	Age	Residence
	M	Burke William H	49	packer	37	here
	N	McPherson Mary F—†	49	real estate	43	"
	O	McPherson Thomas R	49	"	43	"
	R	Hoevelman Mary—†	50	housewife	30	"
	S	Hoevelman William	50	teamster	32	"
	T	Holthaus John	50	upholsterer	57	"
	U	Holthaus Joseph	50	laborer	68	"
	V	Moore Charles	50	"	23	"
	W	Early Harry	52	retired	52	"
	X	Early Mary J—†	52	laundress	52	"
	Y	Sullivan Annie—†	53	housewife	50	"
	Z	Sullivan Timothy C	53	baker	60	"
	A	Burke Bridget—†	53	housekeeper	50	"
	B	Cooper Helen—†	53	"	42	"
	C	Cooper Mary—†	53	clerk	20	"
	D	Engram Lydia—†	53	housekeeper	35	366 Shawmut av
	E	Engram William	53	carpenter	35	366 "
	G	Heffernan Daniel	55	bricklayer	25	200 Col av
	H	Heffernan Frances—†	55	housekeeper	21	200 "
	K	Burke Mary—†	55	"	45	here
	L	Whitehead Elsie—†	55	"	45	"
	M	Whitehead Frank	55	mechanic	22	"
	N	O'Keefe Annie—†	55	housekeeper	62	"
	P	Chaisson Mary—†	56	waitress	58	371 Col av
	R	Chaisson Theodore A	56	locksmith	55	371 "
	S	Costa Jeremiah	56	cabinetmaker	22	Cambridge
	T	Santy Joseph C	56	student	27	328 Shawmut av
	V	Cameron Archibald	58	carpenter	57	here
	W	Coffey Anna—†	58	clerk	23	"
	X	Hosmer Harry P	58	electrician	46	"
	Z	Elias Amelia—†	62	housewife	29	32 Dartmouth
	A	Elias Charles	62	shoemaker	38	32 "
	B	Borsari Colie	62	machinist	25	32 "
	C	Borsari Mary—†	62	housewife	20	32 "
	D	McCabe John	62	laborer	23	464 Shawmut av
	G	Lee Angie—†	68	housewife	60	here
	H	Lee William H	68	electroplater	57	"
	M	Basques Margaret—†	80	housewife	38	"
	N	Garcia Manuel	80	chauffeur	45	"
	O	Grant John	80	laborer	35	"

West Dedham Street– Continued

P	Bennet Hilda—†	80	forewoman	23	130 W Brookline
R	Bennet May—†	80	cook	55	130 "
S	Halloway Arthur	80	engineer	50	130 "
T	Bruce Charles W	80	timekeeper	69	134 Hunt'n av
U	Bruce Emily—†	80	housewife	59	134 "
V	Kiley Elizabeth T—†	84	storekeeper	42	here
W	Fraser Mary—†	86	housekeeper	51	"
X	Fraser Morris	86	hostler	51	"
Y	Bittenhoffer John	88	baker	65	"
Z	Kispert Andrew	88	"	49	"
A	Kispert Rose—†	88	housewife	48	"
B	Kramer Herman	88	baker	22	Germany
C	Kramer William	88	"	23	here
D	Allen Ethel—†	88	maid	34	"
G	Tegnell Anna—†	88	masseuse	21	"
F	Tegnell Annetta—†	88	housewife	38	"
H	Tegnell Ellen—†	88	maid	24	"
E	Tegnell Emel	88	painter	42	"
L	Davis William	92	electrician	37	"
M	Regan James M	92	machinist	48	"
N	Regan Theresa—†	92	housewife	39	"
P	Smith Hannah E—†	92	"	66	"
R	Smith Patrick J	92	riveter	58	"
S	McIsaac Delia J—†	94	housekeeper	49	"
T	McIsaac John J	94	carpenter	50	"
U	Horton Alvira—†	94	housewife	20	579 Col av
V	Horton James	94	assembler	27	579 "
W	Berry Rachel—†	94	housekeeper	70	here
Y	Crowley Lillian—†	96	"	65	"
Z	Maher James	96	shipper	65	"
C	Morrison Granville	98	carpenter	35	Canada
D	Morrison Maud—†	98	housewife	25	"
E	Morrison Roderick	98	carpenter	67	"
H	Interest Barney	100	stonemason	52	here
K	Interest Ethel—†	100	bookkeeper	21	"
L	Interest Rosa—†	100	storekeeper	50	"
M	Brooks Thomas C	101	contractor	58	"
N	Betts Sydney	102	carpenter	60	"
O	Brown Herbert	102	cooper	57	"
P	Case Elias	102	salesman	60	"

Page.	Letter.	FULL NAME.	Residence, April 1, 1926.	Occupation.	Supposed Age.	Reported Residence, April 1, 1925. Street and Number.

West Dedham Street— Continued

R	Colley Florence V—†	102	housewife	52	Stoneham
S	Colley Frank T	102	druggist	57	"
T	Currier Elizabeth—†	102	milliner	28	Burlington Vt
U	Harrington Teana—†	102	clerk	58	here
V	Martines Ethel—†	102	waitress	37	"
W	McIsaac Hector	102	laborer	30	"
X	McIsaac Theresa—†	102	housewife	29	"
Y	O'Connor William	102	painter	45	"
Z	Tapan Mamie—†	102	housekeeper	37	"
A	Wildanger Jacob	102	engineer	47	"
B	Cleary Helen T—†	103	housekeeper	38	"
C	Cleary James J	103	mason	42	"
D	McKennon Sadie A—†	103	operator	47	"
E	Whelan Margaret—†	103	retired	73	"
F	Cranbrook Anna B—†	105	housewife	70	"
G	Cranbrook John H	105	retired	77	"
H	Gorham James	105	janitor	46	"
K	Gorham Mary—†	105	housekeeper	48	"
L	Garrett Bennie	105	chauffeur	28	"
M	Garrett Iva M—†	105	housewife	35	"

Ward 9—Precinct 2

CITY OF BOSTON.

LIST OF RESIDENTS
20 YEARS OF AGE AND OVER

(FEMALES INDICATED BY DAGGER)

AS OF

APRIL 1, 1926

HERBERT A. WILSON, } Listing

JAMES F. EAGAN, { Board.

CITY OF BOSTON—PRINTING DEPARTMENT

Page	Letter	Full Name.	Residence, April 1, 1926.	Occupation.	Supposed Age.	Reported Residence, April 1, 1925. Street and Number.

Cumston Place

A	Clark Annie —†	1	housewife	32	Malden
B	Clark George N	1	laborer	28	"
C	Nelson John	1	"	27	here
D	Noltey Lucille —†	2	laundress	28	"
E	Winkey Robert	2	auto mechanic	32	233 Northampton
F	Diggs Frank	3	brakeman	40	here
G	Grace Manuel	3	laborer	20	New Bedford
H	Jackson Pearl—†	3	houseworker	34	here
K	Davis Marie—†	4	housewife	40	"
L	Parsons Abram	4	laborer	62	"
M	Parsons Susan J—†	4	housewife	50	"
N	Villas Andrew	4	dishwasher	55	"

Cumston Street

S	Betume Joseph	1	carpenter	40	Pennsylvania
P	Dyer Lounana—†	1	housewife	39	here
R	Dyer Septumus	1	laborer	40	"
U	Conklin Herman	2	janitor	20	"
T	Conklin Mary—†	2	laundress	43	"
V	Conklin William	2	postal clerk	22	"
W	Johnson Flossie—†	2	cook	51	"
X	Smith Loretta—†	2	"	28	Wash'n D C
Y	Smith William	2	chauffeur	35	"
Z	Cannon Marion E—†	3	car cleaner	48	here
A	Forone William H	3	laborer	46	"
B	Gray John W	3	mechanic	46	1069 Wash'n
C	Jackson Richard	3	laborer	51	here
D	Hayes Margaret—†	4	housewife	23	543 Shawmut av
E	Hayes Mary—†	4	at home	50	148 Northampton
F	Hayes Stanley D P	4	longshoreman	23	3 Wentworth pl
G	Hayes Vincent	4	"	21	554 Shawmut av
H	Allen Dora—†	5	housewife	67	here
K	Anderson Andreas	5	laborer	45	"
L	Euarkhart Finley	5	retired	65	"
M	Bennett Emma—†	5	laundress	55	57 Rutland
N	Murphy Margaret—†	5	housewife	65	here
O	Winslow Louisa—†	5	"	30	"
P	Casey Frank J	5	teamster	53	222 Shawmut av

2

Cumston Street—Continued

R	Casey Mary—†	5	housewife	43	222 Shawmut av
S	Davis William	5	salesman	55	here
T	Jordan Emma—†	5	at home	70	44 E Brookline
V	Osborn George E	7	janitor	73	here
W	Osborn Mary A—†	7	housekeeper	50	"
X	Docket James	8	janitor	27	Rhode Island
Y	McCloud Turner	8	cook	30	Virginia
Z	Wood Sarah A—†	8	houseworker	60	73 Emerald

Haven Street

A	Conitho Marie—†	1	housewife	50	9 Pembroke
B	Conitho Salvitone	1	retired	70	9 "
C	Paivo Mary—†	2	housewife	25	Maine
D	Paivo Michael	2	counterman	33	"
E	Shaw Frank E	3	steamfitter	44	Franklin N H
F	Bishop David	4	pedler	45	here
G	Featherston Sam W	4	laborer	75	19 Albion
H	Heath Maude M—†	4	housewife	47	here
K	Arsenault Alice—†	5	"	43	"
L	Arsenault Joseph	5	roofer	49	"
N	Holland Wilfred	5	baker	25	"

Newland Street

O	Andrew Nicholas N	75	mixer	32	here
P	Fleming Alice G—†	75	housekeeper	34	"
R	McCall William	75	chef	34	Pennsylvania
T	Garrett Cayde	77	janitor	52	here
U	Flood Munroe J	77	porter	64	"
V	Berg Adele R—†	84	housewife	34	Malden
W	Berg Henry B	84	janitor	34	"
Y	Downes Charles E	88	clerk	59	here
Z	Downes Clara E—†	88	housewife	59	"
A	Clarke Lavenia—†	88½	"	80	"
B	Conner Frank F	88½	painter	58	"
C	Burke Cressida—†	90	housekeeper	52	"
D	Burke Octavius	90	retired	76	"

3

Newland Street—Continued

E	McDonald Margaret—†	90½	laundress	53	here
F	Peterson Alden W	92	student	23	"
G	Peterson Ida C—†	92	housewife	60	"

Pembroke Street

H	Alexander Gabriel	8	manager	42	here
K	Alexander Mary—†	8	housekeeper	51	"
L	Booth Waldo E	8	clerk	25	"
M	Bowser Hazel—†	8	housekeeper	31	"
N	Bowser Roy G	8	clerk	32	"
O	Braitch Frank	8	mechanic	25	29 Lamartine
P	Carpenter Charles E	8	clerk	59	here
R	Colwell Thomas	8	retired	73	35 Main
S	Garvin Michael J	8	printer	35	here
T	Gutta Henry	8	waiter	33	"
U	Hall Burton F	8	clerk	33	"
V	Jiggs Joseph	8	cook	24	Springfield
W	Lenard Arthur	8	steamfitter	30	here
X	MacDonald Robert J	8	manager	45	"
Y	Rauh Carl	8	salesman	32	"
Z	Russell Allen D	8	clerk	54	"
A	Villard Frank	8	special police	63	"
B	Villard Mary—†	8	housekeeper	59	"
C	Courtney Martin H	10	clerk	38	324 Geneva av
D	Duffily James O	10	manager	35	91 River
E	Gise Carl	10	pianist	30	here
F	Hickey Michael J	10	grinder	29	"
G	Kfegh Alex	10	counterman	38	42 Upton
H	Krous Arthur	10	waiter	30	here
K	Monteith Annie †	10	housekeeper	45	"
L	Morrison Daniel A	10	blacksmith	60	"
M	Perry Joseph W	10	cabinetmaker	70	"
N	Quinn John	10	machinist	28	12 Cottage ct
O	Tarry William	10	baker	38	here
P	Task Isreal	10	tailor	46	"
R	Brennan Ella †	12	housewife	24	748 Tremont
S	Brennan William L	12	painter	29	748 "
T	Markis Charles	12	bootblack	29	5 Taylor
U	Markis May †	12	housewife	24	5 "

4

Pembroke Street—Continued

v	Kaints Peter	12	dishwasher	35	5 Taylor
w	Vozkes Anastnos	12	cook	55	5 "
x	Charlmers Charles N	14	expressman	40	60 Falcon
y	Kenneth Ralph	14	machinist	46	here
z	Jones Jennie —†	14	housekeeper	75	"
A	Leary Dennis F	14	janitor	59	"
B	Thompson Palmer C	14	carpenter	38	"
c	Smith Mary A —†	14	housewife	57	"
D	Smith William	14	retired	66	1761 Wash'n

Rutland Street

F	Dalton Helen —†	1	housewife	60	Salem
G	Dalton William	1	painter	60	"
H	Dugan Nora—†	1	at home	55	here
K	Fitzpatrick Stasia —†	1	"	80	"
L	Mahan James	1	mechanic	52	"
M	Sullivan Emily E—†	1	housekeeper	65	"
N	White Blanche —†	1	housewife	43	"
O	White William	1	laborer	46	"
P	Willard Mary—†	1	laundress	50	Lynn
R	Bullard Michael A	2	laborer	54	Vermont
S	Farrell Thomas J	2	chauffeur	29	11 E Springfield
V	Ford Mary B—†	2	housewife	57	31 Vernon
W	Ford Walter H	2	painter	50	31 "
T	Foy Daniel A	2	chauffeur	23	10 Garland
U	Foy Michael	2	laborer	55	10 "
X	Foy Martin E	2	watchman	59	E Weymouth
Y	Foy Mary A—†	2	housewife	54	"
Z	Foy Peter C	2	fireman	62	10 Garland
A	Maxwell Albert G	2	chauffeur	34	33 Neptune rd
B	McDonough Eleanor—†	2	housewife	33	New Jersey
C	McDonough John H	2	auto mechanic	32	"
D	Murray James F	2	laborer	61	1507 Wash'n
E	Norton John F	2	watchman	45	3 Fountain sq
F	Noyes Evelyn M—†	2	housewife	27	80 Worcester
G	Parker Elizabeth M—†	2	elevatorwoman	35	80 "
H	Tansey James J	2	custodian	37	Winchester
K	Segal Catherine—†	3	housewife	30	68 W Concord
L	Segal Louis	3	waiter	35	68 "

5

Rutland Street—Continued

	Letter	FULL NAME.	Residence	Occupation.	Age	Reported Residence
	M	Latham Mary †	3	at home	68	here
	N	Stronach Annie †	3	saleswoman	60	"
	O	Wright George	3	retired	67	"
	P	Pryson Edward	3	laborer	35	"
	R	Hackney Joseph	3	"	28	Salem
	S	Picket Jannet †	3	domestic	29	here
	T	Anthony Angelo	4	salesman	30	54 Rutland
	U	Beard Charles	4	blacksmith	40	Connecticut
	V	Carlson Gustave	4	paperhanger	55	New York
	W	Ellingham Andrew	4	electrician	40	Cambridge
	X	Hartford Frank T	4	painter	48	1 Arlington ter
	Y	Heffernan Leo	4	salesman	29	30 E Canton
	Z	Kelley Charles	4	grocer	45	2 Rutland
	A	McGriskin Arthur	4	watchman	60	196 W Springfield
	B	Scanlon Marion †	4	housekeeper	35	729 Tremont
	C	Raynor Mary †	5	domestic	33	54 Northfield
	D	Raynor Paul	5	barber	38	54 "
	E	Davenport Lillian †	5	domestic	50	231 Northampton
	F	Davenport William	5	merchant	65	231 "
	G	Leskey Everett	5	fishcutter	39	here
	H	Leskey Theresa †	5	housewife	35	"
	L	Allsopp William	6	chauffeur	33	460 Blue Hill av
	M	Brown George	6	garageman	42	Brookline
	N	Callahan Joseph	6	laborer	52	here
	O	Callahan Margaret †	6	housewife	30	24 Reed
	P	Chisholm Trueman	6	icemaker	43	New Hampshire
	R	Connor John F	6	inspector	34	here
	S	Crowley Timothy J	6	retired	72	231 Shawmut av
	T	Daly Mary E †	6	housekeeper	52	Lake View
	U	Davis Margaret	6	factory worker	45	Framingham
	V	Logan Rebecca H †	6	at home	50	here
	W	Maloney Michael J	6	student	34	125 W Concord
	X	Maloney Thomas	6	steward	31	Ireland
	Y	Moore Augusta †	6	housewife	26	Cambridge
	Z	Moore Gus	6	machinist	25	"
	A	Regan James E	6	paver	45	89 St Alphonsus
	B	Kennedy Joseph S	7	molder	27	5 Claremont pk
	C	Kennedy Winnifred †	7	housewife	27	5 "
	E	Holmes Hattie †	7	"	54	here
	G	Doran Wilbur	8	operator	27	60 Austin
	H	White Clarence	8	carpenter	26	Malden

Rutland Street—Continued

K	White Gene—†	8	waitress	22	here
M	Arsonneau Felix	10	decorator	50	8 Rutland
N	Donovan Edward	10	photographer	30	Newton
O	Fenlon Edward	10	retired	60	here
P	Olson Pheobe—†	10	at home	50	114 Longwood av
R	Pendergast Leonard	10	carpenter	34	4 Rutland sq
S	Perry Harry	10	tinsmith	50	here
T	Smith Kenneth	10	teamster	27	Canada
U	Wadleigh Elizabeth—†	10	housewife	26	here
V	Wadleigh Kenneth G	10	salesman	27	"
W	Walker Catherine M—†	10	housekeeper	31	"
X	Carlson Albert	11	machinist	35	329 Shawmut av
Y	Clark Nina—†	11	clerk	22	here
Z	Ferguson Joseph	11	chauffeur	35	"
A	Mack Walter	11	laborer	32	"
B	Marneick Mary—†	11	laundress	40	435 Shawmut av
C	McGarry Nora—†	11	housewife	37	329 "
D	McGarry Thomas J	11	laborer	39	329 "
E	Nolan Catherine—†	11	at home	75	here
F	Rich Antonio	11	merchant	35	"
G	Smith Mary—†	11	laundress	52	"
H	Stoddard Catherine—†	11	cook	45	119 Appleton
K	Walker Rose—†	11	at home	68	here
L	Wheeler Edwin A	11	boxmaker	30	130 Dale
M	Wright Clarence	11	checker	52	here
O	Adams George	12	shoemaker	65	"
N	Allen Albert	12	machinist	30	Milton
P	Camber Florence—†	12	housewife	30	here
R	David Claude	12	waiter	25	Milford
S	Falkins Sterling	12	machinist	45	here
T	Johnson Alfred	12	painter	51	28 Dartmouth
U	Shea Patrick	12	laborer	35	Somerville
V	Sullivan James	12	boilermaker	42	Saugus
W	Wilkinson Joseph	12	mover	30	Malden
Y	Hooker Minnie—†	14	dressmaker	42	Florida
Z	Jones Frances—†	14	housekeeper	26	New York
A	Taylor James	14	policeman	33	here
C	Barry Guy	16	rubberworker	28	"
D	Cooley Catherine—†	16	housekeeper	32	364 Mass av
E	Cooley John	16	cable splicer	30	364 "
F	Doherty Lawrence J P	16	clock examiner	30	Lawrence

Rutland Street—Continued

G	Gandley James	16	cable splicer	52	Worcester
H	Gerathy Arthur	16	counterman	27	Rhode Island
K	Gerathy Muriel—†	16	housewife	24	"
L	Johnson Jerome	16	rubberworker	26	here
M	Mackie Dukie	16	chauffeur	22	N Carolina
N	Waldron Harold P	16	salesman	28	Salem
O	Ward Robert W	16	lineman	52	6 Berkeley
P	Bloom George	18	retired	84	here
R	Cripps Frank	18	houseman	48	Malden
S	Donovan John	18	"	48	here
T	Flynn Annie—†	18	bookbinder	40	"
U	Gallagher George	18	painter	52	Pennsylvania
V	McDonough Carnella—†	18	housekeeper	71	here
W	McLaughlin Ellen—†	18	at home	60	"
X	Murphy Helen—†	18	dressmaker	45	"
Y	Taylor Frank J	18	houseman	42	"
Z	Lyons Ethel—†	20	housewife	35	New York
A	Lyons Henry	20	salesman	36	"
B	Young Cassie—†	20	housewife	25	Vermont
C	Young Osmer M	20	carfinisher	28	"
D	Andrews Aliola—†	20	housewife	37	Maine
E	Andrews Charles F	20	auto mechanic	42	"
F	Marshall Alice—†	22	housekeeper	35	136 Pembroke
G	Marshall James	22	waiter	32	136 "
H	Young Samuel	22	plumber	57	9 "
K	Young Helen—†	22	housewife	66	9 "
L	Phinney Harvey G	22	salesman	43	Rhode Island
M	Phinney Mary E—†	22	housewife	45	"
N	Hamel May—†	24	"	36	Detroit Mich
O	Hamel John E	24	auto mechanic	26	"
P	Dooley John	24	janitor	50	here
R	Hayes Grace F—†	24	housewife	38	7 Worcester
S	Hayes James W	24	clerk	41	7 "
T	Johnson William B	27	merchant	52	Brookline
U	Green George	27	janitor	65	here
V	Armstrong Edna—†	29	housewife	23	202 W Springfield
W	Armstrong Murchie	29	chauffeur	24	202 "
X	Daley William	29	laborer	50	here
Y	Murphy John	29	"	51	13 James
Z	Ralston Lillian—†	29	housewife	26	Bath Me
A	Ralston William	29	engineer	27	"

Rutland Street—Continued

	Letter	Full Name	Res.	Occupation	Age	Reported Residence
	B	Spear Elsie M—†	29	waitress	33	725 Tremont
	C	Swenson Theodore C	29	laborer	60	14 Dana pk
	D	Swift Mary A—†	29	at home	73	725 Tremont
	E	Finocchiaro Anna—†	31	housewife	42	here
	F	Finocchiaro Celia—†	31	stenographer	23	"
	G	Finocchiaro Joseph	31	barber	53	"
	H	Finocchiaro Josephine—†	31	student	20	"
	K	Finocchiaro Salvatore	31	barber	42	"
	L	Buckner Minerva M—†	32	housekeeper	40	"
	M	Jahr Olga—†	32	registrar	25	"
	N	Shadrina Catherine—†	32	librarian	26	Russia
	O	Wentworth Florence—†	32	housekeeper	40	here
	P	Wohlschlagel Dorothy—†	32	piano teacher	20	"
	R	Crowley Daniel	33	laborer	60	"
	S	Eich Joseph M	33	student	22	"
	T	Eich Madeline F—†	33	school teacher	25	"
	U	Eich Mary J—†	33	housewife	57	"
	V	Stromblad Alexander	45	shipper	60	"
	W	Stromblad Alma—†	45	housewife	49	"
	X	Stromblad Astrid I—†	45	stenographer	26	"
	Y	Hartmann France	45	painter	50	"
	Z	Heitzler Joseph	45	decorator	61	"
	A	Heitzler Lena—†	45	housewife	40	"
	B	Bennett Fannie—†	45	at home	62	"
	C	Clark Annie E—†	45	dressmaker	67	"
	D	Gilman John F	45	printer	55	"
	E	Dudley Annie M—†	45	housewife	40	745 Tremont
	F	Dudley Eva F—†	45	at home	58	Bath Me
	G	Dudley Leonard H	45	carpenter	40	745 Tremont
	H	Craig Elizabeth—†	47	waitress	42	here
	K	Feeley Daniel	47	printer	71	76 E Brookline
	L	Fillinginn Whitfield	47	laborer	45	here
	M	Germain Jennie—†	47	cook	60	76 E Brookline
	N	Germain Lester	47	mechanic	22	76 "
	O	Hughes Annie—†	47	housekeeper	50	Newton
	P	Preston Richard	47	musician	54	here
	R	Ramage Doria—†	47	clerk	38	"
	S	Redman Mary—†	47	domestic	30	528 Tremont
	T	Redman Waterl	47	seaman	36	528 "
	U	Williams Julia—†	47	at home	70	here
	W	Bergstrom Simon C	49	machinist	27	"

Rutland Street—Continued

x	Carlberg Aina—†	49	housewife	48	here
y	Carlberg Arthur J	49	machinist	41	"
z	Custepson Helge E M	49	"	30	Bath Me
a	Dysart Robert R	49	auditor	21	"
b	Grau John	49	painter	48	208 W Springfield
c	Lindquist Carl A	49	mechanic	49	196 "
d	MacGregor Albert	49	laborer	23	48 Waltham
e	Rogers John J	49	janitor	57	here
f	Swenson Lars	49	laborer	60	"
g	Clifford Joseph	51	pianoworker	24	"
h	Frederickson Harry	51	"	22	"
k	Freeland James M	51	foreman	31	"
l	Georgafendis James	51	clerk	31	Woburn
m	Larry Victor	51	laundryman	40	86 Waltham
n	Nelson Anton	51	carpenter	25	Somerville
o	Nelson John	51	"	25	"
p	Pappos George E	51	waiter	31	18 St Stephen
r	Riley Thomas	51	"	23	here
s	Rooney Anna L—†	51	bookkeeper	38	"
t	Stevens Cecelia—†	51	housekeeper	35	"
u	Vigilas James	51	waiter	23	"
v	Carr William	53	carpenter	48	"
w	Gilbert Mary W—†	53	housekeeper	47	"
x	Emanuels Joseph	53	watchmaker	69	"
y	Walsh Joseph	53	counterman	24	Somerville
z	Anderson Jeannette—†	55	shoestitcher	25	here
a	Brady Thomas J	55	conductor	49	"
b	Eagan Thomas	55	plumber	49	"
c	Eagan Vera—†	55	cook	31	"
d	Garvey William J	55	porter	33	"
e	Grauman Earnest	55	clerk	45	Salem
f	Grauman Muriel—†	55	"	40	"
g	Grauman Wilhelmina—†	55	housewife	43	"
h	Katschker Edwin	55	molder	21	57 Rutland
k	Katschker Josephine—†	55	seamstress	21	57 "
l	King Florance	55	special police	46	here
m	McCartney David	55	machinist	51	"
n	Munroe Thomas O	55	chauffeur	32	"
o	Peabody Albert F	55	"	47	"
p	Smith Lillian—†	55	waitress	21	Lynn
r	Stevens Herbert J	55	chauffeur	45	here

Page.	Letter.	FULL NAME.	Residence, April 1, 1926.	Occupation.	Supposed Age.	Reported Residence, April 1, 1925. Street and Number.

Rutland Street—Continued

	Letter	Name	Res.	Occupation	Age	Reported Residence
	s	Brady Margaret—†	57	nurse	33	Medford
	t	Burt Margaret—†	57	housewife	35	406 Mass av
	u	Burt Walter J	57	engineer	34	406 "
	v	Graham Ethel—†	57	saleswoman	25	Lowell
	w	Graham James	57	plasterer	29	"
	x	Hurley Sarah—†	57	laundress	22	Bath Me
	y	Manning Catherine—†	57	"	30	30 Upton
	z	Matanzo Raymond	57	clerk	24	Somerville
	A	Mattson Dorothy—†	57	saleswoman	26	14 Dana
	B	Alexander Nettie L—†	58	housekeeper	50	here
	c	Brinell Emma—†	58	at home	65	Brookline
	D	Brown Arthur	58	painter	40	here
	E	Brown Florence—†	58	housekeeper	54	"
	F	Castella Mary—†	58	candymaker	30	"
	G	Goodwin Irving	58	salesman	35	"
	H	Googin Doris—†	58	waitress	25	Rhode Island
	K	McKeane Mary—†	58	laundress	35	here
	L	Powers John	58	window washer	65	"
	M	Rogers Nellie—†	58	housewife	24	"
	N	Rogers William	58	broker	25	"
	o	Shaw Gladys—†	58	waitress	23	Canada
	P	Stewart Gertrude—†	58	"	29	Medford
	R	Walsh Mary—†	58	stitcher	68	Middleboro
	s	Blake Alonco	59	laborer	50	here
	T	Cameron Catherine—†	59	housewife	22	411 Shawmut av
	u	Cameron Clifford	59	teamster	24	411 "
	v	Detter Edward F	59	mechanic	48	here
	w	Durrell Muriel—†	59	clerk	50	"
	x	Linhzes John	59	"	30	"
	Y	McLellan Isabella—†	59	at home	60	"
	z	McLennan Bessie—†	59	housekeeper	52	"
	A	Spaulding Gertrude—†	59	laundress	50	"
	B	Varis Thomas	59	cook	28	Lynn
	c	White Margaret—†	59	laundress	26	45 Rutland
	D	Brown John	60	paperhanger	40	Framingham
	E	Coombs William	60	salesman	33	here
	F	Deardon Harold I	60	contractor	21	"
	G	Deardon Marion I—†	60	housewife	20	N Brookfield
	H	Flunder Ralph	60	paperhanger	38	Everett
	L	McLaughlin Theresa—†	60	seamstress	55	here

11

Page.	Letter.	FULL NAME.	Residence, April 1, 1926.	Occupation.	Supposed Age.	Reported Residence, April 1, 1925. Street and Number.

Rutland Street—Continued

M	Richards Joseph A	60	auto mechanic	42	here
N	Richards Louise K—†	60	housekeeper	45	"
O	Smith Daniel P	60	painter	45	"
O¹	Tirley Samuel	60	retired	76	"
P	Woodie Ardath—†	60	housewife	26	88 Worcester
R	Woodie William I	60	chauffeur	30	88 "
K	Young Emma—†	60	domestic	55	532 Mass av
S	Bennett William	61	baker	48	here
T	Buckley John J	61	machinist	53	"
U	Buckley Margaret H—†	61	housewife	53	"
V	Donlon Mary—†	61	housekeeper	49	73 Rutland
W	Goff Ellen—†	61	seamstress	47	here
X	Johnson Margaret—†	61	housekeeper	42	"
Y	Johnson William	61	baker	32	"
Z	Nichols Horace H	61	teamster	40	56 Clarendon
A	Nichols Mary—†	61	housewife	35	56 "
B	Caput Vera—†	62	factory worker	23	here
C	Cormier John	62	printer	45	21 W Springfield
D	Cushman Elizabeth A—†	62	factory worker	20	40 Ellery
E	Kenney John	62	cab driver	56	104 W Concord
F	McDonnell Dennis	62	machinist	60	10 Highland
G	Murphy Agnes—†	62	stitcher	25	451 Mass av
H	Murphy John F	62	laborer	29	451 "
K	Sirois Pheobe—†	62	factory worker	22	Maine
L	Smiley John F	62	policeman	34	here
M	Smiley Mary B—†	62	housewife	32	"
N	Smith John	62	machinist	38	"
O	Warnock David L	62	auto mechanic	33	1853 Wash'n
P	Warnock Edward	62	"	25	7 Lawrence
R	Wool Denis	62	stagehand	30	here
S	Bowen Patrick	63	plasterer	27	"
T	Gerhard Robert	63	retired	80	"
N	Hardy John	63	carpenter	35	"
V	Harrington Timothy	63	laborer	25	Canada
W	Lyons Mary—†	63	housekeeper	41	here
X	Murphy Cornelius	63	laborer	25	Canada
Y	Neill Patrick F	63	"	26	"
Z	Sullivan Catherine—†	63	waitress	31	here
A	Ahern Mary—†	64	housekeeper	58	139 Albany
B	Cody Beatrice—†	64	housewife	38	here
C	Cody John L	64	shipper	44	"

12

Page.	Letter	Full Name.	Residence, April 1, 1926.	Occupation.	Supposed Age.	Reported Residence, April 1, 1925. Street and Number.

Rutland Street—Continued

	D	Glenville Maria—†	64	nurse	58	675 Tremont
	E	Goodman James F	64	salesman	70	here
	F	Lavin James H	64	machinist	44	"
	G	Luvist Arthur B	64	draftsman	30	137 Mass av
	H	Murphy Mary—†	64	waitress	45	147 Worcester
	K	Murray James J	64	engineer	32	5 Rossmore rd
	L	Nazzan Vincent	64	baker	33	New Hampshire
	M	Ide Emily K—†	65	at home	62	here
	N	Ide George D	65	clerk	74	"
	O	Ide Harriett M—†	65	housewife	68	"
	P	Campbell Garfield	66	mechanic	20	Canada
	R	Campbell Joseph	66	carpenter	21	"
	S	Chamberlain Dudley B	66	waiter	23	here
	T	Chamberlain Frances J—†	66	housekeeper	56	"
	U	Chew Alfred	66	machinist	26	Canada
	V	Chew May—†	66	saleswoman	25	"
	W	Chew William W	66	blacksmith	20	"
	X	Elward Gertrude—†	66	cook	50	Bermuda
	Y	Harrington James	66	clerk	50	here
	Z	Martel Mary—†	66	at home	63	"
	A	McDonell Frederick W	66	dentist	56	"
	B	Neilson Walter	66	cigarmaker	50	"
	C	Blain Christine—†	67	seamstress	38	Lynn
	D	Burke Helen—†	67	domestic	50	here
	E	Collier Loucilla—†	67	clerk	34	"
	F	Downey Madeline—†	67	waitress	20	22 Concord sq
	G	Madden Andrew	67	gardener	42	here
	H	Madden Barbara—†	67	housekeeper	42	"
	K	Schnieder Christopher	67	retired	74	Salem
	L	Schnieder Dora—†	67	housewife	72	"
	M	Southerland Irvin	67	ironworker	30	Bath Me
	N	Worton Joseph	67	clerk	50	653 Mass av
	O	Anderson George	68	houseman	35	W Newton
	P	Doherty John R	68	chauffeur	48	9 Bancroft
	R	Fuller Frank	68	roofer	28	80 W Dedham
	S	Glazer Alice—†	68	factory worker	40	214 Col av
	T	Greely May—†	68	waitress	36	Maine
	U	Hughes Ethel—†	68	domestic	44	443 Shawmut av
	V	Lanno Clifford	68	chef	26	476 "
	W	Pelletier Joseph	68	porter	22	476 "
	X	Perkins Israel	68	painter	53	Cape Cod

13

Rutland Street— Continued

	Y	Reiss Anthony	68	painter	50	46 Upton
	Z	Richards May—†	68	housekeeper	46	10 "
	A	Snyder Philip	68	chef	36	Lowell
	B	Wilson Edward	68	waiter	28	476 Shawmut av
	C	Kenrick Zaidella—†	69	casemaker	36	here
	D	Murphy Elmira C—†	69	housewife	50	482 Mass av
	E	Murphy John H	69	clerk	42	482 "
	H	Matthews Dorothy—†	69	housewife	28	Walpole
	K	Matthews George	69	lineman	30	"
	L	Callahan Charles A	70	stevedore	50	here
	M	Davis Rodman	70	chauffeur	35	"
	N	Dolan Michael F	70	retired	77	"
	O	Gedis Dora—†	70	carpet sewer	45	24 Rutland sq
	P	Hodges Timothy	70	porter	50	here
	R	Kelleher Cornelius	70	garageman	70	"
	S	King Carrie—†	70	housekeeper	40	S Carolina
	T	King Joseph M	70	merchant	52	"
	U	Lee John	70	chauffeur	40	here
	V	Wilbour Alfred B	70	machinist	62	"
	W	Woodman Agnes—†	70	at home	60	"
	X	Wright William J	70	caretaker	45	"
	Y	Lowe Mary—†	71	housekeeper	34	31 Dover
	Z	Lowe Thomas	71	tailor	30	31 "
	A	Penelton Sadie—†	71	cook	30	Cambridge
	B	Berger Theodore	72	fireman	29	here
	C	Gibbons Frank	72	watchmaker	25	"
	D	Hamlin George	72	retired	75	Chelsea
	E	Krajwski Bronistos	72	machinist	36	here
	F	Krajwski Notoa—†	72	housewife	30	"
	G	Manning Louis	72	salesman	32	Malden
	H	McDonald Arthur D	72	telegrapher	55	Milton
	K	McDougall John	72	roofer	29	here
	L	McPhail Anna—†	72	housekeeper	65	"
	M	Mothas Otto	72	cigarmaker	62	"
	N	Robach Florence—†	72	milliner	40	"
	O	Shedd George	72	agent	50	Salem
	P	Stevens Florence—†	72	waitress	30	here
	R	Stevens Raymond	72	painter	28	"
	S	Baker Caroline—†	73	domestic	46	Salem
	T	Berzzran Enoch	73	clerk	28	21 Union pk
	U	Berzzran Oskar	73	"	25	21 "

Page.	Letter.	FULL NAME.	Residence, April 1, 1926.	Occupation.	Supposed Age.	Reported Residence, April 1, 1925. Street and Number.

Rutland Street—Continued

v	Burns Mary—†	73	housewife	40	here
w	Burns Walter	73	salesman	48	"
x	Chapman Garrett S	73	retired	74	"
y	Clark Idella—†	73	checker	38	"
z	Deacks Arthur J	73	cook	52	"
a	Deacks Ila A—†	73	clerk	27	"
b	Dinneen Annie—†	73	nurse	50	704 Tremont
c	Dorr Elsie F—†	73	clerk	30	Bath Me
d	Drew Dulcie—†	73	housewife	37	here
e	Drew Edward	73	mechanic	37	"
f	Gustafson Hugo	73	machinist	27	441 Shawmut av
g	Holmes Malaccie—†	73	at home	83	24 Concord sq
h	Logan William A	73	mechanic	50	Salem
k	McFarland Harold	73	clerk	45	here
l	Pettingill Nathan	73	stevedore	38	46 E Brookline
m	Sawyer Sabina M—†	73	clerk	45	here
n	Wasgatt Jessie G—†	73	housekeeper	66	"
o	Cobe Henry C	74	clerk	50	6 Alvah Kittredge pk
p	Cobe Isreal	74	salesman	65	New York
r	Cobe Louis J	74	clerk	52	6 Alvah Kittredge pk
s	Connell Frank	74	"	49	here
t	Connell Mary—†	74	housewife	44	"
u	Ellsworth Mary—†	74	clerk	26	"
v	Gibson Nellie M—†	74	"	48	"
w	Halpin Sarah—†	74	domestic	60	"
x	Hayes Herbert W	74	chauffeur	48	"
y	Howe Elsie—†	74	clerk	24	5 Columbus sq
z	Irwin Beairsta A	74	real estate	51	here
a	Irwin Marion L—†	74	stenographer	24	"
b	Murray Bert H	74	engineer	35	512 Mass av
c	Ferraro Raffaele	75	laborer	26	173 Warren av
d	Foote Mary E—†	75	at home	74	here
e	Harrington William	75	chauffeur	30	"
f	Larkin Mary J—†	75	nurse	40	"
g	Lewis Margaret—†	75	housewife	34	441 Mass av
h	Shea Nellie T—†	75	housekeeper	49	here
k	Brennan Mathew J	76	salesman	42	87 Worcester
l	Cronin William J	76	laborer	45	19 "
m	Danahy Daniel	76	inspector	70	Malden
n	Hatch Anna C—†	76	at home	61	49 Worcester
o	Hatch George S	76	clerk	46	49 "

Rutland Street—Continued

P	Hill Anna B—†	76	housewife	27	56 Newland
R	Hill James F	76	contractor	34	56 "
S	Lee William	76	agent	50	7 Worcester
T	McGregor Charles	76	laborer	29	85 "
U	McGregor John	76	"	23	Nova Scotia
V	McGregor Laughlin	76	"	27	"
W	McGregor Mary —†	76	buffer	30	85 Worcester
X	Mulino Anna B—†	76	seamstress	46	21 Orange ct
Y	Smith John J	76	electrician	40	87 Worcester
Z	Alberti Joseph A	77	laborer	32	here
A	Alberti Rosie D—†	77	housewife	28	"
B	Cleveland Bridget A—†	77	housekeeper	51	"
C	Cleveland Charles J	77	buffer	53	"
D	Driscoll Cornelius J	77	"	52	Salem
E	Haley Cornelius E	77	teamster	54	here
F	Howard Elizabeth—†	77	housewife	69	"
G	Howard John W	77	chauffeur	47	Lynn
H	Lyng James F	77	buffer	57	here
K	Murphy Elizabeth S—†	77	housewife	43	"
L	Murphy Frank J	77	porter	43	Worcester
M	O'Brien Henry	77	laborer	51	here
N	Erwin Agnes —†	78	waitress	35	"
O	Gaffeny Frank	78	salesman	40	"
P	Goodwin Emery W	78	"	37	"
R	Gould Mary—†	78	laundress	35	Worcester
S	Hartling George	78	carpenter	45	here
T	Mitchel Elnor—†	78	actress	23	New York City
U	Simpson Catherine—†	78	housewife	69	here
U¹	Burnham Walter A	79	cook	49	Bath Me
V	Clare Rita—†	79	stenographer	27	here
W	Clark Theodore E	79	real estate	79	"
X	Flanigan Mary—†	79	at home	73	"
Y	Fraser Angus F	79	painter	24	"
Z	Gillis James	79	molder	24	"
A	Griffin Catherine—†	79	housekeeper	55	"
B	Griffin Deleg	79	tailor	69	"
C	Janetta Lawrence	79	painter	25	"
D	McNeil Angus	79	machinist	24	"
E	Slater Cecilla—†	79	waitress	23	"
F	Brown Lawrence	80	salesman	69	Salem
G	Cox Paul W	80	student	36	64 Hyde Park av

Rutland Street—Continued

H	Franklin Charles	80	waiter	47	here
K	Hines Edward	80	salesman	27	455 Col av
L	Marden Leroy	80	painter	40	here
M	Marden Robert	80	salesman	37	New York
N	Rogers Rosalind—†	80	housekeeper	40	here
P	Quinhian William	80	salesman	45	1779 Wash'n
O	Sherman Alexander	80	"	53	here

Shawmut Avenue

A	Cummings Catherine—†	423	housekeeper	60	here
B	English Andrew J	423	chauffeur	34	"
C	Allen George	423	watchman	54	"
D	Connolly John F	423	salesman	63	"
E	Connolly Margaret—†	423	housewife	56	"
F	O'Brien John	423	clerk	80	"
G	Waitt Harold	423	mechanic	30	"
H	Hasson Charles J	423	fireman	40	Chelsea
K	Jacobs James J	423	baker	63	35 Dover
L	Jacobs Mary— †	423	at home	84	Somerville
M	Jacobs Mary—†	423	housewife	47	35 Dover
N	McCrillis George L	423	watchman	58	here
O	Smith William	423	silversmith	63	35 Dover
P	Taylor William	423	baker	53	35 "
S	Connors Catherine—†	425	clerk	25	Watertown
T	Connors Mary—†	425	dressmaker	27	"
U	Depencier Anna—†	425	laundress	45	23 Upton
V	Depencier Harold	425	pedler	48	23 "
W	Draper Louis	425	laborer	28	1437 Wash'n
W¹	Gamilton Mardiros	425	shoemaker	25	Lowell
X	Kanan George	425	retired	55	here
Y	Kanan George	425	cook	21	"
Z	Kanan Zelfa—†	425	housewife	48	"
A	Lizzate Demerice—†	425	"	27	1437 Wash'n
B	Lizzate Joseph	425	carpenter	25	1437 "
C	Molasky Kazymier	425	"	66	324 Shawmut av
D	O'Neil Thomas H	425	laborer	43	Cambridge
E	Reil Joseph	425	painter	27	108 W Springfield
F	Riley William J	425	mason	46	615 Mass av
G	Cliff Frederica L—†	427	physician	40	here

Page.	Letter.	FULL NAME	Residence, April 1, 1926.	Occupation.	Supposed Age.	Reported Residence, April 1, 1925.
						Street and Number.

Shawmut Avenue—Continued

H	Cliff Leander A	427	physician	78	here
K	McLellan Catherine—†	427	cook	50	"
L	Campbell James M	429	director	47	"
M	Campbell Mary B—†	429	housekeeper	56	"
N	Maher John	429	student	23	"
O	Nechaud Edith—†	429	nurse	23	"
P	Sears Annette—†	429	hairdresser	20	"
R	Abbott Frank	431	cook	53	122 W Concord
S	Barlow Isabelle—†	431	housewife	40	here
T	Barlow Samuel	431	painter	53	"
U	Brown Frank	431	engineer	53	"
V	Delboux Arthur	431	bricklayer	24	Lewiston Me
W	Derany Frederick	431	chef	30	1183 Wash'n
X	Donahue Clarence	431	laborer	48	42 Dover
Y	Gartha Mary—†	431	dressmaker	72	623 Harris'n av
Z	Granville Lillian—†	431	stitcher	60	76 W Newton
A	Ives Emma—†	431	housewife	58	here
B	Ives Patrick	431	laborer	56	"
C	Leger Arthur	431	waiter	22	Canada
D	Marshall Arthur	431	cook	20	Lewiston Me
E	McCranan Catherine—†	431	housewife	47	Melrose
F	McCranan Michael	431	laborer	54	"
G	Murle Catherine—†	431	housekeeper	42	here
H	Rooney Margaret—†	431	"	58	831 Albany
K	White Robert	431	molder	40	Rumford Me
L	Allen Alice—†	433	housekeeper	51	Maine
M	Allen Mary—†	433	waitress	24	"
N	Auley Ellen Y—†	433	at home	55	here
O	Boland George F	433	clerk	26	639 Tremont
P	Caro George	433	mason	34	86 Eustis
R	Cole Sydney M	433	cook	50	18 Hancock
S	Drew Joseph F	433	porter	32	here
T	Drew Regina H—†	433	waitress	31	"
U	Dunn Harry	433	salesman	35	10 Col av
V	Dunn Lulu—†	433	clerk	32	10 "
W	Farrah Frank G	433	carpenter	29	here
X	Farrah Nazara—†	433	housewife	26	"
Y	Hooper Herbert	433	student	35	481 Shawmut av
Z	Lewis Daniel J	433	clerk	35	Everett
A	McClosky Donald	433	student	23	481 Shawmut av

18

Page.	Letter.	Full Name.	Residence, April 1, 1926.	Occupation.	Supposed Age.	Reported Residence, April 1, 1925. Street and Number.

Shawmut Avenue—Continued

	B	Michaelson Alfred	433	cook	20	Sterling
	C	Orfan Michael	433	clerk	42	108 W Springfield
	D	Tarian Ella—†	433	laundress	35	here
	E	Bourque Sarah T—†	435	housekeeper	53	"
	F	Dunn John	435	meatcutter	40	"
	G	Emerson John	435	shoemaker	25	35 Upton
	H	Gester Lea—†	435	housekeeper	30	Nashua N H
	L	Gurron Eula—†	435	housewife	30	here
	K	Gurron John	435	waiter	37	"
	M	Johnson Margaret—†	435	waitress	45	"
	N	Mullen Frederick	435	baker	40	Malden
	O	Owens Louise—†	435	housekeeper	76	here
	P	Rious John	435	carpenter	35	680 Tremont
	R	Rious Lena—†	435	housewife	30	680 "
	S	Sallaway Edwina—†	435	"	20	here
	T	Sallaway James M	435	machinist	25	"
	U	Sullivan Joseph	435	clerk	21	"
	V	Webster Joseph	435	printer	35	80 Appleton
	W	Black Walter	437	cook	25	2 Clifton pl
	X	Kelly John	437	"	32	Melrose
	Y	Kinan Kaleel	437	pedler	24	5016 Wash'n
	Z	Matarazzo Mary—†	437	physician	24	here
	A	McDonald George	437	cook	24	Winthrop
	B	McDougal Hugh	437	piano mover	28	465 Shawmut av
	C	Ryan Thomas	437	waiter	25	Cambridge
	D	Taffae Blanche V—†	437	seamstress	28	Malden
	E	Taffae Sydney B	437	artist	35	"
	F	Generazio Louis F	439	laborer	30	here
	G	Hakim Rosie—†	439	housewife	29	"
	H	Hakim Tom	439	painter	35	"
	K	Hartley Charles	439	"	35	"
	L	Hartley Hattie—†	439	housewife	30	"
	M	Lambert Ellen—†	439	housekeeper	65	"
	N	Campbell Anna—†	441	waitress	33	1 James
	O	Carmichael John	441	carpenter	50	here
	P	Davis Claude J	441	porter	44	Easton N H
	R	Davis Rose—†	441	housekeeper	38	"
	S	Homer Anna—†	441	waitress	25	Norwood
	T	Lally Margaret—†	441	"	30	1 James
	U	Maloof Mary—†	441	housekeeper	40	here
	V	Maloof Sam	441	laborer	40	"

Shawmut Avenue—Continued

w	Nichols Harry	441	laborer	32	Lexington
x	Shaheen Karam N	441	"	34	here
y	Barce Minnie—†	443	housewife	25	1658 Wash'n
z	Barce Walter S	443	engineer	42	1658 "
A	Forsyth Richard	443	fireman	40	76 Rutland
B	Humphrey Bion S	443	cook	22	E Burke Vt
C	King Michael J	443	shipper	45	here
D	Mayen Minervia M—†	443	housekeeper	48	"
E	Mitchell Carroll B	443	fireman	23	Cambridge
F	Mitchell Eva—†	443	housewife	21	"
G	Paton Caroline—†	443	painter	20	Barre Vt
H	Paton Harry	443	engineer	40	"
K	Paton Jennie—†	443	housewife	40	New Hampshire
L	Sheehan Dorothy—†	443	dressmaker	50	606 Tremont
M	Smith John	443	decorator	43	Nantasket
N	Beck Hugh	445	foreman	38	12 Rutland
O	Collins Marie—†	445	housekeeper	40	here
P	Colpitts Frederick	445	laborer	34	Canada
R	Dunne James	445	foreman	44	Chicago Ill
S	Gaw David	445	carpenter	48	here
T	Germany Mary—†	445	housewife	33	"
U	Germany Richard N	445	carpenter	34	"
V	Keyson Horatio F	445	mechanic	60	"
W	Klain Charles E	445	painter	50	"
X	MacGachey Charles H	445	laborer	45	"
Y	MacGachey Jean—†	445	at home	83	"
Z	Maycotte Joseph	445	chauffeur	25	Providence R I
A	Murphy Catherine—†	445	housewife	40	here
B	Murphy John	445	painter	50	"
C	Saiekall Alexander	445	shoeworker	33	119 W Concord
D	Arnesen Charles	446	painter	58	here
E	Frazer Daniel	446	cook	25	47 Warren av
F	Glennen Helen—†	446	housekeeper	48	here
G	Glennen James	446	gardener	51	"
H	Linkoty John E	446	cook	26	"
K	Papas Louis	446	"	36	"
P	Perry Charles	446	stableman	50	Cambridge
M	Wade Michael	446	laborer	65	8 Rutland
N	Anderson Ernest	447	painter	59	here
O	Anderson Matilda—†	447	housewife	51	"
P	Coughlan John H	447	carpenter	58	Bangor Me

Letter	FULL NAME.	Residence, April 1, 1926.	Occupation.	Supposed Age.	Reported Residence, April 1, 1925. Street and Number.

Shawmut Avenue—Continued

R	Duprey Cora—†	447	seamstress	22	here
S	Duprey Margaret—†	447	laundress	24	"
T	Finnerty Martin	447	ironworker	65	"
U	Hammersley Patrick	447	mason	42	Lowell
V	Jardine Lawrence	447	barber	25	Cambridge
W	Klegin Robert	447	real estate	72	here
X	Lignell Gustus	447	fireman	46	"
Y	Linehan Daniel D	447	shoemaker	27	Brockton
Z	Lord Harry	447	mechanic	39	Groton
A	Lord Mary—†	447	housekeeper	32	"
B	McDonald Mary—†	447	housewife	21	Bangor Me
C	McDonald Stephen	447	laborer	23	"
D	Newman Charles	447	chauffeur	33	244 W Newton
E	Newman Margaret—†	447	housewife	32	244 "
F	Donovan Frank	448	salesman	39	here
G	Donovan Louise—†	448	chambermaid	25	"
H	Donovan Mary—†	448	housewife	55	"
K	Fletcher Robert	448	bookkeeper	27	"
L	Hood Marie B—†	448	housekeeper	49	"
M	Kenney Helena—†	448	housewife	50	109 E Newton
N	McCabe Edwin	448	painter	31	here
O	Miller Elizabeth—†	448	stitcher	40	Natick
P	Toney John	448	laborer	55	Malden
R	Brow Joseph	449	lineman	49	here
S	Buckley Bessie—†	449	housekeeper	56	"
T	Buckley Helen—†	449	"	26	"
U	Buckley Mary J—†	449	bookkeeper	25	"
V	Buckley Michael	449	retired	64	"
W	Collins Katherine—†	449	operator	45	"
X	Gould Mary T—†	449	matron	61	"
Y	Hurley Lawrence M	449	laborer	52	89 W Brookline
Z	Paul Thomas	449	lineman	72	98 W Newton
A	Curran Alice—†	450	housewife	27	Brockton
B	Curran Robert	450	brakeman	32	"
C	Frederick Elizabeth—†	450	housekeeper	21	Cambridge
D	Frederick Frank E	450	chauffeur	23	"
E	Hayes Anna—†	450	housekeeper	53	here
F	McCabe Edward	450	painter	31	"
G	McIver Alfred	450	cabinetmaker	46	Portland Me
H	McMorrow Charles	450	laborer	50	9 Bromfield
K	Smith Elizabeth—†	450	saleswoman	50	here

Page.	Letter.	FULL NAME.	Residence, April 1, 1926.	Occupation.	Supposed Age.	Reported Residence, April 1, 1925. Street and Number.

Shawmut Avenue--Continued

	L	Taylor George	450	salesman	60	here
	M	Taylor Harold	450	painter	25	"
	N	Whaler Joseph P	450	"	72	"
	O	Whitney Jesse—†	450	housewife	30	Revere
	P	Whitney John	450	painter	40	"
	R	O'Connell Thomas	451	machinist	54	here
	S	Cosgrove Ambrose S	451	retired	45	California
	T	Fields William F	451	cook	62	22 Milford
	U	Holts Albert J	451	machinist	38	Canada
	V	Howson Margaret—†	451	nurse	35	Chelsea
	W	Kinsmon Benjamin F	451	painter	60	here
	X	Penas Peter	451	cook	25	Cambridge
	Y	Roumaker Francis J	451	upholsterer	24	here
	Z	Spencer Josiah D	451	nurse	54	"
	A	Terrell Helen M—†	451	housekeeper	51	"
	B	Whiting Louis F	451	machinist	51	"
	C	Abrohamiai David	452	cook	35	"
	F	Maijan John	452	laborer	50	"
	D	Maloof Hatem	452	storekeeper	30	"
	E	Maloof Joseph	452	"	40	"
	H	Dodge Agnes—†	453	seamstress	60	Florida
	K	Gray Catherine—†	453	cook	64	38 Gray
	L	Hanna Edith A—†	453	superintendent	41	here
	M	Hobin Annie—†	453	housekeeper	42	7 Milford
	N	Hurley Mary—†	453	"	28	Andover
	O	Kay Lucy—†	453	teacher	41	New York
	P	Lund Florence—†	453	student	29	Brookline
	R	McCormack Carrie—†	453	housekeeper	48	57A Chestnut
	S	Harold Annie—†	456	"	56	here
	T	Kennedy Mary—†	457	saleswoman	52	"
	U	Benson Ethel—†	457	forewoman	21	"
	V	Smith Agnes—†	457	cashier	38	37 Worcester sq
	W	Seelig Emma C †	457	housewife	42	here
	X	Seelig Victor F	457	shipper	42	"
	Y	Edgehill Estelle †	458	housewife	24	"
	Z	Edgehill Herman	458	factory worker	27	"
	A	Paine Clement	458	"	40	"
	B	Paine Inez—†	458	hairdresser	32	"
	C	Brown Anna †	460	housekeeper	33	1413 Wash'n
	D	Brown George J	460	cook	53	1413 "
	E	Connors Daniel	460	laborer	45	Rockland

Letter.	FULL NAME.	Residence, April 1, 1926.	Occupation.	Suppressed Age.	Reported Residence, April 1, 1925. Street and Number.

Shawmut Avenue—Continued

F	Crowley Mabel—†	460	saleswoman	26	Somerville
G	Gallant Albert	460	salesman	45	90 Hunneman
H	Hasson John J	460	gasfitter	56	here
K	Hasson Margaret—†	460	housekeeper	40	"
L	Murray John	460	cook	51	S Framingham
M	O'Brien James	460	"	55	338 Shawmut av
N	Ridge Charles	460	"	26	Springfield
O	Ridge Florence—†	460	housekeeper	34	"
P	Robinson Elizabeth—†	460	at home	84	466 Shawmut av
R	Rodney Mary—†	460	"	59	1 Rutland
S	Vahey John	460	laborer	36	15 Groton
T	Andros Harry	462	painter	45	Portland
U	Bevesly William	462	chef	38	Malden
V	Dungle Ida—†	462	dressmaker	60	5 James
W	Hesnley Charles	462	laborer	45	Los Angeles Cal
X	Maskell Edward	462	"	40	Portland Me
Y	Maskell Mabel—†	462	housekeeper	39	"
Z	Miller Maurice	462	engineer	35	Miami Fla
A	Panobil John	462	chef	40	44 W Newton
B	Snow Jessie—†	462	stitcher	30	Nashua N H
C	Snow Nathan	462	laborer	35	"
D	Sullivan Jeremiah	462	cook	60	308 Shawmut av
E	Sazynsk Nathan	463	retired	69	here
F	Sazynsk Lina—†	463	housewife	55	"
G	Bell Robert	464	laborer	46	Malden
H	Chadwick Charles	464	"	30	"
K	Collman John	464	boxmaker	60	here
L	Deegan Elizabeth—†	464	housekeeper	47	16 Rutland
M	Glynn Edward	464	laborer	40	here
N	Glynn William	464	carpenter	35	"
O	Hardy Watson H	464	butcher	41	16 Rutland
P	Hobbs Ella—†	464	at home	65	here
R	McEachern James	464	dyer	45	"
S	Muldoon Catherine—†	464	at home	50	"
T	Cameron William	465	leather dealer	33	Malden
U	Dragon William T	465	houseman	56	here
V	Gordon Bertha—†	465	housekeeper	38	"
W	Lavochille Homer	465	painter	40	48 Worcester
X	Lavochille Mary—†	465	housewife	28	48 "
Y	McCarthy James	465	gardener	52	63 Concord
Z	Stevens Annie—†	465	housekeeper	63	here

23

Shawmut Avenue—Continued

A	Willett Louis J	465	chef	52	Lynn
B	Devine Micheal M	466	cook	35	here
C	Maloof Helen—†	466	housewife	55	"
D	Maloof Samuel W	466	shoeworker	60	"
E	Mulvey Agnes L—†	466	housewife	35	Hartford Ct
G	Joseph John	468	shoemaker	32	here
H	Joseph Shamas—†	468	housewife	35	"
K	Meaney Josephine—†	468	shipper	49	"
L	Nastorf Anna—†	469	housewife	27	"
M	Nastrof David	469	machinist	31	"
N	Kruntzman Jacob	469	"	32	5 Decatur
O	Kruntzman Katherine—†	469	housewife	30	5 "
P	Boris John	469	salesman	38	here
R	Boris Tina—†	469	housewife	35	"
T	Tebac John	469	painter	28	1196 Tremont
U	Tebac Mary—†	469	housewife	30	1196 "
X	Orr Della—†	475	"	65	here
Y	Venter Margaret—†	475	"	52	126 Berkeley
Z	Venter Max	475	coppersmith	50	126 "
A	Brown Joseph	475	pedler	30	here
B	Brown Rae—†	475	"	30	"
C	Griffin Mae—†	475	housewife	33	68 W Concord
D	Leary John H	475	laborer	66	68 "
E	Mercer Isadore	475	painter	64	here
F	Mercer Joseph	475	machinist	38	"
G	Mercer Lillian—†	475	clerk	24	"
H	Chattack Archie	475	barber	32	529 Col av
K	Chattack Mary A—†	475	housewife	33	529 "
L	Fevenzan John	475	laborer	60	here
M	Fevenzan Mary—†	475	housekeeper	55	"
N	Fevenzan Mary—†	475	bookkeeper	22	"
P	Callahan John	481	teamster	53	"
R	Bush Alex	481	carpenter	54	"
S	Bush Freda—†	481	housewife	54	"
T	Butler Phillip	481	machinist	37	"
U	Cenboy John M	481	inspector	56	45 Holmes av
V	Kelly Daniel J	481	machinist	24	here
W	Roberts John N	481	painter	38	30 Worcester sq
X	Smith James	481	bookbinder	52	here
Y	Stone Alfred	481	electrician	45	41 E Concord

Shawmut Avenue—Continued

z	Stone Bertha—†	481	housewife	34	41 E Concord
A	Caposulili Valentine	483	bricklayer	32	Lynn
D	McNeil Wallace	483	carpenter	47	here
B	O'Connell Ellen—†	483	housewife	53	"
C	O'Connell Julia—†	483	housekeeper	45	"
E	Pulzer Joseph	483	baker	45	Natick
F	Stewart Lawrence	483	carpenter	40	Lynn
G	Allen Robert	485	seaman	22	New York
H	Duskin John	485	packer	48	here
K	Green Ralph	485	seaman	24	New York
L	Holmes George	485	chauffeur	24	here
M	Holmes Lena—†	485	housekeeper	32	"
N	Kaughlin Peter	485	clerk	38	Malden
O	Lynch Catherine—†	485	housekeeper	80	here
P	McCarthy Eugene L	485	bookbinder	52	"
P¹	Mifford Mabel—†	485	housewife	48	Keene N H
R	Slipp Lena—†	485	housekeeper	39	here
S	Thompson Helen—†	485	saleswoman	65	"

Tremont Street

U	Dorney Charles N	664	electrician	35	New Jersey
V	Dorney Edna—†	664	actress	26	"
W	Leenian Charles E	664	real estate	40	725 Tremont
X	Brehant David	664	shipper	44	698 Columbia rd
X¹	Brehant Esta—†	664	housewife	43	698 "
Y	Stevens Bert	664	chauffeur	35	Lenox
Z	Stevens Margaret—†	664	saleswoman	22	"
A	Lewis George	664	steamfitter	29	685 Mass av
B	Cunningham John	666	clerk	74	here
C	Donnelly Elizabeth—†	666	domestic	55	"
D	Ferguson Jane—†	666	housewife	28	"
E	Ferguson William	666	painter	28	"
F	Griffin William	666	retired	56	725 Tremont
G	Reaney Annie—†	666	housekeeper	36	here
H	Ruttle John	666	machinist	62	"
K	Spinos Mike	666	cook	35	187 Warren av
K¹	Vanvouras David	666	chef	35	187 "
L	Yee Sing	666B	laundryman	48	here
M	Boone Annie G—†	668	clerk	23	"

Page	Letter	Full Name.	Residence, April 1, 1926.	Occupation.	Supposed Age.	Reported Residence, April 1, 1925. Street and Number.

Tremont Street—Continued

N	Chapman Raymond	668	clergyman	38	here
O	Drabble Mary E—†	668	housekeeper	54	"
P	Nielsen Walter	668	chauffeur	25	"
R	Roberts Ethel—†	668	housewife	38	Portland Me
S	Roberts Herbert	668	mechanic	36	"
T	Silvers Walter F	668	counterman	23	here
U	Tennant John	668	porter	35	34 Montgomery
Y	Brown Isador E	670	teamster	40	209 Roxbury
W	Brown Myron A	670	cook	23	here
X	Brown Ruth E—†	670	clerk	23	"
Y	Cronin David	670	counterman	23	691 Tremont
Z	Gilmore James H	670	carpenter	39	Lowell
A	Gilmore Mae—†	670	housewife	44	"
B	Greene Edward	670	laborer	38	here
C	Greene Ethel—†	670	housewife	36	"
D	Rogers George	670	tailor	36	"
E	White Ada J—†	670	housekeeper	48	"
F	White George F	670	operator	56	"
G	White James C	670	laborer	25	"
H	Aspro Fred	672	"	46	22 Rutland sq
K	Bergin Dennis J	672	inspector	60	59 Howard av
L	Hunter John	672	printer	45	here
M	Lyons Jennie A—†	672	housekeeper	54	"
N	Lyons John J	672	porter	53	"
O	Nix Albert N	672	clerk	53	"
P	Chadburn Fred C	676	salesman	60	"
R	Cuneo Frank	676	"	50	"
S	Holland Philip	676	machinist	28	"
T	Howe Effie R—†	676	housewife	35	"
U	Howe William A	676	painter	31	"
V	Johnson William F	676	machinist	43	"
W	McDonald Somerland	676	salesman	23	"
X	Murphy Hubert	676	blacksmith	35	"
Y	Kennedy Martin	678	machinist	45	"
Z	Quinlan Catherine—†	678	housekeeper	47	"
A	Quinlan Hammond	678	mechanic	29	"
B	Quinlan Nita—†	678	bookkeeper	27	"
C	Quinlan William	678	painter	55	"
D	Rutt William	678	clerk	21	"
E	Southwick Edward	678	salesman	30	"
F	Starks Hazel—†	678	cashier	26	"

Page.	Letter.	FULL NAME.	Residence, April 1, 1926.	Occupation.	Supposed Age.	Reported Residence, April 1, 1925. Street and Number.

Tremont Street—Continued

	G	Brackett Peter	680	chauffeur	45	here
	H	Campbell William	680	salesman	46	"
	K	Curtis Raymond	680	"	26	"
	L	Ford Frank	680	laborer	32	"
	M	Gagnon Mabel—†	680	saleswoman	38	Providence R I
	N	Georgian Harry	680	chef	39	New York
	O	Golding Edwin	680	photographer	64	here
	P	Hughes William	680	waiter	41	"
	R	Joyce Lawrence	680	painter	26	"
	S	Tobin Jeannette—†	680	housekeeper	43	"
	T	Dowd Timothy	682	lawyer	25	New York
	U	Fenner Walter	682	tel operator	35	here
	V	Fraser Grace—†	682	housekeeper	42	"
	W	Fraser John	682	machinist	43	"
	X	Goodman Robert	682	lawyer	38	New Bedford
	Y	McIsaac Louis	682	laborer	24	here
	Z	Mercer John	682	lather	26	"
	A	Morris Andrew	682	paintmixer	58	761 Tremont
	B	Appleyard Arthur	684	salesman	37	here
	C	Bender Nellie C—†	684	housewife	33	"
	D	Bender William E	684	painter	45	"
	E	Carter Ida G—†	684	inspector	60	"
	F	Cox Thomas H	684	salesman	50	"
	G	Faught Henry	684	"	69	"
	S	Grant James W	684	retired	74	"
	H	Hays Elizabeth—†	684	housewife	50	"
	K	Hays Samuel	684	tel operator	50	"
	L	Kershaw John F	684	druggist	39	"
	M	Moore Rebecca—†	684	housekeeper	40	"
	N	Polak Morris	684	shoecutter	45	"
	O	Sawyer Joseph	684	"	39	"
	P	Sieberg Edith—†	684	housewife	34	"
	R	Sieberg Fred	684	cabinetmaker	39	"
	T	Coughlin Dennis	686	boilermaker	48	1688 Wash'n
	U	Evans John	686	bricklayer	45	here
	V	Henry Mark	686	baker	28	600 Tremont
	W	McLee Augusta	686	cook	47	40 Montgomery
	X	McNeal Arthur	686	carpenter	30	496 Tremont
	Y	O'Brien Leo	686	counterman	22	700 "
	Z	Sheehy Mary—†	686	housekeeper	38	64 Emerald
	A	Amazeen Ada—†	688	waitress	30	here

27

Tremont Street—Continued

B	Dearveau Elias	688	barber	35	96 Pembroke
C	Donovan John F	688	retired	40	14 "
D	Jorgensen Ethel †	688	housekeeper	32	Somerville
E	Jorgensen Nitis	688	chauffeur	35	"
F	McFadden Charles	688	fireman	36	14 Pembroke
G	McIver Allen	688	carpenter	36	78 Worcester
H	Rivers William	688	glazier	40	571 Col av
L	Cotter Albert	690	salesman	25	1829 Wash'n
M	Cox Robert R	690	counterman	45	2 Back
N	Degan William	690	electrician	26	Fitchburg
O	Ford Fred W	690	salesman	21	here
P	Ford John	690	chauffeur	25	Lawrence
R	Gilbert Albert H	690	"	25	53 N Russell
S	Hannigan John	690	"	25	Lawrence
T	Jones Joseph	690	fireman	27	here
U	Nass Emily S †	690	housewife	43	"
V	Povler Joseph	690	student	20	Cambridge
W	Willey Fred	690	chauffeur	45	7 Waltham
Y	Ripley Gertrude †	692	housewife	44	747 Tremont
Z	Bixby Warren	692	painter	45	747 "
A	Clement Alice †	692	waitress	21	New Hampshire
B	Copill Cora †	692	bookkeeper	30	here
C	Haynes Frank	692	machinist	57	"
D	Haynes Gertrude †	692	housekeeper	57	"
E	Lackeye John	692	chauffeur	35	"
F	McGregor John	692	cabinetmaker	60	"
G	McKenzie Annie †	692	domestic	30	"
H	Thompson Celia †	692	seamstress	25	"
K	Thompson Mildred †	692	clerk	23	"
L	Toppan William	692	chauffeur	22	31 Rutland sq
M	Urguart James	692	motorman	45	here
N	Sing Chin	692A	laundryman	54	"
O	Bendell Florence †	694	dressmaker	40	"
P	Blake Kenneth M	694	musician	48	"
R	Currie Harold	694	shoemaker	22	"
S	Griggs Sarah J †	694	housekeeper	50	"
T	McWilliams James	694	shoemaker	50	"
U	Williams Harold C	694	clerk	50	"
V	Williams Mabel	694	housewife	50	"
X	Buckley Julia F †	696	housekeeper	50	"
Y	Buckley Thomas	696	manager	53	"

28

Page.	Letter.	FULL NAME.	Residence, April 1, 1926.	Occupation.	Supposed Age.	Reported Residence, April 1, 1925. Street and Number.

Tremont Street—Continued

z	Chase Mary A—†	696	buyer	51	here
A	Edkins Gertrude M—†	696	compositor	39	"
B	French William M	696	clerk	53	"
c	Grant Anne—†	696	waitress	45	"
c¹	Kendell Gertrude—†	696	saleswoman	29	Randolph
D	Russell William E	696	timekeeper	50	here
E	Russo Frank J	696	floorman	40	"
F	Smith William	696	toymaker	28	"
G	Wise Robert N	696	floorman	55	"
H	Allen Elizabeth J—†	698	housekeeper	60	"
K	Boderick Joseph	698	printer	65	"
L	Breece Dudue W	698	salesman	30	"
M	Howe Mae—†	698	stitcher	45	"
N	Johansen Carl	698	painter	37	"
O	Johansen Lillian—†	698	housewife	25	"
P	Parker Harry C	698	salesman	65	"
R	Pratt Charles A	698	physician	73	"
S	Sawyer Harold	698	brakeman	45	673 Tremont
T	Todd Allen	698	painter	47	here
U	Belediseaw Nelson J	700	cook	25	18 Victory rd
V	Derein Charles J	700	painter	26	here
W	Gaul Bernard C	700	"	21	72 Parkway
X	Gillis James A	700	carpenter	27	Nova Scotia
Y	Kelly Joseph	700	cook	25	3 Concord sq
Z	Lavin Evelyn—†	700	housekeeper	55	here
A	Long Michael	700	laborer	50	497 Mass av
D	Martin Emery M	700	shoemaker	48	Maine
B	Martin George	700	counterman	45	here
C	McLellan Archie	700	carpenter	35	"
E	Berry Ida—†	702	housewife	42	4 Pevear pl
F	Morgan Herberta—†	702	"	20	4 "
G	Morgan Wilfred	702	salesman	20	4 "
H	Robertson Edmund	702	electrician	42	Lowell
K	Robertson Margaret T—†	702	housewife	40	"
L	Burkhart Charles	704	teacher	70	here
M	Cameron Howard	704	lineman	21	Canada
N	Clarke Andrew	704	painter	38	here
O	Doucette Martin	704	carpenter	28	Canada
P	Faulkner Ida M—†	704	housekeeper	42	here
R	Gliane Daniel	704	machinist	20	733 Tremont
S	Habershaw Walter	704	laborer	30	here
T	Tattris John	704	roofer	32	"

Tremont Street—Continued

U	Davidson Amelia—†	706	housewife	28	here
V	Davidson Robert	706	pianoworker	27	"
W	Davidson William	706	retired	64	"
X	Ewen James	706	stonecutter	40	"
Y	Fleming Alexander	706	porter	40	"
Z	Fleming Clifford	706	laborer	38	"
A	Jastowski Bennie F	706	retired	31	"
B	Jastowski Julian	706	teller	64	"
C	Johnson Richard J	706	chauffeur	26	"
D	Lindholm Frank	706	asbestos worker	40	"
E	McGlue Arthur	706	laborer	42	"
F	McGrath Frank	706	pharmacist	44	"
G	Shaw Dial E	706	real estate	28	"
H	Shepard Louis J	706	painter	83	"
K	Walsh James	706	reporter	52	25 Union pk
L	Champlain Odessa C—†	708	clergyman	69	here
M	Champlain Will J	708	"	55	"
O	Crandall Cohen B	708	machinist	55	Pepperell
N	Crandall Delia—†	708	housewife	52	"
P	Gillian George	708	brassmolder	58	here
R	Griffin Daniel W	708	laborer	28	6 Hammett
S	Jewett Henry	708	chauffeur	28	New York
T	Kelly Charles G	708	clerk	54	here
U	Muir George	708	laborer	29	"
V	Ryder Clarence	708	special police	61	"
W	Williams Subina E—†	708	housewife	45	"

Washington Street

A	Russell Clara I—†	1565	housewife	33	1328 Wash'n
B	Russell Clarence H	1565	cook	43	1328 "
C	Langillo Sadie—†	1565	housewife	35	here
D	Peters Lewis	1565	salesman	33	Maine
G	Gianopoulos George	1571	restaurateur	43	here
H	Gianopoulos Jennie—†	1571	housewife	38	"
K	Shoras Charles	1571	counterman	30	"
L	Tsinbogrannis Constantina—†	1571	maid	45	"
M	Trakas Chris	1571	manager	36	"
N	Trakas Georgia—†	1571	housewife	35	"
O	Darling Daniel	1573	meatcutter	28	Everett

Washington Street—Continued

P	Drew John	1573	photographer	32	45 Worcester
R	Gettins James	1573	roofer	50	52 Rutland
S	Montgomery Benjamin	1573	electrician	45	here
T	Short Josephine—†	1573	housekeeper	32	701 Tremont
V	Boisvert Amare—†	1577	housewife	31	Dover N H
W	Boisvert Euchide	1577	laborer	34	New Hampshire
X	Dorothy Danell	1577	"	35	429 Walnut av
Y	Hunt Harvey M	1577	electrician	23	California
Z	Hunt Nellie R—†	1577	saleswoman	50	here
B	Joury Henry	1577	counterman	30	"
C	Joury Pearl—†	1577	housewife	30	"
D	MacLellon Lester R	1577	photographer	32	"
E	Tarvis Annie—†	1577	housekeeper	42	"
A	Tarvis Emanuel J	1577	carpenter	38	"
G	Boggs Albert	1581	elevatorman	45	"
H	Campbell Julia—†	1581	domestic	52	"
K	Doran Edward	1581	mason	60	60 Austin
L	Doran James J	1581	machinist	22	60 "
M	Doran Mary—†	1581	housekeeper	52	60 "
N	Lawrence Nickalos	1581	cook	30	here
O	MacDonald Angus	1581	carpenter	55	"
R	McKay James	1581	waiter	40	"
P	McLellan Hugh	1581	broker	45	"
S	O'Brine Francis J	1581	cook	23	60 Austin
T	Ryan Frank	1581	"	52	here
U	Stewart John	1581	taxi driver	60	"
V	Sullivan Margaret—†	1581	domestic	35	"
W	Thayer Fred	1581	carpenter	45	"
Y	Brown Emily—†	1585	chambermaid	24	7 Burbank
Z	Moran John B	1585	machinist	20	here
A	Moran Mary J—†	1585	houseworker	39	"
B	Calagett William E	1585	agent	50	"
C	Magee Nellie—†	1585	housewife	35	"
D	Jackson Edith—†	1585	housekeeper	32	"
L	Broderick Helen—†	1601	operator	33	"
M	Broderick Julia—†	1601	housewife	53	"
N	Broderick Katherine—†	1601	shipper	29	"
O	Sheehan Nora—†	1601	houseworker	73	"
R	Kelly Lotta B—†	1607	housekeeper	55	"
S	Kelly Marshall E	1607	chauffeur	43	"
X	Newman William	1615A	metalworker	23	"

31

Page	Letter	FULL NAME.	Residence, April 1, 1926.	Occupation.	Supposed Age.	Reported Residence, April 1, 1925. Street and Number.

Washington Street—Continued

	z	Backman Mabel—†	1615A	housewife	33	here
	y	Backman William	1615A	real estate	32	"
	a	Dorsey Anna—†	1615A	housekeeper	50	"
	b	Dorsey Catherine—†	1615A	"	45	"
	c	Dorsey Hughy	1615A	laborer	53	"
	e	Hubbard Etta—†	1621	housekeeper	54	3 Bird
	f	Knowles Mary—†	1621	"	76	20 Clifton pl
	g	Knowles Queenie—†	1621	cashier	29	20 "
	m	Lennox Adelbert	1629	carpenter	35	Lynn
	n	O'Donnell Richard	1629	"	43	56 Newland
	o	Reed Fannie C—†	1629	housekeeper	74	232 Broadway
	p	Sylvester Levna—†	1629	"	60	56 Newland

West Concord Street

	b	Edwards William H	73	laborer	46	Wellesley
	c	Flaherty William	73	"	42	20 Ryan
	d	McCarthy Tresa B—†	73	housewife	65	103 W Springfield
	e	McDonald James	73	machinist	56	448 Shawmut av
	f	Ridder Harry E	73	brakeman	42	103 W Springfield
	g	White Frank	73	painter	50	103 "
	p	Barry Henry	96	chauffeur	25	here
	r	Bell Robert	96	laborer	35	Quincy
	s	Currey Alice †	96	housewife	53	here
	t	Currey Douglas	96	woodmolder	65	"
	u	Ekberg Oscar	96	laborer	48	"
	v	Henry Gertrude—†	96	forewoman	27	35 Concord sq
	w	Miccuche James	96	laborer	54	here
	x	Miccuche Minnie—†	96	housewife	54	"
	y	Powel Harry	96	shipper	54	"
	z	Reed George	96	cook	54	1115 Wash'n
	a	Tucker Miles	96	bookkeeper	50	here
	c	Considine Elmer	98	laborer	40	108 Concord
	d	Haas Elizabeth—†	98	nurse	40	New York
	e	Hodoian Elijah	98	clerk	35	here
	f	Lineston Frank	98	cook	29	New York
	g	Osland Oscar	98	painter	26	here
	h	Raffaty Glades—†	98	housewife	27	"
	k	Waite Allen	98	laborer	31	"
	l	Westcott Evelyn—†	98	housekeeper	54	"

Page.	Letter.	FULL NAME.	Residence, April 1, 1926.	Occupation.	Supposed Age.	Reported Residence, April 1, 1925. Street and Number.

West Concord Street—Continued

	N	Kane Honora—†	100	housekeeper	58	here
	O	Kane Marry—†	100	"	55	"
	P	Lenine Eva—†	100	housewife	27	26 Worcester
	R	McLean Samuel	100	carpenter	35	1413 Shawmut av
	S	Murphy Elibeth—†	100	housewife	28	here
	T	Murphy Patrick	100	fireman	28	"
	U	Quinlan Bridget—†	100	houseworker	30	622 Tremont
	V	Vartanian Margrette—†	100	housewife	45	here
	W	Vartanian Shenabon	100	cook	45	"
	X	Wender Frederick W	100	engineer	58	8 Warren av
	Y	Woods Frank A	101	painter	75	here
	Z	Woods Julliette—†	101	housewife	77	"
	A	Harriss Sarah E—†	101	housekeeper	61	"
	B	Carney Bridget—†	101	cleaner	35	29 Milford
	C	Carney John W	101	laborer	42	29 "
	D	McCray Abbie—†	101	waitress	30	68 W Concord
	E	Eustis William	102	plumber	35	Maine
	F	Gillis Anna—†	102	waitress	25	here
	G	Killen Katheme—†	102	laundress	28	604 Mass av
	H	McDonald Margaret—†	102	housekeeper	38	here
	K	McDonald Mary—†	102	nurse	38	New York
	L	McDonald William	102	clerk	40	here
	M	McInis Frank	102	carpenter	23	"
	N	McInis Henry	102	clerk	20	"
	O	Roberts Clarence	102	chauffeur	28	77 Waltham
	P	Berry Albert	104	laborer	50	Worcester
	R	Berry Bertha—†	104	housewife	50	"
	S	Cole Henry	104	chauffeur	36	65 Rutland sq
	T	Dunlap Harry	104	laborer	25	502 Col av
	U	Dunlap William	104	"	34	502 "
	V	Green Albert	104	"	33	338 Tremont
	W	Green Allice—†	104	housewife	34	338 "
	X	Grignon Joseph	104	cook	35	here
	Y	Grignon Madeline—†	104	housewife	32	"
	Z	Lester Bertrice—†	104	"	23	New York
	A	Lester Earnest	104	laborer	21	"
	B	McCarthy William	104	"	40	here
	C	Bannon Jennie—†	106	cook	43	"
	D	Brint Margaret—†	106	housewife	37	"
	E	Brint William	106	laborer	40	"
	F	Forgett Margaret—†	106	brushmaker	38	"

Page.	Letter.	FULL NAME.	Residence, April 1, 1926.	Occupation.	Supposed Age.	Reported Residence, April 1, 1925. Street and Number.

West Concord Street—Continued

G	Kinney John	106	laborer	47	here
H	Lundin Edith —†	106	painter	22	Malden
K	Lundin Grold	106	"	55	"
L	Manley John	106	electrician	46	here
M	McDonogh Anna —†	106	housekeeper	80	"
N	McDonogh Grace —†	106	nurse	38	"
O	Quinlan James	106	laborer	50	"
P	Roberts Mary —†	106	housewife	37	"
R	Roberts Walter J	106	tailor	50	"
S	Wallace Joseph	106	chauffeur	55	"
T	Corkume Mary —†	108	housewife	22	Cambridge
U	Corkume Raymon	108	mechanic	21	"
V	Lane Anna —†	108	cook	45	Maine
W	Lawlor Lillian—†	108	waitress	30	106 Linden Park
X	McDonogh Elizbeth —†	108	hairdresser	28	167 W Newton
Y	O'Conors John	108	porter	35	52 Waltham
A	Tolman Anna —†	108	housekeeper	43	593 Tremont
B	Tolman Nellie —†	108	waitress	20	593 "
C	Esifforn Florence—†	110	housewife	49	Cambridge
D	Griffen William	110	brushmaker	58	"
E	Halligan John	110	laborer	31	here
F	Hill George R	110	painter	61	"
G	Kerk John C	110	salesman	60	31 W Concord
H	Mitchell Emma M—†	110	housewife	45	447 Audubon rd
K	Mitchell Ralph T	110	salesman	48	447 "
L	Shea Mary —†	110	housewife	71	here
M	Shea Samuel	110	machinist	72	"
N	Stephens Anne E —†	110	housewife	83	1 Glenwood
O	Wentworth Ida—†	110	"	50	here
P	Wentworth Louis	110	manager	49	"
R	Boehler William	112	cook	26	Medfield
S	Bradley Anna —†	112	laundress	65	here
T	Correll Teresa —†	112	houseworker	35	818 Harris'n av
U	Fisher Dorothy —†	112	factory worker	22	here
V	McNulty Rose—†	112	housekeeper	65	Rhode Island
W	Raymen Mary —†	112	hairdresser	28	here
X	Ruane Mary —†	112	housekeeper	44	"
Y	Shea Freida —†	112	cook	39	Medford
Z	Shea Timothy G	112	laborer	26	"
A	Ayer Libbie —†	114	teacher	40	here

34

Page.	Letter	FULL NAME.	Residence, April 1, 1926.	Occupation.	Supposed Age.	Reported Residence, April 1, 1925. Street and Number.

West Concord Street—Continued

B	Cogsinel Gordon	114	retired	65	Concord N H
C	Daily Emily—†	114	houseworker	35	Malden
D	Driscoll Joseph	114	laborer	30	here
E	Farran Maude—†	114	clerk	45	"
F	Glines Anabel—†	114	houseworker	40	"
G	Hansbury Mary—†	114	dressmaker	45	65 Worcester
K	McIsaac Annie—†	114	housekeeper	55	here
L	McIsaac James	114	ironworker	60	"
M	Shungler William	114	cigarmaker	70	"
H	Tobin Edward	114	watchman	65	148 W Concord
N	Volk Lupune	114	cigar stamper	25	New Hampshire
O	White May—†	114	houseworker	30	38 Worcester
P	Penninan Ada M—†	116	at home	72	here
R	Samfan Georgianna—†	116	"	84	"
S	Armstrong Theodore	118	retired	84	"
T	Kiefer Albert L	118	printer	33	"
U	Kiefer Ellen J—†	118	housewife	36	"
V	McPhee Erwin T	118	truckman	34	"
W	McPhee Lydia—†	118	housewife	38	"
X	Connors William	119	cook	30	245 Shawmut av
Y	Cronin John J	119	salesman	53	here
Z	Gammon George	119	clerk	50	"
A	Hickey Clara—†	119	dressmaker	73	"
B	McGrady Anna—†	119	bookbinder	50	138 Terrace
C	McQuaid Mary—†	119	housekeeper	63	here
D	Powers Ella—†	119	boxmaker	37	"
E	Smith Arthur	119	laborer	29	156 Hunt'n av
F	Smith Thomas	119	cleaner	32	17 Lawrence
G	Canton Charles	120	laborer	30	42 Upton
H	Cropsey Earl	120	machinist	35	here
K	Fay Andrew M	120	lineman	60	"
L	Flint Grace—†	120	houseworker	32	427 Blue Hill av
M	Larrabee Arthur	120	cook	26	571 Mass av
N	Mabbett Horace	120	salesman	50	here
O	MacCoubrey James	120	retired	70	"
P	Newhaul Hurbert	120	laborer	30	Lynn
R	Porter Elizabeth—†	120	housekeeper	50	here
S	Soucaros Stelios	120	waiter	32	64 Rutland
T	Allstrom Henry	121	shoeworker	32	here
U	Chambers Clifton C	121	motion pictures	35	New Bedford
V	Coyne Harold	121	shoeworker	33	1890 Wash'n

Page.	Letter.	FULL NAME.	Residence, April 1, 1926.	Occupation.	Supposed Age.	Reported Residence, April 1, 1925. Street and Number.

West Concord Street—Continued

	w	Coyne Marie —†	121	silkworker	30	1890 Wash'n
	x	Deschamps Arthur	121	roofer	41	157 W Concord
	y	Deschamps Blanche—†	121	stitcher	38	157 "
	z	Grimshaw Edyth—†	121	teacher	50	here
	A	Grimshaw Ethel—†	121	housewife	56	"
	B	Halcron William J	121	carpenter	67	"
	C	Losee Sadie—†	121	laundryworker	34	"
	D	Marshall Frank	121	janitor	46	"
	E	Murray Lena—†	121	stitcher	34	11 Haviland
	F	Nickerson George B	121	dairyman	41	here
	G	Nickerson Jennie—†	121	housewife	39	"
	H	Alexander Olga—†	122	waitress	34	153 W Newton
	K	Bootier Anna—†	122	housewife	21	Somerville
	L	Bootier Edward	122	laborer	23	here
	M	Crokes Mary—†	122	housekeeper	35	98 Howard
	N	Crokes Thomas	122	mechanic	40	98 "
	O	Gagnon Thomas	122	shoemaker	39	here
	P	Gibbs Walter	122	laborer	60	"
	R	Johnson Johanna—†	122	nurse	38	Rockport
	S	Johnson John	122	brakeman	40	"
	T	Killeen Helen—†	122	waitress	25	New York
	U	Killeen Thomas J	122	salesman	25	"
	V	Oakes Etta—†	122	housewife	78	508 Mass av
	W	Oakes James	122	mechanic	42	508 "
	X	Walsh Myrtle—†	122	housewife	26	Brookline
	Y	Walsh William	122	tailor	30	"
	Z	Bowen John	123	laborer	45	here
	A	Driscoll Nora—†	123	housekeeper	51	"
	B	Gannett George	123	waiter	30	69 E Dedham
	C	Kennedy Peter J	123	painter	66	Keene N H
	D	McGraw Edward	123	retired	60	Cambridge
	E	Quinn Michael	123	chauffeur	56	here
	F	Finny Elizabeth—†	123	saleswoman	30	Quincy
	G	Bobbins Harry	124	salesman	40	Lawrence
	H	Dwyer Thomas	124	gardener	48	80 Worcester
	K	Gagnon Arthur	124	shoemaker	35	here
	L	Gagnon Mary—†	124	"	26	"
	M	Johnson George	124	counterman	50	624 Mass av
	N	Johnson May—†	124	housekeeper	45	624 "
	O	Mudgett Anna—†	124	"	26	here
	P	Mudgett Richard	124	clerk	30	"

West Concord Street—Continued

R	Nystrom Carl	124	carpenter	25	here
T	Pillsbury Anna—†	124	housekeeper	55	518 Tremont
U	Riggs Minnie—†	124	"	44	523 Col av
V	Riggs Thomas	124	laborer	50	Haverhill
W	Stuart Lina—†	124	clerk	45	523 Col av
S	Taggard Beatrice—†	124	housekeeper	38	here
X	Davis Thomas H	125	waiter	30	866 Tremont
Y	DeMarr Amedie	125	carpenter	40	136 Concord
Z	MacDonald Carolina—†	125	housekeeper	38	Nova Scotia
A	MacDonald Thomas	125	waiter	37	750 Shawmut av
B	Mercier Theophilus	125	wireworker	40	24 Rutland sq
C	Mercier Wilfred	125	carpenter	40	New York
D	Toomey Henery	125	laborer	30	750 Shawmut av
E	Dee Albert F	126	waiter	47	here
F	Dee Eva—†	126	housekeeper	42	"
G	Southwick Anna—†	126	"	80	"
H	Castro Anthony	127	chauffeur	38	"
K	Castro Mandy—†	127	housewife	38	"
L	Courtenay Ellen M—†	127	housekeeper	62	"
M	Courtenay Richard	127	fireman	25	"
N	Gregory Madge—†	127	nurse	37	"
O	Martin Charles	127	"	43	"
P	Martin Rose—†	127	housewife	41	"
R	McGrath Jeramiah	127	machinist	45	
S	Murray Margaret R—†	127	housewife	50	76 Springfield
T	Murray Thomas T	127	papermaker	60	76 "
U	Pritchard Sarah—†	127	at home	70	here
V	Tilden Joel	127	woodturner	65	"
X	Hines Timothy	128	conductor	45	Malden
Y	Lasell Edith—†	128	housekeeper	30	147 W Concord
Z	Lasell Harold J	128	clerk	30	147 "
A	Diamond Henry	128	plumber	35	451 Mass av
A¹	Diamond Minnie—†	128	housekeeper	35	451 "
B	Derocher Mary—†	129	domestic	48	here
C	Dodge Arthur C	129	carpenter	60	"
D	Glynn James	129	laborer	45	53 E Springfield
E	Harrison Arron	129	painter	45	450 Shawmut av
F	Harrison Mabel E—†	129	housewife	55	450 "
G	MacDonald Sarah—†	129	housekeeper	48	here
H	Stanton Peter	129	bookkeeper	42	700 Tremont
K	Ward Thomas	129	laborer	50	here

West Concord Street—Continued

L	Watson John	129	trimmer	49	137 W Concord
M	Adams Charles	130	waiter	28	here
N	Bertram George	130	writer	40	"
O	Donlon John	130	steamfitter	45	"
P	Donlon Nora—†	130	housekeeper	45	"
R	Megan Frank	130	retired	69	"
S	Megan Mary—†	130	housekeeper	58	"
T	Murray Bridget—†	130	"	29	Malden
U	Natsi Thomas	130	printer	31	here
V	Reed Frank	130	laborer	58	118 W Concord
W	Scott William	130	paperhanger	40	here
X	Stergo George	130	laborer	32	"
Y	Cole Cornelius	131	metalworker	23	New Jersey
Z	Doherty Joseph	131	laborer	20	20 W B'way
A	Fallon Catherine S—†	131	housekeeper	45	48 Lexington
B	Fallon James	131	salesman	43	48 "
C	Folger Charles	131	bookkeeper	27	here
D	Grimely John	131	waiter	21	Lawrence
E	Harkin Charles A	131	salesman	26	here
F	Kirby James	131	ironworker	55	"
G	Shea James P	131	printer	45	Winthrop
H	Brown Frank W	132	musician	50	10 Concord sq
K	Cannell Richard	132	clerk	31	Newton Centre
L	Chacheleus Charles E	132	shoemaker	42	here
M	Chacheleus Effameil—†	132	"	42	"
N	Evenhecht Fritz	132	cigarmaker	42	"
O	Hale Anna—†	132	housekeeper	33	"
P	Hale John H	132	janitor	54	"
R	Hartnett William L	132	nurse	28	Medford
S	Lawless Thomas F	132	inspector	46	1667 Wash'n
T	Mephin Bridget—†	132	housekeeper	49	here
U	Mephin Peter	132	machinist	57	"
V	Readman George H	132	engineer	60	"
W	Antonia Marion—†	133	cook	45	Cambridge
X	Cleary Charles	133	pianofinisher	45	35 E Concord
Y	Flaherty Elizabeth J—†	133	housewife	38	here
Z	Flaherty Patrick A	133	retired	38	"
A	Flaherty Thomas J	133	manager	35	Chelsea
B	Leachman William	133	baker	50	here
C	MacDonald Margaret—†	133	domestic	37	46 E Brookline
D	MacDonald Minnie—†	133	checker	40	148 W Concord

West Concord Street—Continued

E	Moses Frank	133	waiter	37	618 Tremont
F	Begg Ina V—†	134	cook	47	here
G	Briery Elizabeth B—†	134	at home	65	"
H	Holmes Vesta L—†	134	housekeeper	48	"
K	Holmes Walter A	134	salesman	64	"
L	Bartlett Chester	135	motorman	35	"
M	Beaudette Arthur	135	manager	27	"
N	Gilarine Ellen—†	135	at home	45	Wellesley
O	Graham Amanda—†	135	housewife	61	here
P	Graham Frank J	135	bricklayer	57	"
R	Hopkirk Jessie—†	135	printer	40	"
S	Kilarney Frank	135	chef	33	70 Rutland
T	Kilarney Lillian—†	135	housewife	31	70 "
U	Tucker Alice—†	135	at home	70	here
V	Watt David	135	piano tuner	61	"
W	Cuspic John C	136	laborer	21	"
X	MacBeth Charles	136	"	35	"
Y	MacDonald Donald N	136	clerk	21	"
Z	MacLean Kenneth	136	carpenter	27	"
A	MacLean Sadie J—†	136	housekeeper	23	"
B	MacLeod Catherine C—†	136	"	60	"
C	MacPherson William	136	chef	60	818 Harris'n av
D	Tingley Anna—†	136	dressmaker	30	Lynn
E	Allen Patrick J	137	shoeworker	35	Medford
F	Burns John	137	laborer	25	Maine
G	Luck Ethel J—†	137	lawyer	24	Cambridge
H	McCloskey John	137	laborer	26	here
K	Prince Mary—†	137	at home	50	"
L	Smith John	137	butler	60	"
M	Smith Mary—†	137	cook	40	"
N	Stewart Mary—†	137	stitcher	40	31 Upton
O	Stott John	137	laborer	25	New Hampshire
P	Toomey Katherine—†	137	at home	55	here
R	Walsh Susan—†	137	housekeeper	35	"
S	Wheeler Bernard	137	laborer	40	"
T	Bruno Wayne	138	student	30	146 W Concord
U	Daniels Jennie—†	138	clerk	21	625 Tremont
V	Fitzabeth Celia—†	138	at home	50	Cambridge
W	Morelli Ernest	138	watchman	31	here
X	Rudy Delia W—†	138	housekeeper	50	"
Y	Westringe Oscar	138	cigarmaker	35	"

Page	Letter	Full Name.	Residence, April 1, 1926.	Occupation.	Supposed Age.	Reported Residence, April 1, 1925. Street and Number.

West Concord Street—Continued

z	Wrichstrom Ellis	138	steamfitter	27	here
A	Doyle Edwin J	139	carpenter	44	271 Hancock
B	Doyle Eva F—†	139	housekeeper	37	271 "
C	Francis Edith —†	139	factory worker	40	here
D	Francis Michael J	139	R R man	44	"
E	Holmes Cora—†	139	housewife	50	577 Mass av
F	Holmes Howard	139	expressman	54	577 "
G	Hudon John	139	mechanic	64	here
H	Lindham Fred	139	machinist	65	173 Tremont
K	MacDonald Sarah—†	139	nurse	35	29 Morton
L	Mooney Agnes—†	139	clerk	39	here
M	Mooney Mary—†	139	"	39	"
N	Waldron Harry A	139	storekeeper	53	"
O	Carr Frank L	140	school teacher	27	43 E Newton
P	Donovan John E	140	manager	48	here
R	Drisko Morton H	140	clerk	28	"
S	MacElroy Thomas H	140	manager	55	"
T	McDonald Nellie—†	140	saleswoman	42	"
U	Metheringham Kate—†	140	storekeeper	47	"
V	Murphy Louise M—†	140	nurse	42	"
W	Nephin Joseph	140	retired	55	"
X	Nephin Julia A—†	140	housewife	54	"
Y	O'Brien Ellen M—†	140	dressmaker	60	"
Z	Phelan Mary V—†	140	at home	62	"
A	Sturgeon Sarah—†	140	laundress	37	"
B	Tarbell Laura—†	140	forewoman	50	
C	Tebo Bertha—†	140	cashier	24	146 W Concord
D	Tebo Irving A	140	salesman	27	146 "
E	Whitcomb Alice C—†	140	dressmaker	63	131 Pembroke
F	Helchie Ernest	141	painter	25	554 Mass av
G	Page Anna—†	141	housewife	21	876 Harris'n av
H	Page Arthur	141	janitor	24	876 "
K	Ricker Harold	141	machinist	28	15 W Dedham
L	Ricker Margaret—†	141	housewife	34	59 Rutland
M	Ricker Minetta—†	141	"	33	15 W Dedham
N	Ricker Ralph	141	painter	37	59 Rutland
O	Wischt Michael	141	laborer	25	Newport R I
P	Bell Elizabeth—†	142	at home	70	here
R	Brown Mabel—†	142	bookkeeper	42	Lowell
S	Calhoun Anna—†	142	nurse	46	here
T	Egan Mary—†	142	bookkeeper	40	"

Page.	Letter.	FULL NAME.	Residence, April 1, 1926.	Occupation.	Supposed Age.	Reported Residence, April 1, 1925. Street and Number.

West Concord Street—Continued

u	Lewis Ethel—†	142	clerk	21	Lynn
v	McCommack Regina—†	142	waitress	33	here
w	McDonough John	142	salesman	32	"
x	McKenna Sarah—†	142	at home	45	"
y	McMartin Edward B	142	engineer	67	"
z	McMartin Helen—†	142	housewife	60	"
A	McMartin Ruth—†	142	postal clerk	30	"
B	Regan Mary—†	142	nurse	45	"
c	True Sarah—†	142	at home	76	"
D	Whitelaw Margarite—†	142	nurse	67	"
E	Beattie Austin	143	vocalist	50	88 W Newton
F	Beattie Mary R—†	143	housewife	48	88 "
G	Crowley Hanah—†	143	housekeeper	50	here
H	Duby Alice—†	143	wool sorter	38	"
K	Nash Thomas	143	teamster	36	"
L	Osterly Bertha—†	143	clerk	50	"
M	Osterly Frank	143	butcher	57	"
N	Udell Frances—†	143	clerk	34	"
o	Young James	143	gardener	26	"
P	Young Margaret M—†	143	housewife	22	"
R	Curry Alice E—†	144	housekeeper	54	"
s	Curry Thomas	144	foreman	56	"
T	Kilbourne Annie C—†	144	buyer	60	"
u	Lendgren Carl V	144	clergyman	28	Chicago Ill
v	Merrifield Prescott B	144	shipper	34	here
w	Risk Sarah J—†	144	housewife	36	"
x	Risk William W	144	lawyer	52	"
y	Sargent Richard T	144	retired	72	"
z	Brookner Carl A W	145	carpenter	53	Stoughton
A	Burns John R	145	druggist	23	10 Concord sq
B	Cummings Catherine—†	145	housewife	45	708 Tremont
c	Franckville Charles M	145	machinist	47	130 W Concord
D	Jessmome Charles H	145	mechanic	25	here
E	Jessmome Joseph	145	"	52	149 W Concord
F	Kanzig Susan—†	145	saleswoman	38	56 E Springfield
G	Kendall George	145	cashier	57	here
H	Lane Thomas	145	inspector	54	"
K	McCarthy John J	145	waiter	35	7 Col sq
L	Slattery Ellen J—†	145	stitcher	38	Brookline
M	Stringer Margaret—†	145	waitress	29	127 W Newton
N	Williams James	145	machinist	35	102 Selden

Page.	Letter.	FULL NAME.	Residence, April 1, 1926.	Occupation.	Supposed Age.	Reported Residence, April 1, 1925. Street and Number.

West Concord Street—Continued

	O	Barker Elizabeth E—†	146	housekeeper	45	here
	P	Barker Guy B	146	clerk	42	"
	R	Beach Gertrude—†	146	checker	42	96 Hunt'n av
	S	Bradley Leon A	146	waiter	28	32 Thane
	T	Fishback Morris	146	cigarmaker	41	here
	U	Flynn Mary—†	146	bookkeeper	27	"
	V	Gaynor Frank R	146	retired	51	Arlington
	W	Hanley Katherine F—†	146	clerk	60	427 Col av
	X	Hollis Harriet L—†	146	bookkeeper	31	here
	Y	Lucas Amelia—†	146	"	31	"
	Z	Maxwell Joseph	146	salesman	25	"
	A	Mulcahy Margaret—†	146	proofreader	38	"
	B	Blair Margaret—†	147	domestic	40	32 Thornton
	C	Brown Ella—†	147	waitress	46	here
	D	Burr Louis	147	shipper	46	"
	E	Donagley Edward	147	rigger	40	"
	F	Gring Ambrose D, jr	147	musician	45	"
	G	Lydoen Catharine—†	147	nurse	51	"
	H	Lydoen John	147	"	50	"
	K	Moore Nellie—†	147	housekeeper	40	"
	L	O'Brien Elizabeth M—†	147	housewife	34	"
	M	O'Brien Patrick J	147	asbestos worker	39	"
	N	Quirk Mary A—†	147	milliner	65	"
	O	Anderson John	148	painter	28	Lynn
	P	Conners Gertrude—†	148	saleswoman	32	Brockton
	R	Larnez Bessie—†	148	houseworker	38	Lowell
	S	Larnez William	148	cigarmaker	45	"
	T	MacDonald Ella—†	148	houseworker	42	here
	U	McCommack Malvina—†	148	at home	75	"
	V	Roseberg Carl	148	laborer	52	"
	W	Athenson Arthur	149	cook	35	Waltham
	X	Hengston John	149	carpenter	40	Lynn
	Y	Higgins Florence—†	149	housekeeper	55	25 Rutland
	Z	Keith Etta W—†	149	housewife	34	19 W Springfield
	A	Keith Havilah	149	machinist	36	19 "
	B	Lehman Addie †	149	at home	53	79 Warren
	C	Meehan James	149	steward	50	here
	D	Moore Harold	149	steamfitter	42	"
	E	Noonan Hazel—†	149	housewife	28	6 Yarmouth
	F	Noonan John	149	boilermaker	31	6 "
	G	Staples George H	149	retired	74	660 Mass av

Page.	Letter.	FULL NAME.	Residence, April 1, 1926.	Occupation.	Supposed Age.	Reported Residence, April 1, 1925. Street and Number.

West Concord Street—Continued

	H	Staples Mary R—†	149	housekeeper	63	660 Mass av
	K	Utz Helen—†	149	artist	30	175 Hemenway
	L	Chew Georgie—†	150	housewife	29	Lowell
	M	Chew James R	150	electrician	30	here
	N	Mack Arthur	150	bricklayer	50	Brockton
	O	Munroe Margaret—†	150	at home	63	here
	P	Murphy Margaret—†	150	dressmaker	35	Lowell
	R	Myer Carl	150	meatcutter	38	here
	S	Seitz Eliza—†	150	at home	65	Lynn
	T	Woods May—†	150	waitress	35	Lowell
	U	Buckley Mollie—†	151	housekeeper	65	here
	V	Francis George	151	retired	79	"
	W	Angel Edward	152	physician	28	"
	X	Byrne Joseph	152	student	23	New York
	Y	Cahill Reta—†	152	nurse	22	Lynn
	Z	Cavanaugh Alice—†	152	laundress	40	here
	A	Coleman Peter	152	laborer	30	"
	B	Conner Thomas	152	salesman	38	"
	C	Hall Helen A—†	152	nurse	28	Providence R I
	D	Havini Alexander	152	laborer	40	Lowell
	E	Lenard Ida—†	152	bowmaker	39	here
	F	Lenard Percy	152	clerk	30	"
	G	Lenard Thomas	152	salesman	44	"
	H	Strout George V	152	retired	55	"
	K	Strout Mary J—†	152	at home	53	"
	L	Upham Robert	152	laborer	68	"
	M	Cronin John	153	shoeworker	40	"
	N	Doane William	153	carpenter	34	Chelsea
	O	Galbert Eugene	153	mechanic	62	here
	P	Hodgkinson William J	153	policeman	35	113 Worcester
	R	Kinsley Jane—†	153	housekeeper	71	here
	S	Mayberry Frank	153	real estate	72	"
	T	Murphy Nellie—†	153	seamstress	70	"
	U	Powers Mary E—†	153	saleswoman	50	"
	V	Powers William T	153	salesman	65	"
	W	Chesley Phoebe L—†	154	nurse	63	"
	X	Elsdalil Conrad	154	pianoworker	27	"
	Y	Graham Isabel M—†	154	housekeeper	51	"
	Z	Graham John F	154	painter	52	"
	A	Hughes Katherine E—†	154	secretary	35	"
	B	Lyons Micheal F	154	druggist	60	"

43

Page.	Letter.	FULL NAME.	Residence, April 1, 1926.	Occupation	Supposed Age.	Reported Residence, April 1, 1925. Street and Number.

West Concord Street—Continued

	c	McClellan Ronald	154	machinist	35	here
	d	McLeod Harry E	154	leather sorter	30	Lynn
	e	Spike Margaret V—†	154	seamstress	50	here
	f	Duddy Charles	155	salesman	54	Gardner
	g	Hudson John	155	cashier	60	here
	h	Jones Frank	155	printer	66	"
	k	Murray Joseph E	155	papercutter	45	"
	l	Oliver Clarence	155	salesman	54	"
	m	Snyder Charles H	155	"	52	"
	n	Snyder Mary A—†	155	housewife	46	"
	o	Andrews Margaret—†	156	clerk	45	"
	p	Andrews William	156	"	20	"
	r	Brooks Louise—†	156	at home	80	"
	s	Conboy Myrtle—†	156	clerk	43	"
	t	Dillon Margaret—†	156	cashier	26	"
	u	Dobson Herbert	156	clerk	47	"
	v	Dobson Kathrine—†	156	housekeeper	45	"
	w	Shanley Micheal	156	engineer	53	"
	x	Shanley Nellie—†	156	housekeeper	48	"
	y	Marcoux Ulric S	157	fireman	27	Webster
	z	Noble Andrew	157	salesman	49	here
	a	Noble Mary—†	157	nurse	50	"
	b	Richenburg Herman	157	machinist	32	4246 Wash'n
	c	Steele Marion—†	157	telegrapher	31	Portland Me
	d	Steele Walter B	157	salesman	34	"
	e	Worley Mary—†	157	housewife	37	here
	f	Worley William	157	machinist	41	"
	g	Young Clara F—†	157	housewife	56	"
	h	Young Ernest M	157	expressman	37	"
	k	Young John B	157	real estate	58	"
	l	Ashworth Harry	158	janitor	40	Fall River
	m	Ashworth Mary—†	158	packer	32	"
	n	Bradley William	158	millhand	21	Scotland
	o	Innes Mary—†	158	cook	45	87 Warren av
	p	Maroney Ida—†	158	agent	40	104 W Concord
	r	McLean Annie—†	158	waitress	34	here
	s	McLean John F	158	electrician	34	"
	t	McLean Mary—†	158	housekeeper	61	"
	u	Watkins Patrick	158	lineman	46	"
	v	Anderson Oscar	160	engineer	35	Quincy
	w	Bishop Ruby—†	160	waitress	30	here

Page.	Letter.	FULL NAME.	Residence, April 1, 1926.	Occupation.	Supposed Age.	Reported Residence, April 1, 1925. Street and Number.

West Concord Street—Continued

	x	Cantello Angelo	160	salesman	34	here
	Y	Green Edward	160	"	28	Newton
	z	O'Connor Walter	160	operator	35	681 Mass av
	A	Smith Nellie—†	160	dressmaker	50	here
	B	Weston Hortense M—†	160	housekeeper	36	"
	C	Winslow Gladys—†	160	waitress	34	"
	D	Brown Thomas	162	laborer	30	Lynn
	E	Carter Augustus	162	painter	29	here
	F	Curtis Florence A—†	162	housekeeper	44	"
	G	Duncan Arthur	162	baker	28	"
	H	Mitchell Olive—†	162	housekeeper	20	Winthrop
	K	Phillips Grace—†	162	clerk	32	Worcester
	L	Smith Gertrude—†	162	housekeeper	25	here

West Haven Street

	M	Williams Thomas	1	coal passer	49	here

West Newton Street

	R	Cherel Harry V	36	shoecutter	51	here
	S	Garvey Margaret—†	36	operator	29	"
	S¹	Gordon Herbert	36	bookkeeper	66	"
	T	Hatt Lottie F—†	36	operator	42	"
	U	Keyser Herbert H	36	salesman	27	"
	V	Levy Anna R—†	36	housekeeper	24	"
	W	Levy Arthur R	36	mechanic	26	"
	X	Linnham Rose—†	36	clerk	42	"
	Y	McCormack John J	36	"	40	"
	z	Mason William H	36	"	53	"
	A	McCabe Sarah J—†	36	at home	72	"
	B	McHugh Anna—†	36	housekeeper	43	"
	C	McHugh James F	36	clerk	39	"
	D	Meehan Frank	36	laborer	33	New York
	E	Moran Martin	36	foreman	28	here
	F	Newcomb Alroy	36	salesman	29	"
	G	Roche William F	36	photographer	38	377 Col av
	H	Stairides Helen S—†	36	clerk	59	here
	K	Sweeney Helen—†	36	"	40	"

45

West Newton Street—Continued

	Letter	FULL NAME	Residence	Occupation	Age	Reported Residence
	L	Bichterman Charles C	37	electrician	37	here
	M	Collins John J	37	chemist	48	"
	N	Fitzgerald Mary E—†	37	housekeeper	48	"
	O	Fitzgerald Maurice E	37	physician	49	"
	P	Garfink Maurice	37	motorman	36	"
	R	Gavin Frank J	37	chauffeur	35	65 Stoughton
	S	McNeil Neil B	37	carpenter	35	here
	T	Mitchell James H	37	retired	65	"
	U	Sandler Frank L	37	boatbuilder	54	"
	V	Sandler Ray F	37	salesman	26	"
	W	Walsh Daniel B	37	clerk	42	"
	X	Gowe George	38	cashier	51	"
	Y	Moore Wilbert	38	teller	42	"
	Z	Moynihan Charlotte—†	38	stenographer	40	46 W Newton
	A	Nash George B	38	wireman	71	70 Green
	B	Rogers John M	38	harnessmaker	58	here
	C	Rogers Mary E—†	38	housekeeper	56	"
	D	Scott William	38	clerk	50	"
	E	Wyman Elsie—†	38	nurse	36	"
	F	Wyman Ralph L	38	waiter	41	"
	G	Anderson Hannah—†	39	housekeeper	62	"
	H	Batchelder Caroline A—†	39	nurse	45	"
	K	Fairbanks Nathaniel	39	shoecutter	35	Portland Me
	L	Grann Gustaf	39	salesman	79	here
	M	Kearins Anna C—†	39	clerk	38	"
	N	Olson Gustaf M	39	upholsterer	43	"
	O	Stevens Leonard R	39	clerk	58	"
	P	Authier Charlotte—†	40	social worker	36	"
	R	Barrows Esther—†	40	"	51	"
	S	Barrows Evelyn L—†	40	teacher	48	"
	T	Blood Ellen F—†	40	social worker	36	"
	U	Collins Nellie—†	40	maid	41	"
	V	Houghton Mabel E—†	40	dietitian	36	"
	W	Kappelle Adella—†	40	cook	50	Nova Scotia
	X	Kefover Roselma—†	40	social worker	41	Uniontown Pa
	Y	Miller Elizabeth—†	40	"	36	here
	Z	Partridge Dorothy—†	40	"	30	Braintree
	A	Shekjerian Flora—†	40	maid	30	Somerville
	B	Smyth Anna L—†	40	social worker	45	Cambridge
	C	Spoor Ruth—†	40	director	46	Watertown
	D	Burtridge Adeline—†	41	houseworker	68	here

46

West Newton Street—Continued

E	Burtridge Helen G E—†	41	clerk	36	here
F	Chesborough Caroline W	41	waitress	59	"
G	Conrad Charles F	41	waiter	53	"
H	Conrad Frances A—†	41	houseworker	51	"
K	Gallagher Margaret A—†	41	housekeeper	59	"
L	Greathead Carrie W—†	41	saleswoman	52	"
M	Keating Jennie—†	41	dressmaker	55	"
N	Keating Julia A—†	41	saleswoman	49	"
O	Leatherwood Paulita W-†	41	housewife	26	44 W Newton
P	Leatherwood Roy F	41	collector	38	44 "
R	LeClaire Alphonse F	41	proprietor	58	here
S	Mackie Thomas J	41	carpenter	71	"
T	McGrath Annie—†	41	houseworker	34	Milton
U	McGrath John J	41	clerk	31	141 Arlington
V	Raymond Isadore	41	"	39	here
W	Rollins Ruth—†	41	"	23	"
X	Sweeney Helen V—†	41	saleswoman	43	20 E Springfield
Y	Sweeney Mary I—†	41	houseworker	53	20 "
Z	Baillageon Louis	42	machinist	27	9 Ringgold
A	Crevier Alcide	42	carpenter	35	here
B	Euinters Marie T—†	42	dressmaker	26	336 Shawmut av
C	Fernald Emma—†	42	housekeeper	70	here
D	Laberge Henry	42	machinist	25	9 Ringgold
E	LeBlane Wilfred	42	painter	21	9 "
F	Miller John H	42	chef	32	565 Col av
G	Mooney George	42	clerk	55	Maine
H	O'Donnell John	42	"	40	74 W Newton
K	Sears Jack	42	waiter	26	here
L	Slysian Alphonsine—†	42	housekeeper	44	"
M	Slysian Antonio	42	machinist	24	"
N	Slysian Edward	42	laborer	20	"
R	Valley Antonio	42	painter	24	Manchester N H
O	Voit Arthur	42	clerk	28	here
P	Voit Ruth—†	42	housekeeper	26	"
S	Warren Anna—†	42	at home	82	"
T	George George	43	retired	75	"
U	George Mary—†	43	housekeeper	70	"
V	Meeter John F	43	laborer	65	"
W	Steward Alice C—†	43	clerk	23	New York
X	Walton John J	43	laborer	25	here
Y	Allen William H	44	retired	78	"

Page.	Letter.	FULL NAME	Residence, April 1, 1926	Occupation.	Supposed Age.	Reported Residence, April 1, 1925. Street and Number.

West Newton Street—Continued

z	Ayool Mary —†	44	housekeeper	42	561 Dudley
A	Fayle Charles H	44	compositor	54	Cambridge
B	Gately Patrick	44	shoeworker	50	20 Louder's lane
C	Homan Harry	44	janitor	34	Maine
D	O'Brien Mary E —†	44	clerk	36	here
E	Bellew Catherine —†	45	packer	24	"
F	Chambers David	45	contractor	46	"
G	Chambers Lillie †	45	housewife	38	"
H	Conroy Margaret —†	45	nurse	38	"
K	Ellis Bernice †	45	waitress	27	"
L	Ellis Philip	45	mechanic	32	"
M	Flemming Margaret —†	45	waitress	28	New York
N	Freeman Mary—†	45	housekeeper	50	74 W Newton
O	Freeman Saul F	45	carpenter	50	74 "
P	Hopkins Ethel—†	45	cashier	25	here
R	Hughes George	45	clerk	60	"
S	Kightlinger Elmer S	45	mechanic	29	10 Radcliffe rd
T	Kightlinger Rae M—†	45	housekeeper	28	10 "
U	Lamont John	45	chauffeur	35	Nantucket
V	McDonald May—†	45	checker	30	here
W	Rohne Louise—†	45	governess	35	"
X	Walsh Mary—†	46	housekeeper	59	"
Y	Walsh Robert	46	clerk	69	"
Z	MacNally Mary F—†	46	"	35	11 James
A	McNally Nora—†	46	housekeeper	65	11 "
B	Bates Caroline †	46	"	66	82 Berkeley
C	DeWitt Mildred—†	46	"	54	here
D	Rewis Emily—†	46	"	41	"
E	Rewis Nellie—†	46	"	42	"
F	Reiser Lottie †	46	"	38	"
H	Riley Edward I	46	chauffeur	35	"
K	Riley Gertrude L—†	46	housekeeper	33	"
L	O'Leary Cornelius	46	clerk	50	"
M	O'Leary Elizabeth—†	46	housekeeper	52	"
N	Sullivan Catherine—†	46	saleswoman	35	"
O	Bryant Henry E	46	salesman	38	"
P	Bryant Perly R	46	chauffeur	30	"
R	Bryant Rosetta—†	46	housekeeper	62	"
S	Brown Enda—†	46	"	41	"
T	Brown Michael I	46	fireman	44	"
U	Hutson Joseph	46	janitor	37	896 Tremont

48

West Newton Street—Continued

v	Smith Evelyn C—†	46	housekeeper	65	here
w	Savoy Isabella—†	46	"	27	419 Shawmut av
x	Savoy Jeremiah	46	laborer	73	419 "
y	Meglue Joseph F	46	salesman	36	here
z	Watso Henry	46	engraver	34	"
A	Watso Ruth—†	46	housekeeper	27	"
B	Doherty Cornelius	46	real estate	56	"
c	Bartels George L	46	cashier	50	27 Union pk
D	Bryant Frank E	46	expressman	28	here
E	Bryant Mary C—†	46	housekeeper	28	"
F	Mullhollow George	46	cook	23	"
G	Baone Mary—†	54	dressmaker	35	25 Peterboro
H	Benway Francis	54	florist	30	here
K	Benway Mary—†	54	housekeeper	28	"
L	Ferris William	54	salesman	29	Waltham
M	Kane Alex	54	nurse	62	here
N	MacGrath John	54	salesman	25	"
O	Martin Arthur	54	carpenter	30	420 Shawmut av
P	Martin Frank	54	"	27	420 "
R	Martin James	54	"	25	New Bedford
S	McDonald Andrew	54	"	40	here
T	Ranzineer Harry	54	butcher	50	11 Concord sq
U	Barcloy Francis J	56	real estate	52	here
V	DesRiviers Ulysses F	56	broker	40	"
W	Kuluci Varmi	56	waiter	35	62 Berkeley
X	Meaney Michael	56	engineer	51	here
Y	Meaney Mivina—†	56	housekeeper	41	"
z	Nawn Edward A	56	carpenter	28	"
A	O'Hare Joseph F	56	clerk	50	"
B	Perrault Charles A	56	salesman	41	Cambridge
c	Rioedan Alice—†	56	bookkeeper	26	1666 Wash'n
D	Sapanos James	56	shoecutter	32	Weymouth
E	Zaloleon John	56	watchman	52	39 P
F	Diamond Nicholas	58	waiter	27	Haverhill
G	Namey Edward	58	shoemaker	36	here
H	Namey Mary D—†	58	housekeeper	33	"
K	Ross Charles	58	chauffeur	35	"
L	Ross George	58	"	30	"
M	Bodge Maud—†	60	clerk	45	Framingham
N	Deorio Frank	60	"	22	176 Eutaw
O	Freeman Gladys—†	60	"	22	15 Dalton

Page.	Letter	FULL NAME.	Residence, April 1, 1926.	Occupation.	Supposed Age.	Reported Residence, April 1, 1925. Street and Number.

West Newton Street—Continued

P	Laprerra Bertha—†	60	housekeeper	36	here
R	Laskey Marie—†	60	clerk	22	38 Horace
S	Mann Harold	60	engineer	28	here
T	Smith Annie—†	60	clerk	23	"
U	Talbot Charles	60	salesman	26	"
V	Thorton Mary—†	60	clerk	24	"
W	Walton Walter	60	salesman	35	"
X	Burns Martin F	61	porter	36	"
Y	Devon Harry E	61	student	24	56 W Newton
Z	Frazer Christine B—†	61	clerk	40	here
A	Freberg Annie E—†	61	maid	64	"
B	Ham Robert F	61	mechanic	28	"
C	Hart Patrick	61	shoe sorter	57	Richmond Va
C¹	Kleacke Annie A—†	61	dressmaker	41	here
D	Levey Harold H	61	student	31	125 Crawford
E	Lyman Henry	61	clerk	56	here
F	McKay William	61	machinist	62	"
G	O'Malley Austin	61	engineer	45	"
H	Redmond Thomas	61	janitor	36	"
K	Rogers Henry P	61	clerk	23	"
L	Ross Charles	61	counterman	25	"
M	Savage Roseanna—†	61	housekeeper	51	"
N	Savage William	61	retired	64	"
O	Steinfield Dedrick	61	master mariner	45	"
P	Terwilliger May—†	61	waitress	36	185 W Brookline
R	Baijajran Moses	62	printer	45	62 Westland av
S	Bowen Margaret—†	62	housekeeper	40	here
T	Brown John	62	electrician	35	Revere
U	Conboy Richard	62	laborer	40	660 Mass av
V	Corkum James	62	"	45	here
W	Fallon Joseph	62	printer	40	"
W¹	Nantes George	62	salesman	35	Worcester
X	Phelan Robert	62	machinist	26	here
Y	Phelan Thomas	62	retired	60	"
Z	Phelan Thomas, jr	62	chauffeur	24	"
A	Abran James E	63	plasterer	34	"
B	Abran Mary R—†	63	housekeeper	22*	"
C	Connolly Margaret—†	63	houseworker	25	"
D	Connolly Patrick	63	clerk	25	Canada
E	Connolly Teresa—†	63	nurse	37	here
F	Doherty James G	63	chauffeur	34	"

	Letter.	FULL NAME.	Residence, April 1, 1926.	Occupation	Supposed Age.	Reported Residence, April 1, 1925. Street and Number.

West Newton Street—Continued

G	Doherty Mary I—†	63	housekeeper	54	here
H	Haley Eral H	63	policeman	33	"
K	Lancaster Harland F	63	student	24	Haverhill
L	Leonard Mary I—†	63	housekeeper	59	here
M	Lynch Mollie—†	63	bookkeeper	33	Somerville
N	Michialowski Valentine	63	student	24	New Britian Ct
O	Murphy John	63	roofer	25	Canada
P	Nelson Carl	63	student	25	Gloucester
R	Paige Margaret —†	63	forewoman	35	here
S	Pauley Jennie —†	63	nurse	35	"
T	Pauley John R	63	tailor	40	"
U	Reid Howard S	63	student	24	Franklin
V	Ronka Encio	63	"	25	Gloucester
W	Walker Bernard S	63	"	25	80 E Concord
X	Whitney Annie—†	63	housekeeper	45	here
Y	Whitney Charles	63	machinist	56	"
Z	Williams Alfred C	63	shipper	30	23 Bowdoin
A	Zalkene George	63	printer	22	Beachmont
B	Deloray Harold	64	engineer	30	666 Tremont
C	Donnelly Richard H	64	chauffeur	40	Maine
D	Noah Amila—†	64	housekeeper	27	123 Berkeley
E	Sheenan John	64	salesman	22	here
F	Sliva John W	64	student	32	Northampton
G	Cronin Hannah—†	65	housekeeper	70	here
H	Hallisey Catherine—†	65	"	60	"
K	Griffin Michael W	65	special police	42	"
L	McLaughlin Edward F	65	salesman	43	"
M	McLaughlin Helen C—†	65	housekeeper	32	"
N	Droogan Agnes P—†	65	operator	30	"
O	Droogan Andrew	65	retired	70	"
P	Droogan Helen J—†	65	tel operator	25	"
R	Droogan Joseph	65	plasterer	45	"
S	Droogan Maria—†	65	housekeeper	62	"
T	Martin Ida E—†	65	masseuse	43	"
U	Pierce Cora—†	65	housekeeper	67	"
V	Bernier Arthur H	66	clerk	20	Lawrence
W	Collins Joseph	66	carpenter	42	here
X	Firewen William	66	shipper	45	Ireland
Y	Hickey Helen—†	66	dressmaker	48	here
Z	Joyce Teresa—†	66	"	45	"
A	Lydon Mary—†	66	housekeeper	39	"

51

West Newton Street—Continued

B	MacLoud William	66	laborer	55	here	
C	Pemberton George W	66	clerk	60	"	
D	Reed William	66	painter	40	"	
E	Schools Carroll	66	hatmaker	30	Milford	
F	Sullivan Henry R	66	operator	34	here	
G	Hyland Catherine C—†	67	housekeeper	50	"	
H	Hyland Joseph P	67	clerk	61	"	
K	Hyland William G	67	mechanic	21	"	
L	Bradley Elva M—†	67	housekeeper	30	"	
M	Bradley Eral A	67	accountant	30	"	
N	Foss Margaret R—†	67	at home	68	"	
O	Williams Edwin	67	clerk	23	New York	
P	Galbraith Gertrude R—†	67	saleswoman	57	here	
R	Smith Florence G—†	67	housekeeper	50	"	
S	Smith Seth H	67	druggist	55	"	
T	MacDonald Julia B—†	67	housekeeper	58	"	
U	Robinson Mary H—†	67	clerk	60	"	
V	Brown Elizabeth A—†	68	housekeeper	43	Burlington Vt	
W	Brown Francis W	68	laundryman	45	"	
X	Degna Gertrude—†	68	clerk	23	here	
Y	Downey Annie M—†	68	housekeeper	41	"	
Z	Hart Bertha—†	68	"	37	Salem	
A	Hart Frederick	68	horseshoer	35	"	
B	Staffore Charles	68	pianomaker	41	Chester N H	
B¹	Winchenbaugh Bessie—†	68	housekeeper	37	"	
C	Winchenbaugh Harold	68	salesman	41	"	
D	Burns James W	70	laborer	40	New York	
E	Burns Rose—†	70	housekeeper	38	"	
F	Callwell Edward	70	porter	65	here	
G	Cort Abbie—†	70	nurse	40	"	
H	Cweig Eleanor—†	70	housekeeper	40	"	
K	Kearn Carl	70	sexton	45	"	
L	MacNeil Edward	70	engineer	28	"	
M	Barillo Angelo	72	laborer	50	"	
N	Carbone Nichols	72	plasterer	35	"	
O	Cummings Mary I—†	72	housekeeper	59	"	
P	Dineen Daniel	72	fireman	51	567 Mass av	
R	Donovan Helen—†	72	tel operator	51	74 W Newton	
S	Floyd Henry	72	clerk	54	here	
T	Garvey Harriet M—†	72	nurse	42	Florida	
U	Garvey John	72	machinist	41	"	

Letter.	FULL NAME.	Residence, April 1, 1926.	Occupation.	Supposed Age.	Reported Residence, April 1, 1925. Street and Number.

West Newton Street—Continued

V	McNeil Jean—†	72	clerk	30	here
W	McNeil Joseph	72	manager	40	"
X	Murphy Hannah—†	72	housekeeper	59	Topsfield
Y	Rodrigure Charlotte—†	72	operator	34	here
Z	Bullard Richard H	74	salesman	29	Milton
A	Cass Emmaline E—†	74	saleswoman	52	here
B	Cummings Shirley A—†	74	housekeeper	32	"
C	MacDonald William	74	salesman	26	"
D	MacDougall William	74	painter	55	"
E	McDonough John	74	laborer	22	Ireland
F	McDonough William	74	"	23	"
G	O'Connor John L	74	carpenter	45	Maine
H	Philbrook Helen—†	74	elevatorwoman	35	154 W Brookline
K	Roast Walter	74	clerk	50	here
L	Crosscup Ella F—†	76	housekeeper	56	"
M	Crosscup George D	76	carpenter	57	"
N	Cushing George D	76	salesman	32	Cambridge
O	Drew Charles	76	porter	58	here
P	Drew Eleanor—†	76	housekeeper	61	"
R	Krogman George A	76	clerk	80	"
S	Milling Jessie—†	76	dressmaker	40	"
T	Milling June—†	76	"	41	"
U	Peterson Annie—†	76	at home	55	"
V	Ross William	76	carpenter	30	"
W	Sargent Mary—†	76	clerk	23	"
X	Smith Lillian A—†	76	maid	26	"
Y	Stephens Martin M	76	retired	52	Needham
Z	Brandt Oscar	78	electrician	50	here
A	Cleary Elizabeth—†	78	saleswoman	28	"
B	Joseph John	78	chauffeur	28	11 Warren
C	Sexton Josephine—†	78	housekeeper	50	here
D	Sheenan Mary—†	78	maid	45	15 Milford
E	Watson Elmer	78	clerk	30	New Hampshire
F	Zaeger Jacob	78	real estate	35	24 Worcester sq
G	Archer Walter I	80	chauffeur	62	Wash'n D C
H	Mason Abbie L—†	80	housekeeper	61	here
K	Mason Forest D	80	carpenter	64	"
L	Mason Raymond B	80	instructor	28	"
M	Menzie Albert	80	patternmaker	45	"
N	Robbins Ruel	80	printer	21	"
O	Brady Patrick	82	elevatorman	55	"

Page	Letter	FULL NAME	Residence, April 1, 1926.	Occupation.	Supposed Age.	Reported Residence, April 1, 1925. Street and Number.

West Newton Street—Continued

	P	Dowleng Fannie †	82	saleswoman	55	here
	R	Fernandes Eli J	82	machinist	56	"
	S	Houghton Suzan †	82	housekeeper	35	125 Pembroke
	T	McKnight Frank	82	salesman	25	Somerville
	U	McKnight Mary †	82	housewife	22	"
	V	Norcross Eliza J †	82	"	75	here
	W	Sheppard Fannie †	82	clerk	33	125 Pembroke
	X	Stewart Edward	82	dentist	38	38 Concord sq
	Y	Anderson Edwin	84	painter	23	here
	Z	Anderson Ivar	84	machinist	20	"
	A	Brogan Robert	84	watchman	51	"
	B	Carlezon Adeline J †	84	housekeeper	64	"
	C	Carlezon Grover	84	chauffeur	35	Phila Pa
	D	Carlson Alfred	84	piano polisher	23	here
	E	Golholm William	84	blacksmith	24	Canada
	F	McPherson Rannie	84	carpenter	40	"
	G	Nordbloom Walfred	84	painter	43	here
	H	Pearson Olaf	84	ironworker	60	"
	K	Sydney John	84	actor	63	Weymouth
	L	Veholm August	84	piano tuner	63	Everett
	M	Volk Caroline †	85	housekeeper	49	here
	N	Volk John H	85	clergyman	49	"
	O	Volk John W	85	electrician	21	"
	P	Volk Martha E J †	85	teacher	23	"
	R	Bacon Mary †	86	housekeeper	41	"
	S	Baker Cathriene †	86	tel operator	40	82 Montgomery
	T	Day Harris	86	nurse	53	here
	U	Herb Anna J †	86	clerk	35	"
	V	McAllister John R	86	auto mechanic	42	"
	W	Morrisson Murdock	86	clerk	20	1133 Tremont
	X	Morse Frank A	86	elevatorman	64	here
	Y	Nadau Lucey †	86	seamstress	40	"
	Z	O'Connor John	86	painter	28	121 W Newton
	A	Paladino Joseph S	86	student	28	Lynn
	B	Planty Harry	86	nurse	42	here
	C	Strasser Charles	86	baker	32	9 Conant
	D	Throwant Bertha †	86	laundress	53	Wash'n D C
	E	Corkern Denzella †	88	dressmaker	40	Canada
	F	Doyle James A	88	cook	25	Gloucester
	G	Grandfield Peter	88	salesman	35	Waltham
	H	Griffith Fredrick	88	cook	50	here

Page.	Letter.	FULL NAME.	Residence, April 1, 1926.	Occupation.	Supposed Age.	Reported Residence, April 1, 1925. Street and Number.

West Newton Street—Continued

K	Leary Cathriene—†	88	hairdresser	25	Somerville
L	Leary William	88	rubberworker	32	"
M	McDonald Annie—†	88	housewife	50	here
N	McDonald David	88	engineer	55	"
O	Miller Mary—†	88	housekeeper	65	Florida
P	Nunes Persis—†	88	clerk	26	Brockton
R	Putnum Lawrence	88	student	21	Maine
S	Smith Charles	88	"	21	"
T	Tahakjian Basikes	88	laborer	70	here
U	Carleton Josephine—†	90	dancing teacher	28	"
V	Carleton Mary—†	90	housewife	55	"
W	Carleton Robert J	90	superintendnet	60	"
X	Dunn James	90	restaurateur	63	"
Y	Murray Mary—†	90	cook	55	"
Z	O'Connor John	90	retired	75	"
A	Rinson Oscar	90	student	22	"
B	Barnes Carrie—†	92	nurse	40	Canada
C	Barnes Hilda—†	92	musician	27	40 Berkeley
D	Campbell Alfred	92	roofer	23	Canada
E	Campbell Calvin N	92	pressman	25	"
F	Colburn Charles	92	dentist	25	New York
G	Coughlan Helen A—†	92	tel operator	32	Brookline
H	Countway Blanch—†	92	clerk	36	124 W Newton
K	Countway Laura—†	92	waitress	39	124 "
L	Donovan May—†	92	typist	25	Vermont
M	Garland Lillian—†	92	"	23	here
N	Gilbs Andrew H	92	salesman	45	"
O	Gilbs Glen E—†	92	housewife	35	"
P	Harris Frank	92	shoecutter	48	189 Warren av
R	Hayes Elizabeth—†	92	clerk	52	here
S	Melanson William	92	insurance agent	35	48 Chestnut
T	Moreway May—†	92	clerk	30	Vermont
U	Smith Margaret A—†	92	dressmaker	63	here
V	Stoneman Edna—†	92	secretary	25	40 Berkeley
W	Beamon Norman D	94	advertising	48	here
X	Brown Ada—†	94	waitress	22	Malden
Y	Copeland Anna—†	94	artist	26	Cochituate
Z	Copeland Jennie—†	94	saleswoman	30	"
A	Cowell Mary—†	94	"	20	Melrose
B	Donovan Elizabeth—†	94	housekeeper	52	here
C	Little Christine—†	94	waitress	20	Waltham

55

West Newton Street—Continued

	Letter	Full Name	Res.	Occupation	Age	Reported Residence
	D	Little Lester	94	druggist	25	Brookline
	E	Pate Martha—†	94	artist	27	Medford Hillside
	F	Powers May—†	94	waitress	35	68 W Canton
	G	Sapier Geroge	94	boilermaker	30	Wellesley
	H	Sheldon Roberta—†	94	artist	30	New York
	K	Westerhood Charles	94	engraver	42	here
	L	Butler Annie D—†	96	clerk	47	"
	M	Carroll Raymond P	96	"	31	"
	N	Coppin Frank H	96	"	20	"
	O	Coppin John H	96	"	23	New York
	W	Ferwas Paul	96	waiter	30	22 Allston
	S	Kelley Annie F—†	96	seamstress	72	here
	T	Nickerson Joseph	96	elevatorman	58	672 Tremont
	U	Sheridan Michael	96	houseman	71	here
	V	Sullivan William H	96	salesman	46	"
	X	Woodworth Harry A	96	printer	47	"
	P	Yarnold George F	96	radio operator	24	"
	R	Yarnold Marietta J—†	96	housekeeper	46	"
	Y	Bagwell Frank	98	cleaner	30	"
	Z	Caron Edward	98	ironworker	36	19 Upton
	A	Daly Andrew J	98	toolmaker	37	here
	B	Daly Gertrude—†	98	housekeeper	43	"
	C	Devito John	98	machinist	32	"
	D	Goodwin Carl	98	waiter	25	Milton
	E	Groll Otta	98	machinist	33	here
	F	Mayberry Ellwood	98	waiter	29	Maine
	G	McDonald John	98	cook	27	Waltham
	H	Poole Amos	98	retired	82	here
	K	Sharp Chester	98	chauffeur	35	Milford
	L	Stanhope Annie—†	98	at home	55	Maine
	M	Stanhope Bertha—†	98	waitress	33	"
	N	Stanhope Fred	98	lumberman	65	"
	O	Stephen Ena—†	98	dressmaker	25	30 Union pk
	P	Tobin Helen—†	98	at home	76	here
	R	Workman James	98	machinist	55	"
	S	Chute Mary A—†	100	nurse	40	"
	T	Ellwood Harry	100	machinist	32	Springfield
	U	McDonald Charles	100	carpenter	66	here
	V	McDonald Jane—†	100	housekeeper	61	"
	W	McDonald John C	100	student	20	"
	X	McPhee Maude—†	100	housewife	35	New York

Page.	Letter.	FULL NAME.	Residence, April 1, 1926.	Occupation.	Supposed Age.	Reported Residence, April 1, 1925. Street and Number.

West Newton Street — Continued

	Y	McPhee Michael	100	carpenter	38	New York
	z	Sheehan Julia—†	100	bookbinder	40	Brookline
	A	Timiny Thomas	100	laborer	44	here
	B	Wagner Lena—†	100	nurse	38	Waban
	C	McInnis Daniel W	102	"	34	Canada
	D	McInnis Hugh C	102	retired	77	here
	E	McInnis Sadie—†	102	housekeeper	26	"

Worcester Street

	G	Clark Edward C	31	machinist	34	Ware N H
	H	Cosgrove Franklin	31	chauffeur	32	here
	K	Cosgrove Gertrude—†	31	waitress	30	"
	L	Dillon William	31	carpenter	52	"
	M	Eaton Royar M	31	machinist	34	Ware N H
	N	Halloran John J	31	butcher	38	41 E Springfield
	O	Harold Bernard	31	machinist	31	here
	P	Hartford Adeline A—†	31	at home	66	572 Mass av
	R	Herbert Samuel	31	painter	35	516 Audubon rd
	S	Hogan Joseph	31	clerk	52	31 Worcester sq
	T	Keane John J	31	steamfitter	50	here
	U	Keane Margaret—†	31	housewife	41	"
	V	McHugh Daniel	31	machinist	52	"
	W	Queeney Peter	31	retired	77	"
	X	Shaunborg Bernord	31	pressman	40	"
	Y	Wilson Forrest L	31	upholsterer	24	40 Worcester
	z	Bancroft Eunice—†	33	dressmaker	70	here
	A	Chase Frances—†	33	seamstress	70	"
	B	McDonald Henry L	33	molder	45	"
	C	Murphy Mary E—†	33	housekeeper	93	"
	D	Percy Roger	33	molder	50	"
	E	Price Hattie—†	33	seamstress	45	"
	F	Shorey Matilda V—†	33	housewife	50	"
	G	Shorey Wilbur S	33	salesman	50	"
	H	Anderson Carl	35	laborer	26	8 Rutland
	K	Bannon Leo	35	counterman	35	here
	L	Bannon Mary—†	35	waitress	31	"
	M	Bishlo Anna—†	35	"	27	"
	N	Derkowski Anthony	35	student	30	"
	O	Gaffey Frank	35	teamster	35	114 Waltham

Worcester Street—Continued

P	Lawrence Catherine—†	35	laundryman	22	14 Posen
R	Lindgren Einar	35	stonecutter	29	16 Worcester sq
S	Ray Bessie—†	35	bottle washer	45	here
T	Strasser Augustus	35	counterman	45	19 Conant
U	Sullivan Jeremiah	35	porter	50	here
V	Tinory Delia—†	35	housewife	29	"
W	Tinory Thomas	35	leather sorter	35	"
X	Care Charles	37	restaurateur	28	Hanover N H
Y	Cogswell Amy—†	37	artist	20	here
Z	Cogswell Myrtle—†	37	housewife	43	"
A	Edwards Charles	37	woodfinisher	60	Newport R I
B	Macaros George	37	restaurateur	45	1699 Wash'n
C	MacDonald Edward B	37	buyer	70	here
D	Malacos Andrew	37	restaurateur	32	"
E	O'Brien William	37	freighthandler	35	"
F	O'Neil William P	37	painter	55	78 W Springfield
G	Richards Ernest A	37	porter	35	here
H	Cadman Leopold	39	machinist	49	Canada
K	Dorey Emma—†	39	at home	65	here
L	Fitzgerald John	39	janitor	60	"
M	Geanako Charles	39	jeweler	28	"
N	Gould Daniel	39	butcher	38	"
O	Gould Hattie—†	39	housewife	33	"
P	Marnes George	39	baker	39	"
R	O'Shea Michael	39	waiter	45	"
S	Shurman Thomas	39	laborer	37	"
T	Thornton Jennie—†	39	hairdresser	30	Wollaston
U	Thornton Joseph	39	rodman	25	"
V	Toole Josephine—†	39	saleswoman	55	36 E Springfield
W	Toole Thomas	39	decorator	60	36 "
X	McDermott Doran G	41	plasterer	36	Wollaston
Y	McDermott Esther—†	41	housewife	27	"
Z	Perry Josephine—†	41	"	23	Atlantic
Z¹	Perry Leslie	41	plasterer	26	"
A	Pettie Anna—†	41	housewife	62	here
B	Pettie John	41	fireman	36	"
C	Pettie Winifred—†	41	stenographer	26	"
D	Frobese Alice M—†	41	tel operator	32	"
E	Frobese Ernest	41	painter	26	"
F	Kerrigan George	41	plumber	21	"
G	Kerrigan Hannah—†	41	housekeeper	51	"

Page.	Letter.	FULL NAME.	Residence, April 1, 1926.	Occupation.	Supposed Age.	Reported Residence, April 1, 1925. Street and Number.

Worcester Street—Continued

H	Antick Joseph	43	clothier	30	45 Worcester
K	Daly Charles	43	laborer	47	here
L	Fales Helen I—†	43	housekeeper	37	"
M	Fales Mary P—†	43	at home	76	25 Leyland
N	Leahmeyer Mary—†	43	waitress	45	here
O	Leahmeyer Sarah—†	43	at home	65	"
P	Moynahan Jeremiah S	43	counterman	30	48 Mall
R	Prior William J	43	salesman	40	86 W Springfield
S	Sizemore James H	43	carpenter	68	8 Pine
T	Spinney Mark R	43	"	50	41 E Springfield
U	Walsh Bartholomew	43	chauffeur	40	here
V	Woodward Belle —†	43	housewife	41	New Bedford
W	Woodward Grover C	43	steward	45	"
X	Anderson Frank	45	machinist	25	here
Y	Connors Mildred—†	45	waitress	23	Connecticut
Z	Letalien Mary—†	45	housewife	33	Cambridge
A	Letalien Peter	45	laborer	44	"
B	MacDonald James	45	"	28	Canada
C	MacDonald Lena—†	45	housewife	26	"
D	Stoddard Mary	45	houseworker	50	50 Concord
E	Waldman Joseph	45	clerk	24	Cambridge
F	James William E	47	electrician	41	Springfield
G	MacDonald Pious	47	molder	43	1 Worcester pl
H	MacMillan Hugh H	47	watchman	47	here
K	MacMillan Ida—†	47	housewife	47	"
L	MacMillian Olive—†	47	clerk	24	"
M	McDuffy Edward E	47	automobiles	43	Worcester
N	McManus Dennis	47	clerk	36	148 Concord
O	McManus Leila T—†	47	nurse	36	148 "
P	Murphy Joseph	47	manager	57	here
R	Ripley Charles	47	cook	55	676 Tremont
S	Stewart Charles	47	machinist	35	here
T	White Arthur E	47	clerk	43	Worcester
U	Yarigle Emery H	47	waiter	40	Somerville
V	Connoly Mary—†	49	cook	55	34 Bradshaw
W	Page Raymond E	49	"	30	Cambridge
X	Page Violet—†	49	housewife	25	"
Y	Staub Elizabeth—†	49	"	50	Braintree
Z	Staub Michael	49	shoecutter	50	"
A	Swift Alice—†	49	saleswoman	50	here
B	Swift Alice P—†	49	"	26	"

Worcester Street—Continued

c	Swift Sarah—†	49	houseworker	21	here
d	Walsh Helen L—†	49	housewife	54	"
e	Bullock Arthur E	51	watchman	50	"
f	Carter Elizabeth M—†	51	at home	65	"
g	Crane William L	51	steamfitter	56	48 Union pk
h	DeWitt Florence M—†	51	waitress	35	Brockton
k	Garrity Arthur	51	salesman	27	Fall River
l	Gregory Josephine—†	51	housekeeper	70	61 Rutland
m	Lee Raymond	51	salesman	25	452 Mass av
n	Nelson Nelse	51	painter	38	12 Union pk
o	Reiser Joseph	51	machinist	45	Lowell
p	Reiser Marie—†	51	housewife	44	"
r	Thompson Mary E —†	51	waitress	46	48 Union pk
s	Drake Edna—†	53	dressmaker	30	here
t	Drake William	53	electrician	49	"
u	Kirby Della—†	53	housewife	22	Maine
v	Kirby John B	53	manager	25	"
w	Magnuson Albert G	53	bridgeworker	51	here
x	Magnuson Axel B	53	canemaker	57	132 Randolph rd
y	Magnuson Hilda L—†	53	housekeeper	62	here
z	McMahan Florence—†	53	housewife	40	"
a	McMahan Thomas	53	machinist	48	"
b	McManus Edward J	53	finisher	41	Malden
c	McManus Minnie—†	53	housewife	50	"
d	Crowley Bridget—†	55	housekeeper	47	here
e	Eagan Margaret—†	55	"	55	"
f	Foster Harriett W—†	55	at home	70	"
h	Klemmer August	59	machinist	49	"
k	Klemmer Hilda —†	59	housewife	39	"
l	Sisson Florence —†	59	"	40	"
m	Sisson Hyman	59	pawnbroker	47	"
n	Chapin William F	61	chauffeur	45	"
o	Dodson Leon M	61	foreman	43	"
p	Dodson Mabel—†	61	housewife	33	"
r	Fitzgerald Ellen G—†	61	waitress	45	40 Gray
s	Flynn Agnes C—†	61	cook	43	69 Worcester
t	Flynn Philip J	61	orderly	44	69 "
u	Fournier Albert	61	chauffeur	20	Maine
v	Fournier Hector J	61	cook	22	"
w	McBride George N	61	salesman	31	1 Dayton av
x	McBride Helen T—†	61	photographer	28	1 "

Worcester Street—Continued

Y	McDonald William F	61	painter	59	75 Worcester
Z	Milla Alice M—†	61	saleswoman	56	here
A	Coffey John R	63	machinist	47	7 Worcester
B	Doyle Ora —†	63	clerk	30	Maine
C	Jacobs Fred	63	photographer	40	here
D	MacKillop Daniel N	63	carpenter	48	Canada
E	MacKillop Effie—†	63	housewife	35	"
F	McLeod Malcom	63	laborer	27	Lynn
G	Perkins Jenny —†	63	saleswoman	45	51 Pembroke
H	Shea Daniel	63	laborer	50	here
K	Smith Rhoda—†	63	brushmaker	22	953 Mass av
L	Swanson Victor	63	stonecutter	45	here
M	Topalian John	63	clerk	35	47 Rutland sq
N	White John J	63	shoeworker	30	34 Regent
O	White William F	63	retired	78	34 "
P	Alexander Elizabeth—†	65	at home	75	27 Hammond
R	Condon William	65	chauffeur	35	New York
S	Elliott James	65	shipper	50	here
T	Elliott Mary—†	65	waitress	37	"
U	Fielding Harry	65	actor	75	"
V	Fielding Margaret—†	65	actress	75	"
W	Fielding Pauline—†	65	"	40	Maine
X	Kelley Frank	65	retired	60	Winthrop
Y	Long Josephine—†	65	housekeeper	33	42 Worcester
Z	Long Roger D	65	electrician	32	42 "
A	Pottie Elizabeth—†	65	waitress	40	here
B	Borening Paul M	67	manager	25	185 Warren av
C	Brietenback Emil J	67	justice of peace	69	120 High
D	Dolan Edna E—†	67	saleswoman	36	here
E	Gillis Ada M—†	67	buyer	36	"
F	Gillis Charles	67	U S customs	40	"
G	Gillis James	67	carpenter	42	"
H	Howerty Anna—†	67	housekeeper	50	Hudson
K	Lester Albert A	67	salesman	50	21 Worcester sq
L	McDougall Mary—†	67	housekeeper	48	here
M	Burns William	69	draftsman	38	Southbridge
N	Butera Michael	69	chef	26	here
O	Carle Marcel	69	waiter	26	282 Col av
P	Devaney John M	69	shoeworker	27	681 Mass av
R	Lemieux Dora—†	69	clerk	24	50 Oak

Page.	Letter.	FULL NAME.	Residence, April 1, 1926.	Occupation.	Supposed Age.	Reported Residence, April 1, 1925. Street and Number.

Worcester Street—Continued

	s	Tomilson Beatrice—†	69	housekeeper	38	563 Col av
	T	Vaughan Ruth—†	69	waitress	32	here
	U	Zimmipen Fred	69	cigarmaker	47	688 Tremont
	V	Broberg Axel W	71	insurance	57	here
	W	Burtey Elizabeth—†	71	cook	41	39 Waltham
	X	Butterfield Martha N—†	71	secretary	45	here
	Y	Hill Herbert	71	conductor	50	45 Rutland sq
	Z	Kelliher William	71	garageman	70	here
	A	Lindstrom Gus	71	stonecutter	25	1619 Mass av
	B	Madsen James	71	artist	45	Worcester
	C	Morrison Annie—†	71	at home	70	28 Worcester
	D	Sakalansky Joseph	71	baker	30	here
	E	Wenerholm Sigrid	71	housekeeper	45	"
	F	Xiday Kinon	71	waiter	42	"
	G	Beane Fred	73	salesman	42	50 Dwight
	H	Buck Anna—†	73	housewife	42	here
	K	Buck Frederick	73	waiter	44	"
	L	Dimetrious George	73	counterman	34	"
	M	Griffin Maurice	73	chauffeur	37	"
	N	Kriticas George	73	counterman	22	59 Dwight
	O	Limberies George	73	candymaker	28	here
	P	McGovern James A	73	starter	28	N Attleboro
	R	O'Rourke Elinor—†	73	waitress	21	1 Tupelo
	S	Pearson Albert	73	waiter	40	57 Appleton
	T	Dugan Delia—†	75	waitress	50	69 Crawford
	U	Dunba Elsie—†	75	stenographer	26	here
	V	Frankowitch Anna—†	75	housekeeper	35	216 Athens
	W	Frankowitch Daniel	75	longshoreman	34	216 "
	X	McGawey Clarence	75	pianomaker	25	263 Shawmut av
	Y	Novack Berig	75	real estate	31	6 Milford
	Z	Rhodes Frank	75	laborer	50	10 Durham
	A	Salidos George	75	counterman	32	92 Pembroke
	B	Smith Arthur	75	printer	33	19 Garrison
	C	Tero Frank	75	shoemaker	31	here
	D	Day Marie—†	77	stitcher	22	701 Tremont
	E	Dufault Edward	77	shoecutter	35	7 Corning
	F	Dufault Henry J	77	"	37	7 "
	G	Edwardson Lowie	77	ironworker	54	here
	H	Edwardson Mary—†	77	housewife	53	"
	K	Eichelberger Jay L	77	manager	62	"

Page	Letter	FULL NAME.	Residence, April 1, 1926.	Occupation.	Supposed Age.	Reported Residence, April 1, 1925. Street and Number.

Worcester Street—Continued

	L	Koppitz Anna—†	77	seamstress	57	here
	M	Mitchell Florence—†	77	shoestitcher	43	"
	N	Morrill Edward	77	machinist	50	59 Rutland
	O	Ryan Michael E	77	laborer	43	here
	P	Sparks Ridgeway E	77	counterman	26	"
	R	Waller Margaret M—†	77	stitcher	20	75 Worcester
	S	Morse Charles H	79	teacher	47	here
	T	Morse Grace A—†	79	housewife	46	"
	U	Adams Richard	81	surveyer	55	"
	V	Elg Gustav	81	machinist	45	Lynn
	W	Gillespie Carrie M—†	81	housewife	40	here
	X	Gillespie Nehemia E	81	teacher	47	"
	Y	Hall John R	81	plumber	55	32 Upton
	Z	Howell Emma L—†	81	bookkeeper	26	here
	A	Lamont Joseph	81	counterman	27	Maine
	B	LeBlanc Anna—†	81	stitcher	24	Lynn
	C	Locke Pearl—†	81	waitress	24	Cambridge
	D	Mahuster Lyda—†	81	teacher	40	here
	E	Rooney Frank	83	watchman	49	"
	F	Rooney Virena—†	83	housewife	51	"
	G	Redigan Edward	83	laborer	48	"
	H	Redigan Nora—†	83	housewife	48	"
	K	Maxwell Nellie—†	83	housekeeper	56	"
	L	Crowell Frank	83	painter	51	"
	M	Bergerron Carrie B—†	83	saleswoman	46	"
	N	Grant Mary—†	83	"	46	"
	O	Nichols Catherine—†	83	housekeeper	61	"
	P	Nichols Fredora—†	83	factory worker	36	"
	R	Hager Bertha—†	83	housewife	73	2085 Centre
	S	O'Brien Mary E—†	83	housekeeper	44	here
	T	O'Brien Thomas F	83	seaman	44	"
	U	Burnham William H	85	chauffeur	32	727 Tremont
	V	White Eva M—†	85	housekeeper	43	727 "
	W	Sullivan Frances—†	85	waitress	25	191 W Springfield
	X	Belfontaine Margaret—†	85	housekeeper	31	here
	Y	Bartlett Bertha—†	85	"	34	"
	Z	Lavery Bernard P	85	grinder	40	36 Newbury
	A	Lavery Margaret—†	85	housewife	47	36 "
	B	Nutter Bernard	85	carpenter	31	New Hampshire
	C	Balch Austin C	85	nurse	47	50 Bickerstaff
	D	Balch Raymond R	85	baker	27	50 "

Worcester Street—Continued

E	Sweet Alice †	85	housekeeper	38	New York
F	Sweet William	85	waiter	34	"
G	Burnham George	85	operator	23	542 Newbury
H	Burnham Louise †	85	clerk	35	542 "
K	Lund Alice †	87	housewife	21	928 Dor av
L	Lund Evan	87	engineer	23	928 "
M	Poole Fred E	87	"	50	27 Worcester sq
N	Erickson Edith †	87	winder	24	94 Chandler
O	Bruce Mary †	87	cementer	27	14 Union Park
P	Cross Margaret †	87	bookbinder	40	Lynn
R	Knapp Anna †	87	laundress	40	here
S	Tracey Katherine †	87	clerk	22	16 Centre
U	Ditmar Harry	87	bookkkeper	28	Somerville
V	Aldron Maude M †	89	housewife	40	Wash'n D C
W	Aldron Thomas	89	salesman	45	"
X	Brown Annie M †	89	housewife	51	92 Worcester
Y	Brown Smith L	89	engineer	51	92 "
Z	Grant Margaret †	89	waitress	45	here
A	Grant William	89	carpenter	60	"
B	Johnson Joseph	89	"	56	"
C	Maddox Sarah †	89	housekeeper	80	"
D	Smith Nora †	89	domestic	40	"
E	Sullivan Martin F	89	laborer	59	28 Worcester
E¹	Wadleigh Carrie †	89	housewife	45	Plymouth
F	White Laura †	89	domestic	40	here
G	Chase Hope †	91	stitcher	30	New Hampshire
H	Chase Stan	91	cigarmaker	35	"
K	Fredrickson Mary †	91	waitress	35	here
L	Haley James J	91	janitor	58	"
M	Lloyd Howard W	91	cabinetmaker	21	"
N	McNiel Charles	91	carpenter	62	92 Worcester
O	Meisel Catherine †	91	at home	80	here
P	Munson Odolph	91	clerk	60	"
R	Ocatabara James	91	cook	24	35 N Margin
S	Papton Ellen D †	91	housewife	62	here
T	Papton Louis M	91	janitor	63	"
U	Turner Frank	91	retired	70	"

Ward 9–Precinct 3

CITY OF BOSTON.

LIST OF RESIDENTS
20 YEARS OF AGE AND OVER

(FEMALES INDICATED BY DAGGER)

AS OF

APRIL 1, 1926

HERBERT A. WILSON, ⎱ *Listing*

JAMES F. EAGAN, ⎰ *Board.*

CITY OF BOSTON – PRINTING DEPARTMENT

Page.	Letter.	FULL NAME	Residence, April 1, 1926	Occupation	Supposed Age.	Reported Residence, April 1, 1925. Street and Number.

Chester Place

	B	Flagg Christopher R	1	caterer	68	here
	C	Keeling Claud	1	laborer	22	Cambridge
	D	Keeling Rosie—†	1	housewife	21	"
	E	Keating John J	2	cook	34	32 Sharon
	F	Donovan James	2	laborer	49	38 Camden
	G	Donovan Margaret—†	2	housewife	46	38 "
	H	Kelley Thomas J	2	stonemounter	60	20 Madison
	M	Harris Walter	5	meatcutter	50	here
	N	Cannon Jesse A	5	laborer	27	"
	O	Taylor Gertrude—†	5	laundress	47	"
	P	Reading Beattie—†	5	housewife	56	"
	R	Rock Philip V	5	laborer	59	"
	T	Gerris Charlena —†	10	housekeeper	48	40 Lenox
	U	Sinotti Amelio	10	manager	52	here
	V	Sinotti Fillmenci —†	10	housewife	47	"
	W	Sinotti Lucy—†	10	"	34	"
	X	Sinotti Nol	10	manager	50	"
	Y	Sinotti Clarentin	10	"	47	"
	Z	Sinotti Peter	10	"	57	"
	A	Luca Grigoris	10	laborer	69	"
	B	Luca Joseph	10	"	40	"
	C	Luca Josephine —†	10	housewife	59	"

Massachusetts Avenue

	E	Calman John H	504	laborer	35	here
	F	Daley Jermiah	504	contractor	38	Waltham
	G	Doherty Bridget —†	504	housewife	36	here
	H	Doherty Joseph	504	foreman	37	"
	K	Doherty Mary —†	504	nurse	26	Gardner
	L	Fallon Margaret —†	504	"	26	"
	M	Fitzgerald Mary —†	504	"	28	"
	N	Fritz Rose—†	504	"	28	"
	O	Howell Sapphire—†	504	waitress	22	Lynn
	P	LaPointe Elizabeth A—†	505	housekeeper	46	here
	R	McIntire Annie W—†	505	housewife	60	"
	S	McIntire Martin J	505	druggist	64	"
	T	Mellon Hugh	505	engineer	60	Framingham

2

Page.	Letter.	FULL NAME.	Residence, April 1, 1926.	Occupation	Supposed Age.	Reported Residence, April 1, 1925. Street and Number.

Massachusetts Avenue—Continued

U	Stewart Margaret J—†	505	housekeeper	54	here
V	Stewart Wetmore A	505	restaurateur	59	"
W	Quinn Anne V—†	505	typist	50	606 Col av
X	Quinn Josephine L—†	505	operator	40	606 "
Y	Daley Charles	507	switchman	42	here
Z	Fitzgibbons James	507	laborer	61	"
A	Fitzgibbons Sadie—†	507	housekeeper	75	"
B	Goldberg Hyman	507	storekeeper	49	164 Magnolia
C	Grady Bertha—†	507	housekeeper	35	here
D	Jenkins Walter	507	clerk	27	Cambridge
E	Jordon Edward F	507	engineer	40	here
F	Kelly Edward	507	mechanic	55	"
G	Lybert Albert	507	cigarmaker	37	"
H	Martin Carlos	507	cook	52	523 Mass av
K	O'Neil James	507	barber	55	here
G	Sergeant Clayton	507	manager	50	"
M	Shorten John	507	mechanic	53	"
N	Tucker Madeline—†	507	maid	27	Portsmouth N H
O	Beauvais Alfred	508	manufacturer	65	here
P	Choate Wesley	508	shipper	34	"
R	Crane Harry	508	hairdresser	50	"
S	DeChamp Ella—†	508	saleswoman	30	"
T	Fiefield Thomas	508	conductor	25	"
U	Gordon Anna B—†	508	housekeeper	44	"
V	Gordon William J	508	engineer	46	"
W	Hunter Annie F—†	508	dressmaker	45	149 Meridian
X	Jordan Mildred—†	508	hairdresser	30	here
Y	Klantgis James	508	agent	35	"
Z	Lothair Aldophis	508	nurse	40	"
A	Stevens Oliver B	508	manager	30	"
B	Stevens Pearl—†	508	at home	25	"
C	Arnold Earle	511	clerk	40	"
D	Beavis Kathleen A—†	511	housekeeper	39	"
E	Beavis Michael F	511	painter	34	"
F	Kempton Frank W	511	machinist	57	"
G	Kilday Helen M—†	511	housewife	59	"
H	Kilday William D	511	clerk	56	"
K	Marine Gunnar	511	"	37	"
L	Nelson Ada M—†	511	operator	32	35 Worcester sq
M	Trayes Cora I—†	511	nurse	33	here
N	Trayes William H	511	physician	46	"

3

Massachusetts Avenue—Continued

o	Withrow Claire—†	511	cashier	24	here
p	Colwell Emma L—†	512	housekeeper	56	"
r	Hamel Anita—†	512	housewife	30	New Hampshire
s	Hamel Oscar	512	barber	40	"
t	James Henry	512	waiter	40	here
u	Niles Charles	512	glazier	51	502 Col av
v	Spears George	512	watchman	44	Lynn
w	Spears Marion— †	512	at home	40	"
x	Weatherbee May—†	512	dressmaker	43	here
y	Weatherbee William	512	woodworker	46	"
z	Cronin Elizabeth—†	514	housekeeper	58	"
a	Jackson Lillian—†	514	dressmaker	40	"
b	McDonald Florence—†	514	nurse	40	"
c	McDonald Katherine—†	514	"	35	"
d	McGrath Mary —†	514	housekeeper	40	"
e	Murphy Sarah - †	514	bookkeeper	22	"
f	Conway James	515	clerk	50	New York
g	Conway Mary —†	515	housekeeper	48	"
h	Forbes Addie - †	515	housewife	44	here
k	Forbes George	515	broker	44	"
l	Harriman Louise—†	515	saleswoman	25	664 Mass av
m	Kelleher Cornelius	515	student	22	197 St Botolph
n	Kimball Stephen	515	"	23	197 "
o	Morgan Alfred	515	salesman	30	Milford
p	Penney Sidney	515	laborer	30	461 Mass av
r	Sullivan Annie—†	515	at home	50	here
s	Sullivan Michael	515	retired	60	"
t	Teehan Adelaide—†	515	housewife	25	"
u	Teehan Dennis	515	laborer	50	"
v	Teehan John	515	mechanic	30	"
x	Bergquist John F	519	tailor	45	"
y	Butler Jennie M—†	519	housekeeper	52	"
z	Butt Augustus	519	carpenter	34	"
a	Danehy Jane - †	519	cook	35	"
b	Danehy Joseph	519	"	35	"
c	Grant Gertrude—†	519	waitress	25	"
d	Holland Albert J	519	salesman	38	Florida
e	Madden Margaret M—†	519	hairdresser	76	here
f	Porter William A	519	manager	43	555 Mass av
g	Randolph Frederick W	519	laborer	35	105 Longwood av
h	Ray Gertrude - †	519	housekeeper	29	725 Tremont

Page	Letter	FULL NAME	Residence, April 1, 1926.	Occupation.	Supposed Age.	Reported Residence, April 1, 1925. Street and Number.

Massachusetts Avenue—Continued

	K	Sliney Chester T	519	mechanic	41	here
	L	Sliney Mary A—†	519	housekeeper	41	"
	M	Tornberg Earle	519	cook	33	"
	N	Wadleigh Charles E	519	mailer	82	"
	O	Wadleigh Minette E—†	519	housekeeper	68	"
	P	Cummings Herbert	520	paperhanger	45	Lowell
	R	Cummings John H	520	"	54	"
	S	Demas Nicholas	520	baker	46	"
	T	Desmond James J	520	trainman	34	Brockton
	U	Dveal Harry	520	cook	43	29 Myrtle
	V	Gardener Delia S—†	520	housekeeper	64	29 "
	X	McCarthy George	520	teamster	50	Lynn
	Y	Morin George	520	salesman	40	New York
	Z	Olsson Ernest	520	cabinetmaker	33	here
	A	Rogers Mary—†	520	waitress	21	268 Bremen
	A¹	Silva Elsie G—†	520	housekeeper	47	685 Mass av
	C	Chapman Ellen—†	521	teacher	50	here
	D	Clements Alice E—†	521	stitcher	45	"
	E	Connery Irving	521	painter	70	"
	F	Drummond Sarah—†	521	at home	80	"
	G	Redington Catherine—†	521	"	80	"
	H	Scollard Mary—†	521	housekeeper	25	"
	K	Shores Lyle	521	pianomaker	40	"
	L	Smith Frederick	521	waiter	58	"
	M	Stepfer Emily—†	521	at home	78	San Francisco Cal
	N	Walker William	521	waiter	45	here
	O	Yates Charles E	521	clerk	48	"
	P	Yates Isabelle C—†	521	housekeeper	48	"
	R	Buckley Cornelius	522	carpenter	41	"
	S	Chamberlain Margaret—†	522	at home	82	"
	T	Dolliver Milton	522	laborer	23	Maine
	U	Moore Alice J—†	522	at home	73	here
	V	Morris Grace M—†	522	dressmaker	47	"
	W	Reed Martha—†	522	hairdresser	35	16 Hemenway
	X	Smith David H	522	clerk	23	Waverley
	Y	Thorne Violet M—†	522	designer	21	here
	Z	Twaddel Bessie—†	522	housekeeper	35	"
	A	Wilson Edward J	522	leatherworker	48	"
	B	Young Francis	522	clerk	21	Maine
	C	Colton Clara A—†	523	"	50	here
	D	Dewar Charlotte—†	523	nurse	40	"

5

Massachusetts Avenue—Continued

E	Foster Joseph	523	clerk	30	here	
F	Godfrey Anne —†	523	"	50	"	
G	Godfrey Lawrence A	523	"	21	Portland Me	
H	Godfrey Ralph A	523	plumber	55	here	
K	Godfrey Rose —†	523	housekeeper	50	Portland Me	
L	Grady John C	523	salesman	40	here	
M	Joy Ray	523	clerk	24	468 Mass av	
N	Larcombe Mary —†	523	"	45	here	
O	Munson Benjamin	523	painter	35	"	
P	Pendelton John	523	"	50	"	
R	Riley Francis	523	"	30	"	
S	Therrier Homer	523	clerk	25	Newark N J	
T	Twombley Carroll	523	cook	25	New Hampshire	
U	Brean Earnest	524	waiter	40	here	
V	Dewight Daniel	524	chauffeur	40	"	
W	Hurley Michael	524	leather sorter	39	"	
X	Molloy John	524	fisherman	36	"	
Y	Moulton Percy C	524	machinist	40	"	
Z	Carr Ethel M —†	525	clerk	27	"	
A	Carr Mary E —†	525	housekeeper	63	"	
B	Carr Rosa B —†	525	"	50	"	
C	Coveney John	525	nurse	28	"	
D	Cranston Frank	525	manager	63	"	
E	Cronan Edwin	525	clerk	58	"	
F	Cronan Edwin V	525	"	27	"	
G	Faunce Charles M	525	broker	60	"	
H	Gardner Frank	525	clerk	27	"	
K	Hall William J	525	painter	43	"	
L	Littlefield Harry	525	cutter	47	"	
M	Rowe Hubert L	525	salesman	45	"	
N	Allard Napoleon	526	patternmaker	35	1323 Wash'n	
O	Black Howard S	526	salesman	49	524 Mass av	
P	Easterbrook Mary A —†	526	housekeeper	55	P E I	
R	Silverman Robert	526	shoecutter	44	here	
S	Vinson Christina —†	526	forewoman	53	229 Longwood av	
T	Felton Charles	527	manager	45	here	
U	Felton Sarah —†	527	housewife	40	"	
V	Frazee Edith —†	527	housekeeper	30	"	
W	Frazee Willis	527	manager	38	"	
X	Gilly James	527	baker	32	399 Mass av	
Y	Guilmette Alice —†	527	housewife	25	here	

Page	Letter	Full Name.	Residence, April 1, 1926.	Occupation.	Supposed Age.	Reported Residence, April 1, 1925. Street and Number.

Massachusetts Avenue—Continued

z	Guilmette Ralph	527	shoeworker	28	here
A	Harper Josephine—†	527	waitress	25	New Jersey
B	Hopper Harry	527	waiter	30	here
c	Jones Irene—†	527	operator	28	"
D	Leslie Sarah—†	527	housekeeper	41	"
E	Morin Grace D—†	527	"	41	"
F	Stiles Everett	527	musician	55	"
G	Wilfred Howard	527	manager	35	"
H	Nibbs Joseph	528	janitor	52	22 Westminster
K	Reed George	528	student	22	22 "
L	Barker John	529	storekeeper	40	here
M	Bearse Leon	529	clerk	25	New Hampshire
N	DeLoria Edna—†	529	stitcher	22	here
O	Fiske Ellen—†	529	at home	55	"
P	Howard William	529	chauffeur	25	"
R	Keating William	529	painter	29	"
S	Marcus Ralph	529	shoeworker	33	141 W Newton
T	Newland Edward	529	solicitor	45	Haverhill
U	O'Niel Albert	529	shipfitter	21	here
V	O'Niel Bartholomew	529	clerk	23	"
W	O'Niel Lawrence	529	painter	24	"
X	O'Niel Mary—†	529	housekeeper	50	"
Y	O'Niel Mary A—†	529	stitcher	31	"
Z	O'Niel Sarah—†	529	"	29	"
A	O'Niel William	529	laborer	57	"
B	O'Niel William	529	"	26	"
C	Williamson Eva—†	529	stitcher	22	"
D	Brown Hernitrude—†	530	housewife	26	"
E	Brown William H	530	manager	27	"
F	Corbett Mary—†	530	coatmaker	66	"
G	Hilt Jennie—†	530	at home	52	"
H	Nixon Margaret—†	530	saleswoman	35	"
K	Owens Frederick	530	waiter	29	Sanford Me
L	Owens Liza—†	530	cashier	20	Sanford Me
M	Porter John	530	teamster	36	here
N	Porter Mae—†	530	forewoman	25	"
O	Ross Dora—†	530	housekeeper	21	"
P	Ross John	530	machinist	26	"
R	Bauer Anna L—†	531	housekeeper	46	"
S	Daley William	531	chauffeur	26	2 Motley
T	Leach John	531	"	30	here

7

Page	Letter	FULL NAME	Residence, April 1 1926	Occupation	Supposed Age	Reported Residence, April 1, 1925. Street and Number.

Massachusetts Avenue—Continued

	Letter	FULL NAME	Res.	Occupation	Age	Reported Residence
	U	Morgan Cora—†	531	clerk	29	New Bedford
	V	Walter Charles R	531	salesman	28	Concord N H
	W	Wustenberg Eric	531	janitor	35	here
	X	Dennehen John M	532	teacher	34	"
	Y	Egan Effie—†	532	houseworker	50	60 Berkeley
	Z	Egan Harvey	532	carpenter	50	60 "
	A	Hinch Harry	532	waiter	35	60 "
	B	Marflett Teresa—†	532	housekeeper	30	60 "
	C	Pantie Katherine—†	532	at home	27	60 "
	D	Whitcomb Lewis	532	porter	37	60 "
	E	Barker Rachel—†	533	housekeeper	36	here
	F	Crooke William A	533	druggist	28	"
	G	McFarlan Curtis	533	waiter	26	"
	H	Brown Helen—†	533	housewife	23	"
	K	Brown Oscar	533	valet	28	"
	L	Diggs Harriet—†	533	saleswoman	40	Newark N J
	M	Carnes George H	534	musician	70	here
	N	Carpenter Harriet C—†	534	at home	75	"
	O	Clapp Calvin S	534	waiter	54	"
	P	Curran Mary C—†	534	housewife	54	"
	R	Dinsmore George F	534	druggist	74	"
	S	Dinsmore Jennie F—†	534	housewife	69	"
	T	Eldridge William A	534	clerk	53	"
	U	James Harold S	534	laborer	35	New York
	V	Lynch Harold L	534	nurse	34	here
	W	McIntyre Addie—†	534	at home	30	"
	X	McLeod Roderick A	534	carpenter	56	"
	Z	Crawford Henry J	536	laborer	45	"
	A	Edwards Anna—†	536	bookkeeper	32	"
	B	McManus John E	536	chauffeur	43	"
	C	Taylor Frederick	536	painter	40	Taunton
	D	Berquist Helen—†	537	waitress	22	here
	E	Berquist John	537	carpenter	25	519 Mass av
	F	Burne Walter	537	tailor	30	here
	G	Collins John	537	mechanic	40	"
	H	Cordella Ina—†	537	cook	27	"
	K	Cousins Mary—†	537	teacher	50	"
	L	Dowd John	537	watchman	50	"
	M	Glover Agnes J—†	537	housekeeper	49	"
	N	Glover Edwin L	537	pressman	56	"
	O	Goddard Henry	537	clergyman	60	"

8

Page.	Letter.	FULL NAME.	Residence, April 1, 1926.	Occupation.	Supposed Age.	Reported Residence, April 1, 1925. Street and Number.

Massachusetts Avenue—Continued

P	Graves Ellen—†	537	at home	60	here
R	Kelley Ambrose	537	pianomaker	50	"
S	LaMarchant Leo	537	barber	60	Canada
T	Lee Robert E	537	cook	40	here
U	Pearly Catherine—†	537	housewife	60	"
V	Pearly Frances—†	537	operator	26	"
W	Sterling Esther—†	537	housewife	26	765 Tremont
X	Sterling William R	537	salesman	36	765 "
Y	Allen Esther—†	538	housekeeper	40	Brockton
Z	Carroll Robert	538	chauffeur	25	here
A	Conway Amy—†	538	at home	50	"
B	Conway George	538	compositor	55	38 W Newton
C	Crawley Harry	538	shoeworker	21	567 Mass av
D	Crawley Lena—†	538	houseworker	21	567 "
E	DeMunzio Vincent	538	musician	30	Providence R I
F	Desjarduis Alfred	538	cook	23	Lynn
G	Jackson Ella—†	538	waitress	23	Brookline
H	Leahy Rosalie—†	538	shoeworker	52	Brockton
K	Moulton Reginald	538	waiter	26	Lynn
L	Murphy Sarah—†	538	houseworker	45	"
M	Princiotto Anthony	538	barber	28	"
N	Princiotto Horace	538	"	30	"
O	Stone Frank	538	merchant	45	567 Mass av
P	Stone Lillian—†	538	at home	35	Lynn
R	Boudreau Charles	539	bookkeeper	25	17 Boyden
S	Callahan Mary T—†	539	at home	37	here
T	Callahan Philip	539	engineer	41	49 Batavia
U	Callahan Stephen J	539	"	38	here
V	Dilliore Delia—†	539	forewoman	60	"
W	Ferareni Ernest	539	retired	60	"
X	Hale William M	539	machinist	60	1761 Wash'n
Y	Hatch Rose—†	539	dressmaker	27	here
Z	Hervey Abbie—†	539	at home	60	"
A	Hildreth Thomas P	539	painter	38	658 Mass av
B	McAlduff George	539	roofer	22	here
C	McAlduff William	539	manager	50	"
D	McGill William C	539	roofer	30	Fall River
E	O'Coneres Paul	539	waiter	25	17 Boyden
F	Poppleton Harold	539	writer	36	here
G	Turner John	539	stonecutter	56	"
H	Coleman Mae—†	540	housewife	47	Lowell

Page	Letter	Full Name	Residence, April 1, 1926	Occupation	Supposed Age	Reported Residence, April 1, 1925. Street and Number.

Massachusetts Avenue—Continued

	Letter	Full Name	Residence	Occupation	Age	Reported Residence
	K	Fennel Patrick	540	machinist	30	68 Savin
	L	Germain Madaline—†	540	bookkeeper	25	Lowell
	M	King Mary—†	540	dressmaker	42	here
	N	Leger Alfred	540	physician	30	"
	O	McGitterich Bartholeman	540	brushmaker	45	678 Mass av
	P	Roed Hunham	540	clerk	35	57 St James
	R	Sidney Louise †	540	waitress	33	75 Worcester
	S	Stone Philip	540	chauffeur	33	here
	T	Zaklicki Alexander	540	shoeworker	40	548 Mass av
	U	Jones Laura A—†	541	social worker	60	here
	V	Monarch Emma E—†	541	housekeeper	60	"
	W	Monarch James	541	janitor	70	"
	X	Phoenix Lydia E—†	541	student	50	"
	Y	Rothennal Bertha M—†	541	"	44	"
	Z	Williams Grace G—†	541	nurse	38	"
	A	Bagley Nellie L—†	542	housekeeper	62	"
	B	Bellie Edward	542	machinist	50	"
	C	Dorr Earl	542	electrician	25	"
	D	Fostmire Emma—†	542	at home	40	"
	E	Long Louis	542	electrician	20	Maine
	F	Lynch John	542	laborer	22	here
	G	McMilken William R	542	packer	52	"
	H	McNamara Patrick	542	manager	42	"
	K	Nickroff Louis	542	machinist	42	"
	L	Rougan Joseph	542	watchman	52	"
	M	Barrows William T	543	cutter	50	14 E Brookline
	N	Burke Barney L	543	waiter	29	Canada
	O	Donnelly Edward M	543	doorman	58	here
	P	Hodge Leroy F	543	janitor	78	"
	R	Kelley Emma —†	543	clerk	22	Canada
	S	Kelley Melvina —†	543	"	25	"
	T	Lee Katherine A —†	543	cook	58	here
	U	Miller Francis G	543	secretary	46	"
	V	Preston William	543	jobber	35	"
	W	Beamish Frank	544	banker	35	"
	X	By John Harry	544	shoecutter	40	"
	Y	By John Marie—†	544	housewife	36	"
	A	Dalton Edward	544	factory worker	24	98 Concord
	B	Dalton Joseph	544	grocer	26	98 "
	B¹	Devaney Joseph	544	"	25	here
	C	Ford Mary —†	544	dressmaker	50	"

10

Page.	Letter.	Full Name.	Residence, April 1, 1926.	Occupation.	Supposed Age.	Reported Residence, April 1, 1925. Street and Number.

Massachusetts Avenue—Continued

D	Gormley William	544	butcher	26	205 Walnut av
E	Harrison James	544	upholsterer	22	41 Lawn
F	Herbert Walter	544	glasscutter	27	here
G	Hughes Patrick	544	mechanic	30	Brookline
H	Long Johanna M—†	544	housekeeper	36	here
K	Long Michael	544	messenger	33	"
L	McCarthy Daniel	544	laborer	22	Canada
M	McCarthy Patrick	544	teamster	30	here
N	McLeod Donald	544	mechanic	22	Brookline
O	Moloney John	544	stonecutter	27	here
P	Moloney Thomas	544	laborer	23	"
S	Rose Alvin F	546	physician	52	"
T	Rose Catherine—†	546	housekeeper	53	"
U	Rose Margarite—†	546	teacher	22	"
V	Rose Marienne K—†	546	"	29	"
W	Buck Edith—†	547	nurse	43	New York
X	Craig Blanche—†	547	housekeeper	40	here
Y	Hopkins Jane M—†	547	"	66	"
Z	Lagerquist Abbie—†	547	cook	67	"
A	Paine Susan—†	547	"	41	"
B	Stevens Jean—†	547	stenographer	57	"
C	Tonneson Carrie—†	547	missionary	67	"
D	Tonneson Marea—†	547	"	51	"
E	Booth William	548	roofer	22	"
F	Canham Leslie	548	meatcutter	25	"
G	Church Frederick	548	carpenter	40	"
H	Collins Andrew	548	meatcutter	40	"
K	Griffin Walter	548	salesman	30	"
L	Howie James	548	"	46	"
M	Howie Jean—†	548	housekeeper	35	"
N	Hubbard Louis	548	millwright	60	"
O	Ladiff William	548	salesman	28	"
P	Whitehurst Nathaniel	548	cook	55	"
R	Bergeron Armand	549	clerk	26	"
S	Descary Hazel—†	549	shoeworker	23	New Hampshire
T	Fienauer John	549	shoemaker	26	"
U	Finnerty John J	549	electrician	33	here
V	Hanley Patrick	549	fireman	33	"
W	Keezer James E	549	plumber	54	"
X	Linehan Daniel J	549	clerk	48	"
Y	Lyons John P	549	"	39	"

Page	Letter	FULL NAME.	Residence, April 1, 1926.	Occupation.	Supposed Age.	Reported Residence, April 1, 1925. Street and Number.

Massachusetts Avenue—Continued

z	McGowan Patrick J	549	motorman	33	here
A	McMahon Joseph A	549	painter	46	"
B	Mirayoer John	549	storekeeper	34	"
C	Nichols Caroline A—†	549	at home	65	"
D	O'Brien Mary C—†	549	housekeeper	42	"
E	Walker William L	549	manager	34	"
F	Zaharaky Andreas	549	porter	35	"
G	Goolsby Catherine—†	550	housewife	55	560 Mass av
H	Goolsby Marion—†	550	waitress	55	560 "
K	Holt Harry	550	porter	46	560 "
L	Jordan Alfred	550	"	35	560 "
M	Myers Franklin	550	physician	39	here
N	Myers Levinie—†	550	housekeeper	46	"
O	Leary George A	551	clerk	32	Springfield
P	Lyons Edward J	551	salesman	65	here
R	Lyons Henry J	551	clerk	24	"
S	Lyons Margaret A—†	551	housekeeper	20	"
T	Lyons Sarah A—†	551	"	60	"
U	Lyons William E	551	salesman	34	"
V	Tlapatse Thomas	551	shoemaker	40	"
W	Towne Louise—†	551	at home	67	"
X	Horton Alfred	552	printer	40	"
Y	Lawrence William S	552	musician	32	"
Z	Rainey Dorothy E—†	552	housewife	34	"
A	Rainey Julian D	552	lawyer	37	"
B	Ridley Lesly	552	tailor	60	"
C	Steward Granville	552	musician	34	"
D	Del Tori John	553	student	35	"
E	Dougherty Charles M	553	"	21	Pennsylvania
F	Morgan Peter	553	bricklayer	37	here
G	Parker Christopher E	553	conductor	65	"
H	Russell Alice A—†	553	clerk	40	"
K	Russell Edmond	553	bricklayer	52	"
L	Thibodeau Irene—†	553	milliner	28	"
M	Johnson Cecil	554	machinist	21	"
N	Johnson John E	554	carpenter	55	"
O	Reid David	554	missionary	58	"
P	Reid Robert	554	reporter	27	"
R	Spaulding Caroline †	554	cook	60	"
S	Barr Arthur	555	chauffeur	28	"
T	Daniels Charles	555	cook	34	"

Page.	Letter.	FULL NAME.	Residence, April 1, 1926.	Occupation.	Supposed Age.	Reported Residence, April 1, 1925. Street and Number.

Massachusetts Avenue—Continued

	U	Daniels Jane—†	555	housekeeper	50	here
	V	Holbrook August A	555	machinist	44	"
	W	Kernova Benjamin	555	upholsterer	30	"
	X	Lewis John	555	dyer	50	"
	Y	Mulcheney Paul	555	student	30	"
	Z	Swanson Alex F	555	mechanic	30	553 Mass av
	A	Comstock Louis	556	photographer	48	here
	B	Crozier William	556	carpenter	48	"
	B¹	Digian Charles	556	machinist	22	"
	C	Hanscom James G	556	janitor	54	130 Dartmouth
	D	Lottele Antonio	556	machinist	35	here
	E	Mason Maria—†	556	saleswoman	46	"
	F	McDonald Archibald	556	carpenter	46	"
	G	Noonan Thomas	556	machinist	51	"
	H	Quinn Cellia—†	556	boxmaker	25	"
	K	Lacey Edward	556	bottlewasher	45	"
	L	Ballentine James, jr	557	nurse	50	Medford
	M	Doncaster George P	557	carpenter	50	here
	N	Ferrie Adam J	557	painter	37	"
	O	Ferrie Harriet—†	557	housekeeper	36	"
	P	Kemper George	557	clerk	25	Ohio
	R	Kemper Harry	557	"	38	here
	S	Lincoln Alvah W	557	meatcutter	69	"
	T	Lincoln Carrie—†	557	housekeeper	67	"
	U	MacLearen Daniel	557	carpenter	22	15 Holyoke
	V	Matherson Sadie—†	557	housekeeper	53	here
	W	Micheals Gertrude—†	557	"	38	"
	X	Micheals Herman	557	cigarmaker	50	"
	Y	Reynolds Annie—†	557	nurse	45	"
	Z	Ruth Catherine L—†	557	housekeeper	55	"
	A	Griggs Ethel—†	558	student	26	"
	B	Harmon Florence—†	558	cook	35	"
	C	Scott Alice—†	558	matron	55	"
	D	Scott Esther D—†	558	bookkeeper	21	"
	E	Carpenter Charles L	559	printer	65	Medford
	F	Kelly Richard J	559	teamster	28	here
	G	Mooney Edward	559	accountant	31	Oklahoma
	H	Peck Anna L—†	559	housewife	39	here
	K	Peck Louis B	559	salesman	42	"
	L	Phippes Mabel—†	559	clerk	20	12 Rutland
	M	Sheehan Maurice F	559	designer	59	here

13

Page.	Letter.	FULL NAME.	Residence, April 1, 1926.	Occupation.	Supposed Age.	Reported Residence, April 1, 1925. Street and Number.

Massachusetts Avenue—Continued

N	Stroyman Maurice	559	merchant	51	589 Tremont
O	Crawford John	560	salesman	30	548 Mass av
P	Crawford Laura—†	560	housekeeper	25	548 "
R	Damon Everett	560	engineer	60	548 "
S	Gray Grace—†	560	saleswoman	42	548 "
T	Gray Harry	560	florist	52	548 "
U	Gregorie Clara—†	560	housekeeper	32	548 "
V	Gregorie Joseph W	560	florist	44	548 "
W	Mathott Camil	560	ironworker	28	548 "
X	Mathott George	560	carpenter	24	562 "
Y	Mathott Semone—†	560	housekeeper	60	562 "
Z	Mathott Wilbur	560	carpenter	22	562 "
A	Miller Harold	560	shipper	26	548 "
B	Miller Jennie—†	560	housekeeper	24	548 "
C	Tucker Emelia—†	560	houseworker	39	here
D	Tucker Frederick H	560	photographer	40	"
E	Vatcher George	560	manager	30	"
F	Vatcher Irene—†	560	saleswoman	32	"
G	Vincent Edward	560	lawyer	23	Lowell
H	Branner Eleanor L—†	561	maid	48	here
K	Commo Dorothy—†	561	stenographer	20	"
L	Gouin Edwin	561	painter	21	Lawrence
M	Long George A	561	inventor	76	here
N	Long Georgeona L—†	561	saleswoman	46	"
O	McDougall Bernard	561	mechanic	20	Canada
R	Meehan Ruth C—†	561	operator	26	here
P	Meehan Thomas F	561	chauffeur	30	"
S	Pantaleone Joseph	561	student	25	New York
T	Pantaleone Steves	561	"	23	Phila Pa
U	Shepherd Frank E	561	porter	67	here
V	Stroyman Maurice	561	salesman	50	"
W	Anderson William	562	expressman	40	61 E Springfield
X	Bushlow William	562	waiter	30	New York
Y	Forbes Melissa—†	562	housekeeper	34	Nova Scotia
Z	Forbes Thomas	562	carpenter	43	515 Mass av
A	Karaywanner James	562	barber	33	153 W Concord
B	Liatlier Frank	562	cigarmaker	35	119 Kendall
C	Monihan Thomas	562	salesman	45	68 Clifford
D	Nelson Winnie—†	562	laundress	45	153 W Concord
E	Simpson Edward	562	salesman	30	65 Dennis
F	Bailey Ida H—†	563	boxmaker	45	474 Mass av
G	Jarvis Frank S	563	clerk	75	here

Page.	Letter.	FULL NAME.	Residence, April 1, 1926.	Occupation.	Supposed Age.	Reported Residence, April 1, 1925. Street and Number.

Massachusetts Avenue—Continued

H	Jarvis Horatio N	563	clerk	56	133 Appleton
K	Jarvis Mary E—†	563	housekeeper	56	133 "
L	Jones Charles	563	machinist	42	Lowell
M	Jones Susan—†	563	housewife	40	"
N	Parker William C	563	clerk	62	133 Appleton
O	Quinlan Annabelle—†	563	cashier	28	534 Glendale av
P	Robinson James W	563	clerk	40	474 Mass av
R	Shea Michael	563	shoemaker	45	133 Appleton
S	Stewart Charles	563	cashier	62	here
T	Stone Grace—†	563	clerk	23	133 Appleton
U	Chan Hoyee—†	564	houseworker	33	here
V	Chan Peter A	564	merchant	43	"
W	Cotter Mary J—†	565	at home	60	"
X	Deasey Catherine—†	565	"	50	"
Y	Erberg John	566	painter	55	"
Z	Geyson Joseph	566	cigarmaker	71	"
A	Hardy William T	566	dishwasher	54	"
B	Planting Charles	566	cook	65	"
C	Darlington Mary E—†	567	clerk	26	Duxbury
D	Drummy Alice—†	567	housewife	27	here
E	Drummey Leo	567	druggist	31	524 Mass av
F	Ford Charles W	567	janitor	31	here
G	Ford Marcia—†	567	housewife	27	"
H	Hilton Bertha E—†	567	housekeeper	58	"
K	Lovejoy Forrest E	567	retired	58	"
L	McKay Nina—†	567	clerk	31	"
M	Shediac Reta—†	567	manager	20	"
N	Whitney Lawrence E	567	custodian	28	"
O	Hilton Fred	569	retired	62	"
P	Price William T	569	real estate	64	"
R	Scott Marion E—†	569	houseworker	34	"
S	Crandall Oscar	570	retired	55	New York
T	Fortune William	570	jaintor	43	47 Worcester
U	Kilburn Fannie—†	570	at home	55	here
V	McDonnell Margaret—†	570	housekeeper	41	63 Worcester
W	McDonnell Marie—†	570	waitress	40	here
X	McGillvarey John	570	lineman	30	"
Y	Perkins George	570	motorman	63	"
Z	Santos Joseph	570	laborer	32	605 Tremont
A	Stetson Walter	570	cashier	51	here
B	Walsh Eugene	570	clerk	25	514 Mass av

15

Page	Letter	FULL NAME.	Residence, April 1, 1926.	Occupation.	Supposed Age.	Reported Residence, April 1, 1925. Street and Number.

Massachusetts Avenue—Continued

	C	Wigner Ross H	570	physician	30	Oklahoma
	D	Wood John J	570	painter	45	here
	E	Armstrong Lyman	571	waiter	32	"
	F	Aurby William	571	U S A	35	"
	G	Black Graham	571	student	20	Nova Scotia
	H	Dakus Joseph	571	janitor	30	134 Gold
	K	Hart Owen B	571	laborer	40	here
	L	Kenney Henry M	571	retired	78	"
	M	Muler Max	571	clerk	30	New Hampshire
	N	Smith Bernice M—†	571	housekeeper	52	here
	O	Sullivan Cornelius	571	retired	75	"
	P	Brickley Melville	572	dentist	57	"
	R	Burhan Sarah—†	572	housekeeper	60	"
	S	Cousins Ella—†	572	at home	69	"
	T	McDonald John	572	fisherman	34	"
	U	McPhee Peter	572	carpenter	60	"
	V	Quigley William	572	helper	68	"
	W	Ralley John	572	laborer	60	"
	X	Tapper Emma—†	572	housewife	70	"
	Y	Vickere Joseph	572	carpenter	34	"
	Z	Walker Minnie D—†	572	housekeeper	60	"
	A	Wallace Phillip	572	laborer	62	"
	B	Alison John	573	janitor	38	"
	C	Dayton Fayette	573	retired	80	"
	D	Fargas Manuel	573	laborer	58	"
	E	Fish Henry C	573	retired	70	New York
	F	Flanagan William M	573	salesman	40	here
	G	Frankam Mary E—†	573	at home	65	78 F
	H	Hackett Charles S	573	clerk	40	Needham
	K	Morgan William	573	"	31	Cleveland O
	L	Sears Sarah—†	573	at home	72	Brookline
	M	Tobey Barbara—†	573	"	52	here
	N	Tobey Samuel E	573	retired	76	"
	O	Wellington Paul	573	clerk	30	New Hampshire
	P	Dunn William	574	carpenter	55	here
	R	Heath Annie I—†	574	housewife	36	"
	S	Heath Leo H	574	tinsmith	35	"
	T	Marr Henry	574	watchman	51	"
	U	Martin Anthony	574	laborer	35	"
	V	Mason Henry	574	fisherman	28	"
	W	Mason Mary—†	574	housekeeper	32	"

Massachusetts Avenue— Continued

x	Schuabe Hugo	574	tinsmith	50	521 Mass av
Y	Carson Mary—†	577	housekeeper	28	here
z	Colleran Patrick J	577	chauffeur	38	"
A	Connell Frances—†	577	at home	50	"
B	Corcancon Walter	577	waiter	25	"
C	Eilertsen Olawa—†	577	housekeeper	52	"
D	Finn Thomas	577	machinist	40	"
E	Glinchy Mary—†	577	cook	50	"
F	Hall Frederick	577	laborer	70	"
G	Hodgkins Jennie—†	577	clerk	50	"
H	Murphy Julia—†	577	housekeeper	51	"
K	O'Neil Lillian—†	577	clerk	27	Quincy
L	Buchin Esther—†	578	housewife	22	here
M	Buchin Harold	578	student	30	New York
N	Gallagher Mora—†	578	waitress	35	8 Blanchard
O	Hardy Virginia—†	578	decorator	35	98 St James av
P	Leslie George	578	carpenter	23	New York
R	Lind John	578	motorman	42	here
S	Lush Alfred E	578	trainman	38	"
T	Parcell William	578	U S N	24	Miami Fla
U	Paton David	578	plumber	25	here
V	Singers Alexander	578	machinist	25	37 Milford
W	Thompson Jean—†	578	housekeeper	52	37 "
X	Ancock Clarence	581	spinner	23	here
Y	Brennon John F	581	laborer	30	"
Z	Fartin Emil A	581	salesman	29	156 E Cottage
A	Goddard Charles F	581	carpenter	45	here
B	Goddard Edith M—†	581	housekeeper	47	"
C	Griffin Gerald A	581	engineer	36	Lynn
D	Griffin Joseph P	581	laborer	46	"
F	Kinner Richard J	581	machinist	34	876 Albany
E	Knight Albert A	581	engineer	22	here
G	Patterson Porter O	581	bookkeeper	46	Lynn
H	Rounds William H	581	engineer	28	181 London
K	Styffe John N	581	"	26	Lynn
L	Anderson Victor A	582	painter	50	here
M	Drew Frances C—†	582	housewife	54	"
N	Gillingham Leonard	582	steamfitter	37	17 Leroy
O	Lee Harry C	582	machinist	32	here
P	McIntyre Garnett M	582	waiter	40	"
R	Meldrum Henry	582	stonecutter	34	Georgia

Massachusetts Avenue--Continued

s	Meldrum Margaret—†	582	housewife	28	Georgia
t	Covell Dorothy —†	585	"	36	532 Mass av
u	Covell Edward	585	fireman	43	532 "
v	Reed Emma—†	585	at home	86	532 "
w	Connolly Edward P	585	chauffeur	32	here
x	Connolly Mary —†	585	housewife	26	"
y	Moran John	585	plumber	30	Salem
z	Dunn Frank	585	clerk	48	here
a	Fossa James	585	agent	48	"
b	Leyden Martin	585	"	62	"
c	Leonard Frank J	585	custodian	44	42 Knoll
d	Leonard Mary F—†	585	housewife	46	42 "
e	Silverman Gertrude—†	585	"	21	63 Edwards
f	Diggs Mabel O—†	586	dressmaker	31	3 Claremont pk
g	Diggs Rebecca—†	586	laundress	57	here
h	Elbury Elizabeth—†	586	at home	63	"
k	French John B	586	waiter	31	"
l	French Marie L—†	586	housewife	34	"
m	Otway Alfred L	586	physician	42	"
n	Otway Muriel A—†	586	housewife	40	"
o	Talbert Joseph	586	barber	53	"
p	Talbert Manda—†	586	housekeeper	37	"
r	Talbert Thomas	586	barber	48	"
t	Quan Henry	588	laundryman	38	"
v	Bickford Frank L	602	chauffeur	35	24 Ellingwood
w	Burham Charles E	602	storekeeper	22	here
x	Fitzgerald Margaret—†	602	houseworker	36	42 Church
y	Morrison Herbert F	602	mechanic	21	New York
z	Morrison Samuel E	602	laborer	23	122 Broadway
a	Morrison Wilfred J	602	"	25	122 "
b	Murphy William O	602	salesman	45	24 Worcester
c	Spellaine Mary M—†	602	houseworker	40	122 Broadway
d	Spellaine Michael J	602	clerk	41	122 "
e	Birmingham Theresa—†	603	at home	49	Salem
f	Ferrillo Chester	603	waiter	27	53 Worcester
g	Ferrillo Ethel —†	603	housewife	26	53 "
h	Harrigan John	603	salesman	35	Bath Me
k	Mildrum James	603	cook	23	32 Union pk
l	Murphy Emily—†	603	saleswoman	25	44 W Newton
m	Murphy James P	603	printer	25	44 "
n	Parles Frederick	603	cook	22	Canada

Page	Letter	FULL NAME.	Residence, April 1, 1926.	Occupation.	Supposed Age.	Reported Residence, April 1, 1925. Street and Number.

Massachusetts Avenue—Continued

o	Pike Ruby—†	603	housewife	24	2 Worcester sq
p	Pike Wilbur	603	counterman	26	2 "
r	Skillings Ida E—†	603	saleswoman	65	Salem
s	Ware Marion—†	603	clerk	23	88 Waltham
t	Ware Olive—†	603	housekeeper	43	88 "
v	Shapiro Harold	605	tailor	55	here
w	Mahoney Daniel	605	laborer	54	50 Winslow
x	Mahoney Julia—†	605	domestic	43	50 "
z	Dahl Anna—†	605	"	48	Salem
a	Olson Alben	605	painter	53	"
c	Brodrick Thomas	608	laborer	34	here
d	Brusso George A	608	machinist	30	27 Smith
e	Leonard Edward	608	janitor	45	623 Col av
f	Leonard Ethel—†	608	houseworker	37	623 "
g	McLean Thomas	608	starter	45	538 Mass av
h	McNeil John	608	waiter	23	here
k	Shaw Ruby—†	608	waitress	26	837 Blue Hill av
l	Gregory Charles	609	clerk	35	101 Oak
m	Kelley Irene—†	609	housewife	25	Salem
n	Kelley Joseph	609	chauffeur	26	"
o	Mulvey Annie—†	609	waitress	35	Lynn
p	Romruak Akem	609	laborer	42	Bath Me
r	Solomon James	609	clerk	52	here
s	Aulenback Albert	612	storekeeper	26	623 Mass av
t	Aulenback Hazel—†	612	housekeeper	45	623 "
u	Carroll Catherine—†	612	"	65	here
v	Dorey Alice F—†	612	at home	60	"
w	Kirby William	612	carpenter	45	623 Mass av
x	Malonson Jennie—†	612	saleswoman	32	623 "
y	McKeon John J	612	salesman	50	Wash'n D C
z	McKirdy Grace—†	612	waitress	45	Beachmont
a	Park Harry	612	salesman	45	623 Mass av
b	Scarbro Bell—†	612	waitress	30	here
c	Sparks Charles	612	chauffeur	30	"
d	Atkinson Goldie H—†	613	housekeeper	28	44 E Newton
e	Atkinson Gordon E	613	manager	29	44 "
f	Atkinson William	613	collector	65	44 "
g	Barrow Regina L—†	613	cashier	21	Arlington
h	Barrow William	613	carpenter	21	"
k	Bowman Elinor—†	613	cashier	25	234 Mass av

19

Massachusetts Avenue—Continued

L	Bowman Harold	613	carpenter	20	234 Mass av
M	Bowman Joseph	613	"	25	234 "
N	Brooks George	613	retired	35	255 Spring
O	Godfrey Aubrey	613	bricklayer	38	44 E Newton
P	Reardon Annie—†	613	housewife	33	Brockton
R	Reardon Daniel J	613	clerk	40	"
S	Balnien Herbert	614	carpenter	25	406 Mass av
T	Barringer Bernard	614	"	52	373 "
U	Benson Carl	614	painter	40	here
V	Benson Elizabeth—†	614	waitress	35	"
W	Dorey Walter E	614	retired	50	612 Mass av
X	Haley Frank	614	clerk	40	here
Y	Jacobs Benjamin	614	salesman	34	113 Harvard
Z	Pearson Annie—†	614	laundress	30	Halifax N S
A	Pearson Clarence	614	laundryman	35	"
B	Smith Eden	614	carpenter	38	573 Mass av
C	Swiker Warren	614	meatcutter	20	Halifax N S
D	Tucker Ruth—†	614	housekeeper	29	here
E	Tucker William	614	clerk	48	"
F	Carry Florence—†	615	waitress	26	Lynn
G	Collins Jeremiah	615	agent	53	here
H	Fidrocki Marie—†	615	housekeeper	27	"
K	Fidrocki William	615	painter	36	"
L	Fife George	615	laborer	25	619 Mass av
M	Green William	615	binder	46	here
N	Holtz Barnett	615	chauffeur	33	"
O	Holtz Florence—†	615	cashier	33	"
P	McKeever George	615	chauffeur	22	673 Mass av
R	McKeever Lestina—†	615	housewife	21	673 "
S	O'Connor Michael L	615	chauffeur	26	106 W Third
T	Page Harry E	615	laborer	25	32 Dartmouth
U	Palardy Henry	615	machinist	27	here
V	Polack Morris	615	cigarmaker	45	627 Mass av
W	Rost George	615	carpenter	46	here
X	Tore Philip	615	storekeeper	28	614 Mass av
Y	Youngquist David	615	laborer	40	here
A	Blake James	617	machinist	35	"
B	Blake Louise—†	617	housewife	27	"
C	Hart Helen—†	617	operator	20	429 Tremont
D	Kaminski Peter	617	electrician	29	here
E	Kaminski Victoria—†	617	dressmaker	22	"

29

Page.	Letter.	FULL NAME.	Residence, April 1, 1926.	Occupation.	Supposed Age.	Reported Residence, April 1, 1925.
						Street and Number.

Massachusetts Avenue—Continued

	F	Kennedy Joseph	617	packer	48	here
	G	Libby Alice —†	617	actress	49	"
	H	Libby Austin	617	counterman	27	"
	K	Moore Christina —†	617	waitress	27	"
	L	Moore Martha—†	617	at home	76	"
	M	Moore William	617	laborer	39	"
	N	Senna Joseph	617	counterman	27	"
	O	Sheehan Timothy	617	plasterer	40	"
	P	Sullivan Catherine —†	617	shoeworker	25	"
	R	Warren William E	617	engineer	35	"
	T	Brown John J	619	mechanic	23	16 Rosedale
	U	Carey George H	619	painter	30	58 W Newton
	V	Carter William	619	mechanic	24	16 Rosedale
	W	Conrad Fay—†	619	waitress	22	698 Mass av
	X	Dowd Thomas F	619	clerk	62	330 Hyde Park av
	Y	Flynn Daniel A	619	boilermaker	41	37 Bradley
	Z	Garaprry Richard	619	steamfitter	26	here
	A	Harrington Benjamin	619	paperhanger	41	8 Meander
	B	Raymond Albert	619	clerk	24	9 Copeland pl
	C	Raymond Lotta—†	619	housekeeper	40	9 "
	D	Raymond William	619	clerk	55	Worcester
	E	Smith Joseph	619	operator	27	181 Vernon
	F	Stell Lillian —†	619	waitress	21	1603 Wash'n
	G	Sullivan Daniel	619	clerk	24	104 E Springfield
	H	Sullivan Mary E—†	619	typist	22	104 "
	K	Vinal Mary J—†	619	housekeeper	32	here
	L	Wilson Irene—†	619	waitress	24	698 Mass av
	M	Wilson Mae— †	619	"	25	698 "
	O	Ackerman David	621	painter	26	19 Appleton
	P	Ahnegren Iven	621	coppersmith	23	Quincy
	R	Alsterberg Florence— †	621	housewife	35	here
	S	Alsterberg Frank O	621	patternmaker	40	"
	T	Alsterberg Frank S	621	retired	70	"
	U	Byers John	621	shoeworker	52	Vermont
	V	Coutere Elmer	621	baker	21	24 Berry
	W	Coutere Forti —†	621	housewife	20	24 "
	X	Cusasfulli Antonio	621	laundryman	23	New York
	Y	Hittle John H	621	cook	34	Malden
	Z	Julian Frank	621	agent	49	here
	A	Lee Annie—†	621	housewife	35	Erie Pa

21

Massachusetts Avenue—Continued

B	Lee Walter	621	mechanic	34	Erie Pa
C	Peterson Gustaf	621	baker	49	104 E Springfield
D	Shalin George	621	machinist	58	here
E	Sherman Edward	621	counterman	28	Lawrence
G	Caffery William	623	clerk	36	here
H	Clark Joseph H	623	salesman	50	"
K	Dyer Lena M —†	623	housekeeper	45	"
L	Feskas James	623	clerk	45	Belmont
M	Lefford George	623	laborer	30	Lawrence
N	O'Leary John	623	"	50	here
O	Stanlasky Alfred	623	salesman	24	Connecticut
P	Terzis Alexander	623	waiter	40	here
S	Mee Sing	626	laundryman	48	"
T	Carron George	627	machinist	35	Lowell
U	Donovan John	627	chauffuer	40	here
V	Engblom Anna— †	627	housekeeper	50	"
W	Kennedy Mary— †	628	"	34	"
X	Kennedy William J	628	dentist	36	"
Y	Salvati Dominic	628	proprietor	35	15 Worcester sq
Z	Salvati Jennie— †	628	housewife	33	15 "
A	Donnelly Mary C—†	628	teacher	45	here
B	Borstein Louis	628	florist	40	68 W Concord
C	Borstein Mamie—†	628	housewife	36	68 "
D	Prior Louis A	628	chauffeur	35	here
E	Welch Margaret— †	628	operator	24	"
H	Spellicy Cornelius	628	agent	56	"
K	Boyle Charlotte R—†	628	housewife	63	1482 Wash'n
L	Driscoll Daniel J	628	salesman	28	194 Boston
M	Fortain William	628	painter	38	1482 Wash'n

Northampton Street

H	Zoes Efstatheos D	143	cook	31	here
K	DeCosta Emonuel	143	"	40	"
L	Carcas Charles	143	"	28	"
N	Jenning Alice— †	145	housewife	38	"
O	Jenning William	145	laborer	34	"
R	Davis John	145	"	48	"
S	Thomas Frank	145	"	30	"
U	Wilson Joan— †	147	housewife	25	65 Lenox

Page	Letter	FULL NAME.	Residence, April 1, 1926.	Occupation.	Supposed Age.	Reported Residence, April 1, 1925. Street and Number.

Northampton Street--Continued

v	Wilson Nathan	147	laborer	30	65 Lenox
w	Rogers Tony	147	"	41	here
x	Whaley Rudolph	147	"	40	"
y	Bozzey Minerva—†	147	housewife	31	"
z	Bozzey Robert L	147	laborer	31	"
b	Rogers Fannie—†	149	cook	33	"
d	Call Emmit	149	laborer	51	"
h	Collier Callie—†	153	housekeeper	27	"
k	Hankinson Eva—†	153	houseworker	35	"
l	Owens James R	153	laborer	26	"
m	Owens Louise—†	153	houseworker	42	"
n	Taylor Lottie—†	153	"	35	"
o	Porter Mary—†	153	cook	31	"
r	Hamilton Isbella—†	155	houseworker	25	"
s	Hamilton Joseph	155	laborer	39	"
t	Stark Robert	155	"	31	"
u	Brown Harry	155	"	50	"
v	Allen William H	155	"	24	85 E Lenox
z	Hard William	157	"	40	here
a	Washington George	157	"	30	"
d	Roy Susan—†	175	housekeeper	69	"
e	Washington Ida M—†	175	housewife	72	"
f	Washington Samuel W	175	retired	78	"
g	Jackson Emanuel	175	waiter	52	"
h	Jackson Lena—†	175	housewife	32	"
k	Hughes Fannie P—†	175	housekeeper	41	"
l	Virginia Clarence C	177	laborer	42	"
m	Virginia Henrietta—†	177	housewife	39	"
n	Proro Daniel	177	oiler	58	"
o	Proro Helen—†	177	housewife	50	"
p	Clay Hattie—†	177	housekeeper	56	"
r	Clay Henry	177	janitor	68	"
s	Fuller Florence—†	177	housewife	40	"
t	Fuller George E	177	chauffeur	43	"
u	Fuller Mary E—†	177	at home	66	"
v	Oxley Albert	179	cook	46	"
w	Oxley Dolorsa—†	179	housewife	38	"
x	Melbourne Hogarth	179	elevatorman	22	"
y	Samuels Cecil	179	waiter	39	"
z	Samuels Martha—†	179	housewife	42	"
a	Turner Florence—†	179	"	39	"

Northampton Street—Continued

	Letter	FULL NAME	Residence	Occupation	Age	Reported Residence
	B	Turner John	179	porter	54	here
	C	Bell Martha—†	179	housewife	28	"
	D	Bell Peter	179	porter	30	"
	E	Carey Lucy—†	181	housewife	30	"
	F	Carey William	181	chauffeur	35	"
	G	Gardner Carrie—†	181	housewife	35	108 Camden
	H	Gardner Joseph F	181	janitor	49	108 "
	K	Newman Ernest	181	"	44	here
	L	Newman Levina—†	181	housewife	50	"
	M	Talbort Hilda—†	181	maid	30	"
	N	Murray Annie—†	181	cook	54	"
	O	Murray James	181	"	55	"
	P	Chambers Roland	225	porter	26	Phila Pa
	R	Davis Sidney	225	waiter	47	here
	S	Johnson Louis	225	laborer	30	184 Northampton
	T	Lee John J	225	chef	32	Phila Pa
	U	Perry Heneeka	225	barber	27	Troy N J
	V	Perry Lucky	225	packer	29	79 Compton
	W	Valro Raymond	225	waiter	26	176 W Springfield
	X	Walton Bessie—†	225	housekeeper	29	here
	Y	Williams George	225	mechanic	26	Camden N J
	Z	Williams Gladys—†	225	chambermaid	24	Attleboro
	A	Benun Edgar	227	waiter	48	Asbury Park N J
	B	Clifton James	227	laborer	50	here
	C	Dukes Rose—†	227	elevatorwoman	20	1 Haven
	D	Gibbons Edward	227	laborer	50	1 "
	E	Gibbons Margaret—†	227	waitress	32	here
	F	Gibbons Victoria—†	227	housekeeper	38	1 Haven
	G	Gross Margaret A—†	227	houseworker	39	here
	H	Gross Margaret H—†	227	at home	68	"
	K	Marks John	227	laborer	49	"
	L	McCann Susan T—†	227	houseworker	37	"
	M	Northern Abram	227	laborer	50	"
	N	Allen James A	229	chauffeur	35	Lawrence
	O	Allen Sadie—†	229	housewife	30	"
	P	Anderson Ruth—†	229	waitress	22	here
	R	Brown Noah	229	elevatorman	45	"
	S	Criggs Charles C	229	watchman	35	"
	T	Hernaiz Julio	229	laborer	25	Pennsylvania
	U	Sanford Ellen—†	229	at home	70	here
	V	Askew Albert	231	chef	40	"

Northampton Street—Continued

w	Canada Turemella—†	231	hairdresser	36	Brockton
x	Delicia Alice—†	231	houseworker	20	16 Windsor
y	Hagbourne Helen—†	231	shoeworker	20	22 Cedar
z	Munns Loretta—†	231	cook	40	New York
a	Norwood John E	231	porter	32	here
b	Riley Ross	231	barber	29	"
c	Slater Edward B	231	laborer	28	Virginia
d	Summerville William B	231	painter	45	98 Bower
e	Allen Alvin B	233	poster	38	here
f	Johnson Alexander	233	laborer	36	"
g	Jones John W	233	"	33	"
h	Lewis Anderson	233	photographer	43	Georgia
k	Luke Edward	233	laborer	40	here
l	Millin Meking	233	"	22	Rhode Island
m	Morris Josephine—†	233	housekeeper	43	here
n	Pierce Charles	233	chauffeur	45	554 Shawmut av
o	Pylburn James A	233	janitor	30	1059 Tremont
p	Robinson George G	233	laborer	70	here
r	Call Clarence	235	waiter	29	8 Hubert
s	Lee Julia E—†	235	masseuse	52	8 "
t	Stewart Mary—†	235	cook	50	33 Camden
u	Sullivan Aaron S	235	mason	40	11½ Wellington
v	Sullivan Louise E—†	235	dressmaker	29	11½ "
w	Brown Beverly	237	janitor	38	here
x	Brown Emily—†	237	housekeeper	48	"
y	Coffer Jacob	237	boilermaker	49	293 Northampton
z	Cousens Eutha—†	237	elevatorwoman	29	here
a	Wilson Frank	237	janitor	40	1204 Tremont
b	Cook Malissia—†	239	cook	49	363 Northampton
c	Fairfax Martha—†	239	elevatorwoman	27	here
d	Hubbard Maceo M	239	student	27	"
e	Ivery George	239	cook	39	"
f	Martin Hattie—†	239	"	26	"
g	St Clair Fredrick D	239	student	23	"
h	Worthy Mabel R—†	239	housewife	40	"
k	Worthy William	239	physician	46	"
l	Jones Albion S	241	clerk	33	"
m	Jones Edwin E	241	porter	32	"
n	Jones Mary E—†	241	housekeeper	70	"
o	Nairne Alfred S	241	dentist	45	"
p	Perkins Daisy L—†	241	maid	47	"

Northampton Street—Continued

R	Pryoy Lee A	241	porter	74	here
S	Gathweight Marvin	243	cook	25	"
T	Grant Alice—†	243	social worker	24	Cambridge
U	Jeffries John	243	bellboy	22	here
V	Liggons Joseph	243	porter	52	"
W	Pinder Algha—†	243	housewife	34	"
X	Pinder Elmer	243	cook	26	"
Y	Sampson Heutis	243	waiter	23	"
Z	Thomas Edward	243	cook	40	14 Westminster
A	Williams Chester	243	"	27	198 W Springfield

Shawmut Avenue

B	Whittredge Clarence	474	laborer	21	here
C	Whittredge Gertrude—†	474	housekeeper	44	"
D	Bemis Catherine—†	474	housewife	41	"
E	Bemis Frederick S	474	machinist	51	"
F	Burm Christopher	474	pianofinisher	56	476 Shawmut av
G	Burm Joseph	474	printer	21	476 "
H	Dunn Bernard	474	elevatorman	23	476 "
K	Hart Rose—†	474	brushfinisher	47	476 "
L	Segee Annie—†	474	housekeeper	59	53 Call
M	Segee Annie—†	474	clerk	21	53 "
N	Segee Ethel—†	474	brushmaker	32	53 "
T	Lunnergan Wallace G	476	brakeman	23	Somerville
R	McKay John F J	476	inspector	43	here
S	McKay Mary A—†	476	housewife	39	"
V	Calusan Frank	476	storekeeper	38	"
X	Dalton Albert	478	carpenter	27	"
Y	Dalton Mary—†	478	housewife	24	"
Z	McLean Hugh	478	laborer	54	"
A	Kiley Sarah H—†	478	housewife	26	"
B	Kiley William J	478	waiter	37	"
C	Foote Edmond A	478	teamster	55	"
D	Foote Rachel M—†	478	housewife	50	"
E	Gavin Annie E—†	478	stitcher	40	"
F	Gavin John F	478	laborer	41	"
G	O'Connell William F	478	steward	39	"
H	Hutchinson Evelyn—†	478	waitress	39	Lawrence

Shawmut Avenue—Continued

K	Hebb James J	478	checker	50	69 Rutland
L	Hebb Mary—†	478	housewife	44	69 "
M	McDonald Ira—†	478	steamfitter	49	here
N	Watkins Grace—†	478	housekeeper	74	"
O	Cone Jennie—†	478	housewife	21	7 Bower
P	Cone William	478	sign painter	31	7 "
R	Waite Mary—†	478	housekeeper	48	Medway
U	Carr Abraham	480	painter	38	here
V	Carr Katherine—†	480	housewife	36	"
W	Selados Catherine—†	480	"	27	"
X	Selados James	480	bootblack	30	"
Y	Sprague Jennie—†	480	housewife	40	1963 Wash'n
Z	Sprague John	480	mechanic	21	1963 "
A	Sprague Thomas	480	"	44	1963 "
D	Pappas Arestede	480	pedler	35	1503 "
E	Pappas Mary—†	480	housewife	35	1503 "
F	Goorno Sarah—†	480	"	40	here
G	Goorno Saul	480	barber	43	"
H	Gooltz Annie D—†	480	housewife	30	"
K	Gooltz Max	480	printer	37	"
L	Pratt Jessie—†	480	housewife	33	"
M	Pratt Roaul	480	mailer	37	"
P	Boyajian Samuel	486	grocer	31	"
R	Ermonian Satenig—†	486	housekeeper	31	"
S	Eemonian Simon	486	barber	36	"
T	Farrenkoph John A	486	chauffeur	20	"
U	Farrenkoph Lena—†	486	housekeeper	49	"
V	Herring Mary L—†	486	waitress	47	"
X	Jones Ethel—†	486	housekeeper	34	"
Y	Jones Rae—†	486	"	20	"
Z	Stetson Leslie	486	inspector	28	Cambridge
E	Vartaman Setrag	496	merchant	37	here
F	Vartaman Victoria—†	496	housewife	33	"
G	Murad Elias	496	grocer	38	151 Albany
H	Murad Rose—†	496	housewife	40	151 "
K	Melcomans Mary—†	496	"	65	here
L	Melcomans Vartan	496	retired	72	"
M	Calusdian Richard	496	grocer	25	"
N	Hazarian Aznive—†	496	housewife	31	"
O	Hazarian Mardage	496	laborer	35	"

27

Letter	FULL NAME.	Residence, April 1, 1926.	Occupation.	Supposed Age.	Reported Residence, April 1, 1925. Street and Number.

Shawmut Avenue —Continued

R	Keel Daniel	499	chauffeur	27	501 Shawmut av
S	McNeal Marie —†	499	domestic	27	here
T	West Abraham	499	porter	46	"
U	West Elizabeth —†	499	hairdresser	36	"
V	Tolliver Ella—†	499	housewife	42	"
W	Tolliver George A	499	porter	54	"
X	Harris Elizabeth —†	499	housewife	20	175 Northampton
Y	Harris William G	499	laborer	28	175 "
Z	Higganbotham Nannie—†	499	housekeeper	46	Cambridge
A	Dockery George	499	waiter	48	here
C	Arthur Nodie	501	operator	20	Walpole
D	Gaines Susan —†	501	housekeeper	31	"
E	Hudnell Harriett —†	501	"	34	7 Rutland
F	Wilder Roy A	501	porter	29	7 "
H	Bryan George H	501	laborer	52	51 Kendall
K	Brown May —†	502	domestic	50	here
L	Whalen Angelina —†	502	housekeeper	47	"
M	Byers Martin B B	503	cook	56	"
N	Dukes Edward	503	salesman	45	"
O	Dukes Etta—†	503	housekeeper	40	"
P	Goodman Estella —†	503	"	27	"
R	Goodman George	503	cook	31	"
S	Gould Josephine —†	503	dressmaker	29	"
T	Grace Lula —†	503	laundress	55	"
U	Grace Walter	503	cook	35	"
V	Taylor Sarah —†	503	housekeeper	31	"
W	Woodfaulk Gutha —†	503	housewife	31	Virginia
X	Woodfaulk James	503	laborer	30	"
Y	Delmore Harry	504	clerk	30	here
Z	Fraser Wilfred H	504	engineer	27	"
A	Pack Irma —†	504	stenographer	21	"
B	Pack Nettie D —†	504	housekeeper	40	"
C	White Charles K	504	clerk	28	"
D	Corner John	505	laborer	50	118 W Springfield
E	Corner Mary —†	505	housewife	48	118 "
F	Elliott Margaret —†	505	"	27	Rhode Island
G	Galvan Avas—†	505	cook	36	17 Rollins
H	Goolsley William	505	clerk	42	103 W Springfield
K	Infante Isadore	505	student	26	New York
L	Joseph Mary —†	505	housewife	25	here

28

Shawmut Avenue—Continued

	Letter	Full Name	Residence	Occupation	Age	Reported Residence
	M	Joseph Michael	505	machinist	30	here
	N	Petterson Miner	505	laborer	28	Chelsea
	O	Rounatie Alphonsus	505	clerk	25	Norwood
	P	Wheeler Henry	505	waiter	30	here
	R	Fitchett Jennie—†	506	laundress	49	"
	S	Lockett Alvira—†	506	cook	80	"
	T	Lockett Elnora—†	506	domestic	50	"
	U	Williams Caroline—†	506	operator	33	"
	V	Willis Bertha—†	506	housewife	57	"
	W	Willis James H	506	engineer	72	"
	X	Coleman Margaret—†	507	housekeeper	40	"
	Y	Johnson Elizabeth—†	507	"	40	"
	Z	Merrill James	507	carpenter	49	"
	A	Merrill Katherine—†	507	hairdresser	47	"
	B	Shaw Louise—†	507	housewife	40	"
	C	Shaw William	507	porter	45	"
	D	Stewart Elizabeth—†	507	hairdresser	35	"
	E	Bourne John S R	508	lawyer	43	"
	F	Goosby Robert	508	metalworker	22	"
	G	Lee George H	508	laborer	41	191 W Springfield
	H	Parris Hiram	508	cook	33	here
	K	Willis Louise M—†	508	housekeeper	42	"
	L	Fitzgerald Mary—†	510	"	40	"
	M	Kelley Nellie—†	510	"	60	Melrose
	N	Leahy Jeremiah	510	laborer	60	here
	O	Mooney Henry	510	carpenter	20	98 W Springfield
	P	Parslow Charles	510	painter	51	here
	R	Parslow Mary—†	510	housekeeper	52	"
	S	Rogers Anna—†	510	housewife	26	"
	T	Rogers Joseph	510	roofer	30	"
	U	Sweeney Harriett—†	510	laundress	40	98 W Springfield
	W	Sarkis Bashara	515	machinist	35	here
	X	Sarkis Mary—†	515	housewife	33	"
	Y	Hilton Charles B	515	roofer	63	1354 Wash'n
	Z	Jackman Annie J—†	515	housekeeper	66	1354 "
	A	Jackman George W	515	printer	45	1354 "
	B	Crane Josephine—†	515	stripper	53	81 W Springfield
	C	Crane Oscar M	515	cigarmaker	48	New York
	D	Dunlap Jennie—†	516	housekeeper	65	here
	E	Fafel Barnett	516	grocer	38	159 W Springfield

Letter	FULL NAME.	Residence, April 1, 1926.	Occupation.	Supposed Age.	Reported Residence, April 1, 1925. Street and Number.

Shawmut Avenue—Continued

F	Fafel Mollie —†	516	housewife	37	159 W Springfield
G	McLaughlin Patrick	516	laborer	50	96 "
H	Sweeney Daniel	516	"	55	96 "
L	DeLong George	518	real estate	53	76 "
M	Haslan Clara—†	518	housewife	36	Malden
N	Haslan Louis W	518	shipper	51	"
O	McDonald Douglas	518	laborer	21	64 Dudley
P	Moses Elvira—†	518	housekeeper	30	30 E Canton
R	Moses Thomas	518	mechanic	31	30 "
S	Ryan Earl	518	carpenter	30	Everett
U	Hall Crispin	520	student	22	New York
V	Hall Denham D	520	physician	36	here
W	Jackson Grace—†	520	laundress	21	"
X	Jackson Jennie—†	520	domestic	70	"
Y	Mitchell Anna—†	520	housekeeper	38	"
Z	Rankin John	520	laborer	35	Brockton
A	Simmons Aurura—†	520	seamstress	30	Everett
B	Lawson Alexander	521	teamster	46	here
C	McDonald James	521	laborer	23	"
D	McDonald John A	521	"	49	"
E	Palligreno Charles	521	teamster	31	"
F	Reid George C	521	coachman	55	"
G	Reid Lydia—†	521	housewife	39	"
V	Green Thomas	539	watchman	56	"
W	Gray Wiley	540	salesman	38	186 Northampton
X	Mason Clyde	540	fireman	22	53 Camden
Y	Mason Jack R	540	"	25	53 "
Z	Hoole Charles	540	chauffeur	35	here
A	Hoole Ruth—†	540	housewife	26	"
B	Mason Ira	540	plasterer	38	"
C	Santos Kathrine —†	542	housewife	38	"
D	Santos Samuel	542	laborer	40	"
E	Searcy Ethel—†	542	housewife	29	"
F	Searcy Margaret—†	542	housekeeper	70	"
G	Searcy Walter	542	mechanic	49	"
H	Mason Leola—†	542	housewife	40	"
K	Mason Leonard	542	paperhanger	40	"
M	Dodge David T	544	inspector	65	"
N	Dodge Mabel F—†	544	housewife	27	"

Shawmut Avenue—Continued

	O	Ellis Catherine—†	544	housekeeper	50	here
	P	Ellis Emma J—†	544	domestic	25	"
	R	Miller Gertrude—†	544	"	35	"
	S	Smith Emma—†	544	housekeeper	28	Malden
	U	Constant Sadie—†	546	domestic	31	Cambridge
	V	Hart Charles	546	shipper	53	Brookline
	W	Johnson Cornelius	546	laborer	42	here
	X	Sakers Annie—†	546	housekeeper	67	"
	Y	Sakers George	546	fireman	63	"
	Z	Shields Martha—†	546	housekeeper	37	1 Chester pl
	A	Shields William	546	janitor	50	1 "
	C	Jones Richard	548	cook	55	here
	D	Mathews William	548	"	35	Brockton
	E	Owens Celia—†	548	housekeeper	50	Everett
	F	Quarell Richard	548	laborer	63	here
	G	Reardon Emma B—†	548	housewife	50	"
	H	Reardon Robert B	548	barber	62	"
	K	Whalen William H	548	laborer	62	Nova Scotia

Stevens Street

	B	Lane Allen	1	porter	30	here
	C	Lane Jewel—†	1	housewife	27	"
	D	Simons James	1	laborer	40	"
	E	Jennings Daniel W	2	retired	70	"
	F	Clark George L	3	laborer	62	"
	G	Devoe Harry	3	janitor	38	113 Harold
	H	Devoe Thomasina—†	3	housewife	35	113 "
	K	Lee Charles	4	porter	29	1 Burbank
	L	Lee Myrtle E—†	4	housewife	29	1 "
	M	Skinner Thomas H	4	waiter	42	16A Camden
	N	Clark Joseph	5	laborer	30	here
	O	Barbadoes Anna M—†	5	stitcher	49	76 Kendall
	P	Gaskin Charles	5	bricklayer	53	here
	R	Gaskin Esther—†	5	housewife	44	"
	S	Cole Maira—†	6	housekeeper	42	57 Pembroke
	T	Edwin Amy—†	6	housewife	27	here
	U	Edwin Stephen	6	laborer	43	"
	V	Young Everett	6	"	38	Cambridge

31

Page	Letter	FULL NAME.	Residence, April 1, 1926.	Occupation.	Supposed Age.	Reported Residence, April 1, 1925. Street and Number.

Tremont Street

	w	Chapman Jane —†	748	housewife	60	606 Tremont
	x	Chapman John	748	retired	65	606 "
	y	Dugan Ethel —†	748	housekeeper	28	Worcester
	A	Fennino Domenic	748	chef	38	New York
	B	Hall Edna—†	748	housewife	38	208 W Springfield
	C	Hall William	748	printer	43	208 "
	D	McFarlane James	748	carpenter	43	11½ Dartmouth
	E	McViney John E	748	"	56	84 W Newton
	F	McViney Katherine—†	748	housewife	52	84 "
	G	Pooley Guy W	748	printer	68	12 Staniford
	H	Silva Anthony	748	chef	45	23 Rutland sq
	K	Smith Clara S—†	748	housewife	52	here
	L	Smith George	748	porter	49	"
	M	Sullivan Eva—†	748	housewife	43	"
	N	Sullivan George	748	marketman	45	12 Durham
	O	Thompson Elizabeth—†	748	dressmaker	34	1125 Tremont
	P	McGrath Francis J	750	clerk	29	here
	R	Smith Hazel M—†	750	housewife	33	"
	S	Smith Peter M	750	physician	50	"
	T	Stockdale Helen—†	750	nurse	25	118 Forest Hills
	U	Beland Anna—†	752	waitress	26	here
	V	Beland Theodore H	752	chauffeur	31	"
	W	Davis Lee W	752	finisher	23	40 Dartmouth
	X	Davis Ruth A—†	752	houseworker	20	40 "
	Y	Hall Joseph	752	chef	66	here
	Z	Landry Adlard	752	boxmaker	30	40 W Newton
	A	Landry Stella—†	752	shoeworker	30	40 "
	B	Picard David	752	"	45	Lynn
	C	Rythen Fritziof H	752	diemaker	54	here
	D	Ruthen Maria J—†	752	housewife	54	"
	E	Shackley Harry	752	clerk	28	"
	F	Shackley Maud E—†	752	laundress	52	"
	G	Shackley William L	752	clerk	25	"
	H	Thimbler Fred	752	cigarmaker	55	Manchester
	K	Thimbler Laura—†	752	shoeworker	40	"
	L	Ashforth Dorothy—†	754	housewife	38	here
	M	Ashforth George H	754	butler	44	"
	N	Burns Katherine—†	754	stitcher	56	"
	O	Crockett Elmer E	754	carpenter	58	"
	P	Crockett Gilbert V	754	chef	21	"

Tremont Street—Continued

R	Cudahy Thomas G	754	laborer	40	102 Chandler
S	Gold Abraham	754	restaurantman	30	here
T	Howard George	754	cook	30	"
U	Lawless William	754	"	38	"
V	Winsor Gilbert	754	operator	51	"
W	Winsor Susanna—†	754	housekeeper	52	"
X	Cronin Anna—†	756	forewoman	40	"
Y	Cronin Earl	756	shipper	28	"
Z	Grant Rose D—†	756	student	34	"
A	Jefferies Margaret—†	756	manager	43	"
B	Jefferies Walter	756	"	36	"
C	Lyons Jeremiah P	756	insurance agent	47	"
D	Maloney Annie—†	756	housekeeper	54	"
E	Maloney Frank	756	garageman	25	"
F	Moore Frank	756	rigger	40	"
G	Peters James	756	cook	36	"
H	Pfefferkorn Harry	756	merchant	36	"
K	Powers Thomas H	756	chauffeur	50	"
L	Reynolds William	756	packer	50	"
M	Bodo Ada R—†	758	hairdresser	35	"
N	Bodo Henry L	758	real estate	35	"
O	Bonderson Carl	758	carpenter	21	84 W Newton
P	Emmanuelson Harry	758	laborer	29	Sweden
R	Gottlander John	758	machinist	29	New York
S	Jelloe Elizabeth—†	758	houseworker	40	243 Charles
T	Leonard Alice O—†	758	housewife	43	here
U	Leonard William H	758	salesman	55	"
V	Nelson Arthur	758	stonecutter	24	22 Warrenton
W	Risberg Carl	758	student	24	Connecticut
X	Risberg John A	758	manager	58	"
Y	Shawno Agnes—†	758	housewife	24	here
Z	Shawno Samuel	758	painter	47	"
A	Smith James	758	cook	35	Andover
B	Tetlow Eva—†	758	"	40	here
C	Ben Charles	760	waiter	50	"
D	Mann Anna—†	760	housewife	47	"
E	Mann Natte	760	waiter	50	"
F	Saunders Charles H	760	"	59	82 Rockland
G	Saunders Cora F—†	760	matron	49	82 "
H	Tucker Artermus T	760	student	23	82 "
K	Brothers Anna—†	760	housekeeper	80	60 W Rutland sq

Page.	Letter.	Full Name.	Residence, April 1, 1926.	Occupation.	Supposed Age.	Reported Residence, April 1, 1925. Street and Number.

Tremont Street—Continued

	L	Cromwell Laura E—†	760	baker	38	32 Wellington
	M	Hutchinson Edith R—†	760	houseworker	26	15 Braddock pk
	N	Jameson Byrdie—†	760	housewife	42	here
	O	Jameson Taylor	760	porter	44	"
	P	Taylor John L	760	"	39	"
	S	Corbin Julia H—†	762	housekeeper	50	600 Tremont
	T	Corbin Peter	762	machinist	55	600 "
	U	Dickey Katherine—†	762	inspector	39	759 "
	V	Hatch Mary E—†	762	housekeeper	81	759 "
	W	Kelley Anna—†	762	waitress	40	141 Worcester
	X	Smith Eva—†	762	housewife	28	Lynn
	Y	Smith William	762	teamster	30	"
	Z	Boyle Philip H	764	gasfitter	40	here
	A	Currie Herbert A	764	porter	50	Newark N J
	B	Dolan Francis H	764	laborer	40	36 Gurney
	C	Duffey James J	764	painter	42	185 W Brookline
	D	Mullen Harry M	764	"	33	29 Pembroke
	E	Purshlow Daniel	764	laborer	52	Cambridge
	F	Sandler Max	764	"	34	Lynn
	G	Hop Charlie	764A	laundryman	52	China
	V	Mathews John H	786	waiter	49	here
	T	Rosser Carrie M—†	786	housewife	25	"
	U	Rosser James T	786	dentist	29	"

Washington Street

	N	York Mary—†	1675	housekeeper	52	here
	O	Sonneman Bessie E—†	1675	housewife	53	"
	P	Sonneman Fred W	1675	policeman	53	"
	R	Barry Mary A—†	1675	housewife	55	"
	S	Barry Mary E—†	1675	typist	21	"
	T	Barry Richard J	1675	clerk	23	"
	U	Stamatos James	1677	grocer	28	"
	V	Stamatos Katina—†	1677	housewife	28	"
	W	Stamatos Nicholas	1677	grocer	34	"
	X	Devine James	1677	detective	45	144 Main
	Y	Gordon Rose—†	1677	housewife	51	here
	Z	Meleady Thomas	1677	laborer	51	"
	A	Sweeney Joseph P	1677	mechanic	42	"
	B	Donovan John J	1677	clerk	34	Lowell

Page.	Letter.	FULL NAME.	Residence, April 1, 1926.	Occupation	Supposed Age.	Reported Residence, April 1, 1925. Street and Number.

Washington Street—Continued

c	Drinan John J	1677	conductor	50	here
D	McAuley Joseph	1677	fireman	53	"
E	Russ Agnes F—†	1677	housewife	50	"
F	Russ Daniel J	1677	motorman	50	"
N	Barbares Franklin B	1699	fireman	34	"
O	Barman Simon C	1699	salesman	62	247 Tremont
P	Belinski Mirko V	1699	musician	59	here
R	Bennett Oliver E	1699	publisher	61	"
S	Branch Charles M	1699	special police	25	Fairmount
T	Campbell John V	1699	watchmaker	48	here
U	Carr Bernice L—†	1699	housekeeper	36	21 Gainsboro
V	Carr George S	1699	nurse	52	21 "
W	Curtin Edward J	1699	real estate	64	here
X	Donovan Charles E	1699	druggist	26	"
Y	Donovan Jeremiah F	1699	"	49	"
Z	Duncan Elizabeth—†	1699	housewife	65	"
A	Ducan James C	1699	engineer	73	"
B	Ganity Robert J	1699	merchant	51	"
D	Goodrich Samuel M	1699	tailor	81	Hanson
C	Gorch Robert A	1699	welder	39	here
E	Hillson Robert A	1699	performer	39	New York
F	Kalb Harry	1699	houseman	71	here
G	Kozadoy David	1699	manager	40	"
H	Ladd John L	1699	clerk	50	"
K	Lane Cora M—†	1699	nurse	57	"
L	Lindeberg Carl J A	1699	foreman	51	Waltham
M	Manning Clara F—†	1699	housewife	60	here
N	Manning Patrick	1699	custodian	65	"
E	Manning Robert F	1699	electrician	29	865 Hunt'n av
P	Mager George W	1699	manager	64	here
R	Messinger William F	1699	agent	81	"
S	Millan George	1699	chauffeur	33	"
T	Penniman Walter H	1699	clerk	48	"
U	Sanbarn Clifton O	1699	meatcutter	59	"
V	Sanbarn Wilfred O	1699	bookkeeper	31	"
W	Saxe George N	1699	storekeeper	46	"
X	Sears Fred H	1699	letter carrier	52	"
Y	Summers Jerom F	1699	insurance agent	42	"
Z	Tatarian Shamodan	1699	storekeeper	33	"
A	Walsh Edward F	1699	agent	50	"
O	Young Florence—†	1745A	nurse	35	Newton

35

Page.	Letter.	FULL NAME.	Residence, April 1, 1926.	Occupation.	Supposed Age.	Reported Residence, April 1, 1925. Street and Number.

Washington Street—Continued

P	Patrick Henry W	1745A	carpenter	43	5 Newcomb
R	White Fay C—†	1745A	housekeeper	44	23 Worcester
S	Bamford Frank L	1745A	clerk	32	56 E Springfield
T	Bamford Respa L—†	1745A	saleswoman	32	56 "
W	Wentworth Mary B—†	1761	housewife	48	New York
X	Wentworth Paul J	1761	student	51	"
Z	Carroll Joseph	1761	salesman	60	here
A	Murphy William H	1761	letter carrier	49	"
B	Nadean Jesse F †	1761	at home	65	"
C	Nadean Mabel L—†	1761	artist	49	"
D	Sexton George F	1761	motorman	60	"
E	Dellacona Alice—†	1761	housewife	36	"
F	Dellacona William L	1761	mechanic	42	"
G	Gandreau John	1761	shoeworker	38	"
H	O'Brien John J	1761	lawyer	44	"
K	Rantuccio Mariannao	1761	barber	43	"
L	Pingree Charles F	1761	teamster	53	Bath Me
M	Pingree Jenney B—†	1761	housewife	55	"
N	Berry Carina †	1761	"	39	Providence R I
O	Berry John	1761	salesman	38	"
P	Burgess Elmira E—†	1761	housewife	60	30 W Dedham
R	Stanicks Joseph	1761	mechanic	33	Salem
S	Stevenson Reta—†	1761	shoestitcher	33	Providence R I
T	Martin Esther K—†	1761	housewife	47	here
U	Martin Joseph A	1761	druggist	47	"
V	Phinney Paul T	1761	clerk	29	"
W	Hoyt Annie—†	1761	at home	73	"
X	Hoyt Charles W	1761	metal worker	44	"
Y	Pierce William R	1761	salesman	68	"
B	Clement Arthur L	1767	shoecutter	30	68 W Concord
C	Clement Dorothy T—†	1767	shoe packer	29	68 "
D	Nichols Harold F	1767	clerk	33	here
E	Callaway Catherine—†	1767	saleswoman	38	"
F	Callaway John	1767	clerk	42	"
G	Chase Harry A	1767	steamfitter	57	135 W Concord
M	Flynn Patrick	1779	clerk	57	605 Mass av
N	Walsh Marion A—†	1779	housewife	28	here
O	Walsh Thomas E	1779	physician	48	"
R	Lavis Bridget E—†	1779	housewife	39	"
S	Lavis Katherine R—†	1779	saleswoman	20	"
T	Lavis William R	1779	chauffeur	39	"

Page	Letter	Full Name.	Residence, April 1, 1926.	Occupation.	Supposed Age.	Reported Residence, April 1, 1925. Street and Number.

Washington Street— Continued

	U	Robertson John	1779	laborer	59	here
	V	Smith Charles A	1779	retired	66	"
	W	Smith Charlotte—†	1779	housekeeper	66	"
	X	Whitham Georgia—†	1779	tel operator	30	"
	Y	Whitham Harold	1779	salesman	38	Brockton
	Z	Ryan Anna A—†	1779	housewife	44	here
	A	Ryan William H	1779	machinist	55	"
	B	Hickey Charles T	1779	steamfitter	47	"
	C	Hickey Josephine—†	1779	housewife	45	"

West Concord Street

	A	Medici Paul	68	janitor	40	here
	B	Medici Justina—†	68	housekeeper	35	"
	D	Marin Joaquinina—†	68	restaurateur	52	1666 Wash'n
	E	Blasi Igidia	68	shoeworker	55	here
	F	Fafibiana Amelia—†	68	housekeeper	28	New Jersey
	G	Fafibiana Frank	68	barber	32	"
	H	Vaughn Anna B—†	68	housewife	43	16 Dover
	K	Campbell Celia—†	68	waitress	24	here
	L	Campbell Lena—†	68	"	24	"
	M	Wood Irene—†	68	"	24	33 Whiting
	N	Wood Myrtle—†	68	"	26	33 "
	O	Moriarty Catherine—†	68	housewife	25	8 Auburn
	P	Moriarty Michael J	68	chauffeur	28	8 "
	R	Benucci Gino	68	laborer	31	here
	S	Benucci Ines—†	68	housekeeper	32	"
	T	Cazzuola Filomena—†	68	"	65	"
	U	Mellonosky George	68	nurse	26	557 Mass av
	V	Vail Henry G	68	"	36	1942 Wash'n
	W	Macomber Henry B	68	contractor	47	Bridgewater
	X	McIntyre John F	68	brakeman	51	here
	Y	McIntyre Mary—†	68	housekeeper	44	"
	Z	Manning Edward F	68	printer	35	"
	A	Manning Ellen—†	68	housewife	37	"
	B	Longchamps Annette—†	68	housekeeper	21	386 Shawmut av
	C	Longchamps Paul	68	roofer	28	386 "
	D	Johnson John	68	carpenter	31	872 Col av
	E	Johnson Natalie—†	68	housekeeper	32	872 "
	F	Dritsas Anna—†	68	"	42	here

37

Page	Letter	Full Name.	Residence, April 1, 1926.	Occupation.	Supposed Age.	Reported Residence, April 1, 1925. Street and Number.

West Concord Street—Continued

	Letter	Full Name	Res.	Occupation	Age	Reported Residence
	G	Dritsas Nicholas	68	coal dealer	55	here
	H	April Henry	68	nurse	33	1942 Wash'n
	K	Mulquinn Francis	68	"	27	1942 "
	L	Stewart Norval	68	"	25	26 Worcester
	M	Lapham Nancy—†	68	housekeeper	27	here
	N	Lapham Sydney	68	manager	31	"
	O	Rowe Catherine I—†	68	housekeeper	30	24 Worcester
	P	Rowe Edward R	68	porter	30	24 "
	R	Coleman John J	68	salesman	24	1767 Wash'n
	S	Coleman Mary V—†	68	housewife	23	1767 "
	T	Cohen Anna—†	68	waitress	43	here
	U	MacDougall Mary—†	68	cashier	29	52 Astor
	V	Reynolds Florence A—†	68	music teacher	27	here
	W	Reynolds William M	68	shipper	70	"
	X	Gillard Alfred	68	manager	23	"
	Y	Gillard James E	68	restaurateur	46	"
	Z	Gillard Lillian—†	68	housekeeper	44	"
	A	Andrews Arthur P	68	merchant	26	"
	B	Andrews John A	68	candymaker	30	"
	C	Zorbas Theodore	68	chauffeur	29	Dedham
	D	Lewis Gertrude—†	68	housekeeper	28	25 Worcester sq
	E	Lewis Joseph L	68	mechanic	32	63 Worcester
	F	Coleman Margaret J—†	68	housekeeper	28	here
	G	Tsacoyeanis Katina—†	68	"	25	81 Brighton av
	H	Tsacoyeanis William	68	grocer	36	81 "
	K	Rowe Thomas R	68	elevatorman	32	474 Shawmut av
	L	Studeley Harriet G—†	68	at home	58	474 "
	M	Brightman Ester—†	68	nurse	22	68 E Concord
	N	Buxton Beatrice E—†	68	"	21	68 "
	O	Edwards Cora E—†	68	"	21	68 "
	P	Foley Frances J—†	68	"	24	68 "
	R	Larsen Hope—†	68	"	22	68 "
	S	Abbot Viola B—†	68	housewife	28	32 Coolidge rd
	T	Abbot Walter H	68	foreman	44	32 "
	U	Waterman Margaret—†	68	housekeeper	55	32 "
	V	Mingo Alexander	68	leatherworker	48	45 Upton
	W	Mingo Colin	68	shoeworker	45	Lynn
	X	Mingo Mysie—†	68	housekeeper	32	"
	Y	Dana George P	68	chauffeur	24	16 Union Park
	Z	Dana May—†	68	tel operator	22	79 E Canton
	A	Diggins Catherine—†	68	housekeeper	43	145 W Concord

West Concord Street—Continued

B	Emmons Olive E—†	68	proofreader	30	145 W Concord
C	Griswold Helen L—†	68	waitress	30	549A Col av
D	McQuillan Bessie F—†	68	housekeeper	45	1746 Wash'n
E	Allison John	78	laborer	60	here
F	Elliot John	78	painter	63	"
G	Flanagan Clara—†	78	laundress	34	"
H	Gallagher Dolly—†	78	powdermaker	25	917 Harris'n av
K	Herbert Arthur	78	blacksmith	65	here
L	Howland Herbert	78	retired	80	"
M	Olsen Ernest	78	laborer	48	"
T	Pring George	78	cabinetmaker	60	"
U	Quinn William	78	laborer	38	"
N	Sanders Edwin	78	"	24	"
O	Sanders Laura—†	78	housewife	23	"
P	Shultz Peter	78	retired	48	"
R	Simmons Mary—†	78	domestic	52	45 Myrtle
S	Simmons Raymond R	78	laborer	50	45 "
V	Wolf John D	80	merchant	79	here
X	Black Garvie A	84	painter	53	"
Y	Black Isabella—†	84	housewife	50	"
Z	Hart Daniel F	84	teamster	54	"
A	Hart Daniel F, jr	84	musician	31	"
A¹	Hart Grace F—†	84	brushfinisher	25	"
B	Hart Margaret—†	84	housekeeper	27	"

West Springfield Street

E	Bennett Fred	76	engineer	55	Malden
F	DeLong George	76	retired	53	3 Rutland
G	DeLong Margaret—†	76	housekeeper	48	3 "
H	Doyle Joseph	76	mason	60	New York
K	Harney Joseph	76	lineman	42	Lynn
L	Harney Winnie—†	76	housewife	34	"
M	Hudon Leo	76	plasterer	25	518 Shawmut av
N	Moreau Idell—†	76	housekeeper	56	42 W Newton
O	Mosher Catherine—†	76	attendant	50	Hull
P	Stuart Edwin	76	laborer	50	Lynn
R	Devine Charles A	83	"	31	Dover N H
S	Flannery Charles F	83	carpenter	38	8 Conant
T	Goodwin William S	83	auto mechanic	43	here

West Springfield Street—Continued

U	Lambert Harry	83	laborer	26	33 Clarendon
V	Lawler James	83	"	45	Cambridge
W	Roche Bernard	83	plumber	35	34 E Springfield
X	Roche Mildred H—†	83	housewife	27	34 "
Y	Mailer Catherine M—†	84	cook	45	517 Col av
Z	King Anna—†	84	housekeeper	44	here
A	King Thomas	84	laborer	55	Hull
B	Schmelling Sophie—†	84	housewife	61	here
C	Schmelling William	84	salesman	39	"
F	Foshay Beatrice—†	84	housekeeper	38	"
E	Foshay Carl	84	painter	40	"
G	Greenwood Nellie—†	84	waitress	50	"
H	Stuart Clara—†	84	housekeeper	35	"
K	Riley Mary—†	84	"	64	"
L	Riley Philip	84	electrician	32	"
R	King William	85	engineer	75	12 Pembroke
O	Mallard Cherles	85	interpreter	39	1900 Wash'n
P	Mallard Cora—†	85	housewife	40	1900 "
S	McGonigle Mary—†	85	seamstress	45	12 Pembroke
T	White Charles	85	carpenter	70	12 "
U	Dakin Charlotte—†	86	housekeeper	50	1309 Wash'n
V	Daniels Daniel	86	laborer	38	here
W	Richards Clement	86	ironworker	43	1309 Wash'n
X	Sullivan Patrick	86	laborer	65	here
Y	Swan Anna A—†	87	housewife	28	"
Z	Swan James L	87	porter	38	"
A	Washington Arnold J	87	chef	48	"
B	Washington Mary E—†	87	housewife	48	"
D	McGlone John J	89	painter	56	"
E	McGlone Lucy E—†	89	housewife	50	"
G	Dean James	89	shoeworker	41	"
H	Bailey John	89	"	42	"
M	Dillon Emma—†	90	housekeeper	80	"
K	Kinkead Edmund C	90	physician	53	"
L	Kinkead Irene—†	90	housewife	29	"
N	Brooks Elizabeth W—†	91	"	35	"
O	Brooks Mason	91	janitor	46	"
P	Jones Henry H	91	laborer	65	"
R	Jones Mary E—†	91	housewife	60	"
S	Byrne Edward F	92	printer	54	"
T	Gibbons Bessie—†	92	telegrapher	23	"

Page.	Letter.	FULL NAME.	Residence, April 1, 1926.	Occupation.	Supposed Age.	Reported Residence, April 1, 1925. Street and Number.

West Springfield Street—Continued

U	Lome Edward	92	carpenter	40	here
V	Mills Lydia—†	92	clerk	50	"
W	Mooney Mary—†	92	housekeeper	50	"
X	Sheafe Charles M	92	cook	52	"
Y	Sullivan Elizabeth—†	92	tel operator	22	"
Z	McKnight Alexander	93	porter	40	"
A	Orr Rosa L—†	93	housewife	38	"
B	Perry John A	93	longshoreman	32	39 Camden
C	Santos Frank	93	"	38	39 "
D	Bowman William	94	repairer	35	Hull
E	Cullen Harry	94	leadburner	31	Lynn
F	Grant Mary—†	94	housewife	45	here
G	Grant William	94	engineer	45	"
H	Manzi Louis	94	molder	43	Hull
K	McCormack Della—†	94	housekeeper	30	Lynn
L	McKenzie Gertrude—†	94	"	32	85 Village
M	Tremas Charles	94	engineer	28	Bayonne N J
N	Budyiloag Weril	95	laborer	35	1119 Wash'n
O	Kasheto John	95	barber	38	304 Bolton
P	Markin Edward	95	painter	30	9 Upton
R	Markin Mae H—†	95	housekeeper	26	9 "
S	Martain Stellar—†	95	factory worker	21	Portland Me
T	Morris Juliet—†	95	"	22	133 W Brookline
U	Barrett Thomas	96	salesman	57	here
V	Caldwell Genevieve—†	96	manicurist	25	"
X	Cunniff John F	96	teamster	57	"
W	Cunniff Katherine—†	96	housekeeper	51	"
Y	Deacon Robert	96	machinist	40	"
Z	Doherty Fannie—†	96	laundress	50	Southboro
A	Fitzgerald Catherine—†	96	housekeeper	33	here
B	Malloy William	96	laborer	57	"
C	McLaughlin James	96	"	27	Ireland
D	McLaughlin John	96	"	27	"
E	McLaughlin Mary—†	96	cook	20	here
F	Murray Mary—†	96	at home	51	613 Mass av
G	O'Callahan Margaret—†	96	cook	20	Ireland
H	Swanson Matilda—†	96	at home	52	here
K	Constock Edward K	97	painter	35	349 Shawmut av
L	Kanan Elias	97	machinist	26	1858 Wash'n
M	Kanan Julia—†	97	housewife	26	1858 "
N	Morely James	97	laborer	26	3 Copley sq

Page	Letter	FULL NAME.	Residence, April 1, 1926.	Occupation.	Supposed Age.	Reported Residence, April 1, 1925. Street and Number.

West Springfield Street—Continued

	Letter	FULL NAME.	Residence	Occupation	Age	Reported Residence
	o	Orlan George J	97	student	25	New York
	p	Tashyatan Thomas	97	baker	35	20 Upton
	R	Courtney Henry L	98	student	21	here
	s	Courtney Lilla D—†	98	housewife	60	"
	T	Courtney Marian L—†	98	teacher	26	"
	U	Courtney Roger D	98	electrician	25	"
	v	Courtney Samuel E	98	physician	62	"
	w	Courtney Samuel E	98	accountant	28	"
	x	Courtney Virginia—†	98	housekeeper	21	"
	y	Emanual Luther	98	student	23	"
	z	Pringle Frank	98	clerk	21	"
	A	Braston Robert	99	laborer	35	Cambridge
	B	Collins William	99	"	30	here
	c	Davis Elige	99	porter	28	"
	D	Edwards Bertha—†	99	housekeeper	49	"
	E	Felton Lewis	99	dishwasher	35	Cambridge
	F	Hamilton Anna—†	99	maid	48	here
	G	Hamilton William	99	printer	50	"
	H	Miles Readmond	99	laborer	64	20 Northampton
	K	Porter Albert	99	salesman	50	10 Parnell
	L	Stewart Thomas	99	porter	25	here
	M	Aline Reginald	100	cigarmaker	24	"
	N	Campbell Thomas	100	laborer	37	"
	o	Bailey Gorden	100	porter	27	New York
	p	Farreall Allwyd—†	100	housekeeper	47	here
	T	Shine Wallie—†	101	housewife	22	Hartford Ct
	U	Shine Walter	101	laborer	26	"
	v	Wells Beatrice—†	101	housewife	30	"
	w	Wells Eddie	101	janitor	23	"
	x	Heck Elizabeth—†	101	housewife	29	here
	Y	Heck St Elmo	101	laborer	27	"
	z	Fowler Victor H	101	cook	28	Sagamore
	B	Brennan James	102	laborer	28	here
	A	Brennan James J	102	blacksmith	58	"
	c	Haskow Charles H	102	watchman	60	399 Northampton
	D	Metcalf Wallace A	102	heelmaker	32	here
	E	Trungren John	102	roofer	38	"
	F	Bailey Armand—†	103	cook	40	395 Northampton
	G	Braxton Gertrude—†	103	housewife	28	760 Tremont
	H	Braxton Major D	103	engineer	35	760 "

Page.	Letter.	FULL NAME.	Residence, April 1, 1926.	Occupation.	Supposed Age.	Reported Residence, April 1, 1925. Street and Number.

West Springfield Street—Continued

K	Jackson Robert	103	laborer	40	Cambridge
L	Johnston John	103	cook	25	9 Lenox
M	Thomaston Cary	103	insuranceman	29	New Jersey
N	Dooley Peter J	104	foreman	53	here
O	Dooley Thomas	104	operator	51	25 Adams
P	Doyle Patrick	104	porter	60	here
R	O'Neil Harry	104	horseshoer	60	"
S	Sullivan Patrick	104	brassmelter	56	"
T	Sullivan Thomas	104	printer	44	"
U	Palmer Walter	105	bellboy	23	Baltimore Md
V	Williams George J	105	painter	48	here
W	Butler Jacob	106	"	55	4 Stevens
X	Butler Minnie—†	106	housewife	38	4 "
Y	Wilson Edna M—†	106	laundress	33	5 "
Z	Kenton Thomas	106	chauffeur	38	163 W Springfield
A	Dorothy Molly—†	108	laundress	53	here
B	Johnson Mary—†	108	storekeeper	30	"
C	McCrea John	108	janitor	59	"
D	Rose John	108	butler	60	"
E	Simmons Albert	108	chauffeur	60	"
F	Hayes Coleman	110	"	28	"
G	Hayes Lillian M—†	110	housekeeper	26	"
H	Miller Beatrice—†	110	"	31	22 Northfield
M	Butler Sarah—†	112	"	55	here
N	Allen Carrie—†	114	"	55	"
O	Baker Isabelle—†	114	"	30	Malden
P	Clark Pauline—†	114	cook	36	here
R	Dickerson Leonard	114	chauffeur	30	"
S	Raysor John	114	barber	24	99 Allston
T	Sheldon Jefferson D	114	janitor	64	here
U	Tyler George	114	"	31	"
V	Brown Alma—†	118	housekeeper	29	"
W	Brown Louis	118	porter	40	"
X	Coleman Bertha—†	118	housekeeper	23	Phila Pa
Y	Coleman Robert	118	laborer	28	"
Z	Johnson Ruth—†	118	housekeeper	28	here
A	Johnson Willard	118	chauffeur	29	"
B	Bamberg Frederick H	133	retired	83	"
C	Bastine Gilman L	133	"	95	"
D	Beede Andrew	133	nurse	51	"
E	Best John J	133	retired	65	77 Worcester

West Springfield Street—Continued

F	Botham Frederick C	133	retired	77	here
G	Brewster John A	133	"	84	"
H	Brown Charles W	133	fireman	68	"
K	Burdon John N	133	retired	82	Gilbertville
L	Burnham Charles E	133	"	78	here
M	Caldwell Margaret—†	133	maid	61	"
N	Calrow Thomas B	133	retired	74	"
O	Canavan Michael J	133	"	77	"
P	Clark Charles H	133	"	80	"
R	Crafts Samuel D	133	"	77	"
S	Dana George A	133	"	87	"
T	Davis William H	133	"	83	"
U	Dennison Gardner	133	"	69	"
V	Dole Sarah G—†	133	nurse	56	"
W	Dyke John	133	retired	72	"
X	Foley Mary W—†	133	maid	36	"
Z	Hale Joseph H	133	retired	78	22 Moreland
Y	Hale William T	133	"	72	here
A	Hall Calmar D S	133	"	69	"
B	Hall Isaac W	133	"	80	"
C	Haskell William A	133	"	91	"
D	Hatheway Stanley N	133	"	76	"
E	Hilliard Haven J	133	"	55	16 Rutland
F	Holland William A. jr	133	"	79	here
G	Howard Thomas H	133	"	78	"
H	Kelton Willard S	133	"	90	"
K	Learnard Horace E	133	"	83	"
L	Lewis George T	133	"	86	"
M	Lorenzo John A	133	"	74	"
N	Luscombe Richard L	133	"	74	19 Myrtle
O	Maloney Katie—†	133	laundress	55	here
P	McLaughlin Annie—†	133	maid	55	"
R	McLaughlin Bridget—†	133	"	22	"
S	McLaughlin Catherine—†	133	laundress	25	"
T	McLaughlin Marjorie—†	133	maid	29	"
U	Merchant James F	133	retired	67	"
V	Olson Charles D	132	"	80	"
W	Perkins Albert F	133	"	81	"
X	Rand Warren B	133	"	79	"
Y	Robinson O'Neil W	133	"	92	"

Page.	Letter.	FULL NAME.	Residence, April 1, 1926.	Occupation.	Supposed Age.	Reported Residence, April 1, 1925. Street and Number.

West Springfield Street—Continued

z	Robinson Robert A	133	retired	94	here
A	Russell John H	133	"	81	"
B	Russell John S	133	"	78	"
C	Sprague Alberto L	133	"	75	507 Col av
D	Stevens Mary A—†	133	superintendent	65	here
E	Stratton William P	133	retired	92	"
F	Sullivan Jeremiah	133	fireman	60	"
G	Tirrell Daniel L	133	retired	87	"
H	Trenholm Margaret—†	133	cook	58	"
H¹	Whittier Mozart	133	retired	86	"
K	Wiswell John L	133	"	80	"
L	Wood John R	133	"	72	"
M	Woodman Arthur L	133	"	70	"
N	Woodruff John	133	"	75	"
O	Worcester Elbridge G	133	"	86	Lakeville
P	Young John L	133	"	65	here
S	Canner Philip	159	laborer	34	Revere
T	Canner Sadie —†	159	housewife	36	"
U	Baker Ruth A—†	159	housekeeper	62	here
V	Middlemass Anna B—†	159	housewife	68	"
W	Middlemass William B	159	weaver	49	"
Y	King Harry	159	batteryman	34	"
Z	King Jannie—†	159	housewife	37	"
A	Selig Moses J	159	foreman	42	"
B	Barrett Leone D—†	159	housewife	24	Phila Pa
C	Bullens Leone D—†	159	housekeeper	47	Brighton
D	Coyne Louise—†	159	"	23	"
F	Strawman Anna—†	159	housewife	33	Lynn
G	Strawman David	159	laborer	35	"
H	Sushman Anna—†	159	housekeeper	34	here
K	Sushman Iseral	159	butcher	48	"
L	Finkalstin Ida—†	159	housekeeper	55	"
M	Finkalstin Ruth—†	159	saleswoman	25	"
N	Finkalstin Sarah—†	159	"	23	"
O	Baker Ruth A—†	159	housekeeper	62	512 Mass av
P	Dandridge George L	160	steward	38	38 Kendall
R	Delaney Anna—†	160	waitress	52	88 Vernon
S	Dewitt Phyllis L—†	160	seamstress	38	88 "
T	Hopkins Mary—†	160	waitress	48	88 "

45

Page.	Letter.	FULL NAME.	Residence, April 1, 1926.	Occupation.	Supposed Age.	Reported Residence, April 1, 1925. Street and Number.

West Springfield Street—Continued

U	Sayles Arthur H	160	steward	37	88 Vernon
V	Sayles Mary L—†	160	housekeeper	33	88 "
X	Ware Theodore	160	waiter	34	Warren O
W	Warner Alfred H	160	architect	43	88 Vernon
Y	White Gertrude—†	160	capmaker	30	88 "
Z	Martin John J	161	printer	51	here
A	Quinn John	161	retired	70	"
B	Quinn Mary E—†	161	housewife	42	"
C	Kanne Esther E—†	161	"	40	"
D	Benjamin Harry S	161	clerk	45	"
E	Benjamin Joseph S	161	"	37	"
F	Benjamin Maurice S	161	chauffeur	46	"
G	Benjamin Tina—†	161	housewife	69	"
L	Ambush Lillian —†	162	housekeeper	22	Everett
M	Bryant Connie—†	162	"	23	Malden
N	Bryant William	162	laborer	35	"
O	Nixon William	162	butler	32	Keene N H
P	Pelham Philip	162	laborer	47	Deer Island
R	Perry Mabel—†	162	housekeeper	36	1059 Tremont
S	Smith Beatrice—†	162	"	25	Everett
T	Allen James E	163	barber	54	here
U	Allen Sarah J—†	163	housewife	58	"
V	Gadham Thomas	163	chef	42	"
W	Green Joseph A	163	janitor	60	"
X	Holmes Joseph V	163	student	50	"
Y	McDonald William	163	chauffeur	50	366 Tremont
Z	Warner Albert W	163	janitor	48	Cambridge
A	Hall Robert	164	cook	30	Maryland W V
B	Hodges Harry	164	teller	50	here
C	Smith Newman	164	clerk	30	"
D	West Edward H	164	janitor	68	"
E	West Sarah—†	164	housekeeper	60	"
F	Covington Josephine—†	165	housewife	40	"
G	Lee Edith—†	165	at home	80	"
H	Reese Jesse	165	laborer	25	"
K	Steward Thomas J	165	porter	34	Cambridge
L	Williams Louise—†	165	maid	26	here
M	Babcock Theodore	166	laborer	30	75 Newland
N	Carrington Rose—†	166	housekeeper	55	here
O	Graham Mabel—†	166	"	39	"

	Letter	FULL NAME.	Residence, April 1, 1926.	Occupation.	Supposed Age.	Reported Residence, April 1, 1925. Street and Number.

West Springfield Street—Continued

	Letter	FULL NAME.	Res.	Occupation.	Age	Reported Residence
	P	Gray Robert	166	laborer	29	229 Northampton
	R	Lopes Peter	166	cook	50	here
	S	Robertson Robert	166	laborer	39	176 W Springfield
	T	Rumbell Mary—†	166	housekeeper	21	Everett
	U	Talbot Anna—†	166	"	72	here
	V	Anderson Joseph	167	janitor	30	Lynn
	W	Downney Gorgia—†	167	cook	22	here
	X	Hanks Murray	167	painter	29	Cambridge
	Y	Smith Caroline—†	167	housewife	35	here
	Z	Smith Hebert	167	laborer	29	"
	A	Smith William L	167	janitor	42	"
	B	Archie Roland	168	operator	30	229 Northampton
	C	Fraction Mary—†	168	housekeeper	48	here
	D	Lenore James	168	fireman	45	"
	E	Lewey Joseph	168	laborer	29	225 Northampton
	F	Sullivan Mary—†	168	domestic	28	3 Woodbury
	G	Williams John	168	mechanic	40	here
	H	Brown Emma—†	170	housekeeper	20	"
	K	Brown William T B	170	engineer	30	"
	L	Brooks Samuel	172	baggageman	28	"
	M	Coffey John	172	laborer	42	"
	N	Johnson Raymond	172	porter	22	"
	O	Thompson Mary—†	172	housekeeper	36	"
	P	Williams Ernest	172	cook	25	Phila Pa
	R	Works Horace	172	laborer	35	here
	S	Bighams John W	174	fireman	26	"
	T	Hutchinson Jennie—†	174	housekeeper	45	"
	U	Jackson William E	174	electrician	27	34 Worcester
	V	Frances George	176	clerk	21	Everett
	W	Holmes James	176	cook	52	353 Col av
	X	Holmes Janie E—†	176	housekeeper	50	353 "
	Y	Jackson Sarah—†	176	cook	49	353 "
	Z	McCorkel Irene—†	176	housekeeper	33	Alexander Va
	A	Seals Mary—†	176	"	30	Delaware
	B	Tabor Joseph	176	porter	30	515 Shawmut av
	C	Waterman Frank L	176	laborer	50	Everett
	D	Wilkins Charles	176	porter	22	Cambridge
	E	Bernier Alfred	178	fireman	38	here
	F	Biggi Lewis	178	salesman	50	"
	G	Blackstone Elizabeth—†	178	housekeeper	65	"

West Springfield Street—Continued

H	Blackstone Ernest	178	cook	35	here
K	Bourasia Louis	178	retired	75	"
K¹	Brown Emma C—†	178	at home	75	"
L	Crumb Charles	178	machinist	45	205 W Springfield
M	Lekso John	178	operator	35	Fitchburg
N	Lekso Louis A	178	student	22	"
O	Marshall Michael	178	clerk	40	here
P	Weymouth Anna—†	178	housekeeper	69	"
R	Whitnen Raymond H	178	laborer	23	Fitchburg

Worcester Street

A	Hummer Alice—†	7	housewife	43	144 Dudley
B	Hummer Harry	7	engineer	48	144 "
C	O'Neil James	7	brakeman	38	New York City
D	O'Neil Lillian—†	7	housewife	26	"
E	Paterio Harry	7	clerk	48	here
F	Stamatopouls Harry	7	"	35	Somerville
G	Lecher Elenora—†	11	housewife	77	here
H	Ryder Ellis	11	porter	39	"
K	Ryder Viola—†	11	nurse	39	"
L	Triplett Mary—†	11	"	45	"
M	Mumby Nora—†	11	housewife	36	"
N	Mumby Robert	11	mechanic	54	"
O	Robinson Herman A	11	clerk	45	"
P	Robinson Mabel—†	11	housewife	40	"
R	Christie Edward	13	laborer	34	"
S	Holgate Margaret—†	13	domestic	34	Cambridge
T	Kettler Benjamin M	13	engineer	60	here
U	Kettler Harriett A—†	13	housewife	52	"
V	Satchell Marion—†	13	domestic	32	"
W	Satterwhite Carrie J—†	13	housewife	30	"
X	Satterwhite William R	13	mechanic	34	"
Y	Beland Flora—†	14–18	stenographer	28	"
Z	Briggs Ella—†	14–18	clerk	43	"
A	Briggs Olive—†	14–18	stenographer	25	"
B	Burnham Alberta—†	14–18	bookkeeper	32	"

Worcester Street—Continued

c	Cooper Emily—†	14–18	student	24	Lynn
D	Drais Lenora—†	14–18	"	26	Findley O
E	Edwards Rachel—†	14–18	bookkeeper	28	Cambridge
F	Ells Gladys—†	14–18	clerk	25	here
G	Elwell Grace—†	14–18	domestic	35	24 Union
H	Gardner Emma—†	14–18	teacher	50	here
K	Hatfield Adelia—†	14–18	milliner	39	"
L	Hersey Ruth E—†	14–18	superintendent	66	"
M	Houghton Eleanor—†	14–18	clerk	21	Elmwood
N	Houston Josephine—†	14–18	matron	66	here
O	Kelley Gertrude E—†	14–18	bookkeeper	28	"
P	Knowles Ruth C—†	14–18	illustrator	24	"
R	Lawton Florence—†	14–18	clerk	32	"
s	Mackay Agnes—†	14–18	stenographer	22	251 Columbia rd
T	Mawson Ella—†	14–18	matron	67	here
U	Meharn Winifred—†	14–18	teacher	40	"
V	Netmore Hazel—†	14–18	student	28	Keene N H
W	Noyes Carrie—†	14–18	clerk	35	here
X	Olderich Mildred—†	14–18	"	21	"
Y	Ostrander Annie—†	14–18	seamstress	40	"
Z	Packard Irene—†	14–18	social worker	26	"
A	Reik Norma—†	14–18	clerk	27	"
B	Seppsla Hilma—†	14–18	"	28	"
C	Shaughnessy Marion—†	14–18	teacher	25	"
D	Snyder Franklin	14–18	janitor	52	"
E	Stokell Charlotte—†	14–18	clerk	33	Needham
F	Swett Marion—†	14–18	"	38	here
G	Tisdale Edith F—†	14–18	proofreader	70	"
H	Townsend Alma—†	14–18	clerk	25	"
K	Upshaytis Mary—†	14–18	milliner	26	75 Evans
L	Usher Sarah—†	14–18	librarian	25	Yarmouth
M	Wheater Mollie—†	14–18	student	26	Albion Mich
N	Wood Edith—†	14–18	stenographer	25	here
O	Chin Sing Yuen	15	laundryman	25	"
P	Yee Bun Wah	15	"	35	"
R	Hurley Michael	17	janitor	40	"
s	Hurley Nellie—†	17	housewife	36	"
T	Betzer Otto	19	machinist	32	86 Worcester
T¹	Boland Carl W	19	salesman	24	Canada
U	Campbell Mary—†	19	housekeeper	54	557 Mass av

Worcester Street —Continued

v	Cronin William J	19	printer	65	5 Worcester sq
w	Doane Edgar E	19	quartermaster	32	Cuba
x	Grant John	19	laundryman	35	1688 Wash'n
y	Harding Fred	19	"	35	1688 "
z	Lane Joseph H	19	engineer	47	32 Worcester sq
A	Ricker Millard	19	florist	39	46 Worcester
B	Shedian Sam	19	salesman	46	658 Mass av
c	Burley Elizabeth—†	20	housewife	45	44 E Newton
D	Hartin James	20	shoemaker	33	24 Rutland sq
E	Hartin Ruth—†	20	housewife	30	24 "
F	Hayes Margaret—†	20	seamstress	50	here
G	Hayes Margaret—†	20	clerk	45	"
H	Linehan Teresa—†	20	dressmaker	40	"
K	Palmer Florence—†	20	housewife	51	7 Regent ct
L	Palmer Irving R	20	elevatorman	53	7 "
M	Roberts Beatrice—†	20	waitress	36	here
N	Biggar Ira	21	teamster	38	Maine
o	Cabral Edward	21	fish dealer	50	Provincetown
P	Cukier Louisa—†	21	housewife	62	Northampton
R	Daley Mary—†	21	nurse	50	8 Worcester sq
s	Driscoll David M	21	clerk	35	Milford
T	Garden John	21	electrician	30	8 Worcester sq
U	Green Etta—†	21	clerk	50	here
v	Mitchell John	21	veterinarian	64	Maine
w	O'Reily Thomas	21	clerk	58	here
x	Sarty Doran	21	longshoreman	25	Maine
y	Shaw Emma—†	21	milliner	36	40 Berkeley
z	Wells Ina M—†	21	stenographer	33	518 Shawmut av
A	Wells Jennie A—†	21	housewife	58	518 "
B	Glidden Carrie J—†	22	housekeeper	61	here
c	Kane Margaret—†	22	demonstrator	36	"
D	Kiezer Gaylon	22	brakeman	42	"
E	Lewis Albert	22	fish cutter	35	"
F	Lewis Mary—†	22	marker	34	"
G	Lewis Walter	22	student	38	20 Worcester
H	Royce Carl M	22	restaurateur	38	139 W Concord
K	Royce Patience M—†	22	waitress	32	139 "
L	Walpole Margaret—†	22	housewife	31	199 Sumner
M	Walpole Walter	22	painter	32	199 "
N	Busch Carrie—†	23	stitcher	22	Florida

Letter	Full Name.	Residence, April 1, 1926.	Occupation.	Supposed Age.	Reported Residence, April 1, 1925. Street and Number.

Worcester Street—Continued

Letter	Full Name.	Res.	Occupation.	Age	Reported Residence
O	Creamer Lillian—†	23	housekeeper	49	here
P	Frances Margaret—†	23	factory worker	40	Newton
R	Glynn Peter	23	polisher	51	298 Dudley
S	Gorham Patrick	23	laborer	28	here
T	Hamil John A	23	clerk	37	New York
U	Homer Charles	23	retired	65	222 Shawmut av
V	Kenney George	23	plumber	29	Cambridge
W	Kenney Mabel—†	23	housewife	24	"
X	Knapp Elizabeth—†	23	housekeeper	47	here
Y	Lawrence Emily—†	23	housewife	34	38 Worcester
Z	Lawrence William	23	mechanic	38	38 "
A	Springer Florence—†	23	domestic	30	New York
B	Wylie Mary—†	23	nurse	50	Plymouth
C	Chinney Godfrey	24	cook	45	here
E	Farmer Ralph	24	operator	43	"
F	Fisher Fred	24	clerk	40	"
D	Gurl Henry J	24	plumber	45	"
G	Kelley Andrew J	24	clerk	35	"
H	McNaughton John A	24	retired	68	"
K	Reno Leo	24	butcher	28	Portland Me
L	Rollf Edward	24	electrician	50	here
M	Tiebeau Irene—†	24	waitress	21	Lowell
N	Willoughby Coral—†	24	housekeeper	43	here
O	Woods Harold E	24	mechanic	28	"
P	Cox James H	25	student	29	"
R	Landry Frank J	25	carpenter	29	Cambridge
S	Malloy Raymond J	25	student	28	here
T	Phinney John	25	painter	41	"
U	Roskowski Stanley	25	machinist	43	"
V	Skonieczny Stanislaw	25	"	45	"
W	Wilkinson William J	25	laborer	34	"
X	Willett Alfred P	25	teacher	34	"
Y	Willett Myrtle—†	25	housewife	29	"
Z	Barlow Fred	26	salesman	45	Leominster
A	Barry Edna—†	26	housewife	23	537 Mass av
B	Barry Russell	26	carpenter	29	537 "
C	Dolan Elizabeth—†	26	cook	29	here
D	Guffrie Bessie—†	26	housewife	30	168 W Newton
E	Guffrie George W	26	salesman	33	168 "
F	Lewis Delia—†	26	housewife	23	here

Worcester Street—Continued

G	Lewis John	26	plasterer	30	8 Hollis
H	Gori Catherine A—†	27	clerk	40	here
K	Landregan John J	27	real estate	41	"
L	Landregan Margaret F—†	27	housewife	50	"
M	Smith Alice A—†	27	"	45	"
M	Smith William J	27	printer	44	"
O	Birson Arthur	28	orderly	28	104 E Newton
P	Blue Malcolm	28	nurse	38	1942 Wash'n
R	Curtis Mark A	28	x-ray man	24	Leominster
S	Gillis Catherine †	28	housekeeper	60	here
T	Hyde William A	28	clerk	58	"
U	Lackey Grover	28	sailor	21	Honolulu
V	MacIntyre Frank	28	nurse	38	here
W	May Annetta E †	28	housekeeper	66	62 Rutland
X	May Henry L	28	clerk	40	62 "
Y	McDonald Colin	28	carpenter	25	75 W Concord
Z	McDougal Gertrude—†	28	maid	23	Canada
A	Parker Walter C	28	sailor	34	Honolulu
B	Sage Wilford J	28	orderly	35	Connecticut
C	McGregor John B	29	carpenter	74	496 Mass av
D	McGregor Nancy M—†	29	housewife	74	496 "
E	Metcalfe Agnes J—†	29	"	29	here
F	Metcalf Alfred E	29	policeman	29	"
G	Missirian Adare—†	29	housewife	21	"
H	Missirian Joseph	29	tailor	30	"
K	Ware Flora—†	29	housekeeper	78	"
L	Ware Margaret—†	29	bookkeeper	35	"
M	Tashjian Aeshalus—†	30	housewife	37	"
N	Tashjian Harutune	30	lecturer	48	"
O	Calusian Hannon—†	30	housewife	72	"
P	Calusian Harutune	30	retired	82	"
R	Ashjian Edith †	30	housewife	20	"
S	Ashjian Jack	30	merchant	26	589 Norfolk
T	Hasekian Charles	30	retired	65	here
U	Hasekian Freda †	30	housewife	56	"
W	Samaras John	30	laborer	46	15 Norwich
X	Samaras Stavrula—†	30	housewife	73	15 "
Y	Banks William S	32	longshoreman	48	here
Z	Grant Julius	32	porter	21	"
A	Lewey William	32	elevatorman	48	"

Worcester Street —Continued

B	Shands Joseph	32	longshoreman	52	here
C	Shands Thomas	32	"	40	"
D	Yates John	32	laborer	77	"
E	Berman Frances —†	34	housekeeper	35	396 Northampton
F	Byers Albert C	34	lumber dealer	38	here
G	Darish John	34	salesman	24	"
H	Joyce Helen —†	34	shoeworker	23	"
K	LaRose Lillian —†	34	nurse	20	19 E Concord
L	White Gerald	34	chauffeur	27	here
M	White Pearl —†	34	housekeeper	24	"
N	Brown Tobis	36	engineer	44	"
O	Carroll Edith F —†	36	housekeeper	44	"
P	Carroll Thomas	36	clerk	24	"
R	Glover Albert R	36	retired	62	"
S	Lotze Henry	36	engineer	32	"
T	Prince Ceraphin	36	shipper	55	"
U	Prince Katherine —†	36	housewife	42	"
V	Whitehead William	36	wireworker	47	"
W	Cody James	38	pipefitter	29	683 Mass av
X	Comelins Sarah —†	38	housewife	25	26 Worcester
Y	Comelins William	38	salesman	28	26 "
Z	Cressman Margaret —†	38	domestic	35	Springfield
A	Greenwood Fred C	38	diemaker	50	34 Worcester
B	Greenwood Margaret —†	38	housewife	25	34 "
C	McGraw William	38	milkman	50	here
D	Riley Minnie —†	38	housewife	45	Taunton
E	Riley Niel	38	lineman	49	"
F	Thurmith Margaret —†	38	housewife	63	here
G	Thurmith Sanford	38	contractor	40	"
H	Thurmith William	38	retired	72	"
L	Austin Mary —†	42	missionary	60	"
M	Cleary Margaret —†	42	housewife	65	"
N	Gilbert Josephine —†	42	stitcher	35	"
O	Hatch Elsie —†	42	factory worker	27	"
P	Hatch Harriet —†	42	housekeeper	60	"
R	Hatch Verna —†	42	nurse	31	"
S	Huelin Lillian —†	42	"	52	"
T	Johnson Annie —†	42	housewife	37	"
U	Johnson Dickerus	42	shoemaker	35	"
V	Kelley Frank	42	carpenter	55	"

Worcester Street - Continued

W	Mason Mary A —†	42	retired	75	here
X	McDonald Jeanette—†	42	"	70	"
Y	Patterson Catherine —†	42	housekeeper	72	"
Z	Patterson John	42	shipper	41	"
A	Robinson Phineas	42	salesman	42	"
B	Scott Joseph R	42	retired	78	"
C	Anderson Anna E —†	44	housekeeper	48	"
D	Buchanon George	44	clerk	47	"
E	Gilbert James C	44	packer	21	619 Mass av
F	Hilbert George	44	carpenter	63	here
G	Hilbert Margaret — †	44	housewife	50	"
H	Morey Elizabeth —†	44	printer	40	Brookline
K	Nystron John	44	mechanic	37	Milton
L	Peterson John	44	painter	45	here
M	Swanson Anna —†	44	housewife	30	Kansas City Mo
N	Swanson Ricker	44	pianoworker	35	"
O	Bozier Elizabeth —†	46	housewife	58	here
P	Bozier James M	46	carpenter	64	"
R	Coffin Mary—†	46	at home	70	Newton
S	Craig Charles	46	salesman	30	New York City
T	Denham Charlotte —†	46	cashier	36	here
U	Kelley George	46	clerk	32	"
V	McKeaggan Alexander	46	mechanic	58	Medford
W	McLeod Barbara —†	46	dressmaker	38	here
X	McLeod Christina †	46	"	39	"
Y	Olive Ella—†	46	seamstress	47	"
Z	Terrio Carrie L—†	46	housewife	60	"
A	Terrio Simon H	46	shipper	59	"
B	Thompson Edward	46	motorman	52	"
C	Wiggin Evelyn †	46	seamstress	38	"
D	Blake Arthur	48	chauffeur	26	122 W Concord
E	Costes Mary †	48	housewife	27	58 W Newton
F	Costes Michael	48	counterman	24	22 Chandler
G	Kirby Anna —†	48	housewife	32	Michigan
H	Kirby Daniel	48	merchant	28	"
K	Menis Nellie †	48	laundress	54	here
L	Morris Lulu †	48	housekeeper	54	"
M	Parquette Alphonso	48	chauffeur	32	122 W Concord
N	Parquette Esther —†	48	housewife	29	122 "
O	Aborn Dorothy †	50	bookkeeper	25	here

Page	Letter.	FULL NAME.	Residence, April 1, 1926.	Occupation.	Supposed Age.	Reported Residence, April 1, 1925. Street and Number.

Worcester Street—Continued

	P	Bean Lester W	50	inspector	30	512 Mass av
	R	Cochrane Richard	50	counterman	58	here
	S	Devine Thomas	50	"	40	"
	T	Hunt Fred	50	electrician	34	Maine
	U	Hunter Mae E—†	50	housewife	60	here
	V	Hunter Samuel C	50	shipper	69	"
	W	Welch Margaret—†	50	housewife	47	"
	X	Welch William J	50	electrician	42	"
	Y	Angelus James	52	baker	35	"
	Z	Doherty Agnes—†	52	housewife	31	"
	A	Higgenbottom Joseph	52	doorman	69	"
	B	Higgenbottom Lucy—†	52	housewife	70	"
	C	Hurley Catherine—†	52	laundress	45	"
	D	Maxim Gertrude—†	52	saleswoman	38	675 Tremont
	E	McNiel Elizabeth—†	52	"	38	here
	F	Murray James	52	pipefitter	41	81 Worcester
	G	Smith Lillian—†	52	housewife	23	Malden
	H	Smith William	52	longshoreman	26	"
	K	Vartabedian Agnes—†	52	housekeeper	50	here
	L	Vartabedian Leo	52	student	24	"
	M	Vartabedian Souren	52	"	28	"
	N	Butterick Mary E—†	54	housekeeper	52	"
	O	Cronin Josephine—†	54	seamstress	45	"
	P	Feely Dell—†	54	buyer	41	"
	R	Feely Helen L—†	54	clerk	32	"
	S	Martel Matilda—†	54	seamstress	45	"
	T	Pappas John	54	counterman	26	"
	U	Pappas Phoebe—†	54	cashier	27	"
	V	Russell Sara F—†	54	at home	77	"
	W	Gardner Frederick H	56	washman	25	"
	X	Gardner Margie W—†	56	housewife	23	"
	Y	Casey Thomas G	56	letter carrier	52	743 Tremont
	Z	Santry Maude E—†	56	stitcher	41	here
	B	Brett Minnie—†	56	stenographer	53	"
	D	Doyle Alice A—†	56	saleswoman	57	"
	E	Chick Jennie—†	56	"	41	"
	F	Fure Gertrude—†	56	"	36	"
	G	Boylston Beulah—†	56	secretary	37	"
	H	Beckswith James	80	porter	55	25 Worcester
	K	Brady Lettie—†	80	packer	45	10 Concord sq

Page	Letter	FULL NAME.	Residence, April 1, 1926	Occupation.	Supposed Age.	Reported Residence, April 1, 1925. Street and Number.

Worcester Street Continued

L	Duhart Alice †	80	laundress	39	54 W Newton
M	Dunlap Evelyn †	80	nurse	25	468 Mass av
N	Gitlen Bernard	80	tailor	47	here
O	Hart Cyle	80	cleaner	30	483 Shawmut av
P	Healey Thomas J	80	conductor	25	42 Woodcliff
R	Hunt Timothy A	80	hatter	55	748 Tremont
S	Irving John	80	chauffeur	24	Canton
T	Kelley Margaret †	80	nurse	25	121 Pembroke
U	McLellen Effie †	80	housekeeper	50	57 Rutland sq
V	Miller Hattie †	80	at home	49	Bolton N H
W	Morrissey Thomas	80	steamfitter	35	Dedham
X	Sullivan Minnie E †	80	housekeeper	44	here
Y	Bertoldi Antonio	82	clerk	43	"
Z	Duboise Ellen †	82	maid	60	748 Tremont
A	Fairchild Catherine †	82	clerk	38	here
B	Hart Daniel	82	laborer	48	3 Sumner pl
C	Kenney Elizabeth †	82	matron	25	Framingham
D	Murray Sadie T †	82	clerk	23	here
E	Murray Sarah J †	82	housekeeper	51	"
F	Swanson Christopher	82	painter	50	"
G	Swansen Gustave	82	piano tuner	48	Cleveland O
H	Brown Florence †	84	bookkeeper	34	Brooklyn N Y
K	Cotton Carlos H	84	salesman	35	7 Midvale rd
L	Cotton Judith B †	84	housekeeper	60	Somerville
M	Derocher William	84	salesman	28	Melrose
N	Gray William	84	butcher	55	here
O	King Archie N	84	shoemaker	42	"
P	Mayhew John P	84	chauffeur	27	"
R	Mayhew Mabel E †	84	housewife	31	"
S	Pine Flora †	84	matron	40	"
T	Prince Gordon R	84	mechanic	26	149 Warren av
U	Welch Brunyatte	84	steward	51	149 "
V	Welch Harriet M †	84	housekeeper	42	149 "
W	Collins Nellie †	86	clerk	35	here
X	Fister Gertrude †	86	shoeworker	35	"
Y	Hirch Edward	86	salesman	50	"
Z	Murphy Bella J †	86	housewife	54	"
A	Murphy Joseph W	86	letter carrier	49	"
B	Roach Stella †	86	clerk	32	"
C	Wetherby Frederick	86	"	55	"

Worcester Street—Continued

	Letter	Full Name	Residence	Occupation	Age	Reported Residence
	D	Weymouth Alwin	86	stonemason	44	here
	E	Sweeney Helen C—†	88	housewife	32	53 White
	F	Sweeney Stephen E	88	carpenter	35	53 "
	G	Carson Aileen G—†	88	housewife	21	890 E Fourth
	H	Carson George A	88	chauffeur	23	252 Tremont
	K	Demes Nora—†	88	housewife	35	here
	L	Demes Oscar	88	baggagemaster	40	"
	M	Bergen Mary—†	88	at home	90	Bangor Me
	N	Pazzetti Charles	88	teacher	30	here
	O	Pazzetti Edith—†	88	housewife	21	"
	P	McKenzie George	88	mechanic	28	"
	R	McKenzie Mary—†	88	housewife	24	"
	S	Cronin Laura—†	88	bookkeeper	38	"
	T	Aldrich Hetbert	88	chauffeur	25	Canton
	U	Aldrich Leone—†	88	housewife	21	Bangor Me
	V	Bolles Mabel—†	88	maid	34	here
	W	Birmingham Michael	90	retired	61	"
	X	Bowes William	90	engineer	40	"
	Y	Boyd Joseph L	90	motorman	55	"
	Z	Breman Charles R	90	chauffeur	50	146 Bunker Hill
	A	Clifford Elina—†	90	stitcher	60	here
	B	Hamilton Olive—†	90	stenographer	22	"
	C	Lyons Alice A—†	90	housewife	21	45 Mercer
	D	Lyons Richard	90	chauffeur	25	45 "
	E	Mason Annie—†	90	at home	55	543 Mass av
	F	McLeod Barbara—†	90	"	78	here
	G	Sherar Chipman S	90	"	62	"
	H	Sherar Elizabeth E—†	90	housewife	49	"
	K	Swan Linda M—†	90	at home	65	698 Tremont
	L	Thomas Minnie A—†	90	nurse	59	here
	M	Wells Nellie—†	90	waitress	30	Lynn
	N	Bartlett Cora B—†	92	housewife	50	Medford
	O	Bartlett Frank A	92	inspector	50	"
	P	Duffy John A	92	clerk	32	"
	R	Farrington Frank C	92	waiter	38	here
	S	Harris Ellsworth I	92	retired	60	Medford
	T	Jones Anna G—†	92	milliner	55	Cambridge
	U	Leamy Margaret—†	92	clerk	42	here
	V	McKinnon Margaret A—†	92	matron	49	453 Shawmut av
	W	Riley Mary E—†	92	clerk	21	Quincy

9–3

Page.	Letter.	FULL NAME.	Residence, April 1, 1926.	Occupation.	Supposed Age.	Reported Residence, April 1, 1925. Street and Number.

Worcester Street—Continued

x	Robb James E	92	mechanic	55	here
y	Robb Mary —†	92	housewife	48	"
z	Waseleska Alla —†	92	student	24	Bangor Me
A	Antill Florence —†	94	housekeeper	40	89 Worcester
B	Antill William F	94	mechanic	53	89 "
c	Brown Wesley C	94	student	25	Malden
D	Cousins Marion —†	94	stenographer	45	here
E	Gibbons Martin J	94	retired	60	240 Blue Hill av
F	Harland Martin	94	carpenter	60	16 Union Park
G	Holman Charles F	94	printer	27	Scranton Pa
H	McAuley John	94	physician	60	here
K	Molinari John	94	laborer	65	3492 Wash'n
L	Moran James J	94	retired	50	48 Worcester
M	Moran William C	94	carpenter	55	48 "
N	Sullivan Daniel A	94	watchman	45	here
o	Williams Frederick W	94	carpenter	45	11 Concord sq

Ward 9—Precinct 4

CITY OF BOSTON.

LIST OF RESIDENTS
20 YEARS OF AGE AND OVER

(FEMALES INDICATED BY DAGGER)

AS OF

APRIL 1, 1926

HERBERT A. WILSON, } Listing

JAMES F. EAGAN, } Board.

CITY OF BOSTON—PRINTING DEPARTMENT

Camden Street

A	Hunt Lelia—†	193	housewife	40	here
B	Hunt Richard B	193	porter	50	"
C	Harris Ruby E—†	193	operator	25	12 Fountain
D	VanTassell Emma—†	193	housewife	65	here
E	VanTassell Standley	193	photo engraver	27	"
F	North Abraham	193	porter	35	"
G	North Alice—†	193	maid	34	"
H	Bennett Peter	195	housewife	27	"
K	Bennett Probidensiu—†	195	"	25	"
L	Maxwell Alberta—†	195	"	26	16 Dilworth
M	Maxwell Benjamin	195	clerk	48	16 "
N	Moshell Myrtle—†	195	maid	27	here
O	Shaw Rufas R	195	carpenter	38	"
P	Bryant Joseph	203	painter	35	"
R	Bryant Maud—†	203	housewife	35	"
S	Mayo Fannie—†	203	"	33	"
T	Mayo Frederick T	203	policeman	39	"
U	Stokes Annie—†	203	housewife	32	25 Marlboro
V	Stokes Romros	203	janitor	34	25 "
W	Taylor Annie—†	205	housewife	42	here
X	Taylor Robert	205	iceman	49	"
Y	Knight Clement P	205	painter	34	"
Z	Knight Susie—†	205	housewife	35	"
A	Jones Catherine—†	205	"	41	"
B	Jones John R	205	starter	43	"

Columbus Avenue

E	Bastey James A	561	leatherworker	72	here
F	Noble John	561	counterman	45	Lynn
G	Faye Lillian M—†	561	housewife	42	10 Sarsfield
H	Faye Maurice F	561	clerk	45	10 "
K	Taylor Ellen—†	561	waitress	28	52 Westland av
L	Frost Maria—†	561	bookkeeper	46	here
M	Connery May B—†	561	waitress	42	"
N	Brawner Josephine—†	561	housekeeper	36	752 Tremont
O	Hencella Mary—†	561	stitcher	50	752 "
R	Arabetgas Elpenike T—†	561	housekeeper	37	here
P	Arabetgas Paul	561	waiter	44	"

2

Page.	Letter	FULL NAME.	Residence, April 1, 1926.	Occupation.	Supposed Age.	Reported Residence, April 1, 1925. Street and Number.

Columbus Avenue—Continued

s	Cassas James P	561	storekeeper	34	here
T	Loursus Anna—†	561	housekeeper	28	30 Worcester
U	Loursus James	561	storekeeper	33	30 "
V	Loursus John	561	"	36	30 "
W	Packard Fred	561	factory worker	50	Lynn
X	Varella Gilbert	561	waiter	67	Cambridge
Y	Varella Luciner—†	561	housewife	63	"
Z	Gorman Frank	563	laborer	38	Somerville
A	O'Melia Patrick F	563	retired	65	here
B	Taylor Harold	563	elevatorman	49	"
C	Dolan Arthur F	563	conductor	32	2 Parker
D	Dolan Edward	563	laborer	37	Somerville
E	Forward Elizabeth—†	563	housekeeper	60	here
F	Young Anne M—†	563	at home	80	10 Sarsfield
G	Yee C Poy	564	laundryman	30	here
H	Yee Showyen	564	"	25	"
K	Wooding James F	564	real estate	41	"
L	Knight Jesse M	564	waiter	50	25 Dundee
M	Knight Judith—†	564	housewife	50	25 "
N	Wright William C	564	mechanic	39	Florida
O	Wooten Gertrude—†	564	housewife	34	here
P	Wooten William	564	musician	49	"
R	Ellerby Ophelia—†	564	houseworker	31	27 Greenwich pk
S	McAllister Elise—†	564	"	20	New York City
T	Parker David	564	cook	22	S Carolina
U	Bell Rose—†	565	housekeeper	59	here
V	Dolan Joseph	565	toolmaker	42	"
W	Sheppard Roy	565	seaman	36	12 Oak
X	Small Catherine—†	565	housekeeper	61	here
Y	Anthersaw Halmer	566	boilermaker	50	"
Z	Bailey Cora—†	566	clerk	39	"
A	Chase Ralph	566	counterman	36	1522 Wash'n
B	Daniel George	566	timekeeper	54	here
C	Foy Lillian—†	566	hairdresser	31	Worcester
D	Fraser Clenn E—†	566	housewife	38	31 Dover
E	Gallant Ellianore—†	566	"	32	79 Rutland
F	Hogan Maude—†	566	clerk	48	here
G	Nehler Justin	566	salesman	38	"
H	Oldride May—†	566	forewoman	55	"
K	Roch Catherine—†	566	tel operator	32	"
L	Tippites Fred	566	advertising	37	Maine

3

Columbus Avenue—Continued

M	White Linnie B—†	566	housewife	53	here
S	Bowen John	568	salesman	27	New York City
T	Buttler George	568	chauffeur	41	here
U	Buttler Joseph	568	spinner	51	Worcester
V	Foley Michael J	568	busboy	21	Canada
W	Fraser William J	568	painter	49	31 Dover
X	Freniere Stella—†	568	housewife	31	Boxford
Y	Kane Evelyn C †	568	"	32	here
Z	Kane James D	568	waiter	35	"
A	Moynighan Edward	568	porter	39	280 Mass av
B	Rodwell Rose—†	568	laundress	35	623 Tremont
C	White John R	568	counterman	41	here
D	Wise Elizabeth—†	568	housewife	30	"
F	Alberto Anthony	570	counterman	35	"
G	Bathall Mary—†	570	housewife	23	708 Tremont
H	Bathall Nelie	570	cigarmaker	30	708 "
K	Dunn John E	570	cook	50	here
L	Goodlin George	570	paperhanger	50	"
M	Kelley John	570	cigarmaker	23	214 Mass av
N	Lemon Eda—†	570	housewife	42	here
O	Lemon Mark	570	cigarmaker	50	"
P	Maddon Elsie—†	570	housewife	24	1 Taylor
V	Maddon John H	570	mechanic	32	1 "
R	Maxwell Sidney F	570	"	25	here
S	Maxwell Viola—†	570	housekeeper	28	"
T	McIntyre Josephine—†	570	usher	23	New York City
U	McIntyre Laura—†	570	saleswoman	28	Canada
W	Papulias James	570	counterman	36	573 Col av
X	Papulias John	570	chef	29	New Hampshire
Y	Adario Joseph	571	salesman	23	New York
Z	Adario Mary M—†	571	housekeeper	21	"
A	White Harland E	571	shoeworker	21	here
B	White Ida M—†	571	housekeeper	41	"
C	Blackman Ducette—†	571	housewife	35	25 Cortes
D	Dodge John	571	tea blender	35	here
E	Lee Emil	571	carpenter	26	8 Dover
H	Baker Mildred—†	571	clerk	23	635 Tremont
K	Clapham Bessie—†	571	housekeeper	27	Providence R I
L	Daley Leroy	571	clerk	25	here
M	McCarthy John J	571	artist	25	7 Gay
N	McCarthy Lilian—†	571	housekeeper	26	7 "

Letter	Full Name	Residence, April 1, 1926.	Occupation	Supposed Age	Reported Residence, April 1, 1925. Street and Number.

Columbus Avenue—Continued

R	Gebo Catherine—†	571	housekeeper	26	Springfield
S	Gebo George	571	garageman	26	"
U	Paine Edith—†	571	housekeeper	27	617 Tremont
T	Paine John C	571	window washer	28	617 "
W	Cashman Bertha—†	571	saleswoman	22	Malden
X	Devine Jacqueline—†	571	housekeeper	21	Somerville
Y	Kennedy Ida—†	571	"	30	here
Z	Kennedy Walter J	571	coremaker	32	"
A	Burns Arthur	571	counterman	26	160 W Newton
B	Fluyer Harry	571	painter	24	here
C	Johnston Richard	571	clerk	30	Canada
N	Jackman Bersford	586	steamfitter	36	here
M	Jackman Edna —†	586	housewife	36	"
O	Simpson Ceavath—†	586	chiropodist	56	"
P	Patterson Carl	586	chauffeur	33	"
R	Whitker Annie—†	586	houseworker	21	32 Hammond
S	Whitker John D	586	steward	27	24 Ball
U	McCaman Fannie—†	588	housewife	38	here
V	McCaman James	588	barber	57	"
W	Lindsey Helen—†	588	seamstress	34	"
X	Lindsey Oliva—†	588	housekeeper	66	"
Y	Chandler Gertrude—†	588	housewife	35	"
Z	Chandler Hurbert	588	waiter	40	"
A	Bell Eliza—†	588	housekeeper	55	550 Shawmut av
B	Bell James	588	porter	58	550 "
C	Larde Maud—†	588	at home	30	550 "
D	Saunders James	590	porter	57	here
E	Saunders Maude—†	590	housewife	45	"
G	Armstrong Cassandra—†	590	"	39	"
H	Bernett Frances—†	590	seamstress	28	Braintree
K	Eggbert Evelyn —†	590	waitress	29	219 W Canton
L	Thurston John	590	carpenter	48	here
M	Thurston Mary —†	590	housewife	39	"
N	Barrows Elwin	590	musician	33	"
O	Robinson Estell—†	592	housekeeper	33	"
P	Robinson Thomas J	592	laborer	35	"
R	Mair Florence—†	592	housewife	32	"
S	Mair Thomas H	592	waiter	34	"
T	Carrillo Marcelino J	592	mover	33	"
U	Carrillo Mary—†	592	housewife	50	"
V	Hodisdon Ucilid	592	laborer	45	"

Page	Letter	FULL NAME.	Residence, April 1, 1926.	Occupation.	Supposed Age.	Reported Residence, April 1, 1925. Street and Number.

Columbus Avenue— Continued

	w	Hopwood Lottie †	592	houseworker	40	here
	x	Williams David R	592	compositor	40	"
	y	Williams Jessie †	592	housewife	38	"
	z	London Frederick J	599	janitor	41	"
	A	London Kate L †	599	housewife	36	"
	B	Nourse Albert	599	painter	52	"
	C	Nourse Bessie †	599	housewife	38	"
	D	Bucklar Annie †	599	"	28	New York City
	E	Bucklar Harry	599	electrician	33	"
	F	Atwood Harry	599	painter	35	82 Appleton
	G	Miller George	599	bookkeeper	48	82 "
	H	Miller Gertrude †	599	housewife	32	82 "
	K	Meyers Leah †	599	saleswoman	36	here
	L	Meyers Solomon	599	salesman	52	"
	M	Bondurent Harry	599	mechanic	34	Gloucester
	N	Bondurent Marion †	599	housewife	27	"
	O	Gray Helen F †	599	"	24	Chicago Ill
	P	O'Toole Thomas	599	manufacturer	36	Springfield
	R	Barrie Marion †	599	waitress	28	286 Col av
	S	Brunell Anna †	599	"	24	Cambridge
	T	Ewing Archibald	599	plasterer	41	here
	U	Ewing Louise E †	599	housewife	41	"
	V	Griffin Annie †	599	saleswoman	36	Belmont
	W	Rassonchine Alla †	599	housewife	25	California
	X	Rassonchine Vladimir V	599	student	26	"
	Y	Roper Albert	599	mechanic	26	56 Rutland
	Z	Roper Ella †	599	saleswoman	28	56 "
	B	Nickerson Guy	599	contractor	42	Portland Me
	C	Nickerson Violet †	599	housewife	23	"
	D	Marks George	599	salesman	38	New Hampshire
	E	Adams Carl	599	mechanic	36	Ohio
	F	Adams Frederick	599	retired	68	"
	G	Adams Margaret †	599	housewife	30	"
	K	Musnitski Peter	599	musician	32	here
	L	Musnitski Sonia †	599	housewife	31	"
	M	Setterland Arthur C	599	mechanic	40	"
	N	Setterland Blanche †	599	housewife	39	"
	O	Cram Henry	599	salesman	34	"
	P	Madden Frank	599	clerk	36	"
	S	Seaver Augustis	599	"	50	"
	T	Seaver Mary A †	599	publisher	39	"

Columbus Avenue — Continued

U	Winn Henry	599	bookkeeper	65	here
V	Winn Isabell—†	599	housewife	48	"
W	Dennison Estella—†	599	"	78	"
X	Peterson Louis W	599	gasfitter	37	54 St Stephen
Y	Peterson Mary E—†	599	housewife	32	54 "
Z	Daniels Annie—†	599	"	41	Arlington
A	Daniels Philip A	599	painter	45	"
B	Brewster John	599	salesman	25	Framingham
C	Brewster Margaret—†	599	housewife	22	"
D	Tanzer Peter	599	tailor	36	here
E	Tanzer Sarah—†	599	housewife	25	"
F	Costello Ella M—†	599	"	40	75 Westland av
G	Costello John J	599	physician	43	75 "
H	Martin Bessie—†	599	housewife	34	49 Astor
K	Martin Leslie	599	mechanic	42	49 "
L	Olsen Pearl E—†	599	housewife	32	Braintree
M	Olsen Russell R	599	salesman	34	"
N	Whitten George	599	printer	23	here
O	Whitten Thersa—†	599	housewife	36	"
P	Whitten William	599	signalman	50	"
S	Brooks Frances M—†	599	housewife	34	Wakefield
T	Brooks Harry	599	U S N	34	"
U	O'Brien Hilda—†	599	housewife	31	New York
V	O'Brien Smith	599	cook	36	"
W	Hanley Georgana—†	599	housewife	32	here
X	Hanley John	599	inspector	38	"
Z	Field Hirta K—†	599	housewife	22	Cambridge
A	Fields Noel H	599	investigator	22	"
B	England Anna—†	599	hairdresser	21	here
C	England Augusta—†	599	clerk	23	"
D	Jones Gladys—†	599	bookkeeper	32	"
E	Jones Mary—†	599	housewife	65	"
F	Jones Samuel	599	retired	79	"
G	Maher Agnes V—†	599	housewife	41	"
H	Maher James F	599	salesman	61	"
K	Fisher Bella—†	599	housewife	35	"
L	Fisher Ernest	599	tailor	52	"
M	Melynn James F	599	engineer	60	"
N	Hall Nellie—†	599	printer	38	"
O	Wing Arthur	599	manager	43	"
P	Wing Mabel—†	599	housewife	45	"

Columbus Avenue—Continued

R	Aicardi Hazel—†	599	housewife	22	Arlington
S	Aicardi James	599	school teacher	28	"
T	Lingoes Estelle—†	599	housewife	24	here
U	Lingoes James	599	furrier	42	"
V	McVickers Annie—†	599	checker	48	394 Mass av
W	White Wilfred	599	chauffeur	23	Haverhill
X	O'Brien Mary E—†	599	housewife	43	83 Worcester
Y	O'Brien Thomas F	599	mechanic	44	83 "
Z	Parker William	599	painter	58	here
A	Wallenta Kenneth	599	salesman	21	Connecticut
C	Harlan Catherine—†	599	waitress	23	520 Mass av
D	Harlan Sarah A—†	599	housekeeper	58	520 "
F	Thurlow Edgar T	599	physician	78	here
G	Thurlow Isabel—†	599	housewife	67	"
H	Stowe Cora A—†	599	bookkeeper	35	"
L	Fitts Ruth A—†	599	agent	60	Rhode Island
M	Bridges May—†	599	saleswoman	52	Maine
N	Taggart Ira—†	599	housewife	32	47 Rutland
O	Taggart Mylie	599	mechanic	38	47 "
R	Zitano Edith—†	606	housewife	34	here
S	Zitano Joseph	606	machinist	35	"
T	Washburn Lillie F—†	606	housewife	68	"
V	Robinson Beatrice—†	606	teacher	36	197 W Newton
W	Dyer Esther—†	606	cashier	25	Maine
X	Sullivan Nora—†	606	housewife	43	10 Anderson
Y	Hyde Frank	606	janitor	46	here
Z	Hyde Mary S—†	606	housewife	34	"
A	Roberts Harry C	606	student	29	1 Cazenove
B	Roberts Robert A	606	"	32	1 "
C	Solliday Levicka—†	606	housewife	38	560 Col av
D	Solliday Robert	606	electrician	42	560 "
E	Fairwether Martha—†	606	at home	73	560 "
F	Granger Mary K—†	606	dressmaker	60	here
G	Wall Margaret—†	606	waitress	47	78 Charles
K	Chase Bertha—†	609	housewife	47	here
L	Chase Leroy E	609	chauffeur	48	"
M	Brennan John M	609	painter	42	"
M¹	Cook Harold F	609	technician	32	"
N	Cook Lydia M—†	609	housekeeper	64	"
O	Cook Mollie—†	609	housewife	36	"
P	Cronin Edward F	609	x-ray man	24	"

Page.	Letter.	FULL NAME.	Residence, April 1, 1926.	Occupation	Supposed Age.	Reported Residence, April 1, 1925. Street and Number.

Columbus Avenue—Continued

R	Rokes Floy—†	609	cook	50	here
s	Spellman Merigold—†	609	pantrywoman	24	Rochester N H
T	Ross Alvenah—†	609	housewife	61	here
U	Ross Henry D	609	printer	55	"
V	Young Ruth—†	609	bookkeeper	37	"
W	Cudelas James	609	butcher	43	"
X	Cudelas Lettia—†	609	housewife	42	"
Y	Frentzos William G	609	fruit	41	557 Col av
Z	Grace Charles J	609	agent	51	here
z¹	MacDonald Hazel R—†	609	nurse	37	Canada
z²	Mallalien Mabel W—†	609	housewife	48	here
A	Chase Edna E—†	609	saleswoman	20	750 Shawmut av
B	Chase Evelyn M—†	609	boxmaker	23	750 "
C	Chase John W	609	shipper	21	750 "
D	Chase Josephine A—†	609	houseworker	44	750 "
E	Chase Robert W	609	plumber	48	750 "
F	Constance Charles P	609	salesman	35	here
G	Constance Gertrude M—†	609	housewife	33	"
H	Constance Thomas E	609	salesman	42	"
K	Bright Lida T	610	piano teacher	54	"
L	Bright William H	610	real estate	52	"
M	Coleman Mary L—†	610	dressmaker	45	"
N	Smith Sarah—†	610	elevatorwoman	42	689 Shawmut av
O	Reynolds Frederick	610	U S A	49	here
P	Reynolds Priscilla J—†	610	housewife	45	"
R	Rothschild Ernest	610	laborer	60	235 Northampton
S	Walker William H	610	elevatorman	23	12 Truro
U	Carrington Darnley	610	porter	27	here
T	Gibson Cecil A—†	610	housewife	34	"
V	Gibson John A	610	shipper	48	"
W	Flu Charlotte S—†	610	housewife	30	"
X	Flu Ewing A	610	porter	27	"
Y	Watkins James T	610	musician	24	"
Z	Canty John C	610	painter	35	23 Braddock pk
A	Fitzpatrick Herbert	610	porter	35	Chelsea
B	Register Ivy—†	610	housewife	24	here
C	Register William	610	porter	26	"
D	Giddens Henry	610	student	28	14 Braddock pk
E	Magauder William C	610	porter	32	here
F	Stewart Carolyn—†	610	manicurist	34	"
G	Chinn Margaret—†	610	housewife	25	"

9

Columbus Avenue—Continued

H	Chinn Pembroke	610	waiter	55	here
K	Chinn Pembroke	610	draftsman	27	"
L	Garnett Jessie—†	612	dentist	28	"
M	Garnett Robert	612	policeman	38	"
N	Hagan Mary—†	612	housekeeper	58	"
O	Jackson Abraham	612	laborer	50	"
P	Jackson Minnie N—†	612	housewife	49	"
R	Norman Maude S—†	612	"	21	"
S	Richards Virginia—†	612	"	36	"
T	Ingliss Annie M—†	612	"	43	12 Dilworth
U	Ingliss Lynch H	612	bellboy	44	12 "
V	Laing Emma—†	612	cook	47	12 "
W	Laing Mary—†	612	housekeeper	69	W Medford
X	Burnett Sidney	612	laborer	28	Cambridge
Y	Chandler Charles	612	carpenter	42	"
Z	Chandler Rosamond—†	612	housewife	40	"
A	Griffith Phillister	612	carpenter	26	"
B	Weeks Nathaniel	612	porter	28	"
C	Lee John L	612	car washer	52	here
D	Lee Maggie—†	612	dressmaker	68	"
E	Stubblefield Mary—†	612	domestic	33	36 Hull
F	Delisser Chrysostomo	612	elevatorman	20	here
G	Jackson Charles	612	mechanic	26	26½ Kendall
H	Lyne Wade	612	"	37	Richmond
K	Rattray James A	612	storekeeper	55	here
L	Rattray Minnie—†	612	housewife	36	"
N	Kennell Mary J—†	612	tel operator	27	"
M	Kennell Winnie—†	612	housewife	53	"
O	Gilmore Edward	613	laborer	35	"
P	Gilmore Joseph	613	metalworker	28	"
R	Tracey John	613	waiter	32	"
S	Chapin Catherine N—†	613	housewife	39	"
T	Chapin Charles A	613	chandeliers	39	"
U	Guess Robert D	613	student	28	"
V	Hamois Adeline †	613	housewife	48	"
W	Hamois Beryl †	613	clerk	27	"
X	Hamois Horace B	613	foreman	50	"
Y	Oxenhorn Emma—†	613	housewife	20	150 Columbia rd
Z	Oxenhorn Morris	613	window washer	33	150 "
C	Koulouris John	613	butcher	39	here
D	Koulouris Vienna—†	613	housewife	28	"

Page.	Letter.	FULL NAME.	Residence, April 1, 1926.	Occupation.	Supposed Age.	Reported Residence, April 1, 1925. Street and Number.

Columbus Avenue—Continued

E	Conkling Marion—†	613	housewife	29	749 Shawmut av
F	Conkling William	613	carpenter	21	749 "
G	Foggie Charles M	614	"	40	81 Humboldt av
H	Foggie Eugenia—†	614	housewife	43	81 "
K	King Albert	614	laborer	61	here
L	King Jennie—†	614	housewife	51	"
M	Wigfall Elizabeth—†	614	housekeeper	90	"
N	McClean Edward	614	mechanic	50	"
O	McClean Eva—†	614	housewife	34	"
P	Hayden Carolyn—†	614	laundress	32	"
R	Hayden James	614	mechanic	42	"
S	Lewis Dorethea—†	614	housekeeper	65	"
T	Lewis Mae—†	614	saleswoman	21	"
U	Burrell Cynthia—†	614	housewife	48	"
V	Burrell Richard T	614	watchman	50	"
W	Burrell Richard T, jr	614	clerk	25	"
X	Cogslill William R	614	barber	63	61 Camden
Y	Haywood Emma—†	614	housewife	44	here
Z	Stewart Lucy—†	614	"	47	"
A	King Bertina—†	614	domestic	22	"
B	Marshall Sarah—†	614	"	35	55 Sterling
C	Taylor Amanda J—†	614	"	49	here
D	Duncan Amanda—†	614	housekeeper	76	New York City
E	Shanks Edward S	614	waiter	32	106 Dartmouth
F	Shanks Marie B—†	614	housekeeper	30	106 "
G	Marks Beatrice—†	615	housewife	48	24 Wellington
H	Marks Charles	615	engineer	55	24 "
K	Marks Margaret—†	615	housekeeper	21	24 "
L	Callahan George W	615	machinist	79	here
M	Quinlan Jane F—†	615	housekeeper	76	"
N	Quinlan Margaret V—†	615	stenographer	37	"
O	Rubin Edna—†	615	housekeeper	33	613 Col av
T	Ritchie Jessie R—†	615	waitress	32	here
U	Dodge Louise A—†	615	stenographer	40	"
V	Foss Ida G—†	616	maid	43	20 Dilworth
W	Foss William A	616	waiter	44	20 "
X	Parker Cora—†	616	maid	38	20 "
Y	King Annie B—†	616	housewife	36	here
Z	King Norris	616	mechanic	35	"
A	Curl Ernestine—†	616	housekeeper	24	Wash'n D C

Columbus Avenue—Continued

Letter	Full Name	Residence	Occupation	Age	Reported Residence
B	Curl Langstod	616	student	26	here
C	Martin Bernice †	616	housekeeper	23	Phila Pa
D	Martin Ernest	616	physician	35	here
E	McClaurin Milton	616	cook	24	"
F	Somers Lottie—†	616	housewife	40	"
G	Tibbs Alma—†	616	housekeeper	30	Connecticut
H	Gibbons James	616	waiter	25	New York
K	Hunt Lydia—†	616	housekeeper	31	here
L	Hunt William H	616	waiter	52	"
P	Edwards Mary A—†	616	housekeeper	59	26½ Kendall
S	Edwards Thomas	616	cook	64	26½ "
M	Miller Ellen O †	616	student	22	26½ "
N	Miller Florence E—†	616	houseworker	20	26½ "
O	Miller John J	616	clerk	29	26½ "
R	Miller Mary I—†	616	houseworker	35	26½ "
T	Brown Harry	616	cook	40	here
U	Brown Lucy A—†	616	housewife	39	"
V	Dawson William	616	cook	57	"
W	Bause Allen	616	laborer	31	"
X	Burke Rose—†	616	bookkeeper	23	"
Y	Johnson Maude—†	616	housewife	31	"
A	McDonald Jennie—†	618	"	45	"
B	McDonald John F	618	mechanic	44	"
C	Inhorn Izzy	618	laborer	35	"
D	Inhorn Yette—†	618	housewife	35	"
E	Mills Julia—†	618	"	30	"
F	Mills Robert	618	janitor	41	"
H	O'Neil Allen P	619	actor	38	"
K	O'Neil James A	619	retired	73	"
L	O'Neil Martha—†	619	housekeeper	72	"
M	Brown Benjamin	619	toolmaker	54	625 Col av
N	Cox Anson G	619	machinist	63	625 "
O	Doughty Frederick	619	elevatorman	60	625 "
P	Hayes John D	619	constable	43	625 "
R	LaRock Bessie—†	619	housekeeper	48	625 "
S	Cox Frances—†	619	waitress	36	here
T	McNamara Bernard	619	foreman	29	"
U	McNamara Elizabeth—†	619	housekeeper	68	"
V	Carrington Iva—†	620	dressmaker	21	616 Col av
W	Hilton Ruth—†	620	"	31	616 "

Page.	Letter.	FULL NAME.	Residence, April 1, 1926.	Occupation.	Supposed Age.	Reported Residence, April 1, 1925. Street and Number.

Columbus Avenue—Continued

	X	Samuels Anthony	620	janitor	65	616 Col av
	Y	Samuels Helen—†	620	housekeeper	56	616 "
	Z	Deins Christine—†	620	housewife	25	here
	A	Gumbs Margaret—†	620	"	29	"
	B	Gumbs Thomas	620	laborer	30	"
	C	James Laura—†	620	houseworker	28	"
	D	Samot Nestor E	620	porter	23	"
	E	Dalton John E	620	real estate	39	19 Wellington
	F	Leroy James	620	electrician	23	here
	G	Riddock Latitia—†	620	houseworker	65	Somerville
	H	Slade Margaret C—†	620	housewife	41	here
	K	Slade Otto	620	fisherman	52	"
	M	Dupont John	622	hatter	42	New York
	N	Tuner Charles	622	chauffeur	42	616 Col av
	O	Washington Julius	622	"	35	616 "
	P	Atkinson William A	622	machinist	45	750 "
	R	Roshar Rose V—†	622	housewife	77	750 "
	S	Smith Sadie R—†	622	housekeeper	45	750 "
	U	Kittredge Margaret—†	623	social worker	50	60 School
	V	Kittredge Robert H	623	electrician	29	60 "
	T	Morrison Luella D—†	623	housewife	31	60 "
	X	Wyman Lillian C—†	623	nurse	49	here
	Y	Lavine Lillian—†	623	housewife	30	599 Col av
	Z	Lavine Samuel	623	butcher	36	599 "
	A	Conway Braxton	623	seaman	31	New York
	B	Gardner Everal	623	cook	32	61 Williams
	C	Gardner Lillian—†	623	"	30	61 "
	D	Banks Alice D—†	623	housewife	48	215 W Springfield
	E	Banks Lawrence H	623	postal clerk	26	215 "
	F	Hollit Thomas	623	longshoreman	48	here
	G	Peterson Madeline—†	623	housewife	48	"
	H	Peterson Nels	623	salesman	70	"
	K	Allen Louise—†	623	housewife	60	"
	L	Fanar Edward	623	inspector	59	"
	M	Griffin Thomas F	623	clerk	60	New York
	N	Monroe Ada—†	625	at home	40	768 Col av
	O	Monroe William	625	porter	44	768 "
	R	Williams Bernard	625	"	26	768 "
	P	Williams Helen—†	625	housewife	22	768 "
	S	Lafferty Patrick	625	carpenter	45	Canada

Columbus Avenue—Continued

T	Hogan Carry—†	625	housewife	28	Cambridge
U	Hogan James	625	salesman	35	"
V	Lewis Loner	625	auto mechanic	33	here
W	Lewis Margaret—†	625	housewife	32	"
Y	Henson Earl A	625	machinist	32	31 Batavia
Z	Henson Pearl †	625	housewife	26	31 "
A	Waterman Noel	625	seaman	42	10 Braddock pk
C	Bussey Isaac	625	porter	28	6 Wellington
D	Storr Leon	625	bellboy	24	Stanford Ct
E	Jackson Sylvia—†	627	at home	87	here
F	Lynch John D	627	chauffeur	40	"
G	Lynch Mary E †	627	housewife	30	"
H	Davis May W—†	627	dressmaker	59	609 Col av
L	Northrup Bernard	627	salesman	50	here
M	Northrup Bessie—†	627	housekeeper	60	"
N	Pasco Charles	627	chef	50	"
O	Penny Francis	627	porter	29	564 Col av
P	Penny Sadie—†	627	housewife	29	564 "
R	Langley James H	627	porter	63	194 Northampton
S	Langley Mary I—†	627	housewife	51	194 "
T	Minton Frank A	627	porter	49	194 "
U	Falawn Mary—†	627	manager	50	Cambridge
V	Benjamin Alice—†	627	housewife	26	146 Worcester
W	Benjamin Launey	627	porter	32	146 "

Dilworth Street

X	Young Arthur	1	porter	28	here
Y	Young Daisy—†	1	housekeeper	54	"
Z	Foreman Arthur B	1	janitor	53	"
A	Hamilton Frances—†	1	housekeeper	42	"
B	Smith Alfred	1	porter	40	"
C	Smith Belle—†	1	housewife	38	"
E	Crite Annanrae—†	2	"	39	977 Tremont
F	Crite Oscar	2	janitor	50	977 "
G	Alexander Cora—†	2	cook	30	32 Wellington
H	Pointer Calvin	2	"	22	4 Clermont
K	Robinson Emma—†	2	laundress	31	33 Kendall
L	Daughtry Ionia—†	3	housewife	35	here

14

Page	Letter	Full Name.	Residence, April 1, 1926.	Occupation	Supposed Age.	Reported Residence, April 1, 1925. Street and Number.

Dilworth Street—Continued

	M	Daughtry William	3	chauffeur	38	here
	O	Hargraves Nancy—†	3	housewife	49	"
	P	Kendall George	3	porter	40	"
	R	Dilworth Samuel	4	fireman	38	389 Northampton
	S	Dilworth Wesley—†	4	cook	28	389 "
	T	Thompson John T	4	barber	35	here
	U	Thompson Mary—†	4	housewife	34	"
	V	Ford Sarah E—†	4	"	48	"
	W	Smith Frank V	4	laborer	34	"
	X	Hunt Cary R	5	mechanic	24	"
	Y	Hunt Hattie O—†	5	housewife	21	"
	Z	Tenney Nellie—†	5	clerk	25	Everett
	A	Tenney Nettie—†	5	housewife	45	"
	B	Wilson Annie C—†	5	"	40	here
	C	Wilson James A	5	waiter	53	"
	D	Pulley Matilda—†	6	housekeeper	50	"
	E	Curtis Agnes—†	6	housewife	26	355 Col av
	F	Curtis Albert L	6	musician	41	355 "
	G	Moore Charles R	6	"	50	55 St Germain
	H	Moore May S—†	6	housekeeper	46	55 "
	K	Reeves Caroline—†	7	operator	22	31 Batavia
	L	Reeves Wilbur B	7	cook	23	31 "
	M	Davis Richard	7	painter	33	80 Rutland sq
	N	Riley Gastrel	7	"	40	here
	O	Wade James	7	chauffeur	37	"
	P	Wade Ursula—†	7	housewife	37	"
	S	Thomas Eva—†	8	"	32	"
	T	Thomas Percy A	8	postal clerk	33	"
	U	Harris Gertrude E—†	8	housewife	40	"
	V	Harris Thomas A	8	chauffeur	63	"
	W	Price Jane R—†	8	maid	40	"
	X	Price Nettie—†	8	cleaner	45	"
	Y	Price Robert E	8	butler	55	"
	Z	Jackson Squire C	9	clerk	34	"
	A	Adams Mary N—†	9	housewife	41	"
	B	Adams Warren J	9	porter	41	"
	C	McGee Blanche—†	9	dressmaker	36	"
	D	McGee Reuben	9	cook	46	"
	E	Clayton Minnie—†	10	houseworker	20	Pennsylvania
	F	Morris Ernest O	10	cook	34	here
	G	Morris Ethel M—†	10	housewife	34	"

15

Dilworth Street—Continued

H	Chambers Joseph R	10	waiter	52	here
K	Chambers Mary M—†	10	housewife	48	"
L	Rickson Daisy O—†	10	"	32	"
M	Rickson Hiram F	10	chauffeur	53	"
O	Oliver George H	11	policeman	36	75 Camden
P	Oliver James A	11	chauffeur	41	75 "
R	Oliver Pauline B—†	11	housewife	25	75 "
S	Davis Blanche—†	11	student	21	here
T	Davis Helen †	11	housewife	46	"
U	Davis William	11	laborer	45	"
V	Callender Agnes—†	11A	housewife	28	"
W	Callender Arthur	11A	waiter	28	"
X	Jordan Julius	11A	porter	33	804 Tremont
Y	Moody Stella—†	11A	housekeeper	30	804 "
A	DeCordova Leopold	12	teacher	35	here
B	DeCordova Theresa—†	12	housewife	25	19 Holyoke
C	Francis Alda—†	12	"	27	here
D	Francis John	12	janitor	43	"
E	Muir Esiah	12	elevatorman	40	"
F	Samuda Albert	12	cook	29	1054 Tremont
G	Marsh Egbert	12	"	38	Newton
H	Marsh Zuida—†	12	housewife	39	"
K	Facey Daniel	14	porter	31	here
M	Forbes Tina—†	14	waitress	28	"
N	Gunter Godfrey	14	porter	32	20 Braddock pk
O	Gunter Marion—†	14	houseworker	28	20 "
P	Richards Albon	14	chauffeur	24	1059 Tremont
R	Richards Mary—†	14	houseworker	22	1059 "
S	Ried Thomas H	15	salesman	38	107 Warwick
T	Sue Grant	15	laborer	39	here
U	Sue Marion—†	15	housewife	37	"
V	Smith Margaret—†	15	"	39	Barnstable
W	Smith William	15	waiter	57	"
X	Best Evelyn C—†	16	housewife	26	here
Y	Best Thomas W	16	bellman	35	"
Z	Carrington Elizabeth—†	16	waitress	31	Somerville
A	Monterro John B	16	laborer	33	64 Westminster
B	Perry Clara—†	16	housewife	33	here
C	Perry Samuel	16	porter	32	"
D	Bryant Charles G	17	laborer	32	"
E	Bryant Eula O—†	17	housewife	26	"

Page.	Letter.	FULL NAME.	Residence, April 1, 1926.	Occupation.	Supposed Age.	Reported Residence, April 1, 1925. Street and Number.

Dilworth Street—Continued

F	Perkins Robert	17	mechanic	34	here
G	Stevens Matthew	17	cook	45	"
H	Stevens Matthew, jr	17	porter	25	"
K	Francis Helen —†	17	housewife	35	"
L	Francis Mary —†	17	"	34	"
M	Cook John M	18	musician	42	"
N	Cook Mary E—†	18	housewife	28	"
O	Johnson Elizabeth—†	18	"	44	"
P	Johnson Robert	18	printer	57	"
R	Dystant Emily—†	18	housewife	40	19 Dilworth
S	Dystant Samuel	18	cook	42	19 "
T	Harrison Emily—†	18	elevatorwoman	22	19 "
U	Benn Hazel S—†	19	housewife	44	41 Cunard
V	Powell Lee A, jr	19	porter	24	701 Shawmut av
W	Williams Clara—†	19	housewife	39	here
X	Williams Samuel	19	cook	38	"
Y	Bailey Mabel —†	19	housewife	37	"
Z	Bailey Theodore	19	laborer	38	"
A	Dyer Catherine—†	20	houseworker	45	"
B	Miller Beatrice—†	20	barber	25	21 Westminster
C	Stokes Georgia—†	20	housewife	49	21 "
D	Stokes Viola	20	barber	31	21 "
E	Clark Rebecca A—†	20	at home	84	here
F	Cruckendle William H	20	elevatorman	74	"
G	Dyett Richard	20	porter	26	"
H	Harris Mabel—†	20	housewife	44	"
K	Johnson Melvina—†	20	dressmaker	20	"
L	Smith Dora—†	21	housewife	48	4A Forest
M	Smith John	21	laborer	52	4A "
N	Goode Clara—†	21	housewife	40	here
O	Goode John L	21	boilermaker	38	"
P	Payton Anita—†	21	housewife	35	"
R	Payton Dudley	21	steward	32	"
S	White Charles	22	laborer	44	"
T	White Martha—†	22	housewife	37	"
U	Johnson David	22	janitor	40	"
V	Knight Aletha—†	22	cook	40	"
X	Lucas Mary J—†	24	dressmaker	50	"
Y	Johnson Helen—†	24	housewife	58	"
Y¹	Johnson John	24	porter	37	"
Z	Adams Bessie—†	24	houseworker	45	"

9—4

Page.	Letter.	FULL NAME.	Residence, April 1, 1926.	Occupation.	Supposed Age.	Reported Residence, April 1, 1925. Street and Number.

Dilworth Street—Continued

| | z¹ | Moore James J | 24 | choreman | 40 | here |
| | z² | Moore Margaret —† | 24 | houseworker | 65 | " |

Massachusetts Avenue

	D	Dalton George D	393	student	29	Weymouth
	E	Dufresne Walter J	393	"	25	479 Mass av
	F	Rangust Olive B—†	393	housekeeper	21	New York
	G	Raugust Walter J	393	seaman	25	Newport R I
	H	Wood Gertrude—†	393	stenographer	39	here
	K	Marsh Eleanor—†	393	bookkeeper	38	"
	O	Lee Anna A—†	393	housekeeper	39	26 Bickerstaff
	P	Lee George E	393	chauffeur	40	26 "
	R	Garrabrant Howard	393	oiler	25	551 Col av
	S	Garrabrant Margaret—†	393	housekeeper	21	551 "
	U	Manchester Lawlor—†	393	"	38	26 Upton
	V	Manchester William F	393	plumber	43	26 "
	X	Bird Elizabeth G—†	393	housekeeper	50	here
	Y	Bird Webster T	393	carpenter	52	"
	Z	Kimball Ira C	393	"	40	N Reading
	A	Kimball Maud V	393	housewife	35	"
	B	Duane Henry	393	carpenter	61	144 Worcester
	C	Duane Vinie—†	393	housekeeper	41	144 "
	E	Sargent May—†	393	housewife	47	44 "
	F	Sargent Walter P	393	salesman	50	44 "
	G	Burden Wilbert A	393	real estate	60	here
	H	Brown Edwin E	393	salesman	52	"
	K	Brown Grace—†	393	housewife	38	"
	L	Chapman Evelyn—†	393	housekeeper	23	109 Peterboro
	M	Chapman Herbert	393	electrician	24	109 "
	M¹	Kinney Asa	393	carpenter	54	Florida
	N	Kinney Thomas O	393	musician	45	"
	O	Flynn Joseph F	393	salesman	34	Lowell
	P	Flynn Mildred—†	393	shoeworker	28	"
	S	Stork Alice—†	393	saleswoman	29	Hopkinton
	T	Stork Robert	393	machinist	31	"
	U	Kidder Caroline—†	393	shoeworker	39	here
	V	Spaulding Mabel M—†	393	"	41	"
	Y	Theriault Edith M—†	394	housewife	24	429 Brookline av
	Z	Theriault George A	394	janitor	29	429 "

Letter	FULL NAME	Residence, April 1, 1926.	Occupation.	Supposed Age.	Reported Residence, April 1, 1925. Street and Number.

Massachusetts Avenue— Continued

B	Bickford Bessie—†	394	repairer	38	Nashua N H
C	Bickford Donald	394	clerk	38	"
D	Stuart Mary G—†	394	housewife	65	here
E	Stuart William L	394	watchman	67	"
F	Worcester Mary M—†	394	housewife	60	"
G	Brody Henry	394	U S customs	28	New York City
H	Carson Harry	394	"	28	"
K	Sealy Fannie—†	394	dressmaker	28	"
L	Donovan Katherine F—†	394	housekeeper	22	25 Lynde
M	Donovan Woolrose J	394	chauffeur	21	13 Bowdoin
P	Turgeon Frank H	394	merchant	60	here
R	Barton William R	394	foreman	48	"
S	Merrill Ethel M—†	394	housewife	22	"
T	Merrill Goodwin I	394	garageman	30	"
U	Boynton Edward P	394	retired	73	"
V	Boynton Paul H	394	salesman	43	"
W	Adler Hannah—†	394	housewife	44	435 Shawmut av
X	Adler Joseph	394	steamfitter	50	435 "
Y	Adler William	394	bricklayer	20	435 "
Z	Hunter Frank W	394	salesman	31	50 Worcester
A	Hunter Gertrude—†	394	housewife	26	50 "
B	Hayward Laura E—†	394	"	58	here
C	Hayward William B	394	trainman	59	"
D	Locke Austin H	394	chauffeur	37	Woolwich Me
E	Hartley Charlotte F—†	394	housewife	23	Brookline
F	Hartley Wilbur G	394	machinist	26	here
G	Searles Susan—†	394	chambermaid	59	"
H	Sheffield Anna—†	394	waitress	29	"
K	Wesson Fulton P	394	mover	31	38 E Springfield
L	Wesson Laura E—†	394	housewife	25	38 "
M	McCarthy Ida—†	394	"	30	Chicago Ill
N	McCarthy John P	394	carpenter	28	"
O	Smith Beatrice M—†	394	artist	25	here
P	Smith Blanch L—†	394	seamstress	46	"
R	Smith Hazel M—†	394	artist	23	"
S	Farr George M	394	printer	44	"
T	Perry Lou—†	394	clerk	46	"
U	Sawyer Nellie—†	394	waitress	27	42 Monadnock
V	Martin Osborn F	394	salesman	51	471 Mass av
W	Carrie Annie T—†	394	housewife	49	49 Astor
X	Carrie Gertrude M—†	394	stenographer	25	49 "

19

Massachusetts Avenue—Continued

Y	Carrie John J	394	student	24	49 Astor
Z	Severance Annie C—†	394	housewife	55	here
A	Severance Frank B	394	special police	66	"
B	Bain Caroline R—†	394	housewife	65	606 Col av
C	Bain Elmer E	394	clerk	38	606 "
D	Bain Norman A	394	retired	68	606 "
E	Duffy Albert J	394	dentist	54	here
F	Kielty John R	394	broker	61	"
G	Swinnerton Nancy W—†	394	housewife	30	"
H	Swinnerton William H	394	auto mechanic	38	"
K	MacCaffery Helen K—†	394	saleswoman	40	"
L	MacCaffery Jean—†	394	stenographer	24	"
M	Griffin Nora C—†	394	saleswoman	44	"
N	Griffin Sarah M—†	394	domestic	32	"
O	Raven Carl R	394	counterman	36	"
P	Rooney John G	394	bricklayer	23	"
R	Easman Ethel J—†	394	waitress	36	"
S	Baisnert Joseph N	395	manager	40	Northampton
T	Deagen Charles L	395	chauffeur	35	Northampton
U	Dears Louise—†	395	forewoman	37	Manchester
V	O'Neill Beranrd	395	printer	20	here
W	O'Neill Lexie	395	janitor	35	"
X	O'Neill Margaret—†	395	milliner	21	"
Y	O'Neill Micheal	395	janitor	45	"
Z	Poirier Grace—†	395	nurse	42	"
A	Ross Reginald	395	tinsmith	22	124 Hanson
B	Wilson Walter H	395	bookkeeper	39	here
C	Wilson William W	395	bookbinder	39	"
E	Dewar Patrick	397	clerk	40	"
F	Downey Francis	397	steamfitter	35	"
G	McDonald Howard	397	chauffeur	21	526 Mass av
H	McDonald James	397	lather	28	here
K	McLeary Howard	397	chauffeur	28	"
L	McManus Thomas	397	musician	30	"
M	O'Day Edith—†	397	housewife	22	"
N	O'Day Francis	397	porter	22	"
O	Rapid James R	397	steamfitter	35	"
P	Fowler Lucy M—†	398	housewife	46	"
R	Fowler William	398	carpet cleaner	68	"
S	Campbell Florence—†	398	dressmaker	47	"
T	Hueston Jessie—†	398	waitress	47	"

Letter	FULL NAME.	Residence, April 1, 1926.	Occupation.	Supposed Age.	Reported Residence, April 1, 1925. Street and Number.

Massachusetts Avenue—Continued

U	Devens William	398	auto mechanic	36	19 Wellington
V	Horn Regina—†	398	housekeeper	60	19 "
W	Murphy John J	398	machinist	41	19 "
X	O'Neil Edward	398	salesman	27	Hingham
Z	Farrington Evlynn—†	399	cashier	26	here
A	Gauthier Adelle—†	399	housewife	67	"
B	Gauthier Adelle—†	399	actress	21	"
C	Gauthier Emile	399	chauffeur	29	"
D	Gauthier Eugene	399	retired	65	"
E	Orville Marie—†	399	checker	40	"
F	Taylor William	399	chauffeur	31	"
K	Edwards Adeline—†	401	factory worker	45	"
L	Edwards George	401	chauffeur	48	"
M	Kneeland Florence—†	401	at home	55	"
N	Kneeland Frank	401	laborer	50	"
O	McDonald Catherine—†	401	waitress	25	"
P	McFarland Julia—†	401	at home	70	"
R	McLoughlan Alice—†	401	stenographer	35	"
S	Penny Grant	401	musician	28	"
T	Relation Joseph	401	barber	49	"
U	Shefferson Lena M—†	401	housewife	49	"
V	Shefferson Russell	401	shipper	22	"
W	Thomas Sherman	401	roofer	27	"
X	Warner Sarah—†	401	chambermaid	68	"
Y	Beattie Harry	403	chef	60	"
Z	DePedro Kay F—†	403	housewife	35	"
A	DePedro Ralph	403	salesman	27	"
B	Kennison Charles W	403	engineer	65	"
C	Kennison Eva M—†	403	housewife	45	"
D	Sachs Nathan	403	merchant	45	"
F	Chase Nathan	405	attendant	55	"
G	Greenberg Samuel	405	salesman	35	"
H	Levine Hyman	405	tailor	45	"
M	Anderson Ernest	406	counterman	35	Worcester
N	Haines Emery	406	machinist	35	Halifax N S
O	Kelley George	406	clerk	33	here
P	Kohler Charles	406	baker	54	"
R	Kohler Sarah †	406	housekeeper	52	"
S	Miller Cheldon	406	painter	28	Cambridge
T	Ransom Aurelius	406	janitor	40	here

Massachusetts Avenue—Continued

U	Astifault Albert	406	molder	40	527 Col av
V	Astifault Anna — †	406	houseworker	33	527 "
W	Broquist David	406	painter	38	65 Westminster av
X	Broquist Sallie — †	406	houseworker	35	65 "
Y	Lee William	406	counterman	38	here
Z	Brown Charles	406	machinist	50	321 Dudley
A	Brown Emma — †	406	housekeeper	40	321 "
B	Keefe Evelyn — †	406	stitcher	32	here
C	Moore John	406	clerk	28	"
D	Hamilton Flory †	406	housekeeper	38	Lynn
E	LeBlanc Agnes — †	406	housewife	27	Halifax N S
F	LeBlanc Desirie	406	carpenter	34	"
G	LeSage Frank E	406	inspector	35	Somerville
H	LeSage Mary C — †	406	housewife	33	"
K	Milne William	406	auto mechanic	36	here
L	Grant Frank	406	chef	37	Eastport Me
M	Ross Norman	406	carpenter	36	here
N	Pennington Oscar	406	policeman	40	367 Mass av
O	Rogers Florence — †	406	waitress	42	102 Westland av
P	Rynar Catherine — †	406	laundress	50	12 Sarsfield
R	Stenson Mazie — †	406	bookkeeper	25	367 Mass av
S	Sutherland Hugh W	406	plumber	44	367 "
T	Sutherland Laura — †	406	housekeeper	49	367 "
U	Bowdenham Hanna — †	406	houseworker	35	105 Edgewood
V	Duncan George W	406	plumber	27	Lowell
W	Snow Alice P — †	406	elevatorwoman	28	105 Edgewood
X	Snow Wallace P	406	electrician	35	105 "
Y	Anderson Ernest	406	inspector	38	here
Z	Barrows Hiram	406	meatcutter	59	"
A	Shepherd Holland	406	salesman	20	"
B	Shepherd May — †	406	housekeeper	52	"
C	Shepherd Wesson L	406	conductor	62	"
D	Agres William	406	chef	30	New Hampshire
E	Kalalekas Demas	406	storekeeper	40	here
F	Martin Charles	406	inspector	37	"
G	Pappas John	406	counterman	37	"
H	Able James	407	carpenter	28	"
K	Gaudet Harry	407	chauffeur	34	"
L	Gaudet Joseph	407	"	36	"
M	Hart Elinor †	407	housewife	35	"
N	Hart George	407	machinist	37	"

22

Massachusetts Avenue—Continued

o	Simons Helen—†	407	cashier	24	here
p	Simons Walter	407	packer	22	"
s	Brawner Joseph P	409	accountant	56	"
t	Delaney Thomas T	409	salesman	39	"
u	Derby Wilbert	409	paperhanger	42	416 Mass av
v	Dugs Inza—†	409	stenographer	21	Canada
w	Ford Charles W	409	cashier	60	here
x	Ford Fannie—†	409	clerk	45	"
y	McKenzie Margaret—†	409	housewife	53	416 Mass av
z	Moylan Edward M	409	machinist	45	416 "
a	Murray George P	409	salesman	40	here
d	Card Horatio S	411	physician	59	"
e	Card Martha O—†	411	teacher	32	"
f	Card Mary E—†	411	housewife	57	"
g	Morrison Josephine C—†	411	"	34	Weymouth
h	Morrison Malcom A	411	laborer	36	"
k	Sefton Harriet E—†	411	at home	59	here
n	Berard Frederick	413	cook	27	410A Col av
o	Gannon Carl	413	baker	28	here
p	Habell Lillian—†	413	housewife	58	"
r	Habell Otto	413	cashier	60	"
s	Jones Alfred	413	steamfitter	38	"
t	Jorden Blanch—†	413	housewife	23	"
u	Jorden Morris	413	cook	39	"
v	Stordy Adia—†	413	housewife	42	"
w	Vanner Blanche—†	413	"	30	"
x	Vanner Ralph	413	cook	35	"
y	Aperstein Bernard	414	student	21	"
z	Bentaman Morris	414	"	22	475 Mass av
a	Brodsky David	414	"	22	90 W Newton
b	Clark Clifford	414	chef	35	Chester Vt
c	Clark Margaret—†	414	housewife	27	"
d	Ginn Theodore	414	salesman	60	here
e	Litman David	414	student	22	Chelsea
f	Locke Donald	414	chauffeur	22	103 Circuit
g	Locke Florence—†	414	housewife	23	103 "
h	Locke Paul	414	mechanic	28	103 "
k	Sison Modesto	414	student	29	Brookline
l	Stern John	414	"	22	21 Chambers
m	Walker William F	414	clerk	30	Sharon
n	White Paul	414	chauffeur	28	Lexington

Page	Letter	FULL NAME.	Residence, April 1, 1926.	Occupation.	Supposed Age.	Reported Residence, April 1, 1925. Street and Number.

Massachusetts Avenue—Continued

O	Dell Julia—†	415	seamstress	40	here
P	Fennessy Harry	415	butcher	30	"
R	Gaudel Henry	415	laborer	45	"
S	Hobson Clarence	415	student	20	"
T	Hobson Mary—†	415	housewife	45	"
U	Holbrook Stella—†	415	seamstress	50	"
V	McKennon Laukie	415	laborer	30	"
W	McMullen Mary—†	415	clerk	23	"
X	McMullen Maude—†	415	"	25	"
Y	DeYoung Gordon	416	mechanic	32	"
Z	Foley Mary—†	416	housekeeper	38	Lynn
A	Foley Norman	416	janitor	43	"
B	Gilligan Edward	416	chauffeur	24	35 Gray
C	Gilligan Eva—†	416	boxmaker	23	35 "
D	Gilligan Mary—†	416	clerk	26	353 Mass av
E	Gilligan William	416	chauffeur	25	353 "
F	Green Everett	416	foundryman	31	Readville
G	Gutterman Max	416	student	20	Brooklyn N Y
H	Johnson Austin	416	clerk	26	here
K	Johnson Dominick	416	painter	28	"
L	Johnson John	416	clerk	27	"
M	Johnson Rita—†	416	housekeeper	22	P E I
N	Havalier Harry	416	student	20	Brooklyn N Y
O	Marion Simon	416	"	22	"
P	Carey Charles J	417	clerk	35	here
R	Cooper Harry	417	manager	35	"
S	Daley John	417	molder	60	"
T	Hoak Raymond J	417	engineer	45	"
U	McDonald Percy	417	patternmaker	47	"
V	Quebec George M	417	barber	55	"
W	Quebec Helen A—†	417	housewife	53	"
X	Rolzhauser Bertha H—†	417	"	57	"
Y	Rolzhauser George F	417	machinist	57	
Z	Brown Royal	418	writer	26	Lebanon N H
A	Nickerson Harold A	418	draftsman	35	Buzzards Bay
B	O'Donnell Mary—†	418	nurse	30	New York
C	Solakian Esther—†	418	physician	50	here
D	Broome Lloyd	419	student	20	"
E	Cyr Valmond H	419	"	20	"
F	Favory Charles H	419	machinist	40	409 Mass av
G	Geary Edward	419	foreman	43	here

Massachusetts Avenue—Continued

H	Sampson Cornelius	419	waiter	22	23 St Germain
K	Shaunesy Mary—†	419	housewife	49	here
L	Yee Yuen	419A	laundryman	52	"
M	Bufford Delphis J	420	shoeworker	40	"
N	Bufford Winifred—†	420	"	36	"
O	Crowley Edyn F	420	steward	21	"
P	McMenimon John J	420	coremaker	38	672A Dudley
R	Portuoy Maurice S	420	student	22	New Bedford
S	Quint Henry F	420	retired	81	Worcester
T	Scott Ralph R	420	salesman	32	Dallas Tex
U	Whelpley Frederick	420	physician	50	here
V	Bohigas Nicholas	421	baker	28	"
W	Boras Charles	421	cook	28	"
X	Cobbeigh Herbert E	421	clerk	50	"
Y	Crawford Charles	421	"	67	"
Z	Crook Lealand	421	machinist	28	"
A	Gifford Ella E—†	421	housekeeper	62	"
B	Grenfell Nevalyn B—†	421	at home	40	"
C	Grenfell Walter E	421	carpenter	44	"
D	Nieh Anton	421	musician	24	"
E	Trott William J	421	barber	52	"
F	Berens Eleanor M—†	422	dancing teacher	60	"
G	Cutello Patrick	422	shoemaker	30	"
H	Dean Alice—†	422	housewife	26	Providence R I
K	Dean Thomas	422	chauffeur	30	"
L	Finneran Patrick J	422	instructor	50	here
M	Fogg Agnes—†	422	housekeeper	45	"
N	Gallagher Mary—†	422	dressmaker	40	423 Mass av
O	LaLeo Ralph E	422	waiter	26	New Bedford
P	LaLeo Rose—†	422	housewife	26	"
R	Ricker Edith—†	422	"	45	Andover
S	Ricker Gladys—†	422	clerk	22	"
T	Ricker Walter	422	plumber	45	"
U	Rodden Herbert T	422	chauffeur	42	Cambridge
V	Sparrow William S	422	tailor	50	here
W	Steele Mary G—†	422	factory worker	26	423 Mass av
Z	Goldstien Samuel	423	merchant	60	here
A	Hourahan Frank	423	actor	23	"
B	Hurley Mary—†	423	housewife	32	"
C	Marshall Donald	423	carpenter	24	"
D	Penalton Carl	423	engineer	27	"

25

Page.	Letter.	FULL NAME.	Residence, April 1, 1926.	Occupation.	Supposed Age.	Reported Residence, April 1, 1925. Street and Number.

Massachusetts Avenue—Continued

E	Ayer Abbie B—†	424	houseworker	70	here
F	Ayer Belle—†	424	"	74	"
G	Ayer Daniel W	424	engineer	66	"
H	Hoyt Ella F—†	424	houseworker	60	"
K	Burns Evelyn—†	425	clerk	22	"
L	Donavan Timothy	425	porter	28	"
M	Higginson Ralph	425	teamster	30	"
N	Hordan Clifford	425	chauffeur	30	"
O	Komier Lena—†	425	milliner	26	"
P	Laurence Catherine—†	425	dressmaker	39	"
R	Parmenter Eva J—†	425	housewife	48	"
S	Parmenter George	425	chauffeur	63	"
T	Perkins Harry	425	salesman	23	"
U	White Everett	425	laborer	42	"
W	Begley Jennie—†	426	clerk	24	342 Beacon
X	Buttler Lillian—†	426	"	27	30 Blue Hill av
Y	Carter Patrick	426	meatcutter	28	Medford
Z	Clyde Henry C	426	student	25	Brookline
A	Condon James	426	painter	51	Cambridge
B	Condon Mabel—†	426	housewife	50	"
C	Cram Gertrude M—†	426	corsetiere	49	here
D	Donovan Kenneth	426	laborer	24	New York City
E	Gormley Anna—†	426	waitress	37	Somerville
F	Hale James E	426	auto mechanic	37	here
G	McDonough William	426	glassmaker	38	"
H	McEllin John	426	boxmaker	42	Providence R I
K	McMahon Catherine—†	426	domestic	48	Brookline
L	VanDusen Charles	426	clerk	22	Barnstable
M	VanDusen Evelyn—†	426	housewife	20	"
N	Anderson Helen—†	427	clerk	35	here
O	Garret Charles	427	"	36	"
P	Hayes Clifford	427	laborer	36	"
R	Lewis James	427	salesman	27	"
U	Cloyd William	429	porter	40	"
V	Dandidge William	429	laborer	35	"
W	Doe Mabel—†	429	housewife	25	"
X	Doe Thomas	429	waiter	32	"
Y	Foster Jefferson	429	"	45	"
Z	Henry Ivan	429	"	36	"
A	Henry Ruby—†	429	housewife	34	"
B	Johnson Robert	429	laborer	32	"

Page.	Letter.	FULL NAME.	Residence, April 1, 1926.	Occupation.	Supposed Age.	Reported Residence, April 1, 1925. Street and Number.

Massachusetts Avenue—Continued

c	Jones John	429	chauffeur	28	here
d	Lee Robert E	429	bellman	60	"
e	McGluen John	429	laborer	30	"
f	Randolp John	429	waiter	60	"
g	Tally Margaret—†	429	housewife	30	"
h	Williamson Ernest	429	waiter	25	"
m	Ambrigo Antonio	431	machinist	30	"
n	Bruno Samuel	431	cook	25	"
o	McCarthy Anna—†	431	housewife	33	"
p	McDonald Arthur	431	laborer	25	"
r	McNeil Andrew	431	candymaker	24	"
s	McNeil Flora—†	431	housewife	50	"
t	Noel Felix	431	laborer	22	"
u	Robinson Anna—†	431	clerk	38	"
v	Robinson Frank	431	laborer	40	"
w	Schmidt Frank	431	baker	35	"
z	Hallett John E	433	pianist	66	"
a	Covitz Benjamin	433	jeweler	47	"
c	Malone Jennie—†	433	housekeeper	45	"
d	Patten Helen—†	433	housewife	45	"
e	Patten Richard W	433	salesman	43	"
f	Bowen Mary—†	433	housekeeper	45	"
g	McLaughlin Grace—†	433	housewife	46	Portland Me
h	McLaughlin Joseph	433	steamfitter	50	"
l	Brady Edward S	434	clerk	22	24 W Dedham
m	Mangan Andrew J	434	laborer	60	24 "
n	Sullivan Mary—†	434	houseworker	35	24 "
o	Thibault Lena—†	434	"	38	24 "
p	Hilderbrandt Max	434	cook	30	here
r	Lord Evelyn A—†	434	houseworker	74	"
s	Reed Evelyn A—†	434	"	44	"
t	Reed James H	434	laborer	55	"
u	Shaw Samuel	434	chauffeur	38	"
v	Walker Ambrose L	434	carpenter	62	"
w	Walker Winnie L—†	434	houseworker	60	"
x	DeSantis Louis A	434	clerk	26	Everett
y	Frazoli Albert	434	"	35	Quincy
z	Gilderbride Walter J	434	"	40	here
a	Gutman Sadie—†	434	houseworker	50	"
b	Hearn David A	434	clerk	40	"

Massachusetts Avenue—Continued

D	Bakurjian Harry	444	counterman	38	Somerville
E	Birmingham Francis	444	salesman	35	here
F	Campbell Percy	444	laborer	40	"
G	Cannon Michael	444	"	25	Malden
H	Coveney James	444	"	26	here
K	Grant William	444	ironworker	34	"
L	Harmond Valma —†	444	clerk	26	"
M	MacKay Margaret —†	444	houseworker	51	
N	Mangnello Eva †	444	clerk	26	Somerville
O	Newhall Eugene H	444	"	67	here
P	Barron Dorothy —†	446	"	25	84 Worcester
R	Boldue Wilfred	446	laborer	46	here
S	Brennan Clara—†	446	housewife	32	"
T	Brennan Frederick	446	laborer	39	"
U	Cranston Ernest W	446	chauffeur	32	"
V	Cranston Rebecca M —†	446	housewife	43	"
W	Gallant Arthur	446	shoeworker	28	"
X	Golden Josephine †	446	housewife	32	"
Y	Golden William H	446	laborer	35	"
Z	Lugrin Frank	446	"	35	Cambridge
A	Lyons James	446	salesman	35	705 Mass av
B	Malinguist Carl	446	painter	36	here
C	Morrilli John	446	salesman	32	675 Mass av
D	Morrilli Louise †	446	housewife	21	675 "
E	Shields Bertha †	446	"	31	Maine
F	Shields John	446	machinist	30	"
G	White Mary †	446	clerk	32	191 Warren av
H	White William	446	laborer	32	191 "
K	Garoyan Gaspard M	447	physician	38	here
L	Henrickson Oscar	447	mason	48	"
O	Baker Augusta —†	449	housewife	53	511 Col av
P	Baker Charles W	449	bookbinder	63	511 "
R	Berry Arthur	449	tel inspector	50	N Weymouth
S	Casey Thomas	449	restaurateur	55	7A Dalton
T	Cox Harry	449	plumber	35	Malden
U	Dikens Clifford	449	chauffeur	31	207 W Springfield
V	McMurrer May †	449	waitress	38	93 Pembroke
W	Balfe Mary A †	450	houseworker	40	here
X	Bolter Clovis A	450	jeweler	55	"
Y	Bolter Sadie M †	450	compositor	52	"
Z	Griffin Anna G †	450	bookkeeper	42	"

Massachusetts Avenue—Continued

A	Griffin Catherine F—†	450	clerk	44	here
B	VanBenshoten Florence—†	450	"	45	"
C	Walther Bertha—†	450	dressmaker	24	"
D	White Anna—†	450	clerk	30	"
E	Croke Joseph	451	mechanic	35	780 E Fourth
F	McCarthy Edward	451	chauffeur	40	556 Mass av
G	McCarthy Helen—†	451	housewife	26	556 "
H	Murphy Anna J—†	451	"	34	556 "
K	Murphy Daniel F	451	shoeworker	48	556 "
L	Sargent May—†	451	waitress	30	473 Cedar
M	Beaton Duncan E	453	manager	32	Lynn
N	Beaton Florrie M—†	453	housewife	22	New York
O	Knapp Laura—†	453	housekeeper	35	here
P	O'Brien James	453	salesman	33	266 Mass av
R	Thompson Joseph G	453	waiter	42	86 Chandler
S	Thompson Maude E—†	453	housewife	43	Cambridge
T	Toma Samuel	453	real estate	40	New York
U	Anderson Julia—†	454	dressmaker	55	here
V	Brennock Jennie—†	454	houseworker	55	"
W	Burns Mary—†	454	waitress	25	"
X	Byron Leo	454	laborer	34	33 Mt Pleasant av
Y	Byron Thomas	454	"	35	33 "
Y¹	Coste Marie G—†	454	housekeeper	39	here
Z	Counihan Elizabeth—†	454	clerk	32	"
A	Counihan Katherine—†	454	dressmaker	35	"
C	Creeran Mary—†	454	houseworker	66	"
D	Cross Mary A P—†	454	at home	80	"
E	Jacobs Harriet F—†	454	seamstress	71	"
F	Lebane Marie—†	454	dressmaker	68	"
G	Lee George	454	clerk	68	"
H	McCabe Margaret—†	454	bookkeeper	30	"
K	Welsh Anna—†	454	houseworker	73	"
L	Welsh Gwendolyne—†	454	clerk	40	"
M	Foote Helen—†	455	housewife	45	"
N	Foote Leverett	455	carpenter	50	"
O	Redding George	455	machinist	70	453 Mass av
P	Redding Louise—†	455	housekeeper	70	453 "
R	Richards Charles	455	manager	30	Cambridge
S	Small Mary—†	455	cashier	35	here
T	Webber Harry	455	real estate	40	"
U	Wendell Anna—†	455	saleswoman	25	New York

Page.	Letter.	Full Name.	Residence, April 1, 1926.	Occupation	Supposed Age.	Reported Residence, April 1, 1925. Street and Number.

Massachusetts Avenue—Continued

v	Boyanton James R	457	retired	73	here
w	Estabrook Herbert H	457	salesman	55	"
x	Laslle Lanphor D	457	publisher	60	Brookline
y	McIsaacs Margaret —†	457	waitress	60	here
z	Parks Marion L—†	457	housewife	57	"
A	Parks Winfield S	457	insurance agent	71	"
B	Delong Ella —†	458	at home	52	"
c	Goulart Jockeen	458	auto repairer	30	"
D	Goulart Joseph	458	patternmaker	39	"
E	Grant Maineland N	458	plumber	49	"
F	Holmes Kenneth	458	laborer	23	Nova Scotia
G	Jarvis Helen—†	458	at home	55	here
H	Jefferies Louis	458	cook	46	417 Mass av
K	MacMurray Frederick	458	salesman	46	1818 Wash'n
L	Marks Nicholas	458	nurse	38	here
M	McAndrews Beatrice —†	458	bookkeeper	24	"
N	McKay Leo	458	electrician	35	"
O	Mulleary Suzance —†	458	at home	45	Newport N H
P	Smith George	458	carpenter	40	12 Harvard
R	Dore Georgiana —†	459	dressmaker	52	here
S	Downey Beatrice M—†	459	housewife	31	"
T	Downey Margaret—†	459	clerk	28	"
U	Downey William J	459	broker	27	"
V	Wright Frank	459	boilermaker	21	"
W	Broderick Annie —†	460	housekeeper	42	"
X	Clay William	460	machinist	65	Lynn
Y	Gilis Walter	460	teamster	40	here
Z	Kelly James J	460	printer	53	Cambridge
A	Kennedy Edward	460	boilermaker	35	here
B	Kennedy Frances —†	460	at home	28	"
C	Mixer Katherine —†	460	waitress	32	"
D	Rich John	460	laborer	45	80 Intervale
E	Roberts Lucy—†	460	shoeworker	36	here
F	Rogers Jennie —†	460	at home	49	"
G	Rogers Melvin	460	automobiles	50	"
H	Summerside Minnie—†	460	dressmaker	70	"
K	Thomas Helen —†	460	real estate	37	"
L	Vicent Edward	460	chauffeur	26	"
M	Wells Uster	460	foreman	50	"
N	Andrews Steven	461	machinist	32	Lynn
O	Burke James F	461	salesman	22	here

Letter.	FULL NAME.	Residence, April 1, 1926.	Occupation	Supposed Age	Reported Residence, April 1, 1925. Street and Number.

Massachusetts Avenue—Continued

P	Lord Irene—†	461	shoeworker	26	Lynn
R	MacIntosh Colin	461	artist	69	Canada
S	MacIntosh Margaret—†	461	housekeeper	65	"
T	Shedd Herman H	461	musician	71	here
U	Shedd Lucy V—†	461	housekeeper	69	"
V	Smith George A	461	clerk	30	"
W	Tetunes Joseph	461	mattressmaker	30	4 Rutland
X	Thompson Florence—†	461	shoeworker	26	Stoneham
Y	Bennett Elizabeth—†	462	housekeeper	50	here
Z	Dodes Stephen	462	laborer	30	Lynn
A	Hall Bertha—†	462	stenographer	48	"
B	Hayes Donald	462	salesman	35	"
C	Houle Archie	462	counterman	22	"
D	Kashian Merias	462	auto repairer	45	
E	Kelly Florence—†	462	buyer	26	New York City
F	Partelow Mary—†	462	saleswoman	34	here
G	Rankin George	462	carpenter	52	Hudson N Y
H	Sheehan Robert	462	farmer	30	Concord
K	Sullivan Daniel	462	ballplayer	28	New Bedford
L	Veaulie Joseph	462	counterman	30	139 W Concord
M	Wolfe Clyde	462	laborer	28	Lynn
N	Young John D	462	cigarmaker	40	here
O	Carpenter George	463	waiter	25	475 Mass av
P	Clark Albert	463	machinist	40	749 Tremont
R	Deviney Delia—†	463	housekeeper	35	St Louis Mo
S	Kilby Dow	463	mechanic	40	64 Pembroke
T	Webber Harry	463	deckhand	35	43 Falmouth
U	Danridge Mary—†	464	at home	59	here
V	Esters Lillian—†	464	saleswoman	26	"
W	Fields Inez—†	464	lawyer	36	"
X	Cloutier Leo	465	chauffeur	29	"
Y	Gonnella Battista	465	waiter	44	"
Z	Joy Dorothy—†	465	nurse	35	Sydney N S
A	Marlow Bernard J	465	caretaker	43	here
B	McSweeney Ella G—†	465	housekeeper	32	493 Mass av
C	Morrill Harold	465	druggist	37	469 "
D	Murphy Margaret—†	465	nurse	30	here
E	Murphy Nellie—†	465	waitress	21	England
F	Potrin Arthur O	465	shoeworker	40	493 Mass av
G	Winslow Jennie E—†	465	housewife	45	here
H	Clara Herbert	466	compositor	35	"

31

Page.	Letter.	FULL NAME.	Residence, April 1, 1926.	Occupation.	Supposed Age.	Reported Residence, April 1, 1925. Street and Number.

Massachusetts Avenue—Continued

K	Daley Elizabeth—†	466	housekeeper	58	here
L	Daley George T	466	foreman	59	"
M	Hayes Matthew A	466	decorator	26	"
N	Hayes May—†	466	housewife	24	"
O	Hickey George N	466	motorman	45	"
P	Jordan Anna—†	466	cook	42	Biddeford Me
R	McCoart Frances—†	466	housewife	25	here
S	McCoart Raymond J	466	manager	34	"
T	McDonald John S	466	salesman	30	Medford
U	McHeffey William E	466	laborer	58	here
V	Merrill George W	466	farmer	72	Biddeford Me
W	Morarity James	466	tailor	35	"
X	Nudett Curtis	466	bookkeeper	'22	here
Y	Patterson Mary F—†	466	housewife	41	474 Mass av
Z	Patterson Robert	466	engineer	50	474 "
A	Price James J	466	counterman	21	Biddeford Me
B	Standish Harriet—†	466	dressmaker	37	514 Mass av
C	Warren Mary—†	466	pianoworker	40	here
D	Dregan Alice—†	467	clerk	40	"
E	Dregan Joseph	467	machinist	40	"
F	Gardener Harold	467	paperhanger	40	"
G	Glennon John	467	retired	64	52 Brook rd
H	Glennon John T	467	nurse	34	New London
K	Marvin Elizabeth—†	467	housekeeper	34	479 Mass av
L	Marvin Frances—†	467	saleswoman	33	479 "
M	Marvin Gertrude—†	467	housekeeper	67	479 "
N	Saunders Everett B	467	seaman	30	England
O	Whalen John A	467	shipper	49	138 W Concord
P	Whalen Mary L—†	467	housekeeper	50	138 "
R	Fiohl Claire—†	468	waitress	32	here
S	Fisher Louise—†	468	"	34	"
T	Lemere Edward	468	waiter	27	"
U	Shadrawy Agnes M—†	468	at home	27	"
V	Shadrawy John M	468	real estate	31	"
W	Smith Agnes—†	468	housewife	27	"
X	Alexsavitsch David	469	shoemaker	40	"
Y	Burke James F	469	salesman	58	"
Z	Buzzell Lena—†	469	dressmaker	35	"
A	Doherty John S	469	piano teacher	29	"
B	Doherty Nora T—†	469	housekeeper	58	"
C	Hall Alice—†	469	clerk	40	"

Page.	Letter.	Full Name.	Residence, April 1, 1926.	Occupation.	Supposed Age.	Reported Residence, April 1, 1925. Street and Number.

Massachusetts Avenue—Continued

D	Hogan James E	469	chauffeur	26	here
E	Jocelyn Walter	469	"	29	"
F	Sims Anna—†	469	waitress	29	"
G	Deplamer Edgar	470	chef	40	"
H	Johnson Edgar	470	agent	30	"
K	Johnson Josephine—†	470	at home	25	"
L	Keith Mary—†	470	"	60	"
M	Kimball Anna—†	470	"	43	25 Rockland
N	Kimball Joseph	470	teamster	45	25 "
O	Lockhart David W	470	carpet layer	42	here
P	Lockhart Loise—†	470	housekeeper	43	"
R	Mallary Mertle—†	470	clerk	24	"
S	Milne Daisy—†	470	bookkeeper	26	"
T	Milne Margaret—†	470	domestic	50	"
U	Moseley Anna—†	470	housewife	62	"
V	Moseley Willard C	470	meatcutter	56	31 E Springfield
W	Everett Alvin O	471	clerk	37	here
X	Foskett Leon	471	shoeworker	45	"
Y	Halcrow Guy	471	mechanic	24	"
Z	Kenner Fred	471	guard	56	"
A	Murphy George S	471	mechanic	29	"
B	Myers Anna—†	471	housekeeper	38	"
C	Wyman Gale	471	mechanic	30	Hartford Ct
D	Alton John	472	laborer	28	here
E	Chick George P	472	motorman	61	"
F	Dawes Helen—†	472	bookkeeper	39	"
G	Garritty Thomas	472	laborer	30	"
H	Goodwin William	472	"	39	"
K	Madden Edward	472	salesman	35	"
L	Mareille Mary—†	472	housekeeper	35	"
M	Norris Clara—†	472	dressmaker	39	"
N	Connors Ellen—†	473	waitress	44	Chelsea
O	Cummings Michael	473	meatcutter	26	here
P	Denieen Lawrence	473	blacksmith	55	"
R	Kelley Dennis	473	motorman	62	"
S	Kille Lawrence	473	foreman	21	"
T	Lenoard Charles R	473	salesman	30	"
U	Lenoard Edward	473	teamster	62	"
V	Lenoard Edward F	473	salesman	36	"
W	Lenoard John J	473	asbestos worker	38	"
X	Lenoard Maria—†	473	housekeeper	50	"

Massachusetts Avenue—Continued

Y	McGreavy Michael	473	policeman	57	here
z	McMannus Edward	473	auto washer	55	"
A	Meheen William	473	conductor	35	482 Mass av
B	O'Brien Joseph	473	auto washer	45	Whitman
c	O'Connor John	473	chauffeur	21	Needham
D	Shawnnessy John J	473	molder	57	here
E	Shawnnessy Joseph F	473	laborer	22	"
F	Connelly Anna—†	474	housekeeper	32	"
G	Connelly Michael	474	laborer	34	"
H	Ducan Thomas	474	painter	50	"
K	Elywood Lena—†	474	waitress	28	"
L	Hayward John	474	laborer	54	"
M	Hutchins Arthur	474	fireman	32	"
N	Marceau William	474	laborer	56	"
O	Marren Mary—†	474	clerk	34	"
P	Moore Agnes—†	474	"	27	"
R	Shorrock James	474	laborer	50	"
s	Sweeney Katherine—†	474	waitress	32	"
T	Brannegan Mary—†	475	housekeeper	60	"
U	Bunskneg Joseph	475	student	23	"
v	Coleman Daniel	475	contractor	49	"
w	Kromise Paul	475	student	23	"
X	McLaughlin Patrick	475	shipper	35	"
Y	Monto Jack	475	student	24	"
z	Stokes Emily—†	475	clerk	60	"
A	Cheeks Alan D	476	dentist	52	
B	Clayton Willard L	476	clergyman	27	Cambridge
c	Handy Alma—†	476	housewife	27	here
D	Handy Nathaniel	476	postal clerk	22	"
E	Lewis David S	476	porter	44	"
F	McCormick Mildred—†	476	domestic	25	"
G	Swan Louis	476	postal clerk	27	"
H	Swan Ruby—†	476	hairdresser	27	"
K	Wilbert Maud—†	476	dressmaker	29	"
L	Anderson Elmer	477	engineer	58	"
M	Fraser Grace—†	477	waitress	21	35 Worcester
N	Hawes Robert	477	painter	45	here
O	Jackson Josephine—†	477	clerk	40	"
P	Jaris Lena—†	477	housekeeper	37	"
R	Lowell Clarence	477	chauffeur	42	"
s	Minnish Starrett	477	fireman	42	501 Col av

Letter	FULL NAME.	Residence, April 1, 1926.	Occupation.	Supposed Age.	Reported Residence, April 1, 1925. Street and Number.

Massachusetts Avenue—Continued

T	Parker Christian—†	477	housekeeper	80	Quincy
U	Parker Frederick	477	laborer	65	"
V	Pinkham Edith—†	477	bookkeeper	32	here
W	Lutek Julia—†	478	at home	31	Lynn
X	Lutek Micheal	478	painter	32	"
Y	Hunter Reta B—†	478	laundress	40	here
Z	Murphy Winefred—†	478	teacher	32	Lowell
A	Coleman Catherine S—†	478	at home	42	594 Tremont
B	Coleman Walter S	478	teamster	39	594 "
C	Winthrop Frank	478	teacher	32	here
D	Winthrop Stella—†	478	"	30	"
E	Bramman Mildred—†	479	social worker	24	New Britain Ct
F	DuPont Grace—†	479	tel operator	23	55 Mass av
G	Fifield William H	479	salesman	50	582 "
H	Gannon Edmund H	479	student	21	Connecticut
K	Golden Daniel L	479	retired	69	"
L	Golden Helen—†	479	housekeeper	38	"
M	MacCrae George	479	carpenter	30	Readville
N	MacCrae John	479	laborer	29	"
O	MacLaughlin Emily—†	479	clerk	21	Maine
P	Nichols Emma—†	479	"	44	582 Mass av
R	Reynolds Walter	479	"	26	Lawrence
S	St Onge Emma—†	479	"	31	21 Rutland sq
T	Thorpe Mary—†	479	tel operator	24	555 Mass av
U	Withan Cora—†	479	clerk	23	Maine
V	Balwin John	480	engineer	50	here
W	Hastings Ethel—†	480	saleswoman	40	"
X	Healey Mary—†	480	at home	40	"
Y	Lyons Ethel—†	480	clerk	35	"
Z	York George W	480	"	52	"
A	York Lennie—†	480	housekeeper	50	"
B	Anderson Carl	482	laborer	27	159 Warren av
C	Brawn Florence—†	482	clerk	21	Quincy
D	Dykins Ralph	482	foreman	32	1271 Col av
E	Mullen John	482	laborer	24	40 Chandler
F	Parker Sadie	482	clerk	25	128 Hanover
G	Reddy Margaret—†	482	houseworker	40	here
H	Salmone Ellen—†	482	housekeeper	37	99 Norway
K	Wooden Richard	482	laborer	20	Maine
L	Wooden Richard S	482	"	50	"
M	Bruce Lillian—†	483	clerk	25	Nova Scotia

35

Massachusetts Avenue—Continued

N	Cederblad Oscar	483	machinist	40	here
O	Craig James P	483	laborer	34	"
P	Dulois Peter	483	waiter	40	"
R	Gordon Augusta †	483	clerk	29	"
S	Grass Louis	483	laborer	37	98 Lenox
T	Hamilton James B	483	waiter	34	26 Milford
U	Hermlund Herman	483	machinist	35	here
V	Leach Katherine †	483	housekeeper	68	"
W	Leach Louise †	483	"	33	"
X	MacCecola George	483	conductor	25	31 Worcester
Y	MacDonald Daniel	483	carpenter	55	here
Z	Smith George	483	plumber	24	"
A	Aulhrturn John	484	polisher	61	"
B	Graham Robert	484	clerk	28	"
C	Jame Kerey	484	machinist	60	548 Mass av
D	Johnson Sven	484	polisher	50	here
E	McMaster Emma L †	484	housekeeper	53	"
F	McMaster Robert	484	chef	57	"
G	Meredith James	484	teacher	61	"
K	Beaudoin Richard	486	manager	21	"
L	Dilis Adrien F	486	cigarmaker	48	"
M	Dilis Elise †	486	housewife	48	"
N	Feeney Frank J	486	laborer	58	"
O	Ickroth Cornelius	486	cigarmaker	52	"
P	Kelley Anna †	486	saleswoman	37	"
R	Kerins James J	486	machinist	23	Salem
S	McLellan Daniel	486	laborer	56	Maine
T	Murphy James E	486	electrician	27	here
U	Murray Ruth †	486	clerk	27	Salem
V	Norberg Carl E	486	machinist	23	518 Shawmut av
W	Petitto John	486	barber	60	518 "
X	Smart George A	486	salesman	46	here
Y	Smith William J	486	merchant	41	Oregon
Z	Smith Winfred J †	486	housewife	42	"
A	Williams Carl	486	machinist	21	518 Shawmut av
B	Ajemian Rose †	487	housekeeper	28	New York
C	Ajemian Lempet	487	tailor	40	"
D	Cady Charles	487	chauffeur	35	here
E	Chausse Anna †	487	bookkeeper	32	"
F	Currier Anna †	487	waitress	30	"
G	Flanagan James	487	laborer	43	"

Massachusetts Avenue—Continued

H	Hickey Maurice	487	laborer	52	here
K	Hickey Michael	487	"	38	"
L	Murphy Jeremiah	487	"	38	"
M	Tebreault Charles	487	"	62	
N	Young Agnes—†	487	waitress	34	"
O	Bizzozew Florence M—†	491	"	22	"
P	Duffey Robert J	491	patternmaker	27	"
R	Feeley John J	491	clerk	30	"
S	Griffin John	491	watchman	81	"
T	Griffin William	491	clerk	39	"
U	Gross Sanford	491	barber	36	"
V	Hughes Lydia—†	491	waitress	33	"
W	Hughes Millard	491	jockey	31	"
X	Lothrope Gus H	491	musician	23	"
Y	Mulvey Adeline M—†	491	clerk	24	"
Z	Pelletier Jean B	491	janitor	51	"
A	Ruzzanenti Catherine—†	491	housekeeper	29	43 Falmouth
B	Ruzzanenti Joseph	491	painter	41	43 "
C	Toms Richard	491	clergyman	72	here
E	MacCallan Betty—†	493	housekeeper	35	"
F	Gray Frederick	493	dentist	23	18 Westford
G	Brownell Byron L	493	millwright	43	here
H	Brownell Margaret L—†	493	housekeeper	31	"
K	Bondi Gus	493	laborer	21	236 Hanover
L	Clattenburg Gertrude—†	493	housekeeper	35	678 Tremont
M	Clattenburg John E	493	machinist	39	678 "
N	McBride Catherine—†	493	housekeeper	31	here
O	McBride Thomas	493	clerk	30	"
P	Bolio Arthur	493	lineman	26	300 Col av
R	Bolio Ella—†	493	housekeeper	40	300 "
V	O'Connor Helen—†	496	"	62	141 Concord
W	Babine Rose—†	496	dressmaker	55	here
X	Bergin Harry	496	metalworker	38	Cambridge
Y	Dempsey Harold	496	foreman	30	here
Z	McClelland Joseph	496	cigarmaker	41	New Hampshire
A	O'Conner John J	496	secretary	48	141 W Concord
B	O'Conner Thomas A	496	bookkeeper	43	141 "
C	Clingan Samuel R	496	salesman	34	here
D	Morin Grace D—†	496	houseworker	40	"
E	Morin William O	496	manager	45	"

Page.	Letter.	FULL NAME.	Residence, April 1, 1926.	Occupation.	Supposed Age.	Reported Residence, April 1, 1925. Street and Number.

Massachusetts Avenue—Continued

	F	Oberg Carl	496	foreman	50	here
	G	Dann George E	496	shadehanger	53	"
	H	Dann Harriet A — †	496	stenographer	60	"
	K	Morrison Alice F— †	496	nurse	65	107 College av
	L	Robinson Arthur G	496	stablekeeper	66	455 Col av
	M	Robinson Margaret C—†	496	housewife	64	455 "
	N	Andrews Gertrude— †	496	milliner	44	here
	O	Morse Anna— †	496	inspector	25	13 Concord sq
	P	Morse Charles	496	foreman	27	13 "
	R	Rich Irma A— †	496	secretary	39	here
	S	Jordan Anna— †	496	clerk	45	833 Beacon
	T	Jordan William K	496	steward	48	833 "
	U	Farr Sarah M— †	496	housekeeper	74	here
	V	Manson Ida M—†	496	"	61	"
	W	Abbett Bernard O	496	paperhanger	50	137 Hutchings
	X	Dorsey Mary—†	496	matron	40	137 "
	Y	Jameson Josephine—†	496	cashier	29	137 "
	Z	O'Connor Margaret—†	496	housewife	46	137 "
	A	Thompson Ernest R	496	motorman	31	137 "
	B	Morrell Rita— †	496	candymaker	22	Maine
	C	Russell Margaret E—†	406	nurse	50	here
	D	Shepard Marie B—†	496	dressmaker	51	"
	E	Higgins Daniel R	496	supervisor	41	"
	F	Lee Harold P	496	salesman	21	Hallowell Me
	G	Turner John K	496	investigator	23	"
	H	Wolff Ellen—†	496	housewife	64	here
	K	Wolff Frank J	496	janitor	70	"

Northampton Street

	K	Adams Nelson L	363	laborer	49	here
	L	DeLeon Albert	363	porter	52	"
	M	Jarratt Homer C	365	real estate	36	"
	N	Lewis Pleasant S	365	waiter	66	"
	O	Tumstall Alexander	365	porter	54	"
	P	Tumstell Lulu B—†	365	domestic	39	"
	R	Bateum William	367	retired	75	"
	S	Ford James	367	laborer	30	Georgia
	T	Lanoe Louise—†	367	housewife	41	here
	U	Miller Fannie—†	367	houseworker	50	Pennsylvania

33

Page.	Letter.	FULL NAME.	Residence, April 1, 1926.	Occupation.	Supposed Age.	Reported Residence, April 1, 1925. Street and Number.

Northampton Street—Continued

	v	Williams Oscar	367	laborer	42	here
	w	Wise Alyisha—†	367	houseworker	35	Pennsylvania
	x	Wise William	367	chauffeur	35	"
	y	Grant William	369	musician	25	Missouri
	z	Towns Rose—†	369	housewife	36	15 Dilworth
	A	Towns William	369	waiter	42	15 "
	B	Taylor Annie R—†	371	housewife	53	here
	c	Taylor Sykes	371	clerk	51	"
	D	Cole Elane—†	371	housewife	30	"
	E	Wisdom Lettia—†	371	houseworker	58	"
	G	Hitchinson Hannah C—†	373	housekeeper	66	"
	H	Hutchinson Rosa M—†	373	"	37	"
	K	Hutchinson Samuel B	373	student	28	"
	L	Larkins Maria H—†	373	housekeeper	86	"
	M	Barbee James E	375	laborer	25	"
	N	Campbell John	375	cook	70	"
	O	Ferguson Mabel G—†	375	dressmaker	26	384 Northampton
	P	Fitchett Mary—†	375	"	38	here
	R	Scott Nathaniel	375	student	24	"
	s	Vickers George	375	clerk	21	"
	T	Beckman Mabel—†	377	maid	42	"
	U	Carter Delia—†	377	"	50	"
	v	Harriston Jesse	377	student	24	"
	w	Johnson Catherine—†	377	maid	45	386 Northampton
	x	Waters Joseph B	377	porter	65	here
	y	Waters Rosenah—†	377	housewife	51	"
	z	Gibbs Louis	379	laborer	23	"
	A	Gibbs William	379	"	52	"
	B	Smith Alexander	379	"	36	26 Wellington
	c	Bell Elijah	381	"	23	here
	D	Manning Jane—†	381	domestic	60	"
	E	White Anna E—†	381	housewife	45	"
	F	White John W	381	clergyman	63	"
	G	Woods Della—†	383	nurse	38	"
	H	Woods Maceo	383	waiter	31	"
	K	Deans Alvin	384	baker	32	Connecticut
	L	Deans Annie—†	384	housewife	24	"
	M	Desmond Arthur J	384	laborer	49	83 Williams
	N	Desmond Catherine—†	384	domestic	31	83 "
	O	Nickols John	384	pedler	28	here
	P	Lee John	385	laborer	56	"

Page.	Letter.	FULL NAME.	Residence, April 1, 1926.	Occupation.	Supposed Age.	Reported Residence, April 1, 1925. Street and Number.

Northampton Street—Continued

	R	Lee Mattie—†	385	housewife	40	here
	S	Johnson Russell S	386	fireman	48	"
	T	Johnson Theresa B—†	386	housewife	36	"
	U	Denbey Martha—†	386	cook	32	"
	V	Bush Aubrey C	386	waiter	41	"
	W	White Joseph T	386	"	41	"
	X	Batchelder Augusta—†	387	housewife	67	"
	Y	Harris Eliza—†	387	matron	40	"
	Z	Hoskins Richard	387	student	40	"
	B	Harris Mary—†	389	houseworker	34	N Carolina
	C	Morris Bertha—†	389	waitress	23	15 Braddock pk
	D	Jones Charles T	389	tailor	34	here
	E	Jones Lillian—†	389	matron	29	"
	F	Randall Elmer	389	waiter	33	"
	H	Doby Preston	391	foreman	41	"
	K	Johnson Frank H	391	teamster	54	"
	L	Keene Sadie—†	391	shipper	27	"
	M	King Beverly	391	chauffeur	30	29 Williams
	N	Wren Ida L—†	391	student	24	here
	O	Peters Agnes—†	392	housewife	34	384 Northampton
	P	Peters George	392	laborer	39	384 "
	R	Faircloud Jestine—†	392	cook	40	here
	S	Gretter Braxton	392	butler	44	"
	T	Gretter Elvia—†	392	housewife	48	"
	U	Bullock Luke	392	laborer	44	"
	V	Bullock Lulu—†	392	housewife	37	"
	W	Brnach George	393	baker	50	"
	X	Briggs Cornelius	393	waiter	50	"
	Y	Briggs Luella—†	393	housewife	49	"
	Z	Usher Lucille—†	393	nurse	26	Kansas
	A	Mills Dorothy—†	394	domestic	27	here
	B	Mills Rufus	394	chef	28	"
	C	Mills Sylvester	394	"	28	"
	D	Alston Emma—†	394	houseworker	50	"
	E	Lovell Malvina—†	394	"	34	"
	F	Foot Earnest	394	porter	44	"
	G	Foot Frances—†	394	housewife	40	"
	H	Richardson Charles B	395	shipper	39	"
	K	Richardson Sarah A—†	395	housewife	65	"
	L	Smite George	395	waiter	25	"
	M	Kalis Irene—†	396	at home	55	"

Page.	Letter.	Full Name.	Residence, April 1, 1926.	Occupation.	Supposed Age.	Reported Residence, April 1, 1925. Street and Number.

Northampton Street—Continued

	Letter	Full Name	Res.	Occupation	Age	Reported Residence
	N	Kalis Manuel	396	cook	27	here
	O	Kulukutas Sophia—†	396	housekeeper	33	"
	P	Kulukutas William	396	cook	33	"
	R	Bowen Guy	396	auto washer	45	"
	S	Bowen Helen—†	396	waitress	21	"
	T	Bowen Mary—†	396	housekeeper	22	"
	U	Bowen Ray	396	contractor	25	"
	V	George John E	396	mechanic	36	"
	W	Richardson Anna —†	396	at home	60	Revere
	X	Virgin Bertha—†	396	housekeeper	44	here
	Z	Garib Favronei—†	396	dressmaker	45	"
	A	Garib George—†	396	elevatorman	46	"
	B	Zimmer George E	396	painter	58	"
	C	Zimmer Isabel C F—†	396	housewife	72	"
	E	Coulanes James	396	shoemaker	45	"
	F	Coulanes Nora—†	396	clerk	45	"
	G	Coulanes Peter	396	retired	48	"
	H	Mavryanis Mary —†	396	housekeeper	49	"
	K	Mavryanis Peter	396	cook	45	"
	L	Arven Anna E—†	396	housekeeper	29	"
	M	Arven David H	396	salesman	31	"
	N	Burtt Gertrude I—†	396	clerk	20	"
	O	Burtt Katherine J—†	396	cashier	62	"
	P	Morris Evelyn—†	396	waitress	24	Brookline
	R	Kaidas Amary—†	396	housekeeper	65	617 Harris'n av
	S	Kaidas Mary—†	396	stitcher	20	617 "
	T	Kaidas William	396	waiter	26	617 "
	U	Goode Ignatius J	396	machinist	62	here
	V	Grendell Dorothy—†	396	housekeeper	37	"
	W	Balkanas Arthur	396	provisions	28	"
	X	Balkanas Nicholas	396	bootblack	32	"
	Y	Gianacopoulos Constantina—†	396	housekeeper	30	"
	Z	Gianacopoulos James	396	counterman	31	"
	A	Finn Alice —†	396	stitcher	21	Lowell
	B	Finn John	396	counterman	23	"
	C	Pappas Charles H	396	cook	31	here
	D	Pappas Elizabeth—†	396	housekeeper	31	"
	E	Giaconmakis Michel E—†	396	cook	36	"
	F	Rempelokis Caliopi—†	396	housekeeper	30	"
	G	Rempelokis Nicholas	396	cook	30	"
	H	Mitchell Anthony	396	counterman	32	"

Page.	Letter.	FULL NAME.	Residence, April 1, 1926.	Occupation.	Supposed Age.	Reported Residence, April 1, 1925. Street and Number.

Northampton Street—Continued

K	Mitchell Christina—†	396	housekeeper	20	New Hampshire
L	Primis Esther—†	396	"	26	Somersworth
M	Primis John	396	cook	30	Somerville
N	Kouyias Harry	396	shoe repairer	32	here
O	Kouyias Pota—†	396	housekeeper	32	"
P	Paraskezas John	396	counterman	38	"
R	Paraskezas Mary—†	396	housekeeper	31	"
S	Geanopulos Sotreos	396	fruit	53	15 Mechanic
T	Geanopulos Virginia—†	396	housekeeper	36	15 "
U	Steuropoulos Christopher	396	fruit	33	15 "
V	Steuropoulos Mary—†	396	housekeeper	20	15 "
W	Carey Charles A	396	steamfitter	34	532 Mass av
X	Carey Jane M—†	396	housekeeper	37	532 "
Y	Karis Bella—†	396	"	27	31 Juniper
Z	Karis Steve	396	bootblack	30	31 "
A	Boutoulakis Irene—†	396	housekeeper	32	435 Col av
B	Boutoulakis John	396	cook	37	435 "
C	Barlas Denitra—†	396	housekeeper	23	here
D	Barlas George	396	waiter	33	"
E	Kelley Thomas D	396	mechanic	56	"
F	McNally Christopher	396	janitor	33	"
G	McNally John W	396	porter	40	"
H	Mitchell Jane—†	396	housekeeper	38	"
K	Mitchell William A	396	steward	39	"
L	Kaya Alexander	396	laborer	26	"
M	Kondailes Valentine	396	waiter	25	"
N	Pappas Anastasia—†	396	housekeeper	60	"
O	Pappas Nicholas	396	retired	74	"
P	Pappas Paul	396	druggist	25	"
R	Panos Helen—†	396	housekeeper	58	8 Ivanhoe
S	Panos Romeo	396	fruit	23	8 "
U	Jomides Aristides	396	"	40	4 E Dedham
V	Jomides Evrobe—†	396	housekeeper	38	4 "
W	Pasco Anna—†	396	"	46	here
X	Pasco Elizabeth—†	396	clerk	21	"
Y	Pasco Nicholas	396	bootblack	53	"
Z	Poulos George	396	waiter	45	"
A	Poulos Sophia—†	396	housekeeper	26	"
B	Kantelis Constantina—†	396	"	26	"
C	Kantelis James I	396	fruit	36	"

Page.	Letter.	FULL NAME.	Residence, April 1, 1926.	Occupation.	Supposed Age.	Reported Residence, April 1, 1925. Street and Number.

Northampton Street—Continued

D	Larkin Clifford V	396	engineer	43	here
E	Larkin Fannie P—†	396	housekeeper	50	"
F	Kountanis George	396	newspaperman	44	"
G	Pasco Daniel	396	bootblack	41	"
H	Pasco Nicoletta—†	396	housekeeper	37	"
L	Stamatello George	396	clerk	20	"
K	Stamatello Harry	396	investigator	24	"
M	Stamatello Ida—†	396	housewife	47	"
N	Stamatello Stamatios E	396	grocer	58	"
O	Stamatello Alexandria—†	396	laundryworker	60	"
P	Stamatello Apostolos	396	laundryman	55	"
R	Stamatello Emorfia—†	396	laundryworker	55	"
S	Carris James	396	fruit	44	"
T	Carris Jane—†	396	housekeeper	31	"
V	Crowell Edward T	396	brushmaker	45	"
W	Crowell Helen F—†	396	housekeeper	43	"
X	Lawson Margaret C—†	396	waitress	38	"
Y	Bean Irving H	396	bricklayer	34	"
Z	Demos George	396	confectioner	25	"
A	Pozes Alexandria—†	396	housekeeper	30	"
B	Pozes Irene—†	396	cashier	22	"
C	Pozes Peter	396	confectioner	44	"
F	Geracoulis Aristra—†	396	housekeeper	45	"
G	Geracoulis Victor	396	restaurateur	28	"
H	Govostes Elizabeth—†	396	laundryworker	52	20 Bickerstaff
K	Govostes Peter C	396	retired	62	20 "
L	Eastman John J	396	manager	59	here
M	Adams Anna E—†	396	housewife	41	"
N	Cotter John J	396	truckman	39	"
O	Ball Charles C	397	student	21	"
P	Ball Charles H	397	laborer	50	"
R	Ball Louise J—†	397	housewife	43	"
S	Strong Robert	397	houseman	28	174 W Springfield
T	Bailey John F	399	elevatorman	25	here
U	Bailey Mary A—†	399	housewife	62	"
V	Bailey Robert H, jr	399	laborer	27	"
W	Bailey Robert H	399	painter	65	"
X	Bailey William G	399	laborer	29	"

Page	Letter	FULL NAME.	Residence, April 1, 1926	Occupation	Supposed Age.	Reported Residence, April 1, 1925. Street and Number.

Tremont Street

z	Coggeshall Mary—†	765	operator	51	479 Mass av
A	DeFiore Frank	765	barber	40	233 Chelsea
B	Little John	765	machinist	45	479 Mass av
c	Seaman Elizabeth—†	765	housekeeper	37	479 "
D	Attaya John	765	waiter	22	Concord N H
E	Attayer Mary—†	765	waitress	21	"
F	Blok Leonard	765	expressman	22	47 Woodlawn
G	Blok Louise—†	765	housewife	23	43 W Newton
H	Fraser Frederick	765	hotel clerk	30	Ludlow
K	Fraser Mary—†	765	housewife	26	"
L	Willet Agnes—†	765	"	25	here
M	Willet Leo H	765	manager	30	"
N	Biggs Frank	767	printer	34	New York
O	Biggs Margaret—†	767	operator	24	Lynn
P	Biggs Maria—†	767	"	31	New York
R	Biggs Robert	767	chauffeur	24	Lynn
S	Doran Elizabeth—†	767	brushmaker	26	Bangor Me
T	Gallagher James	767	counterman	32	Portland Me
U	Gillogly George	767	brakeman	39	New York
V	Gillogly Jessie—†	767	housewife	22	"
W	Kneeland Elsie—†	767	waitress	29	Haverhill
X	Mahoney John	767	cook	24	New York
Y	Messier Ida—†	767	housekeeper	44	here
Z	Ring Irene C—†	767	secretary	21	"
A	Ring William W	767	teamster	46	"
B	Walker Albert	767	cook	40	"
C	Laba Joseph	769	shoemaker	26	251 Springfield
D	Shadrawy Terry M	769	manager	24	Cambridge
E	Festal August	769	baker	38	here
F	Festal Marie—†	769	housewife	38	"
G	Chadbourne Alice—†	769	"	40	Randolph
H	Chadbourne Harold	769	clerk	39	"
K	Cobb Thomas	771	painter	35	179 W Springfield
L	Costopolus Nicholas	771	elevatorman	28	here
M	Cusson Albert	771	clerk	25	New Hampshire
N	Dunning James	771	"	44	here
O	Goodwin Hollis	771	cashier	42	"
P	Marcel Juliette—†	771	waitress	22	548 Tremont
R	Morris Charles	771	packer	45	here
S	Richardson Chester	771	chauffeur	36	773 Tremont

Page.	Letter.	Full Name.	Residence, April 1, 1926.	Occupation.	Supposed Age.	Reported Residence, April 1, 1925. Street and Number.

Tremont Street—Continued

	T	Sharron John L	771	carpenter	38	here
	U	Sharron Mary E—†	771	housewife	44	"
	V	Virgilius Sebastian	771	gardener	32	Medford
	X	Barber Jennie—†	773	waitress	28	Scituate
	Y	Burns Mary—†	773	housewife	28	Malden
	Z	Burns William	773	chauffeur	32	"
	A	Doyle Joseph	773	machinist	44	Detroit Mich
	B	Erickson Frederick	773	clerk	32	Maine
	C	Hickey Lillian—†	773	waitress	35	25 Dartmouth
	D	Kolcoy George	773	cook	28	Lowell
	E	Lavis Charles J	773	chauffeur	38	153 W Newton
	F	Law Eleanor—†	773	waitress	32	153 "
	G	Watt John R	773	hostler	48	25 Dartmouth
	H	Carlson John	775	tailor	39	California
	K	Dexter Rowena—†	775	cook	31	Falmouth
	L	Dugas Albert	775	glazier	30	California
	M	Ferguson Harold	775	chauffeur	22	here
	N	Flaherty Leona—†	775	tel operator	21	21 Haviland
	O	Foster Alfred	775	paperhanger	60	here
	P	Hanson Harry	775	engineer	45	472 Mass av
	R	Keating Annie—†	775	waitress	28	384 Blue Hill av
	S	Markley John J	775	engineer	33	81 Westland av
	T	McDonald Marie—†	775	housekeeper	37	397 Warren
	U	Pantajopolis Arthur	775	retired	35	Canton
	V	Zieck John	775	clerk	32	Rumford Me
	X	Bisbee Ernest S	777	physician	45	here
	Y	Kent Mary A—†	777	housekeeper	50	"
	Z	Kent Mary E—†	777	bookkeeper	26	"

Wellington Street

	E	Valentine Ida M—†	2	housewife	45	683 Tremont
	F	Valentine John B	2	salesman	46	683 "
	G	Taylor Edward E	2	messenger	29	11½ Greenwich pk
	H	Taylor Lillian M—†	2	housewife	30	11½ "
	K	Tuttle George	2	porter	50	here
	L	Rafuse Edith—†	2	busher	38	"
	M	Paine Albert	2	salesman	52	"
	N	Paine Mary—†	2	housewife	52	"
	O	Cook Alice G—†	2	waitress	61	"

45

Page.	Letter.	FULL NAME	Residence, April 1, 1926.	Occupation.	Supposed Age.	Reported Residence, April 1, 1925. Street and Number.

Wellington Street—Continued

R	Larson John W	2	pianoworker	30	here
S	Gaines Ada L—†	2A	housewife	51	"
T	Gaines Jacob S	2A	caterer	55	"
U	Hogan Leon J	2A	student	30	"
V	Howell Ada S—†	2A	dressmaker	41	24 Claremont pk
W	Browne Ethel L—†	2A	housewife	43	here
X	Browne Robert P	2A	steward	40	"
Y	Garrett Eliza—†	2A	housewife	52	"
Z	Garrett Louis	2A	janitor	64	"
A	Garrett Margaret—†	2A	clerk	25	"
B	Garrett Thedoro	2A	laborer	23	"
C	Hill Bertha—†	2A	housewife	39	"
D	Hill Charles W	2A	clerk	40	"
E	Littleton Dorothy—†	2A	teacher	23	"
F	Evans Annie E—†	4	housewife	30	"
G	Evans William H	4	porter	59	"
H	Martin John R	4	waiter	40	"
K	Smith Bruce W	4	"	50	"
L	Winslow William	4	caretaker	50	"
M	Wood Alexander	4	waiter	58	"
N	Merritive John	6	porter	25	S Carolina
O	Sherrier Charles	6	waiter	70	Everett
P	Sydnor Edmund F	6	porter	50	here
R	Sydnor Marie—†	6	housewife	36	"
S	Edwards James	8	cook	35	8 Moreland
T	Foster Cellie E	8	barber	43	here
U	Griffin Mattie—†	8	housekeeper	28	8 Moreland
V	Horton Eunice—†	8	housewife	25	8 "
W	Horton Waldo B	8	policeman	29	8 "
X	McDonell Frederick	8	janitor	37	here
Y	Perkins Eliza C—†	8	laundress	47	"
A	Johnson Florence E—†	12	nurse	30	"
B	Woodruff John	12	porter	30	981 Tremont
C	Woodruff Maud—†	12	housewife	22	239 Northampton
D	Crawford Helen F—†	14	teacher	27	here
E	Crawford Joshua W	14	bail commiss'r	31	"
F	Crawford Mary—†	14	teacher	25	"
G	Crawford Mildred F—†	14	housewife	28	"
H	Wade Arthur W	14	real estate	29	"
K	Wade Mildred L—†	14	housewife	29	"
M	Forbes Elizabeth A—†	18	housekeeper	50	"

Wellington Street—Continued

N	Forbes George W	18	clerk	60	here
O	Westmoreland Isaac C	18	"	40	16 Wellington
P	Westmoreland Marion S–†	18	teacher	30	16 "
R	Browne George W	20	laborer	53	here
S	Browne Henrietta—†	20	housewife	43	"
T	Goodwin Eugene	20	porter	20	"
W	Jackson Burkie—†	22	housewife	36	Fall River
X	Roberson Evylyn—†	22	operator	27	1132 Tremont
Y	Parker Betty L—†	22	housewife	27	20 Wellington
Z	Parker William A	22	porter	34	20 "
A	Barrett Katherine—†	24	housekeeper	38	884 Harris'n av
B	Barrett William	24	casketmaker	23	here
C	Gilmore Theresa—†	24	housewife	39	"
D	Gilmore Timothy	24	chauffeur	43	"
F	Daniels Kitty—†	26	housewife	66	"
G	Moore Walter W	26	cook	40	"
H	Rice Ada—†	26	housekeeper	45	"
K	Wallis Ingraham	26	laborer	45	Everett
L	Jones David D	26	waiter	41	here
M	Jones Jeannette W—†	26	housekeeper	25	"
N	Bourghe Minnie— †	26	houseworker	44	14 Dillworth
O	Millett Alciba	26	waiter	38	295 Col av
P	Page Oscar	26	cook	48	here
R	Booker George	26	waiter	40	"
S	Dickinson Calvin C	26	chauffeur	41	"
T	Dickinson Viola—†	26	housewife	39	"
U	Johnson Edward M	26	elevatorman	27	"
V	Gibson Eugene	32	porter	40	"
W	Jackson William	32	waiter	40	"
X	Mewsome George	32	barber	41	"
X¹	Chin Bow	32	cook	32	"
Y	Haskell George T	32	merchant	28	"
Z	Mon Sectoo	32	waiter	31	"
A	Quan Bow	32	cook	40	"
B	Quan Sing	32	"	32	"
C	Quan Wow	32	"	25	"
D	Gill Florence—†	32	housekeeper	38	"
E	Lewis Margaret—†	32	cook	40	"
F	Melton Joseph M	32	agent	32	"
G	Melton William S	32	porter	34	"
H	Perry Charles W	32	chef	62	123 Warwick

Page.	Letter.	FULL NAME.	Residence, April 1, 1926.	Occupation.	Supposed Age.	Reported Residence, April 1, 1925. Street and Number.

Wellington Street—Continued

	K	Perry Emma—†	32	housewife	49	123 Warwick
	L	Marshall Lillian—†	32	housekeeper	35	here
	M	Broady Charles	32	clerk	33	"
	N	Jeffey Sophie—†	32	housekeeper	40	781 Shawmut av
	O	Keirney David	32	porter	39	799 Tremont
	P	McCoy Margaret—†	32	housekeeper	30	799 "
	R	Coblins Peyton	32	manager	25	78 W Rutland sq
	S	Cooper Turner D	32	waiter	38	here
	T	Walker Olive F	32	chauffeur	35	"
	U	Chiaaris Albert	32	waiter	33	"
	V	Maletskos John C	32	"	42	"
	W	Melsinis George	32	"	30	"
	X	Pappis Constantine	32	"	32	"

West Springfield Street

	Y	Dustin Lloyd	190	sailor	22	here
	Z	Ford Edward	190	chauffeur	32	"
	A	Mercer Philip	190	steamfitter	36	449 Shawmut av
	B	Meredith Frances—†	190	waitress	25	here
	C	Morril Lewis	190	painter	62	140 St Botolph
	D	Pearson Emma—†	190	housekeeper	49	here
	E	Pearson Ernest	190	waiter	49	"
	F	Schelke Emil	190	cigarmaker	45	102 Pembroke
	G	Thomas Kathryn—†	190	waitress	30	here
	H	Beckman John	192	upholsterer	45	207 W Springfield
	K	Buckley Thomas	192	carpenter	38	Maine
	L	Frederick Frank	192	chauffeur	26	Malden
	M	Holden George H	192	real estate	75	here
	N	Lyons William	192	brakeman	69	"
	O	Pelletier Alpha—†	192	housekeeper	45	"
	P	Quinn James A	192	barber	65	"
	R	Urquhart Herman	192	machinist	30	Everett
	S	Blackner Arthur	194	laborer	48	here
	T	Conway Susie—†	194	housewife	24	"
	U	Perry Fred	194	laborer	30	"
	V	Perry Jesse	194	"	39	"
	W	Perry John	194	"	26	"

Page	Letter	FULL NAME.	Residence, April 1, 1925.	Occupation.	Supposed Age.	Reported Residence, April 1, 1925. Street and Number.

West Springfield Street—Continued

x	Perry Lucy—†	194	housekeeper	50	here
y	Perry William	194	laborer	36	"
z	Smith Emmet	194	"	38	"
a	Smith Mamie—†	194	hairdresser	25	"
b	Byork Harold	196	machinist	24	8 Rutland
c	Derry Ernest E	196	mechanic	25	69 Worcester
d	Heron Louise—†	196	forewoman	25	here
e	Johnson Augustus	196	laborer	23	49 Rutland
f	Kindstand Lister	196	"	23	49 "
g	Rancourt Mary—†	196	housekeeper	38	45 Worcester
h	Stewart James	196	rubberworker	53	8 Rutland
k	Yalpas George	196	laborer	40	Hudson
l	Godfrey Mary—†	198	housekeeper	85	here
m	Green Martha M—†	198	"	40	Brookline
n	Penner Margaret—†	198	"	55	here
o	Brice John A	200	porter	49	"
p	Brice Mary E—†	200	housewife	49	"
r	Escley Edward	200	laborer	24	"
s	Mitchell Edward	200	cook	36	"
t	Rudd Mary M—†	200	waitress	25	"
u	Yeard James	200	musician	36	"
v	Bailey Frank	202	mechanic	25	Rhode Island
w	Barlow William	202	radio expert	50	here
x	Bartell Peter	202	laborer	50	Lowell
x¹	Boyle Lucy—†	202	housekeeper	55	New York
y	Brown Tucker	202	shoecutter	52	here
z	Cummings Gene—†	202	waitress	40	693 Tremont
a	Cummings Robert	202	cook	45	693 "
b	Dearborn Mary—†	202	at home	74	here
c	Fitzgerald James	202	laborer	41	86 Warrenton
d	Osgood Edna—†	202	housekeeper	50	here
e	Spooner William	202	upholsterer	65	208 W Springfield
f	Klint Oscar	204	carpenter	43	482 Mass av
g	Kunz Paul	204	painter	66	here
h	Mahoney Recard	204	carpenter	68	"
k	Olson Arel	204	"	55	"
l	Olson Axel R	204	machinist	43	"
m	Olson John	204	mason	53	"
n	Olson Selma—†	204	housewife	55	"
o	Bezanson George	206	porter	28	212 W Springfield

Page.	Letter.	FULL NAME.	Residence, April 1, 1926.	Occupation.	Supposed Age.	Reported Residence, April 1, 1925. Street and Number.

West Springfield Street—Continued

P	Bezanson Mabel—†	206	houseworker	28	212 W Springfield
R	Donley John	206	soldier	40	754 Tremont
S	Downes Gertrude—†	206	houseworker	35	316 Shawmut av
T	Filmore Nettie—†	206	housekeeper	32	762 Tremont
U	Filmore Roderick	206	machinist	32	762 "
V	Ford Henry	206	real estate	38	754 "
W	Hall Harvey	206	carpenter	21	205 W Springfield
X	Hall Mildred—†	206	housewife	20	205 "
Y	Hayes Edward	206	chauffeur	30	205 "
Z	Holmes Frank	206	carpenter	50	E Braintree
A	Holmes Mary—†	206	at home	43	"
B	Riley Bettie—†	206	"	23	Phila Pa
C	Stewart Mary—†	206	stitcher	40	205 W Springfield
D	Stewart Walter	206	laborer	30	205 "
E	Turner John F	206	sailor	45	63 Astor
F	Wortman Bertha—†	206	packer	28	759 Tremont
G	Appleby Irving D	208	milkman	36	101 Dale
H	Appleby Margaret—†	208	housekeeper	36	101 "
K	Bornstein Max	208	cigarmaker	70	24 Angel
L	Keefe Arthur R	208	pressman	48	34 Dover
M	Keefe Pamelia—†	208	housewife	38	34 "
N	Kiley George	208	laborer	30	here
O	Millan Frederick	208	salesman	50	87 Gainsboro
P	Pitlis Arthur	208	cook	25	540 Col av
R	Telfore Thomas	208	retired	77	205 W Springfield
S	George Elizabeth—†	210	housekeeper	40	here
T	George John	210	storekeeper	36	"
U	Palmer George	210	chauffeur	35	"
V	Polsen Gunnar	210	counterman	23	"
W	Porcello Pasquale	210	carpenter	22	"
X	Porcello Rose—†	210	housewife	20	"
Y	Byrne Joseph	212	clerk	27	"
Z	Clark Florence—†	212	housewife	23	Allston
A	Emory Angela—†	212	at home	59	102 W Springfield
B	Fells Samuel	212	expressman	24	563 Mass av
C	Littlefield Villa E—†	212	housekeeper	23	here
D	Littlefield Walter	212	clerk	25	"
E	Lynch Pearl—†	212	maid	24	"
F	Lynch Roy	212	laborer	25	"
G	Rogers Frances—†	212	cashier	28	92 Vernon

Page.	Letter.	FULL NAME.	Residence, April 1, 1926.	Occupation.	Supposed Age.	Reported Residence, April 1, 1925. Street and Number.

West Springfield Street—Continued

H	Shea Frank	212	laborer	28	Connecticut
K	Shea Mary—†	212	stitcher	30	"
L	Withee Albert	212	carpenter	39	Maine
M	Allen Alec	214	blacksmith	26	136 Mass av
N	Flaherty William	214	cook	50	292 W Springfield
O	Furlong Alice—†	214	housekeeper	27	here
P	Furlong Joseph	214	retired	51	"
T	MacLeod George	214	printer	40	"
R	McBride George	214	salesman	50	"
S	McKenna James	214	watchman	27	"
U	Panis John	214	chef	29	"
V	Philips Friendly	214	carpenter	72	"
W	Ryan George	214	chauffeur	40	"
X	Bailey John	216	laborer	30	Watertown
Y	Budreau Leo	216	painter	52	28 Dartmouth
Z	Budreau Mary—†	216	housewife	51	28 "
A	Fiske Dessie—†	216	housekeeper	47	here
B	Hall Edith—†	216	housewife	35	"
C	Lawless Matthew	216	attendant	44	"
D	Lynch James J	216	janitor	48	"
E	Lynch William	216	orderly	22	"
F	Norton James E	216	laborer	65	"
G	Norton Mary C—†	216	housewife	55	"
H	Steve John	216	cook	34	"
K	White Ralph	216	"	22	"
L	Ferdinand George	218	real estate	46	"
M	Ferdinand Margaret—†	218	housekeeper	38	"
O	MacLean Carrie—†	218	domestic	26	New York
N	McKenna Matthew	218	mechanic	30	11 Wellington
P	Rushing William	218	gardener	37	Ohio
R	Walcott Grace—†	218	domestic	23	12 Greenwich pk
S	Warner Ernest	218	mechanic	26	17 Claremont pk
T	Warner Ethel—†	218	housewife	25	New York
U	Dooley Nattie L—†	220	housekeeper	64	here
V	Freeman Nancy R—†	220	"	64	"
W	Howard Bertha F—†	220	"	47	"
X	Howard James T	220	barber	47	"
Y	Jones Harriet A L—†	220	nurse	46	"
Z	Rich Mabel F—†	220	clerk	37	"
A	Rich Robert	220	doorman	45	"

Page.	Letter.	Full Name.	Residence, April 1, 1926.	Occupation.	Supposed Age.	Reported Residence, April 1, 1925.
						Street and Number.

West Springfield Street—Continued

	B	Britt Thomas J	222	conductor	51	here
	c	Deveau Rene	222	waiter	22	"
	D	Fortune Edward N	222	painter	65	"
	E	McCarthy Thomas	222	bookkeeper	73	46 W Newton
	F	Rooney Walter J	222	salesman	66	here
	G	Bell Eliza A—†	224	cook	60	"
	H	Gross Ida B—†	224	dressmaker	42	"

Ward 9—Precinct 5

CITY OF BOSTON.

LIST OF RESIDENTS
20 YEARS OF AGE AND OVER

(FEMALES INDICATED BY DAGGER)

AS OF

APRIL 1, 1926

HERBERT A. WILSON, } Listing

JAMES F. EAGAN, } Board.

CITY OF BOSTON—PRINTING DEPARTMENT

Page.	Letter.	FULL NAME.	Residence, April 1, 1926.	Occupation.	Supposed Age.	Reported Residence, April 1, 1925. Street and Number.

Camden Street

	E	Bond Kenneth	12	laborer	44	46 Sawyer
	F	Booker John	12	"	24	here
	G	Lovey Edward	12	waiter	49	"
	H	Slone Eugenie —†	12	housewife	21	"
	K	Slone Richard	12	papercutter	23	"
	D	Taylor Alice—†	12	housewife	40	"
	L	Taylor Charles	12	laborer	53	"
	N	White Rose—†	14	housewife	25	5 Williams ter
	O	White William	14	laborer	35	5 "
	P	Jarvas Alberta—†	14	housewife	30	10 Connolly
	R	Jarvas Joseph	14	laborer	27	10 "
	T	Johnson Benjamin	16A	"	30	23 Northfield
	U	Johnson Mattie—†	16A	housewife	38	here
	V	Johnson William	16A	chauffeur	30	"
	X	Gibbons Henry	16A	laborer	40	"
	W	Ray Alberta—†	16A	laundress	45	"
	Y	Hicklin Charles	18	mechanic	50	"
	Z	Phenix Benjamin	18	bricklayer	47	"
	A	Barrett Stanley	18	mechanic	29	"
	B	Cunningham Ethel—†	18	housewife	28	"
	C	Cunningham Joselyn	18	mechanic	34	"
	D	Hall Edward	18	painter	36	"
	E	Hall Susie—†	18	domestic	32	"
	G	Sheppard Anna E—†	19	"	60	29 Camden
	H	Peart Ada—†	rear 19	"	40	20 Oak Grove ter
	K	Peart Harriet—†	" 19	"	53	939 Harris'n av
	L	Washington Henry	22	cook	45	here
	M	Tuitt Edward	22	porter	34	"
	N	Tuitt Elsie—†	22	housewife	23	"
	O	Tuitt Frances—†	22	housekeeper	36	"
	R	Blake Oliver	22	laborer	45	"
	U	Jackson Pearl M—†	25	laundress	26	"
	V	Smalls Susan—†	25	"	48	"
	W	Gordon Anna—†	25	"	38	"
	X	Baker Emmaline E—†	26	musician	32	"
	Y	Lattimore Mary—†	26	at home	53	"
	Z	Rivers Arthur	26	laborer	50	36 Ruggles
	A	Smith James	26	"	40	24 Buckingham
	B	Vendelman James	26	waiter	37	23 Woodbury

2

Page.	Letter.	FULL NAME.	Residence, April 1, 1926.	Occupation.	Supposed Age.	Reported Residence, April 1, 1925. Street and Number.

Camden Street—Continued

	D	Shaw John	28	elevatorman	29	here
	E	Shields Lettie—†	28	housekeeper	45	"
	F	Jeffries Thomas	28	laborer	50	"
	G	Ganong May—†	29	laundress	48	"
	H	Buttler George	29	laborer	26	"
	K	Gould Jessie M—†	29	housekeeper	60	"
	L	Chester Sarah E—†	29	domestic	71	"
	N	Floyd Joseph	30	laborer	23	"
	O	Floyd Marie—†	30	housekeeper	56	"
	P	Stewart John	30	cook	35	"
	R	Stephens Louise—†	32	housewife	51	"
	S	Stephens Lucius S	32	waiter	57	"
	T	Shands Jessie—†	33	housekeeper	31	"
	U	Shands William	33	laborer	30	"
	V	Davenport Charles	33	"	55	"
	W	Joyce Anthony	33	"	57	"
	Y	Harrington Charlott E—†	34	at home	72	"
	Z	Scholl Frank E	34	bookkeeper	54	"
	A	Scholl Susie L—†	34	housewife	52	"
	B	Salsman Louise—†	35	housekeeper	63	"
	C	Donovan Emma—†	36	"	49	"
	D	Perry Alice—†	36	laundress	29	"
	E	Smith Elizabeth—†	36	domestic	39	"
	F	Tyler Jane—†	36	housewife	50	"
	G	McPherson Daniel	37	carpenter	45	New York
	H	McPherson Nellie—†	37	domestic	37	"
	K	Dunn William S	37	waiter	51	800 Tremont
	L	Toliver Elizabeth—†	37	domestic	48	800 "
	M	Cook George	37	storekeeper	40	20 Warwick
	N	Cook Lillian—†	37	housewife	30	20 "
	O	French Abbie—†	37	"	30	49 Camden
	O¹	French Herbert	37	laborer	30	49 "
	R	Russell Louis	39	"	34	77 Sterling
	V	Harding John	41	"	32	Pennsylvania
	W	Harding Nellie—†	41	housewife	31	"
	X	Cephas Caroline—†	41	"	30	here
	Y	Cephas Louis	41	laborer	50	"
	A	Robinson Agnes—†	41	housekeeper	50	"
	A¹	Robinson Herbert	41	chauffeur	31	"
	D	Lee Sam	47	laundryman	46	"

3

Page.	Letter.	FULL NAME.	Residence, April 1, 1926.	Occupation.	Supposed Age.	Reported Residence, April 1, 1925. Street and Number.

Camden Street—Continued

E	Prince Edward	49	janitor	34	here
F	Prince Mary—†	49	housewife	30	"
H	Simpson Edward	49	porter	42	"
K	Simpson Minnie—†	49	housewife	50	"
M	Williams James	51	laborer	30	17 Lenox
N	Williams Mary—†	51	housewife	30	17 "
O	Roberson Samuel	51	laborer	35	New York
R	Stephen William	51	"	39	"
P	Thomson Viola—†	51	housewife	35	here
S	Campbell Margaret—†	52	teacher	47	"
T	Cascadolin Catherine—†	52	nurse	25	664 Columbia rd
U	Cassidy Marie—†	52	teacher	30	here
V	Derves Anna—†	52	"	46	"
W	Downey Eleanor—†	52	"	23	France
X	Hanley Mary—†	52	houseworker	21	here
Y	Kazaha Isabelle—†	52	teacher	27	Maryland
Z	Lundy John J	52	engineer	25	Wrentham
A	Lynch Mary—†	52	laundress	51	411 Marlowe
B	Mansini Celiste—†	52	teacher	26	here
C	McCarthy Annie—†	52	seamstress	46	"
D	McDonald Annie—†	52	houseworker	62	"
E	Mylett Mary—†	52	seamstress	63	"
F	Nadeau Annie—†	52	cook	37	13 Hecla
G	Quinliven Rose—†	52	teacher	31	here
H	Raymond Rebecca—†	52	"	26	"
K	Selhorset Anna—†	52	"	41	"
L	Simms Viola—†	52	"	30	"
M	Stewart Helen—†	52	dressmaker	21	"
N	Whalen Annie—†	52	seamstress	38	"
O	Baccus John	53	chauffeur	27	New York
R	Hill Laurice—†	53	housewife	30	here
P	Hill Logan H	53	barber	40	"
S	Perry Estelle—†	53	housewife	35	8 Lenox
T	Perry James	53	laborer	31	8 "
U	Barnard John	57	"	52	160 W Springfield
V	Davis Georgia A—†	57	housewife	47	160 "
W	Harding Thomas	57	laborer	35	160 "
X	Simington Frank T	57	clerk	44	160 "
Y	Alberton Ralph	57	cook	32	160 "
A	Roberson Roy	57	"	29	160 "

4

Page	Letter	Full Name.	Residence, April 1, 1926.	Occupation.	Supposed Age.	Reported Residence, April 1, 1925. Street and Number.

Camden Street —Continued

B	Smith Daniel	57	waiter	26	Lynn
A¹	Buckanan William	57	"	25	160 W Springfield
C	Thomson Peter	57	cook	40	160 "
D	Winn Charles	57	laborer	42	Lynn
E	Denson Carter	59	waiter	32	here
F	Jones Mattie —†	59	housekeeper	48	"
G	Jones Walter J	59	shipper	42	"
H	Stewart John	59	laborer	28	Malden
K	Warner John	59	porter	40	here
N	Alexander Mary —†	61	housekeeper	52	"
O	Alexander Mattie —†	61	"	53	"
P	Wood Irvin P	63	porter	30	"
R	Wood Mary H —†	63	housewife	28	"
S	Davis Elise —†	63	housekeeper	26	108 Camden
T	Whiting Lucy —†	63	"	47	here
V	Polk Benjamin	65	cook	34	"
W	Polk Dora —†	65	housewife	36	"
Y	Craddock Elizabeth —†	65	housekeeper	38	"
X	Craddock George	65	foreman	39	"
Z	Lee Lewis	65	porter	41	"
A	McCree Milton	65	chauffeur	42	"
B	Moses John	65	hatter	27	"
C	Moses Mary M —†	65	housewife	21	"
D	Lindo Robert	65	laborer	35	Malden
E	Luacan Esther L —†	67	housewife	30	here
F	Luacan John R	67	laborer	30	"
G	Cantion Anus	67	"	47	"
H	Parks John J	67	porter	27	"
K	Parks Marrion —†	67	housewife	26	"
L	Fletcher Charles H	69	porter	31	"
M	Fletcher May T —†	69	housewife	32	"
N	Alexander Charles	69	bellman	47	"
O	Turner Linnet —†	69	housewife	32	"
P	Turner Pelmust	69	laborer	42	"
R	Chambers Sarah —†	69	housewife	21	"
S	Chambers Thomas H	69	porter	26	"
T	Walker Eddibill B —†	71	housewife	30	"
U	Walker James	71	mechanic	40	"
V	Shelton John	71	janitor	50	"
W	Jones Austin	71	porter	36	"

Page	Letter	Full Name.	Residence, April 1, 1926.	Occupation.	Supposed Age.	Reported Residence, April 1, 1925. Street and Number.

Camden Street—Continued

x	Jones Bessie—†	71	housewife	36	here
z	Brown Anna A—†	73	"	41	"
A	Brown Thomas E	73	porter	40	"
B	Debinyard Sarah—†	73	cook	58	"
C	Hodges Hamilton	73	teacher	54	"
D	Howard Phillis—†	73	houseworker	51	"
E	Woodest Sylvia—†	73	"	65	"
F	Revere Lewis	74	domestic	65	"
G	Goode Taswell	74	laborer	25	"
H	Bolling Nellie—†	75	housekeeper	36	"
K	Sparrow Arinanna C—†	75	houseworker	85	"
L	Stovall Martha—†	75	student	30	"
N	Kemp Helena—†	76	housewife	47	"
O	Kemp Henry A	76	steward	57	"
P	Kemp Henry A, jr	76	porter	21	"
R	Sparrow Elizabeth J—†	76	housekeeper	59	"
S	Wyatt Sarah—†	77	houseworker	50	299 Beacon
T	Crudup Sallie—†	77	housekeeper	48	here
U	Alvis Fidell	77	laborer	35	"
V	Alvis May—†	77	housewife	32	"
W	Roberts Mosella—†	77	houseworker	40	"
X	Bardouille Aline—†	78	housekeeper	42	"
Y	Bardouille Luke W	78	laborer	42	"
Z	Smith Ella—†	78	housewife	50	668 shawmut av
A	Smith Thomas H	78	waiter	64	688 "
B	Bowen Ida—†	78	domestic	30	here
C	Cabrial Charlie	78	laborer	32	"
D	Hutchinson Wilhemina M—†	78	domestic	42	Brockton
E	Hall Leanna—†	79	cook	29	Nantucket
F	Hall Thomas	79	laborer	29	"
G	White Ethel—†	79	housewife	24	42 Hammond
H	White Frederick P	79	musician	25	42 "
K	Dancay Joseph	79	laborer	30	here
L	Ines Arthur	79	"	29	Cambridge
M	Dent Edith—†	79	housewife	27	here
N	Dent Robert M	79	porter	27	"
O	Skinner Minnie—†	80	housewife	63	"
P	Skinner William A	80	laborer	65	"
R	Murray Hilda—†	80	housewife	32	"
S	Murray Lawrence M	80	laborer	35	"
T	Pyle Gertrude—†	80	domestic	45	759 Cabot

Page.	Letter.	FULL NAME.	Residence, April 1, 1926.	Occupation.	Supposed Age.	Reported Residence, April 1, 1925. Street and Number.

Camden Street—Continued

	U	Reed Mary F—†	81	operator	40	here
	V	Taylor Anna F—†	81	housekeeper	46	"
	W	Bembery Delilah—†	82	at home	57	"
	W¹	Clark Charles	82	janitor	30	236 Ruggles
	X	Clark Sterling	82	plasterer	56	here
	Y	Carr Margaret—†	82	domestic	26	236 Ruggles
	A	Epps Clarence	83	chauffeur	30	21 Claremont pk
	B	Epps Doris—†	83	housewife	23	21 "
	C	Johnson Seth	83	electrician	40	21 Northfield
	D	Munce Estelle B—†	83	houseworker	39	here
	F	Prince Hattie—†	84	housewife	27	"
	G	Prince William A	84	butler	27	"
	H	Feldberg Dora—†	84	housewife	42	"
	K	Feldberg Wolf	84	storekeeper	54	"
	L	Hinderson Charles	85	meatcutter	23	N Carolina
	M	Radcliff Lenna—†	85	housekeeper	30	"
	N	Johnson Warren V	85	janitor	60	here
	O	Williams Ella E—†	85	maid	50	"
	P	Ford Lulbia—†	85	domestic	40	"
	R	Haywood Henrietta—†	85	housekeeper	50	89 Union Park
	S	Alves John	86	laborer	28	Connecticut
	T	Hazard Dora—†	86	housewife	44	1842 Wash'n
	U	Jackson Bessie—†	86	"	40	Connecticut
	V	Lawson Octavia—†	86	"	30	here
	W	Bates Mary—†	86	"	48	"
	X	Harrington Catherine E—†	87	housekeeper	49	"
	Y	Harrington Henry W	87	salesman	54	"
	Z	Harrington Mary A—†	87	housekeeper	51	"
	A	Bradshan Mary E—†	87	"	54	"
	B	Dwyer Annie—†	87	"	54	"
	C	Glenn Magnolia—†	88	"	28	"
	D	Robinson Lucie—†	88	"	44	"
	E	Robinson Robert	88	laborer	58	"
	F	Lewis John	88	"	30	"
	G	Lewis Mary—†	88	housekeeper	25	"
	H	Jackson Irene A—†	89	"	33	"
	K	Jackson Rheoadore	89	porter	32	"
	L	Dugger Joseph	89	"	30	"
	M	Dugger Ruth—†	89	housewife	25	"
	N	Cheeks Edgar	89	laborer	33	"
	O	Cheeks Mable—†	89	housewife	30	"

Page	Letter	Full Name	Residence, April 1, 1926	Occupation	Supposed Age	Reported Residence, April 1, 1925. Street and Number.

Camden Street —Continued

	Letter	Full Name	Res.	Occupation	Age	Reported Residence
	o	Swan Hester E —†	89	housekeeper	49	here
	p	Walker Sarah—†	90	at home	67	"
	r	Reece Annie E —†	90	domestic	48	"
	s	Reece Joseph	90	porter	50	"
	t	Roberts Geneva —†	90	housewife	28	"
	u	Roberts John	90	longshoreman	32	"
	v	Allen William H	91	laborer	69	"
	w	McKinnon Duncan	91	retired	75	"
	x	Taylor Frank E	91	laborer	61	"
	y	Provo Agnes —†	91	housekeeper	35	"
	z	Provo Agnes M —†	91	operator	21	"
	a	Provo Fred	91	machinist	53	"
	b	Gaston David	92	cook	49	"
	c	Davis Lucy—†	92	housekeeper	39	"
	d	Douglas Elizabeth—†	92	housewife	62	"
	e	Harrison Marion—†	92	domestic	27	Phila Pa
	f	Carr Chrisella—†	93	"	30	New York
	g	Forsythe James	93	laborer	30	here
	h	Forsythe Louise—†	93	housekeeper	28	"
	k	Harris Grace—†	93	"	32	"
	l	Jackson Bessie —†	93	"	35	"
	m	Jackson Sam	93	retired	53	"
	n	Randell James	93	janitor	30	"
	o	Smith Frank	93	chauffeur	40	"
	p	Scott Jennie—†	94	housekeeper	52	"
	r	Scott Louis	94	chef	52	"
	s	Williams Evelyn —†	94	housekeeper	30	"
	t	Green Marie —†	94	"	50	"
	u	Augusta William	95	janitor	40	162 W Springfield
	v	Bunn Nettie —†	95	housekeeper	39	162 "
	w	Bunn William	95	janitor	41	162 "
	x	Davis John	95	porter	45	607 Shawmut av
	y	Hanies Alice —†	95	cook	50	129 Warwick
	z	Hearst Daisy —†	95	housekeeper	32	162 W Springfield
	a	Hearst William	95	porter	35	162 "
	b	Nesby Emma—†	95	maid	34	14 Woodbury
	c	Payne Lillian—†	95	laundress	42	162 W Springfield
	d	Turner Charles N	95	cook	48	59 Kendall
	e	Lee Ella M—†	96	domestic	50	here
	f	Pinkney Susan —†	96	housewife	69	"
	k	Smith Inez —†	97	housekeeper	31	198 Northampton

Page.	Letter.	FULL NAME.	Residence, April 1, 1926.	Occupation.	Supposed Age.	Reported Residence, April 1, 1925. Street and Number.

Camden Street—Continued

	L	Smith Minnie —†	97	housekeeper	49	198 Northampton
	M	Page Albert	98	storekeeper	51	here
	N	Page Enindia —†	98	waitress	53	"
	P	Washington Chauncy	98	musician	35	"
	R	Washington Mary—†	98	housewife	65	"
	S	Farrell Emma—†	99	housekeeper	57	"
	T	Hood Elizabeth —†	99	"	52	"
	U	Jones Elizabeth—†	99	"	79	"
	V	Brown Ida—†	99	"	57	"
	W	Hillyer Ross	99	laborer	34	466 Tremont
	X	Dickisson Beverly B	100	engineer	47	here
	Y	Dickisson Ruth—†	100	housewife	30	Everett
	Z	Bowen Bertha—†	100	"	34	here
	A	Bowen Emery M	100	laborer	42	"
	B	Bowen Russell M	100	"	21	"
	C	Brackett Irene L—†	100	domestic	54	"
	E	Hubbard George	101	janitor	45	"
	F	Calender Lillian—†	101	domestic	23	"
	G	Nickerson Della—†	101	housekeeper	50	"
	K	Sloane Eugene	102	laborer	24	"
	M	Cotter Charles	102	"	28	"
	L	Cotter Marion—†	102	housekeeper	24	"
	N	Moore John T	103	cook	26	Pittsfield
	O	Moore Mamie—†	103	housewife	27	"
	P	Eubanks Betrice—†	103	housekeeper	28	here
	R	Eubanks Clarence B	103	laborer	30	"
	S	Banks Albert	104	porter	60	"
	T	Herbert Peter	104	waiter	50	S Carolina
	U	Johnson Stephen	104	"	55	here
	V	Jones Theodore	104	musician	38	"
	W	Keezier Lloyd	104	waiter	38	"
	X	Person Alpha	104	"	40	"
	Y	Reed George A	104	porter	47	"
	Z	Vilian Lenora M—†	104	housewife	39	Georgia
	A	Vilian Philip	104	porter	38	"
	B	Vilian Philip A	104	"	46	"
	C	Thomas Alice B—†	106	domestic	29	here
	D	Wheeler Curtis	106	elevatorman	36	"
	E	Bishop Alfred	106	laborer	39	"
	F	Bishop Isac	106	"	40	"
	G	Bishop Nellie—†	106	housewife	78	"

Camden Street—Continued

H	Higgins Robert J	108	painter	40	here
K	Williams Ida N—†	108	housewife	49	"
L	Mason Estella—†	108	"	31	2 Claremont
M	Mason Thomas	108	manager	32	2 "
N	Lynch Addie—†	108	domestic	42	here
O	Johnson Margaret—†	110	hairdresser	28	27 Northfield
P	Bowles Elsey—†	110	housewife	28	here
R	Bowles Morley	110	mechanic	32	"
S	Haskins Anna—†	110	housewife	29	"
T	Haskins Rufus	110	machinist	35	"
U	Day Ella—†	112	domestic	26	"
V	Johnson Charles	112	chauffeur	39	"
W	Smith Annie—†	112	housewife	48	"
X	Smith James S	112	laborer	48	"
Y	Wheeler Susa—†	112	domestic	22	"
Z	Alexander John J	114	messenger	47	"
A	Alexander Viola—†	114	housewife	37	"
B	Coursey Hattie—†	114	laundress	50	"
C	Green Martha—†	114	domestic	49	"
D	Lewis Meta—†	114	"	38	"
E	Marshall Emma—†	114	"	42	"
F	Merrick Fred	114	porter	45	"
L	Evans Lillian B—†	118	presser	48	"
M	Pennycock Carrie—†	118	domestic	40	"
N	Withers Walter A	118	porter	58	"
P	Goodrum Julia E—†	120	domestic	44	"
R	Johnson Magnolia—†	120	"	30	3 Wirth pl
S	Pritcher Ruth—†	120	"	60	3 "
T	Hornsby Garrett	120	porter	27	Cambridge
U	Hornsby Mattie—†	120	domestic	27	"
V	Williams Hattie—†	120	"	37	688 Shawmut av
W	Davis John	122	laborer	40	783 "
X	Davis Lilian—†	122	housewife	29	783 "
Y	Vantassell Ella—†	122	"	37	3 McLellan
Z	Vantassell John	122	fireman	47	3 "
A	Williams Emily—†	122	housewife	70	here
B	Lambert Rebecca—†	124	domestic	50	"
C	Lambert Washington	124	boxmaker	22	"
D	Loyd Cora—†	124	housewife	39	"
E	Loyd Fountain	124	painter	43	"
F	Loyd Fountain, jr	124	"	21	"

10

Camden Street—Continued

G	Crawford Mary A—†	126	housewife	49	here
H	Walker Charles	126	laborer	50	"
K	Wells Mabel—†	126	housewife	29	"
L	Covington Fletcher	128	painter	40	Florida
M	Covington Henrietta—†	128	domestic	34	"
N	Allen Elizabeth—†	128	housewife	50	here
P	Stephens Ida L—†	130	housekeeper	39	"
R	Stephens William H	130	longshoreman	41	"
S	Forrest William	130	laborer	45	"
T	Jordan Lester	130	longshoreman	27	"
U	Jordan Mary—†	130	nurse	24	"
V	Bennett Constance—†	132	housewife	27	"
W	Bennett Merton	132	chauffeur	31	"
X	Bennett Nathaniel	132	clerk	28	"
Y	Brown James A	132	laborer	44	57 Camden
Z	Brown Mary R—†	132	domestic	41	57 "

Clifton Place

B	Higgins Thomas	1	chauffeur	30	here
C	McGuinness Elisebeth—†	1	laundress	50	"
D	McGuinness John W	1	barber	70	"
E	Calley Charles	2	iceman	21	74 Compton
F	Calley Marion—†	2	housewife	42	74 "
G	Calley Samuel	2	painter	45	74 "
H	Kirnin Alice—†	3	housewife	30	here
K	Wheelock Ellinear—†	3	housekeeper	65	"
L	Wheelcok Frank L	3	roofer	38	"
M	Wheelock Frederick L	3	chauffeur	30	"
N	Wheelock Marion P—†	3	saleswoman	28	"
O	Block Gertrude E—†	4	housekeeper	46	"
P	Teishman Mary E—†	4	at home	65	"
R	Wheelock Lottie—†	5	housewife	42	"
S	Wheelock William J	5	janitor	41	"
T	Flavin Grace—†	5	laundress	35	"
U	Flavin Joseph	5	ironworker	43	"
V	Thompson Della—†	5	hotelworker	26	553 Wash'n
W	Tobin Jane—†	6	housewife	49	here
X	Tobin Mary A—†	6	laundress	23	"
Y	Tobin Patrick F	6	laborer	23	"

11

Page	Letter	Full Name.	Residence, April 1, 1926	Occupation	Supposed Age.	Reported Residence, April 1, 1925. Street and Number.

Clifton Place—Continued

	Z	Johnson Elisebeth—†	6	clerk	21	here
	A	Johnson Winifred—†	6	housekeeper	47	"
	B	Webster Ralph	6	meatcutter	30	"
	C	Maloney Catherine—†	7	housewife	39	"
	D	Maloney Otis	7	printer	39	"
	E	Brenner George S	7	watchman	54	"
	F	Mack Jennie H—†	8	housekeeper	73	"
	G	Fish Alice—†	8	shoeworker	40	"
	K	Daniels Beatrice J—†	9	housewife	30	"
	L	Daniels Harold W	9	mechanic	36	"
	M	McCloud Anna—†	10	housewife	21	"
	N	McCloud John	10	mech dentist	30	"
	O	McCloud Angus J	10	clerk	63	"
	P	McCloud Florence—†	10	housewife	61	"
	R	Boyd James H	11	salesman	23	"
	S	Boyd Margaret M—†	11	packer	21	"
	T	McBride James L	11	"	62	"
	U	McBride Margaret T—†	11	housewife	62	"
	V	Cassidy Nellie—†	12	housekeeper	59	"
	W	Dann August D	12	laborer	43	"
	X	Dann Martha—†	12	housewife	38	"
	Y	Beardsley Bessie—†	13	"	24	"
	Z	Beardsley George	13	porter	26	"
	A	Beardsley Charlotte—†	13	housewife	53	1029 Tremont
	B	Beardsley Elisebeth—†	13	at home	99	1029 "
	C	Beardsley William G	13	laborer	52	1029 "
	D	Black Alexander E	14	shipper	22	here
	E	Harriman Katherine—†	14	laundress	47	"
	F	Bremer William F	14	laborer	35	"
	G	Morrill Fred F	14	teamster	28	"
	H	Morrill Lillian—†	14	housewife	26	"
	K	Ryan Elisebeth—†	14	housekeeper	49	"
	L	Ryan Frank S	14	laborer	24	"
	M	Shea Katherine—†	15	laundress	47	"
	N	Bremer William F	15	clerk	34	"
	O	Leanord Martin A	15	paperworker	56	"
	P	Rauke Katherine—†	15	cleaner	56	"
	R	Rauke Robert	15	ironmolder	49	"
	S	Skidmore Arthur	16	laborer	60	284 Hunt'n av
	T	Thornton Gerald	16	machinist	23	here
	U	Veera Charles B	16	missionary	39	"

Page.	Letter.	FULL NAME.	Residence, April 1, 1926.	Occupation.	Supposed Age.	Reported Residence, April 1, 1925. Street and Number.

Clifton Place—Continued

v	Veera Hattie—†	16	housewife	40	here
w	Fox Lena—†	17	"	25	"
x	Fox Redvers	17	longshoreman	25	"
y	Kennedy Mary—†	17	housewife	48	"
z	Kennedy Thomas	17	waiter	58	"
A	Tanguay Arthur	18	shipper	23	87 Cabot
c	Winters George H	18	carpenter	67	here
d	Winters George W	18	pressman	23	"
e	Winters Mary—†	18	housewife	56	"
f	Kantrowitz Helen F—†	19	"	54	10 Parnell
g	Kantrowitz Maurice	19	salesman	49	10 "
h	Clarke Allen H	19	laborer	52	here
k	Clarke Olive—†	19	housekeeper	79	"
l	Fowler Arthur H	20	printer	41	Dedham
m	Fowler Flossie—†	20	housewife	44	"
n	Constanso Paulina—†	21	"	29	here
o	Constanso Salatore	21	laborer	34	"
p	Meclean Roselina—†	21	housewife	63	"
r	Peterson Mary A—†	21	"	43	"
s	Peterson Oscar	21	storekeeper	42	"
t	Lizio Guy	22	student	31	"
u	Mangano Marie—†	22	housekeeper	55	"
v	Mangano Oreste	22	upholsterer	32	"
x	Stingle Minnie—†	22	housekeeper	50	"
y	Vaughn Freeman	22	carpenter	56	"
A	Gordan Hannah—†	23	clerk	48	"
A¹	Graham Binnie—†	23	housewife	68	"
c	Robinson Margaret—†	23	"	74	"
d	Crowly David F	24	laborer	63	24 Regent pl
e	Crowly Fred E	24	"	21	24 "
f	Crowly Rose—†	24	housewife	50	24 "

Derby Place

h	Cole Edwin W	B	piano tuner	59	here
k	Cole Jenny T—†	B	at home	79	"
l	Cole Nora F—†	B	housewife	53	"

Page.	Letter.	FULL NAME	Residence, April 1, 1926.	Occupation	Supposed Age.	Reported Residence, April 1, 1925. Street and Number.

Derby Place—Continued

M	O'Donnel Edward	B	radio expert	21	here
N	Sair Josephine B—†	B	housewife	45	"
O	Sair Richard	B	piano mover	42	"
O¹	Black Claire M—†	C	clerk	20	"
P	Mullen Mary M—†	C	at home	53	"
R	Perry Jennie L—†	C	housewife	43	"
S	Perry Thomas A	C	mechanic	41	"
T	Nash Annie—†	C	housewife	37	"
U	Nash Earl	C	clerk	37	"
V	Nash William E	C	special police	42	"
W	Barry James W	D	pedler	66	"
X	Grchambault Eugene S	1	steamfitter	58	"
Y	Grchambault Lottie—†	1	housewife	67	"
Z	Fitzgerald Nora—†	2	housekeeper	49	"
A	Murphy Patrick F	2	laborer	48	"
B	Kirnen James	3	baker	27	"
C	Little Agnes—†	4	housekeeper	48	"
D	Chagnon Evelen—†	5	housewife	27	"
E	Chagnon Louis	5	clerk	41	"
F	Tobin John J	6	bricklayer	53	"
H	Howe Annie—†	8	matron	39	"
K	Nichols Amanda—†	8	housewife	26	"
L	Nichols Collier	8	meatcutter	26	"
M	Roberts Annie—†	8	houseworker	52	"
N	Hayden Alice—†	9	housewife	64	"
O	Hayden George H	9	salesman	27	"
P	Hayden Josephine—†	9	clerk	24	"
R	Hayden Theodore F	9	salesman	25	"
S	Rooney Louise—†	10	saleswoman	37	"
T	Stanly James	10	teamster	61	Rhode Island
U	Stanly Elisebeth—†	10	housewife	61	"
V	Wild John	10	retired	72	"
W	Blainy George	11	porter	61	here
X	McCloud George	11	roofer	50	"
Y	McGraw George	11	produce dealer	50	"
Z	O'Brion Frederick	11	laborer	47	"
A	Wall Anna—†	11	housewife	35	"
B	Wall Thomas F	11	salesman	33	"
C	Woodward Louis	11	laborer	40	"

14

Page	Letter	Full Name.	Residence, April 1, 1920.	Occupation.	Supposed Age.	Reported Residence, April 1, 1925. Street and Number.

Dillon Street

D	Coull Isabel—†	1	housewife	50	here
E	Coull John	1	baker	59	"
F	Coull Patrick	1	oiler	26	"
G	McGrail Mary—†	1	housewife	50	"
H	McGrail Mary A—†	1	tel operator	22	"
K	McGrail Thomas	1	laborer	60	"
L	McGrail Thomas, jr	1	chauffeur	21	"
M	Dumwhitie Florance	2	laborer	40	"
N	Dumwhitie Mary—†	2	housewife	38	"
P	Lee Dora—†	3	elevatorwoman	24	"
R	Lee John	3	laborer	22	"
S	Lee Margaret—†	3	housekeeper	60	"
T	Bailey John	4	laborer	47	50 Water
U	Dembey Hanna E—†	4	cook	49	here
V	Austin Vance	4	laborer	40	156 Northampton
W	Frotta Bridgett—†	5	housewife	42	here
X	Frotta Domenico	5	laborer	47	"
Y	Gallagher Catherine—†	6	laundress	23	"
Z	Gallagher Catherine E—†	6	housewife	50	"
A	Gallagher Patrick J	6	chauffeur	53	"
E	Rivey Pauline—†	8	domestic	50	"
F	Reed Ida—†	10	"	45	"
G	Piscatelli Mary—†	10	housewife	59	"
H	Piscatelli Vincenzo	10	laborer	63	"
K	Willis Judith A—†	12	housewife	60	"
L	Willis Roberson C	12	laborer	73	"
M	Maxey William	12	"	49	"
N	Pierce Charles H	12	porter	39	"
O	Dixon Joseph C	13	laborer	39	"
P	Bruce William J	14	porter	57	"
R	Hill Lemuel	14	"	60	"
S	Miles James R	14	laborer	82	"
T	Miles Mary J—†	14	housewife	59	"
U	Harris Frederick P	14	teamster	43	"
V	Harris Mary E—†	14	housewife	37	"
W	Davis Leontine R—†	15	domestic	33	"
X	Johnson Elizabeth V—†	15	"	41	"
Y	Upsheur Julius	15	water tender	48	"
Z	Upsheur Phoebe A—†	15	housekeeper	31	"
A	Washington William S	15	painter	44	"

Page	Letter	FULL NAME.	Residence, April 1, 1926.	Occupation.	Supposed Age.	Reported Residence, April 1, 1925. Street and Number.

Dillon Street—Continued

	B	Jordon George	16	laborer	59	here
	C	Jordon Mamie—†	16	housewife	54	"
	D	Brown Jacob	17	tailor	44	"
	E	Brown Lucretia—†	17	domestic	42	"
	F	Owen Prince	17	laborer	45	"
	G	Simmons John	17	"	51	"
	H	Simmons Rosa—†	17	housewife	44	"
	K	Hart Samuel K	18	laborer	48	"
	L	Lewis Rebecca—†	18	housewife	34	"
	M	Lewis Robert	18	laborer	30	"
	N	McCall William	19	"	37	"
	O	Williams Ruth—†	19	domestic	28	"
	P	Milton Barney	19	storekeper	40	"
	R	World Evelyn D—†	19	housekeeper	45	4 Greenwich
	S	Falden Dora G—†	20	housewife	52	here
	T	Falden Nathanial	20	laborer	45	"
	U	Shefton William H	20	mechanic	49	"
	V	Wilson Carrie—†	20	laundress	35	"
	W	Crocker Anna M—†	21	maid	23	"
	X	Crocker Charles	21	carpenter	48	"
	Y	Crocker Hattie—†	21	housewife	38	"
	Z	Crocker Willie B—†	21	domestic	20	"
	A	Hall Charles	22	laborer	40	"
	B	Hall Mary L—†	22	housewife	30	"
	D	Scott Bessie—†	22	"	21	Phila Pa
	E	Scott Samuel	22	laborer	25	"

Hampton Court

	L	Perkinson John L	1	painter	51	here
	M	Linsley Cloe—†	2	domestic	24	"
	N	Tinsley Edward A	2	janitor	52	"
	O	Tinsley Millie—†	2	housewife	49	"
	P	Turner Nancy E—†	2	housekeeper	82	125 Highland

Lenox Street

	C	Ward Adele M—†	31	housewife	25	here
	D	Ward Charles D	31	caterer	63	"

16

Lenox Street—Continued

Letter	Full Name	Residence	Occupation	Age	Reported Residence
E	Ward Dora—†	31	housewife	58	here
F	Ward George A	31	chauffeur	32	"
G	Ward Louis A	31	"	30	"
H	Ward Marguerite—†	31	housewife	52	"
K	Carr Florence—†	31	laundress	61	"
L	Butler Alice—†	33	housewife	40	"
M	Butler Alonzo A	33	porter	49	"
N	Butler Charles	33	clerk	24	"
O	Brewster Margaret—†	33	housewife	37	"
P	Brewster Richard	33	cook	39	"
R	Gaines John S	33	printer	33	New Bedford
S	Jones Samuel	33	porter	28	"
T	Allen Frederick W	35	chef	60	here
U	Allen Lillian C—†	35	housewife	42	"
W	Odum Mary—†	37	domestic	45	"
X	Tynes Sarah—†	37	"	50	"
Y	White Dorita—†	37	housekeeper	31	"
Z	Haney Liza—†	47	"	67	"
A	Sanford Jennie T—†	47	housewife	58	"
B	Ridley Annie—†	47	houseworker	42	"
C	Jones Evelyn—†	47	housewife	27	43 Compton
D	Jones Robert	47	porter	34	43 "
E	Mack Lulu—†	50	housekeeper	32	here
F	Watson Eva—†	50	"	40	"
G	Hamilton James T	50	laborer	39	10 Sonoma
H	Hamilton Minnie—†	50	housewife	35	10 "
L	Braun Mary—†	50	housekeeper	39	Brookline
M	Collins Charles	50	laborer	32	18 Sawyer
N	Matthews Barney	50	"	27	here
O	Simon Margaret—†	50	housekeeper	31	"
V	Pinzo Michael	59	electrician	25	61 Lenox
W	Creco Frank	59	teamster	25	here
X	Creco Susie—†	59	housewife	22	"
Y	Falcetta Frank	59	teamster	42	"
Z	Falcetta Rose—†	59	housewife	26	"
A	Erickson Alvin	59	chauffeur	25	"
B	Kerr Waldrina—†	59	housekeeper	48	"
C	Griffin Elizabeth—†	61	housewife	33	"
D	Griffin Emanuel	61	painter	40	"
E	Cassetta John	61	laborer	62	"
F	Cassetta Lucy—†	61	housewife	52	"

9—5

Lenox Street—Continued

G	Creco Rosa—†	61	housekeeper	52	here
H	Robinson Mary—†	61	"	41	"
K	Wilson Bernard	61	laborer	52	"
L	McGonigle Elizabeth—†	63	housewife	29	"
M	McGonigle James	63	electrician	33	"
N	McGinley Mary—†	63	housewife	34	"
O	McGinley Michael	63	chauffeur	34	"
P	McLaughlin Daniel A	63	painter	38	Maine
S	Douglas James	65	chef	26	28 Greenwich pk
T	Garrett Susie—†	65	housekeeper	32	28 "
U	Garrett William	65	longshoreman	36	27 Thorndike
V	Eastman Elvine—†	65	housewife	36	36 Northfield
W	Eastman Elzera	65	laborer	30	36 "
X	Wilson Elizabeth—†	65	housekeeper	40	here
Y	Travers Manuel	65	laborer	45	"
Z	Travers Susie—†	65	housewife	32	"
B	Frazier Julia—†	67	housekeeper	43	Beverly
C	Joyner Benjman	67	laborer	43	44 Sawyer
D	Milano Agnes—†	67	housewife	52	6 Connolly
E	Milano James	67	laborer	59	6 "
F	Poindexter Mabel—†	67	housewife	27	here
G	Poindexter Robert	67	janitor	32	"
H	Caddle Doris—†	67	domestic	31	25 Sawyer
K	Caddle Nason	67	laborer	35	25 "
L	Wilson George A	69	"	42	here
M	Wilson Hilda—†	69	housewife	22	"
N	Wilson Rebecca—†	69	"	42	"
P	Rock Ermie—†	69	"	26	"
R	Rock Walter	69	cook	29	"
O	Quill Lela—†	69	domestic	41	"
S	White Elizabeth—†	69	housewife	43	"
T	White Wilson A	69	shipper	40	"
V	Smith Mary—†	71	houseworker	21	New Jersey
W	Mastrorillo Pentlo	71	coal dealer	21	here
X	Greene Edward	71	"	36	Chester Pa
Y	Alres John	71	laborer	22	Plymouth
Z	Andrews Manuel	71	"	44	here
A	Fernandes Frank	71	"	32	Plymouth
B	Fernandes Tony	71	"	35	17 Sawyer
D	Clifford Theresa B—†	73	housekeeper	52	here
E	Welsh Ellen—†	73	"	66	Weston

	Letter.	Full Name.	Residence, April 1, 1926.	Occupation.	Supposed Age.	Reported Residence, April 1, 1925. Street and Number.

Lenox Street—Continued

F	Covalli Dominick	73	laborer	33	Plymouth
G	Covalli Donato—†	73	housewife	30	"
H	Nutting Hannah—†	73	housekeeper	62	599 Shawmut av
L	Connolly Mary—†	75	housewife	60	here
M	Fitzpatrick Katherine—†	75	stenographer	23	"
N	Fitzpatrick Mabel—†	75	tel operator	25	"
O	Cullinan Edward	75	chauffeur	20	"
P	Cullinan Mary—†	75	bookkeeper	23	"
R	Cullinan Mary J—†	75	housewife	53	"
U	Maguire Margaret—†	77	"	60	"
V	Maguire Ralph B	77	mechanic	28	"
W	Martin John	77	cook	25	16 Warwick
X	McCarthy Daniel	77	laborer	23	here
Y	McCarthy Katherine—†	77	housekeeper	42	"
Z	Haley Ellen—†	77	"	38	"
A	Haley Patrick	77	laborer	41	"
B	Shea Helen—†	77	housewife	22	Cambridge
C	Shea Patrick	77	laborer	27	here
E	Cararella Matto	79	"	32	Brockton
F	Cararella Vincenza—†	79	housewife	71	77 Lenox
G	Croke Daniel G	79	laborer	35	here
H	Croke Katherine—†	79	stenographer	21	"
K	Croke Mary—†	79	housekeeper	63	"
L	Lunderville Harry	79	laborer	37	Vermont
M	Moses Harry	79	rigger	31	1821 Wash'n
N	Plant Mildred—†	79	housekeeper	25	Vermont
R	Farrington Frances—†	81	at home	83	41 Cabot
S	Bowen John	81	laborer	49	here
T	Powers Katherine—†	81	laundress	21	"
U	Powers Margaret—†	81	housewife	50	"
V	Powers William	81	laborer	54	"
W	Gauthier Athony	81	bricklayer	50	4 Reed ter
X	Gauthier Celia—†	81	housekeeper	20	4 "
Y	Gauthier Margaret—†	81	"	40	4 "
D	Cunningham Fred A	102	manager	60	here
E	Cunningham Helen M—†	102	housekeeper	57	"
F	Brown Henry	104	janitor	51	"
G	Wilder George H	104	retired	43	"
H	Wilder India—†	104	housekeeper	75	"
K	Farrell Frank H	104	storekeeper	52	"
L	Farrell Mary A—†	104	"	50	"

Page.	Letter.	FULL NAME.	Residence, April 1, 1926.	Occupation.	Supposed Age.	Reported Residence, April 1, 1925. Street and Number.

Lenox Street—Continued

M	Jenkins Gladys—†	104	housekeeper	28	1949 Wash'n
N	Jenkins Mark	104	laborer	29	1949 "
O	Simon Beatrice—†	104	domestic	21	1949 "
P	Williams James V	106	porter	50	19 Newburn
R	Foss James	106	laborer	36	211 Springfield
S	Welsh Martha—†	106	laundress	39	83 Camden
T	McCotty James	106	laborer	34	607 Shawmut av
U	McCotty Margaret—†	106	housekeeper	32	607 "
V	Marston Mathew	106	laborer	38	395 Northampton
W	Marston Rowena—†	106	housewife	34	395 "
X	Scott Charles	108	laborer	42	Cambridge
Y	Scott Cleo—†	108	housewife	30	"
Z	Nelson Harry	108	porter	36	here
A	Nelson Olive—†	108	housewife	34	"
B	Martin Jeremiah	108	laborer	50	"
C	Martin Mary—†	108	housewife	45	"
D	Andrews Hattie—†	108	"	45	"
E	Andrews Manuel	108	laborer	42	"
G	Childs Ella—†	109	housekeeper	53	"
H	Childs Oliver	109	retired	64	"
K	Paradia Louis	109	mechanic	64	"
L	Jones Arthur	109	laborer	41	"
M	Jones Lillian—†	109	housekeeper	30	"
N	Hughes Mabel—†	110	"	47	"
O	Wood Bernice—†	110	housewife	37	106 Lenox
P	Wood John L	110	laborer	50	106 "
R	Ray Addie—†	110	housewife	46	here
S	Ray Josiah	110	waiter	46	"
T	Dickson Alice J—†	110	housewife	39	"
U	Dickson James	110	laborer	39	"
V	Cristiani Frank	111	"	24	21 E Lenox
W	Cristiani Lance—†	111	housekeeper	24	21 "
X	Munnis Delia—†	111	"	46	here
Y	Munnis George F	111	carpenter	62	"
Z	Devine Elizabeth—†	111	housewife	83	"
A	Roach Lawrence E	112	porter	57	"
B	Edward James	112	laborer	36	"
C	Edward Rebecca—†	112	housewife	34	"
D	Jones Lucille—†	112	housekeeper	29	1026 Tremont

Letter	FULL NAME.	Residence, April 1, 1926.	Occupation.	Supposed Age.	Reported Residence, April 1, 1925. Street and Number.

Lenox Street—Continued

E	Rogers Esther—†	112	housewife	43	here
F	Rogers James W	112	porter	44	"
H	Reed Sadie—†	115	housekeeper	39	37 Sterling
K	Badgett Ethel—†	115	domestic	27	82 Ruggles
L	Badgett Joseph	115	laborer	35	37 Sterling
M	Myers Mary L—†	115	housekeeper	51	55 Sawyer
N	Harrell Blanche—†	115	"	24	14 Parnell
O	Harrell Stanley	115	chauffeur	29	14 "
P	Hargrow Edward	115	laborer	52	7 Burke
R	Conwell James	116	"	50	here
S	Higgins Pearl—†	116	housekeeper	22	76 Reed
T	Higgins William	116	laborer	43	76 "
U	Hall Frank	117	"	45	here
V	Henry Sadie—†	117	housekeeper	50	"
W	Henry Walter	117	laborer	24	"
Y	Claybond Rosa—†	117	housekeeper	47	"
Z	Mohamet Hamet	118A	waiter	28	"
A	Mouser Allie	118A	painter	25	"
D	Bolton Anita—†	119	housewife	36	"
E	Bolton George	119	laborer	30	"
F	Bolton Mary G—†	119	housekeeper	61	"
H	Andrews John	119	laborer	29	Onset
K	Reese Lucy—†	119	housekeeper	26	28 Buckingham
L	Hartnett Katherine—†	120	housewife	45	here
M	Hartnett Katherine M-†	120	at home	76	"
N	Hartnett Patrick J	120	operator	49	"
O	O'Reagan Hannah—†	120	at home	75	"
P	Brown Bessie—†	121	housewife	33	32 Sawyer
R	Brown Glen	121	laborer	44	32 "
S	Key John	121	"	35	67 Lenox
T	Key Lila—†	121	housewife	32	67 "
U	Watson Cassie—†	121	"	32	here
V	Watson Joel	121	cook	34	"
W	Lewis Sussie—†	121	housekeeper	37	1304 Wash'n
X	Casey Edward W	122	special police	44	here
Y	Casey Katherine F—†	122	housekeeper	49	"
Z	Casey William A	122	agent	59	"
A	MacCombs Walter	123	laborer	38	"
B	Young Martha—†	123	housekeeper	57	"

21

Page.	Letter.	FULL NAME.	Residence, April 1, 1926.	Occupation.	Supposed Age.	Reported Residence, April 1, 1925. Street and Number.

Lenox Street—Continued

	c	Yerood Davis	123	teamster	38	121 Lenox
	d	Johnson Henry	123	cook	54	here
	e	Morris Alexander	123	barber	64	"
	f	Stokes Anthony	123	laborer	51	927 Harris'n av
	h	Smith Clarence	125	"	32	8 Marble
	k	Smith Lorraine—†	125	housewife	24	8 "
	l	Dennison Jacob	125	porter	36	29 E Lenox
	m	Dolison Jacob	125	"	36	29 "
	n	Conway Anna—†	125	housewife	26	here
	o	Conway Edward P	125	superintendent	32	"
	r	Williams John	127	laborer	38	22 Dartmouth pl
	s	Williams Lornora—†	127	housekeeper	33	22 "
	t	Morthero Antonio	127	laborer	38	20 Willard pl
	u	Morthero Bessie—†	127	housewife	29	20 "
	v	Simkins Mary E—†	127	housekeeper	41	California
	w	Jones Bertha—†	127	"	28	174 Northampton
	f	Marshall Carrie—†	131	housewife	52	here
	g	Marshall Thomas	131	laborer	54	"
	h	Scott Lena—†	131	housekeeper	33	37 Sterling
	k	Brown Josephine—†	131	"	41	here
	l	Lee Gertrude—†	131	operator	21	"
	m	Sidney John D	131	oiler	50	129 Lenox
	n	Sidney Lois A—†	131	housewife	50	129 "
	o	Winston Clarence	131	musician	49	here
	p	Winston Mary—†	131	domestic	40	"
	r	Christian Frank E	131	laborer	44	10 Fairweather
	s	Christian Margaret—†	131	housekeeper	44	42 Northfield
	t	Rogers Sidney R	131	laborer	49	14 Fairweather
	u	DeCotean Charles	131	tailor	30	here
	v	Hoyt Alma—†	131	laundress	28	"
	w	Hoyt William	131	tailor	32	"
	x	Kelley Henrietta—†	131	clerk	23	48 W Canton
	y	Kelley Sarah—†	131	laundress	63	here
	z	Kelley William	131	porter	23	"
	a	Stancy Mary—†	131	cook	60	"
	b	Stancy William	131	laborer	50	"
	c	Dunkley Mary—†	131	housekeeper	28	10 Dartmouth pl
	d	Harrison James	131	cook	37	10 "
	e	Anderson Celestial N—†	131	housewife	35	here
	f	Anderson Charles	131	laborer	34	"

Page.	Letter.	FULL NAME.	Residence, April 1, 1926.	Occupation.	Supposed Age.	Reported Residence, April 1, 1925. Street and Number.

Lenox Street—Continued

	Letter	FULL NAME	Residence	Occupation	Age	Reported Residence
	G	Fordon Bessie—†	131	domestic	35	here
	H	Daley Dora—†	131	housekeeper	45	"
	K	Daley William	131	cook	31	"
	L	Charleston Edward	131	"	30	"
	M	Charleston Maud—†	131	housekeeper	24	"
	N	Thompson Clement	131	laborer	41	"
	O	Thompson Lillian—†	131	housewife	36	"
	P	Lambert Mary—†	131	housekeeper	64	"
	R	Bowden Hattie—†	141	housewife	58	"
	S	Bowden James	141	janitor	53	"
	T	Saunders Thomas	141	"	65	"
	U	Banks Joseph	141	"	45	"
	V	Contee Gladys—†	141	housekeeper	21	"
	W	Contee Mary—†	141	"	54	"
	X	Johnson Julia—†	141	domestic	45	"
	Y	Spicer Annie E—†	141	housewife	39	"
	Z	Spicer Wilson A	141	laborer	53	"
	A	Bland James H	141	ironworker	53	10 Willard pl
	B	Montgomery Mary B—†	141	laundress	42	here
	C	White Hazel—†	141	housewife	33	"
	D	White Walter H	141	stockman	40	"
	E	Terrell Henderson A	141	porter	44	"
	F	Terrell Mabel A—†	141	housewife	43	"
	G	Barnes Lucille—†	141	operator	39	"
	H	Barnes Walter D	141	waiter	38	"
	K	Baccus Lucy—†	141	domestic	45	"
	L	Skinner Robert	141	mechanic	36	"
	M	Taylor Belle—†	141	maid	28	"
	N	Taylor Harry	141	porter	28	"
	O	Barnes Gussie—†	141	seamstress	47	"
	P	Elliott Moses	141	shipper	43	200 Northampton
	R	Nelson Mary E—†	141	housewife	60	here
	S	Nelson Thomas S	141	waiter	51	"
	T	Christy Dorothy—†	141	laundress	24	30 Northfield
	U	Clark Cora—†	141	"	36	here
	V	Clark Samuel	141	cook	45	"
	W	Gloster Lena—†	141	"	49	"
	Y	Vernable Frank	141	laborer	29	227 Newbury
	X	Vernable Glennie—†	141	housewife	32	227 "
	A	Gough Bayard	145	carpenter	53	here

23

Northampton Street

H	Carter Thomas	142	longshoreman	23	Detroit Mich
K	Gray Arthur	142	cook	42	New York
L	Hyman Lena S—†	142	hairdresser	47	786 Tremont
M	Jasper Benjamin G	142	porter	58	38 Willard pl
N	Jasper Mary J—†	142	housewife	71	30 "
O	Jessman William	142	porter	40	30 "
P	Johnson Mary A—†	142	maid	50	Maine
S	Wallace Anson	146	porter	55	here
T	Wallace Louise—†	146	domestic	28	"
V	Jennigs Sarah—†	148	cook	49	50 Sawyer
W	Philip Augustus	148	laborer	70	here
X	Philip Sarah—†	148	housekeeper	62	"
Y	Nobles Marie—†	148	laundryworker	28	140 Northampton
Z	Holmes Luke M	150	physician	33	here
z¹	Russell Alice—†	150	housewife	30	"
A	Russell Frank E	150	laborer	33	"
B	Lucas Daniel	150	caterer	50	"
D	Harris Amanda—†	152	at home	65	Chicago Ill
E	Harris Lee	152	chauffeur	30	here
F	Harris Lillian—†	152	domestic	32	"
G	Russell Alice—†	152	"	32	"
H	Smith William H	152	caterer	53	"
K	Conwell Charles	152	laborer	60	"
N	Curtis Florence—†	160	domestic	28	"
P	Parrish Gladys—†	160	elevatorwoman	25	"
O	Taylor Addie—†	160	laundryworker	44	"
T	Bryant Clarence	168A	waiter	35	610 Shawmut av
U	Bryant Mary—†	168A	housewife	34	610 "
V	Johnson Oliver	168A	bellboy	27	610 "
W	Ridley Mattie—†	168A	housewife	32	610 "
X	Lightfoot Roger	168A	waiter	25	610 "
Y	Brown Matilda—†	172	housewife	44	here
Z	Brown William	172	real estate	49	"
A	Ellis Adarana—†	172	cook	41	"
B	Howland Ernest	172	laborer	54	"
C	Percy James	172	actor	51	"
D	Sabett Robert	172	waiter	50	"
E	Thompson Joseph	172	laborer	63	"
F	Barrows Esther—†	174	housewife	36	"
G	Barrows Manuel	174	laborer	51	"
H	Bonds Albert	176	"	49	"

Page.	Letter	FULL NAME.	Residence, April 1, 1926.	Occupation.	Supposed Age.	Reported Residence, April 1, 1925.
						Street and Number.

Northampton Street—Continued

K	Bonds Elise	176	laborer	24	here
L	Tutts Sulla—†	176	housekeeper	46	"
M	King Bernice—†	178	housewife	33	"
N	King Samuel	178	machinist	46	"
O	Washington Daresy—†	178	housewife	31	"
P	Washington Joseph	178	clergyman	40	"
R	Johnson Edward	180	laborer	36	"
S	Newton Frank	180	"	27	"
T	Newton Luvina—†	180	housewife	23	"
U	Roisten Cora—†	180	"	42	"
V	Roisten John W	180	seaman	47	"
W	Taylor James	180	waiter	37	Lawrence
X	Sulvay David	182	mechanic	27	New Bedford
Y	Sulvay Ethel—†	182	housewife	24	"
Z	Sulvay Katherine—†	182	laundress	23	"
A	Wells Edward	182	chef	40	Maine
B	Freeman William	184	janitor	45	140 W Springfield
C	Harrison Gertrude—†	184	domestic	25	20 Ruggles
D	Jones Harry	184	laborer	25	34 Kendall
E	Jones Mary—†	184	housewife	20	34 "
F	Kennedy May—†	184	housekeeper	32	here
G	Small Edward	184	porter	30	215 W Springfield
H	Smith Cornelius	184	"	28	here
K	Stewart Hugh	184	cook	29	"
L	Thompson George	184	porter	27	"
N	Finney Charles	188	waiter	49	92 Hammond
O	Givens Ida—†	188	waitress	25	here
P	Hill Edward	188	laborer	32	270 Shawmut av
R	Lee William	188	"	24	Vermont
S	Robinson Charles	188	"	23	Maine
T	Tate William	188	"	25	Malden
U	Ward Rita—†	188	domestic	35	New York
V	Ward William	188	laborer	41	"
W	Williams Ida—†	188	housekeeper	60	here
X	Bond Annie—†	190	housewife	33	"
Y	Bond Arthur	190	laborer	22	"
Z	Bond Elbert	190	retired	47	"
A	Bond Elijah	190	laborer	27	"
B	Bond Walter	190	"	21	"
C	Porter Esther—†	190	domestic	43	"
D	Tutts Lulu—†	190	"	45	"

25

Page.	Letter.	FULL NAME.	Residence, April 1, 1926.	Occupation.	Supposed Age.	Reported Residence, April 1, 1925. Street and Number.

Northampton Street—Continued

	E	Williams John	190	presser	21	New Jersey
	F	Darden Lawrence	192	laborer	46	W Virginia
	G	Darden Louise—†	192	housewife	44	here
	H	Hassock Amy—†	192	housekeeper	43	"
	K	Johnson Paul	192	laborer	30	"
	L	Pash Earl	192	student	23	Indiana
	M	Parker Minnie—†	194	housewife	45	here
	N	Parker Powhatan	194	janitor	44	"
	O	Herbert Rebecca—†	194	domestic	22	90 W Springfield
	P	Herbert Thomas	194	attendant	27	90 "
	S	Powell John H	196	clerk	33	72 Sawyer
	T	Powell Mary T—†	196	housewife	34	72 "
	U	Vanderzee Agnes W—†	196	music teacher	30	Marlboro
	V	Gonsalves James	198	laborer	42	Worcester
	W	Gonsalves Mary—†	198	housewife	50	"
	X	Scoltark Adeline—†	198	domestic	38	186 Northampton
	Y	Eveman Emma D—†	198	seamstress	50	Pennsylvania
	Z	Ford Annie—†	198	domestic	54	here
	A	Ford John H	198	mechanic	60	"
	B	Fuller Miranda E—†	200	houseworker	25	"
	C	Lans Annie—†	200	laundress	40	"
	D	Wheeler Clara—†	200	houseworker	65	"
	E	Applewhite Elliott	202	laborer	34	196 Northampton
	F	Baker Theodore	202	longshoreman	20	here
	G	Butler Emily—†	202	houseworker	25	"
	H	Dorsey Toog	202	chauffeur	25	176 W Springfield
	K	McKinnon Fannie—†	202	domestic	24	here
	L	Rush Fred	202	laborer	30	Maine
	M	Rush Marion—†	202	houseworker	24	"
	N	Snow Bertha—†	202	"	28	here
	O	Blount Robert L	204	caterer	47	"
	P	Cuzzens Marguirite—†	204	housewife	35	"
	R	Cuzzens Robert H	204	painter	50	"
	S	Grant Samuel	204	retired	84	57 Kendall
	T	Grant Sarah—†	204	housewife	86	57 "
	U	Overton Chloerellya—†	204	"	33	12 Cunard
	V	Overton Reuben	204	machinist	51	12 "
	W	Randoeph Alma—†	206	maid	28	here
	X	Washington Alice—†	206	"	40	"
	Y	White Charles R	206	waiter	43	"
	Z	White Ruby S—†	206	housewife	36	"

Page.	Letter.	Full Name.	Residence, April 1, 1926.	Occupation.	Supposed Age.	Reported Residence, April 1, 1925. Street and Number.

Northampton Street—Continued

	B	Davis Eva E—†	208	housewife	58	here
	C	Davis George H	208	engineer	60	"
	D	Jackson Rosa—†	208	housekeeper	40	"
	E	Jackson Thomas J	208	porter	43	"
	F	Morris John G	210	mechanic	30	"
	G	Sparrow Mary—†	210	domestic	28	"
	H	Warwick Henry	210	retired	60	"
	K	Thorson Bessie—†	212	housekeeper	51	"
	L	Thorson John O	212	cabinetmaker	72	"
	N	Johnson Lucille—†	212	housewife	25	174 W Springfield
	M	Johnson Luwaugh	212	cook	28	174 "
	O	Johnson Edith—†	212	housewife	37	here
	P	Johnson Willam	212	janitor	37	"
	R	Hodge James	212	laborer	40	42 Kendall
	S	Hodge Martha—†	212	houseworker	40	42 "
	T	Griffin Lauretta—†	214	housewife	47	here
	U	Griffin Milton J	214	roofer	48	"
	X	Carter Carrie—†	214	houseworker	40	"
	Y	Goldston William	216	janitor	50	"
	Z	Manley Celia F—†	216	housewife	42	"
	A	Manley John T	216	mechanic	45	"
	B	Braxton Charles	216	watchman	50	210 Northampton
	C	Taylor John	216	porter	38	here
	D	Harding Edmund	218	waiter	45	"
	E	Harding Malvina—†	218	housewife	36	"
	F	Low Cuthburt	218	laborer	24	"
	H	Howard Cathryn—†	220	housewife	23	New Haven Ct
	G	Howard John	220	car washer	28	"
	K	Kelly Mabel—†	220	housewife	23	N Carolina
	L	Kelly Robert	220	laborer	24	"
	M	Lee Robert	220	chauffeur	35	24 Willard pl
	N	Lee Susie—†	220	housewife	27	24 "
	O	Martin Laura—†	220	housekeeper	47	here
	P	Myrick Bishop	220	chauffeur	22	"
	R	Myrick John S	220	clergyman	50	"
	S	Saunders Judson	220	laborer	28	22 Pembroke
	T	Bland Witham	222	butler	32	Providence R I
	U	Bolling Sarah—†	222	hairdresser	35	here
	V	Shepard William	222	elevatorman	33	"
	W	Simmons Robert A	222	dentist	44	"
	X	Scott Rose—†	224	housewife	20	"

Northampton Street — Continued

Y	Scott Wilfred	224	inspector	27	here
Z	Hobson Agnes—†	224	housekeeper	37	"
A	Howcott John	224	laborer	68	"
B	Howcott Martin L	224	porter	34	"
C	Howcott Mary J—†	224	housekeeper	57	"
D	Crawford Clifford A	224	student	26	"
E	Johnstone Annie—†	224	houseworker	50	"
F	Poss Claudia D—†	224	domestic	44	"

Northfield Street

E	Lewis Edward	11	longshoreman	48	25 Northfield
F	Lewis Emma—†	11	housewife	47	25 "
G	Downing Martha—†	11	domestic	44	16 "
H	Hipps Rebecca—†	11	"	50	17 "
O	Mason Julia—†	11	laundress	45	34 "
K	Smith Louisa—†	11	domestic	48	here
L	Taylor Florence—†	13	"	38	"
M	Cosminski Ella—†	13	laundress	38	"
N	Cosminski Sylvester F	13	cook	42	"
P	Nelson Marian—†	13	waitress	25	34 Northfield
R	Johnson Annie—†	14	housekeeper	70	here
S	Nickolas Elisebeth—†	14	laundress	28	564 Shawmut av
T	Nickolas James	14	paperhanger	34	564 "
U	Washington Frank A	14	mechanic	43	here
V	Washington Marian B—†	14	housewife	29	"
W	Brown Selenia—†	15	"	46	"
X	Brown William H	15	storekeeper	50	"
Y	Lucas Thomas	15	"	48	"
A	Garrett Charles J	16	laborer	50	here
B	Hawkins Margret L—†	16	housewife	50	"
C	Hawkins William F	16	laborer	45	"
D	Dillon Julia—†	16	domestic	30	100 Myrtle
E	Hind Adelaide—†	16	cook	52	here
F	Taylor Susie—†	16	domestic	50	"
G	Seaborn Harry	17	cook	38	"
H	Spencer Mary—†	17	housekeeper	45	"
K	Spencer Peter S	17	caterer	55	"
L	Williams Sadie—†	17	domestic	55	"
M	Harris Boyton	18	laborer	62	"

Page.	Letter.	FULL NAME.	Residence, April 1, 1926.	Occupation.	Supposed Age.	Reported Residence, April 1, 1925. Street and Number.

Northfield Street—Continued

	N	Ashley Rose —†	18	domestic	46	New Bedford
	O	Colbert Mary —†	18	housekeeper	39	32 Northfield
	R	Jenkins Stella—†	18	domestic	33	here
	S	Fickens Robert	19	stevedore	38	"
	T	Muse Pearl —†	19	dressmaker	47	"
	T¹	Robinson Blanche —†	19	hairdresser	33	"
	U	Brown James	19	porter	48	New York City
	V	Brown Viola —†	19	housewife	45	here
	X	Taylor Nellie —†	20	domestic	47	"
	Y	Taylor William	20	laborer	49	22 Northfield
	A	Fernandez Peter	20	"	41	here
	A¹	Fernadez Rebecca —†	20	housewife	24	"
	B	Turner Florence —†	20	laundress	34	"
	C	Martin Jack	21	laborer	28	Marshfield
	D	Smith Samuel	21	"	32	"
	E	Jones Benedict	21	chauffeur	25	here
	F	Mitchell Charles	21	"	32	"
	G	Rainey Sarah —†	21	domestic	65	"
	H	Thomas Clifford	22	laborer	40	26 Woodbury
	K	Williams Ellen —†	22	domestic	26	26 "
	L	Wilson Mamie —†	22	"	22	26 "
	N	Steele Samuel	22	laborer	53	25 Northfield
	O	Steele Sofia —†	22	domestic	71	25 "
	P	Liggett Marion —†	22	"	37	25 "
	R	Nesby Emma —†	23	"	33	14 Woodbury
	S	Nesby Fred	23	laborer	44	14 "
	T	Allen Florence —†	23	cook	38	here
	U	Roderiges John	23	laborer	29	1022 Tremont
	V	Ball James	24	"	34	here
	W	Cruz John	24	"	38	"
	X	Williams Alice —†	24	housewife	43	"
	Y	Johnson Frank	24	janitor	48	"
	Z	Johnson Sadie —†	24	housewife	43	"
	A	Williams John B	24	laborer	49	262 Cambridge
	B	Williams Mary —†	24	domestic	40	262 "
	C	Randolph John L	25	laborer	31	108 W Springfield
	D	Randolph Teresa M —†	25	housewife	28	108 "
	E	Jones Carrie —†	25	housekeeper	64	here
	F	Reeves Thomas	25	laborer	34	"
	G	Washington Charles	26	"	40	"
	H	Wilson Victoria —†	26	housewife	42	"

Page	Letter	Full Name.	Residence, April 1, 1926.	Occupation.	Supposed Age.	Reported Residence, April 1, 1925. Street and Number.

Northfield Street—Continued

K	Brown Fannie—†	26	domestic	50	here
L	Cook Elizabeth—†	26	at home	50	44 Buckingham
M	Davis Lena—†	26	housekeeper	32	98 Camden
N	MacBeth Mamber—†	27	housewife	40	S Carolina
O	Hill Della—†	27	"	27	here
P	Hill William	27	cook	32	"
R	Francis Abraham	27	laborer	54	"
S	Burns Alexander	28	longshoreman	62	"
T	Burns Fannie—†	28	housewife	50	"
U	Richards Charles	28	chauffeur	30	"
V	Richards Eva—†	28	housewife	29	"
W	Amado Joseph S	28	storekeeper	61	"
X	Sisco Christina—†	28	domestic	44	"
Y	Sisco Lee	28	clerk	24	"
Z	Butler Edna H—†	28	domestic	40	"
A	Wells Rosalia—†	28	"	35	"
B	Blakey Benjamin	29	laborer	54	
C	Harrison Margret—†	29	housekeeper	30	52 Sawyer
D	Terry Matthew	29	laborer	37	52 "
E	Singelton Kate—†	29	domestic	29	here
F	Lathrop Ella—†	30	"	58	82 Kendall
G	Lawman Ada—†	30	"	21	here
H	Knapton Henry	30	painter	52	"
K	Knapton Rilla—†	30	housewife	38	"
L	Harris Rosie—†	30	domestic	45	8 Arnold
M	Swan Caroline—†	31	"	81	23 Northfield
N	Swan Louis H	31	waiter	65	23 "
O	Ellison Crafford	31	roofer	27	here
P	Ellison Hattie—†	31	domestic	26	"
R	Cooper Fannie—†	31	laundress	23	"
S	Cooper John H	31	laborer	27	"
T	Brathwaite Bertha—†	32	domestic	25	4 Hubert
U	Gibson Frank	32	tailor	36	here
V	Taylor Cynthia—†	32	domestic	32	Everett
W	Epps Ruby—†	32	"	40	here
Y	Knowlton Grace F—†	33	housekeeper	39	"
Z	Myers James H	33	cook	35	"
A	Smith Arthur E	33	laborer	43	"
B	Smith Margret M—†	33	laundress	49	"
C	Besley Katie—†	33	"	58	38 Newcomb
D	Spencer Letha A—†	34	demonstrator	28	10 Castlegate rd

Letter	FULL NAME.	Residence, April 1, 1926.	Occupation.	Supposed Age.	Reported Residence, April 1, 1925. Street and Number.

Northfield Street—Continued

Letter	FULL NAME.	Residence	Occupation.	Age	Reported Residence
E	Spencer Richard E	34	laborer	37	10 Castlegate rd
F	Baptist Josuah	34	"	45	here
G	Baptist Mary—†	34	domestic	38	"
H	Penn Caroline—†	34	housewife	44	"
K	Penn William H	34	laborer	63	"
L	Reed Cecial	34	"	40	"
P	O'Connell Carl	35	"	45	115 Kendall
S	Washington Sarah—†	36	domestic	40	here
T	Lanier Molly—†	36	housekeeper	49	"
U	Paine Elizabeth—†	36	domestic	40	"
V	Conroy Luther	36	laborer	33	New York City
W	Hockaday Julius P	36	"	36	59 Kendall
Y	Mitchell Arthur	37	"	24	10 Willard pl
Z	Mitchell Lilian—†	37	housekeeper	47	10 "
A	Stewart Charles H	37	laborer	38	19 Notre Dame
B	Stewart Sarah—†	37	housewife	35	19 "
D	Dennis Martha—†	38	domestic	50	here
E	Church Grace—†	38	housewife	50	"
F	Church William H	38	elevatorman	51	"
G	Clifton Emmett	38	painter	27	30 Newcomb
H	Glenn Martha—†	38	domestic	35	here
K	Beauve Bessie—†	39	"	36	"
L	Benton Laurie	39	chauffeur	31	202 Northampton
M	Benton Molly—†	39	housewife	37	202 "
N	Clark Eliza	39	stevedore	52	here
P	Jockson Eliskoz	40	chemist	43	"
R	Taylor Mollie—†	40	domestic	48	"
S	Mitchell Lucy—†	40	"	49	62 Kendall
T	Stewart Milinda C—†	40	"	47	here
U	Merando Bertoldo	41	laborer	30	"
V	Merando Willetta—†	41	housewife	27	"
W	Hill Elsie—†	41	domestic	44	"
X	Wellington Carrie B—†	41	dressmaker	30	"
Z	Boltin Lilian—†	41	domestic	22	Chicago Ill
Y	Brice Diana—†	41	car cleaner	24	104 Lenox
A	Hammilton Jennie—†	42	housekeeper	54	here
B	Robinson Lydia—†	42	at home	74	"
C	Lall Elvira—†	42	housewife	37	"
D	Lall James	42	mechanic	37	"
F	Silvia Joseph	42	longshoreman	39	"
G	Silvia Margret—†	42	domestic	46	"

Northfield Street—Continued

	Letter	Full Name	Res.	Occupation	Age	Reported Residence
	L	Nichols Lucy—†	43	housekeeper	23	572 Shawmut av
	N	Greene Laura—†	43	"	37	here
	O	Lindsay William J	44	laborer	55	"
	P	Lane Benjamin F	44	"	39	"
	R	Lane Estella—†	44	housewife	29	"
	S	Martin Annie—†	44	laundress	47	"
	T	Glover Lettie—†	44	domestic	46	"
	V	Ricker Lillian B—†	45	housekeeper	34	"
	U	Ricker Louis M	45	laborer	37	"
	W	Arthur Amy M—†	45	housekeeper	30	"
	X	Riley Minnie—†	45	"	24	"
	Y	Thomas Rose A—†	45	"	28	"
	A	Allen Abraham	46	laborer	38	"
	B	Allen Emily—†	46	housewife	40	"
	C	Manual Amy E—†	46	domestic	45	"
	E	Williams Lucia	47	janitor	38	40 Northfield
	F	Williams Mary—†	47	housekeeper	39	40 "
	G	Cristiani Annie—†	47	"	38	here
	H	Cristiani Vincenzo	47	laborer	42	"
	K	Allaway Marie—†	47	waitress	26	116 Camden
	L	Bullis Rachel M—†	47	housewife	58	3 Berkeley
	M	Childs Ruby E—†	47	waitress	36	116 Camden
	N	Brown Frederick	48	mechanic	36	here
	O	Brown Mary—†	48	housewife	37	"
	P	Hampton Ernest	48	laborer	40	"
	R	Jennings James	48	janitor	28	"
	S	Peters Nettie—†	48	domestic	35	"
	T	Good Isace	48	laborer	42	"
	V	Carter Robert H	50	cook	30	Brockton
	W	Jones Elsie—†	50	domestic	50	"
	X	Freeman Susa—†	50	housewife	52	here
	Y	Gainsboro Marion—†	50	domestic	38	"
	Z	Gaceson Sarah—†	50	"	56	"
	A	Twohey James	51	janitor	67	57 Northfield
	B	Twohey Madlinene—†	51	housewife	64	57 "
	C	Donnolly Catherine—†	51	housekeeper	26	here
	D	Donnelly William J	51	painter	43	"
	E	Miller Carrie—†	52	housewife	38	"
	F	Taylor Ira—†	52	wagonwasher	35	"
	G	Taylor Lavenia—†	52	housewife	34	"

Northfield Street— Continued

H	Fox Carey	52	chauffeur	35	here
K	Fox Helen—†	52	housewife	32	"
L	Foy Andrew	52	laborer	26	8 Greenwich
M	Foy Marzella—†	52	housewife	21	8 "
N	Hayes Agnes—†	53	housekeeper	34	here
O	Hayes Harold E	53	roofer	32	"
P	Mulcahy Helen—†	53	operator	30	"
R	Mulcahy Mary—†	53	housekeeper	64	"
S	Mulcahy Thomas	53	chauffeur	33	"
X	Smith Emily J—†	55	housekeeper	86	"
Y	Smith George W	55	paperhanger	66	"
Z	Hurley Charles D	55	carpenter	76	"
A	Langan Margarite—†	55	housewife	60	"
B	Cook Ellin T—†	55	housekeeper	60	"
C	Brown Norah—†	56	domestic	38	New York City
D	Liggens Mary—†	56	housewife	53	Youngstown O
E	Sheppard Magmalia—†	56	domestic	58	Everett
F	LeBlanc Thomas W	56	cook	67	here
G	Peterson Clara—†	56	housekeeper	32	"
H	Peterson Isabelita—†	56	domestic	21	"
K	Cobb Susan—†	56	"	53	"
L	Saunders Frederick	56	laborer	45	"
M	Griffin David	57	janitor	28	2002 Wash'n
N	Griffin May—†	57	housekeeper	23	2002 "
O	Green Evelene A—†	57	"	23	Savannah Ga
P	Green Jake	57	laborer	25	"
R	Jones Clarence J	57	postal clerk	29	here
S	Jones Elizabeth M—†	57	housekeeper	29	S Carolina
T	Bailey Mary F—†	57	housewife	28	741 Shawmut av
U	Skinner Estelle—†	57	"	34	15 Claremont pk
V	Lynch Rosella—†	58	housekeeper	53	here
W	Reade William C	58	auctioneer	54	"
X	Johnson Edward	59	chauffeur	39	New York City
Y	Johnson Susan—†	59	clerk	35	"
Z	Wadoski Mary—†	59	housekeeper	36	here
A	Wadoski Peter	59	clerk	40	"
B	Goldsmith Charles	59	florist	63	"
C	Goldsmith Lucy—†	59	housewife	49	"
D	Williams Lucy—†	60	domestic	60	"
E	Williams Thomas	60	clerk	42	"
F	Byron Carrie—†	60	laundress	44	"

Page.	Letter.	FULL NAME.	Residence, April 1, 1926.	Occupation.	Supposed Age.	Reported Residence, April 1, 1925. Street and Number.

Northfield Street—Continued

	L	Brown Elizabeth—†	61	housekeeper	26	77 Newland
	M	Brown Roger S	61	whitewasher	34	77 "
	N	Eliot Irene—†	61	housewife	23	29 Sawyer
	O	Eliot James	61	stableman	29	29 "
	P	Peters Ella—†	62	housewife	48	here
	R	Peters Herbert H	62	janitor	43	"
	S	Beverly John	62	porter	45	"
	T	Jenkins Abbie—†	62	housewife	30	"
	U	Jenkins Seyborn	62	janitor	26	"
	W	Hart Helen N—†	63	housewife	32	32 Corning ct
	X	Hart Thomas H	63	butcher	33	Wakefield
	Y	Hussey Bridget—†	63	housekeeper	43	here
	Z	Hussey James J	63	cutter	45	"
	A	Collier Annie—†	63	housekeeper	33	"
	B	Collier Frank	63	chauffeur	37	"
	C	Wiley Celia—†	64	housewife	39	"
	D	Wiley James	64	laborer	49	"
	E	Day Bruce	64	janitor	60	"
	F	Douglas George	64	laborer	35	"
	G	Gomez John	64	"	38	"
	H	Monteir Jack	64	"	36	"
	K	Smith David P	65	waiter	42	64 Sterling
	L	Smith Mary C—†	65	housewife	41	64 "
	M	Adams Charles	65	laborer	28	43 Northfield
	N	Adams Kathleen L—†	65	housekeeper	29	43 "
	O	Anderson Gerald	65	foundryman	24	14 Cliff
	P	Anderson Viola—†	65	housekeeper	21	176 Warwick
	R	Williams Frank	65	laborer	21	176 "
	S	Gray George R	66	tinsmith	56	here
	T	Screen John	66	musician	30	"
	U	Gray Leo	66	clerk	27	1 Cumston
	V	Gray Ralphia—†	66	housewife	21	1 "
	W	Grant William E	66	waiter	27	here
	X	Savoy Julian	66	"	30	"
	Z	Joseph Hubert	68	chauffeur	37	10 Dartmouth pl
	A	Joseph Laura—†	68	housewife	39	10 "
	B	Robbins Catharine A—†	68	"	35	here
	C	Robbins Richard J	68	stevedore	45	"
	D	Samuel Gordon	68	carpenter	37	"
	E	Charles Emanuel	68	fireman	37	"
	F	Charles Ethel—†	68	laundress	30	"

34

Northfield Street—Continued

G	Baker Louis	69	clerk	37	here
H	Baker Sarah—†	69	housewife	37	"
K	Jackson Kenneth W	69	laborer	26	41 Windsor
L	Jackson Leona M—†	69	housewife	21	41 "
M	Richardson Elizabeth—†	69	housekeeper	35	68 Northfield
N	Boyd Frank	69	laborer	23	68 "
O	Payne Samuel	69	waiter	43	14 Truro
P	Quamo Lamby	69	"	35	here
R	Adams Phillis—†	70	housekeeper	24	99 Warwick
U	Jones Nellie—†	70	nurse	35	12 Kendall
T	Jones Orinda—†	70	at home	73	Canada
V	Dickinson Beatrice—†	70	housewife	37	here
W	Dickinson Lesley	70	stevedore	36	"
X	Michell Fannie E—†	71	housekeeper	48	"
Y	Crawford Catherine—†	71	"	23	"
Z	Johnson Catherine—†	71	housewife	45	"
A	Johnson Cleophas J	71	cook	60	"
B	Taylor Mollie V—†	71	housekeeper	38	40 Northfield
C	Veiza Elizabeth H—†	71	cook	45	here
D	Fenton Alice—†	71	housekeeper	31	"
E	Fenton Samuel	71	laborer	31	"
F	Harris Samuel	72	janitor	41	"
G	Morle Emily—†	72	housewife	49	"
H	Morle Hubert M	72	shipper	48	"
K	Lilly Fredericka—†	72	domestic	27	"
L	Reed Elizabeth—†	72	housekeeper	52	"
M	Lockman Albert	72	laborer	49	"
N	Lockman Belle—†	72	housewife	47	"
O	Clark Samuel R	72	laborer	36	"
P	Ditmar Florence M—†	73	tel operator	35	169 Chestnut av
R	Ditmar William J	73	janitor	66	here
S	McHale John T	73	manager	43	"
T	McHale Ruth M—†	73	housekeeper	31	"
U	Milano Anna—†	73	"	22	65 Northfield
V	Milano Michael	73	laborer	26	65 "
W	O'Handley Joseph P	73	policeman	30	here
X	O'Handley Mary M—†	73	housewife	28	"
Y	Glynn John	73	factory worker	27	"
Z	Glynn Mary—†	73	housekeeper	52	"
A	O'Handley Daniel	75	chauffeur	27	"
B	O'Handley Macolm	75	blacksmith	56	"

Northfield Street—Continued

c	O'Handley Mary—†	75	housekeeper	54	here
d	Green Frank	75	cook	59	"
e	Green Sarah—†	75	housekeeper	43	"
f	Crawford Agnes—†	75	"	55	"
g	Crawford Frank	75	lawyer	62	"
h	Crawford George	75	chauffeur	23	"
k	O'Handley Cornelius J	75	laborer	26	"

Parnell Street

l	Carney Catherine G—†	1	nurse	24	here
m	Carney William F	1	bronzesmith	29	"
n	Fleming Frances M—†	1	forewoman	28	"
o	Powers Peter	1	laborer	47	"
p	Dluty Bella—†	1	housekeeper	28	1232 Blue Hill av
r	Dluty Jacob	1	storekeeper	35	1232 "
s	Smith Hubert A	2	plumber	26	here
t	Smith Mary B—†	2	housekeeper	25	"
u	Smith Michael J	2	salesman	34	"
v	Smith Patrick	2	retired	70	"
w	Day George E	3	machinist	45	"
x	Day John L	3	vulcanizer	23	"
y	Day Mary C—†	3	operator	20	"
z	Day Mary M—†	3	housewife	46	"
f	Kelly Annie—†	6	"	37	"
g	Kelly Michael F	6	porter	38	"
h	Montgomery Mary F—†	7	housekeeper	75	568 Shawmut av
k	Connors Charles	7	carpet cleaner	51	591 "
l	Adams Elizabeth—†	7	housekeeper	35	here
m	Lewis Adline—†	8	housewife	49	"
n	Lewis William A	8	janitor	49	"
o	Steele Frank J	9	glazier	38	"
p	Steele John J	9	carpenter	73	"
r	Peters Mary B—†	9	housekeeper	58	"
t	Cameron Duncan	9	carpenter	65	"
s	Charles Mary—†	9	housekeeper	65	"
u	Stewart Daniel	9	carpenter	50	"
v	Wilson Juanita F—†	10	garmentmaker	35	23 Sawyer
x	Mason Elizabeth—†	11	housekeeper	50	52 Northfield
y	Cross Nina M—†	11	"	33	25 "

	Letter.	FULL NAME.	Residence, April 1, 1926.	Occupation.	Supposed Age.	Reported Residence, April 1, 1925. Street and Number.

Parnell Street—Continued

z	Fowler George W	12	janitor	62	here
A	Fowler Marion M—†	12	housewife	30	"
B	McLellan Delia—†	13	"	54	"
C	McLellan Laughlin	13	carpenter	74	"
D	Doherty Margret—†	13	housekeeper	65	"
E	Doherty Patrick	13	laborer	73	"
F	Steele Daniel	13	carpenter	50	Florida
G	Banks Benjamin J	14	janitor	70	here
H	Kendall Bertha—†	14	laundress	21	"
K	Kendall Sarah—†	14	housekeeper	39	"
M	Hall Elijah	15	laborer	24	22 Newcomb
N	Hall Mary E—†	15	housewife	20	22 "
P	Doherty Mary—†	16	housekeeper	75	here
V	Duffey Margaret E—†	17	"	43	"
T	Ferreira Caroline V—†	17	housewife	41	"
U	Ferreira Joseph E	17	constable	39	"
W	Thomas Elvin	18	laborer	36	67 Lenox
X	Thomas Sarah—†	18	housewife	25	67 "

Sawyer Street

C	Rice Eugene S	3	tel worker	53	here
D	Rice Eva M—†	3	housewife	33	"
E	Barry Philip	3	rubberworker	24	"
F	Barry Rose—†	3	housewife	21	"
G	Maple Elmer	3	mechanic	39	"
H	Maple Sarah—†	3	housewife	55	"
K	Alperen Belle—†	3	"	53	"
L	Alperen David M	3	janitor	55	"
P	McMillan Lillian—†	17	housewife	39	"
S	Andrews Manuel	17	laborer	40	"
T	Fonseca Fred	17	"	29	"
U	Martin Manuel R	17	"	37	California
V	Scott Elizabeth—†	17	housewife	61	here
W	Scott Joseph H	17	seaman	40	"
X	Scott Joseph T	17	cook	70	"
Y	Wright Ida—†	17	housekeeper	37	Augusta Ga
A	Nebblett Emogene—†	17	houseworker	20	here
A¹	Nebblett Ethel—†	17	housekeeper	47	"
C	Junkins Edith—†	21	"	45	"

37

Page.	Letter.	Full Name.	Residence, April 1, 1926.	Occupation.	Supposed Age.	Reported Residence, April 1, 1925. Street and Number.

Sawyer Street—Continued

	D	Chestnut Elizabeth—†	21	housekeeper	52	here
	E	Jett George	21	laborer	40	"
	F	Alves August	21	"	30	5 Holyoke
	G	Alves Earla—†	21	housewife	29	5 "
	H	Andrews Manuel	23	laborer	56	19 Lenox
	K	Gumbs John	23	"	24	here
	L	Vlaun Clara—†	23	laundress	45	"
	M	Binnie John	23	laborer	23	Lawrence
	N	Piano Joseph	23	"	35	Springfield
	O	Bergland Ruth V—†	25	houseworker	27	here
	P	Douglass Stevan	25	postal clerk	29	"
	R	Hackett Sarah M—†	25	housekeeper	40	"
	S	Henstract Rose—†	25	domestic	40	"
	T	Houtman Annie—†	25	"	48	"
	W	Anderson George N	29	laborer	47	795 Tremont
	X	Anderson Mary—†	29	housewife	45	795 "
	Y	Twitchell Jeremiah	29	retired	85	795 "
	A	Lewis Naplien	33A	laborer	44	here
	B	Burries Benjamin	33A	retired	67	"
	C	Burries Mary J—†	33A	housewife	54	"
	D	Weener Lewis	33A	merchant	54	"
	E	Weener Rose—†	33A	housewife	41	"
	F	Noble Isalu—†	39	"	29	"
	G	Noble Wade	39	laborer	48	"
	H	Fox Catherine—†	39	housewife	45	"
	K	Fox Ottoway	39	hostler	46	"
	L	Dwyer Thomas	41	laborer	65	"
	M	James Caroline—†	41	housekeeper	60	"
	N	Bell Viola—†	43	laundress	27	"
	O	Eddison Edward L	43	teamster	42	"
	P	Eddison Laura—†	43	laundress	51	"
	R	McLean Joshua	43	real estate	32	"
	S	Morris John H	45	laborer	28	"
	T	Wells Richard N	45	"	65	"
	U	Wells Susan A—†	45	housewife	59	"
	V	Wells Joseph J	45	painter	24	"
	W	Wells Serena E—†	45	housewife	37	"
	Y	Holmes Marie J—†	47	laundress	51	"
	Z	Reid Sarah—†	47	houseworker	31	
	A	Andrews Carrie—†	49	housewife	46	13 Arnold
	B	Andrews William	49	fireman	52	13 "

38

Letter	Full Name.	Residence, April 1, 1926.	Occupation.	Supposed Age.	Reported Residence, April 1, 1925. Street and Number.

Sawyer Street—Continued

Letter	Full Name.	Residence, April 1, 1926.	Occupation.	Supposed Age.	Reported Residence, April 1, 1925. Street and Number.
c	Ferguson Lucy M—†	49	housewife	42	57 Windsor
d	Ferguson William P	49	laborer	52	57 "
e	Brown Mary—†	49	houseworker	35	here
f	Frazer Joseph	51	retired	60	"
g	Lawson Ramsie—†	51	houseworker	60	"
h	Bean Julia—†	51	"	28	"
k	Rahn Chester	55	laborer	45	522 Col av
l	Thomas Lillian—†	55	housekeeper	42	11 Fairweather
m	Costa Benjamin	55	laborer	42	60 Sawyer
n	Costa Estella—†	55	housewife	40	60 "
o	Butler Elizabeth—†	55	at home	76	here
p	Terry Bertha—†	57	musician	26	"
r	Terry Lullu—†	57	housekeeper	58	"
s	McLinnahan Junino	57	cook	33	N Carolina
u	McLinnahan Lucy—†	57	housewife	26	"
v	McLinnahan Mack	57	laborer	27	"
t	McLinnahan Mary—†	57	housewife	35	"
w	Dixon Mary—†	59	housekeeper	52	here
x	Stevens Maria—†	59	housewife	43	"
y	Stevens Wilson	59	laborer	44	"
z	Dansby Ishmeal	59	clerk	25	New Jersey
a	Hunt Edgar	59	laborer	35	here
b	Rogers Sarah—†	59	houseworker	40	"
c	Fletcher Minnie—†	61	laundress	51	"
d	Jefferson Nora—†	61	seamstress	57	"
e	Crawford Margaret—†	61	housewife	52	"
f	Crawford Nathaniel	61	laborer	53	"
g	Burton Susan—†	63	housekeeper	72	"
h	White Roxielena—†	63	housewife	23	"
k	White William	63	clerk	29	"
l	Louise May—†	65	dressmaker	22	"
m	Turner Kate—†	65	houseworker	69	"
n	Beckett Bertha V—†	65	housewife	32	"
o	Beckett John T	65	pedler	27	"
p	Lops Emma—†	65	housewife	35	38 Sawyer
r	Lops John	65	mason	38	38 "
s	Quarles Anna L—†	67	maid	59	792 Tremont
t	Wilson Beatrice—†	67	housewife	20	792 "
u	Wilson Thomas	67	porter	25	792 "
v	Jackson Dorothy—†	67	maid	25	here
w	Jackson James	67	barber	37	"

Page.	Letter.	FULL NAME.	Residence, April 1, 1926.	Occupation.	Supposed Age.	Reported Residence, April 1, 1925.
						Street and Number.

Sawyer Street—Continued

	X	Dach Inez—†	67	houseworker	47	72A Shawmut av
	Y	Mostow John J	69	real estate	65	here
	Z	Sappho Enc	69	laborer	60	Chicago Ill
	A	Sappho Millie J—†	69	housewife	52	"

Shawmut Avenue

	E	Brooks Alfred	552	porter	68	here
	F	Dean Gerald	552	waiter	34	"
	G	Dean Gladys—†	552	housekeeper	32	"
	H	Johnson Frank	552	laborer	34	25 Woodbury
	K	Farrar Harriot—†	553	nurse	60	here
	L	Alston Ethel—†	554	housekeeper	27	New York City
	M	Alston Henry	554	laborer	29	"
	N	Brooks Maynard	554	longshoreman	26	here
	O	Robinson Jack	554	laborer	52	"
	P	White William	554	hotelworker	45	"
	R	Collins Beatrice—†	555	housewife	45	"
	S	Collins Hebert	555	porter	44	"
	T	Francisco Frank	555	laborer	27	"
	U	Hamlett Aman	555	blacksmith	45	"
	V	Johnson John	555	barber	38	"
	X	Banks Walter	557	junk dealer	40	"
	Y	Gooding Joseph	557	foundryman	35	"
	Z	Jackson Milton	557	fireman	68	"
	A	Marshall Edna—†	557	laundress	40	"
	B	Pelham Charles	557	retired	84	"
	C	Shank James	557	janitor	40	598 Shawmut av
	D	Stokes Isaac	557	truck driver	45	here
	F	Baker Dorothy—†	559	housewife	32	"
	G	Baker George	559	painter	40	"
	H	Baker Susie—†	559	presser	33	"
	K	Cotton Mabel—†	559	housekeeper	34	"
	L	Peters Estelle—†	559	housewife	44	"
	M	Peters George	559	laborer	47	"
	P	Anderson Coleen—†	561A	domestic	25	"
	R	Brown Benjamin	561A	laborer	28	"
	S	Brown Bessie—†	561A	housewife	26	"
	T	Lawrence George	561A	laborer	37	"

Page.	Letter.	FULL NAME.	Residence, April 1, 1926.	Occupation	Supposed Age.	Reported Residence, April 1, 1925. Street and Number.

Shawmut Avenue—Continued

	U	Reginald Henry	561A	cook	35	here
	V	Rutledge Edith—†	561A	housekeeper	35	"
	W	Weeks William	561A	dentist	37	"
	Y	Anderson Rebecca—† rear	562	laundress	38	"
	Z	Anderson Robert "	562	laborer	45	"
	A	Reiff Henry "	562	shipper	33	117 Lenox
	H	Ross Annie—†	581	housekeeper	49	here
	K	Ross Edward	581	steamfitter	55	"
	L	Donovan Cornelius	581	laborer	67	"
	M	Donovan Katherine—†	581	housekeeper	67	"
	U	Marchel Isabell—†	585	"	38	"
	V	Ross Matthew	585	chauffeur	26	"
	W	Frazer Celia—†	585	housewife	34	"
	X	Frazer William	585	laborer	52	"
	D	Holgate Daniel	589	janitor	39	"
	E	Holgate Lavina—†	589	housekeeper	32	"
	F	Steel Catherine—†	589	domestic	33	"
	H	Laws Cecelia—†	589	at home	70	"
	K	Scott Royn—†	589	"	70	"
	L	Scott William	589	janitor	59	"
	M	Davis Anthony	589	machinist	38	"
	N	Hunter Nancy—†	589	housekeeper	55	"
	O	Lovell Dorothy—†	589	housewife	32	"
	P	Lovell Osmyn	589	real estate	35	"
	R	Wilks Clement	589	clergyman	56	"
	S	Wilks Laura—†	589	housekeeper	56	"
	T	Campbell Edgar C	590	laborer	46	48 Sawyer
	U	Lathon George	590	"	55	Hartford Ct
	V	Martin Lena—†	590	domestic	51	48 Sawyer
	D	George Annie—†	599	housekeeper	45	California
	E	George Elizabeth—†	599	student	20	"
	F	George Nickol	599	coppersmith	50	"
	G	Allen Robert E	599	janitor	43	here
	H	Allen Viola—†	599	housekeeper	41	"
	K	Marson Alice—†	599	"	40	"
	L	Marson James E	599	janitor	41	"
	N	Moore Laurae	601	laborer	35	"
	O	Adams Georgana—†	601	housekeeper	60	"
	P	Adams Joseph	601	laborer	30	"
	R	Robinson Mary J—†	601	domestic	36	"

Page.	Letter.	FULL NAME.	Residence, April 1, 1926.	Occupation.	Supposed Age.	Reported Residence, April 1, 1925. Street and Number.

Shawmut Avenue—Continued

s	Hutchinson David	601	waiter	45	here
T	Hutchinson Marinda—†	601	housekeeper	39	"
U	Bailey Freda—†	603	domestic	29	"
V	Small Norman	603	laborer	41	"
W	Patterson Martha—†	603	housekeeper	42	"
X	Morten Lucy—†	603	domestic	40	"
Y	Gaynor Maurice	603	janitor	35	"
Z	McKenzie Alice—†	603	housekeeper	32	"
A	McKenzie Arthur	603	mechanic	46	"
B	Hoard David	605	laborer	39	"
C	Hoard Liza—†	605	housewife	32	"
D	Neely Louis	605	mason	43	"
E	Neely Nora—†	605	housekeeper	35	"
F	Saunders Clemenine—†	605	"	32	"
G	Saunders Leroy	605	cook	33	"
H	Chase Allen	605	laborer	38	"
K	Chase Elizabeth—†	605	housekeeper	32	"
L	Reid Cecelia J—†	607	"	39	"
M	Reid Nathaniel	607	laborer	34	"
N	Bain Jane—†	607	housekeeper	31	"
O	Bain Thomas	607	laborer	42	"
P	Gay Lucy—†	607	domestic	36	"
R	Bibby Maud—†	607	housekeeper	37	85 E Lenox
S	Jordon Thomas E	607	seaman	43	198 Northampton
U	Blake Amelia—†	608A	housewife	29	here
V	Blake Thomas A	608A	janitor	37	"
W	Davis Norwell	608A	clerk	43	"
X	Hawkins Elizabeth—†	608A	housekeeper	46	"
Y	Hawkins Esther—†	608A	domestic	26	"
Z	Wade George	608A	laborer	51	1900 Wash'n
A	Wade Mildred—†	608A	domestic	42	Jersey City N J
B	Spooner Constance—†	609	housekeeper	37	here
D	Jones Carrie—†	609	"	36	"
E	Jones Raymond	609	laborer	40	"
H	Costa Albert E	610A	waiter	40	22 Claremont pk
K	Costa Rachel M—†	610A	housewife	34	22 "
L	Burke John J	610A	laborer	40	88 Hammond
M	Burke Mary E—†	610A	housewife	37	88 "
N	Andrews Linda—†	610A	domestic	26	here
O	Bernard Allabella—†	610A	"	25	"

Letter.	FULL NAME.	Residence, April 1, 1926.	Occupation.	Supposed Age.	Reported Residence, April 1, 1925. Street and Number.

Shawmut Avenue—Continued

P	Lowe Claires—†	610A	domestic	20	New York
R	Wancott Evlina—†	610A	"	42	here
S	Hudson Charles	611	mover	40	"
T	Hudson Joseph	611	porter	47	"
U	Hudson Martha A—†	611	housekeeper	36	"
V	May Clement W	611	engineer	41	"
W	May Inez—†	611	housekeeper	31	"
X	Ellis George W	611	janitor	58	"
Y	Ellis Lucy E—†	611	housekeeper	45	"
Z	Iniss Abraham	611	laborer	42	"
B	Roachford Claudia—†	612A	housewife	32	"
C	Roachford Leslie	612A	real estate	40	"
D	Roberts Erma—†	612A	student	20	Wash'n D C
E	Dyer Litia—†	612A	domestic	42	here
F	Dyer Mary—†	612A	"	20	"
G	Dyer Samuel	612A	laborer	27	"
H	Smith Eunic—†	612A	domestic	34	"
K	Smith Harry	612A	chauffeur	33	"
L	Chandler Edna—†	613	seamstress	38	"
M	Evans William	613	laborer	20	"
N	Beattie Arthur	613	ironworker	41	"
O	Beattie Elinor—†	613	housekeeper	27	"
P	Edwards John T	613	laborer	35	"
R	Edwards Martha—†	613	housekeeper	29	"
S	Reid Earl	613	laborer	27	"
T	Wilson Lora—†	613	housekeeper	35	"
U	Wilson Ralph	613	laborer	37	"
W	Russell Jessie D—†	614A	housewife	54	"
X	Russell William	614A	waiter	55	"
Y	Robinson Beatrice—†	614A	domestic	26	"
Z	Upshur Alberta—†	614A	housewife	42	"
A	Uphur John S	614A	porter	44	"
B	Allston Estella—†	614A	domestic	23	"
C	Gale Joseph	614A	laborer	31	"
D	Henry Reynolds	614A	"	21	"
G	Williams Mertle—†	615	presser	26	Chicago Ill
H	Milbrooks Doris—†	615	housekeeper	43	Atlanta Ga
L	Blanchard Annie—†	616A	"	40	here
M	Blanchard James	616A	laborer	41	"
O	Pateira Manuel	616A	"	40	"

43

Shawmut Avenue—Continued

N	Pena Manuel	616A	laborer	40	New York City
P	Calloway Bertha —†	616A	housekeeper	44	here
R	Calloway Nathaniel	616A	laborer	47	"
S	Medley Samuel E	616A	mechanic	39	"
T	Fitzpatrick Annie —†	617	housekeeper	56	"
U	Fitzpatrick John	617	laborer	30	"
V	Murphy John L	617	polisher	45	"
W	Robbins Viola C —†	617	housekeeper	70	"
X	Whicher Margaret L —†	617	at home	93	"
Y	Haddad Naffie —†	617	"	66	"
Z	Haddad Racheal —†	617	housewife	36	"
A	Haddad Shean A	617	storekeeper	33	"
B	Haddad William A	617	"	39	"
E	Jenkins Ethel —†	618A	housewife	36	"
F	Jenkins Frank	618A	laborer	34	"
G	Dixon Sarah —†	618A	laundress	42	"
H	Dixon William	618A	laborer	54	"
K	Addison Cecil	618A	mechanic	29	"
L	Brown Annie S —†	618A	presser	48	"
M	Zitoli Frank	619	coal dealer	30	"
N	Zitoli Grace —†	619	housewife	24	"
O	Moore Emma A —†	619	at home	78	"
P	Moore Maria L —†	619	housekeeper	80	"
R	Metcalf Edward J	619	laborer	33	7 Flagg
S	Metcalf Mertle —†	619	housewife	32	7 "
Y	Powell Lee A	626	porter	52	here
Z	Buchanan Winifred —†	626	domestic	47	"
A	Brooks Eugenia —A	626	"	45	"
B	Smith Jannia —†	626	cook	50	"
C	Seales Charles H	626A	lawyer	56	"
F	Prailow Eliza —†	630	domestic	22	17 Westminster
G	Prailow William	630	porter	30	17 "
H	Welch Louise —†	630	domestic	38	here
L	Bryan Sarah —†	630	"	38	"
P	Smith Izetta —†	638	laundress	49	"
R	Trotman Lambert	638	teacher	29	"
S	Trotman Lillian —†	638	housewife	27	"
T	Matthews Edna C —†	638	"	49	"
U	Matthews Walter H	638	real estate	50	"

Page.	Letter.	FULL NAME.	Residence, April 1, 1926.	Occupation.	Supposed Age.	Reported Residence, April 1, 1925. Street and Number.

Tremont Street

z	Bailey Cathleen—†	794	cook	30	Wellesley
A	Andrew Leane—†	794	domestic	42	82 Humboldt av
B	Adison Benjamin	796	tailor	26	32 Arnold
C	Adison Lillian—†	796	dressmaker	50	32 "
D	Somerville Robina A—†	796	hairdresser	33	here
E	Armour Rosa B—†	796	housewife	25	"
F	Stamper Bertha—†	796	"	29	622 Col av
G	Stamper James	796	laborer	42	622 "
L	Midelton Benjamin	798	waiter	35	here
M	Midelton Mary —†	798	housewife	25	"
N	Forbes Edward	798	waiter	32	"
O	Forbes Gladis—†	798	housewife	25	"
P	Peters John	798	chef	32	800 Tremont
R	Peters Mabel—†	798	housewife	27	800 "
V	Perkins Irene—†	800	bookkeeper	21	here
W	Perkins Josephine—†	800	housekeeper	42	"
Y	Brown Glifford	802	cook	38	"
Z	Brown Sadie—†	802	housewife	36	"
A	Graham Cora—†	802	domestic	27	Plymouth
B	Lawson Martha—†	802	housekeeper	33	here
C	Scrugge Mary—†	802	domestic	33	"
D	Gowen Ruth—†	804	dressmaker	24	"
E	Moody Anna —†	804	hairdresser	45	"
F	Foster Abraham	806	porter	60	Cambridge
G	Foster Vennie —†	806	housewife	32	"
H	Ecker Harry	806	U S Gov't	29	"
K	Ecker Leona—†	806	housewife	28	"
L	Foster Mary—†	806	domestic	40	104 Dartmouth
O	Stevens Charles	808	factory worker	26	63 Camden
P	Stevens Gertrude—†	808	housewife·	60	63 "
R	Tate Callia—†	808	"	26	here
S	Tate Frank	808	caretaker	32	"
T	Arthur Katherine—†	808	housewife	47	21 W Canton
U	Arthur Samuel	808	janitor	50	21 "
V	Hill Bolton R	810	laborer	33	243 Northampton
W	Hill Inez B—†	810	housewife	34	243 "
X	Jones Luther	810	laborer	28	243 "
Y	Karrigan Arthur	810	muscian	28	here
Z	Karrigan Bessie —†	810	housewife	25	"
A	Williams Anna—†	812	"	34	"

Tremont Street—Continued

B	Williams Edward	812	beef carrier	44	here
C	Londen Alma —†	812	elevatorwoman	28	39 Northfield
D	Webber Lucy—†	812	housewife	36	here
E	Webber Wilfred	812	laborer	36	"
U	Roberts Leontine —†	896	housewife	32	"
V	Roberts Simeon	896	real estate	32	"
W	Saggasse Aurelio	896	shoemaker	62	"
X	Bailey Julia †	896	housekeeper	75	68 Sterling
Y	Scott Charles	896	musician	35	68 "
Z	Scott Louise —†	896	housekeeper	55	68 "
A	Clooke Jeanette —†	896	housewife	30	80 Bowen
B	Phillips Mildred —†	896	domestic	28	31 Cunard
C	Thorpe Daisey—†	896	houseworker	28	129 Lenox
D	Eramian Daniel	896	tailor	39	here
E	Eramian Susie —†	896	housewife	37	"

Washington Street

S	Stavolta Eugenia —†	1821	housewife	41	here
T	Stavolta Stellario	1821	barber	45	"
U	Parkins Marguerite—†	1821	housekeeper	38	127 Myrtle
V	Hardiman James H	1821	insurance agent	53	here
W	Hardiman Mary A—†	1821	housewife	46	"
X	Reed Charles H	1821	baker	59	"
Y	Reed Marie J—†	1821	housewife	53	"
Z	Nagle Mary E—†	1821	housekeeper	42	2 Badger pl
A	Lans Edmund T	1821	fish dealer	68	here
B	Lans Edmund T, jr	1821	janitor	36	"
C	Tataro Mary—†	1821	housewife	28	"
D	Tataro Nathan	1821	foreman	30	"
E	Vondell Henry W	1821	laborer	49	196 Blue Hill av
K	Cecil John A	1829	clerk	47	here
L	Cecil Theresa—†	1829	housewife	37	"
M	Doyle George A	1829	blacksmith	55	"
N	Doyle Margaret—†	1829	housewife	54	"
O	Donohue Joseph P	1829	laborer	29	62 Hampden
P	Donohue Michael P	1829	"	54	62 "
R	Donohue Susan—†	1829	cook	50	62 "
S	Green Corinne—†	1829	housewife	37	here
T	Green Roland	1829	clerk	39	"

Page.	Letter.	FULL NAME.	Residence, April 1, 1926.	Occupation.	Supposed Age.	Reported Residence, April 1, 1925. Street and Number.

Washington Street—Continued

	u	Davis Elizabeth—†	1829	housewife	37	1821 Wash'n
	v	Davis James J	1829	foreman	55	1821 "
	w	Patterson Alexander	1829	window washer	27	30 W Dedham
	x	Patterson Annie—†	1829	housewife	25	30 "
	y	Saccary Alice—†	1829	waitress	27	97 Regent
	z	Saccary Mary—†	1829	"	21	11 Harold pk
	a	Workman Mary—†	1829	laundress	42	here
	b	Johnson Ida C—†	1829	housewife	33	"
	c	Johnson John A	1829	carpenter	35	"
	e	Obst Maurice	1835	merchant	57	"
	l	Moses Frank O	1845	optometrist	56	"
	e	Anderson Thomas	1911	painter	37	Woburn
	f	Gatley Martin M	1911	porter	63	Long Island
	g	Goodwin James	1911	laborer	27	19 E Lenox
	h	Hanley John	1911	stonecutter	48	2 Garfield pl
	k	Harris James E	1911	pedler	54	617 Mass av
	l	McDermott Winnie—†	1911	housekeeper	43	Brookline
	m	Bennett Charles	1913	factory worker	39	18 Roys
	n	Burkett Jesse	1913	teamster	36	here
	o	Fay Martin	1913	laborer	40	Brockton
	p	Hennessey Timothy	1913	rigger	48	here
	r	McDonald Elmira—†	1913	housekeeper	75	"
	s	McEllaney Peter	1913	laborer	50	230 Shawmut av
	t	Norris Katherine—†	1913	houseworker	72	here
	u	Winters Alice—†	1913	"	27	Cambridge
	w	Ahern Michael	1917	mason	60	here
	x	Arbuckle William	1917	laborer	54	11 Derby pl
	y	Blance Nellie—†	1917	houseworker	40	here
	z	Caiger James H	1917	painter	63	Everett
	a	Cashman John J	1917	"	43	28 Vinton
	b	Chocoyne Joseph	1917	carpenter	65	here
	c	Healey Jeremiah	1917	fireman	40	New York
	d	Lane Cornelius V	1917	plumber	53	104 Roxbury
	e	McHale Elizabeth—†	1917	housekeeper	40	here
	f	Mitchell James	1917	laborer	37	8 W Third
	g	Rooney William	1917	teamster	58	here
	h	Ryan Patrick	1917	"	47	"
	m	Brown Adolph	1927	laborer	54	"
	n	Brown Gertrude E—†	1927	housewife	33	"
	o	Perry Gilbert	1927	laborer	53	"
	p	Perry Joseph A	1927	"	23	"

Washington Street—Continued

R	Perry Margaret—†	1927	housewife	45	here	
T	Anderson Bert	1931	porter	50	604 Mass av	
U	Christenson Chris	1931	painter	50	604 "	
V	Comerford Patrick	1931	laborer	50	here	
W	Driscoll Timothy	1931	hostler	60	179 Col av	
X	Duggan Michael	1931	laborer	36	here	
Y	Halligan Mary—†	1931	housekeeper	53	595 Shawmut av	
Z	McPhee Pius	1931	pile driver	60	here	
A	Murphy Michael	1931	laborer	40	Providence R I	
B	Driscoll James	1933	teamster	38	here	
C	McArthur Amos	1933	carpenter	49	"	
D	Welsh Michael	1933	factory worker	53	1 Worcester pl	
E	Whooley John	1933	laborer	41	here	
K	Gaul Carrie—†	1947	domestic	23	564 Shawmut av	
L	Hill Callie—†	1947	houseworker	39	564 "	
M	Carden Alice—†	1947	"	49	here	
N	Jones Columbus J	1947	laborer	36	"	
O	Jones George A	1947	"	32	"	
P	Jones Gertrude P—†	1947	housewife	34	"	
R	Brown Charles B	1947	carpenter	35	"	
S	Brown Ellen—†	1947	housewife	27	"	
T	Jackson Marion W—†	1947	nurse	27	41 Sarsfield	
U	Scottron Georgenia—†	1949	housewife	42	12 Yarmouth	
V	Scottron Thomas O	1949	clerk	41	12 "	
W	Bryant Ella—†	1949	domestic	28	26 Ball	
X	Southerland Eva—†	1949	"	39	26 "	
Y	Wynn James	1949	fireman	28	31 Newcomb	
Z	Wynn Sheldonia —†	1949	housewife	22	13 Hubert	
A	Young Catharine J—†	1949	"	31	here	
B	Young Lewis R	1949	steward	27	"	

Wentworth Place

D	Bush Frank	1	machinist	32	here	
E	Washington Daniel	1	painter	70	"	
G	Bush Mary—†	2	housewife	34	"	
K	Stone Rachel A—†	3	"	40	377 Northampton	
L	Stone Robert	3	porter	43	377 "	

Willard Place

o	Clark Mary—†	2	laundress	50	here
p	Delgarde Gladys G—†	4	housewife	24	"
R	Young Anna V—†	4	"	49	"
s	Young Walter H	4	laborer	45	"
T	Hitchcock George T	8	meatcutter	75	"
U	Hitchcock Margret—†	8	housewife	51	"
V	Gill Frederick	10	porter	38	40 Northampton
X	Hines Peter	10	laborer	40	15 Woodbury
z	White Edith—†	10	housewife	34	Lynn
A	White George	10	molder	34	"
C	Cole Georgiana C—†	10	housewife	30	143 Northampton
D	Cole Thomas H	10	waiter	40	143 "
H	Benson Frank	16	longshoreman	34	here
K	Benson Ivory—†	16	housewife	23	"
L	White Goldie—†	16	clerk	50	"
M	Jackson Hertford	16	engineer	40	"
N	Woods Florence—†	16	housewife	32	"
o	Woods Lewis A	16	laborer	30	"
P	Haynes Holford	18	porter	35	1 Wirth pl
R	Haynes Mabel—†	18	housewife	25	1 "
s	Spranger Mollie—†	18	"	40	here
T	Spranger Vito	18	bootblack	38	"
U	Clark Henry	18	laborer	40	Wash'n D C
V	Clark Mary—†	18	housewife	25	"
W	Collymore Frances—†	20	"	36	here
X	Collymore Reuben	20	janitor	41	"
Y	Bowman Evelyn—†	20	housewife	35	Connecticut
z	Bowman Lee	20	laborer	32	"
A	Lee Arthur H	20	"	43	131 Lenox
B	Lee Sophie—†	20	housewife	29	131 "
C	Scott Mamie—†	20	laundress	25	here
D	Khan Fazal	22	laborer	40	588 Shawmut av
E	Khan Mabel—†	22	housewife	30	588 "
G	Brown Edward C	22	printer	40	108 Hampden
F	Brown Henrietta—†	22	housewife	34	108 "
H	Connors Margret—†	22	clerk	40	here
K	Mendes Elizabeth—†	22	housewife	22	"
L	McBee Charles	23	clerk	54	"
M	McBee Hattie E—†	23	housewife	44	"

Page.	Letter.	FULL NAME.	Residence, April 1, 1926.	Occupation.	Supposed Age.	Reported Residence, April 1, 1925. Street and Number.

Willard Place—Continued

	O	Williams Annie—†	23	housewife	38	here
	P	Williams Walter	24	laborer	42	"
	R	Lee Robert	24	operator	27	"
	S	Lee Susie—†	24	housewife	27	"
	T	Washington Bessie—†	24	houseworker	30	"
	U	Jones Clarence	24	longshoreman	30	"
	V	Jones Edith—†	24	housewife	23	"
	W	Washington Carl	24	longshoreman	32	"
	X	Washington Florence—†	24	housewife	33	"
	Z	McDonald John	25	butcher	25	"
	A	White Doris—†	25	houseworker	31	"
	B	Young James	26	laborer	47	2 Chester pl
	C	Silva Edna—†	26	housewife	23	33 Camden
	D	Silva John	26	laborer	29	33 "
	E	Perry Adeline—†	26	houseworker	30	83 Williams
	L	Pitrofetta Antonio	28	barber	23	here
	M	Pitrofetta Minnie—†	28	housewife	50	"
	N	Pitrofetta Philip	28	barber	59	"
	O	Andrad Joseph A	28	laborer	30	"
	P	Andrad Margaret—†	28	housewife	28	"
	R	Osborne Margaret—†	29	"	23	"
	T	Osborne Deighton C	29	student	30	"
	U	Hunter Eliza—†	30	housewife	36	Virginia
	V	Hunter Henry L	30	laborer	38	"
	W	Milton Emma—†	30	housewife	24	here
	X	Milton James	30	laborer	39	"
	Y	Stoner Marie—†	30	houseworker	33	49 Taber

Wirth Place

	Z	Somerville Gertrude F—†	1	housewife	26	here
	A	Somerville William A	1	painter	31	"
	B	Bush Charles T	1	factory worker	35	590 Shawmut av
	C	Bush Mary E—†	1	housewife	44	590 "
	C¹	Qumont Zackary	1	laborer	29	174 Northampton
	E	Durant Daniel	2	"	40	here
	F	Durant Susie E—†	2	housewife	40	"

Wirth Place—Continued

G	White Ida—†	2	housewife	55	here
H	White Leroy	2	porter	22	"
D	Benjamon Rosaline—†	2	domestic	55	"
K	Gill Viola—†	2	"	33	"
L	Bridges Daisy B—†	3	housewife	34	"
M	Bridges George	3	laborer	35	"
N	Brown Charles A	3	"	38	16 Willard pl
O	Hooker John	3	"	36	16 "
P	Hooker Martha—†	3	housewife	25	16 "
R	Carter Ethel G—†	3	domestic	27	here
S	Gorman Emily—†	3	housewife	24	"
T	Gorman Frank	3	laborer.	35	"

Woodbury Street

U	Morris John E	1	ironworker	42	here
V	Morris Lillian—†	1	housewife	42	"
W	Durr Eliza—†	1	domestic	60	"
X	Campbell Mary A—†	3	"	55	"
Y	Andrews John	3	laborer	48	"
A	Gowan Warren	5	retired	84	"
C	William Joseph A	5	laborer	62	"
D	Berline Moses	7	janitor	35	"
E	Zelowitz Rebecca—†	7	housekeeper	32	"
F	Wilk George	7	laborer	21	"
G	Jones Frances—†	9	domestic	40	79 E Lenox
H	Holder Una—†	9	houseworker	32	1 Concord pl
L	Baysmore Elnora—†	11	domestic	43	104 Kendall
N	Jones William	11	waiter	48	18 Lenox
O	Raynor John	13	trimmer	41	here
P	Raynor Mabel—†	13	housewife	40	"
R	Raynor Isador—†	13	music teacher	26	"
S	Burns William	15	laborer	42	Georgia
Y	Antonicwicz Amelia—†	19	housewife	37	105 Hampden
Z	Antonicwicz Charles	19	junk dealer	38	105 "
A	Holotch Walter	19	"	27	49 Yeoman
B	Casey Gertrude—†	19	laundress	25	Worcester

Woodbury Street—Continued

c	Casey Patrick F	19	longshoreman	34	Worcester
d	Richards George	19	build'g wrecker	41	"
e	Murphy Florence—†	21	houseworker	51	here
f	Thompson Howard	21	laborer	45	"
m	White James	25	"	55	"
n	Silva John	25	"	42	"
o	Pina John	25	"	37	"
p	Lee William	27	"	49	"
r	Turner Agnes—†	27	domestic	35	"
s	Miller Arthur G	27	tailor	53	"
z	Graves Captola—†	35	domestic	45	"
a	Graves Nellie O—†	35	"	29	"
b	Goode Alice A—†	35	housewife	36	18 Arnold
c	Goode Anthony	35	painter	38	18 "
d	White Laura—†	35	domestic	46	here
e	Jones Maude—†	35	"	35	"
f	Jones Thomas	35	laborer	60	"
g	Thorpe Charles	35	"	40	"
h	Thorpe Frances—†	35	housewife	40	"
k	Scott Lucy—†	35	domestic	45	"
l	Stonsio Joseph	35	laborer	24	"
m	Stonsio Mattie—†	35	housewife	24	"
p	Ball Mary—†	39	domestic	52	31 Arnold
r	Moody Delsie—†	39	"	67	31 "
s	Smith Grace—†	39	"	45	here

Worcester Place

t	Flattish Alice—†	1	housekeeper	47	16 Ruggles
u	Flattish George	1	laborer	50	16 "
v	Hart Helen—†	1	housekeeper	68	12 W Dedham
w	Burke Michel	1	teamster	43	here
x	Egan James	1	retired	45	"
y	Maher Frank	1	waiter	38	"
z	McInnes Frederick C	1	innkeeper	45	"
a	McInnes Grace—†	1	at home	69	"
b	McInnes John B	1	laborer	35	77 Cabot
c	Bannan Charles	1	plumber	60	here

Page	Letter	Full Name.	Residence, April 1, 1926.	Occupation.	Supposed Age.	Reported Residence, April 1, 1925. Street and Number.

Worcester Place—Continued

	D	Dewight Charles	1	laborer	50	here
	E	Earl Peter	1	teamster	50	"
	F	Flanigan Richard	1	plumber	50	"
	G	Gimsley Alice—†	1	housekeeper	58	"
	H	Gimsley George	1	clerk	55	"
	K	King Patrick	1	laborer	60	"
	L	McMillian Frank	1	carpenter	51	"
	M	Mitchell Margaret—†	1	housekeeper	45	"
	N	Buckley Joseph	2	laborer	62	"
	O	Buckley Katherine—†	2	housekeeper	54	"
	P	Leonard Thomas	2	laborer	31	"
	R	Turner James	2	lineman	50	1917 Wash'n
	S	Currier Henry J	3	millwright	50	here
	T	Currier Maud—†	3	housewife	39	"
	U	Ingram John	3	laborer	50	"
	V	Miller Thomas	3	foreman	45	"
	W	Powers John	3	teamster	35	764 Harris'n av
	X	Powers Mary—†	3	housewife	36	764 "
	Y	Sheers George	3	packer	45	here
	Z	Sheers Helen—†	3	housekeeper	46	"
	A	Sherrief Helen—†	3	"	40	"
	B	Magill Elizebeth—†	4	housewife	35	116 Longwood av
	C	Magill Robert J	4	cleaner	36	116 "
	E	Woods Mary—†	5	housewife	58	here
	F	Woods William	5	cabinetmaker	61	"
	G	Stearns Albert	5	mover	55	"
	H	Stearns Alice—†	5	housewife	56	"
	K	Sheedy James J	6	porter	38	"
	L	Sheedy Mary—†	6	housekeeper	63	"
	M	Kaplin Abe	7	tailor	50	11 Leverett
	N	Swartz Annie—†	7	housekeeper	42	11 "
	O	Fahey Patrick	8	student	38	72 O
	P	Gould Desiah—†	8	housekeeper	78	here
	R	Gould Leanard W	8	fireman	42	"
	S	Hafferty John	8	teamster	48	Long Island
	T	Kelley Luke	8	jobber	60	15 Haslet
	V	Mosher Francis	8	salesman	64	12 W Canton
	W	Myett Jerome	8	laborer	43	23 Worcester sq
	U	Ryan William P	8	"	61	1931 Wash'n
	W1	Dwyer Warren W	9	elevatorman	60	here

Page.	Letter.	FULL NAME.	Residence, April 1, 1926.	Occupation.	Supposed Age.	Reported Residence, April 1, 1925.
						Street and Number.

Worcester Place—Continued

	x	Geddis Katherine—†	9	housekeeper	56	here
	y	Geddis William J	9	metalworker	58	"
	z	Moble Blanche—†	9	housekeeper	30	"
	A	Moble Clarence	9	glassworker	43	"
	B	Moble Eugene	10	paperhanger	47	"
	C	Cameron Thomas	10	laborer	46	"
	D	Meader Freeman E	10	"	21	Maine
	E	Patrick Helen—†	10	housekeeper	44	here
	F	Kersten William	10	clerk	35	Fort Strong
	G	Lennon Bertha—†	10	stitcher	31	here

Ward 9—Precinct 6

CITY OF BOSTON.

LIST OF RESIDENTS
20 YEARS OF AGE AND OVER

(FEMALES INDICATED BY DAGGER)

AS OF

APRIL 1, 1926

HERBERT A. WILSON, } *Listing*

JAMES F. EAGAN, } *Board.*

CITY OF BOSTON—PRINTING DEPARTMENT

Page.	Letter.	FULL NAME.	Residence, April 1, 1925.	Occupation.	Supposed Age.	Reported Residence, April 1, 1925. Street and Number.

Arnold Street

A	Bissett Charles	1	laborer	40	101 Vernon
B	Bissett Rena—†	1	housewife	39	101 "
C	Lannaville Elmer	1	roofer	50	here
D	Lannaville Olive—†	1	housewife	45	"
E	Betters Mable—†	1	"	25	"
F	Brown Mable—†	1½	"	43	"
G	Jones William	1½	student	28	"
H	Walker Ethel—†	1½	laundress	22	"
L	Gernni Anthony	3	laborer	62	"
M	Gernni Dominic	3	barber	22	"
N	Gernni Mary—†	3	housewife	47	"
O	Kallajian Lazarus S	4	machinist	61	3 E Lenox
R	Hall Catherine—†	6	housewife	37	here
T	Alexander Harry	rear 6	retired	44	"
U	Newman Anna—†	" 6	houseworker	54	Cambridge
W	Hillard Arron	7	laborer	40	New York
X	Hillard Lillian—†	7	housewife	25	"
Y	Facen George	7	laborer	46	here
Z	Hayes Margaret—†	8	hairdresser	34	"
A	Hayes Roland	8	artist	38	"
B	Atkinson George C	8	chauffeur	22	"
C	Williams Emma B—†	8	housewife	30	10 Arnold
D	Williams Gabriel	8	laborer	50	10 "
E	Payne Anna—†	9	housewife	28	13 "
F	Payne Joseph W	9	laborer	50	13 "
H	Lewis Bernard	10	foreman	60	8 "
K	Lewis Eva—†	10	housewife	32	8 "
L	Scott Rebecca—†	11	"	25	here
M	Walker Andrew	11	laborer	40	"
N	Sarno Adelia—†	12	housewife	46	"
O	Sarno Catherine—†	12	bookkeeper	20	"
P	Sarno Guerino	12	merchant	52	"
R	Miles May—†	13	tel operator	24	42 Holyoke
S	Smith Thomas	13	laborer	24	here
T	Hagan Ned	14	"	35	"
U	Hagan Nona—†	14	laundress	59	"
V	Sarno Leo	14	merchant	54	"
X	Moakley Edward H	16	"	65	"
Y	Shinnick Ellen M—†	16	housewife	42	"

2

Letter.	FULL NAME.	Residence, April 1, 1926.	Occupation.	Supposed Age.	Reported Residence, April 1, 1925. Street and Number.

Arnold Street—Continued

z	Johnson Hattie—†	17	laundress	52	here
A	Muncey Henry	17	porter	52	51 Hammond
B	Berry Sarah—†	18	domestic	60	here
c	Brown Jennie —†	18	at home	75	"
D	Gynes Priscilla—†	18	"	52	"
E	Harris Anna—†	18	"	73	"
F	White Pauline—†	18	domestic	66	"
G	Lynch Gertrude—†	19	housewife	38	191 Springfield
K	Jones Annie—†	19½	"	40	here
L	Jones Ezekiel	19½	carpenter	40	"
H	Fling David	19½	laborer	60	"
M	Olmstad Daniel	21	clerk	47	"
N	Olmstad Daniel, jr	21	sculptor	21	"
o	Olmstad Henrietta—†	21	housewife	47	"
P	Meade Henry	22	porter	53	"
R	Renolds Miltilda—†	22	housewife	24	"
s	Smith Catherine—†	23	"	24	"
T	Smith Joseph	23	clergyman	60	"
U	Faulk Annie—†	23	domestic	40	"
v	Faulk Joseph	23	teamster	57	"
w	Steward Edmona—†	23	housewife	40	"
x	Steward James	23	porter	43	"
Y	Dowd Caroline—†	24	operator	27	"
z	Dowd Hazel K—†	24	clerk	28	"
A	Dowd Lotta B—†	24	housewife	49	"
B	Dowd William T	24	laborer	63	"
c	Monthero Albert	25	"	46	"
D	Monthero Ruth—†	25	housewife	40	"
E	Williams Henrietta—†	25	"	46	"
F	Cox Benjamin	25	cook	66	"
G	Cox Mary T—†	25	housewife	62	"
H	Cox William S	25	dentist	43	"
K	Gardner Mary F—†	25	domestic	38	"
L	Thomas Louis	26	laborer	39	"
M	Thomas Vera—†	26	housewife	26	"
N	Green Mary—†	26	"	34	2 Hubert
o	Harris Edward	26	laborer	46	New York
P	Fitzgerald Joseph	27	"	50	here
R	Ward Ada V—†	27	housewife	47	"
s	Ward William N	27	real estate	58	"
T	Walker Charles W	27	laborer	45	Connecticut

3

Page.	Letter.	FULL NAME.	Residence, April 1, 1926.	Occupation.	Supposed Age.	Reported Residence, April 1, 1925. Street and Number.

Arnold Street—Continued

	U	Walker Minie—†	27	housewife	45	Connecticut
	V	Ward Lora M—†	27	"	50	here
	W	Ward Louisia—†	27	"	59	"
	X	Slatter Bessie—†	28	housekeeper	22	48 Phillips
	Y	Howard Catherine—†	28	housewife	51	here
	Z	Howard Roscoe	28	porter	54	"
	A	Wade Robert	28	painter	25	"
	B	Hutchins Levanna—†	29	domestic	47	"
	C	Exum Martha—†	29	"	57	"
	D	Brown Lizzie—†	29	"	30	"
	E	Smith Lizzie—†	30	housewife	47	"
	F	Battle Henry	30	laborer	25	"
	G	Bougia Johanna—†	30	housewife	40	New York
	H	Smith Martina—†	30	"	54	67 Kendall

Ball Street

	L	Lanagen Mary—†	5	domestic	50	1 Derby pl
	M	Dellehanty Johanna—†	5	houseworker	70	here
	N	Louis John	5	blacksmith	40	"
	O	Billings Joseph E	7	machinist	81	"
	P	Campell Rebecca—†	7	housekeeper	76	"
	S	Crosby Ella—†	9	houseworker	47	"
	T	Daniels Henery J	9	watchman	75	4293 Wash'n
	U	Daniels Josephine—†	9	housewife	75	4293 "
	V	Clark Silvester	10	fisherman	62	here
	W	Hart Edwin	10	laborer	38	"
	X	Hart Sophronia—†	10	housewife	40	"
	Y	Eide John	10	laborer	32	Minnesota
	Z	Eide Margaret—†	10	housewife	30	"
	A	Jones Christina—†	10	at home	22	here
	B	Lepine Mary E—†	10	housewife	62	"
	C	Lepine Thomas J	10	laborer	64	"
	D	Sample Emma J—†	10	housewife	26	"
	H	Mullin Annie—†	13	at home	81	"
	K	Americo Francis	13	clerk	36	"
	L	Americo Mary A—†	13	housewife	38	"
	M	Loud Helen—†	14	at home	70	"
	N	Loud John B	14	salesman	28	"
	O	Maloney Edward	14	teamster	26	"

4

Letter.	FULL NAME.	Residence, April 1, 1926.	Occupation.	Supposed Age.	Reported Residence, April 1, 1925. Street and Number.

Ball Street—Continued

P	Maloney Frances—†	14	housewife	30	here
R	Maloney Frank	14	chauffeur	24	"
S	Jones John	15	mechanic	39	"
T	Jones Nellie P—†	15	housewife	35	"
U	Jackson Jessie—†	15	"	45	"
V	Jackson John	15	laborer	50	"
W	Walker Emma—†	15	housewife	52	"
X	Walker John H	15	laborer	50	"
Y	Channell Harry L	16	grocer	65	"
Z	Robinson Annie L—†	16	housekeeper	40	"
A	Widdis Charles E	17	cook	48	"
B	Widdis Lucille E—†	17	housewife	47	"
C	Fitzgerald Edith M—†	18	"	29	"
D	Fitzgerald McFarlane	18	porter	31	"
E	Jones Grace L—†	18	operator	22	"
F	Robinson Rachel—†	19	at home	86	129 W Lenox
G	Skinner Henery	19	painter	45	129 "
H	Skinner Lillian—†	19	housewife	50	129 "
K	Regan John	19	retired	65	here
L	Regan Martha—†	19	housewife	56	"
M	Fendell Stephen	20	watchman	62	"
N	Jackson William H	20	laborer	56	"
O	Jones Emma L—†	20	housewife	49	"
P	Jones Fred	20	painter	50	"
R	Robinson Gertrude—†	20	waitress	42	"
S	Wade Mary—†	21	housewife	34	New York
T	Wade William	21	laborer	38	"
U	Maugh Charles	21	plumber	50	here
V	Maugh Josephine—†	21	housewife	50	"
W	Adams William H	22	porter	42	"
X	Ramsay Clifford	22	waiter	45	"
Y	Wilson George C	22	storekeeper	49	"
Z	Wilson Rebecca H—†	22	housewife	33	"
A	Manley Elnor A—†	23	"	37	"
B	Manley Herman A	23	laborer	37	"
C	Archibald Gerald	24	"	30	"
D	Constantine Florence—†	24	houseworker	63	"
E	Downey Minnie—†	24	"	50	23 Lenox
F	Ford Robert	24	laborer	28	Concord
G	Holland John	24	"	28	New York
H	Pitkins Selina C—†	24	housekeeper	45	here

5

Page.	Letter.	FULL NAME.	Residence, April 1, 1926.	Occupation.	Supposed Age.	Reported Residence, April 1, 1925.
						Street and Number.

Ball Street—Continued

	K	Stith Robert	24	laborer	45	here
	L	Smith Annie L—†	25	waitress	43	"
	M	Whalen Catherine F—†	25	at home	64	"
	N	Carey William B	26	laborer	30	"
	O	Clark Fredrick	26	"	28	6 Windsor
	P	Gregory Preston	26	"	30	here
	R	Horton Lillian—†	26	houseworker	35	363 Northampton
	S	Howard Georgiana—†	26	housewife	25	84 Sterling
	T	Lewis James	26	laborer	28	here
	U	Mitchel Benjamin	26	"	30	1058 Tremont
	V	Morris James	26	"	39	22 Ruggles
	W	Pellington William H	26	"	50	69 Sterling
	X	Buckhanan Robert	27	"	32	here
	Z	Forbs Walter	27	"	37	"
	Y	Lable Benjamin	27	"	30	"
	A	Louis Henery	27	"	29	"
	B	Taylor Charles E	27	"	49	"
	C	Taylor Elizabeth—†	27	housewife	51	"
	D	Anderson Richard R	28	porter	25	"
	E	Bookins Frank G	28	clergyman	55	"
	F	Cooper Anna B—†	28	housewife	49	"
	G	Cooper John E	28	laborer	55	"
	H	Hortgraves Cornilia—†	28	laundress	40	"
	K	Morris Inez—†	28	clerk	26	"
	L	Wheatfall James	28	laborer	27	"
	M	Douglass Catherine—†	29	domestic	35	"
	N	Edward Felicia—†	29	houseworker	60	"
	O	Edward James	29	laborer	32	"
	P	Webb Amelia—†	29	domestic	35	"
	R	Dozier Mary—†	29	houseworker	30	"
	S	Ward Richard	29	laborer	42	"
	T	Brothers Bessie—†	29	domestic	35	55 Kendall
	U	Loon John	29	laborer	75	here
	V	Lopez James	30	clerk	20	"
	W	McQueen Fletcher	30	laborer	55	"
	X	McQueen Minnie P—†	30	housewife	43	"
	Y	Nelson David W	30	laborer	42	Springfield
	Z	Patterson Alice—†	30	domestic	50	here
	A	Spensor Robert	30	waiter	49	"
	B	William John F	30	laborer	43	"
	C	Young Mary—†	30	domestic	45	"

6

Page	Letter	FULL NAME.	Residence, April 1, 1926.	Occupation.	Supposed Age.	Reported Residence, April 1, 1925. Street and Number.

Ball Street—Continued

	Letter	FULL NAME.	Res.	Occupation.	Age	Reported Residence
	D	Steed Abraham	31	lawyer	42	here
	E	Steed Allie—†	31	housewife	37	"
	F	Jones Amy S—†	31	hairdresser	35	"
	G	Reesbey Irene—†	31	domestic	37	649 Shawmut av
	H	Bayne Leonard	32	machinist	38	here
	K	Morton James	32	mechanic	24	"
	L	Nomes Joseph	32	laborer	53	"
	M	Rose Charles	32	"	32	"
	N	Whipple William	32	"	40	28 Ball
	O	Gill Harriet—†	33	domestic	53	32 Sawyer
	P	Pelham Gertrude E—†	33	"	46	here
	P¹	Smith Blanch P—†	33	housewife	37	"
	R	Smith John E	33	machinist	39	"
	S	Wilkie Edward	33	porter	41	"
	T	Wilkie Mary—†	33	domestic	37	"
	U	Cohan John	34	laborer	51	"
	V	Kennedy George	34	"	63	"
	W	Power James J	34	retired	65	"
	X	Yreell Frederick L	34	machinist	57	"
	Y	Yreell John J	34	plumber	21	"
	Z	Yreell Marian—†	34	housewife	45	"

Benton Street

	Letter	FULL NAME.	Res.	Occupation.	Age	Reported Residence
	A	Austin Joseph L	9	meatcutter	47	here
	B	Austin Lelia—†	9	housewife	49	"
	C	Mayers Bessie K—†	9	"	33	"
	D	Mayers David A	9	cook	38	"
	E	Jackson Eliza—†	9	housewife	54	"
	F	Jackson Hugh	9	laborer	50	"
	H	Bell Christopher	11	shoeworker	40	"
	K	Bell Olga—†	11	housewife	39	"
	L	Proctor Charles	11	engineer	49	"
	M	Proctor Louisa—†	11	houseworker	30	"
	N	Eastty Effie I—†	17	clerk	48	"
	O	Krajewski Felix	17	"	57	1037 Col av
	R	DeMontague Lawrence J	19	oiler	31	here
	S	McLeod Sarah—†	19	housekeeper	75	"
	T	Devine Bridget—†	19	housewife	33	Ireland
	U	Devine Micheal P	19	plasterer	30	"

Page.	Letter.	FULL NAME.	Residence, April 1, 1926.	Occupation.	Supposed Age.	Reported Residence, April 1, 1925. Street and Number.

Benton Street—Continued

	v	Taylor Frank	21	letter carrier	47	here
	w	Taylor Margaret M—†	21	housewife	45	"
	x	Perkins George R	21	painter	55	"
	y	Perkins May E—†	21	housewife	45	"
	z	Carey John	21	chauffeur	24	"
	A	Carey Mary G—†	21	boxfinisher	25	"
	B	Carey Nellie—†	21	cleaner	46	"
	c	Roche John	21	paint mixer	47	"
	D	Smithwick Robert	27	janitor	60	"
	E	Smithwick William	27	"	58	"
	F	Kimball Annie—†	27	laundress	47	"
	G	Kelley Mary—†	27	housewife	46	"
	H	Kelley Michael	27	plasterer	49	"
	K	Maher James H	29	laborer	39	"
	L	Maher Julia—†	29	housekeeper	60	"
	M	Maher William F	29	awningmaker	41	"
	N	Kearns Annie—†	29	cigarmaker	26	"
	o	Kearns Cornelius	29	retired	78	"
	P	Kearns Mary—†	29	forewoman	28	"
	R	Cronin Margaret—†	29	housekeeper	52	"
	s	Cronin Timothy	29	janitor	55	"

Camden Street

	w	Fisher Margaret—†	148	housekeeper	36	4 Benton
	w¹	Hutchins Basil F	150	undertaker	52	here
	w²	Perkins Samuel H	150	"	39	"

Columbus Avenue

	F	Jenkins Ella—†	700	hairdresser	43	here
	G	Jenkins Ora C	700	masseur	44	"
	H	Bell Madis—†	700	domestic	22	"
	K	Blakely Attie—†	700	laundress	42	"
	L	Wilson Clara—†	700	houseworker	33	Worcester
	M	Delaney Peter	700	waiter	45	88 Humboldt av
	N	Wade Ethel—†	700	laundress	35	here

8

Letter.	FULL NAME.	Residence, April 1, 1926.	Occupation.	Supposed Age.	Reported Residence, April 1, 1925. Street and Number.

Columbus Avenue—Continued

o	Willox Margaret—†	700	domestic	42	here
p	Francis Annie L—†	702	"	32	37 Kendall
r	Peachey Charles R	702	porter	36	203 Camden
s	Peachey Nettie—†	702	housewife	36	203 "
t	Galloway Rosa L—†	702	housekeeper	45	here
u	White Lillian—†	702	"	40	Brooklyn N Y
v	Clifton James	702	porter	46	here
w	Collins James	702	barber	32	"
x	Johnson Freeman	702	real estate	58	"
y	Anderson Mary—†	704	housekeeper	59	"
z	Robinson Metalda—†	704	clerk	59	"
A	Young Edith—†	704	houseworker	20	"
B	Young Elba—†	704	milliner	22	"
c	Young Laura—†	704	housekeeper	44	"
D	Young Simeon	704	retired	80	"
E	Ash Stanley	704	cook	30	920 Tremont
F	Loveless Mary—†	704	"	50	920 "
G	McAndrew Daniel	704	waiter	40	50 Camden
H	Ridley Ada—†	706	housewife	51	here
K	Ridley Major	706	tailor	50	"
L	Banks Mary E—†	706	housewife	44	"
M	Banks Robert W	706	tailor	53	"
N	Wright Harry L	706	clerk	27	"
o	Wright Jeannette B—†	706	dentist	25	"
P	Hicks Morris J	706	postal clerk	50	1064 Tremont
R	Hicks Nellie V—†	706	operator	37	1064 "
s	Leonard Julia E—†	706	housewife	55	1064 "
T	Pollack Henry J	708	jeweler	34	here
U	Pollack Judah	708	cigarmaker	72	"
v	Pollack Louis J	708	"	43	"
w	Pollack Sarah—†	708	housewife	71	"
x	Milmore Annie—†	708	"	45	"
Y	Milmore Martin	708	real estate	55	"
z	O'Toole Frank J	708	clerk	54	"
A	Brush Felix L	708	sexton	65	"
B	Jewett Wilfred E	708	wireworker	71	"
c	Kane Margaret E—†	708	housewife	51	"
D	Kane Michael S	708	painter	50	"
E	Mahan Thomas F	708	contractor	58	"

9

Page.	Letter.	FULL NAME.	Residence, April 1, 1926.	Occupation.	Supposed Age.	Reported Residence, April 1, 1925.
						Street and Number.

Davenport Street

	G	Hawkins Emma—†	14	housewife	51	here
	H	Hawkins William	14	laborer	54	"
	K	McKenzie Jeremiah	14	chef	44	"
	L	McKenzie Rebecca—†	14	housewife	41	"
	M	Montgomery Alonzo H	14	barber	52	"
	N	Smith Florence J—†	14	housewife	39	"
	O	Smith James N	14	marketman	59	"
	P	Carson Alexander	16	shipper	42	"
	R	Carson William H	16	waiter	45	"
	S	Anderson Laura J—†	16	housewife	36	"
	T	Anderson William H	16	messenger	49	"
	U	Booker Frank	16	porter	46	"
	V	Booker Mary—†	16	housewife	45	"
	W	Carter Edward	18	laundryman	38	"
	X	Carter Louise—†	18	housewife	37	"
	Y	Edwards Mary—†	18	domestic	44	18 Camden
	Z	Harrington Jane—†	18	operator	41	18 Sawyer
	A	Anderson Arnold	18	chef	30	here
	B	Anderson Mattie E—†	18	housewife	25	"
	C	Scott Albert	20	postal clerk	30	"
	D	Holmes Florence H—†	20	housewife	43	"
	E	Holmes Thomas H	20	janitor	47	"
	F	Straughan William	20	porter	59	"
	H	White Mabel—†	22	housewife	33	"
	K	White Sandy	22	janitor	40	"
	L	Grant Catherine—†	22	housewife	33	"
	M	Grant James M	22	bellboy	38	"
	N	Poole Adia—†	24	housewife	27	"
	O	Poole John E	24	barber	31	"
	P	Buckley Georgetta—†	24	housewife	40	"
	R	Buckley James	24	molder	40	"
	S	Johnson Henry	24	janitor	31	"
	T	Johnson Mary—†	24	housewife	39	"
	U	Oliver Elizabeth—†	26	"	32	60 Hammond
	V	Oliver James K	26	operator	42	60 "
	W	Counsel Eliza—†	26	housekeeper	48	here
	X	Brown Helen—†	26	housewife	35	"
	Y	Brown John H	26	shipper	45	"
	Y¹	Landrum Amy L—†	26	domestic	35	"
	Z	Laudrum Elijah	26	car cleaner	30	"
	A	Beal Frank	28	porter	43	"

Page.	Letter.	FULL NAME.	Residence, April 11, 1926.	Occupation.	Supposed Age.	Reported Residence, April 1, 1925. Street and Number.

Davenport Street—Continued

B	Shefton Anna—†	28	housewife	31	here
C	White Adelaid—†	28	housekeeper	63	"
D	White Cora—†	28	domestic	27	"
E	White Philip	28	operator	34	"
F	Slaughter George	28	shipper	47	"
G	Throp Sylvester	28	porter	35	"
H	Whitfield Elizabeth—†	28	housekeeper	55	"
K	Lamb Obeline H—†	28	housewife	35	63 Bainbridge
L	Lamb Richard C	28	waiter	32	63 "

Hammond Street

M	Barmwell Lawrence M	3	laborer	36	19 Dillon
N	Barmwell Susie—†	3	housewife	30	19 "
O	Gatson Jennie—†	3	housekeeper	54	19 "
P	Taylor Sarah—†	3	"	31	here
T	Crawford Mary—†	15	"	50	"
U	Wilson Elizabeth M—†	15	"	60	"
V	Wilson Robert J	15	laborer	36	"
W	Brown Marandi—†	15	domestic	70	Cambridge
X	Crawford Cora—†	15	housekeeper	66	here
Y	Griffin Arthur	16	waiter	63	"
Z	Griffin Minnie—†	15	housewife	42	"
A	Welch Emma—†	17	"	34	"
B	Welch William W	17	janitor	46	"
C	Dorsey Levi W	17	laborer	66	"
D	Dorsey Martha A—†	17	housewife	56	"
E	Terrell Harold M	17	porter	30	"
F	King Rebecca A—†	17	housewife	58	"
G	King William O	17	porter	56	"
H	Wells Harry F	17	postal clerk	31	"
K	Wells Julia A—†	17	housewife	62	"
L	Wells Melvin H	17	fireman	25	"
M	Wells Waverly G	17	paperhanger	64	"
N	Bean Rebecca—†	19	housewife	53	"
O	Bean William C	19	fireman	62	"
P	Brewster Ethel—†	19	housewife	28	"
R	Brewster George	19	porter	38	"
S	Middleton Mary—†	19	housekeeper	39	"
T	Norton Matilda—†	19	housewife	24	32 Yarmouth

Page.	Letter.	FULL NAME.	Residence, April 1, 1926.	Occupation.	Supposed Age.	Reported Residence, April 1, 1925. Street and Number.

Hammond Street—Continued

	U	Norton William	19	laborer	25	32 Yarmouth
	V	Watson James A	19	shoeworker	45	here
	W	Tillman John J	19	clerk	46	"
	X	Tillman Marimetta M—†	19	housewife	46	"
	Y	Leak Ollie—†	21	housekeeper	38	"
	Z	Stevens David	21	laborer	41	"
	A	Hanson Charles	21	"	38	"
	B	Robinson Robert	21	porter	35	"
	C	Robinson Ruth—†	21	housewife	34	"
	D	Blair Phalmer—†	23	housekeeper	51	"
	E	Jones Samuel	23	laborer	35	Phila Pa
	F	Braxton George J	25	"	40	here
	G	Broadus Walter L	25	actor	42	"
	H	Cox Mary V—†	25	housewife	61	"
	K	Cox William G	25	watchman	63	"
	L	Jones Caroline D—†	25	housewife	51	"
	M	Jones John W	25	clerk	29	33 Batavia
	N	Jones Thomas V	25	broker	51	here
	O	Knowles John	25	laborer	24	"
	P	Brown Laura D—†	27	housewife	24	31 Cunard
	R	Brown Richard D	27	broker	43	31 "
	S	Brent Charles	27	laborer	26	Baltimore Md
	T	Brent Laura—†	27	housekeeper	23	"
	U	Watson John	27	laborer	40	here
	V	Watson Martha—†	27	housewife	35	"
	Y	Sharp John K	29	janitor	26	768 Col av
	Z	Sharp Mary—†	29	housewife	26	768 "
	A	Daniels Beatrice M—†	29	housekeeper	42	here
	B	Norman Gladys—†	29	housewife	32	"
	C	Norman Thomas	29	tailor	35	"
	D	Hinds Caesar A	29	engineer	56	1083 Tremont
	E	Hinds Georgia—†	29	housewife	48	1083 "
	F	Foster Edgar	31	laborer	21	here
	G	Redd Samuel J	31	"	49	"
	H	Redd Sarah—†	31	housewife	47	"
	K	Dorsey Ellen—†	31	housekeeper	63	"
	L	Hamilton Harrison	31	porter	34	"
	M	Keeling Margaret—†	31	laundress	53	
	N	Douglas Nora—†	31	houseworker	20	Brookline
	O	Ford Frances—†	31	housewife	39	14 Westminster
	P	Ford James	31	cook	42	14 "

12

Page.	Letter.	FULL NAME.	Residence, April 1, 1926.	Occupation.	Supposed Age.	Reported Residence, April 1, 1925. Street and Number.

Hammond Street—Continued

	R	Meyler Geraldine—†	31	houseworker	24	Maine
	S	Morris Louise—†	31	housekeeper	45	9 Harwick
	U	Jones Benjamin P	33	fireman	48	here
	V	Jones Minnie D—†	33	housewife	37	"
	W	Wright Erdis—†	33	"	24	Georgia
	X	Wright Sarah—†	33	housekeeper	45	here
	Y	Wright William	33	laborer	26	"
	Z	Harding Wesley	33	"	31	928 Tremont
	A	Moore Marie—†	33	housewife	27	928 "
	B	Moore William B	33	painter	35	928 "
	D	McPherson Goldie—†	35	houseworker	29	here
	E	Seivewright Florence—†	35	housekeeper	31	"
	F	Folkes James A	35	janitor	50	"
	G	Folkes Rosetta—†	35	housewife	40	"
	H	Jordan Edward	35	paver	59	"
	K	Jordan Josephine—†	35	housewife	53	"
	L	Warren Florence I—†	35	"	35	"
	M	Warren John H	35	janitor	41	"
	O	Jones Josiah	37	laborer	32	"
	P	Lewis Andrew	37	teamster	32	"
	R	Lewis Elizabeth—†	37	housewife	45	"
	U	Hall Eng	39	laundryman	39	"
	V	Brown George	39	janitor	49	"
	W	Brown Rose—†	39	housewife	45	"
	X	Dixon Ema—†	39	maid	50	"
	Y	Moody Martin O	39	laborer	55	"
	Z	Pernell Mary—†	39	housekeeper	50	"
	A	Barnett Frank	39	porter	35	"
	B	Barnett Ida M—†	39	housewife	30	"
	C	Everett Laura—†	41	dressmaker	45	"
	D	Palmer Edward L	41	cook	64	34 Sawyer
	F	Guppy John A	41	cigarmaker	49	23 Hammond
	G	McClain Ethel—†	41	housewife	29	23 "
	H	McClain John M	41	porter	29	23 "
	K	Brown Aaron	41	laborer	37	Virginia
	L	Brown Edith—†	41	housewife	34	"
	M	Edwards Ruth—†	43	housekeeper	40	New York
	N	Manifold Preston	43	laborer	47	here
	O	Manifold Sarah—†	43	housewife	37	"
	R	Coss Bessie—†	43	"	39	"
	S	Coss Edgar	43	stevedore	46	"

13

Page.	Letter.	FULL NAME.	Residence, April 1, 1926.	Occupation.	Supposed Age.	Reported Residence, April 1, 1925. Street and Number.

Hammond Street—Continued

T	Brisbene Joseph	45	laborer	34	here
U	Brisbene Sarah—†	45	housewife	32	"
V	Cole William E	45	laborer	50	"
W	Harris Kate—†	45	housewife	50	"
X	Harris William	45	laborer	61	"
Y	Graham Gertrude R—†	45	housewife	56	"
Z	Graham Henry I	45	porter	29	"
A	Graham Robert H	45	caterer	63	"
B	Casey Annie—†	45	housewife	24	"
C	Casey Ernest	45	waiter	28	"
D	Fubler Mary E—†	45	housekeeper	50	"
E	Burdett Ruth—†	47	clerk	20	"
F	Burdett Samuel	47	janitor	50	"
G	Bemebroy Carrie—†	47	houseworker	40	"
H	Jonas Ada—†	47	housekeeper	22	Mashpee
K	Robinson Anna—†	47	houseworker	38	Atlantic City
L	Davis Arthur B	47	laborer	28	New Jersey
M	Davis Irene L—†	47	housewife	22	"
N	Harrington Anthony W	47	chef	59	here
O	Harrington Charlotte—†	47	housewife	49	795 Shawmut av
P	Henderson Mack G	47	fireman	39	here
R	Meeks Viola—†	47	housewife	30	97 Camden
S	Meeks William G	47	chef	32	97 "
T	Macroy Jasper	47	repairman	30	110 Kendall
U	Macroy Marion—†	47	housewife	27	110 "
V	Brown Margaret M—†	47	housekeeper	54	40 Hammond
W	Stewart Joseph	47	janitor	23	New York
X	Miller David H	47	operator	32	here
Y	Stewart Martha A—†	47	housekeeper	59	"
Z	O'Brien Cora H—†	47	"	55	"
A	Ray Calvin	48	janitor	40	"
B	Ray Mame—†	49	housewife	37	"
C	Grant Mattie—†	49	"	35	60 Hammond
D	Grant William	49	laborer	35	60 "
E	Parson Dora—†	49	houseworker	43	60 "
F	Parson Laura—†	49	"	29	227 Northampton
G	Julian Mary F—†	49	housewife	40	here
H	Julian Nathaniel	49	clerk	44	"
K	Elliott Ella E—†	49	housewife	42	37 Hammond
L	Elliott Philip H	49	porter	49	37 "
M	Hosten Fannie—†	49	housewife	43	here

14

Page.	Letter.	FULL NAME.	Residence, April 1, 1926.	Occupation.	Supposed Age.	Reported Residence, April 1, 1925. Street and Number.

Hammond Street—Continued

	N	Hosten Joseph	49	waiter	42	here
	O	Houston Thomas	49	porter	45	"
	P	Cheltenham Ella—†	49	housewife	32	"
	R	Cheltenham Tolson	49	waiter	35	"
	S	Corry Nado	49	laborer	29	41 Rose
	T	Coxson Sarah—†	49	housekeeper	40	here
	U	Saunders Melia—†	49	at home	70	"
	V	Taylor Evelyn—†	49	houseworker	26	"
	W	Brown James	49	porter	46	"
	X	Green Ulie	49	chef	42	"
	Y	Burse Albert S	51	musician	31	"
	Z	Burse Beatrice—†	51	housewife	47	"
	A	Burse Veal W	51	laborer	46	"
	B	Dodson James	51	porter	53	"
	C	Dodson Martha E—†	51	housewife	40	"
	D	Henderson Racheal—†	51	housekeeper	52	"
	E	Mandez Frank	51	cook	49	"
	F	Paschall Anna—†	51	housekeeper	84	"
	G	Paschall George	51	butler	42	"
	H	Paschall Martha M—†	51	housekeeper	49	"
	K	Davis James H	53	laborer	45	"
	L	James Richard	53	"	33	666 Shawmut av
	M	James Ursuline—†	53	housewife	34	666 "
	N	Mont John J	53	porter	57	29 Windsor
	O	Keaksmith Peter	53	mason	40	New York
	P	Mendis Frank	53	"	38	here
	R	Pererio Manuel	53	"	44	"
	T	Forbes Lamny	53	porter	32	"
	S	Forbes Lora—†	53	housewife	30	"
	U	Robinson Beatrice—†	53	housekeeper	28	New York
	V	Tyler Minnie K—†	57	housewife	43	here
	W	Tyler William K	57	laborer	43	"
	X	Haynes Mary—†	57	housekeeper	50	"
	Y	Monteiro Manuel	57	laborer	27	15 Parnell
	Z	Pierce Oria—†	57	housekeeper	54	here
	A	Ware Mary A—†	57	houseworker	27	"
	C	Thompson John	59	laborer	29	"
	D	Thompson Marie—†	59	housewife	21	"
	E	Thompson Priscilla—†	59	housekeeper	53	"
	F	Thompson Scippio	59	carpenter	66	"
	G	Brown Joseph H	59	laborer	53	"

15

Hammond Street—Continued

H	Brown Mary C—†	59	laundress	59	here
K	Dixon Emma—†	59	housekeeper	50	"
L	Thompson James W	59	chauffeur	41	"
M	Thompson Maggie—†	59	housewife	38	"
N	Rose Arthur	59	chauffeur	20	"
O	Rose Harriet E—†	59	housewife	46	"
P	Rose Willis W	59	laborer	52	"
R	Rose Willis W, jr	59	chauffeur	21	"
S	Harris Celia—†	61	housekeeper	37	"
T	Foster Clara B—†	61	housewife	35	"
U	Foster William H	61	fireman	45	"
V	Chedeman James	61	laborer	35	New York
W	Miller Thomas	61	clerk	27	872 Col av
X	Redding Walter	63	musician	34	here
Y	White Annie—†	63	housekeeper	53	"
Z	Davis Biedie—†	63	housewife	40	"
A	Davis Thomas	63	painter	49	"
B	Belle Robert	63	laborer	21	"
C	Munroe Paul	63	janitor	23	"
D	Johnson Robert	63	laborer	40	"
F	Stewart Alton J	95	"	35	"
G	Stewart Edith—†	95	housekeeper	35	"
H	Clark Nellie—†	95	domestic	53	"
K	Dewey Milles	95	laborer	52	"
L	Enslow Alice—†	97	housewife	46	"
L¹	Enslow Joseph	97	clerk	54	"
M	Jenkins Lulu—†	97	housekeeper	39	"
N	Langford Victoria—†	97	operator	38	"
O	Fantroy Samuel	97	porter	40	"
P	Webb Mildred—†	97	housekeeper	33	"
R	Edwards Margaret—†	99	houseworker	37	"
S	Knox Minnie—†	99	domestic	54	"
T	Coakley Gabriel	99	painter	60	"
U	Jennings Mary—†	99	houseworker	55	"
V	Armstrong Mary—†	99	housekeeper	68	"
W	Brown Mary—†	99	operator	46	"
X	Smith Howard	99	laborer	32	"
Y	Franklin Ernest B	101	"	39	79 Hammond ter
Z	Franklin Helen F—†	101	housewife	26	79 "
A	Nash Lillian—†	101	housekeeper	36	106 "
B	Patterson Arthur	101	laborer	25	Halifax N S

Hammond Street—Continued

	c	Haskins Alice K—†	101	operator	20	here
	d	Wayne Ethel—†	101	housewife	22	"
	e	Wayne Walter C	101	laborer	25	"
	f	Miller Flossie—†	103	housewife	28	"
	g	Miller James E	103	tailor	26	"
	h	Fraction Elizabeth G—†	103	tailoress	31	"
	k	Warner Viola G—†	103	housekeeper	33	"
	l	Sampson Flora—†	103	housewife	43	"
	m	Sampson William	103	laborer	39	"
	n	Ward Cyril	105	"	36	"
	o	Kahn Harry H	105	clerk	28	"
	p	Kahn Sarah—†	105	housewife	27	"
	r	Gibson Aubrey G	105	lawyer	40	"
	s	Johnson Eleanor—†	107	housekeeper	38	"
	t	Kennedy Charles C	107	laborer	42	"
	u	Brown Chester L	107	"	39	"
	w	Stockwell Fannie M—†	111	housekeeper	53	"
	x	Lyons Mary—†	111	"	50	"
	y	Ebbeson Emma—†	111	housewife	42	"
	z	Ebbeson Paul	111	laborer	46	"
	a	Taws Lillian—†	111	housewife	56	"
	b	Taws William B	111	engineer	74	"
	f	Bailey William	113	laborer	38	"
	g	Ebbeson Anna—†	113	housekeeper	39	"
	h	Swerer George	113	millwright	52	"
	k	Swerer Julie—†	113	housewife	48	"

Hammond Terrace

	a	White Frederick D	77	music teacher	62	here
	b	White Myrtle I—†	77	housekeeper	35	"
	c	Howell Rebecca—†	77	domestic	32	"
	d	Sewell Heneretta—†	77	housekeeper	40	"
	e	Shaw Cecilia—†	77	domestic	26	"
	f	Writh Hattie—†	77	housekeeper	60	1020 Tremont
	g	Franklin Earnest B	79	boilermaker	37	here
	h	Franklin Helen—†	79	housekeeper	34	"
	k	Curran Margaret—†	79	"	46	"
	l	Curran Patrick J	79	blacksmith	52	"
	m	Moore Sarah—†	79	housekeeper	63	"

Page.	Letter.	FULL NAME.	Residence, April 1, 1926.	Occupation.	Supposed Age.	Reported Residence, April 1, 1925. Street and Number.

Hammond Terrace—Continued

N	Greenoway Annie—†	81	housekeeper	32	here
O	Blow Amenda—†	81	"	45	"
P	Blow Ellen H—†	81	waitress	26	"
R	Jones John H	81	manager	32	"
S	Lee Hattie—†	81	housekeeper	55	"
T	Jennings Captolia	83	chef	50	"
U	Jennings Carrie E—†	83	housekeeper	38	"
V	Watson Anna L—†	83	"	27	"
W	Watson Reuben E	83	chauffeur	30	"
X	Smalley Anna M—†	83	housekeeper	56	"
Y	Smalley Charles K	83	brickmaker	66	"
A	Marshall George A	85	pinsetter	30	"
B	Marshall Samuel	85	janitor	56	"
C	Shaw Albert	85	millworker	51	Randolph
D	Thompson Gaston	85	busboy	25	New York
D¹	Palmer Adina—†	85	housekeeper	26	11 Paul
E	Palmer Arnold J	85	dishwasher	28	11 "
F	Knight Charles R	87	porter	22	here
G	Knight Charlotte H—†	87	housekeeper	39	"
H	Brown Bert L	87	porter	30	"
K	Brown Ruthie—†	87	housekeeper	28	"
L	Dockett Bernice—†	87	"	36	"
M	Dockett Josh	87	laborer	38	"
N	Norin Joseph	89	steward	24	"
O	Norin Marslinene—†	89	housekeeper	23	"
P	Williams Hilda B—†	89	"	28	154 Cabot
R	Williams Jacob	89	chef	30	154 "
S	Armstrong Charles	89	porter	40	here
T	Armstrong Marie—†	89	housekeeper	36	"
U	Merande Martin	91	laborer	31	131 Lenox
V	Merande Sadie A—†	91	housekeeper	32	131 "
W	Congord Presley	91	fireman	37	here
X	Jones Lawrence A	91	laborer	40	941 Harris'n av
Y	Tillman Bertha—†	91	houseworker	35	68 Sawyer

Kendall Street

Z	Rotondo Frances—†	4	housewife	20	6 Kendall
A	Rotondo Frank	4	painter	31	58 Shirley
B	Bondfield Cermela—†	4	toymaker	46	here

	Letter	FULL NAME.	Residence, April 1, 1926.	Occupation.	Supposed Age.	Reported Residence, April 1, 1925. Street and Number.

Kendall Street—Continued

	Letter	FULL NAME.	Residence, April 1, 1926.	Occupation.	Supposed Age.	Reported Residence, April 1, 1925.
	c	Celi Grace—†	4	housewife	44	here
	d	Celi John	4	carpenter	54	"
	e	Baldasala Dora—†	4	housewife	31	"
	f	Baldasala James	4	pedler	42	"
	g	Patte Grace—†	4	housewife	35	"
	h	Patte Salvatore	4	laborer	47	"
	k	Luige Louis	6	barber	28	"
	l	Luige Mary—†	6	housewife	41	"
	m	Deucelli Frank	6	pedler	63	"
	n	Deucelli Louise—†	6	housewife	58	"
	o	Kazangian Jack	6	chauffeur	25	"
	p	Darrigo Angelina—†	6	housewife	35	"
	r	Darrigo Dominic	6	pedler	37	"
	s	Simpkin Edward	8	foundryman	40	Georgia
	t	Simpkin Marie—†	8	car cleaner	34	81 Kendall
	u	O'Neil Rose G—†	8	domestic	28	West Indies
	v	White Ida—†	8	housekeeper	27	here
	w	White Jusha	8	machinist	28	"
	x	Flerrinnera Annabell—†	8	housewife	30	"
	y	Flerrinnera Joseph	8	electrician	36	"
	z	James Julius	8	machinist	37	"
	a	James Lottie—†	8	housekeeper	29	"
	c	Whitaker Hattie M—†	9	domestic	39	"
	d	Whitaker Amilia E—†	9	"	47	"
	f	Brown Elvira—†	10	houseworker	36	26 Willard pl
	g	Adams James	10	laborer	37	12 Ball
	h	Adams Mary—†	10	housewife	35	12 "
	k	Hyatt Walter G	10	chauffeur	23	633 Shawmut av
	l	Fields Lucy—†	11	housewife	24	here
	m	Lovell Liza—†	11	"	31	"
	n	Lovell Whitfield	11	teamster	40	"
	o	Franklin Carmelia—†	11	housewife	63	"
	p	Franklin William	11	restaurateur	65	"
	r	Lawrence Andrew J	11	laborer	48	"
	s	Jackson Arthur	11½	foundryman	28	29 Greenwich
	t	Jackson Sara—†	11½	housewife	22	here
	u	Wright Flossy—†	11½	"	28	"
	v	Wright William	11½	baker	29	"
	w	Jefferson Charles	11½	tailor	27	"
	x	Jefferson Matilda—†	11½	housewife	21	"
	y	Williams Anna—†	12	"	21	Florida

Page.	Letter.	FULL NAME.	Residence, April 1, 1926.	Occupation.	Supposed Age.	Reported Residence, April 1, 1925. Street and Number.

Kendall Street—Continued

	z	Williams Verge	12	laborer	49	Florida
	A	Barrett Josephine—†	12	housewife	42	here
	B	Barrett Richard	12	janitor	40	"
	C	Pelham Elizabeth—†	12	domestic	74	67 Windsor
	D	Clark Castello J—†	14	stenographer	21	here
	E	Clark Mary L—†	14	housewife	53	"
	F	Clark Squire	14	engineer	53	"
	G	Smith Annie—†	15	laundress	60	"
	H	Rice Frank B	15	steward	46	"
	K	Rice Marie A—†	15	housewife	45	"
	L	Wood Adie—†	15	"	28	"
	M	Wood Anthony	15	waiter	32	"
	N	Edwards Henry	16	cook	60	"
	O	Edwards Sarah—†	16	housewife	47	"
	P	McBee Esther M—†	16	housekeeper	43	Richmond Va
	R	McBee Russell	16	laborer	32	"
	S	Dockett Robert M	17	"	44	14 Northfield
	T	Dockett Walter	17	checker	21	14 "
	U	Dockett Willie K—†	17	housewife	40	14 "
	V	Miller Joseph D	17	real estate	42	here
	W	Hammond Willimay—†	17	domestic	47	"
	X	Jinkins Virginia—†	18	housekeeper	42	Nantucket
	Y	Pasgrove Bertha—†	18	domestic	42	here
	Z	Archer John	19	janitor	60	"
	A	Felton William	19	bricklayer	45	Bridgewater
	B	Lane Fred	19	chauffeur	34	here
	C	Waiters Eliza—†	19	cook	63	"
	D	Hogart Ethel—†	20	housekeeper	25	116 Camden
	E	Hogart Martin	20	waiter	25	116 "
	F	Lightbourne Dorothy—†	20	stenographer	20	here
	G	Smith John	20	cook	45	New York
	H	Taylor Horace	20	chauffeur	22	here
	K	Thompson Rebecca—†	20	housekeeper	49	"
	L	Vaney James	20	laborer	20	20 Hammond
	M	Bryant Wilbert	21	longshoreman	23	here
	N	Hextall Martha—†	21	housekeeper	45	"
	O	Hyman John	21	plasterer	48	"
	P	Lockhart Gilbert	21	porter	38	"
	S	Phillips Lillian—†	22	housewife	27	"
	T	Phillips William N	22	laborer	33	"
	U	Haywood James	22	longshoreman	26	49 Northampton

Letter.	FULL NAME.	Residence, April 1, 1926.	Occupation.	Supposed Age.	Reported Residence, April 1, 1925. Street and Number.

Kendall Street—Continued

v	Haywood Mary W—†	22	housewife	27	49 Northampton
w	Johnson John I	23	laborer	42	here
x	Johnson Minnie—†	23	housewife	35	"
y	White Dicie—†	23	housekeeper	70	"
z	Days Margaret—†	23	stitcher	36	"
a	Bromwell Estha—†	23	housekeeper	35	"
b	Agustus Enita—†	24	attendant	28	"
c	Alexander Florence—†	24	houseworker	23	"
d	Gilmore Dorothy—†	24	cook	23	Lexington Va
e	Gomes John	24	laborer	30	here
f	Serges Merefit	24	"	35	"
g	Small David	24	"	22	"
h	Smith William	24	"	28	"
l	Johnson Dora—†	25	housewife	43	"
k	Johnson Jacob R J	25	waiter	41	"
m	Marshall Annie W—†	25	housewife	22	29 Kendall
n	Marshall Thomas E	25	cook	28	29 "
o	Meade Christie—†	25	housewife	27	10 Willard pl
p	Meade John	25	laborer	29	26 "
r	Haynes George	26	"	30	here
s	Parks Mildred—†	26	laundress	40	"
t	Spires Nettie—†	26	houseworker	30	"
u	Spires William	26	chauffeur	35	"
v	Johnson James	26	janitor	26	Cambridge
w	Allen Charles	26½	laborer	23	Winchester
x	Bowen Charles A	26½	"	39	"
y	Bowen Sarah—†	26½	housekeeper	27	"
z	Ogilvie George	27	cook	41	68 Ruggles
a	Ogilvie Josephine—†	27	housewife	32	68 "
b	Bobb James	27	pedler	46	here
d	Burt Robert	28	porter	22	"
e	Gilmore Josie—†	28	cook	36	"
f	Warrick Hattie—†	28	housekeeper	45	"
g	Warrick Joseph	28	chauffeur	27	"
h	Warrick Lucy—†	28	housekeeper	24	"
k	Small Edith—†	28	houseworker	29	"
l	Greenwich George	28	baker	69	"
m	Walker Lee	29	laborer	32	"
n	Walker Sallie—†	29	housewife	29	"
o	Byrd Emory	29	laborer	25	"
p	Byrd Mattie L—†	29	housewife	27	"

21

Page.	Letter	FULL NAME.	Residence, April 1, 1926.	Occupation.	Supposed Age.	Reported Residence, April 1, 1925. Street and Number.

Kendall Street—Continued

	R	Ardrey Favorite—†	29	housewife	33	86 Camden
	S	Ardrey Joseph	29	mechanic	43	86 "
	T	Terry Paul R	29	clerk	29	86 "
	U	Berry Arthur	30	laborer	28	New York
	V	Johnson Hazel—†	30	laundryworker	22	1900 Wash'n
	W	Redgick Blanch—†	30	"	26	1900 "
	X	Williams Mary—†	30	maid	51	1900 "
	Y	Julia Ralph	30	laborer	46	here
	Z	Argyle Elizabeth—†	31	laundress	28	4 Fairweather
	B	Simpson Mary E—†	31	housekeeper	34	here
	C	Jackson Moselle—†	32	cook	53	"
	D	Durant Marion—†	32	laundress	55	17 Willard pl
	E	Inniss Clare—†	32	seamstress	28	here
	F	Simpson Mary—†	32	laundress	45	"
	G	White Alfred O	33	compositor	47	"
	H	White Irene E—†	33	housewife	34	"
	M	Spence Elizabeth—†	34	"	47	"
	P	James Mildred—†	35	"	31	11 Oak Grove ter
	R	James Morgan R	35	janitor	40	11 "
	S	Boyd Dorothy—†	35	housewife	22	here
	T	Phillips Lucy—†	35	"	52	"
	U	Snowden Alice—†	35	"	29	"
	V	Snowden William	35	porter	35	"
	X	Robinson George	36	baker	27	33 Kendall
	Y	Robinson Inez—†	36	housekeeper	24	33 "
	Z	Irving Alice—†	36	housewife	35	here
	A	Irving Isreal	36	painter	36	"
	B	Sessoms John W	37	chauffeur	44	37 Lenox
	C	Sessoms Thelma—†	37	housewife	29	37 "
	D	Pachall Anna—†	37	"	40	here
	E	Pachall Boyd	37	waiter	48	"
	F	Grimes Helen J—†	37	housewife	24	8 Oak Grove ter
	G	Grimes William A	37	shipper	28	23 Windsor
	K	Andrews Manuel	38	laborer	34	23 Sawyer
	M	Frank Anna—†	39	housewife	38	here
	N	Frank Henry	39	steward	35	"
	O	Battles William	39	janitor	60	"
	P	Miller Julia—†	39	housewife	40	"
	R	Grewges Lillian—†	39	houseworker	28	"
	S	Grewges Mattie—†	39	"	49	"
	T	Henson Susie—†	40	domestic	39	53 Kendall

22

Page.	Letter.	FULL NAME.	Residence, April 1, 1926.	Occupation.	Supposed Age.	Reported Residence, April 1, 1925.
						Street and Number.

Kendall Street—Continued

	U	Smart Miriam E—†	40	housewife	28	here
	V	Chappell William	40	laborer	47	82 Ruggles
	W	Washington Grant	41	stonecutter	45	here
	X	Lewis James E	41	janitor	53	"
	Y	Lewis Lillian F—†	41	housewife	45	"
	Z	Neal Alonzo C	41	porter	27	"
	A	Hunter Daisey—†	41	housewife	39	"
	B	Hunter Hughie	41	waiter	39	"
	C	Govan Olivia T—†	42	housekeeper	76	"
	D	Phippen Hattie J—†	42	housewife	43	West Newton
	E	Pye Marjorie—†	42	"	23	"
	F	Brannon Fannie—†	42	domestic	26	here
	G	Brannon Garrison	42	fireman	45	"
	H	Hayes Felton	43	student	21	"
	K	Hayes Ola B—†	43	housewife	42	"
	L	Baskin Eldeka—†	43	"	32	"
	M	Baskin James	43	janitor	31	"
	N	Sylvia Amos	43	laborer	22	23 Willard pl
	O	Sylvia Edith—†	43	housewife	21	23 "
	P	Sylvia Joseph	43	laborer	26	23 "
	R	Sylvia Thelma—†	43	housewife	21	23 "
	S	Furman Charley	44	janitor	53	here
	T	Furman Jennie—†	44	housewife	40	"
	U	Campbell Nelson	44	laborer	25	"
	V	Blake Mary E—†	44	domestic	51	61 Fort av
	W	Thornton Ethel L—†	44	stenographer	26	61 "
	X	Lovelace Helen V—†	45	housewife	22	here
	Y	Lovelace Malcom W	45	messenger	22	"
	Z	Matthews Anna V—†	45	housewife	48	"
	A	Matthews George E	45	musician	57	"
	B	Prince Ruth M—†	45	laundress	40	"
	C	Palmer Nanie—†	45	"	82	"
	D	Henry James F	46	real estate	50	"
	F	Langford Henrietta—†	46	chambermaid	24	43 Northfield
	G	Langford Joshua	46	porter	37	43 "
	H	Quarles Arthur	47	"	49	here
	K	Quarles Benjamin	47	laborer	21	"
	L	Quarles Margaret—†	47	housewife	45	"
	M	Quarles Ruth—†	47	clerk	21	"
	N	Austin Druscilla—†	47	housewife	39	"
	O	Austin Mark A	47	clerk	43	"

Page.	Letter.	FULL NAME.	Residence, April 1, 1926.	Occupation.	Supposed Age.	Reported Residence, April 1, 1925.
						Street and Number.

Kendall Street—Continued

P	Thorpe Wilfred I—†	47	domestic	28	here
R	Soloman David	48	mechanic	37	"
S	Soloman Henrietta—†	48	housekeeper	30	"
T	Soloman Marion R—†	48	manager	27	"
U	Soloman Simm	48	retired	73	"
V	Iles Joseph	48	cooper	25	327 Northampton
W	West Mary—†	48	laundress	42	77 Kendall
Y	Shipp Charlotte—†	49	housewife	48	here
Z	Shipp Elijah	49	laborer	63	"
A	Brown Emma—†	49	housekeeper	65	"
B	Sisco Frederick	49	laborer	30	"
C	Alvas Henry	49	"	27	"
D	McIntyre Georgie F—†	50	housewife	46	36 Cabot
E	McIntyre Reud H	50	barber	53	36 "
F	Gooman Samuel W	50	porter	46	here
G	Bogan Bertha—†	50	housewife	25	"
H	Bogan Edward I	50	chauffeur	25	"
M	Robison Arthur J	51	cotton sorter	42	"
N	Allen James H	52	porter	60	"
O	Allen Julia B—†	52	housewife	41	"
P	Allen Leslie N	52	chauffeur	20	"
R	Sumter Daniel	52	longshoreman	55	"
S	Sumter Emily—†	52	housewife	54	"
T	Tilley Alice—†	53	"	36	Cambridge
U	Tilley Charles D	53	clerk	46	"
V	Jeffries Anna—†	53	housewife	32	646 Shawmut av
W	Jeffries Oliver	53	laborer	35	646 "
X	Morrison Ethel—†	53	housewife	24	here
Y	Morrison Joseph	53	chauffeur	26	"
Z	Wiseburg Estha—†	53½	housewife	33	"
A	Wiseburg Samuel	53½	storekeeper	40	"
B	Benley Jeremiah	54	janitor	63	46 Northfield
C	Howard Ethan L	54	bellboy	30	here
D	Howard Willa M—†	54	houswife	29	"
E	Highsmith Mary V—†	54	houseworker	41	"
F	Adams John	55	laborer	35	20 Thorndike
G	Kelley Suzan—†	55	housekeeper	72	here
H	Butcher Edwin	55	laborer	29	184 Northampton
K	Alford Thomas	56	painter	48	here
L	Allen Albert	56	fireman	30	"
M	Belton Carrie R—†	56	housewife	40	"

	Letter.	FULL NAME.	Residence, April 1, 1926.	Occupation.	Supposed Age.	Reported Residence, April 1, 1925. Street and Number.

Kendall Street--Continued

	N	Kelley Charles	56	fireman	41	12 Windsor
	O	Kelley Edith M—†	56	housewife	41	12 "
	P	Loftin Henrietta—†	56	housekeeper	52	48 Kendall
	R	Hall Mollie—†	57	housewife	40	here
	S	Lee Alexander	57	seaman	25	"
	T	Lee Mary—†	57	housewife	24	"
	U	Nash Cora—†	57	housekeeper	45	"
	V	Wilson Winifred—†	58	houseworker	38	"
	W	Quarles Harry	58	cashier	64	"
	X	Quarles Josephine—†	58	housewife	47	"
	Y	Roberts Mattie T—†	58	housekeeper	35	"
	Z	Roberts William H	58	retired	70	"
	A	Dickson Mary—†	59	housewife	52	"
	B	Cunningham John	59	laborer	40	"
	C	Gould Alexander	59	"	42	"
	D	Toneu David	59	teamster	24	"
	E	Smith Mabel C—†	60	housewife	35	"
	F	Baker Carl C	60	janitor	51	"
	G	Baker Mary M—†	60	housewife	41	"
	H	Waters Charles	60	janitor	30	"
	K	Waters Minnie—†	60	houseworker'	50	"
	L	Benson Samuel	61	retired	60	31 Newcomb
	M	Wade William	61	laborer	40	31 "
	N	Jackson Luther	61	machinist	24	here
	O	Jackson Mamie—†	61	housewife	26	"
	P	Jackson Walter	61	laborer	26	"
	R	Ace Juelia—†	61	housewife	48	"
	S	Ace Wanam	61	laborer	21	Georgia
	T	Ace Wanam F	61	"	59	here
	U	Bennett Hattie—†	62	laundress	24	22 Dillon
	V	Bennett Julian	62	laborer	25	22 "
	W	Sewell Nancy A—†	62	houseworker	28	109 Lenox
	Y	Jones Leslie—†	63	housewife	48	here
	Z	Jones William	63	longshoreman	42	"
	A	Gordan Charles	63	janitor	50	"
	B	Jackison Lucy—†	64	housewife	40	"
	C	Jackison William	64	laborer	46	"
	D	Nurse Louise D—†	64	houseworker	30	"
	E	Wilson Ella N—†	64	housewife	25	"
	F	Wilson Saul	64	laborer	30	"

Page.	Letter.	FULL NAME.	Residence, April 1, 1926.	Occupation.	Supposed Age.	Reported Residence, April 1, 1925. Street and Number.

Kendall Street—Continued

G	Buncon Andrew	65	laborer	46	here
H	Roberson Emma—†	65	housewife	21	"
K	Roberson Henry	65	seaman	25	"
L	Sykes Pauline—†	65	housewife	28	24 Notre Dame
M	Sykes Raymond	65	laborer	30	24 "
N	Parker Ruth V—†	66	dressmaker	50	19 Shawmut av
O	Williams Eliza—†	66	houseworker	44	here
P	Gilliam Minnie V—†	66	housewife	45	"
R	Dickerson Elizabeth—†	67	"	58	"
T	Pritchard Richard	67	laborer	52	"
U	Brown James W	68	foreman	44	"
V	Brown Mary A—†	68	housewife	46	"
W	Birt Louis	68	waiter	25	"
Y	Mitchell Steven	69	retired	60	"
B	Lee Elizabeth—†	70	houseworker	63	63 Kendall
C	Lewis Hazel—†	70	laundress	33	60 Cabot
D	Lewis Walter	70	porter	40	60 "
E	Ross Deed	70	laborer	29	54 Kendall
F	Ross Lucy M—†	70	housewife	24	54 "
G	Jones Elizabeth—†	71	"	42	here
H	Waith Bessie—†	71	"	47	"
K	Carnivie Rosco	71	laborer	40	"
L	Daniels Eva K—†	72	seamstress	29	"
M	Greene Lorenzo L	72	piano teacher	26	"
N	Greene Flora M A—†	72	dressmaker	22	New York
P	Jones Charles	73	janitor	60	here
R	Scott David A	74	car cleaner	54	"
S	Scott Lula B—†	74	housewife	43	"
T	Russell Mary—†	74	laundress	42	Providence R I
U	Scott Anna E—†	74	housewife	20	here
V	Scott Milton D	74	chauffeur	22	"
W	Benson Anna—†	75	housekeeper	56	"
X	Benson Anna M—†	75	stenographer	25	"
Y	Benson Frank K	75	expressman	62	"
Z	Benson Mary V—†	75	school teacher	22	"
A	Youngblood Grace J—†	76	housewife	21	1 E Lenox
B	Youngblood Offie D	76	pedler	23	1 "
C	Harris Charles B	76	cook	25	1 Sussex
D	Sake Edmund C	76	porter	29	here
E	Kelley Emily G—†	76	elevatorwoman	25	New York
G	White Hattie—†	77	housewife	48	Camden N J

Page.	Letter.	FULL NAME.	Residence, April 1, 1926.	Occupation.	Supposed Age.	Reported Residence, April 1, 1925.
						Street and Number.

Kendall Street—Continued

H	White William	77	laborer	47	Camden N J
L	Glass Anna—†	78	houseworker	60	here
M	Glass Devela—†	78	housewife	27	"
N	Glass Tillman J	78	oiler	29	"
O	Brown Anna R—†	78	housewife	24	72 Sterling
P	Brown George W	78	longshoreman	30	72 "
R	Edison Annie—†	78	nurse	51	72 "
S	Edison Stephen	78	laborer	54	72 "
T	Johnson Isaac	79	tailor	79	939 Harris'n av
U	Lovey Dorothy M—†	79	housewife	42	here
V	Lovey Harry	79	glazier	40	"
W	Norris Mary V—†	79	housekeeper	48	"
X	Glover Lawrence	80	chauffeur	43	"
Y	Pigott Auslin	80	postal clerk	49	"
Z	Reddish Mary E—†	80	laundress	50	"
A	Reddish William	80	coal dealer	60	"
B	Martin Cora—†	81	housewife	36	Hanover
C	Martin Manuel	81	laborer	36	"
D	Lawrence Ceola—†	81	housewife	26	here
E	Lawrence McCoy	81	laborer	46	"
F	Sewell Henry A	81	mason	40	"
G	Brinkley Sarah—†	82	housekeeper	89	"
H	Thomas Elma G—†	82	laundress	62	"
K	Thomas Walter	82	laundryman	70	"
L	Dickerson Sarah E—†	82	houseworker	51	"
N	Antoine Archibald	83	machinist	39	116 Camden
O	Taylor Martha—†	83	housewife	50	172 Kendall
P	Jenkins Eva L—†	83	dressmaker	35	544 Shawmut av
R	Oakes Clara L—†	84	secretary	40	here
S	Oakes Gertrude—†	84	housekeeper	45	"
T	Cassell Jane—†	85	housewife	52	"
U	Fortune Catherine—†	85	"	61	"
V	Purnell Annie M—†	85	housekeeper	55	"
W	Purnell Ida—†	85	"	62	"
X	Parker Elijah	87	janitor	65	"
Y	Parker Emily—†	87	housewife	55	"
Z	Ward John T	87	laborer	35	"
A	Ward Lila—†	87	housewife	37	"
B	Avertt Helen—†	88	"	32	"
C	Avertt James	88	porter	36	"
D	Keyes Gladys—†	88	housewife	21	85 W Rutland sq

Page.	Letter.	FULL NAME.	Residence, April 1, 1926.	Occupation.	Supposed Age.	Reported Residence, April 1, 1925. Street and Number.

Kendall Street—Continued

	Letter	FULL NAME	Residence	Occupation	Age	Reported Residence
	E	Keyes Robert H	88	waiter	27	85 W Rutland sq
	F	Leggons Savinia—†	88	laundress	45	here
	G	Redd Georgie C—†	89	housewife	49	"
	H	Redd William	89	janitor	60	"
	K	White Charles	89	laborer	45	"
	L	Williams Fannie—†	89	housewife	50	Omaha Neb
	M	Batson John C	90	laborer	36	here
	N	Batson Julia—†	90	housewife	27	"
	O	Hector Lillian—†	90	cook	45	"
	P	Gist Casper	90	retired	22	40 Williams
	R	Gist Sinnie—†	90	houseworker	40	40 "
	S	Jeter James E	90	laborer	36	40 "
	T	Jones Carrie H—†	91	housewife	52	588 Shawmut av
	V	Williams Frank	91	laborer	27	36 Northfield
	W	Williams Lulu—†	91	housewife	39	36 "
	X	Cole John W	92	teamster	68	31 Ball
	Y	Cole Susan F—†	92	houseworker	38	41 Hammond
	Z	Luiton William	92	janitor	36	46 Kendall
	A	Kitchener Thaddias	93	printer	45	here
	B	Slawson Harriette—†	93	housekeeper	30	"
	E	Alves Louis	95	laborer	45	Duxbury
	F	Green Edna—†	95	housekeeper	32	here
	G	Bascom Elizabeth M—†	96	housewife	58	"
	H	Bascom James E	96	engineer	55	"
	K	Reid Faith—†	96	cook	25	109 Boylston
	L	Reid John	96	"	27	109 "
	M	Woods Ozie L—†	96	housewife	31	here
	N	Woods Samuel P	96	laborer	36	"
	O	Jameson Elizabeth—†	97	housewife	60	"
	P	Houston William F	98	janitor	41	"
	R	Townes Abraham	98	shipper	63	"
	S	Townes Mary E—†	98	housewife	52	"
	T	Hall Allen J	99	cook	50	124 Canton
	U	York Arthur	99	"	33	here
	V	Patrick William L	100	janitor	73	"
	W	Wilson Mary V—†	100	cook	48	"
	X	Oxley Benjamin T	100	car cleaner	51	"
	Y	Singleton Julia—†	100	laundress	34	"
	Z	Grace Mary—†	101	housekeeper	60	367 Northampton
	A	Sharp Emma—†	101	housewife	42	here
	B	Sharp John L	101	porter	50	"

28

Page.	Letter.	Full Name.	Residence, April 1, 1926.	Occupation.	Supposed Age.	Reported Residence, April 1, 1925. Street and Number.

Kendall Street—Continued

	c	Bailey Margaret G—†	102	housekeeper	45	here
	d	Bland Charles	102	postal clerk	39	505 Col av
	e	Rogers Annie—†	102	laundress	44	48 Williams
	f	Augustus Elijah	103	porter	48	here
	g	Augustus Jennie—†	103	housewife	44	"
	h	Henry Robert	103	cook	39	"
	k	Johnson Margaret—†	103	housewife	66	18 Dilworth
	l	Brown Rebecca—†	104	housekeeper	38	here
	m	Brown Samuel C	104	elevatorman	45	"
	n	Smith Margaret—†	104	housekeeper	65	"
	o	Stokes Leola—†	104	housewife	21	"
	p	Stokes Thomas	104	barber	29	"
	r	Middleton Henry	105	cook	25	"
	s	Middleton Jerry	105	carpenter	38	"
	t	Roberts Florence—†	105	housewife	55	"
	u	Royal William H	105	porter	37	"
	v	Stone Charles	105	"	55	"
	w	Andrews Ida—†	106	housewife	22	4 Smith av
	x	Andrews Manuel	106	laborer	29	4 "
	y	Roderick Manuel	106	"	59	4 "
	z	Baker Charles N	106	chemsit	22	here
	a	Dancy Julia—†	106	houseworker	50	"
	b	Dancy Ruth—†	106	laundress	28	"
	c	Donahue Lawrence	106	waiter	25	"
	d	Murphy Berry	107	"	54	"
	e	Gibson Peter	107	elevatorman	50	"
	f	Woods Rebecca—†	107	housewife	33	"
	g	Adams Henry H	108	laborer	32	9 Yarmouth
	h	Floyd Bertha P—†	108	domestic	34	here
	k	Lawrence Mattie F—†	108	houseworker	38	11 Northfield
	l	Adams Marina P—†	108	domestic	53	here
	m	Nelson Barbara—†	108	"	54	"
	n	Nelson Percy	108	waiter	34	"
	o	Maison Claudia—†	108	domestic	39	"
	p	Phillips Elizabeth G—†	109	maid	21	"
	r	Phillips Jefferie B	109	counterman	24	"
	s	Phillips Lawrence L	109	porter	31	"
	t	Phillips Susan E—†	109	housewife	49	"
	u	Young John H	110	janitor	51	69 Sawyer
	v	Young John H, jr	110	molder	25	Readville
	w	Young Rose A—†	110	housewife	43	69 Sawyer

Page.	Letter.	FULL NAME.	Residence, April 1, 1926.	Occupation.	Supposed Age.	Reported Residence, April 1, 1925. Street and Number.

Kendall Street—Continued

x	Jones Jack	110	laborer	53	57 Camden
y	Jones Roberta—†	110	housewife	32	57 "
z	Young Frederick	110	molder	28	Readville
A	Young Gladys J—†	110	housewife	24	"
B	Reddick Marion—†	112	"	36	20 Hampshire
c	Reddick Zachariah	112	mechanic	36	20 "
D	Hutson Daisy—†	112	housewife	30	67 Williams
E	Hutson Frederick	112	janitor	31	67 "
F	Mitchell Bell—†	112	laundress	29	28 Holyoke
G	Jackison Anna S—†	112	houseworker	39	20 Hampshire
H	Foster Paul R	114	cook	38	78 W Rutland sq
K	Powell Abbie—†	114	houseworker	52	10 Kendall
K¹	Middleton Lottie—†	114	"	32	here
L	Middleton Louis B	114	carpenter	32	"
M	Freeman Frank	114	janitor	35	N Carolina
N	Freeman Lula—†	114	housewife	32	"
O	Howard Cora—†	114	"	48	"
P	Martin Albert	119	laborer	58	66 Hammond
R	Martin Lucy—†	119	housewife	50	66 "
S	Flint Walter J	119	clerk	49	here
T	Alcorn Louise—†	119	"	27	66 Westminster
U	Brown Una—†	119	"	30	66 "
V	Camiell Clemaunce—†	119	housewife	55	here
W	Camiell Leon	119	cigarmaker	57	"
X	Leylekian Leo	119	student	30	"
Y	Leylekian Nekdar—†	119	housewife	32	"
Z	Ganjian Ajaviu—†	119	"	36	"
A	Ganjian Toros	119	laborer	35	"
B	Kasabian Aroosyak—†	119	housewife	30	"
C	Kasabian Manoog	119	tailor	38	"
D	Grinidge Arora—†	119	housewife	32	1204 Tremont
E	Grinidge Charles	119	kitchenman	24	1204 "
F	Grinidge James O	119	laborer	36	1204 "

Lenox Street

c	Waterhouse Abbie—†	144	housekeeper	31	here
D	Waterhouse Joseph B	144	mechanic	37	"
E	Burke Clevland	144	cook	30	"
F	Burke Griffith—†	144	maid	26	Newton

	Letter.	Full Name.	Residence, April 1, 1926.	Occupation.	Supposed Age.	Reported Residence, April 1, 1925. Street and Number.

Lenox Street—Continued

	Letter	Full Name	Res.	Occupation	Age	Reported Residence
	G	Butter Josephine—†	144	piano teacher	56	here
	H	Dorsey Bishop	144	musician	56	"
	K	Gales George	144	waiter	45	"
	L	Foster Frederick M	144	blacksmith	30	1204 Tremont
	M	Foster Lillian—†	144	housewife	34	1204 "
	N	McAlvin Herbert K	144	laborer	41	here
	O	McAlvin Margaret A—†	144	housekeeper	73	"
	P	McAlvin William A	144	clerk	45	"
	R	Harris Edward	144	laborer	42	"
	S	Hubert Arthur	144	janitor	54	"
	W	Kelly Cora—†	156	housekeeper	35	"
	X	Ross Edward	156	porter	46	"
	Y	Dingee John P	156	carpenter	54	"
	Z	Johnson Grace—†	156	domestic	39	"
	A	Pelletier Joseph B	156	roofer	47	"
	B	Reid Laura E—†	156	housekeeper	33	69 Sterling
	C	Reid Philip A	156	laborer	47	69 "
	D	Beal Edward A	156	janitor	68	here
	E	Beal Laura M—†	156	housewife	59	"
	F	Hill James	156	janitor	41	"
	G	Robinson Isabell—†	156	domestic	37	"
	H	Innes Bertha—†	156	housekeeper	47	"
	K	Innes Leonard W	156	sailor	42	"
	L	Adams Jane—†	156	housekeeper	35	"
	M	Adams William	156	laborer	32	"
	N	Moralles Olivia—†	156	waitress	22	11½ Greenwich pk
	O	Moralles Tony	156	barber	23	11½ "
	P	William Preston B	156	musician	41	here
	R	Johnson Christine—†	156	housekeeper	64	"
	S	Purdon Philip A	156	paperhanger	54	"
	T	Pollard George	156	clerk	37	"
	U	Pollard James	156	metalworker	35	"
	V	Pollard John	156	chauffeur	31	"
	W	Pollard Joseph	156	teamster	43	"
	X	Pollard Mary—†	156	housekeeper	64	"
	Y	Belton John	156	laborer	31	106 Lenox
	Z	Keelang Blanche—†	156	waitress	24	106 "
	A	White Benjamin	156	proprietor	38	here
	B	Wilson Margaret—†	156	housekeeper	46	106 Lenox
	C	Bryon Elinora—†	156	"	56	101 Hammond
	D	Bryan John J	156	porter	49	101 "

31

Page	Letter	Full Name.	Residence, April 1, 1926.	Occupation.	Supposed Age.	Reported Residence, April 1, 1925. Street and Number.

Madison Street

	K	Spanley Edward	3	barber	35	here
	L	Skanley Gabriel	3	retired	79	"
	M	Spanley Susie—†	3	housekeeper	23	"
	N	Lynch Alice—†	5	"	41	"
	O	Lynch John J	5	chauffeur	44	"
	P	Thompson Mary E—†	5	housekeeper	44	"
	R	Thompson Stephen J	5	polisher	48	"
	S	Wlash John J	7	constable	70	"
	T	Walsh Emily G—†	7	housekeeper	50	"
	U	Casey Elmer	9	laborer	49	"
	V	Casey Mary—†	9	housekeeper	45	"
	W	Hammond Annie—†	11	at home	72	"
	X	Hammond James	11	painter	73	"
	Y	Richards Agnes E—†	11	domestic	54	"
	A	Smith Henry C	13	waiter	53	8 Marble
	B	Smith Margaret—†	13	housekeeper	45	8 "
	C	Favere Alice—†	15	"	58	here
	D	LaPoint William	15	salesman	22	"
	E	McCue Frank M	15	painter	40	"
	F	Baker Berry	17	laborer	26	"
	G	Bowden John R	17	waiter	40	"
	H	Declue James	17	janitor	36	"
	K	Wilson Isaac	17	porter	29	"
	L	Gaskins Emma—†	19	laundress	45	42 Newcomb
	M	Gaskins Peter	19	laborer	42	42 "

Sawyer Street

	P	Moore Jane—†	2	laundress	65	here
	R	Wideman Carrie—†	2	housewife	47	"
	S	Wideman John	2	plasterer	47	"
	T	Boon Angline—†	4	housekeeper	65	"
	U	Washington Ganville	4	laborer	21	Richmond Va
	V	Young Lillian—†	4	matron	34	here
	W	Childs Hattie—†	6	houseworker	57	"
	X	King Kizzanie—†	6	housekeeper	67	"
	Y	Dudy Cora—†	6	"	58	"
	Z	Dudy Louis	6	laborer	55	"
	A	Burrill Frances M—†	6	housekeeper	80	"

32

Sawyer Street—Continued

B	Thompson Harry A	8	laborer	54	here
C	Thompson Mary —†	8	housewife	45	"
D	McCollum Jennie B—†	8	laundress	48	82 Camden
E	Price Emma—†	8	cook	33	here
F	Tarres Florence—†	10	laundress	25	17 Sawyer
G	Bernard Isabel—†	10	housewife	43	here
H	Lamson Alice—†	10	laundress	44	"
K	Mathews Florence—†	10	dressmaker	31	"
L	Housell William H	12	laborer	38	6 Stevens
M	Johnson Lillian—†	12	housekeeper	40	6 "
N	Frohman Marvis V—†	12	laundress	55	here
O	Riley Rebter—†	12	housekeeper	77	1968 Wash'n
P	Thomes Florence—†	12	laundress	54	1968 "
R	Baker Michael	14	fireman	40	here
S	Baker William	14	laborer	28	"
T	Cox Thomas	14	janitor	25	"
U	Inniss Ella—†	14	housewife	40	"
V	Inniss Lester	14	laborer	57	"
W	Reves Naomi †	14	laundress	24	New York
X	Reves Novel	14	laborer	23	"
Y	Henderson Mary—†	16	domestic	40	here
Z	Lee Eula—†	16	laundress	42	"
A	Collins Frank	18	laborer	65	"
B	Collins Mary—†	18	housewife	53	"
C	Coff Bula—†	18	housekeeper	36	42 Hammond
D	Collins Samuel H	18	laborer	26	Lynn
E	Engermann Daniel	18	"	33	646 Shawmut av
F	Engermann Margaret—†	18	laundress	32	646 "
G	Smith Charles	20	janitor	30	here
H	Smith Mary—†	20	housewife	28	"
K	Pena Frank	20	laborer	38	25 Sawyer
M	Hewings Ethel—†	22	housewife	42	here
N	Hewings Richard	22	laborer	45	"
O	Braxton Alice—†	22	housewife	58	"
P	Long Margaret—†	22	laundress	41	"
R	Scott Amelia—†	22	"	60	"
S	Fry Estasla—†	24	"	42	"
T	Hamilton Susan—†	24	"	54	"
U	Dickinson Archie A	24	janitor	47	"
V	Dickinson Grace—†	24	housewife	40	"

Sawyer Street—Continued

W	Dickinson Sarah A—†	24	housekeeper	63	7 Parnell
X	Benders Joseph E	26	laborer	22	6 Fairweather
Y	Hargett Gertrude—†	26	housewife	23	30 Sawyer
Z	Hargett James	26	janitor	33	30 "
A	Douglas Albert	26	laborer	31	12 "
B	Douglas Ethel—†	26	housewife	26	12 "
C	Jennett Carrie—†	28	houseworker	46	here
E	Nickens Louisea—†	28	housekeeper	48	"
F	Nathalio Elizabeth—†	30	housewife	30	93 Springfield
G	Nathalio Francis	30	laborer	30	93 "
H	Brown George M	30	musician	33	17 Sawyer
K	Brown Nannie B—†	30	houseworker	53	here
L	Brown Walter J	30	laborer	27	"
M	Barrows John	30	"	40	"
O	Pratt Frances—†	32	housekeeper	35	83 Kendall
P	Lupes Isaac	32	laborer	41	125 Lenox
R	Young Mildred—†	32	housekeeper	39	125 "
S	Devoe Thomas H	34	painter	40	38 Newcomb
T	Tribee Elizabeth—†	34	housekeeper	40	38 "
V	Ripley Isaac	36	retired	92	here
W	Young George	36	cook	64	"
X	VanRiper George	36	chauffeur	47	3 E Lenox
Y	VanRiper Margaret—†	36	housewife	28	3 "
Z	Green Hattie—†	36	housekeeper	41	here
A	Curry Domingo	38	laborer	38	156 Northampton
B	Curry Fannie—†	38	housewife	37	156 "
C	Pope Nellie—†	38	laundress	23	156 "
D	Dias Thomas	38	laborer	43	here
E	Ramos Arthur	38	barber	27	93 W Springfield
F	Jones Maude—†	40	houseworker	41	70 Northfield
G	Murphy Andrew	40	laborer	29	66 Kendall
H	Murphy Virginia—†	40	houseworker	29	66 "
K	Simmons Corrine—†	40	housekeeper	41	70 Northfield
L	Wilson Mary—†	40	cook	25	Lincoln
M	Calwell Rose—†	40	houseworker	35	here
N	Bell Margaret A—†	42	housekeeper	70	"
O	Hodges Charles W	42	oiler	31	"
P	Thompson Elnore—†	42	laundress	24	"
R	Gross Herbert	42	pedler	31	"
S	Gross Louise—†	42	housekeeper	74	"

Page	Letter	Full Name.	Residence, April 1, 1926.	Occupation.	Supposed Age.	Reported Residence, April 1, 1925. Street and Number.

Sawyer Street—Continued

T	Cannon Oliver	44	laborer	50	40 Sawyer
U	Irving Fannie—†	44	housekeeper	34	here
V	Wilson Aric	44	laborer	47	"
W	Lee Erna—†	44	cook	34	17 Kendall
X	Sylvester Helen—†	44	waitress	27	7 Claremont pk
Y	Johnson David	46	painter	50	here
Z	Williams Charles M	46	laborer	42	"
A	Williams Dorothy—†	46	housewife	24	"
B	Bond Laura—†	46	houseworker	50	"
C	Bright Lucy—†	48	"	28	Norfolk Va
D	Burton Ethel—†	48	laundress	35	here
E	Dukes Earla—†	48	housewife	32	Savannah Ga
F	Dukes Fred	48	waiter	41	"
G	Hicks Nathan	48	longshoreman	47	"
H	Hicks Sarah—†	48	houseworker	47	here
K	Brown William H	50	fireman	54	83 Sterling
L	King Anna—†	50	housewife	60	here
M	King Fitzherbert	50	porter	56	"
N	Bowden Joseph	50	"	71	"
O	Gordon Josephine—†	50	houseworker	58	"
P	Morrison Mary—†	52	"	48	"
R	Harris Ellen—†	52	housewife	30	"
S	Harris Emmett	52	laborer	30	"
U	Wimbley Adolph	54	butler	29	19 Parnell
V	Wimbley Jack	54	chauffeur	26	19 "
W	Wimbley Rose—†	54	housewife	27	19 "
Y	Elzey Blanche—† .	54	houseworker	40	here
Z	Brodey Daniel	56	laborer	70	Cambridge
A	Hamilton Jessie L—†	56	waitress	27	here
B	Hamilton Mary C—†	56	housekeeper	65	"
C	Munsey Millie—†	58	houseworker	40	Salem
D	Upshure Annie—†	58	laundress	50	here
E	Walker William	60	laborer	29	Cambridge
F	Whitfield Anna—†	60	houseworker	40	38 Sawyer
G	Ming Henry	60	retired	50	here
H	Still Gertrude—†	60	housewife	31	"
K	Freeman Annie—†	62	"	35	59 Sawyer
L	Freeman George H	62	chauffeur	36	59 "
M	Richardson Anna—†	62	houseworker	38	102 Hammond
N	Jeffriess Delia—†	62	"	47	here
O	Eichelburger Annie—†	64	housewife	59	"

Sawyer Street—Continued

P	Eichelburger Lawrence A	64	porter	61	here
R	Foye Floyd M	66	steward	26	1868 Centre
S	Foye Mary—†	66	houseworker	20	here
T	Nobles Estell—†	66	"	32	"
U	Nobles John	66	laborer	26	"
V	Nobles Mims	66	"	58	"
W	Nobles Victoria †	66	housewife	45	"
X	Lynch George W	68	porter	43	127 Lenox
Y	Bell John	68	laborer	27	55 Kendall
Z	Bell Viola—†	68	housewife	25	55 "
B	Ansel Mary—†	70	housekeeper	71	here
C	Cuff Gilbert S	72	laborer	25	"
D	Johnson Charles H	72	"	49	"
E	Johnson Sarah L—†	72	housewife	44	"
G	Robinson George	72	laborer	60	"
H	Marriott Stella—†	72	housewife	32	New York
K	Marriott William H	72	porter	49	"
L	Cousins Blanche †	72	housewife	35	14 E Lenox
N	Tines Bessie—†	72	houseworker	20	39 Sterling
O	Tines John H	72	laborer	21	39 "
P	Bivans George	72	"	29	52 Kendall
R	Booker Norman	72	waiter	70	Baltimore
S	Grace Alexander	76	porter	38	100 Sawyer
T	Grace Sylvina †	76	housewife	28	100 "
U	Farrier Irene—†	76	"	30	here
V	Farrier William	76	janitor	30	"
X	Johns Joseph A	76	"	32	"
W	Johns Reburtha—†	76	housewife	31	"
Y	Gilliard Katherine M—†	78	housekeeper	25	"
Z	Evans Otts	78	painter	36	"
A	Williams David	78	barber	42	"
B	Williams Sylvina—†	78	housewife	46	"
C	Tavada Louis	80	laborer	36	"
D	Tavada Philis †	80	housewife	36	"
E	Kennedy Jane—†	80	"	31	"
F	Kennedy Walter	80	pedler	42	"
G	Buchanan Dena †	80	houseworker	20	"
H	French Indie—†	80	housewife	25	"
K	French Vincent	80	laborer	31	"
L	Barnes George L	82	chief	42	"
M	Barnes Ida— †	82	housewife	32	"

Page.	Letter.	FULL NAME.	Residence, April 1, 1926.	Occupation.	Supposed Age.	Reported Residence, April 1, 1925. Street and Number.

Sawyer Street—Continued

	N	Griffith James	82	porter	36	here
	O	Griffith Ruth—†	82	housekeeper	31	"
	R	Williams James	90	meatcutter	46	"
	S	Jones Henry	92	cook	48	"
	T	Jones Marie—†	92	housewife	44	"
	U	Rand Ruby	92	carpenter	52	Cambridge
	V	Ferguson Jessie—†	94	stripper	75	here
	W	Kneeland Estelle—†	94	"	45	"
	X	McFadden Edith—†	94	pantrywoman	40	"
	Z	Howard John B	96	retired	57	"
	Y	Howard Ella L—†	96	housekeeper	43	"
	A	Buckner George W	98	machinist	54	"
	B	Crawley Charles N	98	cook	47	"
	C	Crawley Mary J—†	98	housewife	42	"
	D	Yates John	100	janitor	54	"
	G	Berry Anna J—†	102	housewife	48	"
	H	Berry John H	102	cook	61	"
	K	Clark Richard A	102	porter	46	Lynn

Shawmut Avenue

	M	Springer Beatrice—†	627	housewife	35	here
	N	Clark Ollie	629	chauffeur	34	Brookline
	O	Jackson Blanche—†	629	houseworker	34	1022 Tremont
	P	Wilson Mary—†	629	nurse	27	New York
	R	Hawkins Amelia—†	631	houseworker	69	39 Northfield
	S	Jackson Anna—†	631	laundress	44	68 Sterling
	T	Kirton Christine—†	631	housewife	48	here
	U	Kirton Clemmouth	631	porter	23	"
	V	Kirton Nathaniel	631	fireman	60	"
	W	Jackson Elizabeth—†	633	laundress	30	68 Sterling
	X	Jackson William	633	chauffeur	31	68 "
	Y	Collymore Alice—†	633	housewife	35	665 Shawmut av
	Z	Collymore Joseph	633	longshoreman	37	665 "
	A	Barrett Samuel	635	pedler	42	here
	B	Jessamy Bertha—†	635	storekeeper	36	"
	C	Gainey Flordie—†	635	housewife	20	N Carolina
	D	Fainey William	635	porter	22	"
	E	Jones Arthur A	637	chauffeur	39	here
	F	Jones Elizabeth—†	637	housewife	46	"

Page.	Letter.	FULL NAME.	Residence, April 1, 1926.	Occupation.	Supposed Age.	Reported Residence, April 1, 1925. Street and Number.

Shawmut Avenue—Continued

G	Jones George B	637	chauffeur	41	here
H	Jones Julia I— †	637	housewife	31	"
M	Yee Foo	641	laundryman	65	"
L	Yee Hing Foo	641	"	23	"
N	Giavamiello Catherine-†	643	housewife	34	"
O	Giavamiello Dominick	643	coal dealer	36	"
P	Amendolare Joseph	643	"	54	"
R	Amendolare Rose— †	643	housewife	49	"
S	Festino James	643	coal dealer	34	"
T	Festino Raffella—†	643	housewife	24	"
V	Tempesta Frank	645	coal dealer	30	"
W	Tempesta Madalena—†	645	housewife	27	"
X	Veleta Angelina—†	645	domestic	58	"
Y	DeTully Anna— †	645	housewife	21	"
Z	DeTully Constantino	645	ice dealer	29	"
A	Solmena Andy	645	coal dealer	48	"
B	Solmena Mary— †	645	housewife	48	"
C	Zero John	645	coal dealer	43	"
D	Zero Phelmena— †	645	housewife	35	"
E	Bryant Abram A	646	shoemaker	73	"
F	Howard Virginia— †	646	domestic	44	"
G	Faulk Effie— †	646	housewife	21	"
H	Faulk Robert	646	electrotyper	25	"
K	Francis Emily—†	646	cook	45	"
L	Jeffries Coy	646	laborer	26	"
M	Jeffries Lena—†	646	laundress	23	"
N	Braxton Joseph B	646	porter	22	"
O	Braxton Margaret E—†	646	housewife	22	"
P	Johnson Lorie	646	laborer	24	Alabama
R	Johnson Mary—†	646	housewife	23	"
S	Thompson Martha—†	646	laundress	23	
T	McDavid Lucinda—†	647	housewife	60	11 Arnold
U	McDavid Phillys	647	roofer	66	New York
V	Strong Clarence	647	messenger	21	here
W	Strong Sadie— †	647	laundress	34	"
X	Wallace George A	647	inspector	37	9 Windsor
Y	Wallace Susan C— †	647	housewife	30	here
Z	Young John W	647	cleanser	25	Hartford Ct
C	Munroe Isaac	649	laborer	50	here
D	Munroe Isabella— †	649	housewife	52	"

Page.	Letter.	FULL NAME.	Residence, April 1, 1926.	Occupation.	Supposed Age.	Reported Residence, April 1, 1925. Street and Number.

Shawmut Avenue—Continued

E	Waller Charles	649	laborer	23	21 Windsor
F	Walker Hazel—†	649	housewife	22	83 Westminster
G	Williams Fannie—†	649	laundress	55	here
K	Josey Sally—†	651	"	44	40 Newcomb
L	Baker George W	651	porter	48	5 Chester pl
M	Thompson Rose—†	651	housewife	31	5 "
P	Fordham Percy	653	policeman	35	here
R	Guilford Harriet—†	653	domestic	87	"
S	Manning Lucille—†	653	maid	31	"
T	Mulligan Peter	653	porter	25	"
U	Richardson Susie—†	653	housekeeper	35	"
V	Watts Lucy—†	655	housewife	48	Canada
W	Watts Ormond	655	laborer	48	"
X	Sehouse Minnie B—†	655	laundress	33	here
Y	Forsythe Alfred U	655	laborer	49	"
Z	Forsythe Mary—†	655	housewife	36	"
K	Mason Ella—†	660	"	36	"
L	Mason John T	660	painter	56	"
N	Gray Emma—†	660	housekeeper	39	"
O	Gray Ralph	660	machinist	40	"
P	Fletcher Herbert	660	chauffeur	31	"
R	Fletcher Marion—†	660	housekeeper	34	"
S	Campbell Gertrude—†	662	"	30	44 Kendall
T	Oliver Mamie E—†	662	"	34	here
U	Oliver Watt S	662	foreman	44	"
V	Bemberry Edward W—†	662	at home	62	"
W	Bemberry Elizabeth—†	662	housewife	50	"
X	Knox Ira L	662	waiter	63	"
Y	Knox Margaret E—†	662	housekeeper	40	"
Z	Henry Elonzo	664	barber	35	"
A	Henry Rose—†	664	housewife	26	"
B	Jones Katie—†	664	domestic	37	19 Camden
C	Richerson Etta—†	664	"	31	19 "
D	Minor Ella—†	664	"	45	5 Marble
E	Minor Thomas	664	janitor	47	5 "
F	Hurd Josephine—†	664	housewife	45	here
G	Fay Mamie—†	666	housekeeper	40	"
H	Burns Edgar	666	laborer	35	"
K	Burns Joseph A	666	janitor	37	"
L	Burns Sarah—†	666	housekeeper	66	"

Shawmut Avenue—Continued

M	Bias Rosa †	666	domestic	39	here
N	Brooks Lillian †	666	"	35	"
O	Chisholm Marie †	666	"	33	"
P	Gumes Edna †	666	"	41	"
R	Gumes Minnie †	666	"	39	"
T	Williams Eustis J	670	porter	48	"
U	Williams Rose †	670	dressmaker	38	"
V	Toomer Alice †	670	housekeeper	51	"
W	Johnson Harry A	670	laborer	42	"
X	Johnson May †	670	housekeeper	41	"
Z	Williams Albert	672	laborer	42	"
A	Williams Mildred †	672	housekeeper	40	"
B	Sikes Georgiana †	672	"	40	"
C	Sikes James	672	laborer	41	"
D	Howard Frank	672	janitor	33	"
E	Howard Laura †	672	housewife	30	"
F	Gavin Arthur	672	painter	40	"
G	Gavin Martha †	672	housekeeper	39	"
H	Barton Francis L	673	cook	40	"
K	Barton Sallie H †	674	dressmaker	40	"
L	Scott Elizabeth †	674	housekeeper	26	"
M	Scott Stephen	674	cook	31	"
N	Alcorn Marie †	674	housekeeper	30	"
O	Alcorn William	674	janitor	27	"
R	Rochester Alice †	676	hairdresser	43	"
S	Rochester Edmund	676	waiter	41	"
T	Jefferson Carl P	676	porter	52	New York
U	Jefferson Margory †	676	housekeeper	38	"
V	Fletcher Albert	676	chef	41	here
W	Fletcher Madeline †	676	housekeeper	42	"

Smith Avenue

Z	Ford John	1	janitor	57	here
A	Ford Susie †	1	housekeeper	53	"
B	Tyler William	1	laborer	65	"
D	Foster Annie B †	2	housekeeper	33	"
E	Foster Benny M C	2	expressman	34	"
F	Gamble Carrie †	2	housekeeper	30	"
G	Gamble Harry	2	laborer	35	"

Smith Avenue—Continued

M	Pinto Cyril	6	laborer	27	here
N	Pinto Gladys —†	6	housekeeper	24	"
O	Maddox Charlotte —†	6	"	39	12 Howard
P	Maddox John H	6	chef	40	12 "
R	Callander Leslie	6	laborer	30	here
S	Callander Rebecca —†	6	housekeeper	31	"

Tremont Street

Y	Hawkins Stanley	795	janitor	48	here
Z	Polk Gladias —†	795	domestic	21	"
A	Polk Lillian —†	795	maid	23	"
B	Polk Mabel A —†	795	domestic	53	"
C	Benn Bernard N	795	clerk	45	Brookline
D	Benn Edith —†	795	domestic	38	"
E	Cameron Egbert	795	porter	30	192 Northampton
F	Cox Thomas R	795	dentist	50	here
G	Lucas Louise —†	795	domestic	35	"
H	Drysdale Gertrude —†	795	"	45	Brockton
K	Hasbrook Hattie —†	795	housewife	55	here
L	Hasbrook John A	795	janitor	68	"
M	Gomez Bessie —†	795	housewife	35	30 Braddock pk
N	Gomez Manuel	795	laborer	38	30 "
O	Hasbrook Emma R —†	795	housewife	42	here
P	Hasbrook Ernest W	795	laborer	39	"
R	Hailstalk John H	795	waiter	68	"
S	Mickens Mattie —†	795	housekeeper	45	"
T	Barnett Sadie —†	799	"	45	612 Col av
V	Barnett Stephen	799	porter	46	612 "
W	Hicks Richard	799	clerk	45	New Jersey
X	Grant Minnie —†	799	housekeeper	45	here
Y	Welles Albert	799	mechanic	43	"
Z	Welles Anna —†	799	housewife	45	"
A	Welles Sarah —†	799	at home	77	"
B	Lucas Ralph	799	taxi driver	45	"
C	Hall Ella E —†	801	housekeeper	55	"
D	Hall Simon J	801	retired	67	"
E	Lynch Luther	801	tailor	45	"
F	Lynch Robbie —†	801	housewife	45	"
G	Bruen William N	801	chauffeur	35	"

Page	Letter	Full Name.	Residence, April 1, 1926.	Occupation.	Supposed Age.	Reported Residence, April 1, 1925. Street and Number.

Tremont Street—Continued

H	Ponteaux Margaret —†	801	housewife	52	here
K	Ponteaux William P	801	waiter	45	"
L	Foster Ida—†	801	domestic	45	"
M	Greene Hattie R—†	801	"	40	"
O	Lynch Annie B—†	803	seamstress	65	"
P	Wimby Ida—†	803	"	40	"
R	Williams Eva—†	803	laundryworker	44	"
S	Thornton Josephine—†	803	domestic	44	"
T	Thornton Martha—†	803	maid	49	"
U	Crick Irene—†	803	laundress	28	6 Williams ter
V	Crick Keizia—†	803	houseworker	44	6 "
W	Crick Stella—†	803	maid	22	6 "
X	Harris Arthur	803	laborer	40	6 "
Z	Counte Frank	805	waiter	42	here
A	Foster Walter	805	lawyer	48	360 Mass av
D	Blackwell Rose—†	813	housekeeper	45	here
E	Bryant Ferrela—†	813	housewife	30	"
F	Bryant Ralph O	813	cook	33	"
G	Payne Daisy—†	813	housekeeper	35	"
H	Payne Humphrey	813	waiter	40	"
P	Amos Annie K—†	924	housewife	34	125 Cabot
R	Amos William W	924	furniture	39	125 "
S	Druitt William H	924	janitor	39	125 "
T	Gray Ethel M—†	924	housekeeper	35	959 Tremont
U	Gray Hubert C	924	waiter	38	959 "
V	Gray Randall R	924	bellboy	36	959 "
W	Gray Susie—†	924	housekeeper	30	959 "
A	Nobles John	928	longshoreman	26	66 Sawyer
B	Reid Ethel—†	928	domestic	27	803 Tremont
C	Buckner Lewarance L	928	waiter	54	here
D	Foster Paul A	928	proprietor	38	"
E	Summons Hattie—†	928	housekeeper	39	"
F	Summons Robert	928	laborer	49	"
H	Lewis Alexander	928	baker	32	894 Tremont
K	Lewis Antionett—†	928	housekeeper	27	894 "
M	Steward Charles G	932	dentist	50	here
N	Steward Maude T—†	932	housekeeper	43	"
O	Manokey Jeremiah	932	waiter	66	"
P	Manokey Josephine—†	932	housekeeper	52	"
R	Bonnella Albert W	932	elevatorman	40	"
S	Bonnella Margaret—†	932	housekeeper	38	"

Page	Letter	FULL NAME.	Residence, April 1, 1926.	Occupation.	Supposed Age.	Reported Residence, April 1, 1925. Street and Number.

Tremont Street—Continued

	Letter	FULL NAME.	Residence April 1, 1926.	Occupation.	Supposed Age.	Street and Number.
	T	Hogeland Ferdinand	932	chef	40	here
	U	Hogeland Leile—†	932	housekeeper	38	"
	V	Yee Jim	934	laundryman	58	Somerville
	Y	Jones Hamilton	936	waiter	35	here
	Z	Smith John S	936	"	48	"
	A	Smith Mary F—†	936	housekeeper	42	"
	B	Thompson James A	936	printer	24	"
	C	Thompson Sevana M—†	936	domestic	46	"
	F	Christian Clara B—†	940	dressmaker	45	"
	G	Conyers James	940	postal clerk	26	"
	H	Conyers Sarah—†	940	waitress	24	"
	K	Edwards Ardell C—†	940	matron	36	"
	L	Morse Annie M—†	940	housekeeper	55	54 Sawyer
	M	Coles Anna E—†	940	domestic	52	here
	N	Lawton Emma J—†	940	"	48	"
	P	Dinsmore Rosetta—†	944	housekeeper	45	"
	R	Grooms Grace F—†	944	"	39	"
	S	Grooms James E	944	janitor	45	"
	T	West James	944	laborer	70	"
	U	West Lillian—†	944	operator	30	"
	V	West Mary—†	944	housekeeper	65	"
	W	West William	944	laborer	62	"
	X	Boghosian Kainer—†	944	houseworker	60	"
	Y	Boghosian Mary—†	944	housekeeper	60	"
	D	Kalpakdzian Levan	944	garageman	27	"
	Z	Kalpakdzian Matilda—†	944	dressmaker	29	"
	B	Foster Eliza—†	948	housekeeper	63	"
	C	Foster Helen—†	948	"	45	"
	D	Fawn Ruth—†	948	domestic	37	"
	E	Harvey Cordelia—†	948	housekeeper	47	605 Shawmut av
	F	Harvey Grace P—†	948	domestic	30	here
	G	Carey Minnie—†	948	"	28	30 Sussex
	H	Hayes Clifford	948	guard	24	30 "
	K	Hayes Frances M—†	948	housekeeper	22	30 "
	O	Jennings Sadie—†	957	housewife	44	13 Hubert
	P	Johnson Taylor	957	retired	70	13 "
	R	Dotson Clarence	957	laborer	39	here
	S	Dotson Ellen—†	957	housekeeper	45	"
	T	Brown John	957	porter	45	"
	U	Washington Anna B—†	957	housekeeper	50	"
	V	Washington Ella—†	957	domestic	22	"

Tremont Street— Continued

z	Martin Clifton	959	laborer	26	68 Ruggles
A	Martin Margaret — †	959	housekeeper	55	68 "
B	Wright Mary — †	959	"	26	68 "
C	Blocker Mary — †	959	"	50	here
D	Barron William D	959	laborer	22	"
E	Carpenter Estelle — †	959	housekeeper	42	"
G	Bishop Cora †	961A	"	54	"
H	Bishop George	961A	laborer	26	"
K	Bishop Grace— †	961A	housewife	24	"
L	McFarlane Catherine— †	961A	"	21	17 Hubert
M	McFarlane Hannah— †	961A	"	24	24 Northfield
N	McFarlane Hubert	961A	laborer	23	24 "
O	McFarlane Wilfred	961A	"	32	24 "
P	Mahan Daisy †	961A	manicurist	38	here
R	Mahan Margaret †	961A	waitress	48	"
S	Lyons Mary †	963	housekeeper	66	"
T	Lyons Mary E †	963	housewife	32	"
U	Lyons Patrick J	963	B F D	33	"
V	Clifford Eleanor †	963	housewife	27	"
W	Clifford Frank	963	salesman	36	"
Z	Markley Edward D	965	"	41	107 Cabot
A	Markley Vivian †	965	housewife	31	107 "
B	Rogers Jennie †	965	waitress	60	here
C	Coulis Esther †	965	housekeeper	70	"
D	Coulis Peter	965	tailor	38	"
E	Coulis Sarah †	965	housewife	35	"
G	Norian John	967	shoemaker	60	"
H	Norian Rose — †	967	housewife	52	"
O	Gibson Olive — †	971A	domestic	45	"
P	Campbell Bessie †	971A	"	41	"
R	Campbell William H	971A	porter	30	"
S	Johnson Arthur A	971A	salesman	36	"
T	Tines Edith T †	971A	domestic	25	2 Dartmouth pl
U	Williams Jennie †	971A	housekeeper	30	2 "
V	Williams Vivian C	971A	laborer	29	2 "
X	Jones James L	973A	"	30	53 Ruggles
Y	Jones Mary †	973A	housewife	42	53 "
Z	Forbes Irene †	973A	domestic	35	40 Windsor
B	Gray Gladias J †	973A	clerk	21	Worcester

Page.	Letter.	FULL NAME.	Residence, April 1, 1926.	Occupation.	Supposed Age.	Reported Residence, April 1, 1925. Street and Number.

Tremont Street—Continued

	Letter.	FULL NAME.	Residence	Occupation.	Age	Reported Residence
	A	Lambert Blanche—†	973A	housewife	29	here
	C	Lambert William	973A	laborer	48	"
	D	Conaway George	973A	undertaker	40	"
	E	Myles Mildred—†	973A	housewife	31	"
	G	Schaffer Albert	975A	cook	45	"
	H	Trott Arthur A	975A	carpenter	29	New York City
	K	Trott Frederick S	975A	machinist	38	66 Hammond
	L	Trott Olivia—†	975A	housewife	36	66 "
	M	Steward Minnie—†	975A	"	33	here
	N	Steward William A	975A	porter	34	"
	P	Clements Forrest A	977A	waiter	24	"
	R	Clements Roland W	977A	porter	36	"
	S	Reid Dora M—†	977A	housewife	48	"
	T	Reid William B	977A	mechanic	42	"
	U	Moore Alice M—†	977A	dressmaker	21	1029½ Tremont
	V	Moore Alonzo J	977A	tailor	45	1029½ "
	W	Moore Alonzo J, jr	977A	porter	22	1029½ "
	X	Moore Annie J—†	977A	housekeeper	41	1029½ "
	Y	Moore Herbert H	977A	porter	24	1029½ "
	Z	Brown Mary—†	977A	domestic	35	981A "
	A	Hathaway Helen—†	977A	housewife	40	981A "
	B	Hathaway William E	977A	waiter	45	981A "
	D	Chase Anna—†	979A	housewife	35	here
	E	Chase James R	979A	laborer	35	"
	F	Widgeon Adelaide—†	979A	housekeeper	53	"
	G	Widgeon Wilson B	979A	waiter	62	"
	H	Mano Avdis Z	979A	salesman	50	"
	K	Mano Paris—†	979A	housewife	34	"
	M	Carrington Maud—†	981A	dressmaker	41	"
	N	Carrington William R	981A	musician	42	"
	O	Davies Dorothy—†	981A	domestic	40	"
	P	Davies Thomas	981A	carpenter	29	"
	R	Nelson Eunice—†	981A	housewife	27	"
	S	Nelson James	981A	laborer	48	"
	T	Gordon Samuel S	981A	waiter	43	"
	U	Hill Joseph C	981A	laborer	30	"
	V	Sides Bertie M—†	981A	housewife	31	"
	W	Sides George A	981A	laborer	35	"

Washington Street

Y	Otley Emma—†	1957	housewife	39	here
Z	Otley Joseph	1957	laborer	51	"
A	Wright Alice—†	1957	housewife	42	"
B	Wright Mosse L	1957	engineer	55	"
C	Benders Ester—†	1957	housewife	25	"
F	Kentil Edward	1957	laborer	45	"
D	Robinson Catherine—†	1957	housekeeper	31	"
E	Robinson Emile	1957	laborer	34	"
G	Lewis Charles	1959	retired	32	"
H	Lewis Susie—†	1959	housewife	28	"
K	Taylor Julia—†	1959	"	35	1 Sussex
L	Stokes Bessie—†	1959	"	34	here
M	Ingerman Gertrude—†	1959	"	27	29 Ball
N	Ingerman Isaiah	1959	molder	29	29 "
O	Smith Arthur W	1959	porter	44	here
P	Smith Mary K—†	1959	housewife	36	"
R	Walker Bertha—†	1959	"	30	106 Kendall
S	Walker Ira	1959	machinist	28	here
T	Ellis Albert	1959	janitor	35	"
U	Boye Richard	1959	laborer	55	26 Flagg
V	Reid Fannie—†	1959	housewife	51	here
W	Reid William E	1959	porter	50	"
Y	Crossen William	1963	laborer	22	"
Z	Davis Jetson	1963	"	44	"
A	Davis Sarah—†	1963	housewife	38	"
B	Bird Charles	1963	laborer	25	1842 Wash'n
C	Mitchell Annie T—†	1963	housewife	39	1842 "
D	Walker Lucinda—†	1963	"	45	here
E	Walker William	1963	laborer	40	"

Westfield Street

L	Hyde James	2 & 4	janitor	35	here
M	Ray Percy	2 & 4	clerk	57	"

Woodbury Street

R	Wickham Sarah—†	4	domestic	72	here
S	Sims Anna—†	6	housekeeper	38	"
T	Robinson Lottie—†	6	"	41	"
U	Akins Ellen—†	6	"	29	"
V	Sheppard William	8	laborer	67	"
W	Warbington Rebecca—†	8	housekeeper	42	"
X	Warbington West	8	laborer	38	"
Y	Sampson Bert M	8	"	23	"
Z	Sampson Rose—†	8	housekeeper	60	"
D	Pohorecki Antoni	12	real estate	52	"
E	Pohorecki Catherine—†	12	housewife	48	"
F	Adams Andrew E	12	real estate	54	"
G	Perechodauch Filimon	12	cook	46	"
H	Bosick John	12	freighthandler	25	Shirley Centre
K	Fedorezk Joseph	12	factory worker	72	"
M	Smiley George	14	laborer	28	here
N	Smiley Ruth—†	14	housekeeper	28	"
O	Robinson Mary—†	14	"	40	"
P	Hart Bessie—†	16	"	33	20 Woodbury
R	Watkins Susie—†	16	cook	55	here
S	Jordan Ursula—†	16	housekeeper	29	Cambridge
T	Bendisher Florence—†	18	housewife	30	Springfield
U	Bendisher John	18	laborer	29	"
V	Rernitzski Elizabeth—†	18	housekeeper	46	here
W	Rernitzski John	18	laborer	22	"
X	Rernitzski Michael	18	"	50	"
Y	Cook Aron	20	"	38	"
Z	Wiggin Ned	20	"	60	"
A	Winn Mitchell	20	cook	24	"
C	Godfrey Frank	22	laborer	51	"
D	Sheppard Grace—†	22	housekeeper	24	"
E	Sheppard Raymond	22	laborer	24	"
F	Jones William	22	paperhanger	45	"
L	Asbury Charles	26	laborer	52	"
M	Johnson George	26	"	48	"
O	Flemmings David	26	"	38	4 Sanford pl
P	Holder Eva—†	28	housekeeper	29	here
R	Holder James	28	laborer	35	West Indies
S	Holder Edith—†	28	housekeeper	36	"

Woodbury Street—Continued

T	Holder Hurbert	28	laborer	39	here
U	Johnson Ella M—†	30	housekeeper	30	"
V	Johnson James M	30	boilermaker	34	"
W	Hunt William H	30	laborer	42	"
X	Jones William	30	janitor	42	"
Y	Asquith Pearl—†	30	housekeeper	27	"
Z	Asquith Rupert	30	plasterer	31	"

Ward 9—Precinct 7

CITY OF BOSTON.

LIST OF RESIDENTS
20 YEARS OF AGE AND OVER

(FEMALES INDICATED BY DAGGER)

AS OF

APRIL 1, 1926

HERBERT A. WILSON, } Listing

JAMES F. EAGAN, } Board.

CITY OF BOSTON—PRINTING DEPARTMENT

Cabot Street

A	Palinquist Alma B—†	34	seamstress	55	here
B	Palinquist Elmer J	34	carpenter	22	New York
C	Nobles Matty—†	36	housewife	25	here
D	Nobles Minis	36	laborer	28	"
E	Nobles Laura—†	36	houseworker	35	"
G	Doherty John	38	grave digger	28	Ireland
H	Kelly Annie—†	38	at home	75	here
K	Prunty Rose—†	38	housewife	64	"
L	Prunty Stephen	38	porter	64	"
M	Whiteside Annie—†	38	housewife	35	"
N	Johnson Margaret—†	40	"	56	290 Com av
O	Johnson Marion—†	40	housekeeper	68	290 "
P	Larson Arthur	40	manager	23	here
R	Larson Caroline A—†	40	housewife	64	"
S	Larson Hans	40	laborer	65	"
T	Larson Reidan	40	mechanic	30	"
U	Peels Geneva—†	42	houseworker	57	"
V	White Florence—†	42	housewife	23	"
W	White Wilbert H	42	baker	25	"
Y	White Annie—†	44	houseworker	44	112 Northampton
Z	Kelsey Carrie—†	44	"	35	here
A	Kilday Duncan	44	storekeeper	32	"
B	Lovelace Barbara—†	44	housewife	45	"
C	Lovelace Robert	44	porter	44	"
D	Lewis Charles	46	carpenter	35	"
E	Lewis Molly—†	46	housewife	30	"
F	Davis Annie—†	46	laundress	40	"
G	White Annie—†	46	houseworker	50	50 Kendall
H	Russell Arthur	46	porter	44	1930 Wash'n
K	Sisto Antonio	48	pedler	44	here
L	Sisto Mary—†	48	housewife	41	"
M	Harris Esther—†	48	"	24	Winthrop
N	Harris James	48	painter	28	"
O	Frances Eleanor—†	48	houseworker	35	here
P	Travers Geneva—†	48	housewife	40	Winthrop
R	Travers Harry	48	painter	42	"
S	Farrio Lucy—†	50	houseworker	50	here
T	Hillman Clifton	50	laborer	60	"
U	Nichols Lucy—†	50	houseworker	30	Cambridge
V	Porter Mary—†	50	"	30	8 Arnold

2

Page.	Letter.	FULL NAME.	Residence, April 1, 1926.	Occupation.	Supposed Age.	Reported Residence, April 1, 1925. Street and Number.

Cabot Street—Continued

W	Spurill Verlean—†	50	housewife	22	53 Camden
X	Spurill William	50	waiter	24	53 "
Y	Mouradian Marnos—†	52	housewife	38	here
Z	Mouradian Moosik	52	shoemaker	38	"
A	Trauma Charles	52	"	35	"
B	Trauma Rose—†	52	housewife	22	"
C	Connor Julia A—†	52	"	61	"
D	Connor Mary E—†	52	shoeworker	40	"
G	Hurley Catherine—†	54	housekeeper	20	"
H	Hurley Patrick	54	laborer	45	"
K	Foley Catherine T—†	54	housewife	45	"
L	Foley Timothy D	54	laborer	46	"
M	Donovan Catherine—†	54	cashier	21	"
N	Donovan Margaret—†	54	houseworker	45	"
O	O'Neil Hannah—†	54	housewife	65	152 Cabot
P	O'Neil Timothy	54	retired	66	152 "
R	Nustrullo Vincenzo	56	storekeeper	50	here
S	Walker Emily S—†	56	housewife	26	"
T	Walker George H	56	laborer	32	"
U	Haltiwanger Mattie—†	56	housewife	27	18 Cunard
V	Haltiwanger Perry	56	laborer	27	18 "
W	Jackson Ada—†	56	housekeeper	44	here
X	Jackson Alonzo	56	laborer	23	"
Y	Maldero Antonio	58	pedler	28	"
Z	Maldero Mary—†	58	housewife	23	"
A	Wise Carrie—†	58	houseworker	30	"
B	DeSuze Claude	58	cook	44	"
C	DeSuze Hattie—†	58	housewife	56	"
D	Swan Albert	58	laborer	35	"
E	McDonald Mary—†	60	houseworker	34	"
F	Maldlio Mary—†	60	"	66	"
G	Maldlio Stella—†	60	housewife	20	"
H	Maldlio Veto	60	pedler	35	"
K	Smart Winifred—†	60	housekeeper	29	18 Hubert
L	Smart William	60	laborer	35	19 Windsor
M	Wilson Mary M—†	60	housewife	35	here
N	Wilson Robert W	60	insurance agent	39	"
O	Pringle Margaret—†	62	houseworker	50	52 Cabot
P	Dasho Peter T	62	real estate	51	here
R	Dasho Sophie—†	62	housewife	37	"
S	Keefe Helen—†	62	houseworker	34	"

3

Cabot Street—Continued

T	Keefe Patrick	62	foreman	60	here
U	Malone Dennis J	64	laborer	31	"
V	Malone Hannah—†	64	housewife	65	"
W	Malone William D	64	finisher	61	"
X	Mason Nellie—†	64	housewife	43	"
Y	Mason Samuel N	64	laborer	53	"
Z	Sheehan Mary—†	64	housewife	46	"
A	Sheehan Thomas	64	laborer	48	"
B	Harris George G	66	auto repairer	43	"
C	Harris Mary W—†	66	housewife	38	"
D	Harrington Frank	66	chauffeur	39	"
E	Harrington Hannah—†	66	housewife	38	"
F	Johnston Catherine—†	66	"	39	"
G	Johnston David	66	longshoreman	40	"
H	Dempsey Johanna—†	68	houseworker	53	"
K	Foley Catherine—†	68	demonstrator	23	"
L	Foley David	68	laborer	58	"
M	Foley Hannah—†	68	housewife	56	"
N	Holton Mary—†	68	houseworker	45	"
O	Cooke Maude C—†	70	"	79	"
P	Ingersoll Mary—†	70	"	45	"
R	Hart Jennie—†	70	housekeeper	71	"
S	Anderson Julia C—†	70	houseworker	54	"
U	Blackman Charles	74	janitor	65	"
V	Blackman Robert T	74	"	55	"
W	Goodman Jennette P—†	74	houseworker	61	"
X	Peterson Emma—†	74	housewife	26	"
Y	Peterson Joseph	74	janitor	31	135 Cabot
A	Anderson Albert N	84	longshoreman	43	38 Cunard
B	Anderson Mamie—†	84	housewife	38	38 "
C	Taylor Edna J—†	84	houseworker	36	31 Westminster
D	Guinder Jane E—†	94	"	63	here
E	Guinder Sarah J—†	94	housekeeper	85	"
F	Janeves Mary—†	rear 94	houseworker	41	"
G	Rauch Augusta—†	94½	chambermaid	55	"

Greenwich Street

H	Hinton Barbara—†	2	houseworker	38	47 Hammond
K	Hinton Charles	2	porter	53	47 "

4

Page.	Letter.	FULL NAME.	Residence, April 1, 1926.	Occupation.	Supposed Age.	Reported Residence, April 1, 1925. Street and Number.

Greenwich Street—Continued

	L	Brooks Ellen J—†	2	housewife	30	here
	M	Brooks James L	2	cook	41	"
	N	Christmas Edward B	2	chauffeur	26	29 Ball
	O	Christmas Mary T—†	3	housewife	25	W Medford
	P	Lockwood Lettia—†	4	cook	47	38 Williams
	R	Tyler Mildred—†	4	housewife	23	here
	S	Tyler William K	4	letter carrier	22	"
	T	Herbert Florence—†	4	houseworker	20	"
	U	Herbert William	4	elevatorman	22	"
	V	Reed Hattie—†	4	housewife	47	"
	W	Wright Rhoda C—†	6	houseworker	30	"
	X	Jackson Lillian—†	6	housewife	22	"
	Y	Jackson Mortimer	6	postal clerk	21	"
	Z	Woodfork Agnes M—†	6	housewife	37	"
	A	Woodfork George N	6	porter	44	"
	B	Barbour Cecelia—†	7	housekeeper	45	"
	C	Henry Cornelia—†	7	houseworker	48	787 Shawmut av
	D	Stewart Gladys—†	7	factory worker	24	783 "
	G	Davis Hugh F	7	laborer	45	11 Dartmouth pl
	F	Gibson John A	7	porter	37	11 "
	E	Rankin Florence—†	7	housewife	26	11 "
	H	Johnson Edward S	8	woodcarver	24	Phila Pa
	K	Johnson Ivy—†	8	housewife	20	"
	L	Warner Gertrude—†	8	"	26	here
	M	Warner Walter	8	cook	41	"
	N	James Nathan	8	porter	43	"
	O	James Therza—†	8	housewife	42	"
	P	Casneau Alice A—†	9	dressmaker	59	"
	R	Morrill Martha A—†	10	housekeeper	45	"
	S	Foreman Nannie B—†	11	domestic	48	14 Ceylon
	T	Foreman Salvorian	11	engineer	55	14 "
	U	Smith Laura A—†	11	domestic	50	here
	V	Elliott Joseph R	12	R R man	57	"
	W	Elliott Margaret—†	12	housewife	56	"
	X	Bryant John	13	laborer	45	55 Greenwich
	Y	Bryant Lelia—†	13	housekeeper	57	here
	Z	Bryant Moses	13	cement finisher	59	"
	A	Bailey Isaac S	14	chauffeur	39	"
	B	Reed Margaret E—†	14	hairdresser	32	"
	C	Wilson Nettie—†	14	elevatorwoman	25	"
	D	Callis Alexander	15	mason	27	34 Fayette

5

Greenwich Street—Continued

E	Thomas Grace—†	15	housewife	46	here
F	Wilson David S	15	cook	44	"
G	Allen Charles	16	"	39	"
H	Allen Frances W—†	16	laundress	70	"
H¹	Allen Helen—†	16	houseworker	30	"
K	Carter Howard	17	repairer	21	"
L	Miller Josephine—†	17	laundress	69	"
M	Wynn Mary E—†	17	houseworker	50	"
N	Asken Martha—†	18	"	72	"
O	Dupree Alfred	18	clerk	22	766 Shawmut av
P	Dupree Estella—†	18	houseworker	23	here
R	Forsythe Sadie—†	18	manager	37	"
S	Wiche John	18	"	23	"
T	Bishop Harriett E—†	19	housekeeper	61	"
U	Jeter Lillian C—†	19	"	44	"
V	Jeter Samuel M	19	cook	44	"
W	Thomas Lottie A—†	20	housekeeper	40	"
X	Browning Richard E	21	chauffeur	45	25 Warwick
Y	Browning Rose—†	21	housewife	36	25 "
Z	Clayton Samuel	21	chef	40	here
A	Farrell Eva—†	21	housewife	34	"
B	Farrell Robert	21	longshoreman	38	"
C	Hill Bessie M—†	22	housewife	49	"
D	Hill James E	22	machinist	48	"
E	Crawford Annie B—†	23	housewife	32	"
F	Crawford Henry E S	23	porter	35	"
G	Howard Herman	23	"	36	"
H	Dedox Abbie—†	24	houseworker	31	"
K	Lee Lucy—†	24	housewife	40	"
L	Lee Riley A	24	porter	55	"
M	Jones Charles M	25	"	50	"
N	Jones Sylvia—†	25	housewife	48	"
O	Simpson Amy—†	26	"	29	"
P	Simpson William	26	chauffeur	40	"
R	Brown Joseph	27	waiter	53	"
S	Good Walter B	27	porter	59	"
T	Edwards Mollie—†	28	housewife	43	"
U	Edwards Wilbur	28	waiter	53	"
V	Somerville Cora L—†	29	stockwoman	25	"
W	Williams Hannah J—†	29	housewife	32	"
X	Williams James	29	porter	50	"

Letter.	FULL NAME.	Residence, April 1, 1926.	Occupation.	Supposed Age.	Reported Residence, April 1, 1925. Street and Number.

Greenwich Street—Continued

Letter.	FULL NAME.	Residence, April 1, 1926.	Occupation.	Supposed Age.	Reported Residence, April 1, 1925. Street and Number.
Y	Tillman Ellis D	29	waiter	51	here
z	Tillman Rose B—†	29	housewife	47	"
A	Davis Julian	30	cook	31	"
B	Davis Mattie—†	30	maid	21	"
C	Stubbs Frank S	30	clergyman	50	"
D	Stubbs Mattie—†	30	housewife	48	"
E	Kirton Vincent	31	cutter	32	121 W Lenox
F	Jones Viola—†	31	stitcher	31	Bermuda
G	Murray Berisford	31	cleanser	37	here
H	Lewis Elizabeth C—†	32	dressmaker	27	"
K	Sharp James F	32	watchman	65	"
L	Sharp Maria J—†	32	housekeeper	63	"
M	Talbert Dora—†	33	maid	42	"
N	Pleasant Florence—†	33	housewife	57	"
O	Pleasant William N	33	porter	49	"
P	Gooding Constance—†	34	housewife	41	"
R	Gooding William A	34	waiter	41	"
S	Jackson Blanche E—†	35	clerk	27	"
T	Jackson Eugene A	35	shipper	52	"
U	Jackson Richard A	35	postal clerk	53	"
V	Jackson Sarah J—†	35	housekeeper	75	"
W	Harris James	36	garageman	33	612 Col av
X	Harris Mabel—†	36	housewife	28	612 "
Y	Tattoon Fannie—†	37	housekeeper	28	here
z	Williams Frank	37	porter	48	"
A	Taleaferro Delia—†	38	housewife	48	"
B	Taleaferro Samuel A	38	car cleaner	59	"
C	Warrick Eugene	39	porter	26	"
D	Warrick Ida—†	39	housewife	27	"
E	Roach Ethel L—†	39	"	29	"
F	Roach James	39	machinist	37	"
G	Briggs Louis	39	laborer	33	"
H	Briggs Susie—†	39	housewife	30	"
K	Jones Lucius J	40	retired	38	"
L	Haskins Frank	41	salesman	48	"
M	Haughton Charles J	41	porter	63	"
N	Haughton Rachel O—†	41	dressmaker	49	"
O	Quander James L	41	laborer	33	17 Braddock pk
P	Poindexter John	43	elevatorman	21	here
R	Poindexter Lucille—†	43	housekeeper	52	"

7

Greenwich Street—Continued

s	Poindexter Lucille H—†	43	hairdresser	25	here
T	Poindexter Thomas	43	laborer	56	"
U	Reddick Eliza L—†	45	housewife	44	"
V	Reddick Robert H	45	manager	44	"
W	Manley Joseph	47	porter	22	N Carolina
X	Reid John D	47	"	35	2 Greenwich
Y	Reid Lavinia—†	47	housewife	32	2 "
Z	Richie Ella W—†	49	"	55	here
A	Richie William T	49	postal clerk	56	"
B	Johnston Grace C—†	51	housewife	53	"
C	Johnston William A	51	postal clerk	64	"
D	Cunningham Isabella—†	53	lecturer	49	New York
E	Jones Sarah—†	53	housewife	50	here
F	Jones William	53	laborer	60	"
G	Prichett Bernard N	53	porter	29	"
H	James Augustus	55	manager	54	"
K	James Ida B—†	55	housewife	52	"
L	Wong Julius	57	laundryman	32	16 Oxford

Hammond Street

N	McClennan Harriet W—†	6	social worker	26	here
O	Ridley Constance—†	6	"	28	"
P	Sullivan Mary D—†	6	"	23	"
R	Anderson Carrie—†	10	tailoress	50	"
S	White Alta—†	10	housewife	38	"
T	White Thomas	10	steward	42	"
U	Ebron Mary—†	10	laundress	53	"
V	Parrish Hattie—†	10	"	69	"
W	White Dera—†	10	housewife	41	"
X	White George	10	driller	46	
Y	Braxton Ernest	12	mover	33	15 Greenwich pk
Z	Braxton Ruth—†	12	housewife	21	22 School
A	Bovell Ruth—†	12	laundress	26	83 Sterling
B	Silvey Cornelia E—†	12	housewife	43	here
C	Silvey James M	12	chauffeur	41	"
D	Rowland Susie—†	12	laundress	47	"
E	Haywood Laura—†	12	"	47	"
G	Broxton Annie—†	14	"	48	"
H	Venable Polly A—†	14	domestic	78	"

Hammond Street—Continued

K	Venable Sarah—†	14	laundress	39	New Hampshire
L	Randolph Gladys—†	14	housewife	50	here
M	Randolph Thomas	14	waiter	48	"
N	Wheeler Alice L—†	14	housewife	32	"
O	Wheeler Joseph M	14	bellman	35	"
P	Fernandez Grace —†	16	storekeeper	38	"
R	Fernandez Lawrence	16	mover	34	"
S	Pelmer Alexander	16	elevatorman	25	"
T	Suggs Edward	16	teamster	54	"
U	Nellon Esther—†	16	housewife	48	"
V	Nellon Peter F	16	laborer	51	"
W	Raymond Sherman R	16	porter	65	"
Z	True Herbert	24	janitor	60	175 Ruggles
A	True Jennie —†	24	housewife	47	175 "
B	Hall Charles	24	brass polisher	29	here
C	Hall Grace—†	24	housewife	28	"
D	Bennett Ella A—†	24	domestic	85	"
E	Briggs Della—†	24	housewife	60	"
F	Briggs Lucius A	24	painter	74	"
G	Hearn Alice J—†	24	nurse	54	"
H	Carroll Bridget A—†	24	laundress	46	"
K	Kennedy Leo F	24	clerk	23	"
L	Kennedy Thomas	24	painter	59	"
M	Burnett Robert C	24	musician	40	"
N	Hatch Elizabeth—†	24	housewife	55	"
O	Hatch George L	24	furniture	60	"
P	Brosseau Henry	24	clerk	38	"
R	Brosseau Josephine—†	24	domestic	68	"
S	Barks Julia—†	24	housekeeper	38	135 Cabot
T	Manning Margaret—†	24	hairdresser	27	21 Worthington
U	Nichols John	24	clerk	31	here
V	Nichols Mary—†	24	housewife	31	"
W	Whitaker Benjamin F	24	watchman	36	"
X	Whitaker Margaret A—†	24	laundress	50	"
Y	Nyberg Albert	24	chauffeur	29	"
Z	Nyberg Emma—†	24	housekeeper	65	"
A	Clark Rhoda V—†	24	baker	55	"
B	Hopkins Charles C	24	clerk	54	"
C	Hopkins Cyril L	24	"	28	"
D	Hopkins Madaline—†	24	housekeeper	25	"
E	Doherty Mary E—†	24	dishwasher	37	"

9

Hammond Street—Continued

F	Marshall Frank	24	laborer	22	23 Downing
G	Marshall John	24	"	26	23 "
H	Marshall Katherine M—†	24	domestic	62	29 "
K	McCarthy Mary—†	24	housekeeper	40	here
L	Buckhalz Flora—†	24	"	41	"
M	Lind Albert A	24	chauffeur	21	"
N	Lind Blanche C—†	24	housewife	39	"
O	Wood Eva M—†	24	"	28	291 Eustis
P	Wood Robert H	24	janitor	42	291 "
R	Clifford Charles	24	baker	60	here
S	Weitz Sadie—†	24	laundress	40	"
T	Rogers Emiline—†	24	housekeeper	37	"
U	Rogers Phillip	24	janitor	35	"
V	Hall Jennie A—†	24	housewife	40	"
W	Hall Robert L	24	chauffeur	40	"
Y	Ferguson Hattie—†	24	housewife	28	14 Dana pl
Z	Ferguson William	24	machinist	29	14 "
B	Dalton Ernest E	24	clerk	21	602 E First
A	Dalton Ethel M—†	24	houseworker	42	602 "
C	Perkins Joseph	24	electrician	30	here
D	Williams Lillian—†	24	housewife	27	119 Ruggles
E	Williams William	24	mover	32	119 "
F	Texeria Martha—†	32	housewife	44	here
G	Texeria Peter	32	laborer	49	"
H	Hodge Josephine—†	32	maid	21	"
K	Hodge Katherine—†	32	laundress	42	"
L	Dixon William	32	waiter	22	"
M	Jackson Eric	32	porter	26	"
N	Jackson Hilda—†	32	housewife	27	"
O	Jones Shelley	32	waiter	42	"
P	Starr Bessie E—†	32	housewife	39	"
R	Starr Eugene S	32	waiter	38	"
S	Curtis Frederick	32	janitor	50	"
T	Curtis Laura—†	32	domestic	60	"
U	Lane Edward	32	porter	25	"
V	Lane Howard	32	"	24	"
W	Brown Augustin	32	laborer	25	New Jersey
X	Whiting Farris	32	"	32	615 Shawmut av
Y	Whiting Mildred—†	32	housewife	28	615 "
Z	Dixon Frank	32	carpenter	26	101 Hammond
A	Johnson Clarence	32	waiter	25	101 "

Letter.	FULL NAME.	Residence, April 1, 1926.	Occupation.	Supposed Age.	Reported Residence, April 1, 1925. Street and Number.

Hammond Street—Continued

B	Johnson Louise—†	32	housewife	22	101 Hammond
C	Brandford Ada—†	32	cook	40	Sagamore
D	Hutchinson Georgia—†	32	houseworker	30	"
E	Byars Albertena—†	34	housewife	32	37 Hammond
F	Byars George E	34	chauffeur	34	37 "
G	Crawford Charles	34	waiter	53	67 Ruggles
H	Crawford Charles, jr	34	chauffeur	25	67 "
K	Crawford Julia—†	34	housewife	52	67 "
L	Moran Julia—†	34	"	22	67 "
M	Moran William	34	waiter	24	67 "
N	Lawrence Malcolm	34	houseman	24	here
O	Watson Frances—†	34	domestic	45	"
P	Agnew Milton—†	34	recorder	24	"
R	Milton Cliford P	34	porter	22	"
S	Oliver Henry B	34	mechanic	21	"
T	Scott Ella M—†	34	housewife	43	"
U	Scott John A	34	manager	54	"
V	Barnes Mary—†	34	cook	30	371 Northampton
W	Moore Nancy—†	34	housewife	31	3 Wentworth pl
X	Moore Thomas	34	laborer	30	3 "
Y	McClain Alonso	34	steamfitter	25	here
Z	McClain Gertrude—†	34	housewife	24	"
A	McClain Martha—†	34	"	52	"
B	McClain Thomas	34	retired	60	"
C	Baptist Luther	34	clerk	31	614 Columbus av
D	Ellis Sarah—†	34	domestic	38	here
E	Lawrence Ferdinand	34	cook	26	"
F	Lawrence Vera—†	34	housewife	21	"
G	Munroe Catherine—†	34	domestic	45	"
H	Poindexter Emma—†	34	houseworker	45	"
K	Williams Cordelia—†	34	"	40	"
L	Reid Clementina—†	36	housewife	34	"
M	Reid Joseph B	36	cook	38	"
N	Cropp Jane G—†	36	houseworker	58	"
O	Cropp William H	36	waiter	58	"
P	Gunn Mary—†	36	nursemaid	64	"
R	Lindsey Bertha—†	36	musician	34	"
S	Smith Wilhemina—†	36	laundress	32	"
T	Campbell Lucy—†	38	housewife	28	"
U	Campbell Washington	38	laborer	28	"
V	Thompson Edward	38	"	30	"
W	Thompson Jennie—†	38	laundress	29	"

11

Page.	Letter.	FULL NAME.	Residence, April 1, 1926.	Occupation.	Supposed Age.	Reported Residence, April 1, 1925. Street and Number.

Hammond Street—Continued

	X	Harris Malvina —†	38	housekeeper	55	here
	Y	Mason Edward	38	laborer	40	"
	Z	Mason Rebecca —†	38	laundress	29	"
	A	Campbell Sylvanus	38	porter	40	"
	B	Samuels John	38	janitor	33	"
	C	Samuels Wilhelmina —†	38	housewife	33	"
	D	Durant Joseph	38	waiter	55	11 Burbank
	E	Durant Sarah —†	38	housewife	38	11 "
	F	Calden John J	40	watchman	70	20 Mall
	G	Calden Rosetta —†	40	housewife	39	20 "
	K	Manning Bertha S —†	40	"	30	here
	L	Manning Junian R	40	watchman	32	"
	N	Wentworth Clarence A	42	porter	43	"
	O	Crawford Anna D —†	42	housewife	22	"
	P	Crawford Joshua A	42	clerk	24	"
	R	Newton Ella M —†	42	houseworker	47	"
	S	Bryant Foster	42	cook	46	"
	T	White Charlotte A —†	42	housewife	31	"
	U	White James R	42	clerk	34	"
	V	Brewster Lillian —†	42	maid	45	"
	W	Roddy Matilda —†	42	domestic	36	95 Camden
	X	Ware Anna E —†	42	houseworker	59	here
	Y	Ware Joseph H	42	clerk	36	"
	Z	Holt Jennie A —†	42	housewife	24	"
	A	Holt William J	42	chauffeur	26	"
	B	Ransell Hattie —†	60	houseworker	40	"
	C	Singleton Thomas	60	laborer	35	59 Ruggles
	D	Williams Lucy —†	60	houseworker	56	here
	E	Dunbar Ethel —†	60	housewife	29	"
	F	Dunbar Hezekiah	60	laborer	31	"
	G	Hickson Henry	60	dishwasher	28	40 Hammond
	H	Hickson Lillian —†	60	laundress	25	40 "
	K	Atwell Louise —†	60	cook	32	671 Shawmut av
	L	Noel Thomas M	60	grocer	42	25 Hammond
	M	Jackson Charles D	60	musician	31	here
	N	Kent Albert	60	laborer	35	"
	O	Washington Florence —†	60	musician	31	"
	P	Chisholm Ethel —†	60	housewife	23	29 Kendall
	R	Chisholm Theodore	60	cook	25	29 "
	S	Joseph James E	60	"	31	here
	T	Joseph Narcissa —†	60	housewife	29	"

12

Hammond Street —Continued

u	Williams Louis E	62	chauffeur	36	here
v	Williams Winifred—†	62	hairdresser	29	"
w	Grammer William H	62	clerk	51	"
x	Johnson Henson T	62	porter	46	"
y	Johnson Sadie H—†	62	housewife	49	"
z	Dunbar Agnes C—†	62	maid	52	"
a	Louden Esther B—†	62	clerk	39	"
b	Peniston Ely	62	janitor	47	"
c	Price Amelia M—†	62	housewife	31	"
d	Price Thomas S	62	steamfitter	32	"
e	Johnson Mary C—†	66	domestic	40	"
f	Farrington Charlotte E-†	66	laundress	44	"
g	Hayes Jesse A	66	janitor	54	"
h	Hayes Josephine—†	66	housewife	50	"
k	Carter Lalia M—†	66	"	29	"
l	Carter Lytcott T	66	clerk	35	"
m	King William	66	seaman	24	"
n	Moore Arthur	66	"	49	133 Sterling
o	Moore Dorothy E—†	66	housewife	34	here
p	Moore William H	66	seaman	48	"
r	Greene Chesterfield H	66	broker	58	"
s	Gray Lucy—†	66	laundress	44	"
t	Pollack Louise—†	66	domestic	46	"
u	Stewart Lillian—†	66	hairdresser	50	New Jersey
v	Henderson Joseph	66	painter	38	here
w	Henderson Simeon	66	cook	32	"
x	Cass Marshall	68	mechanic	33	"
y	Cass Melnea—†	68	housewife	31	"
z	Wright Frederick D	70	porter	44	"
a	Wright Julia B—†	70	housewife	38	"
b	Hawkins Lee	72	tailor	40	"
c	McIlvaine Grace—†	72	housewife	38	"
d	McIlvaine John F	72	proprietor	49	"
e	Richardson Leon	72	barber	55	"
g	Butler Adelle V—†	76	housewife	44	"
h	Butler John A	76	beltmaker	47	"
k	Broadis Raymond	78	porter	25	33 Flagg
l	Brown Frank	78	barrel hooper	36	29 Albion
m	Brown Jessie—†	78	housewife	33	29 "
n	Potter Bessie—†	78	"	34	125 Lenox
o	Potter Nathaniel L	78	porter	43	33 Flagg

13

Hammond Street— Continued

R	Monroe Catherine A—†	86	housewife	62	here
S	Monroe Paul	86	waiter	60	"
T	Carter Alice D—†	86	housewife	45	"
U	Carter William H	86	teamster	60	"
V	Whiting Mary L—†	86	housewife	44	"
W	Whiting Willis	86	chef	53	"
X	Allen Jasper	86	machinist	50	165 W Springfield
Y	Allen Mary P—†	86	housewife	40	165 "
Z	David Martha—†	86	domestic	41	here
A	Jones Elizabeth—†	86	"	33	"
B	Douglas Catherine M—†	88	housewife	39	679 Shawmut av
C	Douglas William Z	88	laborer	35	679 "
D	Jones Dillie—†	88	housewife	47	16 Davenport
E	Jones James F	88	porter	56	16 "
F	Krauser Mary—†	88	dressmaker	44	Cambridge
G	Thomas Eliza—†	88	housekeeper	24	Pennsylvania
H	Thomas Granderson	88	cook	27	"
K	DeLemos Alma F—†	88	dressmaker	31	458 Shawmut av
L	DeLemos Tusto F	88	decorator	39	458 "
M	Phillips Cecile B—†	88	housewife	31	37 Braddock pk
N	Phillips Robert T	88	barber	32	104 Hammond
O	Allyne Celia—†	90	housewife	33	here
P	Allyne William	90	porter	34	"
R	Crawford John	90	lawyer	66	"
S	Rice Margaret—†	90	housewife	48	"
T	Johnson Anthony	90	engineer	40	110 Camden
U	Johnson Edna—†	90	housewife	37	110 "
V	Mead Hattie—†	90	domestic	35	here
W	Spinola Charles	92	laborer	41	"
X	Spinola Eleanora—†	92	housewife	37	"
Y	Holland Louis H	92	porter	65	"
Z	Saunders Ada—†	92	housewife	45	"
A	Caine Ella—†	92	"	41	"
B	Caine Shellie F	92	porter	43	"
C	Lee Aurelia—†	92	clerk	24	"
D	Tavares Edith—†	92	housewife	25	10 Village
E	Tavares Philip	92	laborer	35	40 "
F	Wade Addie—†	94	domestic	40	here
G	Wade Henry	94	porter	40	"
H	Munroe Louisa M—†	94	housekeeper	73	"
K	Washington Daniel	94	engineer	59	"

14

Letter	Full Name.	Residence, April 1, 1926.	Occupation.	Supposed Age.	Reported Residence, April 1, 1925. Street and Number.

Hammond Street—Continued

L	Brown John	94	janitor	59	37 Windsor
M	Nichols Matilda—†	94	laundress	40	36 Kendall
N	Upshur Josephine—†	94	domestic	48	36 "
O	Tomlin Hattie—†	94	"	36	here
P	Tomlin Thomas	94	waiter	40	"
R	Fowler Jacob	96	porter	75	810 Tremont
S	Dooley Edward	96	waiter	32	5 Carlton pk
T	Dooley Ruth—†	96	housewife	26	5 "
U	Wheaton Maude—†	96	domestic	41	8 Smith av
V	France Lalia—†	96	"	48	here
W	Wanzo John F	96	waiter	60	"
X	Gibson George D	96	porter	40	"
Y	Gibson Mary—†	96	housewife	43	"
Z	Mosby Mary—†	96	cook	50	"
B	Greene Harry	102	porter	35	"
C	Snowden Martha—†	102	housekeeper	29	"
D	Almieda Gregory	102	laborer	40	"
E	Almieda Mazie—†	102	housewife	31	"
F	Boles Beatrice—†	102	housekeeper	48	61 Hammond
G	Ward Esther—†	102	housewife	21	here
H	Ward James	102	cook	24	"
K	Carter Grace A—†	102	housekeeper	65	"
L	Horne Nellie E—†	102	maid	41	"
M	Lewis Walter F	102	cook	44	"
N	Price John W	102	porter	26	"
O	Tappin Helen—†	102	stitcher	30	"
P	Lane Mongeila—†	102	domestic	28	Brookline
R	Williams Catherine W—†	104	waitress	43	here
S	Johnson Charles S	104	waiter	52	"
T	Johnson Lucile B—†	104	housewife	40	"
U	Carter Henry A	104	meatcutter	42	18 Hubert
V	Carter Mary—†	104	housewife	33	15 "
W	McKay Bessie—†	104	domestic	45	Newton
X	Pettyjohn Isiah	106	cook	52	here
Y	Pettyjohn Nellie—†	106	housewife	40	"
Z	Prioleau John	106	chauffeur	30	115 Lenox
A	Simms Idalia E—†	106	laundress	26	115 "
B	Simms Margaret—†	106	domestic	60	here
C	Folkes Amanda V—†	106	housewife	25	15 Dilworth
D	Folkes McDonald	106	painter	26	15 "
E	Brown Dora—†	108	laundress	34	90 Fenway

Page.	Letter.	FULL NAME.	Residence, April 1, 1926.	Occupation.	Supposed Age.	Reported Residence, April 1, 1925. Street and Number.

Hammond Street—Continued

	F	Brown Samuel	108	car washer	38	90 Fenway
	G	Boles Alice—†	108	maid	53	here
	H	O'Neal Louise—†	108	waitress	48	"
	K	Wilkinson Gertrude—†	108	houseworker	33	"
	L	Williams Jennie—†	108	cleaner	43	"
	M	Black Isadora—†	108	housewife	29	"
	N	Black Peter F	108	porter	33	"
	O	Samuels Wilfred	108	"	30	"

Shawmut Avenue

	V	Mytz Sarah—†	665	houseworker	60	50 Lenox
	W	Green Fannie—†	665	"	47	N Carolina
	X	Midget Lincoln	665	waiter	45	122 Camden
	Y	Flowers Mabel—†	665	houseworker	37	Reading
	Z	Wallace Annie—†	665	"	36	38 Hammond
	B	Taylor Harriet—†	667	waitress	27	27 Garden
	C	Williams Ivan	667	waiter	21	here
	E	Boyd Madeline—†	667	housewife	25	40 Warwick
	F	Boyd William E	667	laborer	27	New Hampshire
	G	Weirs Maria—†	667	domestic	56	41 Sarsfield
	H	Coleman George	667	laborer	42	here
	K	Williams Marsh—†	667	domestic	48	Florida
	N	Thompson Atles	669	laborer	43	here
	O	World Gordon	669	"	35	21 Dilworth
	P	Brown Victoria—†	669	housekeeper	65	here
	R	Davenport Lillian—†	669	domestic	51	"
	S	Logan Marie—†	669	housekeeper	40	New York
	T	Musenden Sarah—†	669	"	37	here
	W	Graham Clarine—†	671	housewife	26	"
	V	Graham Frederick E	671	laborer	29	"
	X	O'Bryant Edward	671	porter	25	22 Kendall
	Y	O'Bryant Elsie T—†	671	housewife	21	22 "
	Z	Duggan Mabel—†	671	domestic	26	33 "
	A	Allen Marietta—†	671	"	34	here
	B	Bishop Florence—†	671	laundress	30	"
	C	Nables Norther	673	painter	25	520 Shawmut av
	D	Walker Josephine—†	673	domestic	25	Putnam Ct
	E	Wilkins Charles	673	laborer	21	N Carolina
	F	Smith James T	673	waiter	52	49 Sterling
	G	Woods Minerva—†	673	domestic	33	49 "

Shawmut Avenue—Continued

H	Shirley Ziphora—†	673	domestic	38	here
K	Warren Amelia—†	673	"	38	"
N	Dudley Edward	679	janitor	50	Brookline
O	Dudley Rebecca—†	679	housewife	39	"
P	Howard Cora—†	679	domestic	53	N Carolina
R	Johnson Eugenia—†	679	housewife	38	62 Williams
S	Johnson John W	679	cook	48	62 "
T	Bryant Clarence	679	waiter	36	here
U	Bryant Eliza—†	679	domestic	59	"
V	Bryant James H	679	waiter	57	"
W	Tate Marion—†	679	domestic	31	"
X	Warren Benjamin	679	laborer	36	"
Y	Moffitt Julia—†	681	housewife	49	875 Harris'n av
Z	Moffitt William	681	laborer	51	875 "
A	Gaines Emma—†	681	at home	46	here
B	Lopes Catano	681	laborer	36	3 Warwick
C	Stokes Edward C	681	porter	46	here
D	Waddell Arthur B	681	"	34	"
E	Waddell Bessie—†	681	housewife	54	"
G	Burrill Ethel M—†	683	"	30	"
F	Burrill Rolins	683	shoeworker	41	"
H	Johnson Alexander	683	ironworker	56	"
K	Jordan Minnie L—†	683	domestic	47	"
L	Kenney David D	683	laborer	57	"
M	Flowers Gertrude L—†	683	domestic	49	"
N	Flowers Lee	683	cook	54	"
O	Headley Charles	683	messenger	46	"
P	Simmons Elizebeth—†	683	at home	56	"
R	Simmons Willis	683	laborer	67	"
S	Henry John F	685	butcher	67	"
T	Henry Mary A—†	685	at home	69	"
U	Smith Joshua	685	porter	26	"
V	Smith Lorina—†	685	housewife	25	"
W	Cleland John M	685	laborer	41	"
X	Cleland Marie—†	685	housewife	36	"
Y	Jones Louis	685	laborer	25	Wash'n D C
Z	Jones Mary—†	685	housewife	25	"
A	Jones Rebecca—†	685	domestic	45	here
B	Brinson Edgar	685	janitor	21	81 Humboldt av
C	Henry Birdie—†	685	housekeeper	21	31 Windsor
D	Henry Charles A	685	clerk	21	31 "

9—7

Page.	Letter.	FULL NAME.	Residence, April 1, 1926.	Occupation.	Supposed Age.	Reported Residence, April 1, 1925. Street and Number.

Shawmut Avenue—Continued

	E	Jordan Beatrice—†	687	housewife	29	here
	F	Jordan Ernest	687	porter	29	"
	G	Coles Ethel H—†	687	housewife	34	"
	H	Coles William C	687	porter	40	"
	K	Donaldson Herbert	687	waiter	55	"
	L	Donaldson Mary—†	687	housewife	44	"
	M	Carney Albert F	687	laborer	39	"
	N	Carney Julia—†	687	housewife	29	"
	O	Terrell Joel	687	porter	55	"
	R	Shaw Albert	689	student	24	"
	S	Shaw Harvey B	689	"	22	"
	T	Shaw Jessie—†	689	music teacher	46	"
	V	Alexander George	689	cook	24	"
	W	Johnson Daniel	689	laborer	30	"
	X	Johnson Gussie—†	689	domestic	45	"
	Y	Johnson Hagar—†	691	housewife	40	"
	Z	Johnson Louis	691	laborer	41	"
	A	Davis Charles	691	painter	52	"
	B	Davis Pattie—†	691	housewife	50	"
	C	Brisbane Rosa—†	691	domestic	31	693 Shawmut av
	D	Jones Gustav	691	laborer	38	here
	E	Myers Mamie—†	691	housekeeper	34	"
	F	Smith Hyman	691A	tailor	47	"
	G	Parker Beatrice—†	693	housewife	33	"
	H	Parker Moses	693	laborer	32	"
	K	Robinson Benjamin F	693	"	38	"
	L	Robinson Viola J—†	693	housewife	32	"
	M	Robinson Clara—†	693	"	41	"
	N	Robinson William	693	janitor	45	"

Sterling Street

	R	Eayes Etta—†	53A	storekeeper	54	here
	S	Eayes Harrison H	53A	"	58	"
	T	Thomas Anna—†	53A	domestic	27	"
	U	Brown Rose—†	55	housewife	70	"
	V	Cook Ella—†	55	domestic	49	"
	W	Cook George	55	cook	39	"
	X	Strother Ida L—†	55	housewife	51	"
	Y	Strother William J	55	porter	57	"

	Letter.	FULL NAME.	Residence, April 1, 1926.	Occupation.	Supposed Age.	Reported Residence, April 1, 1925. Street and Number.

Sterling Street—Continued

	Letter.	FULL NAME.	Residence, April 1, 1926.	Occupation.	Supposed Age.	Reported Residence
	z	Cook Frank	55	painter	60	here
	A	Cook Isebella—†	55	housewife	55	"
	B	Lee Gladys—†	61	"	39	"
	C	Lee John H	61	porter	44	"
	D	Bell Alice—†	61	housewife	49	63 Sterling
	E	Bell Ervan	61	baker	35	63 "
	F	Bush Adam	61	glazier	30	here
	G	Bush Susan—†	61	housewife	25	"
	H	Burckmeyer Clarence	63	metalworker	55	"
	K	Burckmeyer Lucie H—†	63	housewife	35	"
	L	Godfrey William	63	fireman	40	29 Westminster
	M	Lourie Harry	63	waiter	41	here
	N	Paine Cecelia—†	65	housewife	42	"
	O	Paine Joshua	65	porter	46	"
	P	Wood Caroline—†	65	housekeeper	59	"
	R	Daniels Kate—†	65	laundress	42	"
	S	Moore James	65	engineer	54	"
	T	Bryant James	67	clerk	47	"
	U	Bryant Rose—†	67	housewife	49	"
	V	Nelson Elizabeth—†	67	domestic	47	"
	W	Nelson Ella—†	67	dressmaker	38	"
	X	Freeman George	67	porter	46	"
	Y	Freeman Sarah—†	67	housewife	46	"
	z	Ringwood Alice S—†	69	"	41	85 Sterling
	A	Ringwood Homer G	69	chauffeur	28	85 "
	B	Ringwood John A	69	laborer	52	85 "
	C	Fowler Gussie—†	69	housewife	39	here
	D	Fowler Lang	69	fireman	40	"
	E	Butcher Charles	69	blacksmith	45	3 McLellan
	F	Turner Emma—†	69	laundress	42	here
	G	Ford Elizabeth —†	71	domestic	40	"
	H	Keizer Edith—†	71	housewife	21	"
	K	Keizer Milton	71	laborer	21	"
	L	Freeman Ella—†	71	housewife	37	"
	M	Freeman Melvin	71	laborer	38	"
	N	Gable John	71	chauffeur	21	"
	O	Cassidy Gustav	73	janitor	27	"
	P	Harris James	73	paperhanger	29	New York City
	R	Jackson Dora—†	73	housewife	67	here
	S	Jackson William B	73	machinist	27	"
	T	Gaines Rose—†	75	at home	67	2 Arnold

Sterling Street—Continued

U	Perkins Harry	75	laborer	39	2 Arnold
V	Perkins Louise—†	75	housewife	36	2 "
W	Beckett Henry C	75	laborer	38	21 Hubert
X	Beckett Susie—†	75	domestic	36	21 "
Z	Buckley Charles	77	cook	37	here
A	Buckley Florence E—†	77	housewife	34	"
B	Merchant Adolphus	77	compositor	48	"
C	Mier Paul E	77	mechanic	33	"
D	Crowder Lorenia—†	77	housewife	45	"
E	Crowder Walter	77	glazier	48	"
F	Diggs Charles H	79	barber	67	"
G	Diggs Mary—†	79	housewife	60	"
H	Calb Annie—†	79	domestic	40	"
K	Calb James	79	laborer	36	"
L	Rowe Elizabeth—†	79	housewife	48	"
M	Gilmore Frederick H	81	laborer	33	116 Lenox
N	Gilmore Sarah F—†	81	clairvoyant	50	116 "
P	Stewart Saloman A	81	musician	29	10 Fabyan
R	Bryan Annie—†	81	laundress	53	92 Camden
S	Hawkins Junius	81	longshoreman	29	92 "
T	Walden Charles	81	laborer	50	New York City
U	Johnson Thomas L	81	"	53	here
V	Morgan John	83	chauffeur	34	12 Harwich
W	Morgan Leroy—†	83	domestic	32	12 "
X	Bouvell Louis	83	laborer	36	here
Z	Johnson Annie—†	85	housewife	57	"
A	Johnson Edward	85	laborer	59	"
B	Thompson Sophia S—†	85	at home	54	9 Arnold
C	John Alfred	85	laborer	29	12 Marble
D	Martin Beatrice—†	85	housewife	28	18 Williams
E	Martin Wilfred	85	laborer	25	18 "
G	Leslie Idora—†	87	housewife	34	here
H	Leslie Moseley	87	riveter	36	"
K	Montier Helen—†	87	housekeeper	33	610 Col av
M	Cummings Harriett—†	89	domestic	50	here
N	Burns Florence—†	89	"	39	"
O	Peters George	89	laborer	54	"
R	Harrison Evelyn—†	101	housewife	24	665 Shawmut av
S	Harrison Joseph	101	laborer	29	64 Westminster
T	Davis Susan—†	101	domestic	39	19 Hubert
U	Davis Thomas	101	freighthandler	45	19 "

Sterling Street—Continued

v	Wilson Catherine —†	101	housewife	49	here
w	Wilson Charles H	101	stockman	45	"
x	Wilson Charles M	101	clerk	21	"
y	Cosgrove Elizabeth —†	103	bookbinder	22	"
z	Cosgrove Helen—†	103	finisher	24	"
a	Cosgrove John J	103	laborer	29	"
b	Cosgrove Joseph T	103	"	55	"
c	Cosgrove Sarah J—†	103	housewife	52	"
d	Cooney Elizabeth—†	103	"	59	"
e	Cooney John F	103	laborer	65	"
f	Cooney Thomas R	103	chauffeur	30	"
g	Griffin Anna—†	103	clerk	20	"
h	Griffin Hannah—†	103	housewife	53	"
k	Griffin John F	103	clerk	26	"
l	Griffin Mary—†	103	housekeeper	29	"
m	Giffin Patrick	103	stonemason	58	"
n	Eayrs Laura A —†	105	at home	77	"
o	Jordan Charles F	105	retired	70	"
p	Miller Ellen R —†	105	at home	81	"
r	Kelly John	105	manager	50	"
s	Arale Matilda —†	107	housewife	26	"
t	Arale Romelda	107	chef	27	"
u	Auderiola Gevana	107	cook	38	"
v	Bendea Feletez	107	"	40	"
w	Ruckatalad Frances—†	107	housewife	33	"
x	Nicholson Alexander	107	real estate	64	"
y	Collins Albert	109	clerk	43	"
z	Collins Teresa—†	109	housekeeper	42	"
a	Curley Catherine—†	109	saleswoman	49	"
b	Curley William E	109	baker	62	"
d	Stysanian Mary—†	109	housekeeper	55	"
e	Sawyer Mary B—†	109	housewife	54	"
f	Sawyer Stephen A	109	teamster	65	"
g	Janjigian Hagop	109	tailor	36	"
h	Janjigian Jennie—†	109	housewife	20	"
k	Mariganian Helen—†	109	"	38	"
l	Mariganian Martin	109	butcher	44	"
m	Kuzirian John	109	clerk	24	"
n	Jonjegian Sangan	109	tailor	28	"
o	Jonjegian Yera—†	109	housewife	26	"
p	Ashukian Oscar	109	butcher	30	"

Page	Letter	FULL NAME.	Residence, April 11, 1926.	Occupation.	Supposed Age.	Reported Residence, April 1, 1925. Street and Number.

Sterling Street— Continued

R	Epkarian Avdies	109	butcher	35	here
s	Epkarian Reta—†	109	housewife	30	"
T	Zartarian Anna—†	109	"	54	"
U	Zartarian John	109	dishwasher	60	"
V	Elman Ida—†	109	housekeeper	44	"
W	McAllister Mary E—†	109	domestic	58	"
X	Gamble Arthur	109	laborer	31	136 Sterling
Y	Gamble Daisy—†	109	housewife	29	136 "
Z	Marigian Helen—†	109	"	37	here
A	Marigian Martin	109	laborer	44	"
B	Shoals Flossie—†	109	housewife	34	52 Westminster
C	Shoals George	109	painter	34	52 "
D	Johns Arthur	109	crane operator	29	457 Shawmut av
E	Johns Marie—†	109	housewife	35	457 "
F	McMullen Mary—†	109	"	48	12 Marble
G	Lecesne Margaret—†	109	housekeeper	50	15 Hubert
K	Winn Delia—†	133	"	34	146 Cabot
L	Winn Fredrick	133	janitor	52	146 "
M	Calhoun Viola—†	133	domestic	36	41 "
N	Crawford James	133	laborer	37	Lynn
O	Morris James	133	butler	40	41 Cabot
P	Anderson Jacob	133	molder	27	14 Cliff
R	Roy Herbert	133	cook	22	14 "
S	Brown Josephine—†	133	housekeeper	26	131 Lenox
T	Warren Robert	133	bellboy	27	131 "
U	Gibbons Eliza—†	133	housekeeper	52	133 Cabot
V	Sims John	133	laborer	28	133 "
W	Sims Margaret—†	133	housekeeper	33	133 "
X	Griffin Vietta—†	133	domestic	20	Pennsylvania
Y	Platt William	133	laborer	26	"
Z	Burrell Lester	135	salesman	46	here
A	Collins Nellie—†	135	housekeeper	65	"

Sussex Street

B	Heggie George M	1	chauffeur	44	91 W Rutland sq
C	Heggie Lucinda M—†	1	housewife	31	91 "
E	Paul Dora—†	4	clerk	38	here
F	Paul Isadore	4	storekeeper	32	"

Letter.	FULL NAME.	Residence, April 1, 1926.	Occupation.	Supposed Age.	Reported Residence, April 1, 1925. Street and Number.

Sussex Street—Continued

G	Davis Eddie	4	laborer	34	48 Cabot
H	Thomas Martha—†	4	housekeeper	33	48 "
K	Gilbert Ada—†	5	"	33	here
L	Gilbert Venie—†	5	domestic	40	"
M	Heggie Alice—†	6	"	35	16 Linwood
N	Heggie Philip	6	chauffeur	42	16 "
O	Stubbs Julian R	7	clerk	42	here
P	Stubbs Marion B—†	7	housewife	39	"
R	Smith Clyde	8	laborer	35	"
S	Smith Flora—†	8	domestic	25	"
T	O'Brien Ella M—†	9	housewife	50	"
U	O'Brien James E	9	cook	52	"
V	Blair Temperance—†	10	housekeeper	45	"
W	Mason Laura A—†	10	domestic	27	"
X	Lovett Alice—†	11	elevatorwoman	30	"
Y	Lovett Emma—†	11	hairdresser	36	"
Z	Lovett Ethel—†	11	elevatorwoman	36	"
A	Ellison Judge	12	janitor	36	"
B	Ellison Lottie—†	12	domestic	26	"
C	Whaley Beatrice—†	14	housewife	40	"
D	Whaley James	14	storekeeper	64	"
E	Hathaway Rose—†	16	domestic	33	"
F	Webb Dorothy—†	16	bookkeeper	21	"
G	Jordan Clifford C	18	inspector	35	"
H	Jordan Florence L—†	18	housewife	35	"
K	Perry Margaret—†	22	domestic	45	"
L	Watkins Charles J	24	cook	60	18 Cunard
M	Watkins Nannie—†	24	housewife	50	18 "
N	Chapman Lula—†	26	"	30	W Virginia
O	Chapman Oscar	26	postal clerk	36	here
P	Harris Edward L	28	expressman	57	"
R	Jones Arthur H	28	laborer	36	"
S	Jones Emma—†	28	housewife	40	"
T	Thompson Israel	30	waiter	43	88 Hammond
U	Thompson Mattie—†	30	housewife	42	88 "
W	Hoyett Hamilton	34	carpenter	45	here
X	Anderson Julia C—†	36	cook	48	"
Y	Sands Hanna—†	38	housekeeper	60	"
Z	Sands Louis	38	cook	41	"

Warwick Street

A	Smith Ruby—†	1	housewife	29	here
B	Smith William J	1	glazier	48	"
C	Warren Dora L—†	1	housewife	39	"
D	Warren George	1	shipper	42	"
E	Parker Addie V—†	1	housewife	48	"
F	Parker Samuel K	1	janitor	46	"
G	Alston Catherine—†	3	housewife	31	91 Hammond
L	Miller Laura—†	3	housekeeper	54	31 Holyoke
H	Mitchell Joseph S	3	lawyer	34	here
K	Mitchell Lucy—†	3	housewife	27	"
M	Callender Leslie	3	salesman	30	New York
N	Jackson Jane—†	3	domestic	34	here
O	Frie Bessie—†	5	housewife	24	"
P	Frie Carroll H	5	chauffeur	31	"
R	Dorsey William	5	porter	29	194 Northampton
S	Murray Beatrice R—†	5	housewife	27	503 Shawmut av
T	Murray Clyde D	5	shoeworker	26	503 "
U	Hendricks Thomas	5	porter	29	616 Col av
V	Smith Addie—†	5	hairdresser	39	here
W	Smith Walter	5	waiter	43	"
X	Morris Oscar W	7	clerk	21	"
Y	Pryor Frank D	7	janitor	38	"
Z	Pryor Mary E—†	7	housewife	40	"
A	Holmes Daniel	7	laborer	39	"
B	Walker Ruth—†	7	housewife	31	"
C	Walker William	7	porter	31	"
D	Lawson Frank M	7	auto mechanic	42	Brookline
E	Lawson Ora M—†	7	housewife	44	"
F	Galloway Guy A	9	laborer	22	here
G	Peacheey Elizabeth—†	9	laundress	37	"
H	Peacheey Flossie—†	9	"	44	"
K	Peacheey William H	9	porter	44	"
L	Thompson Elizabeth—†	9	laundress	51	Malden
M	Dunston Etta—†	9	"	45	here
N	Hathway Joseph	14	porter	43	"
O	Hathway Julia—†	14	housewife	40	"
P	Nelson Lulu—†	14	milliner	26	"
R	Winter Christopher S	15	clerk	55	"
S	Winter Nellie P—†	15	housewife	43	"
T	Walthers Marion C—†	16	"	29	"

Page.	Letter.	FULL NAME.	Residence, April 1, 1926.	Occupation.	Supposed Age.	Reported Residence, April 1, 1925. Street and Number.

Warwick Street—Continued

	U	Walthers William	16	foreman	30	here
	V	Smothers Edward	17	waiter	53	"
	W	Smothers Maud—†	17	housewife	39	"
	X	Harris John H	18	steward	44	"
	Y	Harris Mary F—†	18	housewife	65	"
	Z	Harris Samuel H	18	waiter	73	"
	A	Jackson Raymond C	18	clerk	27	Cambridge
	B	Hankinson Myrtis L—†	19	housewife	40	here
	C	Hankinson Thomas B	19	porter	50	"
	G	Goode Alfrieda—†	20	housewife	41	"
	H	Hoodfolk Carroll	20	laborer	49	"
	K	Warrington Malcom	20	carpenter	57	"
	L	Warrington Mary—†	20	domestic	48	"
	M	Ham Emily—†	20	"	40	"
	D	Campbell Agnes E—†	21	housewife	42	"
	E	Campbell Arthur E	21	waiter	44	"
	F	Bird Lillian—†	21	nurse	40	"
	N	Graves John	23	fireman	44	"
	O	Graves Mary E—†	23	housewife	42	"
	P	Goode John W	23	waiter	45	"
	R	Goode Lavinia—†	23	housewife	43	"
	S	Somervill Louisa—†	23	laundress	56	"
	T	Somervill Sandy	23	laborer	61	"
	U	Bowden Beanjamin G	24	porter	56	"
	V	Bowden Sarah—†	24	housekeeper	51	"
	W	Hanson Sarah A—†	24	at home	79	"
	X	McKinney Virginia B—†	24	cook	54	"
	Y	Wilson Margaret M—†	24	housewife	25	"
	Z	Wilson Theodore L	24	auto mechanic	26	"
	A	Elliot George E	25	car cleaner	45	"
	B	Jackson Caroline—†	25	housewife	45	"
	C	Jackson Walter	25	cook	47	"
	F	Paschall Aida V—†	26	housewife	33	"
	G	Paschall William H	26	porter	43	"
	H	Powell Harold	26	"	27	"
	K	Powell Imogene—†	26	operator	25	"
	L	Hallowell Isabella—†	26	domestic	56	"
	M	Brown Arthur N	27	dentist	27	"
	N	Brown Clark F	27	porter	62	"
	O	Brown Laura P—†	27	housewife	52	"
	P	Brown William F	27	dentist	31	"

Page	Letter	Full Name.	Residence, April 1, 1926.	Occupation.	Supposed Age.	Reported Residence, April 1, 1925. Street and Number.

Warwick Street—Continued

	R	Jackson Carolina—†	27	housekeeper	73	25 Warwick
	S	Spriggs Georgie L—†	28	laundress	62	here
	U	Lattimore Alphonzo L	28	porter	47	"
	T	Lattimore Andrew B	28	physician	43	"
	V	Lattimore Mary A—†	28	housewife	71	"
	W	Branch Charles	29	shoemaker	39	109 Lenox
	X	Branch Zuleka—†	29	housewife	32	Bahama Islands
	Y	Anderson Lilleth—†	29	"	27	72 Ruggles
	Z	Anderson Sydney L	29	cook	27	72 "
	B	Byndlos Lillian—†	30	housewife	26	58 Cabot
	C	Byndlos Peter	30	laborer	27	58 "
	E	Harold Arthur B	30	longshoreman	40	here
	F	Sneed Robert	30	porter	56	"
	G	Merchant Ernest	31	chiropodist	53	"
	H	Merchant Sadie—†	31	dressmaker	45	"
	K	Martin Ruth—†	31	housewife	23	Phila Pa
	M	Jones Mattie—†	32	laundress	35	here
	N	White Eva—†	32	"	42	47 Hammond
	O	Harris Sadie—†	32	"	35	here
	R	Davis Ida B—†	33	"	55	"
	S	Russell Allen	33	porter	55	"
	S¹	Russell Emma—†	33	laundress	45	"
	T	Cumberbatch Evelyn—†	33	housewife	24	"
	U	Cumberbatch Fred S	33	tailor	30	"
	V	Williams Edna—†	33	laundress	27	Cambridge
	W	Haynes Isom W	34	janitor	52	here
	X	Haynes Julia—†	34	housewife	52	"
	Y	French George M	35	fireman	37	8 Middlesex
	Z	French Lillian L—†	35	housewife	30	8 "
	A	Baldwin George	35	painter	45	here
	B	Baldwin Julia—†	35	housekeeper	47	"
	C	Mayon Amy—†	35	housewife	37	"
	D	Mayon James	35	cook	42	"
	E	Moore Mary E—†	36	hairdresser	50	"
	F	Berry Archibald	37	druggist	39	"
	G	Berry Edna M—†	37	housewife	29	"
	H	O'Brien John	37	undertaker	61	"
	K	Grant Florence—†	37	housewife	31	"
	L	Grant Thomas	37	laborer	46	"
	M	Butler Emily J—†	38	domestic	25	"

Letter	FULL NAME.	Residence, April 1, 1926.	Occupation.	Supposed Age.	Reported Residence, April 1, 1925. Street and Number.

Warwick Street—Continued

N	Joseph Norman C	38	porter	25	810 Tremont
O	Smith Maude T—†	38	housewife	42	here
P	Childs Benjamin	39	bellman	37	"
R	Childs Nettie—†	39	housewife	37	"
S	Childs Oscar C	39	bellman	45	"
U	Valentine Mary—†	39	domestic	54	"
V	Willis Joseph	39	chauffeur	42	"
W	Smith Mabel—†	40	housekeeper	25	"
X	Smith Nannie—†	40	domestic	45	"
Y	Holmes Jessie—†	40	"	33	"
Z	Harris Carrie A—†	41	housekeeper	50	"
A	Whitter Agatha—†	42	housewife	28	13 Oak Grove ter
B	Whitter James	42	laborer	38	13 "
C	Byrdsong John W	42	porter	54	here
D	Byrdsong Pauline—†	42	housewife	41	"
E	Marshall John C	43	porter	56	"
F	Roper Lottie L—†	43	housewife	27	"
G	Roper William L	43	mechanic	28	"
H	Piggot Kathleen—†	44	factory worker	21	61 Williams
K	Stuart Alexander	44	porter	34	here
L	Stuart Hilda—†	44	housewife	32	"
N	Merchant Evelyn—†	45	housekeeper	35	"
O	Harris Anna M—†	45	housewife	40	"
P	Williams Alberta—†	46	teacher	25	"
R	Williams Alexander	46	laborer	55	"
S	Williams Alexander, jr	46	"	23	"
T	Williams Isabell—†	46	housekeeper	56	"
U	Williams Mamie—†	47	"	35	"
V	Flagg Rosa—†	47	"	65	"
X	Bagby Betty—†	48	"	50	"
Y	Bagby Sterling	48	porter	55	"
Z	Wentworth Bessie—†	48	elevatorwoman	50	40 Cedar
A	Read Alice D—†	49	housekeeper	45	here
B	Smith Rosa—†	49	"	54	"
C	Collins Evelyn—†	49	housewife	28	"
D	Collins Ralph	49	porter	30	"
F	Davis Tilly J—†	51	waitress	49	"
G	Minton Charles A	51	messenger	39	"
H	Minton Mabel L—†	51	housewife	38	"
K	West Willis	51	porter	53	"

27

Page	Letter	FULL NAME.	Residence, April 1, 1926.	Occupation	Supposed Age.	Reported Residence, April 1, 1925. Street and Number.

Warwick Street—Continued

	L	Edmondson George	51	waiter	51	here
	M	Edmondson Maud—†	51	housewife	34	"
	N	Rideant Thomas	53	porter	42	10 Marble
	O	Valantine Bertha—†	53	domestic	55	10 "
	P	Valantine Ethel—†	53	elevatorwoman	31	10 "
	R	Lewis Florence L †	53	housekeeper	48	here
	T	Willis Georgine—†	55	housewife	36	"
	U	Willis Henry A	55	waiter	39	"
	X	Pauley Charles F	59	machinist	27	"
	Y	Pauley Mary E—†	59	housewife	21	"
	Z	Bisbee Anna—†	59	"	31	45 Winchester
	A	Bisbee Charles A	59	janitor	46	45 "
	B	Hill Temple—†	64	houseworker	63	here
	C	Sherrill Luella—†	64	laundress	42	"
	D	Hector Annie—†	64	cook	57	630 Shawmut av
	E	Steward Barbara—†	64	houseworker	29	630 "
	F	Kyser John F	64	janitor	49	here
	G	Kyser Marion—†	64	housewife	30	"
	H	Washington Adeline B—†	66	nurse	44	"
	K	Doleber Codelia—†	66	houseworker	44	"
	L	Payton Annie—†	66	housewife	44	"
	M	Payton Frank	66	laborer	50	"
	N	Lindsay Florence †	68	houseworker	35	"
	O	Williams Pauline—†	68	housewife	33	"
	P	Williams Theodor	68	cook	33	"
	S	Levatt Elma—†	69	housewife	37	"
	T	Levatt Valantine	69	weaver	35	"
	U	Watkins Belle—†	69	houseworker	30	"
	V	Watkins Massie	69	porter	32	"
	W	Gibson Ethel—†	69	domestic	35	"
	X	Gardner Myrtle †	69	elevatorwoman	36	132 Sterling
	Y	Pollard Jennie †	69	housewife	34	here
	Z	Pollard Lisle	69	cook	32	"
	A	White Vera †	69	housewife	30	"
	B	Brown John B	69	laborer	65	Long Island
	C	Dixon Nicholas	69	janitor	56	here
	D	McLean Bessie †	69	housewife	40	"
	E	McLean Henry	69	laundryman	35	"
	G	Taylor Edith †	69	housekeeper	48	"
	H	Lehtonen Agust, jr	69	pianomaker	30	"

Page	Letter	Full Name.	Residence, April 1, 1926.	Occupation.	Supposed Age.	Reported Residence, April 1, 1925. Street and Number.

Warwick Street—Continued

	K	Lehtonen Agust	69	retired	75	here
	L	Lehtonen John	69	painter	69	"
	M	Lehtonen Sophie—†	69	housewife	69	"
	O	Norris Gertrude—†	69	"	40	"
	P	Norris James	69	waiter	44	"
	R	Johnson Margaret—†	69	laundress	49	Cambridge
	S	Williams Charles	69	painter	69	here
	T	Williams Sadie—†	69	laundress	69	"
	U	Gaboural Sarah—†	70	houseworker	59	"
	V	Russell Ella L—†	70	operator	29	"
	W	Ferriabouch Estelle H—†	70	housewife	41	"
	X	Ferriabouch Prince	70	attendant	41	"
	Y	Brennen John S	70	shipper	31	"
	Z	Brennen Lena—†	70	housewife	30	"
	A	Collins Leroy	71	stevedore	30	60 Hammond
	B	Collins Sadie—†	71	housewife	25	60 "
	C	Jones Cora—†	71	laundress	42	80 Windsor
	D	Powell Wilber	71	porter	38	80 "
	E	Booker Marie—†	71	maid	27	399 Northampton
	F	Wells Mabel—†	71	housewife	31	666 Shawmut av
	G	Cutting Alberta—†	71	"	30	here
	H	Downes Rosa—†	71	domestic	39	"
	K	Reed Arthur B	73	painter	54	Bridgeport Ct
	L	Reed Margaret M—†	73	housewife	41	"
	N	Butcher James N	73	hairdresser	32	Medford
	M	Butcher Nina T—†	73	housewife	27	"
	O	Robinson Louise—†	73	"	38	here
	P	Robinson Steven	73	laborer	37	"
	R	Wilson Irene—†	73	factory worker	25	21 Oak Grove ter
	S	Daniels Hubert	73	porter	27	Halifax N S
	T	Daniels Rosa—†	73	housewife	24	"
	U	Yagjian Richard	73	baker	45	here
	V	Yagjian Rose—†	73	housewife	38	"
	X	Aylanian Manoog	73	carpetmaker	33	"
	Y	Aylanian Warthoohea—†	73	housewife	33	"
	Z	Smith Charles H	73	porter	23	24 Claremont pk
	A	Smith Winifred—†	73	housewife	26	24 "

Page.	Letter.	FULL NAME.	Residence, April 1, 1926.	Occupation.	Supposed Age.	Reported Residence, April 1, 1925. Street and Number.

Westminster Street

c	Gibbs Addie—†	11	housewife	43	here
d	Wood Ethel—†	11	stockwoman	25	"
e	Wood Mollie—†	11	maid	52	"
f	Ross Ellen—†	11	housekeeper	31	69 W Lenox
g	Ross John	11	porter	48	69 "
h	Johnson Vaiche	11	chauffeur	33	here
k	Thomas Joseph E	11	waiter	60	"
l	Thomas Lillian—†	11	housewife	26	"
m	Smith Ellen—†	11	barberess	25	"
n	Smith Gertrude—†	11	maid	45	"
o	Brown Mary—†	11	houseworker	46	"
p	Hopkins Annie—†	11	housekeeper	44	"
r	Hopkins John T	11	stableman	50	"
s	Bunting Charles	11	laborer	32	35 Cunard
t	Bunting Ione—†	11	housekeeper	24	35 "
u	Wilson Amy—†	11	"	29	35 "
v	Wilson Patrick	11	laborer	29	35 "
w	Ayers John E	11	waiter	63	here
x	Pittido Carrie L—†	11	laundress	55	"
y	Baker Ada—†	11	houseworker	43	"
z	Webb Arzulia L—†	12	housekeeper	31	"
a	Webb Marion L	12	postal clerk	44	"
b	Green Daniel	12	porter	43	"
c	Green Lucy—†	12	housekeeper	42	"
d	Flint Cumphery—†	12	"	46	"
e	Brown Edna—†	12	domestic	39	"
f	Morris Alice—†	12	"	41	"
g	Patrick Esther—†	12	housekeeper	33	"
h	Patrick William E	12	porter	34	"
k	Cannady Samuel	12	laborer	26	"
l	Simms Beatrice E—†	12	dressmaker	36	"
m	Plantt Augusta—†	12	at home	38	"
n	Wilkerson Edith—†	12	housekeeepr	25	"
o	Wilkerson Harold C	12	musician	29	"
p	Hicks Emma—†	12	laundress	47	"
r	Ragland Moses	12	chef	52	
s	Bowen John	14	porter	32	77 Newland
t	Bowen John W	14	fireman	52	90 Camden
u	Bowen Reba—†	14	housekeeper	30	77 Newland

Page.	Letter.	FULL NAME.	Residence, April 1, 1926.	Occupation.	Supposed Age.	Reported Residence, April 1, 1925. Street and Number.

Westminster Street—Continued

v	Bell Betty —†	14	laundress	50	77 Newland
w	Smith William	14	baker	22	77 "
x	Everett Fanny—†	14	housekeeper	57	here
y	Johnson William P	14	porter	34	"
z	Walker Diley—†	14	laundress	35	"
A	Varrs Anna—†	16	housekeeper	83	"
B	Varrs Joseph A	16	laborer	31	"
c	Varrs Linona—†	16	laundress	53	"
E	Pasachell John E	16	porter	41	"
D	Pasachell Luella —†	16	housekeeper	38	"
F	Greenway Jane—†	16	"	50	"
H	Christmas Peter P	17	porter	60	"
K	Peary Moses	17	steward	41	"
L	Peary Rosa—†	17	housekeeper	37	"
M	Mathew Frederick	17	chauffeur	28	"
N	Hill Edward	18	mechanic	44	"
O	Hill Ethel —†	18	housekeeper	34	"
P	Farrior Elizabeth—†	18	laundress	62	"
R	Smith Cliffton	18	janitor	23	"
S	Smith Frances—†	18	laundress	49	"
T	Fray James	19	trucker	48	"
U	Landron Rebecca—†	19	housekeeper	57	4 Claremont ct
W	Worrell Lester A	20	engineer	42	here
X	Worrell Mable—†	20	housekeeper	35	"
Y	Terry Karen—†	20	laundress	47	"
Z	Cornish Augusta—†	20	housekeeper	25	"
A	DeCosta Manuel	21	laborer	42	New Bedford
B	Mills Rhoda—†	21	housekeeper	40	New Jersey
c	Coleman Abraham	21	porter	60	here
D	Tillman Emily—†	21	housekeeper	35	Maine
E	Tillman Wayne	21	janitor	41	"
F	Holmes Alfred	22	laborer	29	Lynn
G	Holmes Viola—†	22	domestic	22	"
H	Proyor Andrew	22	tailor	33	here
K	White Charles	22	laborer	24	"
L	White Edith—†	22	housekeeper	25	"
M	Lewis Byrd C	23	laborer	49	"
N	Lewis Jennie F—†	23	housekeeper	45	"
O	Boden Caroline—†	23	"	75	"
P	Morris Robert J	23	lawyer	56	"

Page.	Letter.	FULL NAME.	Residence, April 1, 1926.	Occupation.	Supposed Age.	Reported Residence, April 1, 1925. Street and Number.

Westminster Street—Continued

	R	Smith Edward L	23	waiter	39	here
	S	Smith Lora F—†	23	housekeeper	28	"
	T	Unas Daisy—†	24	"	38	"
	U	Unas Henry	24	truckman	41	"
	V	Irving Elizabeth J—†	24	domestic	29	"
	W	Mattier Clarence J	24	laborer	44	"
	X	Mattier Ellen—†	24	housekeeper	31	"
	Y	Bryant Ada—†	25	"	40	"
	Z	Bryant Frank	25	porter	50	"
	A	Bryant John	25	musician	22	"
	B	Bryant Mark	25	"	26	"
	C	Glover Alice—†	26	at home	63	783 Shawmut av
	D	Glover Royal	26	porter	25	783 "
	E	Riley Ida—†	26	hairdresser	32	783 "
	F	Barrows Myrene—†	26	laundress	30	here
	G	Hazard Bertha—†	26	housekeeper	30	"
	H	Hazard John	26	porter	53	"
	K	Hartfield Fanny—†	27	housekeeper	29	"
	L	Hartfield Richard	27	meatcutter	30	"
	M	Monroe Bertha—†	27	housekeeper	30	"
	N	Monroe Weldon	27	tailor	30	"
	O	Tucker Edward	27	porter	37	"
	P	Tucker Mary—†	27	housekeeper	33	"
	R	Underwood Charles W	28	boiler maker	45	"
	S	Underwood Marion S—†	28	housekeeper	22	"
	T	Crockett Marie—†	28	at home	22	"
	U	Crockett Samuel	28	porter	26	"
	V	Stokes Bernice—†	28	housekeeper	20	"
	W	Stokes Frank	28	machinist	28	"
	X	Miller Berkley	29	waiter	38	"
	Y	Miller Lotta—†	29	housekeeper	34	"
	Z	Thornton Rosa K—†	29	"	49	82 Sterling
	A	Thornton William	29	teamster	54	82 "
	B	Ware Addie—†	29	housekeeper	35	here
	C	Jackson Sara E—†	30	"	52	"
	D	Brown Lucy—†	30	cook	45	"
	E	Johnson Rose—†	30	laundress	38	172 Northampton
	F	Smith Peter	31	laborer	30	8 Burbank
	G	Alston Eary	31	"	43	here
	H	Marks Leopold	31	porter	31	"

32

Letter.	Full Name.	Residence, April 1, 1926.	Occupation.	Supposed Age.	Reported Residence, April 1, 1925. Street and Number.

Westminster Street—Continued

K	Marks Marion—†	31	housekeeper	52	here
L	Jackson Albert	33	laborer	22	Utah
M	Johnson Ella—†	33	housekeeper	46	here
N	Johnson Wilford	33	chauffeur	41	"
O	Nelson Mable—†	33	housekeeper	28	63 Williams
P	Nelson Maston	33	tailor	26	63 "
R	Green Mary J—†	33	housekeeper	45	18 Dartmouth
S	Green Reginald	33	laborer	48	18 "
T	Hudson Elizabeth—†	35	housekeeper	48	here
U	Hudson Garland	35	janitor	55	"
V	Bridget Isabella—†	35	laundryworker	48	"
W	Miller Eva S—†	35	waitress	28	"
X	Bracy Charlotte—†	35	housekeeper	39	65 Ruggles
Y	Bracy Paul S	35	porter	41	65 "
Z	Harris Agusta—†	48	at home	85	82 Sterling
A	Page Hartlett—†	48	housekeeper	45	82 "
B	Page Jerry	48	laborer	40	82 "
C	Wiggins Albert C	48	bottler	36	here
D	Wiggins Leila—†	48	housekeeper	30	"
E	McDonald Bertha—†	48	"	32	"
F	McDonald Frederick	48	janitor	40	"
G	Whitley Bessie—†	48	housekeeper	38	"
H	Whitley Robert	48	rigger	40	"
K	Reid Emma—†	51	domestic	36	103 Camden
L	Reid William R	51	porter	45	103 "
N	Dworkis Bernard	51	tailor	40	here
O	Dworkis Goldie—†	51	housekeeper	39	"
S	Clancey Francis S	53	plumber	33	"
T	Clancey Helen F—†	53	housekeeper	30	"
U	Ellman Caroline—†	53	"	75	"
V	Ellman Florence L—†	53	clerk	30	"
W	Donovan James F	53	"	47	New York
X	McLaughlin May E—†	53	cleaner	58	44 Beacon
Y	Lunderville Ernest	55	bookbinder	31	here
Z	Lunderville Lucy—†	55	houseworker	29	"
A	Jeffrie Henretta—†	55	laundress	45	34 Village
B	Jeffrie John	55	laborer	47	34 "
C	Trouit Mary—†	55	cook	54	110 W Lenox

Page.	Letter.	FULL NAME.	Residence, April 1, 1926.	Occupation.	Supposed Age.	Reported Residence, April 1, 1925. Street and Number.

Windsor Street

E	Wallace Victoria—†	9	domestic	40	here
F	Perry Bessie B—†	9	housekeeper	36	"
G	Price Malinda E—†	9	domestic	56	"
H	Loggans George F	9	janitor	40	"
K	Richardson Susie—†	9	seamstress	38	"
L	Barber Clara—†	9	domestic	50	32 Greenwich pk
N	Branch Annie—†	11	housewife	48	2½ Clayton pl
O	Branch William	11	janitor	47	2½ "
P	Routh Charles H	11	cementfinisher	39	here
R	Williams Louise—†	11	housekeeper	29	82 Ruggles
S	Williams Nickolan	11	cook	47	82 "
T	Jackson Edward	13	porter	41	here
U	Jellison Thomas	13	chauffeur	32	"
V	Routh Hattie M—†	13	housekeeper	35	"
W	Troupe Claybourne	13	porter	28	"
X	Covington William	14	plasterer	47	"
Y	Williams Amadelo—†	14	domestic	29	"
Z	Williams Bertha—†	14	hairdresser	42	"
A	Joseph Ivy A—†	14	housewife	26	106 Dartmouth
B	Joseph LeBlanc H	14	porter	38	106 "
C	Woods Fannie E—†	14	elevatorwoman	48	here
D	Betts Sadie M—†	14	domestic	34	"
E	McKnight Bessie—†	14	"	27	"
F	Scott Annie F—†	14	housewife	44	"
G	Scott Robert E	14	grocer	53	"
H	Taylor William N	14	policeman	29	"
K	Gale Charles	14	porter	34	"
L	Gale Mary—†	14	housewife	32	"
M	Nixon James	14	cook	41	"
N	Nixon Margaret S—†	14	housewife	34	"
O	Nixon Welton	14	porter	21	"
P	Isaacs Louise C—†	14	housewife	38	"
R	Isaacs Robert H	14	janitor	58	"
S	Spencer Daniel	14	expressman	62	"
T	Spencer Marion—†	14	housewife	52	"
U	Wright Libbie—†	14	domestic	39	"
V	Williams Mary—†	14	housewife	38	New York
W	Williams Thomas J	14	porter	45	"
X	Boyce Isreal F	14	laborer	40	65 Sawyer
Y	Hopson Bessie—†	14	housekeeper	44	65 "

34

Letter.	FULL NAME.	Residence, April 1, 1926.	Occupation.	Supposed Age.	Reported Residence, April 1, 1925. Street and Number.

Windsor Street—Continued

Letter.	FULL NAME.	Residence, April 1, 1926.	Occupation.	Supposed Age.	Reported Residence, April 1, 1925. Street and Number.
z	Harrison Lillian—†	14	housewife	31	28 Davenport
A	Harrison Quillar	14	mechanic	31	28 "
B	Irons Gertrude C—†	14	domestic	36	100 Camden
c	Poole Eva T—†	14	dressmaker	30	Brookline
c¹	Sheldon Ray N	14	musician	36	Everett
D	Cook Gertrude—†	15	clerk	28	80 Hammond
E	Harris Ada—†	15	housewife	25	53 Windsor
F	Harris Milton	15	elevatorman	32	53 "
G	McCarter Betty—†	15	housekeeper	68	here
H	Price Charles H	15	coal passer	48	"
K	Price Ella—†	15	housewife	47	"
L	Reynolds Robert	16	painter	65	49 Hammond
M	Reynolds Robert, jr	16	cook	36	49 "
N	Wooley Muriel V—†	16	housewife	31	here
O	Wooley Timothy S	16	foreman	43	"
P	Wynn Floyd	16	chauffeur	26	3 Wellington
R	Wynn Mary E—†	16	housewife	31	3 "
S	Johnston Edward	17	laundryman	24	here
T	Johnston Ethel—†	17	housewife	28	"
U	Hill Daisy—†	17	housekeeper	71	"
V	White James	17	porter	30	"
W	White Suzie—†	17	domestic	20	"
X	Dukes David	18	student	28	Pennsylvania
Y	Harris Catherine E—†	18	housewife	46	here
Z	Harris Samuel A	18	pedler	34	"
A	MacNeill Lilly M—†	18	nurse	30	"
B	Manuel Clifford B	18	porter	45	"
c	Saxton George T	18	radios	35	"
D	Reed Annie—†	19	housekeeper	80	"
E	Schenck Jerome D	19	cleaner	48	"
F	Schenck Ruth—†	19	houseworker	44	"
G	Cromady Lucy—†	19	housewife	33	"
H	Cromady William	19	laborer	37	"
K	Moore Charles	19	porter	68	"
K¹	Moore Lucy—†	19	dressmaker	45	"
L	Albury Walter	20	student	30	"
M	Bovell Estelle—†	20	housekeeper	36	"
N	Grant Egbert	20	engineer	56	"
O	Prescod James	20	agent	44	"
P	Vanhse Alonzo	21	porter	61	"
R	Vanhise Julia A—†	21	housewife	45	"

Page.	Letter.	Full Name.	Residence, April 1, 1926.	Occupation.	Supposed Age.	Reported Residence, April 1, 1925. Street and Number.

Windsor Street—Continued

	s	Lee Theadore	21	machinist	55	here
	u	Borden John F	22	janitor	25	"
	v	Francis Esther L—†	22	dressmaker	43	"
	w	Lattimer Henry J	22	student	22	"
	x	Lattimer Martha R—†	22	housewife	60	"
	y	Lattimer Peter	22	janitor	79	"
	z	Lattimer William B	22	"	27	"
	a	Rivers Esther L—†	22	housekeeper	28	"
	b	Rivers George W	22	porter	28	"
	c	Butts Helen J—†	23	domestic	24	78 Hammond
	d	Butts Mary F—†	23	housekeeper	60	78 "
	f	Hibbler Charles	23	insurance agent	55	here
	g	Francis Agat R	24	engineer	48	"
	h	Francis Laura A—†	24	housewife	45	"
	k	Scholar Mabel—†	24	housekeeper	28	"
	m	Robinson Julia—†	25	housewife	40	"
	n	Robinson Samuel B	25	fireman	51	"
	o	Lucas Margaret—†	25	housewife	25	Wilmington
	p	Lucas Palmer	25	cooper	25	"
	r	Robinson Mary—†	25	domestic	20	here
	s	Taylor George	25	janitor	25	41 Windsor
	t	Taylor Mary—†	25	domestic	25	41 "
	v	Johnson Virginia J⁕—†	26	laundress	33	66 Sterling
	u	Jones Ella S—†	26	housewife	36	here
	w	Jones William H	26	clergyman	53	"
	x	Blair Mildred B—†	27	waitress	24	Cambridge
	y	Janifer Ruth—†	27	domestic	27	"
	z	Harris Jessie M—†	27	housekeeper	29	here
	a	Stanfield Booker T	27	houseman	22	"
	b	Brown Charles S	28	machinist	33	"
	c	Brown Ethel D—†	28	housewife	31	"
	d	Ferguson Charlotte J—†	28	laundress	31	"
	e	Ferguson Thomas A	28	laborer	33	"
	f	Peart Phylis V—†	28	domestic	23	"
	g	Simpson Ruben	28	laborer	34	"
	h	Thompson Edith R—†	28	maid	29	"
	k	Price Charles H	29	waiter	60	"
	l	Stevens Ida—†	29	housekeeper	60	"
	m	Murphy Charles	29	dishwasher	32	"
	n	Meiser Sarah—†	29	laundress	53	"
	o	Padmore Julian	29	seaman	34	"

Page.	Letter.	FULL NAME.	Residence, April 1, 1926.	Occupation.	Supposed Age.	Reported Residence, April 1, 1925. Street and Number.

Windsor Street—Continued

	P	Todd Wilbur	29	clerk	25	554 Shawmut av
	R	Ditmus Edward A	30	retired	84	here
	S	Raynor Bessie—†	30	housewife	40	"
	T	Raynor George H	30	teamster	46	"
	U	Raynor George L	30	laborer	21	"
	V	Raynor Hazel G—†	30	housewife	21	"
	W	Gillard Mary—†	31	domestic	35	"
	X	Adams Cassie—†	31	housewife	48	"
	Y	Adams William	31	hostler	50	"
	Z	Burris Frank	31	watchman	52	"
	A	Burris Lucy—†	31	housewife	50	"
	B	Carrick Harry E	32	janitor	41	14 Windsor
	C	Durbin Hannah A—†	32	housewife	50	here
	D	Durbin Jesse O	32	janitor	50	"
	E	Leland Daniel T	32	retired	88	"
	H	Andrews Adolphus	33	laborer	44	"
	K	Andrews Edith—†	33	housewife	32	"
	L	Hopes Mary—†	34	housekeeper	56	"
	M	Brisbane Henry C	34	laborer	39	"
	N	Crowley Harry W	34	waiter	58	706 Col av
	O	Gibson Hattie—†	34	laundress	47	672 Shawmut av
	P	Porter Joseph A	34	houseman	72	here
	R	Ruthdly Gussie	34	laborer	21	77 Sterling
	S	Summer John E	34	porter	52	here
	T	Hoskins Eugene	35	cook	48	"
	U	Hoskins Josephine—†	35	housewife	44	"
	V	Harris Adam	35	porter	35	"
	W	Harris Leola—†	35	domestic	20	"
	X	Belmont Edith—†	35	laundress	44	"
	Y	Willis Carrie D—†	36	housewife	54	"
	Z	Willis Thomas	36	clergyman	60	"
	B	Carden Irene—†	36	laundress	28	14 Windsor
	A	Coffey Etta—†	36	domestic	38	New York
	C	McIntee Raymond	36	laborer	32	516 Shawmut av
	D	Midgett William W	36	meatcutter	46	here
	E	Rose Charles S	36	laborer	24	59 Hammond
	F	Smith Bessie—†	36	domestic	27	Virginia
	G	Harris Clara—†	37	housekeeper	56	here
	H	Harris Enoch	37	laborer	56	"
	L	Collier Joseph	37	lecturer	48	"
	M	Connolly Laura—†	38	housewife	46	"

Page	Letter	FULL NAME.	Residence, April 1, 1926.	Occupation.	Supposed Age.	Reported Residence, April 1, 1925. Street and Number.

Windsor Street Continued

N	Connolly William	38	laundryman	55	here
O	Gardner James	38	butler	34	"
P	Gardner Virginia—†	38	cook	29	"
R	Smith Lucy—†	39	housewife	65	"
S	Smith Peter	39	chiropodist	69	"
T	Hunt Rebecca—†	39	domestic	50	"
U	White Berlin	39	ballplayer	25	"
V	White Madeline—†	39	housewife	20	"
W	Smith John E	39	policeman	32	"
X	Smith Lillian M—†	39	housewife	49	"
Y	Duguid Fitz	40	laborer	40	138 Pleasant
Z	Forbes Beatrice—†	40	housewife	25	here
A	Forbes William W	40	porter	35	"
B	Hadrick Edward T	40	"	28	"
C	Hadrick Virginia—†	40	cook	56	"
D	Mills Florence—†	41	housewife	44	"
E	Byers Bertha—†	41	domestic	45	53 Windsor
F	Byers Gladys—†	41	dressmaker	23	53 "
G	Wilson Lottie—†	41	domestic*	28	here
H	Trottman Edith V—†	42	housewife	35	"
K	Trottman Samuel	42	porter	37	"
L	Sealey Conrad F	42	janitor	30	"
M	Sealey Keturah—†	42	housewife	37	"
N	Lloyd Henry M	42	porter	33	"
O	Lloyd Rose L—†	42	housewife	36	"
P	Barsky Freda—†	43	"	35	"
R	Barsky Samuel	43	storekeeper	42	"
S	Mosson Albert	43	mover	43	"
T	Mosson Sybil—†	43	housewife	32	"
U	Rainey Dorothy A—†	44	presser	25	"
V	Rainey Ernest J	44	porter	24	"
W	Rainey Ethel D—†	44	maid	23	"
X	Rainey Sarah W—†	44	housekeeper	46	"
Y	Caines Irwin	44	laborer	35	"
Z	Caines Sarah—†	44	housewife	29	"
A	Rosen Jennie—†	44A	"	30	"
B	Rosen Joseph	44A	storekeeper	33	"
D	Bizzell Frank	50	chauffeur	36	"
E	Drake Nina—†	50	domestic	32	"
F	Lee Anthony	50	porter	45	"

Windsor Street —Continued

G	Lee Josephine V—†	50	housewife	36	here
H	Van Charles	50	chauffeur	25	"
K	Hester Beulah S—†	52	housewife	30	4A Forest
L	Hester William H	52	clergyman	37	4A "
M	Hamilton Mollie—†	53	laundress	40	here
N	Cook Elizabeth—†	53	housekeeper	40	Phila Pa
O	Manley Hugh	53	laborer	35	13 Delle av
P	Armstrong Henry	54	janitor	49	635 Shawmut av
R	Dennis George W	54	laborer	62	here
S	Dennis Minnie—†	54	housewife	46	"
T	Forsyth John	54	janitor	47	"
V	Jacklin Douglass	54	cook	25	679 Shawmut av
U	Jacklin Florence—†	54	housewife	21	679 "
W	Jacklin Leon V	54	porter	23	679 "
X	Jones Cora—†	55	housewife	50	here
Y	Jones Melvin	55	cook	55	"
Z	Tarry Delia—†	55	housewife	49	"
A	Tarry Nathanial	55	carpenter	53	"
B	Bullock Katherine W—†	56	housewife	41	"
C	Bullock Mathew W	56	lawyer	43	"
D	Kane Carrie—†	57	housewife	28	"
E	Kane Marcus	57	chauffeur	40	"
F	Vanderzee John	57	waiter	38	"
G	Mitchell Ellen L—†	58	housewife	65	"
H	Mitchell Frank L	58	letter carrier	65	"
K	Simmons Bessie R—†	58	housewife	36	"
L	Simmons Jack C	58	porter	42	"
P	Hall Harriet C—†	60	housewife	42	"
R	Hall John B	60	physician	49	"
S	Bradley Thomas	61	janitor	50	30 Warwick
T	Payne Clarence	61	waiter	35	here
U	Payne Rebecca—†	61	housewife	32	"
V	Elliot Cora—†	61	"	40	"
W	Elliot Grant	61	watchman	45	"
X	Reddick Cornelius T	63	porter	38	"
Y	Reddick Ruthina F—†	63	housewife	30	"
Z	Adams Amos	63	stableman	35	"
A	Adams Gertrude—†	63	housewife	31	"
B	Ball Carrie—†	65	housekeeper	57	"
F	Ball Newton L	65	musician	26	"
G	Davis Mae—†	65	housewife	36	"

Page.	Letter.	FULL NAME.	Residence, April 1, 1926.	Occupation.	Supposed Age.	Reported Residence, April 1, 1925. Street and Number.

Windsor Street—Continued

H	Davis Willie L	65	choreman	37	here
C	Polstor Charles	65	longshoreman	26	"
D	Ross Harriet E—†	65	housewife	23	"
E	Ross Robert D	65	clerk	24	Swampscott
K	Reddick Eliza T—†	67	student	24	here
L	Reddick Katherine R—†	67	hairdresser	41	"
M	Reddick Luke R	67	porter	40	"
N	Reddick Nancy A—†	67	housekeeper	63	"
O	Jones Eugene	69	cook	60	686 Shawmut av
P	Rickson Dora—†	69	domestic	50	here
R	Williams James E	69	porter	59	"
S	Williams Josephine—†	69	housekeeper	21	"
T	Williams Louisa—†	69	housewife	55	"
U	Williams Louisa—†	69	cook	23	"
V	Ball Loulie—†	71	housekeeper	49	"
V¹	Ball Newton	71	janitor	65	"
W	Preston Lulu—†	71	elevatorwoman	45	"
X	Vas Joaquim	71	machinist	32	"
Y	Vas Marie—†	71	factory worker	33	"
Z	Francis Richard J	73	clerk	42	384 Northampton
A	Francis Ruby L—†	73	housewife	33	384 "
B	Roberts Emily—†	73	hairdresser	35	here
C	Hopkins Constance—†	73	student	22	"
D	Hopkins Edgar	73	cook	28	"
E	Foster Martha A—†	75	dressmaker	57	"
F	Jackson James E	75	laborer	56	"
G	Jackson Mattie—†	75	housewife	56	"
H	Poole Jesse	75	laborer	46	38 Warwick
K	Jones Henrietta—†	77	housewife	47	here
L	Jones Robert W	77	porter	58	"
M	Miller Robert	77	"	46	"
N	Washington Mary—†	77	car cleaner	25	"
O	Oliver Bessie—†	79	housewife	44	"
P	Oliver Charles C	79	shipper	48	"
R	Evans Leo	80	mechanic	32	196 Northampton
S	Evans Marie—†	80	housewife	30	198 "
T	Evans Milton	80	chauffeur	28	Cambridge
U	Johnson Herman	80	physician	37	Everett.
V	McIntree Sadie—†	80	housekeeper	25	17 Claremount pk
W	Miller Beatrice—†	80	domestic	22	33 Lenox
X	Miller Mahala—†	80	"	20	33 "

40

	Letter	FULL NAME.	Residence, April 1, 1926.	Occupation.	Supposed Age.	Reported Residence, April 1, 1925.
						Street and Number.

Windsor Street—Continued

	Letter	FULL NAME.	Residence	Occupation	Age	Reported Residence
	y	Newton Jeanette—†	80	housewife	32	12 Sawyer
	z	Newton William	80	longshoreman	50	12 "
	A	Russell Edgar	80	seaman	38	27 Northampton
	B	Russell Elsie—†	80	housewife	35	26 "
	C	Cantas Bertha—†	81	domestic	45	here
	D	Branco Tony	83	millhand	27	38 Conant
	E	Bruce Cora B—†	83	housekeeper	50	here
	F	Keene Alice—†	83	domestic	36	"
	G	Lindsey Anna S—†	83	florist	42	"
	H	Manley Essie—†	83	domestic	34	"
	K	Phillips Fitz R	83	laborer	40	"
	L	Santiago Frank	83	millhand	27	38 Conant
	N	Taylor Charlotte—†	96	housewife	46	here
	O	Taylor Edward W	96	porter	58	"
	P	Belt Charles C	96	barber	59	"
	R	Belt Hattie M—†	96	housewife	49	"
	S	Turnage Alexander A	96	porter	42	"
	T	Turnage James	96	student	22	"
	U	Turnage Margaret—†	96	housewife	42	"
	V	Marks Ida—†	97	"	48	"
	W	Marks Samuel	97	coal dealer	48	"

9—7

41

Ward 9—Precinct 8

CITY OF BOSTON.

LIST OF RESIDENTS
20 YEARS OF AGE AND OVER

(FEMALES INDICATED BY DAGGER)

AS OF

APRIL 1, 1926

HERBERT A. WILSON, } Listing

JAMES F. EAGAN,   } Board.

CITY OF BOSTON—PRINTING DEPARTMENT

Page.	Letter.	FULL NAME.	Residence, April 1, 1926.	Occupation.	Supposed Age.	Reported Residence, April 1, 1925. Street and Number.

Benton Street

	A	Harris Ckarles	4	laborer	29	2 Smith av
	B	Wilson Percy	4	chauffeur	24	here
	C	Harris Harold L	4	poster	31	"
	D	Henry Ireene —†	4	laundress	25	"
	E	Frye Hortense —†	4	housewife	26	44 Cabot
	F	Frye Leighton B	4	grinder	35	44 "
	G	Finch James H	6	clerk	52	here
	H	Lewis Irene N —†	6	housewife	32	"
	K	Lewis Jerome	6	laborer	35	"
	L	Bower Mary —†	6	laundress	35	"
	N	Johnson William H	8	mason	52	"

Burke Street

	P	McCoy Lillian —†	4	dressmaker	29	here
	R	Miller Mary —†	4	laundress	32	"
	S	Peterson Adolph F	5	cementworker	53	"
	T	Peterson Hanna —†	5	storekeeper	•44	"
	U	Speaker Fred B	5	laborer	42	Pennsylvania
	V	Speaker Lillian —†	5	housewife	39	"
	W	Geary Hilland E	7	laborer	38	11 Claremont pk
	Y	MacKey Emily —†	7	housewife	33	9 Burke
	Z	MacKey James	7	operator	47	9 "
	D	Evans Simeon	16	laborer	32	Florida
	E	Brathwaite Violet —†	16	houseworker	35	here
	F	Roberts Carlisle	16	busboy	21	"
	G	Daniels Frederick	16	helper	39	"
	H	Daniels Lillian —†	16	housekeeper	32	"
	K	Miller Fannie I —†	16	housewife	32	"
	L	Miller Robert	16	clerk	44	"
	M	Reid Joanna —†	16	domestic	28	"
	N	Foreman Frank S	18	barber	31	107 Hammond
	O	Prince Etta - †	18	waitress	22	31 Eustis
	P	Upshure Gertrude —†	18	houseworker	27	39 Camden
	R	Upshure Mary —†	18	housewife	30	39 "
	S	Brown May —†	18	waitress	30	50 Cabot
	T	High James	18	clerk	30	2 Westfield
	U	Smalls Fannie —†	18	housewife	30	here
	V	Williams Nellie —†	18	"	25	"

2

Letter.	Full Name.	Residence, April 1, 1926.	Occupation.	Supposed Age.	Reported Residence, April 1, 1925. Street and Number.

Cabot Street

W	Jackson Thomas	29	laborer	51	Brockton
X	Smith Martha—†	29	laundress	42	here
Y	Taylor Chris	29	truckman	30	205 Camden
C	Bazemose James W	41	chauffeur	48	here
D	Bazemose Rosa B—†	41	housewife	47	"
E	Whiting Alice—†	41	domestic	34	"
F	Whiting James	41	porter	39	"
G	Lopez Alfred	41	laborer	41	"
H	Santos Alice—†	41	housekeeper	31	"
K	Santos Charles	41	laborer	33	"
L	Campbell John B	43	cook	48	"
N	Murphy Mary A—†	67	housewife	72	"
O	Murphy Thomas E	67	chauffeur	72	"
P	Stark Etta E—†	67	housewife	37	"
R	Stark William F	67	finisher	44	"
S	Saperstein Anna G—†	67	clerk	24	"
T	Saperstein Frances—†	67	"	31	"
U	Saperstein Hyman	67	shoemaker	68	"
V	Saperstein Mary—†	67	clerk	23	"
W	Saperstein Nathan	67	shipper	25	"
X	Saperstein Rose—†	67	housewife	61	"
Y	Wall Bertha E—†	69	"	34	53 Haskins
Z	Wall Joseph F	69	clerk	38	53 "
A	Rudinger Rudolf	69	cook	63	here
B	Rudinger Sophia—†	69	housewife	62	"
C	Tobbe Theadore H	69	baker	31	"
D	Lehan Ellan T—†	69	houseworker	62	"
E	Lehan Florence G—†	69	clerk	27	"
F	Salisbury Arthur L	75	gasfitter	49	"
G	Salisbury Catherine S—†	75	housewife	54	"
H	Salisbury Frederick G	75	shoeworker	22	"
K	Burns Margaret—†	76	waitress	50	"
L	Vail Margaret C—†	75	housewife	27	Brookline
M	Mooza Alexandria—†	75	"	45	here
N	Mooza Roman—†	75	baker	46	"
O	Martin Rosanna—†	77	houseworker	35	"
P	Tanwalt Dora—†	77	housewife	67	"
R	Tanwalt Henry	77	laborer	65	"
T	Thompson Fannie—†	79	saleswoman	48	"

3

Cabot Street—Continued

u	Conlon Hattie—†	79	saleswoman	48	here
v	Gordon Emma—†	79	houseworker	72	"
w	Donahue Bridget—†	81	matron	55	"
x	Donahue Frances—†	81	cigarworker	25	"
y	Donahue John J	81	chauffeur	30	"
z	Donahue Mary—†	81	housewife	28	"
A	Foley Edward	81	chauffeur	25	"
B	Chioccola John	81	shoemaker	45	52 Cabot
c	Dahlbeck Annie—†	81	housewife	54	here
D	Dahlbeck Axel	81	baker	48	"
G	Allen Graham—†	99	housewife	32	"
H	Allen Joseph N	89	grocer	37	"
K	Graham Carrie—†	99	housewife	20	80 Rutland sq
L	Graham James	99	porter	23	80 "
M	Blair Annie—†	99	domestic	51	here
N	Victor Eliza—†	99	houseworker	74	"
o	Anderson Agnes S—†	101	housewife	50	"
P	Anderson Carl	101	lineman	45	"
R	Greene Charles W	101	musician	33	"
s	Greene Katheryn M—†	101	stenographer	29	"
T	Greene Raymond F	101	chauffeur	25	"
U	Greene William	101	retired	63	"
V	Greene William F	101	chauffeur	31	"
w	Marr Lillian V—†	101	housewife	28	"
x	Marr Raymond A	101	actor	28	New York
Y	Bowden Emma E—†	101	at home	67	25 Mt Ida rd
z	Johnson Alvhild—†	101	housewife	31	here
A	Johnsen Gunnar	101	painter	25	"
c	Davis Joseph	109	laborer	21	70 Sterling
D	Davis William	109	"	26	54 Sawyer
E	Davis Anna—†	109	housewife	29	54 "
F	Davis Mary—†	109	houseworker	20	70 Sterling
H	Harrison John	109	laborer	46	here
L	Scanlon Frank	113	chauffeur	27	"
M	Towle Bessie—†	113	housekeeper	21	Cambridge
N	Lanciano Peter	115	laborer	34	5 Oswego
o	Lanciano Yvonne—†	115	housewife	26	5 "
P	Conboy Catherine G—†	115	forewoman	49	here
R	Mahoney Agnes F—†	115	housewife	52	"
s	Mahoney John J	115	carpenter	66	"

Page	Letter	FULL NAME.	Residence, April 1, 1926.	Occupation.	Supposed Age.	Reported Residence, April 1, 1925. Street and Number.

Cabot Street—Continued

	T	Cameron James S	117	shipper	27	here
	U	Cameron Mary F—†	117	housewife	24	"
	V	Goodwin Anna F—†	117	"	25	"
	W	Goodwin William R	117	machinist	30	"
	X	McKenna Delia—†	117	housewife	48	"
	Y	McKenna Francis	117	retired	55	"
	Z	McKenna Margaret—†	117	stitcher	23	"
	A	Byrnes Anna—†	119	housewife	26	"
	B	Byrnes Delia—†	119	"	53	"
	C	Byrnes James F	119	steamfitter	22	"
	D	Byrnes James R	119	teamster	49	"
	E	Raedy Catherine C—†	119	brushmaker	25	"
	F	Raedy Charles A	119	clerk	24	"
	G	Raedy Joseph A	119	retired	64	"
	H	Dadmun Eva—†	121	housekeeper	38	"
	K	Lackware William	121	roofer	36	"
	T	Ensko Agnes—†	135	housewife	28	66 Hampshire
	U	Ensko Michael F	135	motorman	29	66 "
	V	Carmichael Albert E	135	clerk	21	here
	W	Carmichael Emma—†	135	housewife	51	"
	X	Carmichael Ernest	135	clerk	50	"
	Y	Carmichael Sybel—†	135	"	22	"
	Z	Bergman Mary W—†	135	dressmaker	70	"
	A	Fowler George A	135	painter	53	"
	B	Pelkington Sarah—†	135	at home	79	"
	C	Widdup Eva C—†	135	houseworker	49	"
	D	Audonian Harry	135	laborer	36	"
	F	Croke James F	137	"	50	"
	G	Hogan Agnes G—†	137	saleswoman	34	"
	H	Hogan Charles A	137	mechanic	32	"
	K	Hogan John E	137	laborer	52	"
	L	Hogan Joseph S	137	porter	42	"
	M	Hogan Mary E—†	137	housekeeper	49	"
	N	Hogan William H	137	painter	45	"
	O	Staffiere Anna M—†	141	housewife	30	1123 Harrison av
	P	Staffiere Roco	141	laborer	31	1123 "
	R	Islas Rudolph	141	factory worker	40	Somerville
	S	Kadakas William	141	laborer	38	here
	T	Nenn Charles	141	mechanic	30	"
	U	Nenn Vera—†	141	housewife	30	"
	V	Chesley Arthur	143	carpenter	59	"

5

Page.	Letter.	FULL NAME.	Residence, April 1, 1926.	Occupation.	Supposed Age.	Reported Residence, April 1, 1925.
						Street and Number.

Cabot Street—Continued

	w	Chesley Margaret M—†	143	housewife	39	here
	x	Killoran Margaret—†	143	"	35	"
	y	Killoran Patrick	143	laborer	36	"
	z	Taylor Anna E—†	143	housekeeper	51	"
	A	Taylor Joseph H	143	retired	65	"

Columbus Avenue

	c	Allen Sadie—†	748	waitress	27	here
	D	Smith Estelle—†	748	housewife	37	"
	E	Smith William E	748	waiter	48	"
	F	St Hilaire Edward C	748	chauffeur	35	"
	G	Wooten Daniel L	748	garageman	42	"
	H	Wooten Delia I—†	748	housewife	34	"
	K	Kelley David	748	waiter	25	"
	L	Saunders Rena—†	748	housewife	39	"
	M	Craig Lillian G—†	750	nurse	36	"
	N	Craig Septimus E	750	real estate	38	"
	O	Ham Gregg	750	porter	33	6 Dilworth
	P	Ham Nannie J—†	750	housewife	45	6 "
	R	Frazer Bernice—†	750	"	31	here
	S	Frazer Charles G	750	chef	37	"
	T	Busch Charles L	752	porter	57	"
	U	Busch Rowella—†	752	domestic	40	"
	V	Foster Charlotte—†	752	housekeeper	48	"
	W	Thompson Burnett	752	machinist	37	"
	X	Thompson Sibyl C—†	752	housewife	27	"
	Y	Burnett Amos H	752	clerk	52	"
	z	Burnett Catherine—†	752	housewife	38	"
	A	Colston Flora—†	768	houseworker	28	14 Windsor
	B	Lypen Ethelbart	768	real estate	28	here
	C	Parker Flora—†	768	housekeeper	60	Ohio
	D	Nelson Fredrick H	768	drug clerk	32	here
	E	Nelson Yvonne—†	768	housewife	28	"
	F	Perkins Carl	768	galvanizer	25	Cambridge
	G	Buchanan Hubert	768	porter	40	29 Hammond
	H	Buchanan Ruth E—†	768	housewife	33	29 "
	K	Harris Eliza—†	768	houseworker	62	29 "
	L	Walker Charlotte M—†	768	housewife	36	176 Springfield
	M	Walker William P	768	porter	38	176 "

Page.	Letter.	FULL NAME.	Residence, April 1, 1926.	Occupation.	Supposed Age.	Reported Residence, April 1, 1925. Street and Number.

Columbus Avenue—Continued

N	Black Brenda—†	768	housewife	26	here
O	Black James S	768	galvanizer	38	"
P	Granum Cyril	768	porter	32	"
R	Granum Louise—†	768	housewife	29	"
S	Gordon Joseph H	768	chef	39	23 Dundee
T	Gordon Mildred—†	768	housewife	28	23 "
V	Baumgardner Victoria—†	768	student	22	here
W	Dixon Catherine—†	768	housewife	42	"
X	Dixon Herbert	768	chauffeur	42	"
Y	Gordon Lillian—†	768	houseworker	52	"
Z	Brown Dora—†	768	housewife	31	"
A	Brown Walter	768	porter	38	"
D	Sampson Clarence E	772	salesman	46	"
E	Sampson Minnie E—†	772	housewife	42	"
F	Nantias Algea J	772	roofer	21	"
G	Nantias Napoleon	772	cigarmaker	57	"
H	Nantias Odina—†	772	housewife	55	"
K	Pappas Eva—†	772	"	45	422 Tremont
L	Pappas John	772	waiter	48	422 "
M	Marshall Catherine—†	774	housewife	57	here
N	Marshall Fredrick O	774	watchman	74	"
O	Grebstein Elizabeth—†	774	housekeeper	24	"
P	Grebstein Richard	774	weaver	53	"
R	Sullivan James P	774	chauffeur	23	"
S	Sullivan John J	774	"	24	"
T	Sullivan Margaret—†	774	housewife	52	"
U	Sullivan Patrick	774	chauffeur	54	"
V	Davis Peter	776	tailor	32	Georgia
W	Gibson Karl	776	"	39	Phila Pa
X	Day George F	776	waiter	34	Maryland
Y	Day Mary I—†	776	housekeeper	49	"
Z	Pierce Pearl—†	776	housewife	27	"
A	Pierce Wallace	776	porter	33	"
B	Segal Charles	778	storekeeper	34	here
C	Segal Jennie—†	778	housewife	28	"
D	Evora Alvaro J P	813	laborer	44	"
E	Evora Florence—†	813	housewife	36	"
F	Straub John S	813	machinist	36	431 Mass av
G	Straub Maud C—†	813	housewife	39	431 "
H	Casey Helen—†	813	waitress	43	here
K	Casey James J	813	electrician	45	"

Columbus Avenue—Continued

L	Casey Josephine—†	813	waitress	47	here
M	Casey Mary—†	813	housewife	35	"
N	Collins William F	815	laborer	36	6 E Dedham
O	Cook Clara H—†	815	housekeeper	40	6 "
P	McGaw William	815	retired	72	6 "
R	Emery Laura—†	815	housewife	28	136 Pembroke
S	Emery William C	815	woodworker	45	136 "
T	Cavanaugh William	815	hostler	36	here
U	Martin Charles C	815	laborer	24	"
V	Martin Della—†	815	housewife	49	"
W	Martin Henry J	815	mattressmaker	52	"
X	Karlson Winslow	819	coach	34	"
Y	Cusick Catherine M—†	819	housewife	28	"
Z	Cusick Herbert J	819	printer	25	"
A	Jones Hazel—†	819	housewife	48	"
B	Jones Robert P	819	telegrapher	52	"
E	Modestino Rose —†	834	housekeeper	55	"
F	McKay Joseph W	834	brakeman	59	"
G	McKay Nellie B—†	834	housewife	57	"
H	Hubbad Charles L	834	forester	38	"
K	Hubbard Jessie M—†	834	housewife	40	"
L	Francis Helen S—†	836	"	20	"
M	Francis Herbert W	836	chauffeur	25	"
N	Barry Margaret A—†	836	housekeeper	80	"
P	Raney Laura—†	836	housewife	31	"
O	Raney Louis	836	machinist	33	"
S	McNeil Francis J	853	clerk	35	"
T	McNeil Margaret E—†	853	housewife	35	"
U	Banch Thomas J	853	fireman	46	"
V	Murray Theadore—†	853	messenger	20	"
W	Clark Emily —†	583	laundress	32	Chelsea
X	Saunders Hannah—†	853	housewife	56	here
Y	Saunders John T	853	fireman	70	"
Z	Gray Manuel	855	chauffeur	30	"
A	Gray Mary—†	855	housewife	31	"
B	Fickias Caroline—†	855	forewoman	34	"
C	Fickias Eva—†	855	stitcher	27	"
D	Fickias George W	855	letter carrier	31	"
E	Fickias Louise—†	855	housekeeper	35	"
F	Fickas Philip	855	gardener	66	"
G	McNicholas John J	855	policeman	33	109 Vernon

Page.	Letter.	FULL NAME.	Residence, April 1, 1925.	Occupation.	Supposed Age.	Reported Residence, April 1, 1925. Street and Number.

Columbus Avenue—Continued

H	McNicholas Margaret E—†	855	housewife	25	109 Vernon
K	Allen George E	856	porter	47	here
L	Baylor Emma —†	856	houseworker	34	290 Newbury
M	Coleman Charles	856	chauffeur	45	here
N	Desmond Anna H—†	856	housekeeper	33	"
O	O'Connell Edith F—†	857	housewife	25	164 Old Colony av
P	O'Connell Michael J	857	cook	29	2 Ewer
R	Hare Josephine R—†	857	housekeeper	25	30 Sarsfield
S	Dowd Christina E—†	857	housewife	25	here
T	Dowd Lawrence V	857	bookkeeper	27	"
U	Hare Theresa K—†	857	operator	20	30 Sarsfield
V	Hutchins Edith —†	860	housewife	43	106 Alexander
W	Hutchins Joseph	860	chef	33	106 "
X	Kgergard Paul	860	painter	32	New York
Y	Galatas Edith—†	860	housewife	28	here
Z	Galatas Louis	860	druggist	34	"
A	Regan Irene—†	860	housewife	28	"
B	Regan Wilbert F	860	machinist	42	"
C	Gardner Albert	860	clerk	27	Chicago Ill
D	Moulton Jeffry	860	electrician	27	1845 Dor av
E	Moulton Ruth M—†	860	housewife	22	1845 "
F	Ruel Harriet—†	860	"	23	here
G	Ruel Hubert N	860	operator	28	"
H	Morrison Hattie—†	860	tel operator	33	Canada
K	McCarty Josephine—†	860	forewoman	42	here
L	Preston Grace—†	860	housewife	47	"
M	Preston Leroy W	860	chauffeur	35	"
N	Kuegel Ernest	860	"	27	"
O	Kuegel Florence—†	860	housewife	25	"
P	Gardner Sadie—†	864	saleswoman	36	"
R	Sgolin William	864	chauffeur	23	Martha's Vineyard
S	Cunningham Eva—†	864	housewife	24	here
T	Cunningham James J	864	superintendant	27	"
U	Cunningham Louise—†	864	tel operator	24	"
V	Cunningham Michael J	864	chauffeur	28	"
W	Scott Clara M—†	864	housewife	25	735 Tremont
X	Scott Fred W	864	welder	26	735 "
Y	Ruel Evariste	864	taxi driver	25	here
Z	Ruel Margaretto—†	864	housewife	23	"
A	Lavery James M	864	chauffeur	41	"

9

Page.	Letter.	FULL NAME.	Residence, April 1, 1926.	Occupation.	Supposed Age.	Reported Residence, April 1, 1925. Street and Number.

Columbus Avenue—Continued

	B	Lavery Mary K—†	864	housekeeper	39	here
	C	Burnside David	864	salesman	29	"
	D	Burnside Dorothy—†	864	housewife	25	"
	E	Manza Anthony A	864	teamster	33	"
	F	Manza Grace E—†	864	housewife	34	"
	G	Turner Cary L—†	864	"	40	"
	H	Turner Herbert N	864	garage maker	42	"
	K	Boyle Joseph	864	longshoreman	24	117 D
	L	Doyle Helen—†	864	housekeeper	32	Worcester
	N	McDonald John	864	longshoreman	28	142 Bowen
	M	Quinn Robert	864	"	40	260 Shawmut av
	O	Slamin Harriett S—†	868	housewife	29	24 Julian
	P	Slamin John A	868	clerk	29	24 "
	R	Mulcahy Alice I—†	868	housewife	39	15 Holborn
	S	Mulcahy Michael B	868	clerk	41	15 "
	T	Barry Anne—†	868	housewife	37	here
	U	Barry Leonard S	868	ironworker	37	"
	V	Miliotis George	868	cook	27	Ipswich
	W	Miliotis Margarett—†	868	housewife	27	"
	X	Lambert Sophie—†	868	housekeeper	65	11 Marble
	Y	Sullivan Arthur M	868	repairman	42	11 "
	A	Pike Bertha O—†	868	shoe packer	32	1188 Col av
	B	Pike Catherine—†	868	housewife	54	1188 "
	C	Pike Eva W—†	868	shoeworker	30	1188 "
	D	Pike Mary E—†	868	stitcher	24	1188 "
	E	Kenney Catherine—†	868	housewife	25	1188 "
	F	Kenney Peter L	868	chauffeur	25	1188 "
	G	Zollinger Harry J	868	"	32	864 "
	H	Zollinger Rose—†	868	housewife	35	864 "
	K	Hanson Edmund	868	cigarmaker	41	here
	L	Hanson Marie—†	868	housewife	42	"
	M	Sole Agnes—†	872	"	26	unknown
	N	Sole Harry	872	ironworker	37	"
	O	Maminas John G	872	janitor	50	here
	R	Campbell Ethel—†	872	housewife	28	"
	S	Drokas Charles	872	waiter	25	"
	T	Drokas Peter	872	clerk	27	"
	U	Kokos James	872	waiter	28	"
	V	Kokas Lena—†	872	housewife	33	"
	W	Lalonde Edward	872	waiter	26	"
	X	Voutsas Lucia—†	872	housewife	24	Greece

Page.	Letter.	FULL NAME.	Residence, April 1, 1926.	Occupation.	Supposed Age.	Reported Residence, April 1, 1925. Street and Number.

Columbus Avenue—Continued

	Y	Vantslas Pericles	872	proprietor	37	80 Chandler
	z	French Alice—†	872	housekeeper	35	555 Mass av
	B	Brunton Ethel—†	872	waitress	28	here
	D	Green Elma W	878	storekeeper	28	"
	E	O'Neil Mary—†	880	housewife	30	"
	F	O'Neil Thomas	880	caretaker	37	"
	G	Lord Mary—†	902	housewife	35	"
	H	Lord William	902	laborer	30	"
	K	Newell Chaucey P	902	chef	47	Rhode Island
	L	Newell Katherine A—†	902	housewife	47	"
	M	Smith Ruth—†	902	"	58	here
	N	Yukumsky Adam	904	shoeworker	30	223 Wash'n
	O	Yukumsky Emma—†	904	housewife	28	223 "
	P	Conway Annie—†	904	at home	73	50 Thorndike
	R	Fay Mary—†	904	laundress	38	50 "
	S	Cashman Ellen—†	904	housekeeper	64	Pittsfield
	T	Stasis Anna—†	906	housewife	54	2 Weston pl
	U	Stasis Benjamin	906	laborer	60	2 "
	V	Sennott Harry J	906	machinist	40	here
	W	Sennott Mary F—†	906	housewife	32	"
	X	Riley Alice—†	906	"	43	"
	Y	Riley William L	906	custodian	45	"
	Z	Garvey Annie F—†	908	housewife	56	"
	A	Garvey George H	908	finisher	56	"
	B	Lynch Catherine—†	908	laundress	48	"
	C	Banks James P	908	waiter	50	"
	D	Olson Johanna—†	910	at home	75	"
	E	Murphy Catherine—†	910	dressmaker	60	"
	F	Johnson Josephine—†	910	laundress	57	"
	G	Buckley Catherine—†	912	clerk	42	"
	H	Johnson Anna—†	912	laundress	62	New York
	K	Blance Robert	912	engineer	50	E Northfield
	L	Sullivan Dennis	914	stableman	45	here
	M	Tracy John	914	laborer	50	"
	N	Soronson Mary—†	914	laundress	87	"
	O	Fowler Catherine E—†	916	"	65	1241 Col av
	P	Fowler Mary E—†	916	"	42	1241 "
	R	Phillips Lucy—†	916	shoeworker	40	61 Whittier

Page.	Letter.	Full Name.	Residence, April 1, 1926.	Occupation.	Supposed Age.	Reported Residence, April 1, 1925. Street and Number.

Coventry Street

	U	Marshall Carry—†	7	housewife	58	18 Burke
	V	Marshall James	7	clerk	32	18 "
	W	Jumper Ruth—†	7	housewife	20	here
	X	Jumper Sally—†	7	"	55	"
	Y	Jumper Samuel	7	clerk	26	"
	Z	Anderson Gladys—†	7	housewife	39	61 Camden
	A	Anderson James	7	engineer	49	61 "
	B	Johnson Ella—†	7	housewife	39	8 Benton

Cunard Street

	D	Rosen Benjamin	3	laborer	24	here
	E	Rosen Bessie—†	3	housewife	45	"
	F	Ahoyian Harry	3	shoeworker	39	"
	G	Ahoyian Satenig—†	3	housewife	27	"
	H	Cohan Abraham	3	tailor	32	"
	K	Cohan Celia—†	3	housewife	27	"
	L	Brust Mary—†	5	"	40	1196 Tremont
	M	Brust Theodore W	5	laborer	51	1196 "
	N	Pahigian Armen	5	salesman	39	here
	O	Pahigian Derkin—†	5	housewife	35	"
	P	Baldin Mamie—†	5	domestic	24	18 Burke
	R	Christian Joseph F	5	laborer	51	18 "
	S	Smith Ottile—†	5	housewife	38	18 "
	T	Butler Nora—†	7	"	32	here
	U	Butler William	7	shoeworker	33	"
	V	Alaimo Ida—†	7	housewife	32	"
	W	Alaimo Joseph	7	tailor	41	"
	X	Ashjian James	7	shoeworker	30	"
	Y	Ashjian Rose—†	7	housewife	68	"
	Z	Burke Mary—†	8	"	48	"
	A	Burke Patrick J	8	laborer	50	"
	B	Burke William P	8	clerk	20	"
	C	Gardner Agnes—†	8	housewife	58	"
	D	Gardner Agnes E—†	8	packer	20	"
	E	Gardner Edward A	8	watchman	58	"
	F	Lynch John	8	laborer	59	"
	G	Lynch Joseph P	8	carpenter	24	"
	H	Lynch Mary T—†	8	bookkeeper	21	"

12

Cunard Street—Continued

	K	Lynch Teresa—†	8	housewife	51	here
	L	Lightfoot Cecile—†	9	domestic	24	120 Bower
	M	Lightfoot Wilber	9	porter	25	New York
	N	Makel Florence—†	9	housewife	45	394 Northampton
	O	Makel Luther	9	laborer	48	394 "
	P	Pierce Edward L	9	"	50	39 Sarsfield
	R	Pierce Viola—†	9	housewife	55	39 "
	T	Carney Olivia T—†	10	"	34	here
	U	Carney William L	10	laborer	37	"
	V	Gardner Florence—†	10	housekeeper	39	"
	W	Gardner John	10	porter	40	"
	X	Montgomery Rebecca—†	10	housewife	53	"
	Y	Montgomery William	10	porter	57	"
	B	Price Charles H	12	retired	75	"
	C	Price Charles H, jr	12	policeman	40	"
	D	Price Sophia C—†	12	housewife	66	"
	E	Price George R	12	porter	54	"
	F	Price Julia—†	12	housewife	49	"
	G	Dickerson Hattie L—†	12	housekeeper	46	"
	H	Gates Ella—†	12	domestic	40	"
	K	Still Edwin	12A	printer	62	"
	M	Atus Annie—†	18	housewife	35	Brockton
	N	Atus Roy	18	laborer	34	"
	O	Rue Isabella—†	18	housewife	31	28 Westminster
	P	Rue John A	18	laborer	36	28 "
	R	Wilson Claude	18	porter	29	105 Hammond
	S	Wilson Cyril	18	laborer	27	105 "
	T	Williams Laura—†	18	housewife	55	here
	U	Williams Rachel—†	18	domestic	31	"
	V	Lumpkins George W	18	clerk	35	Washington
	W	Lumpkins Nancy—†	18	housewife	33	"
	X	Chisholm Elizabeth—†	18	domestic	25	here
	Y	Fletcher George	18	laborer	35	"
	Z	Miller Herbert	18	"	40	"
	A	Fountain Wilhemina—†	18	domestic	30	unknown
	B	King Sallie—†	18	"	60	32 Cunard
	C	Simpson Henry	18	laborer	22	here
	D	Simpson Myrtle—†	18	domestic	27	"
	E	Price Mary—†	18	tailoress	36	27 Greenwich
	F	Wright Mathew	18	laborer	35	32 Newcomb
	M	Edmondson Samuel J	30	"	41	here

13

Page.	Letter.	Full Name.	Residence, April 1, 1926.	Occupation.	Supposed Age.	Reported Residence, April 1, 1925. Street and Number.

Cunard Street—Continued

	N	Hill Paralee—†	30	domestic	35	here
	o	Hill William M	30	laborer	50	"
	P	Kelly William J	30	"	50	1059 Tremont
	R	Henderson Charles	30	porter	57	here
	s	Henderson Helen—†	30	housewife	74	"
	T	Stephens Katie—†	30	"	47	"
	u	Stephens William	30	laborer	65	"
	v	Cotton Alice E—†	31	domestic	37	"
	w	Birsh William	31	laborer	59	"
	x	James Arthur	31	"	35	"
	y	James Nancy—†	31	housewife	61	"
	z	Brown Thomas	31	laborer	50	"
	A	Gallimore Johana—†	31	domestic	42	"
	B	Offley Pearl—†	31	"	27	33 Cunard
	c	Offley Robert C	31	porter	29	33 "
	D	Williams Annie—†	31	housewife	23	8 Sawyer
	E	Williams Redding	31	laborer	41	8 "
	F	Watts Mary—†	31	domestic	43	Hartford
	G	Tines Edith—†	31	"	44	Brookline
	H	Tines Robert	31	laborer	22	Halifax N S
	K	Dixon Cecil	31	porter	42	here
	L	Dixon Stella—†	31	housewife	39	"
	M	Ray Carrie—†	31	domestic	27	"
	N	Ray Earl	31	chauffeur	28	"
	o	Pitt Eva—†	32	domestic	38	"
	P	Dennison Jacob	32	porter	32	"
	R	Dent Mary—†	32	housekeeper	28	"
	s	Ferguson William	32	chauffeur	26	"
	T	Brannon Edward	32	laborer	54	87 Sterling
	u	Dorsey Catherine L—†	32	housekeeper	23	87 "
	v	Haynes Mary—†	33	domestic	33	here
	w	Belle Arnold	33	laborer	33	"
	x	Belle Marguerite—†	33	housewife	33	"
	y	Crowell Edward	33	waiter	24	New Bedford
	z	Smith Wilbur	33	laborer	43	Providence R I
	A	West Maude—†	33	domestic	30	Woburn
	B	Chase Gladys—†	33	"	25	Newport R I
	c	Moore David	33	laborer	25	9 Burke
	D	Wright Elnor—†	33	at home	26	9 "
	E	Gaynor Josiah	33	carpenter	31	186 Northampton
	F	Gaynor Loretta—†	33	housewife	26	186 "

14

Cunard Street—Continued

K	Bornstein Anna—†	34	housekeeper	21	here
H	Bornstein Louis	34	tailor	52	"
L	Osborne Raymond T	34	chauffeur	22	"
M	Reevs Fannie—†	34	housewife	45	"
N	Reevs John A	34	laborer	46	"
O	Ayers Lucian	34	student	24	Wash'n D C
P	Simmons Bessie—†	34	housewife	41	here
R	Simmons George	34	laborer	42	"
S	Simmons Percey	34	clerk	22	"
T	Parrish Isabelle—†	35	housewife	23	980 Tremont
U	Parrish William I	35	laborer	24	980 "
V	Hall Anna—†	35	domestic	50	here
W	Hall Lucy—†	35	waitress	22	"
X	Page Ethel - †	35	"	25	"
Y	Milton Elizabeth—†	35	housewife	30	"
Z	Milton William	35	laborer	25	"
A	Brown James	35	"	32	92 Westminst'r
B	Scoltock Eva - †	35	housewife	32	712 Shawmut av
C	Scoltock Florence—†	35	domestic	32	92 Westminst'r
D	Scoltock John	35	laborer	31	712 Shawmut av
F	Carver Margaret A—†	36	housewife	63	here
G	Carver Michael F	36	janitor	72	"
H	Waterhouse Eugene	36	laborer	38	"
K	Waterhouse Julia—†	36	housewife	24	"
L	Hill Lee	36	retired	42	Springfield
M	Hill Mary—†	36	housewife	35	"
N	Pierce Alice W—†	36	milliner	24	here
O	Pierce Emerson J	36	clerk	26	"
P	Pierce Frances E—†	36	elevatorwoman	22	"
R	Pierce Mattie W—†	36	housewife	52	"
S	Meyers Margaret—†	37	domestic	40	"
T	Addison Angeline G—†	37	housewife	42	"
U	Addison Marion W	37	gardener	52	"
V	Juitt Eva—†	37	domestic	24	"
X	Lynch Julia—†	38	"	45	"
Y	Short Benjamin	38	laborer	35	"
Z	Wingood Arnold	38	"	38	12 Northfield
A	Wingood Etoile—†	38	domestic	37	12 "
B	Jackson Bertha—†	38	housewife	32	here
C	Jackson Edward	38	laborer	44	"
D	Wilson Daniel F	39	waiter	42	"

15

Cunard Street—Continued

Letter	Full Name	Residence	Occupation	Age	Reported Residence
E	Wilson Matilda—†	39	housewife	35	here
F	Langford Joseph	39	laborer	42	"
G	Montgomery John J	39	watchman	35	81 Highland Park
H	Smith Florence—†	39	domestic	39	here
K	Francis Chester H	39	laborer	28	"
L	Francis David E	39	janitor	60	"
M	Francis Henrietta—†	39	domestic	52	"
O	Greenidge Joseph	41	laborer	45	44 Warwick
P	Greenidge Vivian—†	41	housewife	29	44 "
R	Clarke Samuel	41	laborer	53	here
S	Clarke Zelma—†	41	housewife	43	"
T	Mitchell Agnes—†	41	"	22	Nova Scotia
U	Mitchell Harry	41	laborer	24	"
V	Smith Edward H	42	clerk	35	here
W	Smith Nellie E—†	42	housewife	30	"
X	Graves Mary—†	42	at home	60	Wash'n D C
Y	Newkirk Frances—†	42	domestic	40	here
Z	Nichols Lottie L—†	42	housewife	34	"
A	Nichols Robert L	42	attendant	34	"
B	Brown Edith—†	42	student	21	17 Greenwich pk
C	Jackson Jennie—†	42	presser	45	here
D	Jones Alice—†	42	housewife	47	"
E	Jones Bernard H	42	painter	46	"
F	Scott Sallie—†	42	domestic	34	"
G	Weston Lulla—†	42	"	50	"
H	Cross Marie—†	42	"	60	"
K	Mitchell John	42	porter	59	"
L	Smith Marion—†	42	domestic	32	"
M	Bell Julius	42	laborer	55	"
N	Bell Mollie—†	42	housewife	40	"
O	Carney Harry F	42	attendant	42	"
P	Carney Jennie—†	42	housewife	42	"
R	Dabbs William	42	laborer	22	"
S	Pankin Nannie—†	42	domestic	46	"

Drew Place

Letter	Full Name	Residence	Occupation	Age	Reported Residence
T	Brown Charlotte—†	1	housewife	49	here
U	Horton Mary—†	1	cashier	34	3 Drew pl
V	Brown Robert H	1	painter	48	here

Page.	Letter.	FULL NAME.	Residence, April 1, 1926.	Occupation.	Supposed Age.	Reported Residence, April 1, 1925. Street and Number.

Drew Place—Continued

	w	Eldridge William	1	mechanic	50	here
	x	O'Neil Mary —†	2	housewife	64	"
	y	O'Neil Richard	2	inspector	77	"
	z	Copper Celica —†	2	seamstress	50	"
	a	Holmes Arvilla L—†	3	housewife	44	"
	b	Holmes Stephen	3	hostler	45	"
	c	Leadbetter Lavina—†	3	domestic	53	22 Wellington
	g	Novack Antonio	4	rubberworker	48	here

Feiling Place

	h	Hoffman Emma—†	1	housewife	45	here
	k	Hoffman Paul	1	baker	55	"
	l	O'Brien Alice —†	2	brushmaker	21	"
	m	O'Brien Edward	2	teamster	49	"
	n	O'Brien Louise—†	2	housewife	50	"
	o	McCarthy Daniel	3	chauffeur	51	"
	p	McCarthy Margaret—†	3	housewife	44	"
	r	Boos Fritz	4	baker	43	43 Weston
	s	Boos Mary—†	4	housewife	35	43 "
	t	Lucca Giatano—†	4	"	34	33 Clark
	u	Lucca Maurio	4	baker	44	33 "

Grinnell Street

	v	Vaugh Maud—†	6	housekeeper	36	99 Warwick
	w	Brinkert Emma F—†	6	stitcher	21	here
	x	Brinkert Emma—†	6	housewife	49	"
	y	Brinkert Richard	6	chauffeur	54	"
	z	Steward John B	8	painter	33	83 W Rutland sq
	a	Steward Marion—†	8	housewife	31	83 "
	b	Henry Christina—†	8	"	35	1059 Tremont
	c	Henry George T	8	chauffeur	53	1059 "
	d	Schlappi Christian	8	carpenter	60	here
	e	Schlappi Jacob	8	machinist	30	"

Hammett Street

F	Paul Anna—†	1	nurse	36	here
G	Paul Charles M	1	piano tuner	36	"
H	Walsh James M	1	laborer	24	"
K	Walsh Joseph	1	"	59	"
L	Walsh Nora—†	1	housewife	58	"
M	Harrington Edward J	1	conductor	36	3 Hammett
N	Harrington Mary M—†	1	housewife	30	3 "
O	Sullivan Catherine—†	1	clerk	22	3 "
P	Sullivan Margaret—†	1	"	28	3 "
R	Sullivan Mary—†	1	housewife	40	3 "
S	McRae Isabella—†	3	housekeeper	43	35 Haskins
T	Morrison Anna—†	3	at home	77	35 "
U	Monahan Margaret—†	3	housewife	50	here
V	Monahan Michael	3	laborer	50	"
W	Chapple Catherine—†	3	housewife	22	"
X	Chapple Thomas E	3	foreman	25	"
Y	O'Hara Bridget—†	3	housewife	42	"
Z	O'Hara Patrick	3	laborer	53	"
B	Honway Gertrude—†	4	packer	25	"
C	Honway Patrick	4	watchman	64	"
D	Bowen Lydia M—†	4	clerk	28	"
E	Sweetzer Clarence H	4	chauffeur	31	"
F	Sweetzer Florence M—†	4	housewife	59	"
G	Sweetzer Williard M	4	watchman	57	"
H	Lynch Jeremiah	4	clerk	50	"
K	Lynch Joseph M	4	decorator	26	"
L	Totten Edward A	4	clerk	26	"
M	Totten Helen T—†	4	housewife	23	"
N	Morgan Alma M—†	5	"	32	"
O	Morgan Ross C	5	painter	32	"
P	Fitzgerald John	5	chauffeur	35	7 Hammett
R	Fitzgerald Mary K—†	5	housewife	34	7 "
S	Carroll Mary C—†	5	"	30	here
T	Carroll William F	5	chauffeur	31	"
U	Murphy Patrick L	5	plumber	33	74 Mallet
V	Poirier Joseph T	5	carpenter	34	8 Goldsmith pl
W	Poirier Margaret—†	5	housewife	25	7 "
X	McNamara Thomas F	6	real estate	50	here
Z	Waterman Charles T	6	broker	38	"
A	Waterman George A	6	clerk	28	"

18

Page.	Letter.	FULL NAME.	Residence, April 1, 1926.	Occupation.	Supposed Age.	Reported Residence, April 1, 1925. Street and Number.

Hammett Street—Continued

B	Waterman Helen—†	6	clerk	23	here
C	Waterman Mary J—†	6	housewife	63	"
D	Waterman Phillip	6	clerk	21	"
E	Forrest John	6	laborer	62	"
F	Forrest Margaret—†	6	housewife	63	"
G	Power Margaret—†	6	"	56	"
H	Power William P	6	laborer	59	"
K	Reagan Elizabeth—†	6	waitress	48	"
L	Handren John F	6	laborer	34	"
M	McManus Isabella—†	6	housewife	55	"
N	Frieburger Julia C—†	6	"	24	934 Col av
O	Frieburger William F	6	chauffeur	25	934 "
P	McNamara Margaret B—†	6	housekeeper	36	934 "
R	Muliero Elizabeth B—†	6	"	26	934 "
S	Muliero Matthew C	6	machinist	26	934 "
T	Skelly Mabel—†	6	housewife	40	here
U	Skelly Thomas	6	chauffeur	45	"
V	Breslin James E	6	laborer	34	"
W	Breslin Mary—†	6	housewife	32	"
X	Griffen Ellen—†	6	domestic	58	"
Y	McDonald James E	6	chauffeur	27	"
Z	McDonald Mary—†	6	housewife	29	"
A	Ash Helen M—†	6	"	46	"
B	Ash Solomon	6	engineer	46	"
C	Gillis Robert	6	janitor	62	"
E	Gallagher Frank	6	laborer	65	"
F	Gallagher James	6	"	62	"
G	McLeod Catherine—†	7	housewife	38	9 Weston pl
H	Prance John H	7	engineer	42	here
K	Prance Mary A—†	7	housewife	40	"
L	Beck Henry	7	laborer	76	"
M	Beck Herbert E	7	fireman	45	"
N	Beck Marion—†	7	housewife	65	"
O	White Francis J	7	insurance agent	33	"
P	White Margaret V—†	7	housewife	31	"

Howe Court

R	Agoian Yartg	1	storekeeper	38	here
S	Garabedian Oscar	1	laborer	65	"

Page.	Letter.	FULL NAME.	Residence, April 1, 1926.	Occupation.	Supposed Age.	Reported Residence, April 1, 1925. Street and Number.

Howe Court—Continued

T	Garabedian Sultan—†	1	housewife	65	here
U	Mousechian Arshalous—†	1	"	41	"
V	Mousechian Nahabed	1	rubberworker	41	"
W	Scanlon Catherine A—†	2	housekeeper	59	"
X	Scanlon Francis J	2	chauffeur	32	"

Newbern Court

Y	Henry Jane—†	3	domestic	72	here
Z	Price Eliza—†	3	"	72	"

Newbern Street

A	MacGregor Mary E—†	15	housewife	29	here
B	MacGregor Willard	15	guard	35	"
C	Small James	15	chauffeur	35	"
D	Small Theresa—†	15	domestic	33	"
E	Wallace Clara—†	15	housekeeper	55	"
F	Wallace Watson	15	laborer	60	"
G	Frye Mary F—†	15	housekeeper	54	New York
H	Mill Moses	15	laborer	30	"
K	Gross Anna L—†	16	housewife	52	here
L	Gross Joseph D	16	baker	53	"
M	Gross George H	16	electrician	25	"
N	Gross Matilda A—†	16	dressmaker	20	"
O	Wolf Emma P—†	16	housewife	50	"
P	Wolf Philip J	16	baker	54	"
R	Bamberry Mary—†	17	domestic	45	80 Williams
S	Nelson Thomas	17	laborer	62	80 "
T	Wilkinson Margaret L—†	18	housewife	39	here
U	Wilkinson Thomas	18	janitor	53	"
V	Garland Louise—†	18	housekeeper	32	"
W	McKay Mary—†	18	laundry worker	60	"
X	Kelly Annie—†	18	housekeeper	72	"
Y	Clay Frank	19	auto washer	65	"
Z	Smith Albert	19	laborer	50	"
A	Smith Mary—†	19	housewife	48	"
B	Smith Mary V—†	19	"	34	"

20

Newbern Street—Continued

c	Smith William E	19	auto mechanic	47	here
d	Williams Alfred	19	fireman	23	16 Hubert
e	Williams Lacie L.	19	laborer	20	19 "
f	Williams Lewis	19	"	62	19 "
g	Williams Mary A—†	19	housewife	58	19 "
h	Almond Anna —†	19	domestic	34	here
k	Almond Fred	19	chauffeur	30	"
m	Moxley Edward J	19	watchman	42	"
n	Moxley Edward J	19	elevatorman	21	"
o	Moxley Gertrude—†	19	domestic	34	"
p	Cavil William E	19	actor	23	"
r	Connor Catherine C— †	19	domestic	63	"
s	Kenny Annie—†	23	housewife	48	"
t	Kenny Emily- †	23	clerk	21	"
u	Kenny Frances A—†	23	hairdresser	27	"
v	Kenny Frederick A	23	expressman	50	"
w	Gouleas Archileas	23	laborer	41	11 Palmer
x	Gouleas Hannah—†	23	housewife	47	11 "
y	Davis Fred	23	steamfitter	38	here
z	Peterson Martin	23	painter	46	"
b	Mason Ethel— †	26	housekeeper	36	"
c	Mason Ralph	26	teamster	38	"
d	Vanible Martha —†	26	factory worker	36	"
e	Lee Eliza—†	27	housekeeper	88	"
f	Lee Sarah E— †	27	houseworker	40	"
g	Mason Alice—†	28	housekeeper	27	"
h	Mason Henrietta—†	28	"	46	"
k	Smith George	28	car cleaner	27	"
l	Reed Alonzo	30	porter	31	"
m	Reed Harriett—†	30	housewife	42	"
n	Hadley Gertrude—†	31	"	29	"
o	Hadley William	31	porter	32	"
p	Williams Richard	32	boilermaker	27	"
r	Williams Viola—†	32	housewife	31	"
s	Healey Catherine—†	34	housekeeper	49	"
t	Healey John	34	painter	47	"
v	Rosen Amelia E—†	36	stenographer	21	"
w	Rosen Charles F	36	machinist	27	"
x	Rosen John	36	"	52	"
y	Rosen Mary E—†	36	housewife	52	"
z	Koff Victoria—†	38	storekeeper	60	"

21

Page.	Letter.	FULL NAME.	Residence, April 1, 1926.	Occupation.	Supposed Age.	Reported Residence, April 1, 1925. Street and Number.

Pratt Court

	B	Broph Jane—†	1	housewife	52	10A Cabot
	C	Broph William	1	laborer	21	here
	D	McKenna John T	1	chauffeur	31	New York City
	E	Gallagher Mary—†	2	at home	61	here
	F	Rose Elizabeth—†	2	housewife	38	"
	G	Wiggin James	2	shoecutter	65	"
	H	McFarland James F	3	shipper	30	"
	K	McFarland Pauline—†	3	housewife	28	"
	L	Winkler Charles	4	painter	57	"
	M	Winkler Gertrude—†	4	housewife	48	"
	O	Buck Eulalia M—†	5	"	46	"
	P	Buck James	5	foreman	33	"
	N	Crandall Henry	5	clerk	66	"
	R	Irwin Sadie—†	6	domestic	41	320 Longwood av
	S	Simmons Mary E—†	6	housewife	57	here

Ruggles Street

	Y	Barker Jennette—†	173	social worker	57	here
	Z	Channel Bertha—†	173	housekeeper	41	104 Seaver
	A	Channel Horace L	173	sexton	65	104 "
	B	Channel John W	173	teacher	43	104 "
	C	Crowe Ella—†	173	missionary	70	here
	D	Gascarro Elizabeth—†	175	housewife	37	47 Weston
	E	Gascarro John	175	laborer	40	47 "
	F	Ross Alexander	177	chauffeur	23	here
	G	Ross Bessie—†	177	housewife	46	"
	H	Ross Hugh	177	chauffeur	22	"
	L	Mudge Charles R	199	laborer	53	"
	M	Mudge James J	199	vocalist	24	Missouri
	N	Mudge Mary B—†	199	housewife	50	here
	O	Mudge Mary V—†	199	saleswoman	21	"
	T	Brown Josephine—†	205	housekeeper	28	7 Weston pl
	U	Nickerl Anna—†	205	"	53	here
	V	Riley Alice—†	205	laundry worker	55	818 Harrison av
	Y	Raney Lillian—†	207	dressmaker	49	here
	W	Brown Charles	207	longshoreman	42	"
	X	Brown Ella—†	207	housewife	53	"

Letter.	FULL NAME.	Residence, April 1, 1926.	Occupation.	Supposed Age.	Reported Residence, April 1, 1925. Street and Number.

Sarsfield Street

C	Devlin Annie—†	7	housewife	52	here
D	Devlin Joseph F	7	packer	49	"
E	Collins Mary—†	7	clerk	44	"
F	Anderson Celia—†	7	laundress	46	"
G	Berry Margaret—†	8	housewife	30	Somerville
H	Berry Stanley	8	chauffeur	35	"
K	Donoghue James	8	"	26	here
L	Donoghue Mary—†	8	housewife	22	"
M	Reid Sadie—†	8	"	45	"
N	Reid William	8	laborer	55	"
P	Steere Helena—†	10	housekeeper	60	"
R	Boyle Bridget H—†	10	housewife	38	894 Hunt'n av
S	Boyle David P	10	garageman	41	894 "
T	Launders Catherine—†	10	domestic	37	894 "
U	Leser Dorothy—†	10	bookbinder	29	here
V	Leser Laura—†	10	housekeeper	60	"
W	Leser Madin—†	10	bookbinder	26	"
Y	Fay Julia C—†	11	at home	75	"
Z	Fay Richard J	11	clerk	41	"
A	Fay Sarah C—†	11	housewife	44	"
B	Gagne Alice M—†	11	"	48	"
C	Gagne Francis X	11	clockmaker	48	"
D	Hatfield Gertrude—†	12	housekeeper	44	"
E	Hatfield William	12	laborer	47	"
F	Knight Henry W	12	chauffeur	21	"
G	Gilgunn Thomas	12	laborer	23	Ireland
H	Ryter Alice—†	12	stitcher	34	here
K	Dowling Bridget—†	12	housekeeper	50	115 Worcester
L	Dowling Edward J	12	laborer	27	115 "
M	Jones Fannie—†	13	housekeeper	42	here
N	Smart Annie—†	13	domestic	36	48 Northfield
O	Wright Alverine—†	13	housewife	24	here
P	Wright Tobe W	13	porter	30	"
R	Davis Lulu—†	13	car cleaner	36	"
S	McGee Harriett—†	13	housekeeper	90	"
T	Doyle May—†	14	dressmaker	50	"
U	Regan Daniel J	14	laborer	60	"
V	Regan Hannah—†	14	housewife	60	"
W	Regan James A	14	chauffeur	31	"

23

Sarsfield Street—Continued

Letter	Full Name	Res.	Occupation	Age	Reported Residence
x	Morris Florence—†	14	laundress	55	here
z	Crockett Ethel V—†	15	housewife	23	19 Cottage av
A	Crockett Mitzel	15	porter	24	19 "
B	Freeman Bertha—†	15	cook	42	here
C	Marshall Ruth—†	15	stitcher	32	New York
D	Randolph Francis L	20	janitor	65	here
E	Randolph Ralph C	20	checker	30	"
F	Randolph Rose—†	20	housewife	62	"
H	Merrill Frederick H	24	clerk	53	"
K	Westwood Esther—†	24	stenographer	24	"
L	Westwood Nettie A—†	24	housekeeper	55	"
M	Westwood Walter	24	plumber	62	"
N	Maurice Mae—†	27	domestic	37	"
O	McCannell Alexander	27	clerk	39	"
P	McCannell Bertha—†	27	housewife	38	"
R	Arvidson Elizabeth—†	27	housekeeper	38	142 Gray
S	Arvidson Eugene	27	engineer	40	142 "
T	Hannaford Georgie—†	29	forewoman	40	here
U	Gloster James P	29	machinist	51	"
V	Gloster Rose—†	29	housewife	46	"
W	Hastings Frederick	29	laborer	46	"
X	Hastings Mary—†	29	housewife	46	"
Y	Johnson Allen A	30	laborer	45	421 Dudley
Z	Johnson Alma C—†	30	housewife	62	119 Cedar
A	Johnson Eric M	30	elevatorman	64	816 Shawmut av
B	Azevado Emanuel S	30	cook	29	here
C	Azevado Helen—†	30	housewife	27	"
D	Kelley Catherine—†	30	"	38	199 Vernon
E	Murray Bessie—†	30	clerk	40	199 "
F	Dragon Annie—†	32	housekeeper	30	New Hampshire
G	Dragon Frederick C	32	painter	33	"
H	Peterson Samuel	32	cook	55	Connecticut
K	Peterson Sarah—†	32	housekeeper	65	here
L	Larkin Andrew	32	fireman	47	"
M	Larkin Sarah—†	32	housewife	42	"
N	Paige Raul	36	machinist	31	"
O	Taintor Loring	36	painter	52	"
P	Taintor Mary—†	36	housekeeper	62	"
R	Howard Frank A	36	engineer	62	196 Vernon
S	Tobey Charles A	36	chauffeur	23	Maine
T	Tobey Mabel—†	36	housewife	21	196 Vernon

Page.	Letter	FULL NAME.	Residence, April 1, 1926.	Occupation.	Supposed Age.	Reported Residence, April 1, 1925. Street and Number.

Sarsfield Street—Continued

	U	Connolly Emma —†	36	laundress	37	here
	V	Grindrod Helen—†	38	housewife	31	"
	W	Grindrod William	38	salesman	28	"
	X	Thompson Anna —†	38	housewife	50	"
	X¹	Thompson William	38	plumber	52	"
	Y	Brinkert Catherine —†	38	housewife	27	"
	Z	Brinkert Herbert	38	chauffeur	27	"
	A	Johnson Louise—†	39	domestic	26	Arlington
	B	Lawrence Richard B	39	cook	26	93 W Springfield
	C	Ramos Gertrude —†	39	housewife	36	here
	D	Ramos Manuel F	39	chauffeur	34	"
	E	Dunkley Edith —†	39	housekeeper	47	"
	F	Touhey James	40	laborer	44	"
	G	Touhey Mary —†	40	housewife	33	"
	H	Dulong Helena —†	40	"	30	"
	K	Hart Edward P	40	chauffeur	24	"
	L	Hart Mary E —†	40	housewife	58	"
	M	Hanson Catherine —†	40	"	22	190 Blue Hill av
	N	Hanson James A	40	auto mechanic	28	190 "
	P	Binzy Delia —†	41	housekeeper	42	here
	R	Philips William H	41	cook	63	"
	S	Holmes Mary R —†	41	housekeeper	37	"
	T	McKenna Joseph	41	waiter	56	"
	U	Saunders Catherine —†	42	housewife	32	94 W Newton
	V	Saunders Charles	42	plumber	38	94 "
	W	McGee Catherine —†	42	housewife	47	44 Sarsfield
	X	McGee Charles, jr	42	switchman	49	44 "
	Y	Eliott William A	42	blacksmith	23	Canada
	Z	Hardiman Mary —†	42	shoeworker	23	New York
	A	Murphy Mary —†	42	housewife	50	here
	B	Lumbard Clyde	44	boxmaker	25	178 Cabot
	C	McDougall Ellen —†	44	housewife	56	here
	D	McDougall Sadie —†	44	bookbinder	29	"
	E	Murphy Patrick J	44	blacksmith	62	"
	F	Mayer Celia —†	44	stitcher	35	"

Sterling Street

	G	Walker Phoebe —†	142	domestic	71	here
	H	Dorsey Lucy —†	142	"	57	"

Page.	Letter.	FULL NAME.	Residence, April 1, 1926.	Occupation.	Supposed Age.	Reported Residence, April 1, 1925. Street and Number.

Tremont Street

	B	Woods Eral	968	janitor	30	Cambridge
	C	Wilson Margaret—†	968	housewife	40	here
	D	Wilson Oliver	968	janitor	38	"
	E	Hardwick Allen	968	laborer	25	"
	F	Hardwick Fredericka—†	968	housewife	25	"
	G	Reid Mabel—†	968	"	40	"
	K	Francis Charles E	972	fireman	29	"
	L	Francis Emma—†	972	housekeeper	57	"
	M	Mason James W	972	laborer	44	"
	N	Foster Mabel—†	972	housewife	30	Cambridge
	O	Foster Thomas	972	waiter	38	"
	P	Lew Harry	974	laundry worker	25	here
	S	Robinson Margaret—†	976	housekeeper	55	Cambridge
	T	Smith Gennie—†	976	"	53	here
	V	Parish Lucindie—†	980	"	49	"
	W	Mitchell Albert	980	porter	35	"
	X	Williams Henry	980	laborer	56	"
	Y	Williams Ida B—†	980	housewife	50	"
	Z	Adams Gabrial	980	porter	45	"
	A	Adams Zelma—†	980	housewife	20	"
	C	Anonie Eda—†	984	"	28	New York
	D	Anonie Robert	984	porter	33	"
	E	Lake Marrian—†	984	housewife	28	here
	F	Lake Samuel	984	janitor	30	"
	L	Russell Charles J	987	stevedore	50	"
	M	Russell Ethel G—†	987	housewife	48	"
	N	Cheltenham Albert	987	janitor	38	"
	O	Cheltenham Reginald	987	"	36	"
	P	Manley Ella—†	987	domestic	25	"
	S	Channer David	988	physician	39	"
	T	Channer Mertel—†	988	housewife	28	"
	U	Padmore Clifford	988	porter	42	"
	V	Padmore Lottie—†	988	housewife	35	"
	W	Nelson Anna—†	988	housekeeper	40	"
	X	Walker William	988	porter	30	"
	Y	Robinson George	989	longshoreman	45	"
	Z	Flint Elijah	989	retired	82	Nova Scotia
	A	Hunt Ellen—†	989	domestic	42	here
	B	Stokes Helen M—†	989	housewife	38	"
	C	Stokes James B	989	waiter	37	"

26

Tremont Street—Continued

G	Henson Francis A	991	musician	35	here
H	Williams Sadie—†	991	domestic	34	"
K	Ferguson Mary—†	991	"	62	"
L	Wyatt James	991	paperhanger	40	5 Burke
M	Niles Hattie—†	992	housekeeper	40	Cambridge
N	Thompson Doctor	992	waiter	49	here
O	Thompson Harriett—†	992	housewife	45	"
P	Lewis Vance	992	laborer	35	"
S	Jenkins George W	994	assembler	25	"
T	Jenkins Henry J	994	laborer	59	"
U	Jenkins Mabel—†	994	housewife	53	"
V	Jenkins Mabel M—†	994	factory worker	28	"
W	Jenkins Robert W	994	shoeworker	21	"
X	Farrell Delia—†	994	housewife	43	"
Y	Farrell Malachy	994	laborer	42	"
Z	Holland Charles F	994	nickelplater	47	"
C	Coughlin Catherine—†	998	clerk	44	"
D	McCauley Cecilia F—†	998	housewife	26	"
E	McCauley John	998	laborer	68	"
F	McCauley Joseph H	998	"	34	"
G	Milmore Amenda E—†	998	housewife	43	"
H	Milmore James J	998	retired	53	"
K	Milmore Vivian G—†	998	school teacher	22	"
L	Haskard Arthur R	998	engraver	22	"
M	Haskard Hannah M—†	998	housewife	55	"
N	Haskard Harold J	998	receiver	30	"
O	Haskard Walter G	998	clerk	55	"
P	Murray Alice—†	998	housekeeper	40	"
R	Murray James	998	laborer	35	"
S	Douglass Alfonzo C	999	student	41	"
T	Winn Mattie—†	999	domestic	30	"
U	Hayes Hattie—†	999	"	45	"
V	Slaughter Frank	999	gardener	75	"
Y	Fletcher Florence R—†	1003	housewife	60	1016 Tremont
A	Blair David K	1003	porter	39	Medford
B	Lee Mary G—†	1003	housewife	48	4 Burke
C	Lee Walter E	1003	waiter	58	4 "
D	Turner Rose—†	1003	saleswoman	23	4 "
E	Fay John P	1004	bookkeeper	58	here
F	Finnan Margaret E—†	1004	housekeeper	63	"

Tremont Street—Continued

T	Holiday Helen—†	1015	housewife	30	here
U	Holiday Lewis	1015	porter	46	"
W	Carter Cleora—†	1016	housewife	36	"
X	Carter James	1016	chauffeur	41	"
Y	Jones Annie—†	1016	housekeeper	32	Cambridge
B	Crawford Catherine L—†	1019	housewife	59	here
C	Crawford Edward J	1019	clerk	25	"
D	Crawford Frank E	1019	packer	64	"
E	Crawford Jennett E—†	1019	operator	33	"
F	Goodwin Frank C	1019	manager	30	"
G	Goodwin John E	1019	chauffeur	31	"
H	Goodwin Mary—†	1019	housekeeper	53	"
K	Berry Archabald J	1019½	druggist	39	"
L	Berry Edna M—†	1019½	housewife	28	"
M	Davis Rosa—†	1019½	cook	39	45 Warwick
N	Chappelle Lenora—†	1019½	maid	37	45 "
R	Joseph Manuel	1022	laborer	35	here
S	Joseph Ruth—†	1022	housewife	29	"
V	Henderson Albert	1022	porter	34	"
W	Henderson Harriett—†	1022	housewife	25	"
Z	Parker John	1025	janitor	49	"
A	Parker Nellie V—†	1025	housewife	43	"
B	Chandler Helen—†	1025	clerk	23	"
C	Williams Ella—†	1025	housewife	55	"
D	Williams Frank	1025	janitor	60	"
E	Brown Bertha J—†	1025	hairdresser	40	"
F	Brown Elsie W—†	1025	chiropodist	22	"
G	Piper Richard T	1025	clerk	25	"
H	Spikes Sallie—†	1026	housekeeper	29	Cambridge
K	Miller Linydia W—†	1026	housewife	40	here
L	Miller William C	1026	porter	48	"
M	Clifton Florance—†	1026	housekeeper	39	"
N	Hanscome Pheba—†	1026	"	69	"
O	Brown Margie—†	1026	dressmaker	29	"
P	Gray Margaret—†	1026	domestic	35	"
R	Rolston David W	1026	porter	49	"
U	Bolling William	1026	janitor	35	"
V	Sansford Helena—†	1026	housewife	43	"
W	Sansford Preston	1026	porter	44	"
X	Yates Harvey B	1027	policeman	34	"
Y	Yates Winton T—†	1027	housewife	31	"

Tremont Street—Continued

z	Turner Blanche —†	1027	housewife	27	here
A	Turner Charles W	1027	porter	39	"
E	Moore Alice M—†	1029½	dressmaker	21	"
F	Moore Alonzo J	1029½	tailor	44	"
G	Moore Alonzo J	1029½	porter	21	"
H	Moore Annie J—†	1029½	housekeeper	41	"
K	Moore Herbert H	1029½	porter	23	"
L	Adams Claude	1029½	druggist	56	41 Hammond
N	Berry Charlotte E—†	1031	housewife	35	here
O	Berry George A	1031	laborer	59	"
R	Wallace John A	1031	fruit dealer	62	"
W	Bowles Calvin C	1037	student	33	"
X	Bowles Cassandia A—†	1037	housewife	25	"
Y	Bowles George T	1037	manager	28	"
z	McCloskey Anna—†	1047	housewife	33	"
A	McCloskey Arthur J	1037	electrician	34	"
B	McDonough Annie—†	1037	housewife	60	"
C	McDonough James J	1037	chauffeur	28	"
D	McDonough John	1037	laborer	64	"
E	McDonough John C	1037	chauffeur	27	"
F	McDonough Mary M–†	1037	forewoman	29	"
G	McDonough Theresa C-†	1037	boxmaker	26	"
H	Lewis Arthur O	1037	brassfinisher	45	"
K	Lewis Margaret A—†	1037	housewife	42	"
L	Curtiss Felix	1037	steamfitter	37	"
M	Curtiss Sophie R—†	1037	housewife	39	"
N	DeRosa Charles T	1037	printer	40	"
O	DeRosa Julia —†	1037	housewife	71	"
P	O'Rourke Bridget —†	1037	housekeeper	61	"
R	O'Rourke John	1037	metalworker	22	"
S	O'Rourke Margaret —†	1037	forewoman	32	"
T	O'Rourke Mary —†	1037	clerk	34	"
U	O'Rourke Micheal J	1037	chauffeur	29	"
V	Lewis Elbridge C	1037	painter	31	Nashua N H
W	Lewis Mary E—†	1037	housewife	37	"
A	Nordling Alfreda M—†	1043	"	59	here
B	Nordling Charles O	1043	undertaker	55	"
C	Crawshaw Charles	1043	retired	60	"
D	Nelson John P	1043	engineer	46	6 Fort av
E	Nelson Mary M—†	1043	housewife	44	6 "
G	Lattimore Minnie—†	1045	glovemaker	20	here

Tremont Street—Continued

H	Lattimore Nellie—†	1045	car cleaner	36	here
K	Micheals Minnie—†	1045	housekeeper	37	"
L	Erickson Carl F	1045	waiter	46	"
M	Miller Edward S	1045	baker	29	32 Arnold
N	Miller Roslyn—†	1045	housewife	22	32 "
O	Tyler John W	1045	chauffeur	30	32 "
P	Trent Estelle—†	1045	housewife	30	101 Ruggles
R	Trent Rudolf L	1045	janitor	28	101 "
S	Albert Ellie—†	1045	domestic	32	21 Westminster
T	Ward Harriett—†	1045	housewife	29	here
U	White Elizabeth B—†	1045	laundress	53	"
V	White Lillian R—†	1045	attendant	20	"
W	Adams Walter C	1045	teamster	52	"
A	Wadsworth John	1050	porter	64	"
B	Davis Nellie—†	1050	housekeeper	40	"
D	Ponce Ethel M—†	1051	housewife	35	37 Cunard
E	Ponce Richard R	1051	porter	33	37 "
F	Foster Ellen T—†	1051	nurse	73	here
G	Foster Thomas A	1051	porter	39	"
H	Rodger Charles A	1051	marketman	47	"
K	Rodger Elizabeth—†	1051	housewife	39	"
L	Kirkland Cornelia—†	1051	maid	23	"
M	Wilson Lula V—†	1051	laundress	43	"
N	O'Donnell William J	1051	machinist	58	1029½ Tremont
O	Beard Francella—†	1051	housewife	37	53 Windsor
P	Beard John	1051	painter	36	53 "
R	Wells Curtis	1051	clerk	34	31 Cunard
T	Lashley Ella—†	1052	housewife	48	here
U	Lashley William	1052	porter	56	"
W	Jones Elizabeth J—†	1053	housewife	38	"
X	Jones Robert J	1053	janitor	52	"
Y	Foster William J	1053	teamster	31	New York
Z	Hoffman Edward	1053	laborer	50	here
A	Minters Aurelius	1053	porter	40	"
B	Stith Frank E	1053	machinist	34	"
C	Stith Zizmore—†	1053	housewife	29	"
D	Gray Arthur	1053	bellboy	28	"
E	Naaman Mary—†	1053	waitress	29	"
F	Johnson Helen—†	1053	housewife	29	59 Williams
G	Johnson Richard J	1053	baker	30	21 Hammond
H	Lindsay John	1053	machinist	32	here

Page	Letter	FULL NAME	Residence, April 1, 1926.	Occupation	Supposed Age	Reported Residence, April 1, 1925. Street and Number.

Tremont Street—Continued

	Letter	FULL NAME	Residence	Occupation	Age	Reported Residence
	K	Lindsay Mary—†	1053	housewife	40	here
	P	Hevin Anna—†	1059	"	24	"
	R	Hevin Cesiel	1059	porter	22	"
	S	Clark Minnie—†	1059	factory worker	50	779 Shawmut av
	T	Kildare Grace—†	1059	housewife	29	44 Cabot
	U	Simmons Frank	1059	chauffeur	25	779 Shawmut av
	V	Conway Abby P—†	1059	laundryworker	61	here
	W	Francis Charles M	1059	laborer	35	"
	X	Brooks Elsie—†	1059	domestic	21	"
	Y	Jones Charles H	1059	porter	36	"
	Z	Jones Fannie—†	1059	housewife	25	"
	A	White Millicent—†	1059	housekeeper	31	"
	B	White Reginald	1059	porter	42	"
	C	Pollard Edward	1059	baker	28	"
	D	Pollard Etheline—†	1059	housewife	27	"
	E	Campbell Francis	1059	houseworker	45	742 Shawmut av
	F	Owen Lillian—†	1059	waitress	27	742 "
	G	Morrison Louis	1060	teamster	42	here
	H	Davis Bessie—†	1060	housewife	32	New York
	K	Davis Morris	1060	tailor	32	"
	L	Graham Francis	1060	laborer	40	48 Westminster
	M	Graham Julia—†	1060	housewife	40	48 "
	N	ODonnell Bella—†	1060	"	44	11 Benton
	O	O'Donnell Charles	1060	laborer	47	11 "
	P	Lee Lurcellia—†	1060	housewife	35	here
	R	Lee Robert	1060	laborer	37	"
	S	Vass Melteda—†	1060	housewife	36	52 Northfield
	T	Vass Paul	1060	laborer	36	52 "
	U	Brown Harold W	1060	porter	22	here
	V	Greene Allen J	1060	chauffeur	51	"
	W	Green Mary P—†	1060	housewife	41	"
	Z	Wong Gin	1062	laundryworker	45	"
	D	White Terry	1064	janitor	42	"
	B	Foy Jeremiah	1064	"	44	"
	C	Foy Lena—†	1064	housewife	44	"
	H	Holloway Roberta—†	1066A	housekeeper	40	"
	K	Howard Elizabeth—†	1066A	housewife	37	"
	L	Howard Francis	1066A	porter	50	"
	N	Allen Sarah—†	1068	housewife	39	127 W Lenox
	O	Allen William	1068	laborer	42	127 "
	P	Allen Charlett—†	1068	housekeeper	35	here

Tremont Street—Continued

A	Johnson Dora—†	1080	housekeeper	40	here
B	McIntyre Larnie	1080	newsdealer	27	"
C	McIntyre Larnie J	1080	clerk	57	"
D	McIntyre Martha—†	1080	housewife	48	"
E	Price Ida—†	1080	"	38	"
F	Price Windfield	1080	clerk	43	"
H	Mitchell Fredrick	1081	laborer	28	"
K	Mitchell John	1081	machinist	40	"
L	Mitchell Margaret	1081	stitcher	30	"
M	Mitchell Mary—†	1081	housewife	60	"
N	McCarthy James J	1081	postal clerk	21	"
O	McCarthy Mary A—†	1081	housekeeper	56	"
R	Brophy Annie—†	1081	housewife	46	"
S	Brophy Richard T	1081	clerk	21	"
T	Brophy Thomas R	1081	pipefitter	52	"
P	Cairnes Thomas G	1081	janitor	41	"
U	Finneran John	1081	laborer	54	"
V	Morgan Anna J—†	1081	clerk	23	"
W	Morgan Bridget A—†	1081	housewife	49	"
X	Morgan Mary A—†	1081	clerk	20	"
Y	Shortall Ellen—†	1081	housekeeper	50	"
Z	Shortall Margaret—†	1081	weaver	21	"
A	Foley John	1081	laborer	21	"
B	Foley Mary—†	1081	housewife	52	"
C	Foley Mary T—†	1081	forewoman	23	"
D	Foley Patrick D	1081	laborer	53	"
E	Connolly James H	1081	janitor	57	"
F	Small Agnes T—†	1081	houseworker	52	"
K	Whitlock Ella—†	1083	domestic	46	3 Sussex
L	Whitlock Fannie—†	1083	housekeeper	70	3 "
M	Zollinger Edwin	1083	helper	23	here
N	Zollinger John	1083	cabinetmaker	50	"
O	Zollinger Matilda—†	1083	housewife	48	"
P	Zollinger Walter	1083	chemist	30	"
R	Burton Olive †	1083	housewife	35	"
S	Burton Roland	1083	elevatorman	40	"
T	Sango John	1083	student	26	"
U	Rivers Mary—†	1084	housekeeper	68	"
V	Olive Dora—†	1084	domestic	35	Cambridge
W	Anderson Alice—†	1084	"	40	here
Y	Schwartz Alice—†	1086	housewife	55	"

Tremont Street—Continued

A	Schwartz Frank J	1086	locksmith	75	here
B	Schwartz Hellen—†	1086	clerk	22	"
C	Schwartz Philip G	1086	chauffeur	25	"
D	Miller Hazel B—†	1086	housewife	36	"
E	Miller Lawrence L	1086	painter	31	"
F	Reynolds Leslie—†	1086	domestic	52	"
G	Vass John	1086	laborer	25	34 Cabot
H	Vass Peter	1086	"	27	34 "
M	MacNeill Mary L—†	1090	housewife	28	here
N	MacNeill Ralph M	1090	chauffeur	36	"
O	Emerson John	1090	mason	45	"
P	Emerson Vena—†	1090	housewife	38	"
R	Hoy Mary—†	1090	housekeeper	58	"
S	Tailor Paul	1090	laborer	25	Cambridge
T	Kalkhoven Chrestine—†	1090	housewife	38	here
U	Kalkhoven John	1090	laborer	40	"
B	Long Henry	1096	painter	27	Lawrence
C	Butler George E	1096	electrician	37	24 Hammond
D	Butler Nettie—†	1096	housewife	42	24 "
O	McCauley Mertel—†	1104	"	33	1 Motley
P	McCauley Willard H	1104	laborer	31	1 "
R	Hand Edward	1104	painter	60	here
S	Hand Elizabeth—†	1104	housewife	54	"
W	Hutchons Margaret—†	1106A	housekeeper	40	41 Weston
Y	Popp Marie—†	1108½	"	75	here
Z	Popp Pauline—†	1108½	clerk	41	"
A	Lynch Edward J	1108½	watchman	53	"
B	Lynch Mary E —†	1108½	housewife	49	"
G	Edora Joseph	1117	salesman	42	"
H	Edora Regina —†	1117	housewife	34	"
K	Cox James E	1117	machinist	51	"
L	Cox Nellie—†	1117	housewife	45	"
M	McCormack Alice —†	1117	houseworker	35	Lowell
N	McCormack William	1117	printer	32	"
O	Thompson Frederick B	1117	chauffeur	41	Waltham
P	Thompson Leonora—†	1117	housewife	36	"
R	Irwin Edward J	1117	janitor	50	here
S	Irwin Frances E	1117	laborer	21	"
T	Irwin Louise J —†	1117	housewife	20	89 Union Park
U	Irwin William G	1117	chauffeur	23	here
V	Drobach Mary—†	1117	housekeeper	47	"

9—8

Page.	Letter.	FULL NAME.	Residence, April 1, 1926.	Occupation.	Supposed Age.	Reported Residence, April 1, 1925. Street and Number.

Tremont Street—Continued

w	Gillow Helen—†	1117	housewife	41	4 Sumner pl
x	Gillow James	1117	foreman	42	4 "
Y	Westwood Lillian—†	1117	cashier	30	6 Hammett
z	Derderian Minas	1117	laborer	39	here
A	Sunukjian Aznio —†	1117	housewife	29	"
B	Sunukjian John	1117	shoe repairer	42	"
c	Kalayan Mary—†	1117	housekeeper	52	"
D	Ashjian Eva—†	1118	housewife	30	198 Cabot
E	Ashjian Sarkas	1118	shoeworker	36	198 "
F	Bean Johania K—†	1118	housewife	58	here
G	Bean Thomas	1118	laborer	58	"
K	Reyden Alice —†	1120	housewife	45	Malden
L	Reyden John	1120	restaurantman	53	"
N	Coombs Cecil	1122	clerk	25	here
O	Francis Gertrude—†	1122	housewife	44	"
P	Francis James C	1122	restaurantman	50	"
R	McQuiney Patrick	1122	laborer	40	"
s	Newman Charles	1122	shoeworker	37	"
v	Hop Kee	1124A	laundryman	56	"
x	Jones Mary —†	1125A	housewife	32	"
Y	Jones Pearl H —†	1125A	clerk	33	"
z	Coldrick Arthur	1125A	shipper	52	"
A	Thayer Effie D —†	1125A	housekeeper	47	"
B	Halajian Dickran M	1125A	shoeworker	35	"
c	Halajian Zartoohie—†	1125A	housewife	23	"
D	Karapoloian Mihran	1125A	baker	49	"
E	Bent Cecil	1125A	auto finisher	24	24 Frothingham av
F	Coleman Leman	1125A	printer	20	here
G	Durling Celia †	1125A	factory worker	42	"
H	Niles Henry	1125A	meatcutter	38	25 Leland
K	O'Toole Anna T—†	1125A	housewife	34	here
L	O'Toole James N	1125A	chauffeur	32	"
M	Kirkorian Aznif—†	1125A	housewife	28	"
N	Kirkorian Malcon	1125A	tailor	36	"
O	Hathaway Adeline A—†	1125A	housewife	32	"
P	Hathaway James E	1125A	mechanic	39	"
R	Tompson Louise †	1125A	forewoman	39	"
s	Lefkofsky Bertha †	1125A	housewife	42	"
T	Lefkofsky Solomon	1125A	coal dealer	44	"
U	Lowell Rhoda—†	1126	housewife	38	"
v	Lowell Walter	1126	chauffeur	38	"

34

Tremont Street—Continued

W	Farren James J	1126	laborer	46	5 King ter
X	Farren Mary B—†	1126	housewife	46	5 "
E	Panzone Michele	1133A	shoemaker	49	here
F	Vayo Josephine—†	1133A	housekeeper	48	"
G	Hathaway Catherine F-†	1133A	"	68	"
H	Hathaway Harold J	1133A	chauffeur	32	"
K	Hathaway Helen J—†	1133A	housewife	24	"
L	Adams Mary—†	1130A	housekeeper	45	"
M	White Francis C	1133A	chauffeur	25	2 Church pl
N	White Kathleen G—†	1133A	housewife	30	here
O	Brayn Joseph	1133A	fireman	28	175 Popular
P	Brayn Minnie—†	1133A	housekeeper	30	175 "
R	Morrison Mary—†	1133A	housewife	53	48 Ivy
S	Fornaro Nicholas	1133A	chauffeur	46	here
T	Fornaro Rose—†	1133A	housewife	32	"
U	Desmond Eleanor—†	1133A	factory worker	35	"
V	Walsh George J	1133A	chauffeur	38	"
W	Walsh Margaret A—†	1133A	housewife	38	"
B	Smith Catherine E—†	1137A	housewife	52	"
C	Smith Joseph H	1137A	creameryman	58	"
D	Pendergast Ellen—†	1137A	housekeeper	66	1133A Tremont
E	Sullivan Alice—†	1137A	saleswoman	27	1133A "
F	Telelyjian Lucy—†	1137A	housewife	23	here
G	Telelyjian Sookes	1137A	manager	30	"
H	Goldsmith Abraham G	1137A	cigarmaker	48	"
K	Goldsmith Margaret—†	1137A	operator	38	"
L	Walsh Charles W	1137A	chauffeur	43	"
M	Walsh Lavinia C—†	1137A	housewife	45	"
N	Minerva Kathleen—†	1137A	"	25	"
O	Minerva Micheal	1137A	steamfitter	34	"
P	Door Norman	1138	retired	70	"
R	Scott Lottie—†	1138	housekeeper	34	"

Walpole Street

H	Badeaux Louis	17	tailor	60	here
K	Budd Gabrealle N—†	17	dressmaker	51	"
L	Hill Caroline—†	17	housekeeper	82	40 Village
M	Watkins John C	17	operator	69	here
N	Wilkshelms Mary E—†	17	housewife	79	"

Walpole Street—Continued

Letter	Full Name	Res.	Occupation	Age	Reported Residence
o	Wilkshelms Willehemina—†	17	operator	41	here
p	Law Mary—†	17	domestic	30	"
r	Law Steven	17	janitor	40	"
s	Rowland Mary—†	17	domestic	29	"
t	Franklin Margrete—†	17	housewife	63	Maine
u	Franklin Mildred—†	17	domestic	26	"
v	Kent Ella—†	17	"	33	here
w	Portas Gertrude—†	17	"	28	Maine
x	Portas Joseph	17	cook	27	"
y	Stokes Alice—†	17	domestic	43	"
z	Phillips Alonza	17	laborer	24	here
a	Vaughan Mary—†	17	laundress	45	"
b	Jackson Arite	17	clerk	32	"
c	Jackson Clemon E	17	musician	27	"
d	Jackson Jentry	17	clerk	29	"
e	Jackson Larinda—†	17	"	21	"
f	Jackson Samuel E	17	waiter	59	"
g	Jackson Susan E—†	17	housewife	55	"
h	Jackson William J	17	waiter	25	"
k	Vaun Edith—†	17	maid	28	129 Warwick
l	Vaun Gladys—†	17	housekeeper	22	127 "
m	Vaun Hazel—†	17	marker	20	129 "
n	Martin Bertha—†	17	housewife	45	here
o	Martin George	17	painter	20	"
p	Martin Solomon	17	porter	49	"
r	Chaviz Elma—†	22	waitress	23	"
s	Woodward Edgar	22	mechanic	50	"
t	Woodward Irene—†	22	housewife	42	"
u	Anderson John	22	motorman	22	"
v	Davis George	22	porter	37	"
w	Davis Patricia—†	22	domestic	25	"
x	Berd James	23	chauffeur	40	Georgia
y	Gibbs Fannie—†	23	domestic	40	here
z	Gibbs William	23	mover	40	"
a	Watts David	23	waiter	45	"
b	Birch Mattie—†	23	housewife	38	"
c	Birch Robert	23	janitor	45	"
d	McQuene Nellie—†	23	domestic	50	"
e	Flowers Clara—†	23	housewife	33	Connecticut
f	Flowers Frank	23	waiter	45	here
g	Flowers James	23	laborer	39	Connecticut

Walpole Street—Continued

H	Flowers Lulu—†	23	housewife	47	here
K	Best Charlotte—†	23	hairdresser	23	"
L	Best Gertrude—†	23	housewife	55	"
M	Best Ida—†	23	elevatorwoman	27	"
N	Best Rufus	23	porter	50	"
O	Goodman Luella—†	23	milliner	40	"
P	Chappell Martha—†	23	janitress	41	"
R	Catlin Avis—†	23	waitress	20	"
S	Catlin St Aubin	23	clerk	30	"
T	Greenidge Beatrice—†	23	housewife	56	"
U	Greenidge Grant	23	laborer	49	"
V	Ward Lila—†	23	houseworker	28	"
W	James Bruce	23	chauffeur	25	"
X	James Irene—†	23	housewife	23	"
Y	Williams George V	23	laborer	32	"
Z	Williams Julia—†	23	housewife	44	"
A	Meyers Joseph D	24	clerk	56	"
B	Meyers Selina E—†	24	housewife	47	"
C	Marshall Anne—†	24	waitress	45	"
D	Marshall Archie	24	waiter	53	"
E	Pinto Cyril	24	clerk	24	"
F	Robinson Adassa—†	24	housewife	32	"
G	Robinson William	24	waiter	29	"

Weston Place

H	Knight Annie—†	1	storekeeper	62	here
K	Morton Bessie—†	2	housewife	52	110 Kneeland
L	Morton Joseph J	2	laborer	29	110 "
M	Fink Edward	3	longshoreman	32	here
N	Fink Richard	3	laborer	30	"
O	Rothwell James	3	superintendent	38	"
P	Rothwell Mary—†	3	housewife	38	"
R	Doherty Catherine—†	4	"	42	191 Cabot
S	Doherty James	4	laborer	39	191 "
T	Hassett James	4	"	54	here
U	Hassett Mary—†	4	housewife	56	"
V	Barry John	5	laborer	26	"
W	Barry Mary—†	5	housewife	27	"
X	Bell Catherine—†	5	"	66	"

Page.	Letter.	FULL NAME.	Residence, April 1, 1926.	Occupation.	Supposed Age.	Reported Residence, April 1, 1925. Street and Number.

Weston Place—Continued

	Y	Bell Charles G	5	plasterer	59	here
	Z	Brooks Lila—†	6	domestic	46	"
	A	Burke Anna—†	6	"	45	"
	B	Gratch Clara—†	7	housewife	57	43 Prentiss
	C	Gratch Frank	7	janitor	68	43 "
	D	Pitzold Catherine—†	7	housewife	20	here
	E	Pitzold William H	7	laborer	25	"
	F	Anderson Thomas	8	carpenter	60	"
	G	Robinson Eva—†	8	housewife	54	"
	H	Hooton Alvin C	9	painter	53	208 Springfield
	K	Hooton Gertrude J—†	9	housewife	46	208 "
	L	Rice Elizabeth —†	9	"	51	191 Cabot
	M	Rice Henry H	9	engineer	38	191 "
	N	Pitzold Harriett—†	10	stenographer	28	here
	O	Pitzold Lena—†	10	housewife	49	"
	P	Pitzold William H	10	retired	49	"
	R	McBurney Samuel	11	teamster	34	"
	S	McBurney Cynthia—†	11	housewife	33	"
	T	Dooley Andrew F	11	laborer	49	"
	U	Dooley Isabella—†	11	housewife	43	"
	V	Anderson Anna—†	12	"	43	"
	W	Anderson Earnest	12	laborer .	21	"
	X	Anderson Gustaf	12	"	47	"
	Y	McAdams John	13	retired	82	"
	A	Kennedy Thomas	14	laborer	60	"
	B	Kelly Bridget—†	14	housewife	53	"
	C	Kelly Catherine E—†	14	shoe stitcher	29	"
	D	Kelly John	14	laborer	63	"
	F	McGregor James	15	"	64	13 Weston pl
	G	McGregor Mary—†	15	housewife	54	13 "
	H	Tingley Clara—†	16	clerk	30	here
	K	Tingley Eunice—†	16	domestic	38	"
	L	Tingley Lydia—†	16	clerk	42	"
	M	Godsoe Herbert P	16	laborer	44	"
	N	Godsoe Mary C—†	16	housewife	35	"
	O	Carroll Louis J	17	laborer	30	"
	P	Carroll Pauline—†	17	housewife	36	"
	R	Fitzpatrick John F	17	plumber	53	"
	S	Fitzpatrick Joseph F	17	painter	58	"
	T	Fitzpatrick Mary A—†	17	at home	87	"
	U	Simmons Pearl—†	18	housewife	30	"

38

Weston Place—Continued

	v	Driscoll Joseph	18	chauffeur	24	here
	w	Harrington Catherine—†	18	housewife	53	"

Weston Street

	x	Russo Angello	22	barber	38	here
	y	Russo Bertha—†	22	housewife	35	"
	z	Dwyer Maurice	22	chauffeur	32	13 School
	A	Girigoshian Jacob	22	barber	32	20 Gertrose
	B	Girigoshian Margaret—†	22	housewife	27	20 "
	c	Jefferson Catherine—†	23	"	25	here
	D	Jefferson Clarence	23	porter	27	"
	E	Andrews Elnora—†	23	clerk	31	"
	F	White Sarah—†	23	housewife	49	"
	G	Winn Fannie—†	23	"	26	"
	H	Winn Norman H	23	painter	35	"
	K	Covell Anna—†	27	housewife	40	"
	L	Covell Lee	27	chauffeur	44	"
	M	Anderson Leah—†	27	housewife	55	"
	N	Anderson Peter	27	carpenter	60	"
	o	Kemmett Alice—†	28	housewife	40	"
	P	Kemmett William C	28	laborer	46	"
	s	Sheedy Minnie—†	29	housewife	40	"
	T	Sheedy Thomas	29	buffer	42	"
	U	Sheedy Thomas	29	clerk	23	"
	w	Tibbs Etta—†	33	housewife	42	"
	x	Tibbs Oscar W	33	mechanic	45	"
	Y	Washington Frederick A	33	laborer	53	"
	A	Allen Elizabeth—†	35	housewife	42	"
	B	Blunt Ruth—†	35	"	27	33 Kendall
	c	McDonald Alexander J	35	cook	53	here
	D	Pinckney Helen—†	35	housewife	24	63 Sawyer
	E	James Ella—†	35	laundress	42	here
	F	Brothers Louis	37	steward	30	"
	G	Brothers Martha—†	37	housewife	32	"
	H	Chase Herbert	37	cook	30	1051 Tremont
	K	Chase Loretta—†	37	domestic	25	1051 "
	L	Jones Mattie—†	37	laundress	43	here
	N	Goddard Anna—†	41	housewife	24	23 Newbern
	o	Goddard Lawrence	41	clerk	27	23· "

		FULL NAME.	Residence, April 1, 1926.	Occupation.	Supposed Age.	Reported Residence. April 1, 1925. Street and Number.
	P	Mudge William F	41	retired	69	here
	R	German Harold A	41	laborer	24	"
	T	Carty Annie G—†	45	housewife	41	"
	U	Carty Henry J	45	roofer	45	"
	V	Carty Mary—†	45	clerk	21	"
	W	Aldrich Louise—†	47	stitcher	30	671 Parker
	X	Murray Arthur P	47	painter	55	671 "
	Y	Murray Mary L—†	47	housewife	54	671 "
	Z	Scherer Henrietta—†	47	saleswoman	21	671 "
	A	Scherer Joseph	47	chauffeur	21	671 "
	B	Furkhard Alice M—†	49	saleswoman	22	here
	C	Furkhard Fannie—†	49	housewife	45	"
	D	Carey Thomas F	49	plumber	59	"
	E	Ford Barbara V—†	49	housewife	52	"
	F	Ford Thomas F	49	buyer	23	"
	G	Ford Walter L	49	draftsman	25	"
	K	Fulson Bridget M—†	49	housewife	55	"
	H	Walsh Richard D	49	machinist	25	"
	L	McAvoy Hannah F—†	55	housewife	45	"
	M	McAvoy Patrick J	55	laborer	50	"
	N	Winthrop Charles	55	clergyman	35	"
	O	Smith Emma—†	57	housekeeper	58	"
	U	Downing Edward J	63	painter	53	"
	V	Downing Ellen—†	63	at home	80	"
	W	Downing George H	63	painter	45	"
	X	Downing Michael J	63	printer	50	"
	Y	Raiklen Jennie—†	65	housewife	40	"
	Z	Raiklen Michael	65	painter	40	"
	A	O'Brien Catherine E—†	66	tel operator	20	"
	B	O'Brien James F	66	gasfitter	50	"
	C	O'Brien Mary—†	66	housewife	49	"
	D	King Robert	68	roofer	42	76 Weston
	E	Gill Flora—†	68	housewife	37	here
	F	Gill William	68	laborer	42	"
	G	Gleason Arthur	68	chauffeur	42	"
	H	Gleason Margaret—†	68	housewife	67	"
	K	McKay Elizabeth—†	68	domestic	60	"
	L	Cady Francis	69	electrican	43	"
	M	Connelly Thomas	69	conductor	35	"
	N	Crowell James	69	packer	55	"
	O	Dawes Peter	69	roofer	42	"

Weston Street—Continued

Page.	Letter.	FULL NAME.	Residence, April 1, 1926.	Occupation.	Supposed Age.	Reported Residence, April 1, 1925. Street and Number.

Weston Street—Continued

P	Dorbe Ernest	69	machinist	38	here
R	Gatt Rodney	69	elevatorman	27	"
S	Wood John	69	teamster	55	"
T	Wheelock Florence—†	72	clerk	24	"
U	Wheelock Nellie—†	72	housewife	74	"
V	Linden Delia—†	72	"	38	"
W	Linden William H	72	laborer	40	"
X	Fleming Ellen—†	74	housewife	60	"
Y	Sheehan Catherine—†	74	"	60	"
Z	Doherty Frank	76	teamster	50	61 Northfield
A	Wadman Sydney	76	laborer	60	Brookline
B	McAvoy Anna—†	76	housewife	53	61 Northfield
C	Coffey Thaddeus	76	janitor	41	31 Eastburn
D	Coffey Catherine—†	76	housewife	31	31 "

Ward 9–Precinct 9

CITY OF BOSTON.

LIST OF RESIDENTS
20 YEARS OF AGE AND OVER

(FEMALES INDICATED BY DAGGER)

AS OF

APRIL 1, 1926

HERBERT A. WILSON, } *Listing*

JAMES F. EAGAN, } *Board.*

CITY OF BOSTON—PRINTING DEPARTMENT

Adams Place

E	Johnson Dorothy—†	20	housewife	33	here
F	Johnson Fredrick	20	laborer	34	"
G	Ferrigan Delia—†	20	housewife	54	"
H	Ferrigan Michael J	20	retired	65	"
K	Thomas Ellen—†	22	housewife	50	"
L	Thomas Louis	22	gateman	68	"
M	Thomas Louis	24	chauffeur	24	"
N	Thomas Margaret—†	24	housewife	23	"
O	Timyno Antonia—†	24	housekeeper	70	"
P	Timyno Raymond	24	clerk	42	"
R	Timyno Theresa—†	24	housewife	28	"
S	Debro Peter	26	shoeworker	34	"
T	Garris Johanna—†	26	housekeeper	78	"
U	Scholimero Louis	26	stonecutter	40	"
V	Kuhan William F	26	printer	57	"
W	Luca John	26	teamster	32	"
X	Seculla Vincent	26	tailor	42	"
Y	Trssell Catherine—†	28	housewife	39	"
Z	Trssell Francis	28	tailor	56	"
A	Nelson Alford	28	laborer	40	"
B	Nelson Berrell—†	28	housewife	21	"
C	Brewster Levinia—†	28	housekeeper	38	"
D	Edman Emma—†	28	housewife	29	"
E	Edman Jacob	28	cook	35	"
F	Griffith Louise—†	28	housekeeper	28	"
G	Pickett Percy	28	laborer	20	"
H	Thomas Peter	28	"	25	Cambridge
K	Freedman Ellen—†	28	housekeeper	70	here
L	Freedman James	28	clerk	41	"
M	Gordan Felix	28	painter	26	"
N	Gordan Ina—†	28	housewife	26	"
O	Leslie Lynden	28	porter	22	"

Auburn Street

P	Carr Harriet—†	6	houseworker	35	here
R	Chasleston James	6	barber	40	New York
S	Esgray Robert	6	expressman	60	here
T	Blackman Matilda—†	6	houseworker	29	"

Auburn Street—Continued

Letter	FULL NAME	Residence	Occupation	Age	Reported Residence
U	Ferris George H	8	mover	49	here
V	Ferris Margaret—†	8	housewife	43	22 Gurney
W	Moore Margaret—†	8	"	39	22 "
X	O'Connell George G	8	expressman	22	6 Monument av
Y	O'Connell Helen—†	8	cashier	21	22 Gurney
Z	Fallen Catherine—†	8½	housewife	35	here
A	Fallen Patrick	8½	machinist	36	"
B	Byron Michael J	8½	lithographer	45	"
C	Chenette Alice V—†	8½	housewife	42	"
D	Chenette Louis L	8½	chauffeur	47	"
E	Buckley Catherine—†	8½	housewife	47	"
F	Buckley James	8½	laborer	48	"
G	Rankin Robert	8½	pinboy	23	"
H	Conners Margaret C—†	10	housewife	50	"
K	Conners Richard	10	builder	55	"
L	Madden Mary E—†	10	dressmaker	60	"
M	Kufman Pearl—†	14	housewife	32	"
N	Kufman Philip	14	butcher	42	"
O	Milder Elizabeth—†	14	housewife	45	19 Oak Grove ter
P	Milder Joseph	14	coal dealer	55	19 "
R	Daly Emma L—†	16	housewife	48	here
S	Daly Henrietta A—†	16	housekeeper	46	"
T	Daly Margaret L—†	16	operator	44	"
U	Daly Ruth V—†	16	clerk	33	"
V	Daly Thomas A	16	plasterer	48	"
W	McDaniel Agnes—†	18	domestic	43	47 Hammond
X	McDaniel William	18	laborer	48	47 "
Y	Thompson Annie R—†	18	housewife	50	here
Z	Thompson Charles A	18	fireman	58	"
A	Gettings Bella—†	20	coatmaker	36	"
B	Gettings Catherine—†	20	milliner	35	"
C	Gettings Jane—†	20	saleswoman	40	"
D	King Delia J—†	20A	seamstress	35	"
E	McCloskey Annie F—†	20A	housewife	42	3 Linden av
F	McCloskey Edward	20A	jeweler	50	3 "
G	McKernan Patrick	20A	custodian	43	here
H	Mooney Margaret—†	20A	housewife	28	25 Auburn
K	Ward Barbara—†	20A	"	62	here
L	Ward John F	20A	bricklayer	60	"
M	Ward Mary A—†	20A	stenographer	30	"
N	Ward Michael	20A	secretary	26	"

3

Auburn Street—Continued

O	Mouradian Edward	22	electrician	36	here
R	Archibold Annie E—†	24	housewife	52	"
T	Archibold Annie E—†	24	tel operator	21	"
U	Archibold George N	24	motorman	55	"
S	LeBon Dorothy—†	24	housewife	23	"
P	Magee Bernard H	24	constable	54	1188 Col av

Cabot Street

V	Ardenaur Fredrick	98	painter	44	here
W	Wise Frank	98	mechanic	33	"
X	Wise Victor	98	"	59	"
Y	Rollins Julia—†	98	housewife	49	"
Z	Rollins William	98	laborer	51	"
A	Williams Eva—†	rear 108	housewife	24	"
B	Williams Leroy	" 108	clerk	26	"
C	Dotson Emma—†	" 108	domestic	49	99 Cabot
D	Irving Srena—†	" 108	"	43	here
E	Innis Charlotte—†	" 108	"	51	"
F	Howell Rose—†	" 108	"	55	"
G	Husband Rufus	" 108	carpenter	59	"
H	Jeffers Ernest	" 108	cook	43	"
K	Yee Eva—†	110	houseworker	36	"
L	Raymond Joseph D	110	painter	34	1118 Tremont
M	Raymond Leona E—†	110	housewife	33	1118 "
N	Wise Adam E	110	chef	51	here
O	Malone Johanna—†	110	housewife	72	"
P	Malone Michael F	110	blacksmith	64	"
R	Armstead Emma—†	112	housewife	40	"
S	Armstead William	112	grocer	45	"
T	Braxton Henrietta—†	112	domestic	47	24 Newcomb
U	Hudson Ella—†	112	"	45	here
W	Stevens Elizabeth—†	124	housewife	34	"
X	Stevens Joseph	124	cook	42	"
Y	Lucas Louis A	124	janitor	33	"
Z	Lucas Minnie—†	124	housewife	29	"
A	Dozier Bertha—†	126	housekeeper	43	"
B	Prevoa Fannie—†	126	waitress	31	"
C	Hamm Gladys—†	126	houseworker	32	76 Westminster

4

Letter.	FULL NAME.	Residence, April 1, 1926.	Occupation	Supposed Age.	Reported Residence, April 1, 1925.
					Street and Number.

Champney Place

E	Turner David	1	carpenter	41	2 Clifton pl
F	Turner Martha—†	1	housewife	43	2 "
G	McLaughlin Anna—†	2	housekeeper	55	here
H	McLaughlin Edward	2	mechanic	25	"
K	McLaughlin James	2	mover	21	"
L	McLaughlin James R	2	auto painter	46	"
M	Colson Howard	3	clerk	66	105 Linden Park
N	Colson Jennie—†	3	storekeeper	60	105 "
O	Scully Edward T	4	chauffeur	34	14 Auburn
P	Scully Florence M—†	4	housewife	31	14 "
R	Doran Joseph P	5	chauffeur	44	here
S	Doran Sadie—†	5	housewife	39	"
T	Doran William	5	shipper	21	"
U	Wylie Millie—†	6	housewife	52	334 Tremont
V	Wylie Standish E	6	painter	51	334 "
W	Purtell Catherine L—†	7	housewife	34	50 Reed
X	Purtell James F	7	chauffeur	37	50 "
Y	Skinner Eva—†	8	housekeeper	41	here
Z	Skinner James	8	salesman	44	"
A	Callahan Catherine—†	9	housewife	50	1031 Wash'n
B	Crowley Michael	9	cementfinisher	58	1931 "
C	Lewis William A	9	carpenter	53	New Hampshire
D	Maher Anna—†	10	wardmaid	62	here
E	Maher Anna J—†	10	clerk	24	"
F	Maher Helen R—†	10	"	22	"
G	O'Tooel Mary E—†	10	housewife	28	"
H	O'Toole Thomas J	10	metalworker	30	"

Goldsmith Place

K	Young Fanny—†	1	housekeeper	37	26 Ruggles
L	Young James	1	laborer	40	26 "
M	Boyce Ella H—†	1	housekeeper	43	here
N	Boyce William H	1	machinist	50	"
O	McDonnell Catherine—†	1	housekeeper	35	"
P	McDonnell Daniel	1	laborer	46	"
R	Finn John J	3	"	24	77 Lenox
S	Finn Margaret—†	3	housekeeper	60	77 "
T	Redia Arther J	3	janitor	42	here

5

Goldsmith Place—Continued

U	Redia Catherine—†	3	housekeeper	40	here
V	Pierce Sadie—†	3	"	37	"
W	Pierce George N	3	painter	34	"
Y	Munroe Clarence E	5	"	40	"
Z	Munroe Eliza E—†	5	housekeeper	37	"
A	Phelan William B	5	chauffeur	38	"
B	O'Connor Theresa M—†	5	clerk	23	2 Cambridge
D	Rene Joseph A	6	carpenter	40	here
E	Rene Yeline—†	6	housewife	39	"
F	Ayres John S	6	leathercutter	41	"
G	Ayres Mary—†	6	housewife	39	"
H	Driscoll John E	7	laborer	27	"
K	Driscoll Margaret—†	7	housekeeper	26	"
L	DeCorsey Margaret A—†	7	"	65	"
N	DeCorsey Michael	7	painter	67	"
M	McShea Mary E—†	7	housekeeper	34	"
O	Benson Anna J—†	7	bookkeeper	24	"
P	Benson Anna M—†	7	housekeeper	59	"
R	Benson Ester V—†	7	student	22	"
S	Benson Frank W	7	superintendent	26	"
T	Benson Jenny A—†	7	housekeeper	30	"
U	Benson Martin	7	pianomaker	63	"
W	McMarsters Charles	8	woodworker	41	"
X	McMarsters Rose M—†	8	housewife	31	"
Y	Seles Earl	8	dentist	20	Nova Scotia
Z	Stowe Alice—†	8	clerk	20	77 Worcester
A	Conkey Gertrude—†	9	"	51	here
B	Riggs Hattie E—†	9	housewife	55	"
C	Deon Raymond	9	fishcutter	51	"
D	Jacob Caroline—†	9	housewife	89	"
E	Jacob Philip F	9	machinist	63	"

Hubert Street

G	Hollinside Marie—†	1A	matron	40	here
H	Powell Annie E—†	1A	houseworker	37	"
K	Conover Grace E	1A	housekeeper	49	"
L	Conover Harvey	1A	shipper	21	"
M	Conover Marion G—†	1A	social worker	23	"
N	Conover Mildred L—†	1A	dressmaker	25	"

Letter.	FULL NAME.	Residence, April 1, 1926.	Occupation.	Supposed Age.	Reported Residence, April 1, 1925. Street and Number.

Hubert Street—Continued

O	Johnson Wendell S	1A	watchman	59	here
P	Hicks Pearl	2	housewife	28	"
R	Hicks Samuel	2	carpenter	36	"
S	Greene William H	2	janitor	39	"
T	Brady Esther F—†	2	housewife	47	"
U	Brady Suzanne E—†	2	"	82	"
V	Avery Alice—†	2	laundress	28	11 Winthrop
W	Banks Lennie—†	2	domestic	31	70 Sterling
X	Blake Horatio	2	janitor	42	61 Fort av
Y	Clarke Lillian—†	2	housewife	35	here
Z	Clarke Reginald M	2	laborer	40	"
A	Walker Joseph W	2	waiter	74	"
B	Walker Margaret—†	2	housewife	63	"
C	Selby Beatrice A—†	2	housekeeper	32	"
D	Selby William H	2	clerk	54	"
E	Fauntleroy Harry	2	retired	96	"
F	Fauntleroy James	2	chauffeur	33	"
G	Fauntleroy Mary—†	2	at home	73	"
H	Fauntleroy Odie—†	2	clerk	26	"
K	Fauntleroy Sophia—†	2	"	24	"
L	Lowe Daisy—†	3	housewife	33	"
M	Lowe Frank	3	foreman	33	"
N	Benjamin John	3	laborer	48	"
O	Benjamin Ruth—†	3	laundress	47	"
P	Coles James C	3	elevatorman	38	"
R	Coles Margaret—†	3	domestic	38	"
S	Bethune Arthur E	4	porter	24	"
T	Campbell Florence—†	4	housewife	30	"
U	Campbell Henry	4	seaman	32	"
V	Lambertson Colin	4	laborer	40	"
W	Revis James	4	chauffeur	38	"
X	Revis Jennie—†	4	housewife	34	"
Y	Allen Florence—†	4	"	54	"
Z	Allen Horace	4	musician	34	"
A	Jones Allen	4	porter	39	"
B	Terry Abigo—†	4	domestic	48	"
C	Hudson Earnest	4	cook	32	"
D	Hudson Elizabeth—†	4	housewife	30	"
E	Harvey Allen	4	butcher	52	"
F	Harvey Constance—†	4	housewife	27	"
G	Bean Agnes—†	4	domestic	50	"

7

Hubert Street — Continued

H	Bodie Eva —†	4	dressmaker	49	here
K	Bodie June—†	4	clerk	21	"
L	Bouling Alfred	4	waiter	50	"
M	Chandler Maude—†	4	cook	30	"
N	Smith Alberta—†	4	"	38	"
O	Smith Margaret—†	4	domestic	24	"
P	George Mollie E—†	5	"	41	"
R	Hester Henry	5	laborer	41	"
T	Coppin Ketrah—†	5	housewife	38	"
U	Coppin Samuel	5	porter	39	"
V	Calloway Edward	6	"	28	"
W	Calloway Rosella—†	6	housewife	24	"
X	Smith Benjamin	6	painter	31	"
Y	Smith Edith—†	6	housewife	29	"
Z	Fauntleroy Mary—†	6	"	40	"
A	Bradshaw Violet—†	6	laundress	24	"
B	Joseph Frances—†	6	"	38	"
C	Bonito Frank	6	cook	52	"
D	Bonito Margaret—†	6	housewife	46	"
E	Jordan Louise—†	6	"	30	1121 Harrison av
F	Jordan Ormie	6	janitor	30	1121 "
G	Jackson Esther—†	6	domestic	33	here
H	Dennison Philip J	6	elevatorman	50	77 Emerald
K	Davis Alonzo	7	molder	32	here
L	Davis Kathleen—†	7	housewife	30	"
M	Williams Laura—†	7	domestic	55	"
N	McKenzie Mary—†	7	laundress	45	572 Shawmut av
O	Jones Richard	8	cook	36	here
P	Brodie Elizabeth—†	8	domestic	32	"
R	Brake Gerald	8	janitor	28	New York
S	Shepherd Gordon	8	laborer	25	here
T	Anderson John E	8	glazier	57	"
U	Anderson Mary E—†	8	housewife	55	"
V	Sollie Henry	8	laborer	58	"
W	Jones Beatrice—†	8	housewife	33	"
X	Jarvis Clifford	8	molder	27	"
Y	Jarvis Ethel—†	8	housewife	28	"
Z	Jarvis Priscilla—†	8	"	24	"
A	Jarvis Rufus	8	chauffeur	25	"
B	Pride Estella—†	8	housewife	46	"
C	Pride William G	8	laborer	45	"

Page.	Letter.	FULL NAME.	Residence, April 1, 1926.	Occupation.	Supposed Age.	Reported Residence, April 1, 1925. Street and Number.

Hubert Street—Continued

D	Lewis Annie M—†	8	housewife	50	here
E	Lewis James M	8	clerk	49	"
F	White Edgar	8	porter	36	19 Savin
G	Tolliver Charlie	9	painter	50	here
H	Tolliver Lucy—†	9	domestic	50	"
K	Johnson Abby M—†	9	housewife	59	84 Williams
L	Johnson James E	9	laborer	64	84 "
M	Thompson Lena—†	9	domestic	50	3 Woodbury
N	White Robert A	9	laborer	33	84 Williams
O	Douglin Adraiana—†	9	housewife	38	here
P	Douglin Benjamin	9	fireman	39	"
R	Granville Augustus A	10	laborer	42	"
S	Granville Emma L—†	10	housewife	40	"
T	Summers Henrietta—†	10	"	35	"
U	Summers James H	10	machinist	45	"
V	Benjamin Annie—†	10	cook	55	"
W	DaLomba Barbara—†	10	housewife	20	"
X	DaLomba Julius	10	chef	27	"
Y	Arthur Bertha—†	10	domestic	20	Brookline
Z	Hamblin Elizabeth—†	10	"	50	1204 Tremont
A	Williams Fitz A	11	sandblaster	43	10 Hubert
B	Williams Harriet M—†	11	housewife	35	10 "
C	Gately Annie—†	11	"	63	here
D	Gately Thomas	11	laborer	64	"
E	Lee Annie—†	11	housewife	41	"
F	Lee James	11	laborer	42	"
G	Medley Earl	12	"	43	"
H	Medley Edna—†	12	housewife	42	"
K	White Elizabeth—†	12	"	36	"
L	White George	12	clerk	50	"
M	Binyard Frank	12	"	21	26 Ball
N	Josephs Clara C—†	12	housewife	28	here
O	Josephs John	12	laborer	30	"
P	Josephs Rebecca—†	12	domestic	23	"
R	Clarke Hyacinth—†	13	"	21	"
S	Oxley Martha—†	13	housewife	50	"
T	Aird Mary—†	13	domestic	35	"
U	Jessamy Clarice—†	13	"	38	"
V	Small Carrie—†	13	housewife	36	"
W	Small Jake	13	coal dealer	42	"
X	Ramseur Ruah—†	14	laundress	27	180 Northampton

Page.	Letter.	FULL NAME.	Residence, April 1, 1926.	Occupation.	Supposed Age.	Reported Residence, April 1, 1925. Street and Number.

Hubert Street—Continued

	Y	James Charles	14	laborer	40	here
	Z	Cabral Frank	14	"	38	65 W Lenox
	A	Cabral Louise—†	14	housewife	35	31 "
	B	Jeter Frederick J	14	porter	35	1060 Tremont
	C	Jeter Leota G—†	14	laundress	26	1060 "
	D	Hunter Willis	15	retired.	70	36 Sawyer
	E	Yates Julia—†	15	domestic	50	100 "
	F	Yates Marion—†	15	laundress	22	100 "
	G	Greene Annie—†	15	housewife	38	here
	H	Greene Burt	15	laborer	40	"
	K	Munroe Bessie—†	15	housewife	34	"
	L	Monroe Joseph	15	porter	40	"
	M	William Willie M	15	laborer	21	"
	N	Meranda Dorothy—†	16	housewife	32	10 Willard pl
	O	Meranda Frank	16	laborer	33	10 "
	P	Minot Levi	16	cook	35	here
	R	Thompson Alfred	16	"	39	"
	S	Thompson Katurah—†	16	housewife	36	"
	T	Roberts Emma—†	16	domestic	45	1060 Tremont
	U	Roberts Matildy—†	16	housewife	64	1060 "
	V	Caines Ebenezer	17	laborer	37	here
	W	Caines Phebe—†	17	housewife	28	"
	X	Lerner Jennie—†	17	"	42	"
	Y	Lerner Leopold	17	retired	50	"
	Z	O'Brien John	17	janitor	45	W Indies
	A	Parker Isaac	18	laborer	31	here
	B	Parker Nancy—†	18	housewife	23	"
	C	Ward Carrie—†	18	domestic	41	"
	D	Ward Joseph A	18	laborer	42	"
	E	Gambel Frederick	18	carpenter	34	"
	F	Sanford Lawrence	18	clerk	20	"
	G	Smith Marion—†	18	domestic	49	"
	H	Gomes Eloine—†	18	housewife	34	"
	K	Gomes Emanuel	18	laborer	36	"
	L	Hunt Dora—†	18	domestic	40	Brookline
	M	Mars Margaret—†	18	"	20	Sharon
	N	Thomas John T	18	paperhanger	60	here
	O	White George	18	laborer	47	"
	P	White Mary E—†	18	housewife	43	"
	R	Emery Lester M	18	laborer	24	S Weymouth
	S	Kountz Asa B	18	janitor	59	here

Madison Street

T	Bowles Daniel F	2	packer	56	here
U	Bowles Elizabeth—†	2	houseworker	22	33 Linden Park
V	Bowles Marhsal J	2	laborer	24	here
W	Murphy Mary M—†	2	houseworker	56	"
X	Arnold Frank G	2	salesman	72	"
Y	Garbrini Sarah—†	2	houseworker	65	1101 Harrison av
Z	Love Anna J—†	2	housewife	33	8 Sterling
A	Love Charles	2	engineer	44	8 "
B	McGloin Anna M—†	2	housewife	23	8 Madison
C	McGloin Edward	2	printer	25	8 "
D	Sullivan Helen—†	4	houseworker	66	here
E	Pierce Emma—†	4	"	66	"
F	McIntyre Robert E	4	sign painter	45	"
G	O'Brien Bridget C—†	4	housewife	66	"
H	Wilson Albert	4	janitor	66	Quincy
K	Cook Mary E	4	housewife	48	here
L	Ziegler Michael	4	laborer	69	"
M	Dern Blanch E—†	6	housewife	22	8 Madison
N	Dern Herman A	6	clerk	21	8 "
O	Sullivan John F	6	laborer	39	here
P	Sullivan Julia—†	6	housewife	36	"
R	Wilson Thomas H	6	painter	61	"
S	Wilson Victoria J—†	6	housewife	57	"
T	Daley George J	6	janitor	39	217 Albany
U	Daley Mary F—†	6	housewife	46	217 "
V	Dean Emma—†	8	"	48	here
W	Cammet Henry B	8	laborer	71	"
X	Cook Mary—†	8	houseworker	38	Lynn
Y	Cashman Gertrude B—†	8	housewife	28	127 Moreland
Z	DeVenosa Clara—†	10	"	54	here
A	DeVenosa Gustave	10	decorator	60	"
B	Allen Ellen—†	10	housewife	64	"
C	Allen Frank B	12	baker	32	"
D	Allen Henry B	12	tinsmith	26	"
E	Allen Margaret—†	12	clerk	21	"
F	Collins Mary B—†	12	housewife	41	22 Madison
G	Collins Patrick J	12	foreman	42	22 "
H	Plaisted Ida E—†	14	housewife	51	here
K	Simons Ethel L—†	16	"	37	"
L	Simons Rubin W	16	mechanic	36	"

11

Madison Street — Continued

M	Cutter Elizabeth — †	16	housekeeper	57	here
N	Cutter William O	16	engineer	70	"
O	Stanley Mary E — †	16	housewife	63	5 Ball
P	Toomey Frank	18	engineer	30	here
R	Segee Emily — †	18	housewife	63	"
S	McCulloch Effie D — †	18	"	59	"
T	McCulloch Ester G — †	18	clerk	33	"
U	Glancey James H	20	barber	55	"
V	Glancey Mary L — †	20	housewife	54	"
W	Kirk Isabella — †	20	"	40	"
X	Kirk William	20	rigger	45	"
Y	Bassett Catherine — †	20	housewife	50	Milton
Z	Seiferth Lewis P	22	shoecutter	41	here
A	Seiferth Mildred G — †	22	housewife	39	"
B	Thornton John A	22	shipper	38	"
C	Thornton Lillian M — †	22	housewife	39	"
D	Henery William	24	chauffeur	21	Foxboro
E	Donahue John	24	laborer	40	here
F	Donahue Mary — †	24	housewife	38	"
G	Davis Elizabeth — †	26	housekeeper	43	"
H	Davis Ernest	26	mover	38	New York
K	Clinton Nickolas	26	truckman	27	here
L	Hackett Catherine R — †	26	housewife	84	"
M	Holland Robert W	26	laborer	47	"
N	McCormack Archie	28	carpenter	58	Lynn
O	Domigan Louise — †	28	houseworker	42	here
P	Domigan Richard	28	painter	45	"
R	McGrath Delia — †	30	housekeeper	40	27 O
S	McGrath William	30	laborer	50	here
T	Ladd Catherine F — †	30	stenographer	21	"
U	Ladd John T	30	chauffeur	20	"
V	Ladd Mary E — †	30	housewife	52	"
W	Ladd William	30	painter	48	"
X	Murphy Francis J	32	janitor	45	185 Dudley
Y	Vieno Bernard	32	baker	29	989 Col av
Z	Vieno Jenny — †	32	housewife	29	989 "

Marble Street

A	Dumas Luther	1	laborer	43	here
B	Dumas Mary — †	1	housewife	44	"
C	Fonville George	1	laborer	58	"

Marble Street—Continued

D	McGhee Jerry	1	laborer	21	here
E	Lee Howard J	1	"	21	"
F	Lee Rebecca P—†	1	housewife	57	"
G	Lee Samuel B	1	steward	58	"
H	Williams Ernestine—†	2	housewife	28	1 Concord pl
K	Williams Henry	2	mechanic	30	1 "
L	Withers Byron R	2	elevatorman	23	here
M	Withers Helen—†	2	"	21	"
N	Withers Mattie—†	2	factory worker	37	"
O	Mason Elenor—†	3	matron	47	"
P	McKane Alice W—†	3	physician	57	"
R	McKane Cornelius	3	clerk	28	"
S	McKane William F	3	fireman	23	"
T	Woodby William B	3	gardener	68	"
U	Badgett Henry	4	laborer	33	"
V	Hubbard Fred	4	retired	62	40 Newcomb
W	Hubbard Susan—†	4	laundress	48	40 "
X	Johnson Charles H	4	porter	54	here
Y	Tyler Carrie—†	5	housewife	32	Virginia
Z	Tyler Warren	5	longshoreman	35	"
A	Walker Clara—†	5	housewife	26	"
B	Walker James	5	longshoreman	33	"
C	Blake Lillian—†	8	cook	35	here
D	Jackson Herbert	8	baker	30	"
E	Jackson Mary—†	8	housewife	27	"
F	Burewl Ida—†	8	"	35	607 Shawmut av
G	Burewl Payton	8	chauffeur	40	607 "
H	Johnson Pauline—†	9	housewife	27	here
K	Johnson Peter J	9	chauffeur	28	"
L	Christmas John	9	porter	24	54 Windsor
M	Christmas Rita—†	9	housewife	22	54 "
P	Read Maggie—†	10	"	42	Virginia
R	Read Violet—†	10	houseworker	22	"
S	Young John D	10	waiter	39	here
T	Young Mary E—†	10	housewife	34	"
U	Jackson George L	11	retired	64	"
V	Jackson Maud E—†	11	housewife	64	"
W	Chapman Andrew L	11	machinist	38	525 Mass av
X	Chapman Gertrude A—†	11	secretary	30	here
Y	Jackson Marion M—†	11	"	26	"
Z	Fitzgerald Charles	11	trainman	51	"

Page	Letter	FULL NAME	Residence, April 1, 1926	Occupation	Supposed Age	Reported Residence, April 1, 1925. Street and Number.

Marble Street Continued

	Letter	FULL NAME	Res.	Occupation	Age	Reported Residence
	A	Haskell Sarah —†	11	cashier	34	here
	B	Kemp Duncan J	11	expressman	42	"
	C	Black Edna —†	11	domestic	26	18 Hubert
	D	Cisco Jane —†	11	elevatorwoman	39	75 Ruggles
	E	Martin Gertrude —†	11	domestic	31	75 "
	F	Turner Reginald	11	plasterer	28	New York
	G	Schottmiller John F	11	porter	46	111 Ruggles
	H	Schottmiller Mary A—†	11	housekeeper	35	111 "
	K	Margosian Annie—†	11	housewife	30	here
	L	Margosian Onnic	11	furrier	40	"
	M	Kickal Anthony	11	coatmaker	34	"
	N	Kickal Nellie —†	11	housewife	35	"
	P	Ellison Henry	11	laborer	31	218 W Springfield
	R	Ellison Jose —†	11	housewife	29	218 "
	O	Groves Edward E	11	laborer	40	Brookline
	S	Jackson Arthur L	11	fireman	29	113 Cedar
	T	Jackson Florence —†	11	housewife	26	113 "
	U	Ahigian Haysue	11	merchant	30	here
	V	Ahigian Victoria —†	11	housewife	24	"
	W	O'Connor John	11	laborer	56	"
	X	Heggie John F	11	chauffeur	47	17 Wachusett
	Y	Jackson Bertha —†	11	housewife	39	here
	Z	Jackson Fred	11	chauffeur	37	"
	A	Foley Margaret G —†	11	stenographer	44	"
	B	Foley Thresa —†	11	bookkeeper	41	"
	D	Nichols Florence—†	12	waitress	32	528 Mass av
	E	Nichols Ostranda —†	12	housewife	54	528 "
	F	Baltusus Raymond	12	restaurateur	33	here
	G	Skahnites Charles	12	oiler	39	"
	H	Shaknites Veronica —†	12	houseworker	37	"
	K	Williams Richard	12	molder	27	71 Warwick
	L	Williams Westmeath—†	12	housewife	36	71 "
	M	Kelley Gertrude —†	12	houseworker	37	here
	N	Kelley James J	12	motorman	40	"
	O	Nugent James W	12	painter	60	"
	P	Black Edna—†	12	houseworker	27	18 Hubert
	R	Cisco Janey—†	12	elevatorwoman	40	75 Ruggles
	S	Martin Gertrude —†	12	houseworker	38	75 "
	T	Turner Reginald	12	plasterer	28	New York City
	U	Anderson Beatrice—†	12	houseworker	24	here
	V	Anderson Clara —†	12	student	22	"

Page.	Letter.	FULL NAME.	Residence, April 1, 1926.	Occupation.	Supposed Age.	Reported Residence, April 1, 1925. Street and Number.

Marble Street—Continued

	W	Anderson McKerrow	12	laborer	26	here
	X	Burns Anna—†	12	houseworker	35	"
	Y	Earley George	12	boilermaker	38	19 Newburn
	Z	Earley Rose—†	12	houseworker	43	19 "
	A	Peterson Harriet—†	12	"	21	19 "
	B	Jolley James J	12	waiter	38	12 Braddock pk
	C	Wright Ethel—†	12	houseworker	35	1051 Tremont
	D	Drury Maria—†	12	at home	64	here
	E	Nugent Annie—†	12	"	68	"
	F	Lee Emma—†	12	houseworker	38	31 Ball
	G	Lee William E	12	clerk	51	31 "
	H	Priven Maurice	12	laborer	45	here
	K	Priven Rebecca—†	12	houseworker	40	"
	L	Privern Samuel	12	carpenter	21	"
	M	Argoomanian Zaker	12	storekeeper	45	"
	N	Minasian Hagop	12	"	37	"
	O	Jones Evelyn—†	12	housewife	33	"
	P	Jones Joseph	12	laborer	37	"
	R	Lipson Betty—†	12	bookkeeper	20	"
	S	Lipson Eva—†	12	clerk	22	"
	T	Lipson Flora—†	12	housewife	50	"
	U	Lipson Louis	12	cobbler	52	"
	V	Brown Elizabeth—†	12	domestic	40	72 Warwick
	W	Brown Lottie M—†	12	housewife	26	72 "
	X	Brown Mary F—†	12	laundress	42	72 "
	Y	Jackson Este le—†	12	housewife	26	83 Williams
	Z	Jackson Harold E	12	laborer	28	83 "
	z¹	Bennett Leroy	12	steamfitter	30	here
	z²	Bennett Lorraine—†	12	housewife	27	"

Ruggles Street

	A	Eklund Elmer	9	machinist	36	Millis
	B	Eklund Harriet—†	9	housekeeper	36	"
	C	LaFleur Edward	9	machinist	22	"
	D	Polson Joseph	9	roofer	26	Pennsylvania
	E	Seifirth Charles L	9	chauffeur	49	here
	F	Seifirth Mary E—†	9	housekeeper	44	"
	G	White Catherine—†	9	"	55	"

Ruggles Street —Continued

H	White Silvia —†	9	bookkeeper	20	here
K	Brewster Sarah E—†	11	leather sorter	42	"
L	Soper Arthur W	11	butcher	58	"
M	Billings Edward G	11	steamfitter	36	"
N	Billings Minnie A —†	11	housekeeper	36	"
O	Bullock Annie—†	11	clerk	47	"
P	Skidmore Frank	11	salesman	38	8 Goldsmith pl
R	Skidmore Jane —†	11	housekeeper	65	here
S	Rogers Agnes —†	13	waitress	38	"
T	Rogers Percy	13	baker	37	"
U	Flagg Aida —†	13	housekeeper	55	"
W	Cadigan Cornelius	13	mason	43	"
X	Cadigan Dennis	13	retired	86	"
V	Killian Catherine —†	13	housekeeper	45	"
Y	Smith Arthur J	15	repairman	30	"
Z	Smith Edward E	15	plumber	25	"
A	Smith Sadie F —†	15	housekeeper	40	"
B	Hetherington Elizabeth —†	15	saleswoman	34	"
C	O'Toole Charles F	15	auto mechanic	44	"
D	O'Toole Elizabeth M —†	15	housekeeper	86	"
E	O'Toole John H	15	ironmolder	55	"
F	O'Toole Mazie —†	15	clerk	36	"
G	Stone Hyman	15	carpenter	60	"
H	Stone Joseph H	15	salesman	26	"
K	Stone Mary —†	15	housekeeper	51	"
L	Stone Samuel L	15	clerk	21	"
M	Lee George	24	laundryman	53	"
N	Grace Catherine —†	24	housekeeper	32	40 Vine
O	Grace William F	24	steamfitter	37	40 "
P	Meadows Ernest F	24	painter	49	here
R	Roth John E	24	watchman	51	"
S	Glynn Alice —†	26	tel operator	21	969 Col av
T	Glynn William	26	salesman	23	7 Goldsmith pl
U	Rogers Elizabeth —†	26	housekeeper	51	here
V	Rogers Frank	26	carpenter	59	"
W	Rogers Frank	26	mechanic	26	"
X	Rogers Joseph	26	"	28	"
Y	Partridge Frederick	26	vulcanizer	31	"
Z	Partridge Margerie L—†	26	housekeeper	29	"
B	Young Cloris —†	28	"	34	34 Cliff
C	Young Elmer	28	laborer	33	34 "

Ruggles Street—Continued

F	Burgess Mary †	36	laundress	37	here
G	Suggs Ella M †	36	housekeeper	53	"
H	Harris Laura †	36	"	55	66 Cabot
N	Hezlitt Emily W †	41	"	64	here
O	Hezlitt William H	41	clerk	66	"
P	Archibald Carl	41	watchman	40	England
R	Archibald Iris †	41	housekeeper	29	"
S	Zito Eugene	41	pressman	36	here
T	Zito Linnie †	41	housekeeper	29	" .
U	Malone Silvester	41	bookkeeper	27	"
V	O'Brien Edward	41	storekeeper	44	"
W	O'Brien Elizabeth †	41	housekeeper	44	"
X	Hageman John	41	bookkeeper	42	"
Y	Hallgren Karl A	41	pianomaker	48	"
Z	Hallgren Sigrid E †	41	housekeeper	34	"
A	Kelley Beatrice †	41	"	44	Revere
B	Kelley Charles	41	clerk	59	"
C	Huckle Mabel E †	41	bookkeeper	20	1 Champney pl
D	Laverty Margaret †	41	forewoman	40	1 "
E	Johnson Benjamin	50	pharmacist	40	here
F	Johnson Edith S †	50	housekeeper	38	"
G	Reed Hattie †	50	"	37	"
H	Washington Lillian †	50	"	21	Sheridan
M	Scruggs Marionette †	53	"	31	here
N	Charlton Venus †	53	housewife	22	New York
O	Charlton William	53	longshoreman	25	"
P	Flowers Mary C †	53	housekeeper	55	here
S	Johnson Frederick	58	repairman	30	"
T	Johnson Helena †	58	laundress	42	"
U	Daley Mildred †	58	housekeeper	34	"
V	Herbert Amada †	58	"	42	"
W	Gittens Florence A †	58	"	45	"
X	Gittens John J	58	longshoreman	47	"
Z	Busquine Caroline †	59	housewife	38	"
A	Busquine Joshia	59	painter	40	"
B	Young Elsworth †	59	housewife	23	"
C	Young Herbert	59	chauffeur	24	"
D	Rollins Hattie †	59	housewife	30	"
E	Rollins Thomas	59	janitor	30	"
F	Chinn John T	60	attendant	44	"
G	Chinn Maud M †	60	elevatorwoman	34	"

9—9

17

Page.	Letter	FULL NAME	Residence, April 1, 1926.	Occupation.	Supposed Age.	Reported Residence, April 1, 1925. Street and Number.

Ruggles Street—Continued

		FULL NAME		Occupation.	Age	Residence
	H	Robbins Collie—†	60	housekeeper	54	here
	K	Jennott Alphonso	60	porter	31	16 Braddock pk
	L	Jennott Viola—†	60	housekeeper	31	16 "
	M	Jennott Wilfred	60	laborer	27	16 "
	N	Dyer George	60	waiter	60	here
	O	Lowther Pattie A—†	60	cook	57	"
	R	Lord Edward	61	clerk	40	Maine
	S	Sheilds Agnes—†	61	housewife	27	here
	T	Sheilds Jessie	61	janitor	42	"
	U	Wright Mabel—†	61	housewife	31	"
	V	Yarby Cenderilla—†	61	housekeeper	44	Cambridge
	W	Humphrey Clara—†	62	none	23	Worcester
	X	Humphrey Harold	62	truckman	25	"
	Y	Paris Charles K	62	janitor	40	here
	Z	Paris Clara—†	62	housekeeper	45	"
	A	Cummings Evelina O—†	62	"	30	"
	B	Cummings Sidney S	62	tailor	31	"
	C	Parker Liza—†	62	housekeeper	46	"
	F	Johnson George	63	cook	35	"
	G	Cannon Alice—†	63	housekeeper	41	"
	H	Rose Manuel	63	cook	30	"
	K	Cox Ada—†	63	housewife	34	"
	L	Cox Thomas	63	longshoreman	44	"
	M	Vostead Clovas	63	janitor	30	"
	N	Vostead Susan—†	63	housewife	28	"
	P	Lincey Ada F—†	63	"	29	"
	R	Lincey John A	63	clerk	30	"
	S	Robinson Elija—†	63	waiter	44	"
	T	Robinson Pinkie—†	63	housewife	39	"
	U	Whitehead Laurie—†	63	housekeeper	51	"
	V	Whitehead Lincoln	63	janitor	24	"
	W	Gray Gladys—†	64	elevatorwoman	22	"
	X	Mont Natale	64	"	24	"
	Y	Mont Maud—†	64	housekeeper	46	"
	Z	Mont Walter	64	carpenter	63	"
	A	Stewart Charles A	64	mechanic	41	"
	B	Stewart Irene G—†	64	housekeeper	38	"
	C	Husbands Bentide—†	64	"	29	"
	D	Husbands Wilbrit	64	porter	29	"
	F	O'Brien Cora—†	65	housekeeper	49	"
	G	O'Brien Manuel	65	retired	78	"

18

Ruggles Street—Continued

H	Greggs Harriet—†	65	housekeeper	38	here
K	Corban Jestine—†	65	housewife	31	"
L	Corban John	65	tailor	31	"
M	Mablet Edna—†	65	domestic	23	"
N	Chase Mary—†	66	housekeeper	28	"
O	Yett Mary J—†	66	"	36	Sawyer st
P	Dell Ella—†	66	"	31	here
R	Dell Thomas	66	cook	38	"
S	Parsons Ephraim A	66	"	42	"
T	Parsons Reaver L—†	66	"	29	"
U	Moore Coleman	67	porter	25	"
V	Moore Gwendolyn—†	67	housewife	23	"
W	Walker Arlean—†	67	"	38	61 Ruggles
X	Walker William	67	longshoreman	45	61 "
Y	Nelson Avery	67	chauffeur	21	here
Z	Nelson Florence—†	67	housekeeper	47	"
A	Nelson Jeannette—†	67	elevatorwoman	22	"
B	Mason Leonard	67	porter	21	"
C	Mason Martha—†	67	housewife	20	"
E	Benders Mary—†	68	laundress	41	77 Ruggles
F	Benders Pearl—†	68	at home	20	77 "
G	Benders William H	68	laborer	50	77 "
H	Santos Ethel—†	68	housekeeper	34	76 "
K	Santos Frederick	68	laborer	38	76 "
L	James Cornelius	68	cook	25	564 Shawmut av
M	James Mary E—†	68	housekeeper	24	564 "
O	Thom Bertha—†	69	housewife	40	Cambridge
P	Thom Edward	69	carpenter	42	"
R	Lewis Fitzgerald	69	cook	38	21 Hubert
S	Lewis Menvela—†	69	housewife	34	21 "
T	Granger Margaret—†	69	"	29	here
U	Skerrett Sarah—†	69	housekeeper	40	"
V	Webb Sarah—†	69	"	40	"
W	Lewis Charles W	69	porter	41	"
X	Lewis Julia—†	69	housewife	34	"
Y	Green Elizabeth—†	69	"	24	"
Z	Green James	69	longshoreman	36	"
A	Cook Harriett—†	69	housewife	48	"
B	Cook William R	69	porter	58	"
C	Griffeth Dudley	69	"	45	"
D	Thorpe Clifford	69	"	53	"

Ruggles Street—Continued

E	Thorpe Gladis—†	69	housekeeper	20	here
F	McFarland Florence—†	69B	"	50	"
G	Kantrobitz Hattie—†	73	housewife	42	"
H	Kantrobitz Nathaniel	73	clerk	42	"
K	Carman Bert	73	waiter	26	"
L	Carman Ivy—†	73	housewife	22	"
N	Watson Charles R	75	laborer	48	"
O	Watson Elizabeth G—†	75	housewife	47	"
P	Cooper Gennie—†	75	"	47	"
R	Cooper George	75	clerk	53	"
S	Carhlun Ella—†	75	housekeeper	25	72 Ruggles
T	Madrey Elizabeth—†	75	housewife	30	72 "
U	Madrey Samuel	75	longshoreman	29	72 "
V	Dewey Effie—†	77	housewife	31	here
W	Dewey William	77	porter	45	"
X	Miller Lillian—†	77	housewife	38	"
Y	Miller Samuel	77	janitor	50	"
B	Cahouette Marie †	95	housekeeper	38	"
C	Irving Gladis—†	95	housewife	29	"
D	Irving Robert	95	steamfitter	33	"
F	Simons Louis	95	tailor	44	"
G	Simons Sarah †	95	housewife	38	"
N	Squire Hattie †	101	"	55	"
O	Squire John	101	stonecutter	69	"
P	Wilson Joseph	101	chauffeur	38	"
R	Pritchett John	101	metalworker	27	"
S	Pritchett Mary †	101	housewife	22	"
T	Holden Martha †	101	housekeeper	46	"
W	Pine Gertrude †	105	housewife	24	"
X	Pine Joseph	105	laborer	42	"
Y	Robinson Gertrude—†	105	housewife	50	"
Z	Robinson Nathaniel	105	retired	58	"
B	Bloom Bertha †	107	stitcher	40	762 Shawmut av
C	Alpert Bessie †	107	clerk	21	here
D	Madden Lillian †	107	housekeeper	48	"
E	Gilman Jennie †	107	storekeeper	68	"
F	Morris Inez †	109	housewife	37	5 Winthrop pl
G	Montell Estina †	109	"	44	8 Hubert
K	Johnson Abethel †	111	"	22	9 "
L	Johnson Charles	111	tailor	27	Detroit Mich
M	Smith Jemima †	111	domestic	47	28 Sawyer
R	Terres Georgiana—†	117	housewife	25	Providence R I

Ruggles Street—Continued

s	Terres John	117	laborer	25	Providence R I
T	Robinson Henry D	117	elevatorman	53	here
U	Robinson Margaret—†	117	housewife	56	"
V	Robinson Margaret L—†	117	clerk	25	"
W	Rogan Bernard F	117	laborer	31	"
X	Rogan Mary E—†	117	housewife	24	"
Y	Arsenlut Joseph	119	laborer	30	"
Z	Arsenlut Sophie—†	119	housewife	49	Canada
A	Arsenlut Tillie—†	119	"	26	here
B	Fillmore Jessie—†	119	stitcher	27	754 Tremont
C	Fillmore Walter	119	boilermaker	34	754 "

Shawmut Avenue

G	Christmas Lucinda—†	686	domestic	24	N Carolina
H	Davis Alice—†	686	houseworker	24	here
K	Davis Charles	686	clerk	34	"
L	Davis Henry	686	"	26	"
M	Davis John	686	painter	52	"
N	Davis Lulu—†	686	housewife	35	"
O	Love Leah—†	686	domestic	26	New York City
P	Oliver Malissia—†	688	hairdresser	38	57 Windsor
R	Perham Nannie—†	688	domestic	50	W Medford
S	Rhodes Elizabeth—†	688	housewife	50	here
T	Rhodes Frank	688	porter	56	"
U	Ross Minnie—†	688	houseworker	30	"
V	Anderson Martha—†	690 & 692	"	56	14 Windsor
W	Hamilton Anna—†	690 & 692	"	52	Detroit Mich
X	Washington Charles	690 & 692	waiter	37	14 Windsor
Y	Redmond Earl	690 & 692	student	20	here
Z	Stevens Richard	690 & 692	cigarmaker	65	"
A	Stevens Sarah—†	690 & 692	housewife	60	"
B	Goode Jesse	690 & 692	real estate	55	"
C	Goode Mary A—†	690 & 692	housewife	28	Hyannis
D	Weaver Dorothy—†	690 & 692	domestic	20	here
E	Weaver Louise—†	690 & 692	"	56	"
F	Hodges Lottie L—†	690 & 692	maid	48	"
G	Martin Ida H—†	690 & 692	at home	71	"
H	Richardson Earnest	690 & 692	laborer	33	"
K	Crump Anna E—†	690 & 692	maid	54	"

Page	Letter	FULL NAME.	Residence, April 1, 1926.	Occupation.	Supposed Age.	Reported Residence, April 1, 1925. Street and Number.

Shawmut Avenue—Continued

	L	Crump Thomas A	690 & 692	waiter	52	here
	M	Edwards Gilbert	690 & 692	"	31	"
	N	Carey Daisy—†	690 & 692	housewife	45	"
	O	Carey James	690 & 692	barber	50	"
	R	Dadson Ralph	694	laborer	30	Phila Pa
	S	Perry Florence L—†	694	hairdresser	44	here
	T	Perry Minda—†	694	housekeeper	66	"
	U	Pinheiro Don J	694	physician	53	"
	V	Brito Joseph	696	laborer	27	10 Burbank
	W	Dias Manuel	696	operator	43	23 Ball
	X	Domes Victor	696	"	29	29 Sterling
	Y	Jackson Halline B—†	696	housewife	33	here
	Z	Jackson Lucius M	696	clerk	42	"
	A	March Eddie	696	watchmaker	27	"
	B	Martin Antonio	696	operator	34	"
	C	Williams Nellie—†	696	maid	22	29 Sterling
	D	Taylor George H	698	retired	69	here
	E	Taylor Martin	698	chauffeur	28	"
	F	Taylor Mary—†	698	housewife	23	1081 Tremont
	G	Taylor Samuel E	698	chauffeur	30	here
	K	Clagg Carrie—†	699	housekeeper	46	"
	L	Johnson Coline—†	699	housewife	45	"
	M	Johnson Jermiah	699	janitor	47	"
	N	Smith Blanch E—†	699	housewife	31	"
	O	Smith Herman	699	porter	32	"
	P	Warbington Rebbeca—†	701	housewife	42	8 Woodbury
	R	Warbington West	701	longshoreman	38	8 "
	S	Timberlake Edward J	701	porter	40	here
	T	Timberlake Eva B—†	701	housewife	38	"
	U	Thomas Albert M	701	longshoreman	31	"
	V	Thomas Rose—†	701	housewife	31	"
	W	Smitherman John E	701	janitor	34	Cambridge
	Y	Sisco Gertrude—†	703	housewife	35	here
	Z	Sisco Isacc	703	painter	44	"
	A	Mitchell Laurie—†	703	housewife	31	"
	B	Mitchell Rufus	703	longshoreman	55	"
	C	Sparrow Joseph M	703	janitor	38	"
	D	Strother Louisa M—†	703	housewife	29	70 Westminster
	E	Strother William L	703	porter	33	70 "
	F	Paretchanian Hagop	704	clerk	50	here
	G	Paretchanian Vartanoosh—†	704	housewife	40	"

· 22

Page.	Letter.	FULL NAME.	Residence, April 1, 1926.	Occupation.	Supposed Age.	Reported Residence, April 1, 1925. Street and Number.

Shawmut Avenue—Continued

H	Harriman Bertha—†	704	housewife	45	here
K	Harriman Clarence	704	carpenter	50	"
L	Paretchanian Albert	704	student	20	"
M	Paretchanian Arron	704	clerk	55	"
N	Paretchanian George	704	electrician	23	"
O	Paretchanian Takuhe—†	704	housewife	50	"
P	Sealey Ella M—†	705	housekeeper	38	"
R	Wolf Bertha—†	705	"	45	"
S	Harrell Cular—†	705	housewife	22	"
T	Harrell Leon	705	janitor	30	"
U	Hasbruck Marie—†	705	housekeeper	31	"
X	Quow Edna—†	707	housewife	50	"
Y	Quow Fredrick J	707	cook	58	"
Z	Anglin George	707	janitor	27	Cambridge
A	Harris Lula—†	707	housekeeper	57	here
B	Coodloe Rose—†	708	waitress	25	669 Shawmut av
C	Johnston Clarendon C	708	cook	28	here
D	Johnston Elizabeth—†	708	housewife	23	"
E	Gordon Ernest I	708	waiter	32	"
F	Gordon Louise E—†	708	housewife	35	"
G	Jordan James	708	laborer	33	"
H	Nelson Rose—†	708	domestic	35	"
M	Jilkes Ernest	710	waiter	47	"
N	Jilkes Hilda—†	710	housewife	44	"
O	Coleman James A	710	fireman	59	"
P	Coleman Nannie F—†	710	housewife	45	"
R	Simmons Clarence A	710	painter	36	"
S	Simmons Lillian—†	710	housewife	39	"
U	Giragosian John	711	shoeworker	56	"
V	Kazarian Martin	711	"	53	"
W	Cook Lena—†	711A	housekeeper	55	"
Z	Nason Mary—†	713A	"	31	"
A	Green Jacob	714	clerk	57	"
B	Green Jacob, jr	714	"	20	"
C	Green Viola—†	714	housewife	50	"
D	Rutherford James	714	salesman	62	34 Windsor
E	Ferguson Conrade	714	clerk	41	here
F	Ferguson Mary E—†	714	housewife	38	"
G	Fortune Harold	714	waiter	24	"
H	Willard Mary—†	714	houseworker	65	"
L	Holston Carrie—†	715	"	30	"

Shawmut Avenue Continued

M	Holston Nina —†	715	housekeeper	28	here
N	Ball Carrie—†	716	houseworker	70	"
O	Ball William	716	laborer	50	"
P	Porter Pauline —†	716	laundress	57	"
R	William Angie—†	716	houseworker	57	"
S	Bynoe Edner—†	716	housewife	29	"
T	Bynoe John	716	laborer	30	"
U	Bynoe Louise—†	716	domestic	28	"
V	Foster Earnest—†	716	"	31	"
Z	Young Ashton	718	laborer	29	720 Shawmut av
A	Young Milicent —†	718	housewife	29	720 "
B	Paul Avis M—†	718	"	23	here
C	Paul William H	718	chauffeur	27	"
D	William Alice M—†	718	houseworker	47	11 Benton
G	Smith Harold S	719	janitor	31	12 Marble
H	Smith Lester P	719	clerk	27	72 Sawyer
K	Smith Lucy E—†	719	housekeeper	62	72 "
L	Smith Conway C	719A	laundryworker	38	28 E Lenox
M	Smith Glates—†	719A	housewife	30	28 "
N	Gordon Mary I—†	720	"	30	here
O	Gordon Robert	720	barber	46	"
R	West Charles C	720	cook	35	"
S	Haffler James	720	steelworker	39	11 Westminster
T	Haffler Mable—†	720	housewife	24	here
X	Harris William E	722A	laborer	45	"
Y	Kadish Abraham	722A	tailor	41	"
Z	Kadish Fannie—†	722A	clerk	21	"
A	Kadish Sarah—†	722A	houseworker	71	"
B	Kadish Sarah—†	722A	housewife	42	"
E	Deane Mary R H—†	724A	domestic	26	"
F	Hinton Margaret—†	724A	"	48	"
G	Selby Sarah J—†	724A	"	60	"
H	Burns William H	724A	laborer	48	"
K	Ramsey Sarah —†	724A	domestic	47	"
N	Hill Catherine M—†	726½	housewife	59	"
O	Hill Robert S	726½	porter	72	"
P	Lincoln Beulah H—†	726½	waitress	37	"
R	Brown Alice—†	726½	domestic	49	"
S	Brooks Florence E—†	726½	housewife	33	"
T	Brooks Robert E	726½	chauffeur	35	"
U	Alberts Hettie K—†	726½	houseworker	52	21 Windsor

24

Shawmut Avenue— Continued

v	Harmon Clarence	726½	molder	45	Portland Me
w	Harmon Mary—†	726½	housewife	47	"
c	Smith Charles	732	laborer	28	32 Ball
d	Jones William	732	clerk	22	here
e	Rollins Roger	732	steamfitter	23	Everett
f	Lightbourne Jane—†	732	housewife	44	W Medford
g	Lightbourne William L	732	contractor	42	"
h	Galloway Ella—†	732	domestic	48	here
k	Jackman Edward	732A	laborer	48	"
l	Jones Ethel—†	732A	housewife	26	"
m	Mohan Eaton	732A	seaman	32	"
n	Mohan Marion—†	732A	housekeeper	35	"
p	Jackman Edward D	736	laborer	39	"
r	Maughn Eustes	736	"	35	"
s	Maughn Mirian—†	736	housewife	35	"
t	Jones Ella—†	736	"	29	W Indies
u	Jones William	736	laborer	35	"
y	McLean Daniel M	741	janitor	45	here
z	McLean Fannie B—†	741	housewife	42	"
a	Wilson Sarah L—†	741	"	38	"
b	Wilson William B	741	chauffeur	39	"
c	Hatfield George E	741	janitor	54	"
d	Hatfield Rose—†	741	housewife	64	"
e	Brown Mary—†	741	housekeeper	40	"
f	Ritichen Robert	741	barber	42	"
g	Kelley Estel	741	laundryman	35	"
h	Skiner Marie—†	741	housekeeper	75	"
k	Collymore Beatrice—†	741	housewife	46	67 Ruggles
l	Collymore Edwin	741	cooper	49	67 "
m	Lee Ella—†	742	housewife	40	here
n	Lee Owen	742	clerk	45	"
o	Smith Clarone A—†	742	housewife	27	"
p	Smith Joseph E	742	porter	29	"
s	Goodman Madison	742	laborer	29	29 Wellington
t	Goodman Mary B—†	742	houseworker	43	29 "
x	Cox Veora—†	744	domestic	23	N Carolina
y	Fay Andrew	744	laborer	26	8 Greenwich
z	Fay Marzella—†	744	housewife	21	8 "
b	Ritchardson Eva—†	745A	"	20	84 Walnut av
c	Ritchardson Percy S	745A	chauffeur	27	84 "
d	Lewis Claristine—†	745A	housewife	27	64 Williams

Shawmut Avenue—Continued

E	Lewis Everard	745A	cook	28	64 Williams
F	Williams Juanita —†	745A	housekeeper	42	here
K	Hunter Emma W †	746	housewife	71	"
L	Hunter Henry	746	salesman	72	"
M	Collins Timothy	746	electrician	28	"
N	Hurley Margaret—†	746	housewife	28	702 Mass av
O	Hurley Thomas	746	wire stripper	39	702 "
P	Woodman Hyman	746	storekeeper	45	here
R	Allen Howard	746	woodworker	28	"
S	Brydges Howard	746	welder	30	"
T	Brydges Margaret —†	746	housewife	30	"
U	Collins Louise—†	746	"	24	"
V	Allen Mary —†	746	"	28	"
W	Allman Bessie —†	746	"	41	"
X	Allman Philip	746	watchmaker	40	"
Z	Cranston Mary †	746	housewife	25	"
A	Cranston William	746	clerk	26	"
B	Muyse Joseph L	746	fisherman	44	"
C	Muyse Minnie J —†	746	housewife	37	"
D	Colburn Christie —†	747	housekeeper	40	"
E	Scott Marie O †	747	housewife	32	"
F	Scott Wallace	747	porter	34	"
G	Ross Annie—†	747	housewife	50	"
H	Ross Clifton R	747	janitor	22	"
K	Ross Robert L	747	cook	51	"
M	Wilson Bertha —†	749	housekeeper	28	"
N	Wilson William R	749	cook	30	"
O	Farnham Adell F —†	749	housewife	48	"
P	Farnham Louis S	749	porter	52	"
S	Archbald Eldora †	749	housekeeper	62	"
T	Archbald Harry W	749	carpenter	23	"
U	Shepard Catherine E —†	749	housekeeper	30	"
V	Shepard Nathaniel	749	painter	28	"
X	McEachen Julia —†	750	rugmaker	45	1 Canton pl
Y	MacPharland Catherine—†	750	housewife	37	1 "
Z	Sinclair William D	750	packer	38	1 "
A	Barsell Margaret †	750	housewife	31	Melrose
B	Barsell William	750	clerk	33	"
C	Burgess Andrew	750	freighthandler	38	here
D	Burgess John E	750	janitor	44	"
E	Hartman Christie A —†	750	houseworker	49	"

Page.	Letter.	FULL NAME.	Residence, April 1, 1926.	Occupation.	Supposed Age.	Reported Residence, April 1, 1925. Street and Number.

Shawmut Avenue – Continued

F	Nicholson Daniel P	750	shoelaster	33	here
G	Wasson John J	750	electrician	24	"
H	Doherty Annie —†	750	houseworker	37	"
K	Doherty Patrick J	750	shoeworker	38	"
L	Coughlin Michael J	750	shipper	50	"
M	Gass Simon	750	casemaker	46	"
N	Hamblin Mary E —†	750	houseworker	49	"
O	Hamblin Warren H	750	shipper	45	"
P	McKinnon Christine —†	750	waitress	21	"
R	McKinnon Merdie —†	750	"	28	"
S	Pervey Anna M—†	750	houseworker	25	Braintree
T	Nickerson Jennie —†	750	milliner	45	here
U	Rounighan Jack	750	machinist	35	19 St Francis de Sales
V	Sharkey Winnie—†	750	housekeeper	37	37 Batavia
W	Sneed Violet E—†	751	"	28	here
X	Tanner Annie V—†	751	housewife	41	"
Y	Tanner Thomas E	751	clerk	41	"
Z	Gardner Benna —†	751	housewife	42	96 Hammond
A	Gardner Latrobe C	751	porter	44	96 "
B	Brooks Elinor—†	751	housekeeper	45	here
C	Brooks Eral H	751	porter	27	"
D	Brooks Walter E	751	waiter	45	"
H	Hewlett Allen L	757	cook	30	"
K	Hewlett Eleanor —†	757	housewife	52	"
L	Hewlett James T	757	student	25	"
M	DeLong Minnie A—†	757	housekeeper	54	"
N	Gibbon Annie C—†	757	"	47	"
P	Blair Lillie—†	759	housewife	48	"
R	Blair Walter J	759	waiter	49	"
S	Hogan Alice M—†	762	dyeworker	24	"
T	Sisco Mary E—†	762	houseworker	67	"
U	Sisco Moses	762	porter	35	17 Windsor
V	James Anna—†	762	housewife	30	here
W	James Henry	762	laborer	40	"
X	Berry Willis	762	"	44	"
Y	Berry Winnifred—†	762	housewife	42	"
Z	Bloon Samuel	762A	shoeworker	55	"
A	Dane Mary S—†	763	housekeeper	80	"
B	Wiggin Gertrude A—†	763	"	60	"
C	Daner Albert E	763	paperhanger	63	"
D	Dustin Eliza—†	763	housekeeper	60	"

Shawmut Avenue Continued

E	Nelson Alice †	763	at home	60	here
F	Smith James	763	retired	64	"
G	Hills Catherine †	764	clerk	55	"
H	Austin Lizzie †	764A	houseworker	78	"
K	Johnson John	764A	cementworker	42	"
L	Washington Annie U †	764A	housewife	33	"
M	Washington William A	764A	porter	34	"
N	Bowen Mary A †	764A	housewife	54	"
O	Frye Edith M †	764A	"	29	"
P	Frye Jerry L	764A	janitor	53	"
R	Reece Albert	766	tailor	38	"
S	Boyde Eugene	766A	clerk	35	"
T	Boyde Mary †	766A	housewife	33	"
U	Selven Edger B	766A	mover	27	Everett
V	Selven Tamar †	766A	housewife	23	"
W	Ethridge Amy F †	766A	"	52	here
X	Ethridge Columbus A	766A	clerk	49	"
Z	Remy Clarence	770	laborer	29	"
A	Remy Rhoda †	770	housewife	28	"
B	Drakes Charles	770	laborer	42	"
C	Drakes Ruth †	770	housewife	33	"
D	Prescott Reynolds	770	porter	49	"
E	Waid Helen †	770	houseworker	70	"
G	Hoyt Stewart E	772	collector	63	"
H	Plenty Helen †	772	housewife	36	"
K	Plenty Robert P	772	clerk	43	"
L	Davis Clarence J	772	carpenter	37	"
M	Davis Cora †	772	housewife	36	"
O	Hooper Alice †	774	"	38	"
P	Hooper Nathaniel	774	shipper	49	"
R	Tony Florence †	774	domestic	40	"
S	Tony George	774	laborer	43	"
T	Grant Bessie †	774	houseworker	33	"
U	Lopes James	774	laborer	36	"
V	Santos Henry	774	"	32	"
Z	Brooker Frank E	rear 780	roofer	53	"
A	Forester Jessie †	" 780	housewife	39	"
B	Forester John L	" 780	laborer	52	"
C	Harriston Sallia †	781	housewife	35	Cambridge
D	Harriston William	781	porter	45	"
E	Jordan Frederick	781	teamster	46	here

Shawmut Avenue—Continued

F	Smith Robert A	781	janitor	33	here
G	Wilson Jennie F—†	781	housekeeper	58	"
H	Allison Kenneth	781	janitor	29	"
K	Allison Lottie A—†	781	housewife	24	"
L	Doyle Catherine—†	782	"	40	"
M	Doyle Patrick	782	laborer	48	"
N	Meroth Catherine U—†	782	cashier	23	"
O	Meroth Joseph	782	porter	69	"
S	Parker James	783	fireman	80	"
T	Taylor Codelia—†	783	housekeeper	50	"
U	Taylor Fredrick	783	clerk	28	"
V	Brown Jessie—†	783	housekeeper	44	"
W	Brown Richard	783	janitor	50	"
X	Deshun Jennette—†	783	at home	78	"
Y	Taylor Lillian—†	783	domestic	30	"
Z	Debmann Isac	784	machinist	35	"
A	Taylor Ada M—†	784	housewife	47	"
B	Taylor William H	784	machinist	46	"
C	Thompson Lucie—†	786	housewife	57	"
D	Thompson Walter B rear	786	barber	53	"
E	Franklin Charles	787	chauffeur	31	"
F	Franklin Jennie—†	787	housekeeper	55	"
G	Kilduff Louis V	788	laborer	34	"
H	Kilduff Mary E—†	788	housewife	34	"
K	Goldspring Arden L	788	bellboy	52	"
L	Kearns Margaret—†	788	at home	60	"
M	Kearns Michael	788	laborer	72	"
O	Gould Francis	792	"	22	"
P	O'Hara Mary E—†	792	housewife	39	"
R	O'Hara William J	792	janitor	39	"
S	Gould Annie—† rear	792	housewife	48	"
T	Gould Charles F "	792	knitter	20	"
U	Gould Charles H "	792	machinist	53	"
V	Gould Esther—† "	792	saleswoman	23	"
W	Wright George M	793	janitor	68	"
X	Wright Nettie—†	793	housewife	62	"
Y	Serrington Camille—†	794	domestic	35	Swampscott
Z	Serrington Isaac G	794	salesman	41	"
A	Serrington William	794	chemist	42	"
B	Hardy Henry	794	laborer	45	here
C	Hardy Lillian—†	794	housewife	45	"

Shawmut Avenue—Continued

D	Stewart George E	794	waiter	53	here
E	Stewart Mary E—†	794	domestic	52	"
F	Tucker Isadora E—†	794	housewife	50	"
G	Tucker William H	794	fireman	58	"
H	Lawson Ethel M—† rear	794	housewife	42	"
K	Lawson Frank E "	794	mechanic	42	"
L	Lawson John V "	794	retired	78	"
M	Carter Robert L	795	fireman	31	"
N	Carter Sadie C—†	795	housewife	34	"
O	Nevels Mattie—†	795	housekeeper	46	"
P	Barnforth Bernard	796	clerk	29	"
R	Fitzgibbons John	796	laborer	59	"
S	Brennan John	796	"	50	"
T	Brennan Louise—†	796	housewife	39	"
U	Young Daniel I	796	carpenter	60	"
V	Burrel Anthony	799	cook	50	New York
W	Carter James	799	janitor	60	here
X	Wricks Baylor	799	waiter	59	"

Sterling Street

D	Taylor Inez—†	28	housewife	50	here
E	Taylor William H	28	caterer	35	"
F	Chase Gertrude—†	28	housewife	42	"
G	Chase Reginald	28	pipefitter	44	"
H	Guilford James E	28	waiter	41	"
K	Guilford Mamie—†	28	housewife	38	"
L	Byars Dolly—†	29	houseworker	46	147 Northampton
M	Ewing Watson	29	painter	49	Quincy
N	Francis John	29	kitchenman	40	here
O	Francis Sarah—†	29	housewife	29	"
R	Johnson Charles A	29	barber	35	Providence R I
S	McGill George	29	kitchenman	40	here
U	McLaughlin Sarah—†	29	maid	30	68 Williams
T	McLean Lucy—†	29	houseworker	60	11 Windsor
P	Quow Orie—†	29	domestic	50	here
V	Redmond Charles W	29	real estate	39	"
W	Redmond Viola—†	29	housewife	40	"
X	Robinson Ralph	30	student	28	"
Y	Thompson Clara—†	30	housekeeper	53	"

Sterling Street—Continued

		FULL NAME.	Res.	Occupation	Age	Reported Residence
	z	Thompson Estelle—†	30	laundress	22	here
	A	Freeman Arthur L	30	chauffeur	32	"
	B	Freeman Edward M	30	mover	58	"
	C	Freeman Rosella—†	30	housewife	62	"
	D	Belgrade Mary—†	30	domestic	67	10 Willard pl
	E	Douglas Beatrice—†	30	laundress	39	10 "
	F	LeCain Selina W—†	31	domestic	94	here
	G	Outing Charles	32	chauffeur	22	2002 Wash'n
	H	Outing Janie—†	32	housewife	50	2002 "
	K	Outing Napoleon	32	laborer	49	2002 "
	L	Chisholm Mary J—†	33	housewife	41	here
	M	Chisholm William H	33	baker	46	"
	N	Jones Harry H	34	porter	38	810 Tremont
	P	Richards Isabella—†	35	housewife	58	here
	R	Richards Samuel	35	laborer	60	"
	S	Brown James W	36	janitor	76	"
	T	Jackson Annie O—†	36	housewife	59	"
	U	Jordan Charles	36	laborer	29	Lynn
	V	Watkins George	36	florist	36	18 Hampshire
	W	Watkins Helen—†	36	operator	33	18 "
	A	Diggs Ella—†	38	laundress	68	6 Fairweather
	B	Paul Mary—†	38	domestic	50	Lynn
	C	Robinson Esther—†	38	laundress	40	here
	D	Williams Isaac	38	retired	84	"
	E	Young Julia—†	38	housekeeper	74	"
	F	Hudlin George A	39	chauffeur	29	27 Ball
	G	Hudlin Ina—†	39	housewife	28	27 "
	H	Kezirian Kirkor	39	factory worker	55	here
	K	Kezirian Taguie—†	39	housewife	40	"
	M	Singleton May—†	40	houseworker	32	"
	N	Singleton Smeo	40	ironmolder	34	"
	P	Burgess Arthur	41	laborer	45	"
	R	Burgess Florence—†	41	laundress	48	"
	S	Erving Adelaide—†	41	houseworker	23	46 Northfield
	T	Murray David	41	laborer	29	Cambridge
	U	Murray Lillian—†	41	houseworker	28	"
	V	Watkins Bertie L—†	43	housewife	50	here
	W	Watkins Robert P	43	janitor	55	"
	Y	Montgomery Robert A—†	43	operator	23	41 Sterling
	A	Hoyt Martha E—†	49	housewife	45	Cambridge
	B	Hoyt William	49	fireman	59	"

Sterling Street—Continued

c	Mann Gertrude A—†	49	housewife	21	Medford
d	Mann James N	49	fireman	26	New York
e	Davis Judson W	49	cook	50	92 Camden
f	Davis Lucy J—†	49	housewife	40	92 "
k	Woodis Arthur S	58	electrician	38	here
l	Woodis Nellie—†	58	housewife	34	"
m	Doherty Catherine N—†	60	domestic	76	"
n	Dunn Robert E	62	laborer	40	"
o	Durrell Albert S	62	advertising	49	"
p	Patterson Gertrude J—†	62	nurse	43	"
r	Scholder Nathaniel	62	painter	46	"
t	Morgan Lunette—†	64	housewife	25	12 Harwich
u	Morgan Robert	64	shipper	26	12 "
w	Arnold Elizabeth—†	66	laundress	40	here
x	Arnold Marion—†	66	"	23	"
y	Johnson Martha—†	66	houseworker	27	32 Wellington
z	King Bessie—†	66	laundress	26	32 "
b	Chesterfield John D	68	plasterer	78	123 Cabot
c	Cooper Jenney C—†	68	laundress	30	123 "
d	Bray Nannie—†	68	domestic	62	665 Shawmut av
e	Johnson Robert M	68	waiter	52	665 "
g	Davis Joseph	70	porter	21	6 Arnold
h	Davis Mary—†	70	housewife	21	6 "
k	Carson Louise—†	70	houseworker	38	40 Williams
m	Parris Evelyn—†	72	factory worker	32	1 Newcomb
n	Lightler Edna—†	72	houseworker	30	1 "
o	Robinson Fannie—†	72	laundress	45	133 Sterling
p	Anderson Hattie B—†	72	housewife	43	here
r	Anderson Leroy	72	cook	45	"
s	Crute William	74	caretaker	38	"
t	Crute Kizzie—†	74	houseworker	40	"
w	Williams Beulah—†	76	laundress	34	17 Newburn
x	Jackman Willy B—†	76	cook	42	84 Sterling
y	Jones Mary—†	78	housewife	25	here
z	Jones Samuel	78	laborer	27	"
a	Seymour Susan—†	78	laundress	51	"
b	Seymour Thomas E	78	real estate	47	"
c	Ponton Edward	78	waiter	52	115 Lenox
d	Taylor Belle—†	78	houseworker	58	here
e	Leary James	80	laborer	50	"
f	McAully Jessie—†	80	housekeeper	50	"
g	Wallace John	80	mover	60	"

Last	Letter	FULL NAME.	Residence, April 1, 1926.	Occupation.	Supposed Age.	Reported Residence, April 1, 1925. Street and Number.

Sterling Street—Continued

H	Ming Catherine—†	80	laundress	28	119 Kendall
K	Fitzgerald Lacey	80	laborer	40	here
L	Cooper Hattie B—†	82	laundress	42	25 Oak Grove
M	Dillard James	82	laborer	46	S Carolina
N	Gaines Thomas	82	teamster	52	627 Shawmut av
O	Springer James	82	laborer	42	627 "
R	Robinson Minnie A—†	84	laundress	50	33 Westminster
S	Richardson Annie M—†	84	housewife	44	here
T	Richardson Edward T	84	steward	53	"
U	Eller Sarah—†	84	laundress	39	"
V	Beckett Lillian G—†	84	housewife	28	"
W	Beckett William F	84	policeman	30	"
X	Wilson Annabella—†	84	housewife	50	651 Shawmut av
Y	Wilson Oscar G	84	shipper	50	651 "
Z	Paul Edward L	84	letter carrier	30	here
A	Paul Hildred—†	84	housewife	30	"
B	Moore Josephine—†	84	"	37	"
C	Moore Theodore	84	mover	36	"
D	Caldwell Lillian—†	84	housewife	36	"
E	Caldwell Walter G	84	porter	41	"
F	Henry Robert C	130	tailor	37	"
G	Donaldson Leola J—†	132	housewife	46	"
H	Donaldson Lyman B	132	musician	23	"
K	Donaldson Samuel B	132	cook	45	"
L	Henry John R	132	waiter	30	5 Warwick
M	Henry Lucille—†	132	housewife	29	5 "
N	Newton Dorothy—†	132	teacher	23	here
O	Newton Herbert	132	letter carrier	21	"
P	Newton Olivia—†	132	housekeeper	49	"
R	Eaton George J	134	waiter	44	"
S	Eaton Maude L—†	134	housewife	33	"
T	Feurtado Florence—†	134	"	35	"
U	Feurtado Harry	134	shipper	35	"
V	Lewis Emma L—†	134	housewife	36	"
W	Lewis George W	134	welder	39	"
X	Armstrong Sarah—†	134	domestic	55	"
Y	Gordon George	134	porter	47	"
Z	Hector Leona—†	134	domestic	23	"
A	Stewart Gladys—†	134	"	21	"
B	Greggs Charles L	136	laundryman	35	385 Northampton
C	Greggs Ethel E—†	136	housewife	45	385 "

9—9

Page.	Letter.	FULL NAME.	Residence, April 1, 1926.	Occupation.	Supposed Age.	Reported Residence, April 1, 1925. Street and Number.

Tilden Place

	E	Hansen Hans J	1	carpenter	67	here
	F	Underwood Frances—†	1	nurse	48	"
	G	Quigley Joseph B	1	teamster	47	"
	H	Quigley Mary A—†	1	housekeeper	42	"
	K	Cranston Cora—†	2	domestic	61	"
	L	Clark John A	2	electrician	32	"
	M	Graham Lewis H	2	steamfitter	38	"
	N	Graham Margaret A—†	2	housewife	38	"

Vernon Street

	R	Furman Evangeline—†	23	clerk	24	here
	S	Furman Samuel V	23	salvation army	62	"
	T	Rand Josephine—†	23	housekeeper	22	87 Vernon
	U	Carleton Ethel M—† rear 25	housewife	23	here
	V	Carleton Harry G " 25	merchant	39	"
	W	Beals Edna A—† " 25	waitress	24	1273 Tremont
	X	Beals Helen T—† " 25	nurse	49	1273 "
	Y	Kirby Margaret M—† " 25	housewife	24	5 Newhall
	Z	Kirby William M " 25	chauffeur	28	5 "
	A	Callahan Catherine A—†	27	housekeeper	67	here
	B	Colley Gertrude T—†	27	collector	31	"
	C	McLean Arthur S	29	policeman	29	11 Marble
	D	Sexton John T	29	"	27	11 "
	E	Callahan Frank	29	foreman	38	here
	F	Callahan Hilma—†	29	housewife	31	"
	G	Curran Anna M—†	31	"	20	20 Kent
	H	Curran Charles L	31	laborer	20	20 "
	K	Field Chester	31	chauffeur	22	23 Marcella
	L	Field Chiquita M—†	31	saleswoman	27	23 "
	M	Field Daisy—†	31	"	21	23 "
	N	Field Sadie—†	31	"	35	23 "
	O	Barron Margaret—†	35	housekeeper	60	here
	P	Gilday Anna K—†	35	"	29	"
	R	Gilday Maude L—†	35	clerk	31	"
	S	Miey Thomas	35	storekeeper	66	"
	T	Cronan Daniel	39	chauffeur	28	21 Palmer
	U	Murray John	39	"	22	Cambridge
	V	Torrie Charlotte—†	39	housekeeper	50	here

Vernon Street—Continued

w	Torrie William H	39	manager	55	Canada
x	McBarron Charles H	45	blacksmith	63	here
y	McBarron Edward L	45	clerk	45	"
z	McBarron Sarah—†	45	housewife	65	"
A	Kelley William J	47	longshoreman	36	"
B	Giroux Albert	47	chauffeur	48	"
c	Giroux Florence—†	47	saleswoman	34	"
D	Hawkins Catherine—†	47	housewife	28	"
E	Hawkins William O	47	fireman	31	"
F	Griffin John J	49	musician	56	"
G	Griffin Priscilla J—†	49	housewife	41	"
H	Kelley Mary—†	49	"	37	"
K	MacDonald Catherine—†	49	housekeeper	60	"
L	MacDonald Joseph J	49	bookbinder	45	"
M	McGowan Jennie—†	49	egg packer	57	53 Havre
N	Cryer Ellen—†	49	housekeeper	67	here
O	Pellow Anna—†	49	clerk	25	"
P	Wiley Elizabeth—†	49	dressmaker	47	"
R	Wiley Georgiana—†	49	"	22	"
T	Murphy Dennis	51	retired	52	"
U	Murphy Edward P	51	bricklayer	26	"
v	Kelley Alice M—†	51	housewife	22	99A Roxbury
w	Wright Lillian M—†	51	"	44	here
x	Wright George W	51	carpenter	50	"
y	O'Brien John T	53	chauffeur	33	69 Decatur
z	O'Brien Theresa A—†	53	housewife	33	69 "
A	Walsh Jennette—†	53	"	44	237 Cabot
B	Walsh Jeremiah F	53	laborer	49	237 "

Warwick Street

D	Harrison Susie—†	95	houseworker	49	here
E	Johnson Harry	95	fireman	45	"
F	Morris Viola—†	95	houseworker	31	61 Camden
G	Midgett Ella B—†	95	domestic	20	here
H	Midgett Mary—†	95	houseworker	50	"
K	Munroe Constance—†	95	housewife	30	12 Cliff
L	Munroe William H	95	waiter	34	12 "
M	Thomas Daniel	95	porter	37	here
N	Thomas Ethel—†	95	housewife	35	"

Warwick Street – Continued

o	McCain Eliza †	97	housewife	45	here
P	McCain George	97	painter	46	"
R	Blunt Augustus	97	porter	51	"
s	Blunt Carrie †	97	housewife	40	"
T	Senhouse Betrice †	97	houseworker	34	82 Williams
U	Harris George B	97	porter	46	here
V	Harris Kate O †	97	housewife	39	"
W	Johnson Joseph	97	janitor	40	"
X	Weir Ernestine †	99	housewife	34	718 Shawmut av
Y	Weir John	99	expressman	38	718 "
z	Fernandez Anthony	99	laborer	26	here
A	Fernandez Mildred †	99	housewife	23	"
C	Gregory Edith †	99	clerk	21	115 Warwick
D	Gregory Thomas	99	painter	47	115 "
E	Gregory Virginia †	99	housewife	36	115 "
F	Pasek Albert	99	sign painter	40	here
G	Pasek Anna †	99	houseworker	68	"
H	Pasek Frank	99	polisher	42	"
K	Pasek John	99	machinist	38	"
L	Nalbandian Harootune	99	shoemaker	55	"
M	Nalbandian Helen †	99	housewife	37	"
N	Shukloian Mark	99	rug dealer	36	"
o	Shukloian Sara †	99	housewife	60	"
P	Lewis Matilda †	99	candymaker	44	106 Hammond
R	Lewis Thomas A	99	shoeworker	40	106 "
s	Smith Hazel †	99	houseworker	22	106 "
T	Montier Della †	rear 99	housewife	33	8 Benton
U	Montier Sidney W	" 99	janitor	33	8 "
V	McLoud Margaret †	" 99	houseworker	29	here
W	Clapp Alex	" 99	laborer	22	Cambridge
X	Clapp Margaret †	" 99	housewife	21	"
Y	Clapp George	" 99	laborer	26	Richmond Va
z	Clapp Julia †	" 99	houseworker	25	"
A	Randolph Laura †	" 99	"	32	here
B	Montier Clarence	" 99	janitor	23	23 Hubert
C	Montier Vera †	" 99	housewife	21	23 "
D	Choolfaian James E	" 99	carpenter	35	here
E	Choolfaian Mary †	" 99	housewife	32	"
F	Lincoln Clifford H	" 99	painter	42	"
G	Wilson Frank	" 99	cook	55	"
H	Jackson Mary R †	105	housekeeper	54	"

Page.	Letter.	FULL NAME.	Residence, April 1, 1926.	Occupation.	Supposed Age.	Reported Residence, April 1, 1925. Street and Number.

Warwick Street — Continued

K	Roberts Emma —†	105	housekeeper	25	here
L	Roberts Harold	105	chauffeur	27	"
M	Diggen Emma L †	107	housekeeper	52	"
N	King Charles	107	painter	55	"
O	Smith Cathaleen E —†	107	houseworker	32	Richmond Va
P	Smith Robert D	107	laborer	33	"
R	Emery William H	109	physician	77	here

Washington Street

W	Whitney Frederick	2049	starter	58	here
X	Whitnery Herbert	2049	laborer	54	"
Y	Whitney Margaret —†	2049	houseworker	61	"
Z	Donahue Edward	2049	druggist	48	"
A	Donahue Mary V —†	2049	housewife	43	"
B	Kenney John J	2049	laborer	47	"
L	Authouse Ella —†	2075	housewife	45	121 St Stephen
M	Authouse Hartio	2075	fishcutter	50	121 "
N	Powers Mabel —†	2075	housewife	28	10 Ball
O	Powers Peter	2075	roofer	30	10 "
P	McDermott George J	2075	"	30	here
R	McDermott Lucretia —†	2075	housewife	30	"
T	Gorman Elizabeth F—†	2079	"	28	"
U	Gorman Ray D	2079	tel worker	28	"
V	McGee Catherine A †	2079	bookbinder	34	"
W	McGee John F	2079	guard	40	"
X	McGee Theresa D —†	2079	tel operator	24	"
Y	Malley Jessie —†	2079	houseworker	41	23 Hanson
A	Thorn Carl F	2083	chauffeur	33	here
B	Thorn Elizabeth K—†	2083	housewife	32	"
D	O'Keefe Bartholomew H	2083	clerk	47	5 Palmer pl
E	O'Keefe Florence L—†	2083	housewife	38	5 "
F	O'Keefe William H	2083	clerk	22	5 "
G	Boltz George	2085	"	35	here
H	Boltz Mary—†	2085	housekeeper	66	"
K	Boltz Walter F	2085	clerk	28	"
L	Shay John	2085	salesman	23	"
M	Murphy Albert S	2085	fireman	38	"

Page.	Letter.	FULL NAME.	Residence, April 1, 1926.	Occupation.	Supposed Age.	Reported Residence, April 1, 1925. Street and Number.

Washington Street—Continued

N	Murphy Evelyn G—†	2085	housewife	36	here
O	Griffen James P	2085	gilder	25	"
P	Griffen Sadie—†	2085	housewife	28	"
K	Barry Thomas J	2145	laborer	48	"
L	Burke Thomas J	2145	buyer	35	"
M	Conklin George J	2145	bookkeeper	76	"
N	Donovan Dennis	2145	mover	40	"
O	Enslow Charles J	2145	clerk	28	3 Anita ter
P	Laundria Sophie—†	2145	housewife	38	here
R	Laundria William D	2145	clerk	41	"
S	MacCorther Angus	2145	carpenter	75	"
T	McGready Patrick	2145	clerk	40	Dedham
U	Meehan James	2145	watchman	75	here
V	Moore William	2145	painter	45	"
W	O'Brien Patrick J	2145	chauffeur	24	"
W¹	Quaid Dennis	2145	salesman	44	"
X	Roache James	2145	painter	45	Brockton
Y	Rourke William J	2145	"	50	"
Z	Saunders Barnet	2145	salesman	30	here
A	Slason George	2145	clerk	61	"
B	Steeves Frank	2145	"	50	144 Dudley
C	Turpin Benjamin	2145	chauffeur	24	726 Com av
D	Wall William	2145	foreman	57	New York
G	Buckley James	2161	policeman	29	here
H	Buckley Madeline—†	2161	housewife	26	"
K	Meyerstein Carl	2161	janitor	44	"
L	Meyerstein Etta—†	2161	housewife	50	"
M	Marshall Mary F—†	2161	"	45	"
N	Marshall Walter T	2161	plasterer	53	"
O	Venner Doris—†	2161	shoeworker	35	63 Smith
P	Baer Caroline—†	2161	at home	71	here
R	Baer Emma C—†	2161	bookkeeper	45	"
S	Oliver Marion V—†	2161	pressfeeder	28	"
T	Sumner Frank	2161	ironworker	38	12 Stanwood
U	Sumner Maud A—†	2161	housewife	41	12 "
V	Reed Charles W	2161	chauffeur	57	here
W	Reed Susan A—†	2161	housewife	55	"
X	Severi James	2161	painter	40	Plymouth
Y	Severi Margurite—†	2161	housewife	40	"
Z	Colbert Bertha—†	2161	"	38	here
A	Colbert John E	2161	letter carrier	47	"
B	LePage Nepolian	2161	special police	62	Brookline

Washington Street—Continued

C	Dickenson Lillian—†	2161	seamstress	44	Texas
D	Hall Thomas	2161	chauffeur	24	U S A
E	McDonald William T	2161	steamfitter	55	here
F	Sugrue Mary—†	2181	stitcher	47	"
G	Brown Avery	2161	stableman	65	"
H	Brown Ella—†	2161	housewife	55	"
K	Brown Myrtle—†	2161	stenographer	30	"
L	Papen Theodore F	2161	shipper	62	"
M	Connelly Mary—†	2161	nurse	53	"
N	Fitzgibbons James	2161	clerk	50	New York City
O	Fitzgibbons May—†	2161	housewife	45	"
P	Best Ida M—†	2161	clerk	23	Somerville
R	Bryce Nettie M—†	2161	manager	43	"
S	McNulty John	2161	woodcarver	59	237 Dudley
T	Raymond Rose A—†	2161	housewife	42	237 "
U	Raymond Walter F	2161	painter	57	237 "
V	Remick Vianna—†	2161	shoeworker	27	here
W	Worth Gertrude—†	2161	housewife	29	"
X	Worth Herman	2161	dentist	29	"
Y	Holland Bertha M—†	2161	cashier	36	"
Z	Rogers Hilda A—†	2161	hairdresser	36	"
A	Sideleau Arthur L	2161	chauffeur	30	"
B	Sideleau Dorris—†	2161	housewife	29	"
C	Paine Susan J—†	2161	at home	60	"
D	Bettinson Helen—†	2161	houseworker	30	New York
E	Campbell Catherine—†	2161	saleswoman	70	here
F	Whooley Morgan	2161	chauffeur	29	New York
G	Hamlin Florence—†	2161	clerk	28	here
H	Harriman Donald	2161	mechanic	35	"
K	Johnson Derinder—†	2161	housewife	58	"
L	Johnson William H	2161	motorman	56	"
M	Abner Manuel S	2161	woodworker	63	"
N	Abner Mary—†	2161	housewife	57	"
O	Fisher Charles H	2161	retired	83	"
P	Thomas Manuel	2161	steward	65	"
R	Vretos Betrice—†	2161	housewife	30	1 Columbus sq
S	Vretos Nicholas	2161	chef	33	1 "
T	Ainsley John	2161	painter	59	here
U	Holland Maud—†	2161	housekeeper	45	"
V	Latham Alice—†	2161	housewife	35	"
W	Latham Parker	2161	fisherman	38	"

Westminster Street

A	Bethune Elizabeth—†	64	cook	35	here	
B	Bethune Owen F	64	builder	34	"	
D	Breckleton Clarence G	64	cutter	32	"	
E	Breckleton Evelyn—†	64	housekeeper	28	"	
F	Jackson Florence K—†	66	"	46	"	
G	Jackson James T	66	decorator	43	"	
H	Shearer Charles F	66	porter	27	125 Warwick	
K	Shearer Marguarite—†	66	housekeeper	25	125 "	
L	Perry Eleanor—†	66	"	29	67 Williams	
M	Alcorn Harold	68	houseman	35	66 Westminster	
N	Alcorn Hettie—†	68	housekeeper	57	here	
O	Ward James H	68	laborer	32	"	
P	Ward Mabel—†	68	housekeeper	29	"	
R	Young Bertha—†	68	laundress	33	"	
S	McCoat Daisy—†	70	"	28	"	
T	Williams Mabel—†	70	"	46	"	
U	Leake Flirlie	70	laborer	21	948 Tremont	
V	Leake Ruby—†	70	laundress	23	948 "	
W	Miller Mossie—†	70	dressmaker	25	948 "	
X	Bowden Ernest	70	machinist	30	here	
Y	Bowden George E	70	hotelman	35	"	
Z	Bowden Mary—†	70	housekeeper	62	"	
A	Turner Mary E—†	72	housewife	49	"	
B	Simmonds Ethel—†	72	dressmaker	38	"	
C	Simmonds Lydie—†	72	housekeeper	70	"	
D	Simmonds Mabel—†	72	dressmaker	25	"	
E	Douglas Ernest	72	cook	30	Newport R I	
F	Harris Sadie—†	72	domestic	29	Attleboro	
G	Gupton William	72	cook	52	Maine	
K	Hutchins Elizabeth—†	74	houseworker	43	here	
L	Hutchins Jeremiah	74	R R man	62	"	
M	Fields Ada—†	74	housekeeper	25	693 Shawmut av	
N	Robinson George	74	postal clerk	33	555 "	
O	Robinson Pearl—†	74	hairdresser	28	555 "	
P	Bennett Annie—†	74	cook	63	here	
R	Franklyn Sadie—†	74	laundress	55	"	
S	Gupton William	74	porter	50	32 Newcomb	
T	Hapewell Jennie—†	74	cook	66	here	
U	Harris Sadie—†	74	housekeeper	29	32 Newcomb	
V	Brown Esther—†	76	housewife	23	2½ Clayton pl	

Page.	Letter.	Full Name.	Residence, April 1, 1926.	Occupation.	Supposed Age.	Reported Residence, April 1, 1925. Street and Number.

Westminster Street—Continued

Letter.	Full Name.	Residence	Occupation.	Age	Reported Residence
w	Brown William B	76	mechanic	27	2½ Clayton pl
x	Campbell Gertrude—†	76	waitress	28	555 Shawmut av
y	Johnson Clarister—†	76	clerk	25	655 "
z	Johnson Phebe—†	76	housekeeper	56	655 "
A	Gordon Luceil—†	76	housewife	30	here
B	Gordon Rupert	76	cook	28	"
C	Robert Alfred J	84	porter	60	36 Buckingham
D	Robert Gerald	84	laborer	47	71 Warwick
E	Robert Mary E—†	84	housekeeper	46	71 "
F	Frank Adina—†	84	"	28	87 Reed
G	Frank John	84	laborer	28	87 "
H	Burnett Luverne	84	carpenter	33	664 Shawmut av
K	Burnett Sadie—†	84	at home	24	664 "
L	Glasgow Irene—†	84	cook	25	here
M	Glasgow Jennie T—†	84	maid	50	"
N	Cheek Pennie—†	86	housekeeper	22	78 Kendall
O	Cheek William	86	laborer	27	78 "
P	Dorsey Charlotte—†	86	dressmaker	37	here
R	Ellis Arthur	86	longshoreman	43	"
S	Ellis Mabel—†	86	housekeeper	34	"
T	Paris Charles	88	elevatorman	34	"
U	Paris Sarah—†	88	housekeeper	57	"
V	Gold Bessie—†	88	"	35	"
W	Gold Morris	88	pedler	48	"
X	Isles Catherine—†	88	housewife	23	726 Shawmut av
Y	Isles John H	88	cook	29	726 "
Z	Soper John	90	laborer	35	101 Hammond
A	Pena Lillian—†	90	at home	28	924 Tremont
B	Pena Manuel J	90	laborer	33	924 "
C	Perry Laura—†	90	at home	65	924 "
D	Calaway James	90	laborer	24	Springfield
E	Hogue Carrie—†	90	housewife	24	79 Emerald
F	Hogue Lawrence H	90	porter	41	79 "
H	Furtado Josephine—†	92	laundress	35	here
K	Furtado Peter	92	laborer	35	"
L	Cidolit Virginia—†	92	housekeeper	35	463 Appleton rd
M	Jackson Lillian—†	92	cook	42	41 Camden
N	Walker Loretta—†	92	housekeeper	20	41 "
O	Walker William	92	machinist	24	41 "
P	Robinson James R	92A	carpenter	42	Monponsett
R	Robinson Mabel—†	92A	housekeeper	33	"

Page.	Letter.	FULL NAME.	Residence, April 1, 1926.	Occupation.	Supposed Age.	Reported Residence, April 1, 1925. Street and Number.

Westminster Street—Continued

s	Carter Mary—†	94	laundress	58	here
t	Gilmore Beatrice—†	94	waitress	25	"
u	Monroe Alfred A	94	porter	36	55 Warwick
v	Monroe Ophelia—†	94	housekeeper	28	55 "
w	Davis Edward	94	steamfitter	45	here
x	Davis Leila—†	94	at home	24	"
y	Haggie Mildred—†	96	housekeeper	33	"
z	Haggie Pleasent D	96	paperhanger	46	"
A	Foster Christina—†	96	laundress	58	19 Hubert
B	Foster Walter	96	taxi driver	34	19 "
c	Gordon Florence—†	96	housekeeper	52	1 Smith av
D	Pitman William C	96	porter	53	1 "

Weston Street

F	Butler Shermont	9	chauffeur	23	23 Thorndike
G	Sopes Viola—†	9	maid	30	Lawrence
H	Williams Daisy H—†	9	factory worker	22	here
K	Williams Minnie A—†	9	housekeeper	38	"
L	Williams Susie A—†	9	factory worker	21	"
M	Wilson Richard A	11	laborer	44	165 W Springfield
N	Casciottolo Frank	11	porter	32	here
P	Casciottolo Generoso	11	laborer	62	"
O	Casciottolo Joseph	11	"	21	23 Newburn
R	Casciottolo Mary—†	11	housewife	56	here
s	Casiciottolo Michael	11	pianoworker	34	"
T	Bornner Elma—†	11	housewife	24	"
U	Bornner John H	11	steamfitter	29	"
V	Berge Susan—†	13	laundress	57	"
W	Berge Walter	13	porter	39	"
X	Smith Harold F	13	boilermaker	46	"

Williams Street

D	Benjamin William	18	laborer	39	here
E	Bishop Iris—†	18	domestic	26	6 Williams ter
F	Bramble Rose—†	18	"	39	here
G	Dyer Alice—†	18	housewife	30	"
H	Dyer Joseph R	18	chauffeur	37	"

42

Page.	Letter.	FULL NAME.	Residence, April 1, 1926.	Occupation.	Supposed Age.	Reported Residence, April 1, 1925. Street and Number.

Williams Street—Continued

	K	Gaynor Eliza— †	18	domestic	50	here
	L	Miller John	18	seaman	25	"
	M	Miller Sarah— †	18	domestic	29	"
	N	Putnam James	18	cook	25	"
	O	Putnam Louise— †	18	domestic	28	1111 Harrison av
	P	Rickets Nina—†	18	"	28	here
	R	Sweeney Marie—†	18	"	22	72 Ruggles
	T	Owens Arminta—†	20	housewife	38	here
	U	Owens James T	20	barber	42	"
	W	Haskins Roger E	22	waiter	40	"
	X	Haskins Roger E, jr	22	clerk	20	"
	Y	Haskins Sallie A—†	22	housewife	50	"
	A	Brown Thomas K	24	baker	57	"
	B	Goodman Annie—†	24	houseworker	50	"
	D	Goodman Milford	24	fisherman	42	"
	C	Goodman Tassie—†	24	housewife	50	"
	E	Healey Agnes—†	24	domestic	35	"
	F	Mulroy Martin J	24	salesman	34	10 Alleghany
	G	Ransdon Frank	24	teamster	58	10 Greenville
	K	Carey Michael	26	millhand	68	here
	L	Keddy John W	26	painter	64	"
	M	Lukes James	26	teamster	45	"
	N	McHugh Bernard	26	clerk	37	"
	O	Miller Henry G	26	laborer	70	"
	P	Connor Johanna—†	28	houseworker	73	"
	R	Connor John J	28	clerk	48	"
	S	Shea Helen T- †	28	at home	47	"
	T	Guard George	30	clerk	42	"
	U	Mathew John	30	"	25	"
	U¹	Mathew Teresa— †	30	housewife	22	"
	V	McKenna Bernard	30	seaman	24	"
	W	McKenna Teresa—†	30	houseworker	56	"
	X	Mirrell Mary—†	30	dressmaker	32	"
	Y	Kelley Emily K—†	32	housewife	47	"
	Z	Kelley Michael	32	retired	70	"
	A	Reardon Anna M—†	32	saleswoman	32	5 Hammett
	B	Readon Catherine—†	32	houseworker	60	5 "
	C	Christian Matilda—†	34	at home	70	here
	D	Christian Peter	34	clerk	45	"
	E	Christian Rose—†	34	domestic	40	"
	F	Christian Susie—†	34	housewife	38	"

43

Williams Street — Continued

G	Davis Everett W	34	carpenter	38	here
H	Davis Gertrude —†	34	domestic	38	"
K	Ganaway Marie —†	34	seamstress	40	"
L	Henry Joseph	34	laborer	38	"
M	Barber Frances —†	36	clerk	62	"
N	Copp Hazel M —†	36	houseworker	30	Wash'n D C
O	Dale Annie —†	36	clerk	28	here
P	Foster Enid J —†	36	houseworker	20	716 Shawmut av
S	Lindsey James H	38	florist	40	here
T	Schuyler James	38	seaman	27	"
U	Schuyler John T	38	mechanic	23	"
V	Schuyler Mary E —†	38	housewife	51	"
W	Schuyler Thomas G	38	manager	63	"
Y	Younger Fred	40	porter	25	29 Walnut
Z	Younger Vernice —†	40	housewife	25	29 "
A	Morris Robert C	40	laundryworker	22	W Newton
B	Morris Ruth E —†	40	housewife	20	"
E	Hossack Adle —†	59	houseworker	52	here
F	Hossack Dora —†	59	domestic	23	"
G	Dudley Annie —†	59	housekeeper	40	"
H	Price Christopher C	59	porter	47	"
K	Price Clifford E —†	59	housewife	40	"
L	Robinson Robert O	59	waiter	36	"
M	Grant George	60	laborer	46	"
N	Thompson Leslie E	60	porter	31	"
O	Thompson May —†	60	housewife	26	"
P	Brown Robert	60	waiter	41	"
R	Brown Sophie —†	60	housewife	38	"
S	Lewis Claremont	61	janitor	29	"
T	Lewis Edwardine —†	61	housewife	29	"
U	Nelson Isadore —†	61	"	34	"
V	Nelson William	61	laborer	36	"
Y	Jefferson Emma B —†	62	housewife	53	"
Z	Jefferson William H	62	waiter	58	"
A	Archer Alexander	62	laborer	33	698 Shawmut av
B	Archer Annie —†	62	housewife	29	698 "
C	Robinson Anna B —†	62	"	28	here
D	Robinson Herbert	62	cook	29	"
E	Schwartz Morris	63	carpenter	46	"
F	Schwartz Rose —†	63	housewife	45	"
H	Barnett Irine —†	63	domestic	22	"

44

Williams Street—Continued

	K	William Zillia—†	63	housewife	35	here
	N	Garet Louise—†	64	domestic	34	"
	O	Gall Herman	64	porter	29	"
	P	Gall Lillian—†	64	housewife	32	"
	R	Wiggins Livina—†	64	domestic	39	"
	S	Knight Adella—†	66	housewife	72	"
	T	Knight Charles	66	laborer	44	"
	U	Mathew Cicilan—†	66	domestic	38	New York City
	V	Strashun Fannie—†	66	housewife	39	here
	W	Strashun Harry	66	pedler	46	"
	X	Diggs George	66	laborer	45	7 Arnold
	Y	Diggs Jessie—†	66	housewife	35	7 "
	A	James Charles	67	laborer	27	Cambridge
	B	James Elouise—†	67	housewife	24	"
	C	Chapman Emma—†	67	"	48	here
	D	Chapman Nies	67	laborer	53	"
	E	Clark Celia—†	68	housewife	40	"
	F	Clark Ralph	68	porter	42	"
	G	Clark Anna—†	68	housewife	33	"
	H	Clark John	68	laborer	35	"
	K	Rodnitsky Bertha—†	68	houseworker	55	"
	L	Johnson Arthur B	69	porter	39	"
	M	Johnson Eugene H	69	housewife	35	"
	O	Palmer Mabel—†	69	housekeeper	28	"
	P	Palmer Walter	69	shipper	28	"
	R	Harrison Ada—†	70	domestic	49	"
	S	Clark Mary—†	70	housewife	40	"
	T	Clark Samuel	70	laborer	42	"
	U	Gladden Viola—†	70	housewife	22	28 Anderson
	V	Gladden Walter	70	laborer	24	28 "
	W	Barton Edward A	71	mason	50	here
	X	Barton Ritchel—†	71	housewife	48	"
	Y	Lambert James J	71	teamster	48	"
	Z	Lambert Lucy—†	71	laundress	48	"
	A	Goodridge Allen W	71	porter	31	"
	B	Goodridge Stella—†	71	housekeeper	26	"
	C	Mahoney Agnes J—†	72	at home	64	"
	D	Rue Agnes L—†	72	housewife	32	"
	E	Reed Elizabeth—†	72	"	48	"
	F	Reed William H	72	janitor	49	"
	G	Brown Thomas	72	porter	75	"

Williams Street — Continued

H	Sewell George A	72	carpenter	38	here
K	Sewell Sadie —†	72	housewife	38	"
L	Clark William J	73	porter	28	99 Warwick
M	Griffith James	73	stevedore	39	here
N	Griffith Phylis —†	73	housekeeper	37	"
O	Chapman Olive —†	73	housewife	26	"
P	Smith Henrietta —†	74	"	32	"
R	Smith Theophile	74	laborer	39	"
S	Simonds Lydia—†	74	at home	70	W Indies
T	Simonds Mary —†	74	domestic	24	"
U	Wilson Eva †	74	"	25	"
V	Morrison Louis	74	teamster	50	here
W	Newton Tempie—†	74	housekeeper	29	"
X	Yauborough Mattie —†	74	domestic	50	"
Y	Gough Jessie †	75	housewife	39	"
Z	Gough Lorinzo	75	laborer	42	"
A	Gough Madline †	75	domestic	21	"
B	Jacobs Ora —†	75	housewife	44	"
C	Johnson Dora —†	75	housekeeper	46	"
D	Philips David M	75	laborer	41	"
E	Johnson Charles	76	chauffeur	26	"
F	Johnson Josephine —†	76	housewife	24	"
G	Goldstein Annie —†	76	"	35	"
H	Goldstein Myer	76	real estate	37	"
K	Smith Mary —†	76	housewife	32	"
L	Smith Robert H	76	laborer	34	"
M	Bowen Atta †	77	housewife	33	"
N	Bowen Leonard	77	laborer	46	"
O	McCreary James	77	"	40	"
P	Williams Cora —†	77	housekeeper	41	"
R	Jackson James A	77	laborer	53	"
S	Jackson Lula—†	77	housewife	38	"
T	Brown Catherine L —†	78	domestic	56	716 Shawmut av
U	Brown Alfred	78	laborer	44	here
V	Brown Margaret —†	78	housewife	48	"
W	Noble Laura A †	78	"	38	"
X	Noble Paul J	78	fireman	52	"
Y	Ferri Michael	79	laborer	34	"
Z	Ferri Pauline —†	79	housewife	34	"
A	Thomas John	79	laborer	47	"
B	Thomas Melteda —†	79	housewife	35	"

Page.	Letter.	FULL NAME.	Residence, April 1, 1926.	Occupation.	Supposed Age.	Reported Residence, April 1, 1925. Street and Number.

Williams Street—Continued

c	Mims Emma—†	79	housewife	36	here
d	Mims Henry	79	laborer	37	"
e	Drury Mary E—†	80	housewife	45	199 Vernon
f	Drury William F	80	cook	46	199 "
g	Mahoney Josephine—†	80	housekeeper	47	199 "
h	Freeney John W	80	janitor	48	here
k	Newton Annie—†	80	housewife	39	"
l	Newton Henry	80	porter	40	"
m	Brien Mildred—†	81	housekeeper	52	"
n	Marsh James	81	laborer	39	"
o	Morrison Annie—†	81	domestic	26	"
p	Reddick Preston	81	laborer	25	"
r	Reddick Stephen	81	porter	64	"
s	Reddick Stephen	81	laborer	21	"
t	Reddick Viola—†	81	housewife	47	"
u	Thomas Frances—†	81	housekeeper	29	"
v	Hannon Margaret—†	82	domestic	32	"
x	Foskey Clarissa—†	82	housewife	42	"
y	Foskey Harvey	82	packer	43	"
w	Gomes Gladys—†	82	domestic	20	
z	Mayers Allister	82	mechanic	40	21 Hubert
a	Mayers May—†	82	housewife	30	21 "
b	Purcell Ora—†	83	"	25	here
c	Reed John J	83	cook	25	"
d	Reed William F	83	laborer	50	"
e	Thomas John	83	waiter	44	"
f	Thomas Mary—†	83	housekeeper	42	"
g	Thomas Isolene—†	83	housewife	38	"
h	Thomas James	83	waiter	39	"
k	Emerson Dorothy—†	83	housewife	30	"
l	Emerson George	83	laborer	40	"
m	Brumand Griffith	83	"	36	"
n	Hinds Ester—†	83	housekeeper	42	"
o	White Emma—†	83	"	38	"
p	Paul George	83	carpenter	32	"
r	William John	84	laborer	48	"
s	William Mary—†	84	housewife	42	"
t	Johnson Carrie—†	84	at home	48	"
u	Richardson Mabel—†	84	domestic	26	"
v	William John H	84	porter	39	"
w	William Lucille—†	84	housewife	30	"

47

Page	Letter	FULL NAME.	Residence, April 1, 1926.	Occupation.	Supposed Age.	Reported Residence, April 1, 1925. Street and Number.

Williams Street—Continued

x	Earle Martha—†	86	domestic	37	here
y	Drayton Charles	86	actor	33	"
z	McGirt Moses	86	elevatorman	34	"
A	McGee George	86	cook	29	136 Sterling
B	McGee Gertrude—†	86	housewife	23	136 "

Williams Street Terrace

c	Kelly Alfred	1	cook	40	here
D	Kelly Sarah—†	1	housewife	30	"
E	Benjamin Mary E—†	2	houseworker	36	"
G	Allen Ida—†	2	housewife	24	"
H	Allen John	2	laborer	24	"
F	Simmonds Annie—†	2	domestic	26	"
K	Fernands Frank	2	grocer	38	"
L	Fernands Jenny †	2	housewife	22	"
M	Monty David H	3	laborer	51	"
N	Perry Robert	3	"	43	"
O	Emerson Charles	3	cooper	45	"
P	Emerson Inez †	3	housewife	38	"
R	Carney Sophie—†	3	domestic	32	84 Williams
V	Santos Emma A †	5	housewife	39	here
W	Santos John J	5	barber	43	"
X	Greer Robert	5	carpenter	36	2 Chester pl
Y	James Florence †	5	dressmaker	35	Brookline
Z	Fergus Abraham	5	laborer	29	here
A	Fergus Margaret †	5	housewife	28	"
B	Jones Edward	6	laborer	34	"
C	Jones Mamie †	6	housewife	28	"
D	Walcott Esther †	6	"	40	"
E	Walcott Hezekiah	6	tailor	40	"
G	Johnson Florence A †	7	housewife	39	"
H	Johnson James M	7	machinist	48	"
K	Bradley Jennie †	7	houseworker	59	"
L	Mason Arabella †	7	maid	49	"
M	Blackman Alice G—†	8	housewife	35	"
N	Blackman Sydney	8	laborer	42	"
O	Young August †	8	housewife	44	"
P	Young Byron	8	mechanic	21	"
R	Harris Daniel C	8	painter	31	"

Page.	Letter.	FULL NAME.	Residence, April 1, 1926.	Occupation.	Supposed Age.	Reported Residence, April 1, 1925. Street and Number.

Williams Street Terrace—Continued

s	Young Marietta—†	8	housewife	30	here
t	Falcelano Domenick	9	laborer	54	"
u	Jones Essie—†	9	housewife	27	"
v	Jones Walter E	9	laborer	37	"
w	Brown Martha—†	9	domestic	38	"

Winthrop Place

x	Cole Albert	4	restaurateur	40	2161 Wash'n
y	McGee Annie A—†	4	housewife	52	here
z	McGee George J	4	barber	56	"
a	MacDonald Ada—†	4	stitcher	51	"
b	MacPherson Eunice B—†	4	houseworker	22	Newton Centre
c	Shapiro Celia—†	4	housekeeper	67	here
d	Uroff Max	4	real estate	38	"
e	Macomber Grace—†	4	housewife	24	Abington
f	Macomber Stanley	4	machinist	24	"
g	Farrington Joseph W	4	gasfitter	48	here
h	Farrington Mary E—†	4	housewife	84	"
k	Hull Alta M—†	4	"	46	"
l	Hull Tullis W	4	conductor	34	"
n	Schultz Frederick	4	salesman	39	"
o	Schultz Margaret F—†	4	housewife	31	"
m	Wetmore Hazel B—†	4	inspector	26	"
p	Bowes Marion E—†	5	housewife	38	"
r	Bowes Whileminia V—†	5	maid	42	"
s	McSwain Florence—†	5	clerk	27	"
t	Orea Alfred	5	waiter	43	"
u	Cross Emma—†	6	housewife	44	"

Ward 9—Precinct 10

CITY OF BOSTON.

LIST OF RESIDENTS
20 YEARS OF AGE AND OVER

(FEMALES INDICATED BY DAGGER)

AS OF

APRIL 1, 1926

HERBERT A. WILSON, } *Listing*

JAMES F. EAGAN, } *Board.*

CITY OF BOSTON—PRINTING DEPARTMENT

Auburn Place

A	Adams Charlie	2	painter	68	here
B	Crocker William	2	carpenter	47	"
C	Sellon Christen —†	2	housekeeper	61	"
D	Sellon Henry D	2	car repairer	73	"
E	Sellon Henry D, jr	2	salesman	24	"
F	Sellon William H	2	letter carrier	36	"
G	Wolfe Mable E —†	2	stenographer	37	"
H	Farbush Florie —†	4	domestic	26	Cambridge
K	Wheary Frederick	4	laborer	44	52 Westminster
L	Issenberg Pearl—†	4	housewife	39	here
M	Issenberg Solomon	4	clerk	40	"
N	Greenstein Joseph L	4	"	40	"
O	Mogalson Ida —†	4	housekeeper	51	"
P	Mogalson Mary —†	4	bookkeeper	20	"

Auburn Street

R	Miller Henry	3	clerk	45	here
S	Miller Mary —†	3	housewife	41	"
T	O'Connell Margaret E —†	3	"	50	"
U	O'Connell Marion V—†	3	bookkeeper	28	"
V	O'Connell Patrick J	3	printer	54	"
W	O'Connell William	3	"	34	16 Lamont
X	Meas John	3	retired	79	here
Y	Minkle Flora T —†	3	housewife	52	"
Z	Minkle Florence J—†	3	stenographer	25	"
A	Minkle Helen K—†	3	"	27	"
D	McEttrick Helena—†	5	housewife	43	18 Auburn
C	McEttrick John J	5	laborer	40	18
E	Burke Catherine —†	5	"	57	here
F	Burke Gertrude —†	5	stitcher	22	"
G	Burke Jeremiah	5	laborer	57	"
H	Burke Theresa —†	5	clerk	24	"
K	Burke Walter	5	conductor	21	"
L	Curran Agnes—†	5	housewife	49	"
M	Curran George E	5	stage manager	50	"
N	Truda Frank	5	musician	46	"
O	Singer Esther—†	7	housewife	48	"
P	Singer Samuel	7	janitor	50	"

2

Page.	Letter.	FULL NAME.	Residence, April 1, 1926.	Occupation.	Supposed Age.	Reported Residence, April 1, 1925.
						Street and Number.

Auburn Street—Continued

	R	Wiseman Louis	7	laborer	36	here
	S	Wiseman Rebbecca—†	7	housewife	26	"
	T	Frank Gertrude—†	rear 7	"	23	"
	U	Frank William	7	salesman	23	"
	V	Richter Alexander	11	student	21	23 Haskins
	W	Richter Jacob	11	storekeeper	52	23 "
	X	Richter Rose—†	11	housewife	50	23 "
	Y	Glick Ida—†	11	bookkeeper	20	here
	Z	Glick Maurice	11	meatcutter	50	"
	A	Glick Rebbecca—†	11	bookkeeper	22	"
	B	Glick Rose—†	11	housewife	40	"
	C	Burke Adelaide R—†	11	school teacher	26	"
	D	Burke Edward J	11	installer	33	"
	E	Burke Frank J	11	lawyer	40	"
	F	Burke Helen K—†	11	school teacher	25	"
	G	Burke Mary E—†	11	clerk	39	"
	H	Burke Timothy J	11	retired	70	"
	K	Harrington Josephine—†	11	housewife	41	"
	L	Murray Stanley R	11	chauffeur	29	"
	M	Gleason Agnes—†	13	clerk	25	"
	N	Gleason Margaret—†	13	"	22	"
	O	Gleason Martin	13	bricklayer	58	"
	P	Gleason Nora—†	13	housewife	59	"
	R	Colby Joseph	13	printer	31	"
	S	Gleason Catherine—†	13	housewife	28	"
	T	O'Neil Edward J	15	salesman	31	2 Kensington
	U	Raftery Aileen T—†	15	teacher	21	here
	V	Raftery Evelyn P—†	15	stenographer	23	"
	W	Raftery Marie N—†	15	teacher	25	"
	X	Egan Margaret F—†	19	clerk	33	162 Cabot
	Y	Egan Molly A—†	19	"	28	162 "
	Z	Egan Sallie V—†	19	"	25	162 "
	A	Egan Sarah F—†	19	housewife	63	162 "
	B	Egan Lawrence C	19	asbestos worker	36	here
	C	Egan Margaret—†	19	housekeeper	27	"
	D	Leiberman Maurice	19	steamfitter	27	"
	E	Canavan Isabella V—†	21	clerk	24	"
	F	Canavan John H	21	chauffeur	31	"
	G	Canavan Mary A—†	21	housewife	51	"
	H	Wallace Hilda—†	21	"	30	"
	K	Wallace James	21	laborer	32	"

3

Page.	Letter.	FULL NAME.	Residence, April 1, 1926.	Occupation.	Supposed Age.	Reported Residence, April 1, 1925. Street and Number.

Bicknell Avenue

	L	Belinger Cornelia —†	1	houseworker	43	29 Westminster
	M	Burton Jessie	1	expressman	54	58 Ruggles
	N	Chandler Mabel —†	1	houseworker	24	58 "
	O	Peters Edith—†	1	"	34	72 Sawyer
	P	Jones Gertrude—†	3	"	30	4 Fairweather
	R	Lewis John	3	laborer	55	Virginia
	S	Washington Bessie—†	3	houseworker	24	"
	T	Dixon Christina —†	3	housewife	28	7 Fairweather
	U	Dixon Edward L	3	laborer	47	7 "
	V	Hammock Ethel —†	5	cook	43	New York
	W	Odom Henry	5	fireman	41	33 Westminster
	X	Odom Sarah—†	5	housewife	33	33 "
	Y	Mulcahy Edward	6	carpenter	21	here
	Z	Mulcahy Katherine—†	6	houseworker	23	"
	A	Mulcahy Mary—†	6	housewife	50	"
	B	Currian Lida—†	6	"	49	"
	C	Currian Thomas H	6	salesman	62	"
	D	Johnson John	6	clerk	64	"
	E	Butler Richard F	6	"	49	"
	F	Rae Mary E—†	6	operator	50	"
	G	Peterson Hannah M—†	8	housewife	67	"
	H	Peterson Herman Oscar	8	car repairer	68	"
	K	Peterson Walter O	8	wireworker	38	"
	L	Lewis Lavenia M—†	8	houseworker	55	"

Cabot Street

	N	Hiitt Annie L—†	226	housewife	21	Portland Me
	O	Hiitt Ernest H	226	metalworker	40	"
	P	Alpert Israel M	226	storekeeper	38	here
	R	Alpert Tillie M—†	226	housewife	34	"
	S	Johnson Jennie—†	226	"	30	"
	T	Johnson Meeka	226	shipper	35	"
	U	O'Brien Anna—†	226	housewife	24	Worcester
	V	O'Brien George F	226	machinist	29	"
	X	Burns John	235	laborer	38	New York
	Y	Davey Frank	235	plasterer	58	192 Vernon
	Z	McBrine Bernard	235	laborer	38	here

Page.	Letter.	FULL NAME.	Residence, April 1, 1926.	Occupation.	Supposed Age.	Reported Residence, April 1, 1925. Street and Number.

Cabot Street— Continued

A	McBrine Ellen—†	235	housewife	40	here
B	McDermott Michael	235	laborer	58	192 Vernon
C	Murphy Margaret—†	235	housewife	42	28 Terrace
D	Murphy Michael	235	laborer	52	28 "
E	Steel Albert	237	chauffeur	32	Providence R I
F	Steel Lillian—†	237	housewife	32	"
G	Fisher James	237	plumber	52	Cleveland O
H	McGam John	237	teamster	26	here
K	McGam Mary—†	237	housewife	60	"
M	Snow Herbert W	240	telegrapher	34	715 Tremont
N	Snow Ruth M—†	240	housewife	28	715 "
O	Hart Mary A—†	240	"	37	here
P	Hart Patrick J	240	car inspector	40	"
R	Hughes Bridget A—†	240	housewife	38	"
S	Hughes Patrick J	240	fireman	37	"
U	Campbell Catherine—†	242	housewife	52	"
V	Campbell Martin J	242	carpenter	56	"
W	Campbell William M	242	clerk	20	"
X	Harron Bridget—†	242	housewife	75	"
Y	O'Melia Patrick	242	laborer	56	"
Z	O'Melia Ruth—†	242	school teacher	21	"
A	Daley Marie—†	242	housewife	40	69 Linden Park
B	Kenney John F	243	electrician	26	4 Linden av
C	Kenney Mary F—†	243	housewife	24	4 "
D	O'Toole Mary—†	243	"	23	here
E	O'Toole Patrick	243	meatcutter	26	"
F	Burke Mary—†	243	housewife	36	1195 Tremont
G	Burke Mathew	243	laborer	46	1195 "
H	Burke Thomas	243	"	25	118 Broadway
K	McDermott Stephen	243	stableman	50	1195 Tremont
L	Taylor Catherine—†	245	housewife	27	3829 Wash'n
M	Taylor William	245	repairman	32	3829 "
N	Carey Elizabeth—†	245	housewife	32	here
O	McGuire Elizabeth—†	245	"	40	"
P	McGuire Michael	245	engineer	40	"
R	Burns Ellen J—†	250	housewife	65	"
S	Burns Esther—†	250	clerk	23	"
T	Burns John F	250	retired	68	"
U	Burns Sadie—†	250	at home	26	"
V	Fusco John	rear 251	laborer	47	123 Cabot
W	Fusco Mary—†	" 251	housewife	45	123 "

5

Cabot Street—Continued

x	Reina Alexander	rear 251	chauffeur	25	123 Cabot
y	Reina Joseph	" 251	laundryworker	23	123 "
z	Biondi Frank	" 251	barber	22	here
A	Raymond Phillip	" 251	masseur	61	"
B	Raymond Pietrina—†	" 251	housewife	49	"
D	Sargent George A	257	storekeeper	60	39 Cambridge
E	Norton Edward M	258	fruit	53	here
F	Joyce Catherine—†	259	housewife	48	"
G	Joyce Frank T	259	elevatorman	50	"
H	Gaffney Mary—†	259	waitress	30	"
K	Gaffney Thomas	259	chef	35	"
L	Devine Sarah—†	259	housewife	60	"
N	Jordan Mary—†	259	"	60	"
P	Creedon John	262	laborer	49	63 Longwood av
R	Creedon Mary—†	262	housewife	55	63 "
S	Frizzell Annie—†	262	"	34	194 Cabot
T	Frizzell John	262	chauffeur	35	194 "
U	Good Bridget—†	rear 262	housewife	72	here
V	Melia James	" 262	laborer	59	New Hampshire
W	Comeau Annie—†	" 262A	housewife	35	here
X	Comeau Louis	" 262A	laborer	36	"
Z	Bishop Blanche—†	263	clerk	23	"
Y	Bishop Edward	263	porter	44	"
A	Bishop Margaret—†	263	housewife	29	"
B	Cass Martha F—†	263A	"	32	"
C	Cass Michael J	263A	conductor	38	"
D	Willett Charles	263A	auto mechanic	47	Canada
E	Willett Margaret—†	263A	housewife	44	"
F	O'Connell Margaret—†	264	"	45	here
G	O'Connell Michael	264	laborer	50	"
H	DeAngelo Angelina—†	265	housewife	48	"
K	DeAngelo Domonic	265	bricklayer	53	"
L	Harrington Catherine M—†	265	stenographer	25	"
M	Harrington Edward G	265	salesman	24	"
N	Harrington Eileen N—†	265	stenographer	29	"
O	Harrington Ellen J—†	265	clerk	40	"
P	Harrington Mary M—†	265	housewife	37	"
R	Harrington Patrick J	265	car repairer	60	"
S	Harrington Patrick L	265	policeman	32	"
U	Carson Emma A—†	266	housewife	49	"

	Letter.	FULL NAME.	Residence, April 1, 1925.	Occupation.	Supposed Age.	Reported Residence, April 1, 1925. Street and Number.

Cabot Street—Continued

v	Carson Walter	266	mechanic	26	here
w	Carson William	266	laborer	59	"
y	Green Mary G—†	rear 267	housewife	45	"
z	Green Sylvester "	267	storekeeper	35	"
c	Wohlgemuth Frank	271	chauffeur	39	"
d	Wohlgemuth Mary—†	271	housewife	39	"
e	Gallagher Mary A—†	271	"	32	"
f	Gallagher Patrick F	271	chauffeur	35	"
g	Sullivan Daniel	273	tel worker	21	"
h	Sullivan Jeremiah J	273	laborer	58	"
k	Sullivan Mary—†	273	housewife	56	"
l	Boyle Ella—†	273	"	37	"
m	Boyle Simon	273	manager	42	"
n	McLean John W	273	chauffeur	36	"
o	McLean Mary E—†	273	housewife	34	193 Cabot
p	McDonald Francis Joseph	273	mopmaker	27	3 Motley
r	McDonald Mary—†	283	housewife	26	3 "
t	May Arthur James	283	clerk	21	here
s	May James J	283	watchman	54	"
u	May Marion—†	283	housewife	53	"
v	Hayes Gertrude—†	283	"	29	3 Motley
w	Hayes Patrick W	283	laborer	29	3 "
x	Tate Elizabeth—†	283	housewife	60	3 "
y	Houlihan Annie—†	285	"	44	here
z	Houlihan John	285	shipper	20	"
a	Houlihan Michael	285	harnessmaker	56	"
b	Mulrean Helen—†	285	stitcher	24	"
c	Mulrean Lillian—†	285	housewife	61	"
d	Turley Lillian—†	285	collector	30	"
e	Murray James J	285	laborer	51	"
f	Murray Nellie—†	285	housewife	39	"
g	McKinnon Cornelius	287	carpenter	54	"
h	McKinnon Georgiana—†	287	housewife	50	"
k	McKinnon John E	287	clerk	21	"
l	McKinnon Joseph A	287	shipper	20	"
m	Diggins Margaret—†	287	housewife	27	"
n	Diggins Michael	287	plasterer	38	"
o	O'Leary Margaret—†	287	housewife	48	"
p	O'Leary Margaret E—†	287	bookkeeper	22	"

7

Page.	Letter.	FULL NAME.	Residence, April 1, 1926.	Occupation.	Supposed Age.	Reported Residence, April 1, 1925. Street and Number.

Haskins Street

s	Bassin Elizabeth—†	12	housewife	74	here
T	Bassin Nathan	12	retired	50	"
U	Haliday Mattison	12	chauffeur	29	29 Kendall
V	Haliday Maud—†	12	housewife	23	29 "
W	Silverman Harry	12	chauffeur	25	here
X	Silverman Peggy—†	12	housewife	23	"
Y	Thompson Beatrice—†	14	clerk	35	13 Weston
Z	Thompson Joseph	14	janitor	40	13 "
A	Eizzard Lena—†	14	saleswoman	37	43 Kendall
B	Simper Lillian—†	14	housekeeper	38	here
C	Barrie Catherine—†	14	housewife	29	40 Sterling
D	Barrie Simon	14	bricklayer	37	40
E	Depteplite Bertha—†	14	dressmaker	36	here
F	Campbell George P	20	finisher	64	"
G	Donahue Mary—†	20	housekeeper	51	"
H	Callahan Daniel H	22	retired	70	"
K	Callahan Katherine—†	22	finisher	38	"
L	Callahan Sarah—†	22	housewife	70	"
M	Gervais Agatha P—†	24	"	62	"
N	Gervais Louis L	24	repairer	28	"
O	Gervais Mariette P—†	24	stenographer	22	"
P	Gervais Theresa E—†	24	skiver	23	"
R	Gervais Triffle	24	repairer	62	"
S	Goldis Joseph	30	carpenter	40	"
T	Goldis Rose—†	30	housewife	29	"
U	Baker Louis	30	collector	60	"
V	Baker Molly—†	30	housewife	56	"
W	Whipple Catherine—†	34	"	21	"
X	Whipple Thomas	34	laborer	24	"
Y	Buckley John J	34	lather	50	"
Z	Kelley Elizabeth—†	34	forewoman	55	"
A	Kelley Louise E S—†	34	stenographer	28	"
B	Kelley Mary R—†	34	housewife	30	"
C	Rogers Jack J	36	cook	37	"
D	Rogers Lillian L—†	36	housewife	27	"
E	Binders Corrinne—†	38	"	22	"
F	Binders George F	38	machinist	50	"
G	Binders Susie D—†	38	housewife	47	"
H	Binders William E	38	chauffeur	23	"
L	Ransom Amy—†	40	housewife	37	720 Shawmut av

8

Haskins Street—Continued

M	Hawkins Corinne—†	42	housewife	27	35 Northfield
N	Morton Eleanor—†	42	"	27	74 Ruggles
O	Morton Joseph	42	laborer	28	74 "
P	Gould Joseph	44	"	22	New York
S	Hoffman Aaron	44	butcher	60	here
R	Hoffman Anna—†	44	housewife	44	"
T	Callahan Dennis	44	laborer	56	"
U	Callahan Mary—†	44	housekeeper	54	"
V	Wisnevsky Ludmila—†	46	housewife	41	"
W	Wisnevsky Richard	46	stockman	50	"
X	Roache Agnes L—†	46	tel operator	22	"
Y	Roache Bessie—†	46	housewife	41	"
Z	Roache James H	46	machinist	44	"
A	Girrvirr Ellen M—†	54	housewife	55	"
B	Girrvirr Francis E	54	salesman	27	"

Kent Street

C	McGrath John R	6	grocer	57	1260 Dor av
D	McGrath Viola L—†	6	housewife	46	1260 "
E	McHale John	6	attendant	53	here
F	McHale Mary—†	6	housekeeper	87	"
G	DesRoche Lewis W	6	stock clerk	24	"
H	DesRoche Prosper	6	carpenter	55	"
K	DesRoche Rose—†	6	housewife	52	"
L	Brindley Emma—†	9	"	55	"
M	Brindley George	9	helper	54	"
N	Kelley Helen—†	9	factory worker	26	882 Parker
O	Kelley Russell L	9	fireman	28	882 "
P	McPeck Elizabeth I—†	9	laundress	60	930 Col av
R	Woods Louisa—†	9	shoeworker	38	930 "
S	Houlihan Ellen—†	11	houseworker	37	here
T	Higgins Catherine—†	11	housewife	48	"
U	Flynn Annie M—†	11	clerk	23	"
V	Flynn Catherine F—†	11	housewife	46	"
W	Flynn Helen J—†	11	clerk	21	"
X	Kelley Mary—†	12	hotelworker	35	20 Kent
Y	Raynor Celia—†	12	waitress	35	20 "
Z	Bostrom Josephine—†	12	housewife	47	here
A	Bostrom Victor E	12	engineer	40	"

Kent Street—Continued

B	Carey Catherine—†	12	housewife	53	here
C	Carey Elizabeth—†	12	tel operator	22	"
D	Mackey Patrick W	13	engineer	63	"
E	Kennedy Francis E	13	janitor	67	"
F	Kennedy Hanna E—†	13	housewife	60	"
G	Kennedy Joseph A	13	freighthandler	25	"
H	Kennedy Walter I	13	clerk	20	"
K	King Charles H	13	"	20	"
L	King Jenny—†	13	housewife	43	"
M	King John F	13	laborer	44	"
N	Mackey Lawrence	13	student	21	"
O	Cook Annie M—†	15	housewife	50	Providence R I
P	Cook Herbert C	15	surveyor	23	"
R	Breen Daniel F	15	repairman	42	here
S	Breen Mary E—†	15	housewife	38	"
T	Currie Elizabeth R—†	15	clerk	20	"
U	Currie Josephine—†	15	houseworker	46	"
V	Kelley Helen—†	16	housekeeper	62	"
W	Bradley Helen—†	16	boxfinisher	23	Ireland
X	West Nora—†	16	housewife	28	here
Y	West Robert	16	repairman	30	"
Z	Semler Sophia A—†	17	housewife	31	"
A	Freher Dennis	17	piano mover	50	"
B	Freher Frances—†	17	housewife	44	"
C	Scanlon Catherine A—†	17	"	55	"
D	Scanlon Lillian—†	17	saleswoman	29	"
E	Scanlon Thomas J	17	factory worker	36	"
F	Scanlon William F	17	tel worker	28	"
H	Curran Ellen E—†	20	houseworker	47	"
K	Hartford Edward M	20	tel worker	41	"
L	Riley Anna—†	20	hotelworker	50	754 Fifth
M	Kelley Helen—†	21	silkfinisher	53	here
N	Kelley Maria E—†	21	housekeeper	61	"
O	Greenan Josephine C—†	21	housewife	32	"
P	Greenan William B	21	chauffeur	33	"
R	McKenna Catherine C—†	21	housewife	34	"
S	McKenna John	21	repairman	40	"
T	Fitzgerald Elizabeth—†	22	clerk	45	"
U	Fitzgerald Martha †	22	housewife	80	"
V	Fitzgerald Mary—†	22	teacher	37	"
W	Crawford William T	24	elevatorman	52	85 Eustis

Page.	Letter.	FULL NAME.	Residence, April 1, 1926.	Occupation.	Supposed Age.	Reported Residence, April 1, 1925. Street and Number.

Kent Street—Continued

G	Crawford Elizabeth—†	24	housewife	35	85 Eustis
X	Cass Catherine V—†	24	"	46	here
Y	Cass Robert H	24	letter carrier	50	"
Z	McNeill Louis	24	painter	39	"
A	McNeill Mary A—†	24	housewife	38	"
B	Sullivan Eugene	26	laborer	42	"
C	Sullivan Mary—†	26	housewife	39	"
D	Coffey Beatrice—†	26	"	38	"
E	Coffey Jeremiah	26	postal clerk	43	"
F	Hurley Celia L—†	26	housewife	39	"
G	Hurley William J	26	laborer	39	"
H	Lowenhielm Carl G	31	retired	65	"
K	Townsend Frak N	31	salesman	54	"
L	Morse Luel—†	31	housekeeper	75	"
M	Moore Anastasia—†	32	housewife	62	"
N	Moore Thomas	32	laborer	62	"
O	Moore William F	32	shoeworker	28	"
P	Mallory Anna—†	32	operator	24	Everett
R	Mallory David H	32	granitecutter	54	"
S	Mallory Lola B—†	32	housewife	42	"
T	Kennedy Anna S—†	32	"	26	here
U	Kennedy Thomas F	32	policeman	26	"
V	Kennedy William R	32	chauffeur	28	"
W	Feeley Elizabeth—†	rear 33	housewife	52	"
X	Feeley Henry	" 33	salesman	54	"
Y	Finnerty William	" 33	steamfitter	35	"
Z	Perham Lila J—†	" 33	housekeeper	62	"
A	Perham William	" 33	painter	29	"
B	White Sara F—†	" 33	retired	72	"
C	Herbert Charles D	34	chauffeur	25	66 Ruggles
D	Herbert Gladys—†	34	factory worker	23	66 "
E	Herbert Lettie—†	34	laundress	49	66 "
F	Jameson Katherine A—†	35	housewife	27	29 Valentine
G	Jameson Paul	35	carpenter	26	29 "
H	Hoare Eugene J	35	laborer	39	1 Rockland
K	Hoare Mira—†	35	housewife	38	1 "
L	Watson Dudley	37	carpenter	32	here
M	Watson Evelyn—†	37	housewife	29	"
N	Miller Leana—†	37	houseworker	43	"
O	Robinson Alberta J—†	37	housewife	25	"

11

Kent Street—Continued

P	Robinson George E	37	porter	29	here
R	Foreman Matilde—†	37	houseworker	45	65 Lenox
S	Flaherty Louis	38	machinist	49	here
T	Flaherty Mary—†	38	housewife	44	"
U	Schaffer Frank	40	cigar packer	66	"
V	Schaffer Pauline—†	40	stenographer	26	"
W	Steinberg Anna—†	40	housewife	42	New Jersey

Lamont Street

X	Boyle Annie K—†	8	housewife	45	here
Y	Boyle Robert F	8	garageman	47	"
Z	Drury Annie B—†	8	housekeeper	41	"
A	Hurly Agnes—†	8	housewife	28	"
B	Hurly William	8	laborer	28	"
C	Bragan Mary J—†	9	housekeeper	60	"
D	Woodward Ada B—†	9	bookkeeper	37	"
E	Woodward Joseph	9	retired	79	"
F	Woodward Matilda—†	9	housewife	70	"
G	Woodward Victor E	9	finisher	35	"
H	Woodward Annie V—†	9	housekeeper	48	"
K	Abrams Etta—†	10	housewife	34	"
L	Abrams Joseph	10	merchant	41	"
M	Goldsmith Harry H	10	"	54	"
N	Ruprecht Helen G—†	12	housewife	22	"
O	Ruprecht Joseph D	12	inspector	28	"
P	O'Brien Mary —†	12	housekeeper	30	"
R	Stuke Regina E—†	12	"	26	"
S	Stuke Robert E	12	boxmaker	27	"
T	Blanchard Lawrence	12	salesman	20	"
U	Blanchard Sarah—†	12	housekeeper	40	57 St Francis de Sales
V	Hartigan Marguerite J—†	13	housewife	29	here
W	Hartigan William J	13	policeman	30	"
X	Flynn Abbie—†	13	at home	65	"
Y	Flynn Annie E—†	13	operator	31	"
Z	Flynn John J	13	packer	35	"
A	Flynn Mary E—†	13	housewife	26	"
B	Hannon Alice C—†	13	stenographer	24	"
C	Hannon Helen A—†	13	instructor	27	"
D	Hannon Joseph T	13	mechanic	25	"

Page.	Letter.	FULL NAME.	Residence, April 1, 1926.	Occupation.	Supposed Age.	Reported Residence, April 1, 1925. Street and Number.

Lamont Street—Continued

E	Hannon Mary A—†	13	housewife	53	here
F	Hannon Patrick J	13	laborer	62	"
G	Hannon Walter	13	"	21	"
H	Vierkent Charles	14	teamster	50	"
K	Vierkent Charles, jr	14	shipper	20	"
L	Vierkent Julia—†	14	housewife	45	"
M	Vierkent Mary—†	14	laundress	25	"
N	Smith Albra	14	laborer	41	25 Field
O	Smith Catherine—†	14	housewife	43	68 "
P	Smith Cecil	14	laborer	39	68 "
R	McGregor Agnes—†	14	saleswoman	20	here
S	McGregor Bessie—†	14	housekeeper	27	"
T	McGregor Georgina—†	14	car cleaner	51	"
U	Cyr Jesse A	16	painter	42	"
V	Cyr Mary A—†	16	housewife	40	"
W	Chase Dorothy F—†	16	"	25	"
X	Chase Frederick G	16	last turner	27	"
Y	Moore Irene G—†	16	housekeeper	21	"
Z	Moore James	16	retired	70	"
A	Moore Mary A—†	16	clerk	20	"
B	Kenney Nora—†	19	housewife	26	"
C	Kenney Patrick	19	laborer	28	"
D	Rooney Annie—†	19	housewife	35	"
E	Rooney John J	19	repairer	38	"
F	Manning Bridget—†	19	at home	75	"
G	Manning Katherine—†	19	waitress	42	"
H	Manning Mary E—†	19	nursemaid	28	"
K	Cunningham Daniel J	21	laborer	23	"
L	Fay William E	21	"	39	4 Circuit
M	Minkel Anna G—†	21	housekeeper	33	here
N	Minkle Harry F	21	printer	34	"
O	Ganters Marie—†	21	cook	41	"
S	Halesky Julia—†	21	stitcher	40	"
P	Hazelstein Mary A—†	21	housekeeper	69	"
R	Hazelstein Theresa—†	21	"	43	"
T	Campbell Dennis	24	fireman	50	"
U	Campbell Margaret—†	24	housewife	45	"
V	Brookfield George	24	chauffeur	31	781 Parker
W	Brookfield Mary—†	24	housewife	26	781 "
X	Daly James W	28	mechanic	27	here
Y	Fallon Agnes L—†	28	housekeeper	22	"

Lamont Street—Continued

z	Fallon Annie M—†	28	housekeeper	55	here
A	Fallon Edward F	28	clerk	23	"
B	Fallon James E	28	auditor	26	"
C	Fallon John J	28	mechanic	30	"
D	Murray Patrick	28	laborer	45	
E	Callahan William A	28	teamster	28	42 Calumet
F	Hinchey Joseph	28	laborer	40	2464 Wash'n
H	Hurd John B	30	carpenter	60	here
G	Hurd Mary J—†	30	housewife	59	"
K	Jackson Margaret—†	30	"	29	93 Marcella
L	Jackson Victor	30	electrician	31	93 "
M	Ducey Charles	35	milkworker	26	11 Lamont
N	Ducey Loretta—†	35	housewife	25	here
O	Gilvery Agnes—†	35	"	31	Somerville
P	Gilvery Donald	35	retired	79	"
R	Gilvery Donald H	35	carpenter	37	"
S	Gilvery Mary—†	35	housewife	75	"
T	Healley Annie—†	35	stitcher	40	here
U	Kelley Esther A—†	35	housewife	42	"
V	Kelley James W	35	letter carrier	51	"
W	Backlund John E	36	painter	33	"
X	Backlund Lydia—†	36	housewife	33	"
Z	Johnson Abbie—†	36	laundress	55	"
A	Neeman Bessie—†	36	"	56	"
A¹	Fennelly Mary—†	36	matron	40	"
B	Gould Cecil	37	waiter	32	"
C	Gould Elsie A—†	37	housewife	30	
D	Flaherty Michael J	37	clerk	36	2 Dabney pl
E	Gallagher James	37	laborer	54	263 Cabot
F	Gallagher James F	37	salesman	31	263 "
G	Gallagher Joseph P	37	chauffeur	25	263 "
H	Gallagher Lawrence J	37	laborer	21	263 "
K	Gallagher Mary—†	37	housewife	53	here
L	Brennen John A	38	teamster	38	21 Bartlett
M	Brennen Marie—†	38	housewife	41	21 "
N	St Lawrence Andrew J	38	floorlayer	59	here
O	St Lawrence Margaret—†	38	housewife	46	"
P	St Lawrence Mary—†	38	clerk	24	"
R	St Lawrence William	38	printer	22	"
S	Fetler Betty—†	38	housewife	45	7 King ter
T	Fetler Charles	38	laborer	50	7 "

Page.	Letter.	FULL NAME.	Residence, April 1, 1926.	Occupation.	Supposed Age.	Reported Residence, April 1, 1925. Street and Number.

Lamont Street—Continued

	U	Klinger Carl	39	weaver	25	here
	V	Kolbe Helen—†	39	housewife	28	"
	W	Kolbe Walter	39	weaver	33	"
	X	Rohner Elsie—†	39	milliner	26	Germany
	Y	FitzGibbons Joseph T	39	electrician	35	here
	Z	FitzGibbons Mary E—†	39	housewife	33	"
	A	Donnelly James	39	laborer	34	"
	B	Donnelly John	39	chauffeur	34	"
	C	Donnelly Mary—†	39	housewife	26	"
	D	Goslin James E	40	foreman	40	"
	E	Goslin Lena—†	40	housewife	40	"
	F	Housman Hyman	40	agent	26	"
	G	Housman Rachel—†	40	housewife	25	"
	H	Fahmery Agnes—†	40	"	55	"
	K	Flannery John J	40	salesman	59	"

Linden Avenue

	A	Noseworthy Mary—†	2	packer	27	19 W Brookline
	B	Noseworthy Matthias	2	boilermaker	32	19 "
	C	Swift Elizabeth V †	2	housewife	33	1125 Tremont
	D	Swift Leonard T	2	letter carrier	40	1125 "
	E	Welsh Mary F—†	2	wardmaid	58	74 Fenwood rd
	F	Gardner Anthony	2	chauffeur	28	here
	G	Gardner Mary—†	2	stenographer	23	"
	H	Kenney Geroge	4	real estate	51	"
	K	Kenney John F	4	electrician	25	"
	L	Kenney Mary—†	4	housewife	23	"
	M	Molinelli George	4	chauffeur	27	"
	N	Molinelli Mary—†	4	housewife	55	"
	O	Molinelli Peter	4	extract maker	65	"
	P	Murray Elizabeth—†	4	housewife	68	"
	R	Murray Mary E—†	4	stenographer	32	"
	S	Davis Annie A—†	6	housewife	47	"
	T	Davis Herbert L	6	electrician	59	"
	U	Mahoney Dennis	6	storekeeper	50	"
	V	Athridge Alexander D	6	steamfitter	30	37 Lamont
	W	Athridge Mae—†	6	saleswoman	22	37 "
	X	Athridge Michael F	6	clerk	22	37 "
	Y	Mubrean Annie—†	6	typist	28	37 "

15

Page.	Letter.	FULL NAME.	Residence, April 1, 1926.	Occupation.	Supposed Age.	Reported Residence, April 1, 1925. Street and Number.

Linden Avenue—Continued

	z	Long Charles E	8	counterman	29	here
	A	Long Ethel M—†	8	housewife	24	"
	B	Jackson Elizabeth—†	8	"	35	"
	c	Jackson Guy W	8	teamster	35	"
	c¹	Harrington Barbara E—†	8	housewife	37	"
	D	Harrington Joseph T	8	laborer	37	"

Linden Park Street

	E	Gallaher Lawrence	1	laborer	21	37 Lamont
	F	Lufkin Annie—†	1	housewife	49	here
	G	Lynch Mary—†	1	factory worker	21	6 Kent
	H	McCawley Eliza J—†	1	housekeeper	74	here
	K	McLean Collins F	1	carpenter	55	1518 Dor av
	L	Ryan James	1	laborer	26	Brookline
	M	Witteridge Arthur	1	auto trimmer	64	here
	N	Bentley John D	7	laborer	65	72 Dudley
	O	McDonald Ronald	7	carpenter	41	Brookfield
	P	Nolan Dunkin F	7	laborer	26	18 Ray
	R	Nolan Marion—†	7	housewife	20	18 "
	S	Brennan John J	9	elevatorman	51	here
	T	Dolan Annie—†	9	salesman	40	"
	U	Donahue Margaret M—†	9	housekeeper	36	"
	V	McDonald Annie—†	9	"	80	"
	W	McDonald Thomas W	9	laborer	57	"
	X	Murphy Henry M	9	retired	70	"
	Y	Norton Thomas	9	porter	55	"
	z	Evelyn Donald	11	checker	45	"
	A	Evelyn Mary D—†	11	housekeeper	50	"
	B	Horan Ellen—†	11	housewife	45	"
	c	Giombrinis Galomo	13	porter	39	"
	D	Keenan Michael	13	"	33	6 Newark
	H	Duffley Catherine—†	23	housewife	46	here
	K	Duffley Charles W	23	plasterer	53	"
	L	Keney Thomas F	23	pianoworker	56	"
	M	Quinlan Dennis F	25	laborer	32	"
	N	Quinlan Helen—†	25	housewife	32	"
	O	Timmins Arthur D	25	policeman	33	"
	P	Timmins Elizabeth J—†	25	housewife	38	"
	R	O'Neill Bessie—†	25	"	30	"

16

	Letter	FULL NAME.	Residence, April 1, 1925.	Occupation.	Supposed Age.	Reported Residence, April 1, 1925. Street and Number.

Linden Park Street—Continued

Letter	FULL NAME	Res.	Occupation	Age	Reported Residence
s	O'Neill John	25	roofer	25	here
T	Mahoney Anna T—†	27	housewife	29	"
U	Mahoney William R	27	expressman	29	"
V	Owens Catherine E—†	27	housewife	41	"
W	Owens David M	27	attendant	48	"
X	Dunne Ellen—†	27	nurse	40	"
Y	Flannery Mary—†	27	housewife	53	"
Z	Flannery Michael	27	blacksmith	55	"
A	Flannery William	27	elevatorman	21	"
B	Conroy Daniel J	29	printer	35	482 Brookline
C	Conroy Elizabeth E—†	29	housewife	33	482 "
D	McElwain Daniel O	29	letter carrier	48	here
E	McElwain John J	29	"	20	"
F	McElwain Mary M—†	29	saleswoman	22	"
G	Walsh Arthur J	29	salesman	20	"
H	Walsh Gertrude A—†	29	housewife	41	"
K	Walsh Harold R	29	machinist	22	"
L	Walsh Richard L	29	tool grinder	42	"
M	Gately John C	31	laborer	59	"
N	Gately John J	31	shoeworker	23	"
O	Gately Maria †	31	housekeeper	54	"
P	Keane Patrick	31	laborer	45	"
R	McCarthy John	31	"	63	"
S	Rice Arthur	31	porter	24	"
T	Coffee Mary—†	33	stenographer	22	"
U	McManus Ellen—†	33	factory worker	26	"
V	Ryan Mary—†	33	housekeeper	64	"
W	Turner Charles	37	laborer	35	Somerville
X	Turner Ellen—†	37	housewife	32	"
Y	Connors Francis	37	chauffeur	21	here
Z	Connors Nellie—†	37	housewife	49	"
A	Brennan Mary—†	37	"	29	185 Highland
B	Brennan Thomas J	37	laborer	28	185 "
C	Judge Lillian—†	39	housekeeper	31	here
D	Judge Peter	39	chauffeur	26	"
E	Walsh Annie—†	39	housewife	54	"
F	Walsh Hilbert	39	laborer	22	"
G	Walsh Patrick	39	steamfitter	60	"
H	Tatoff Mary—†	39	housekeeper	50	"
K	Hart James J	41	mechanic	36	35 St Francis de Sales

9—10   17

Linden Park Street- Continued

L	Hart Nora E—†	41	housewife	30	35 St Francis de Sales
M	Gleason John	41	laborer	22	here
N	Gleason Joseph	41	"	32	"
O	Gleason Mary—†	41	housekeeper	54	"
P	Gleason Nellie—†	41	saleswoman	28	3 Malbon pl
R	Gleason Richard	41	clerk	30	here
T	Burns Emma—†	43	storekeeper	53	"
U	Burns Mary—†	43	clerk	32	"
V	Harrington Dennie P	43	"	26	38 Lamont
W	Mulkern Martin J	43	cutter	29	38 "
X	Mulkern Mary A—†	43	housewife	28	38 "
Y	Burg Annie—†	43	housekeeper	55	here
Z	Miller Gertrude—†	43	factory worker	29	"
A	Miller Herbert	43	chauffeur	27	"
B	Miller Esther E—†	45	housewife	42	"
C	Miller Lester	45	carpenter	44	"
E	Martin Thomas	45	laborer	62	"
D	Melia Patrick	45	barber	72	"
F	Curley Elizabeth A—†	45	inspector	49	"
G	Curley Florence—†	45	"	45	"
H	Good John F	45	B F D	42	"
K	Good Mary A—†	45	housekeeper	41	"
L	Dunlea Charles J	47	waiter	30	"
M	Dunlea Margaret—†	47	housewife	38	"
P	Garry Edward J	47	pedler	22	147 Vernon
R	Garry John J	47	laborer	60	Saxonville
N	Hillary Edward G	47	chauffeur	26	here
O	Hillary Grace H—†	47	housewife	26	"
T	Morrison Elise—†	47	"	43	"
S	Morrison James	47	motorman	47	"
U	Dillon John P	49	salesman	30	"
V	Richards Grace—†	49	housewife	24	"
W	Richards John H	49	paperhanger	36	"
X	Hill Henry G	49	retired	66	"
Y	Hill May—†	49	housewife	66	"
Z	Totman Elizabeth—†	49	"	55	"
A	Totman George E	49	machinist	60	"
B	Totman Ruth—†	49	secretary	25	"
C	Totman William F	49	clerk	31	"
D	Murphy William J	51	lineman	35	1287 Mass av
E	Savage Anna M—†	51	housewife	35	1287 "

18

Linden Park Street—Continued

F	Weiner Max	51	cobbler	55	here
G	Weiner Morris	51	brushmaker	23	"
H	Weiner Rose—†	51	housewife	52	"
K	Neitlich Ida—†	51	"	30	"
L	Neitlich Isreal	51	steamfitter	30	"
M	Moore Charles E	53	policeman	37	"
N	Moore Sarah A—†	53	housewife	30	"
O	O'Brien John P	53	teamster	48	"
P	O'Brien Mary—†	53	housewife	40	"
R	O'Brien Thomas F	53	roofer	21	"
S	O'Brien Walter P	53	clerk	23	"
T	Rich Sarah—†	53	laundress	31	"
U	Walsh Anna E—†	53	bookkeeper	23	"
V	Walsh Mary—†	53	housewife	54	"
W	Walsh Mary V—†	53	clerk	26	"
X	Walsh Thomas	53	laborer	58	"
Y	Walsh Thomas J	53	salesman	22	"
Z	Walsh William J	53	clerk	20	"
A	Andries Joseph A	63	machinist	29	"
B	Andries Kathleen C—†	63	housewife	28	"
C	Heath Agnes—†	63	"	47	"
D	Heath Ernest	63	electroplater	47	"
E	Walsh Beatrice M—†	63	housewife	45	"
F	Walsh Patrick E	63	steward	52	"
G	Smith Margaret—†	65	housewife	38	34 Whitney
H	Smith Thomas	65	mason	48	34 "
K	Ward Ellen—†	65	housekeeper	68	here
L	Ward John F	65	porter	32	"
M	Ward William H	65	elevatorman	40	"
N	Fitzgerald Margaret—†	65	housewife	30	"
O	Fitzgeral Wallace	65	shoemaker	34	"
P	Burke Helen—†	67	housewife	25	"
R	Burke Martin	67	chauffeur	25	"
S	Gettins Mary—†	67	waitress	32	"
W	Driscoll Ruth—†	67	shoeworker	29	"
X	Driscoll William	67	roofer	29	"
T	Fitzgerald Anna E—†	67	housekeeper	60	"
U	Fitzgerald David E	67	steamfitter	34	"
V	Fitzgerald Winifred—†	67	shoeworker	24	"
Y	Gallagher Annie—†	67	housewife	49	65 Linden Park
Z	Gallagher Thomas	67	plasterer	45	65 "

Page	Letter	FULL NAME.	Residence, April 1, 1926.	Occupation.	Supposed Age.	Reported Residence, April 1, 1925. Street and Number.

Linden Park Street—Continued

	A	Fernandes Ethel M—†	69	housewife	23	here
	B	Fernandes Manuel H	69	chauffeur	29	"
	C	Carey Elizabeth A—†	69	housewife	47	"
	D	Carey Walter L	69	plumber	48	"
	E	Carey Walter L, jr	69	letter carrier	25	"
	F	Hayes Francis B	69	machinist	29	"
	G	Hayes James P	69	porter	32	139 Pembroke
	H	Hayes Margaret T—†	69	housekeeper	23	here
	K	Hayes Timothy	69	retired	73	"

Oak Grove Terrace

	L	Banks Mary L †	4	housewife	32	here
	M	Banks Otis P	4	clerk	34	"
	N	Walker Adeline †	4	housewife	30	7 Warwick
	O	Walker Robert	4	cook	35	7 "
	R	Barboza Angline †	6	housewife	34	here
	S	Barboza Domingo	6	laborer	42	"
	T	Murray Westly	6	"	30	83 Sterling
	U	Webb Henry	6	porter	36	here
	V	Webb Marie †	6	housewife	36	"
	W	Gunderinay Fannie—†	6	cook	40	Brockton
	X	Holland Aletha M †	6	housewife	32	here
	Y	Manley Charles B	6	painter	46	"
	Z	Holman Luter	7	barber	47	"
	A	Holman Mora †	7	housewife	37	"
	B	Scott William J	7	janitor	50	"
	C	Chapman Ada †	7	housewife	24	"
	D	Chapman Whitfield	7	porter	26	"
	E	Chase Lambert	7	waiter	20	New Jersey
	F	Hyatt George W	8	porter	51	here
	G	Hyatt Helen M †	8	houseworker	45	"
	H	Callender Ida †	8	"	34	Cambridge
	K	Callender James	8	laborer	39	"
	L	Semedo Domingos L	8	"	36	here
	M	Semedo Rose L †	8	housewife	36	"
	N	McDonald Evelyn—†	9	"	22	Brookline
	O	McDonald Murdock	9	special police	24	29 Oak Grove ter
	P	Sykes Harry	9	baker	36	Cambridge
	R	Sykes Howitt †	9	housewife	36	"

Letter	Full Name	Residence, April 1, 1926.	Occupation.	Supposed Age.	Reported Residence, April 1, 1925. Street and Number.

Oak Grove Terrace Continued

Letter	Full Name	Residence, April 1, 1926.	Occupation.	Supposed Age.	Reported Residence, April 1, 1925. Street and Number.
s	Burke Oliver	10	porter	40	here
T	Burke Viloer —†	10	housewife	36	"
U	DaVeiga Mardline J	10	laborer	37	"
V	Goms Dick	10	"	40	"
W	Rice Thomas	10	"	40	Providence R I
X	Vaz Janiario P	10	"	37	here
Y	Mendelewitz Joseph	10	baker	47	"
Z	Mendelewitz Lena —†	10	housewife	41	"
A	Tobey Eller —†	11	"	43	"
B	Tobey Eugene	11	laborer	49	Cambridge
C	Beckford Lillian —†	11	domestic	35	here
D	Russell Eliza—†	11	"	54	"
E	Hart Sarah—†	12	"	44	"
F	Christopher Mildred —†	12	housewife	22	61 Williams
G	Christopher William	12	laborer	32	61 "
H	Mascoll Louise—†	12	domestic	32	here
K	Kennedy Louise —†	12	housewife	29	"
L	Kennedy William	12	cook	26	"
M	Messie Lottie —†	12	"	30	"
N	Davis John W	13	laborer	41	15 Sarsfield
O	Davis Mara —†	13	housewife	40	15 "
P	Govan Cain	13	chauffeur	28	Delaware Md
R	Govan Carrie —†	13	housewife	29	"
T	Hoyte Rhoda —†	14	"	40	here
S	Hoyte Robert	14	laborer	50	"
U	Thompson Rhoda —†	14	dressmaker	20	"
V	Weeks Jason	14	laborer	26	"
W	Weeks Rhoda —†	14	domestic	44	"
X	Grace Ima —†	14	housewife	25	29 Willard pl
Y	Grace Julsee	14	laborer	23	29 "
Z	Lewis Mable —†	15	housewife	38	here
A	Lewis William H	15	laborer	40	"
B	Osborne James	15	waiter	38	"
C	Lopes Carl	15	laborer	52	"
D	Montro Dannie —†	15	"	25	"
E	Perry Manuel	15	"	39	"
F	Varella Jose C	15	"	49	"
G	Shepard Bessie —†	16	housewife	42	"
H	Shepard Samuel M	16	clerk	43	"
K	Gray Emmer —†	16	housewife	25	19 Hubert
L	Gray Shirrill	16	clerk	28	19 "

Page.	Letter.	FULL NAME.	Residence, April 1, 1926.	Occupation.	Supposed Age.	Reported Residence, April 1, 1925. Street and Number.

Oak Grove Terrace—Continued

N	Evans Margaret †	17	housewife	40	here
O	Evans Walter	17	longshoreman	42	"
P	Cohen Freda—†	17	houseworker	26	"
R	Cohen Herman D	17	painter	26	"
S	Meyer George J	17	baker	55	"
T	Meyer Henry G	17	printer	25	"
U	Meyer Louis A	17	baker	24	"
V	Meyer Sophie—†	17	housewife	48	"
W	Mapp Marie—†	18	domestic	24	"
X	Newsome Edith †	18	housekeeper	38	Medford
Y	Newsome John	18	laborer	31	"
Y¹	Matti Linford	18	"	25	Newton
Z	Matti Tolerance—†	18	houseworker	30	"
B	Cesmeau Syldster	19	ironworker	29	61 Ruggles
C	Hagan Maud—†	19	domestic	43	44 Sawyer
D	Lomax Lillian—†	19	housewife	33	96 Westminster
E	Cooper George W	19	teacher	72	here
F	Cooper Nellie E—†	19	housewife	62	"
G	Goldstein Harry	20	tailor	38	"
H	Goldstein Rose—†	20	housewife	39	"
K	Rhoden Alice—†	20	houseworker	60	47 Sawyer
L	Rhoden Anna—†	20	housewife	30	47 "
M	Rhoden Walter	20	laborer	41	47 "
N	Smith James	20	electrician	40	here
O	Wilson Reginald	21	laborer	22	"
P	Wilson Violet—†	21	housewife	30	"
R	Jackson Howard T	21	laborer	24	664 Shawmut av
S	Jackson Pauline M—†	21	housewife	22	664 "
T	Douglass George	21	longshoreman	28	here
U	Douglass Mary—†	21	housewife	29	"
V	Douglass Monterman	21	laborer	22	"
W	Desmond Emily—†	22	housewife	39	30 Arnold
X	Desmond William H	22	laborer	45	30 "
Y	Johnson Elizabeth—†	22	housewife	47	33 Yarmouth
Z	Johnson William	22	cook	35	33 "
A	Barry John	23	laborer	47	54 Sawyer
B	Brister Stanley	23	"	36	54 "
C	Walsley Adie—†	23	housewife	50	54 "
D	Bowen Etta—†	23	"	20	here
E	Bowen George	23	laborer	21	"
F	Murray Jervis—†	23	housewife	25	66 Warwick

22

Oak Grove Terrace—Continued

	G	Murray Mortimer	23	laborer	29	66 Warwick
	H	Thompson Kenneth	23	"	22	27 Kendall
	K	Gersberg Sidney	25	storekeeper	38	Cambridge
	L	Gersberg Sylvia—†	25	housewife	30	"
	M	Shore Rose—†	25	houseworker	55	"
	N	White Agnes—†	25	housewife	23	218 W Canton
	O	White William	25	chauffeur	28	218 "
	P	Pearlstein Annie—†	25	housewife	35	here
	R	Pearlstein Joseph	25	pedler	37	"
	S	Grabousski Adams P	27	clerk	42	43 Fay
	T	Grabousski Vromicea—†	27	housewife	43	43 "
	U	Zeaser James	27	janitor	35	here
	V	Zeaser Josephine—†	27	housewife	34	"
	W	Michael Emil F	27	fireman	34	"
	X	Michael Florence—†	27	housewife	31	"
	Y	Badgett Alice—†	29	"	29	"
	Z	Badgett William	29	cook	35	"
	A	McDonald Catherine E—†	29	housewife	53	"
	B	McDonald Hugh R	29	laborer	65	"
	C	McDonald John M	29	baker	23	"
	D	Rock Undine C—†	29	houseworker	23	Newton
	E	Rock Zuleka—†	29	domestic	26	here

Prentiss Place

	F	Wheeler Helena—†	2	housewife	45	283 Cabot
	G	Wheeler Helena M—†	2	saleswoman	21	283 "
	H	Wheeler John F	2	janitor	49	283 "
	K	Donnelly Thomas	3	laborer	50	here
	L	Ernshaw Celia—†	3	housewife	50	"
	M	Ernshaw John E	3	shoeworker	21	"

Roxbury Street

	X	King Frances B—†	81	housewife	40	here
	Y	King Thomas H	81	commissioner	56	"
	Z	Faour John	81	janitor	59	"
	A	Faour Rose—†	81	housewife	47	"
	B	Torrente Marica—†	81	houseworker	46	"

Page.	Letter.	FULL NAME.	Residence, April 1, 1926.	Occupation.	Supposed Age.	Reported Residence, April 1, 1925. Street and Number.

Roxbury Street—Continued

c	Torrente Michael	81	candymaker	28	here
d	Burton Eunice—†	81	perforator	23	"
e	Cook William G	81	foreman	46	"
f	Sawtell Christina—†	81	housewife	59	"
g	Sawtell John S	81	elevatorman	56	"
h	Brewster Harold A	81	chauffeur	29	"
k	Brewster Helen L—†	81	housewife	28	"
l	Sheehan Joseph W	81	chauffeur	46	"
m	Sheehan Mary E—†	81	housewife	33	"
n	White Marion—†	81	"	29	"
o	White Thomas	81	conductor	31	"
p	Murtagh Jennie—†	81	shoeworker	33	"
r	Murtagh Mary—†	81	housewife	45	"
s	Murtagh Thomas	81	chauffeur	45	"
t	McKenna James	83A	stableman	50	"
v	Mooney Anthony	83A	laborer	50	"
w	Mooney Mary—†	83A	houseworker	56	"
x	Norton John	83A	laborer	32	"
y	Brady Catherine—†	83A	houseworker	60	"
z	Brady Elizabeth—†	83A	waitress	28	"
a	Brady James H	83A	weaver	32	"
b	Brady John T	83A	machinist	35	"
c	Brady Martha A—†	83A	at home	28	"
d	Brady Michael F	83A	machinist	26	"
e	Bartlett Margaret—†	85	housewife	25	Chelmsford
f	Bartlett Robert	85	machinist	25	"
g	Edgerton David	85	auto repairer	28	here
h	Shepeard Mary—†	85	houseworker	50	"
k	Dana Dora—†	85	housewife	55	"
l	Dana Hyman	85	laborer	66	"
o	Howarth Mary—†	87A	houseworker	68	"
p	Walsh Edward F	87A	salesman	30	"
r	Walsh Lillian—†	87A	housewife	29	"
s	Harris Catherine V—†	87A	"	27	"
t	Pyne Catherine—†	87A	"	63	"
u	Pyne Edward	87A	laborer	66	"
v	Brinkert Catherine—†	93	housewife	30	"
w	Brinkert William C	93	repairer	33	"
a	Butler Catherine—†	99A	housewife	38	43 Linwood
b	Butler Edward	99A	chauffeur	38	here
c	Harding Carrie A—†	99A	housewife	58	"

Page.	Letter.	FULL NAME.	Residence, April 1, 1926.	Occupation	Supposed Age.	Reported Residence, April 1, 1925. Street and Number.

Roxbury Street—Continued

	D	Harding George M		99A painter	58	here
	E	Buzzell Josephine —†		99A laborer	33	Beachmont
	F	Perry Mary V—†		99A artist	28	193 London
	G	Rogers Frank V		99A retired	69	193 "
	H	Rogers Morris V		99A laborer	32	193 "
	K	Rogers Reita—†		99A housewife	26	193 "
	L	Ferris Hattie—†		99A laundress	55	here
	N	Rehm Charles W	rear 99	teamster	44	"
	O	Rehm Frank W	" 99	plumber	74	"
	M	Tilt Benjamin F	" 99	printer	45	"
	P	Tilt Mary J—†	" 99	housewife	42	"
	R	Tilt William H	" 99	finisher	20	"
	S	Carty Ann—†	103	at home	76	"
	T	Ehmons Agnes—†	103	operator	22	"
	U	Ehmons Annie—†	103	housewife	47	"
	V	Ehmons Charles F	103	painter	46	"
	W	Ehmons Leo	103	teamster	24	"

Ruggles Street

	A	Lerry Lorena C—†	70	housekeeper	71	here
	B	Russell Lorena L—†	70	"	29	"
	C	Russell William F	70	electrician	29	"
	D	Crosby Lottie —†	70	housekeeper	31	"
	E	Crosby Wells	70	laborer	35	"
	F	Lasee Manuel M	70	"	30	"
	G	Manuel Isiac	70	porter	45	"
	H	McGirt Joseph H	70	storekeeper	55	"
	K	McGirt Nancy J—†	70	housekeeper	54	"
	L	McLearn Margaret—†	70	"	68	"
	N	Burns Annie B—†	72	"	39	"
	O	Burns Robert	72	janitor	40	"
	S	Brown Irine A—†	72	housekeeper	44	"
	R	Coleman Harry	72	laborer	25	"
	P	Deryton Benjamin	72	"	22	"
	T	Deryton Lucy—†	72	housekeeper	21	"
	U	Robeson Mary E—†	72	"	29	"
	V	Thomas Samuel H	72	janitor	46	"

Ruggles Street—Continued

W	Pierce Blanche A—†	74	housekeeper	45	here
X	Pierce Charles H	74	engineer	50	"
Y	Susie Frank	74	laborer	38	"
Z	Vass Henery	74	"	36	"
A	Maddox Charles	74	"	25	"
B	Maddox Mable—†	74	housekeeper	23	"
C	Alston Jennie E—†	76	"	25	Winthrop
D	Alston Samuel K	76	laborer	34	"
E	Campbell Cristena—†	76	domestic	20	17 Camden pl
F	Green Elizabeth—†	76	housekeeper	26	17 "
G	Green Henry G	76	sailor	40	17 "
H	Rainey Douglas P	76	laborer	49	here
K	Saunders Annie—†	76	housekeeper	52	"
N	Shaffer Fanny—†	78	"	46	"
O	Ruggles Harold E	78	porter	22	"
P	Ruggles Lorraine—†	78	housekeeper	28	"
R	Blitt Louis	78	shoemaker	49	"
S	Blitt Rose—†	78	housekeeper	38	"
U	Johnson Ethel M—†	82	"	29	"
V	Johnson Robert	82	laborer	44	"
W	Sultis Edith—†	82	housekeeper	29	96 Westminster
X	Anderson James	82	waiter	28	unknown
Y	Brown William G	82	porter	39	New York
Z	Young Blanche O—†	82	housekeeper	42	here
A	Young Silas	82	laborer	40	"
B	Buttler Helen E—†	82	housekeeper	47	"
C	Buttler Nathan S	82	chauffeur	44	"
D	Bold Charles	82	musician	31	19 Northampton
E	Mustasky Herman	72	watchmaker	43	here
F	Mustasky Sadie †	82	housekeeper	39	"
G	Washington Alfretta—†	82	"	25	"
H	Washington Archie	82	porter	27	"

Saint Francis de Sales Street

L	Homes Leroy E	7	chauffeur	22	here
M	Norwood Clifton W	7	mechanic	34	"
N	Norwood Maude L—†	7	housekeeper	28	"
P	DelMonte August	7	laborer	25	10 Third
R	DelMonte Gladis †	7	housekeeper	24	10 "

Page.	Letter.	FULL NAME.	Residence, April 1, 1926.	Occupation.	Supposed Age.	Reported Residence, April 1, 1925. Street and Number.

Saint Francis de Sales Street—Continued

	s	Kane Mary—†	7	housekeeper	53	10 Third
	T	Cunniff Bridget—†	12	"	64	here
	U	Perry Hannah—†	15	houseworker	45	456 D
	V	Quigley Margaret—†	15	"	53	here
	Z	Maloney George	17	brakeman	21	"
	A	Lynch Lillian F—†	18	saleswoman	27	40 St Francis de Sales
	B	Stevens Frank J	18	policeman	62	48 Alpine
	C	Stevens Lillian L—†	18	housekeeper	33	48 "
	D	McDonald Susana—†	18	"	30	223 Cabot
	E	Main Harold D	19	machinist	29	here
	F	Main Mary—†	19	housekeeper	28	"
	G	Egan Helen—†	19	"	56	"
	H	Egan Mary—†	19	"	60	"
	K	Hassion Nora—†	19	at home	60	"
	L	Folan Bridie—†	19	houseworker	30	"
	M	Ducett Joseph	19	advertising	26	Chelsea
	N	Curran Mary A—†	20	housekeeper	57	here
	O	Atkins Hellen A—†	20	housewife	21	"
	P	Atkins John W	20	carpenter	29	"
	R	McHowell Charles A	20	machinist	23	"
	S	McHowell Velma L—†	20	housewife	20	"
	T	Patch Love—†	20	nurse	24	"
	V	Gellwet Henry	31	laborer	56	"
	W	Gellwet Margaret—†	31	housewife	50	"
	X	McGraw Edith M—†	31	housekeeper	75	"
	Y	McGraw Hugh E	31	laborer	46	"
	Z	McGraw Mildred E—†	31	usher	20	"
	A	Hurley Jeremiah J	31	laborer	39	10 Frothingham av
	B	Hurley Mary L—†	31	housekeeper	77	10 "
	C	Fisher James	32	laborer	43	Canada
	D	Fisher Ruth—†	32	housewife	43	"
	E	Tower Lillian H—†	32	"	31	4 Langdon
	F	Tower Walter E	32	roofer	36	4 "
	H	Bishop George H	33½	plasterer	35	Maine
	K	Bishop Lena M—†	32½	housewife	25	"
	L	Morton Douglas R	32½	waiter	29	here
	M	Morton Emma—†	32½	housewife	28	"
	N	Donohue James P	33	fireman	40	"
	O	Mullen John J	33	painter	56	"
	P	Mullen Mary J—†	33	housewife	50	"
	R	Fisher Norah P—†	34	"	21	4 May

Page	Letter	Full Name.	Residence, April 1, 1926.	Occupation.	Supposed Age.	Reported Residence, April 1, 1925. Street and Number.

Saint Francis de Sales Street—Continued

	s	Fisher Thomas F	34	inspector	22	here
	t	Looby Agnes M —†	34	housewife	39	55 Westminster
	u	Looby Matthew J	34	laborer	52	55 "
	v	Burns Mary F †	34	housewife	27	157 Highland
	w	Burns Robert F	34	chauffeur	27	157 "
	x	Hartigan Mary E —†	35	housewife	39	here
	y	Hartigan Thomas H	35	meatcutter	38	"
	z	O'Connor Nora —†	35	domestic	55	34 St Francis de Sales
	b	Faro Rose †	36	housewife	25	166 Staniford
	c	Faro Toni	36	laborer	26	166 "
	d	Burns Annie M —†	36	housewife	29	2 Highland pl
	e	Burns Henry P	36	salesman	33	2 "
	f	Otto Edward J	38	laborer	37	21 Downing
	g	Temple Catherine M —†	38	housewife	40	21 "
	h	Temple Robert C	38	laborer	42	21 "
	k	Noonan Annie —†	38	housewife	46	here
	k	Noonan Michael	38	teamster	45	"
	l	Noonan Michael J	38	policeman	22	"
	m	Welch Margaret —†	38	laundress	50	"
	n	Bowler Nora —†	40	waitress	44	"
	o	Miles Ellen E —†	40	housekeeper	74	"
	p	Welsh Margaret—†	40	"	51	"
	r	Walters Anna —†	40	housewife	45	"
	s	Walters Oliver	40	cook	50	"
	t	Redmond Mary —†	44	housewife	47	188 Cabot
	u	Redmond William	44	manager	48	188 "
	v	Ginty James J	44	laborer	47	here
	w	Ginty Mary—†	44	housewife	41	"

Shawmut Avenue

	x	Lancaster Helen A —†	803	housekeeper	46	here

Vernon Court

	n	Doherty Anna —†	1	domestic	38	44 St Francis de Sales
	o	Denning Bessie M—†	2	housewife	38	here
	p	Denning Edward J	2	electrician	48	"

Page.	Letter.	FULL NAME.	Residence, April 1, 1926.	Occupation.	Supposed Age.	Reported Residence, April 1, 1925. Street and Number.

Vernon Court—Continued

	R	Maguire Michael	2	chauffeur	33	984 Col av
	S	McCarthy Frank	3	shoeworker	34	here
	T	McCarthy Susan A—†	3	housewife	39	"

Vernon Place

	U	Hurston George M	2	salesman	49	here
	V	Hurston Mary M—†	2	housewife	32	"
	W	Goldman Edith—†	2	"	35	"
	X	Goldman Morris	2	storekeeper	37	"
	Y	Mardden Mary—†	2	laundress	35	"
	A	Kirkell Anna—†	4	housewife	31	"
	B	Kirkell Frank	4	laborer	39	"
	C	Hill Edith L—†	4	housewife	28	"
	D	Hill John	4	laborer	35	"
	E	Costin William	6	"	79	"
	F	Lamkin James	6	"	30	"
	G	Lamkin Jane—†	6	housewife	73	"
	H	Sullivan Beatrice—†	6	saleswoman	23	"
	K	Sullivan John J	6	student	21	"
	L	Sullivan John L	6	teamster	49	"
	M	Sullivan Margaret—†	6	housewife	47	"
	N	Tansey Agnes M—†	6	bookkeeper	25	"
	O	Tansey Mary B—†	6	houseworker	48	"
	P	Tansey Thomas T	6	chauffeur	22	"

Vernon Street

	R	Waite Mary P—†	46	at home	40	here
	S	Greenberg Dora—†	46	housewife	54	"
	T	Greenberg Helen—†	46	bookkeeper	27	"
	U	Greenberg Philip	46	junk collector	55	"
	V	Greenberg Sarah—†	46	domestic	22	"
	W	Baker Harry	46	junk collector	49	"
	X	Baker Samuel	46	paper dealer	21	"
	Y	Baker Sarah—†	46	housewife	47	"
	Z	Calahan Cornelius	48	teamster	24	"
	A	Calahan Gladys—†	48	housewife	20	"

29

Vernon Street—Continued

B	Stackpole Mable —†	48	stitcher	39	here
C	Boire Alphons E	48	retired	81	15 Kent
D	Boire Joseph R	48	insurance agent	43	15 "
E	Boire Mary A—†	48	housewife	44	15 "
F	Snyder Ida —†	48	"	45	here
G	Snyder Louis	48	junk collector	75	"
H	Curtian Mary —†	48A	domestic	65	8 Ward
K	Curtian Matthew	48A	laborer	21	8 "
L	Fallon Bernard J	50	hostler	42	here
M	Murry Mary E —†	50	houseworker	46	"
N	Foster Mary J —†	50	housewife	57	105 Vernon
O	Foster William B	50	laborer	58	105 "
P	Taitel Morris	50	junk collector	40	here
R	Taitel Polly—†	50	housewife	39	"
U	Price Louis	50	clerk	30	"
T	Price Margaret —†	50	housewife	26	"
S	Saul George W	50	piano mover	50	Providence R I
V	Manning Francis—†	52	houseworker	46	here
W	Staples Joseph A	52	salesman	58	"
X	Kaplan Joseph	52	laborer	50	"
Y	Kaplan Rachel—†	52	housewife	48	"
Z	Landy Dera —†	52	"	36	"
A	Landy Frank	52	salesman	39	"
B	Butler Robert V	52	mechanic	45	"
C	Butler Sadie F—†	52	housewife	35	"
E	Halidy James	60	laborer	58	"
F	Halidy Mary —†	60	domestic	22	"
G	Halidy Sousan —†	60	housewife	49	"
H	Bowen Matilda —†	60	houseworker	39	96 Lenox
K	Terrofirre Andrew	60	laborer	29	here
L	Terrofirre Mary—†	60	housewife	33	"
M	Hinds Beatrice —†	60	"	44	"
N	Hinds Frederick	60	clergyman	49	"
O	Cassidy Annie M—†	66	at home	75	"
P	Cassidy Florence—†	66	housewife	41	"
R	Cassidy John B	66	undertaker	49	"
S	Burton Elizabeth A —†	70	housewife	44	"
T	Burton Florence I —†	70	waitress	21	"
U	Burton William H	70	mechanic	42	"
V	Dunn Annie—†	70	housewife	48	"

Page.	Letter.	Full Name.	Residence, April 1, 1926.	Occupation.	Supposed Age.	Reported Residence, April 1, 1925. Street and Number.

Vernon Street—Continued

	w	Dunn John T	70	special police	24	here
	x	Dunn Patrick F	70	laborer	59	"
	y	Wineberg Lena—†	76	housewife	59	"
	z	Wineberg Philip	76	tailor	59	"
	a	McCarthy Elizabeth—†	76	housewife	40	"
	b	McCarthy James	76	clerk	21	"
	c	McCarthy Timothy	76	laborer	50	"
	d	Franklin Charles M	76	chauffeur	40	"
	e	Franklin Sarah F—†	76	housewife	35	"
	f	Reinherz Jennie—†	78	"	34	"
	g	Reinherz Louis	78	salesman	40	"
	h	White Edger L	78	shipfitter	38	"
	k	White Grace A—†	78	housewife	36	"
	l	May Dorothy—†	78	bookkeeper	29	"
	m	May Lena—†	78	"	26	"
	n	May Max	78	retired	66	"
	o	May Sarah—†	78	housewife	67	"
	p	MacLeod Donald J	80	chauffeur	47	"
	r	MacLeod Jennette A—†	80	housewife	47	"
	s	Leacy Annie M—†	80	clerk	23	"
	t	Leacy Duncan	80	carpenter	55	"
	u	Leacy James F	80	clerk	25	"
	v	Leacy Mary A—†	80	housewife	47	"
	w	Wixon Orrin H	80	seaman	52	"
	x	Wixon Tresia—†	80	housewife	36	"
	z	Brook Herbert M	82A	carpenter	41	"
	a	Brooks Julia A—†	82A	housewife	40	"
	b	Adams Julius J	84	piano mover	58	"
	c	Adams Mary A—†	84	housewife	55	"
	d	Mahoney Hazel G—†	84	"	20	77 Clayton
	e	Mahoney John J, jr	84	shipper	24	115 Cabot
	f	Mulrey Rose—†	84	at home	40	here
	g	Chamberlain Frederick	86	teamster	59	"
	h	Chamberlain Mary E—†	86	housewife	55	"
	k	Arenge Arthur	86	plumber	25	"
	l	Arenge Josephine I—†	86	housewife	27	"
	m	Abraham Frederick	86	teamster	59	"
	n	Abraham Mary E—†	86	housewife	54	"
	o	Austin Alice—†	87	nurse	22	Dover N H
	p	Bounelli Annie—†	87	maid	55	382 Main
	r	Boyle Katherine—†	87	cook	46	28 Linden

Vernon Street —Continued

s	Corkum Irene —†	87	nurse	25	here
t	Czuj Esther —†	87	"	22	Turners Falls
u	Daniels Edgar	87	bookkeeper	23	England
v	Doherty Gertrude —†	87	nurse	41	Westfield
w	Duffy Margaret A —†	87	"	27	37 Train
x	Early Frank	87	laundryman	55	here
y	Edwards Dorothy —†	87	nurse	32	818 Harris'n av
z	Egan John	87	houseman	35	here
A	Euait Gertrude —†	87	nurse	22	Quincy
B	Gardner Margaret F —†	87	superintendent	37	Greenfield
C	Herwitz William	87	house officer	24	Revere
D	Hughes Nora —†	87	nurse	23	86 Cushing av
E	Huntoon Florence —†	87	"	21	Adams
F	Leahy Annie —†	87	laundress	35	here
G	Lorimer Hazel —†	87	nurse	26	"
H	McLoughlin Mary —†	87	maid	60	41 Northampton
K	McNultry Helen —†	87	nurse	23	Dover N H
L	Paris William	87	house officer	25	Chelsea
M	Parkinson Mary —†	87	nurse	41	Gloucester
N	Porter Ruth —†	87	clerk	23	here
O	Post Lillian —†	87	maid	35	New Brunswick
P	Stinson Edna —†	87	nurse	24	202 W Newton
R	Toohey Josephine —†	87	"	40	here
s	Wood Beatrice —†	87	housekeeper	24	41 Berkeley
T	Daniel Carry —†	88	housewife	40	3 Chester pl
U	Daniel Milton	88	mechanic	32	3 "
V	Franz Edward J	90	police officer	27	here
W	Franz Elizabeth —†	90	housewife	65	"
X	Franz Henry S	90	fireman	31	"
Y	Franz Mary —†	90	bookkeeper	32	"
Z	Franz Sabina E —†	90	"	40	"
A	Franz Sebastian	90	retired	65	"
B	Cleary James	92	painter	36	"
C	Cleary Sadie —†	92	housewife	34	
D	LaRochelle George E	92	chauffeur	28	107 Munroe
E	LaRochelle Josephine C —†	92	shoeworker	28	107 "
F	McGreever Daniel A	92	student	21	here
G	McGreever Katherine —†	92	housewife	48	"
H	Moran Elmir W	92	mechanic	24	49 Brook av
K	Moran Francis	92	"	20	Everett
L	Green Susan —†	94	at home	78	101 Camden

Page.	Letter.	FULL NAME.	Residence, April 1, 1926.	Occupation.	Supposed Age.	Reported Residence, April 1, 1925. Street and Number.

Vernon Street —Continued

M	Shelton Edna E—†	94	clerk	21	101 Camden
N	Shelton Fannie B—†	94	housewife	58	101 "
O	Shelton Flossie—†	94	bookkeeper	22	101 "
P	Shelton Hazel B—†	94	dressmaker	25	101 "
R	Shelton Howard J	94	shipper	27	101 "
S	Shelton Philip T	94	chauffeur	26	101 "
U	Shelton William L	94	janitor	60	101 "
T	Boyde Lucinda—†	94	domestic	45	101 "
V	Kunan Helen V—†	96	housewife	29	here
W	Kunan Thomas W	96	fireman	30	"
X	Miasnick Minnie—†	96	housewife	30	"
Y	Miasnick Samuel	96	storekeeper	38	"
Z	Daly Joseph W	96	chauffeur	24	3 Worcester sq
A	Rich Catherine A —†	96	housewife	29	here
B	Rich Frank P	96	teacher	35	"
C	Concannon Martin F	rear 97	butcher	67	"
D	Smith Francis A	" 97	reporter	28	"
E	Smith Helen E—†	" 97	housekeeper	43	"
F	Smith Mathew J	" 97	retired	69	"
G	Thibodeau Gladys—†	98	housewife	25	New Hampshire
H	Thibodeau Henery	98	mason	24	"
K	Trib Jennie—†	98	housewife	50	here
L	Trib Morris	98	junk collector	60	"
M	Shapirio Iseral	98	"	46	"
N	Shapirio Sadie —†	98	housewife	40	"
O	McMahon Annie F—†	99	housekeeper	62	"
P	McMahon Charles H	99	clerk	35	"
R	McDevitt John J	99	printer	41	"
S	Smith Bertha A—†	99	housewife	38	"
T	Smith Lawrence A	99	letter carrier	37	"
U	Dunn Charles F	100	papercutter	34	"
V	Dunn Mary F—†	100	housewife	37	"
W	Scott Isabella—†	100	at home	75	"
X	McBride Catherine —†	100	clerk	58	"
Y	Doyle James C	102	barber	28	226 Cabot
Z	Hacket John	102	plumber	31	Medford
A	Jesso Mary—†	102	houseworker	43	226 Cabot
B	Taylor Richard	102	laborer	30	here
C	Taylor Sarah—†	102	housewife	26	"
D	Brown Howard	102	seaman	33	"
E	Brown Olga—†	102	housewife	35	"

9—10

Page.	Letter	FULL NAME.	Residence, April 1, 1926.	Occupation.	Supposed Age.	Reported Residence, April 1, 1925. Street and Number.

Vernon Street—Continued

G	Cornirre Flauna—†	102	housewife	33	here
F	Cornirre James D	102	tailor	37	"
H	Connell Margaret T—†	116	housekeeper	58	"
K	Davison Nora—†	116	housemaid	57	"
L	Deasey William T	116	clergyman	54	"
M	Keenan Joseph J	116	"	30	Brookline
N	Lydon Patrick J	116	"	43	here
O	Begley Teresa—†	122	teacher	29	"
R	Dooling Mary A—†	122	"	31	"
S	Fitzgerald Genevieve—†	122	"	26	"
T	Jones Delia A—†	122	"	53	"
U	Kelley Mary—†	122	"	26	"
P	O'Connor Mary—†	122	housekeeper	35	"
V	Raymond Marie A—†	122	teacher	42	"
W	Roche Elizebeth—†	122	"	45	"
X	Ward Delia—†	122	"	35	"
Y	Whelton Teresa L.—†	122	"	30	"
Z	Kelley Mary—†	124	laundress	56	"
A	Kelley Nellie—†	124	retired	51	"
B	Ford Harry	124	bookkeeper	30	"
C	Gilmartin William	124	laborer	24	"
E	Gomley Catherine M—†	130	housewife	52	"
F	Gomley Elizabeth M—†	130	bookkeeper	23	"
G	Gomley James F	130	machinist	21	"
H	Gomley Michael P	130	stableman	35	"
K	Coulter Sarah—†	130	housewife	32	"
L	Coulter Thomas S	130	carpenter	34	"
M	Olsen Oagot—†	130	housewife	33	Norway
N	Olden Siguard	130	carpenter	34	Watertown
O	Thursen Oscar	130	seaman	33	Norway
P	Caffee William	134	leatherworker	44	here
R	Earley Bernard J	134	shipper	23	"
S	Earley Delia—†	134	houseworker	54	"
T	Earley John F	134	chauffeur	26	"
U	Driscoll Cornilious	134	laborer	25	"
V	Driscoll Timothy J	134	lawyer	23	"
W	Murphy Anna—†	134	housewife	54	"
X	Murphy Frank	134	electrician	21	"
Y	Murphy Joseph	134	painter	52	"
Z	Murphy Mary—†	134	tel operator	27	"
A	Carrino Felix	134	chauffeur	32	"

34

Page.	Letter.	FULL NAME.	Residence, April 1, 1926.	Occupation.	Supposed Age.	Reported Residence, April 1, 1925. Street and Number.

Vernon Street—Continued

	B	Carrino Minnie—†	134	housewife	25	here
	C	Chiolo Susie—†	136	"	50	65 Longwood av
	D	Chiolo Thomas	136	laborer	55	65 "
	E	DiManni John	136	shipper	21	65 "
	F	Gurney Charles	136	painter	42	121 Vernon
	G	Gurney Winnifred—†	136	housewife	38	121 "
	H	Hangis Loretta—†	136	"	38	11 Haskins
	K	Hangis Louis	136	shoecutter	38	11 "
	L	Kelley Thomas	136	rubberworker	51	11 "
	M	Muehlberger Albert C	138	salesman	22	74 Jamaica
	N	Muehlberger John	138	clerk	30	74 "
	O	Muehlberger Philipina—†	138	houseworker	55	74 "
	P	Hunt Bessie K—†	138	housewife	31	here
	R	Hunt James J	138	laborer	37	"
	S	Rose Elizabeth A—†	138	housewife	30	"
	T	Rose James F	138	chauffeur	30	"
	U	MacLain Agnes A—†	140	housewife	30	Providence R I
	V	MacLain Kenneth J	140	painter	48	"
	X	McCormick Mark	140	florist	33	here
	W	McCormick Mary—†	140	saleswoman	32	"
	Y	O'Hara Hugh	140	chauffeur	28	"
	Z	Curtis Anna G—†	140	clerk	21	"
	A	Curtis Hanna G—†	140	housewife	53	"
	D	Long Jenneth—†	142	"	25	46 Springfield
	B	McLaughlin Edward	142	teamster	36	671 Mass av
	C	McLaughlin Margaret—†	142	housewife	23	671 "
	E	Haggerty Charlott M—†	142	"	37	here
	F	Haggerty William J	142	porter	51	"
	G	Clark Hugh	142	laborer	63	"
	H	Clark Mary—†	142	clerk	29	"
	K	Clark Winnie—†	142	housewife	63	"

Washington Place

	L	O'Connor Francis J	8	laborer	52	here
	M	O'Connor Francis V	8	salesman	23	"
	N	O'Connor Nora—†	8	housewife	49	"
	O	O'Connor Walter J	8	machinist	21	"
	P	Powell Edward F	8	chauffeur	27	"
	R	Powell Mary E—†	8	housewife	27	"

Washington Place—Continued

Page.	Letter.	Full Name.	Residence, April 1, 1926.	Occupation.	Supposed Age.	Reported Residence, April 1, 1925. Street and Number.
	s	Cronin Mary A—†	9	saleswoman	50	here
	t	Gustafson Ellen—†	9	housewife	40	"
	u	Gustafson John	9	janitor	46	"
	v	Walsh Joanna—†	9	houseworker	70	"
	x	Clifford Mary J—†	9	housewife	36	"
	w	Clifford Patrick F	9	insurance	38	"
	y	McDonough Elizabeth—†	10	housewife	29	580 River
	z	McDonough James	10	machinist	31	580 "
	A	Gray Henry	10	retired	55	here
	B	Keilty Helen—†	11	housewife	35	"
	c	Keilty John	11	laborer	42	"
	D	Hegarty Joseph P	11A	chauffeur	30	"
	E	Hegarty Mary—†	11A	housewife	24	"
	F	Hartnett Annie—†	11A	laundress	48	6 Maple pl
	G	Hartnett John	11A	longshoreman	44	6 "
	H	Hartnett John W	11A	retired	79	6 "
	K	Madden Francis W	12	boilermaker	35	here
	K¹	Madden Margaret—†	12	housewife	34	"
	L	Burg Carl R	12	shipper	25	43 Linden Park
	M	Burg Marion—†	12	housewife	22	43 "
	N	Femino Flora—†	14	"	35	here
	o	Femino Leo	14	barber	39	"
	P	Vanni Adelmo	14	caster	37	"
	R	Vanni Palma—†	14	housewife	32	"
	s	Fiander Edgar F	15	shipper	21	"
	T	Fiander John	15	porter	56	"
	U	Fiander Selena—†	15	housewife	50	"
	v	Hailer Frederick C	16	druggist	27	"
	w	Hailer Theresa C—†	16	housewife	23	"
	x	Cardella Joseph N	16	barber	68	"
	y	Cardella Lena E—†	16	saleswoman	25	"
	z	Cardella Mary I—†	16	housewife	57	"
	A	Flynn Anna—†	17	"	35	10 Wash'n pl
	B	Flynn James	17	laborer	34	10 "
	c	Goodwin Frank	19	policeman	38	here
	D	Watson Edward J	19	boxmaker	50	"
	E	Nickerson Addie—†	20	housewife	34	"
	F	Nickerson Lionel	20	laborer	40	"
	G	Wollman Anna—†	20	housewife	34	"
	H	Wollman Paul	20	painter	30	"

Ward 9—Precinct 11

CITY OF BOSTON.

LIST OF RESIDENTS
20 YEARS OF AGE AND OVER

(FEMALES INDICATED BY DAGGER)

AS OF

APRIL 1, 1926

HERBERT A. WILSON, } *Listing*

JAMES F. EAGAN, } *Board.*

CITY OF BOSTON—PRINTING DEPARTMENT

Cabot Street

A	Schlecht Hans	136	florist	26	Germany
B	Schlecht Mary—†	136	housekeeper	32	"
C	Smith Frances—†	136	housewife	27	here
E	Jackson Jennie—†	142	housekeeper	59	"
F	Hudson Catherine—†	146	housewife	85	"
G	Hudson Edward	146	retired	87	"
L	Daley Mary—†	150	housewife	69	"
M	McCabe Margaret—†	150	"	52	89 Worcester
N	McCabe Thomas F	150	porter	56	89 "
O	Ward Mary—†	152	housewife	64	9 Weston pl
P	Ward Thomas	152	laborer	71	9 "
R	LeBlanc Emma—†	152	housewife	23	New York City
S	LeBlanc Victor	152	lineman	38	"
T	Harris Nathaniel	154	laborer	26	26 Arnold
U	McDonald Charles	154	carpenter	30	here
V	McDonald Rosetta—†	154	housewife	29	"
W	Jones Minnie—†	154	domestic	45	Cambridge
Y	Bryan Adelaide A—†	157	houseworker	57	here
Z	Bryan Albert S	157	cook	22	"
A	Bryan Norman A	157	laborer	25	"
B	Lake Rose L—†	157	housewife	37	"
C	Wolff Herbert L	157	watchman	48	"
D	Wolff Rosetta A—†	157	houseworker	46	"
E	Peterson Charles C	159	laborer	52	"
F	Peterson Grace A—†	159	at home	45	"
G	Peterson Ruby I—†	159	houseworker	25	"
H	Davis Mordecia A	159	laborer	32	"
K	Parks Adelaide L—†	159	houseworker	36	19 Peterboro
L	Parks James A	159	laborer	38	19 "
O	Palmer Elizabeth B—†	161	houseworker	45	here
P	Palmer George L	161	electrician	57	"
R	Galligher Catherine R—†	161	houseworker	40	"
S	Galligher Hugh	161	laborer	44	"
T	Gwynn Mattie—†	161	houseworker	50	"
U	Norian George	162	chauffeur	21	5 Cunard
V	Benner William H	162	mariner	53	Maine
X	Owen Anna E—†	162	factory worker	36	984 Col av
W	Shakalouyos George	162	mechanic	30	23 Green
Z	Kenney Catherine—†	163	housewife	41	here
A	Kenney John	163	laborer	47	"
A¹	Minton John J	163	"	48	"

Cabot Street—Continued

	B	Minton Mary —†	163	houseworker	45	here
	C	Minton Mary E—†	163	saleswoman	22	"
	D	Walsh Catherine G—†	163	houseworker	50	"
	E	Walsh James M	163	machinist	23	"
	F	Walsh John J	163	laborer	30	"
	G	Walsh Luke F	163	carpenter	25	"
	H	Carr Alfred N	164	upholsterer	20	"
	K	Carr Helen M—†	164	saleswoman	22	"
	L	Carr Nellie F—†	164	housewife	50	"
	M	Carr Norman F	164	salesman	28	"
	O	Calderara Charles A	164	teamster	36	"
	N	Calderara Mary E—†	164	housewife	30	"
	P	Brickley Anna G—†	164	operator	28	"
	R	Brickley Edward F	164	B F D	31	"
	S	Brickley Grace K—†	164	operator	23	"
	T	Brickley Mary E—†	164	housewife	50	"
	U	Brickley Thomas F	164	laborer	55	"
	W	Goode Daniel L	168	cableworker	24	19 Whittier
	X	Goode Marie V—†	168	housewife	22	19 "
	Y	Young Bradford J	168	watchman	71	here
	Z	Young Mary—†	168	housewife	70	"
	A	Meegan Mary—†	168	"	50	"
	B	Meegan Thomas	168	expressman	35	"
	C	Landin Anna—†	170	housewife	81	"
	D	Landin John	170	ironworker	78	"
	E	Eagan Margaret—†	170	housekeeper	55	Cambridge
	F	Bergen Ellen—†	170	"	72	here
	G	Bergen Henry	170	teamster	34	"
	H	Bergen Mary—†	170	housewife	31	"
	K	Hardy Charles	174	storekeeper	60	"
	L	Hardy Laura—†	174	clerk	21	"
	M	Pender Anna—†	174	housekeeper	33	"
	N	Pender James E	174	machinist	70	"
	O	Pender James J	174	installer	30	"
	P	Smith Franklin	174	machinist	68	"
	T	Athans Helen J —†	177A	housekeeper	28	"
	U	Athans James S	177A	manufacturer	48	"
	V	Velonias Arthur C	177A	laborer	27	"
	C	Poitress Eva M—†	181	houseworker	21	"
	D	Poitress Mary S—†	181	clerk	22	"
	E	Poitress Mathew	181	machinist	47	"

3

Cabot Street—Continued

F	Poitress Sarah A—†	181	houseworker	45	here
G	Curtin Anna—†	182	housewife	28	"
H	Curtin John J, jr	182	laborer	31	"
K	Neary John H	182	inspector	38	"
L	Curley William J	182	laborer	32	"
M	Kenney Catherine A—†	182	operator	42	"
N	Kenney Mary T—†	182	"	46	"
P	Kelly Helen J—†	184	housewife	30	"
R	Kelly Martin H	184	mechanic	32	"
S	Behnke Dell F—†	184	housewife	29	"
T	Behnke Frederick W	184	machinist	29	"
U	Behnke Hilda—†	184	boxmaker	22	"
V	Clonan Coleman J	184	plasterer	53	"
W	Stillman Flora L—†	185	houseworker	37	"
X	Stillman Frank J	185	laborer	36	"
Y	Haggerty John J	185	"	32	"
Z	Haggerty Josephine V—†	185	houseworker	35	"
A	McElwain Elizabeth—†	185	bookkeeper	24	29 Linden park
B	Carter Lawrence	185	laborer	32	here
C	Furey James H	185	"	43	"
D	Furey Margaret M—†	185	houseworker	42	"
E	Leahy John H	187	chauffeur	35	"
F	Leahy Margaret T—†	187	houseworker	36	"
G	Shapiro Doris—†	187	housekeeper	56	"
H	Shapiro Louis	187	junk dealer	25	"
K	Shapiro Maurice	187	"	58	"
L	Shapiro Samuel	187	"	33	"
M	Gordon Manuel	187	laborer	31	"
N	Gordon Sarah—†	187	housekeeper	29	"
O	MacLean Alexander	188	shipper	35	Canada
P	MacLean Lillian—†	188	housewife	26	"
R	Webber Anna—†	188	"	51	1 Church pl
S	Webber Henry R	188	painter	45	1 "
T	Doherty Alice—†	189	houseworker	42	here
U	Doherty Catherine J—†	189	clerk	22	"
V	Boyre Alma—†	189	stitcher	38	134 Halleck
W	Proctor Nettie M—†	189	shoeworker	44	here
X	Palmer Samuel	191	laborer	50	7 Vernon
Y	Martin William H	191	"	59	here
A	Sullivan Catherine—†	192	housewife	37	"
B	Sullivan Patrick J	192	contractor	44	"

Page.	Letter.	FULL NAME.	Residence, April 1, 1926.	Occupation.	Supposed Age.	Reported Residence, April 1, 1925. Street and Number.

Cabot Street—Continued

	Letter	FULL NAME	Residence	Occupation	Age	Reported Residence
	c	Rose James C	192	motorman	43	here
	D	Rose Nora—†	192	housewife	45	"
	E	Walton John E	192	gardener	51	"
	F	Walton Mary E—†	192	housewife	49	"
	G	Foster Ida J—†	193	houseworker	47	896 Albany
	H	Foster Stephen R	193	laborer	47	896 "
	K	Miller James	193	machinist	43	9 Church pl
	L	Miller Margaret W—†	193	houseworker	56	9 "
	R	McQuinn Nadine—†	196	housewife	35	9 Rollins
	S	McQuinn Richard	196	laborer	52	9 "
	T	Kilduff Ellen F—†	196	housewife	42	here
	V	Kilduff Joseph F	196	chauffeur	21	"
	U	Kilduff Joseph T	196	"	46	"
	W	Riley Frederick	196	"	35	"
	X	Riley Mary J—†	196	housewife	72	"
	A	Butley Thomas P	214	mechanic	36	558 E Second
	B	Cluney James L	214	chauffeur	28	6 Linden av
	c	Curley Annie M—†	214	housewife	50	here
	D	Curley Daniel J	214	agent	51	"
	E	Curley Joseph R	214	fireman	30	"
	F	Curley William F	214	clerk	26	"
	G	Giovennelle Martin J	214	chauffeur	28	15 Linden
	H	Gogan Francis	214	plasterer	56	here
	K	Holden George W	214	gasfitter	45	29 Alpine
	L	Kelley Louis F	214	clerk	24	7 Dallas pl
	M	Kelley William H	214	chauffeur	22	7 "
	N	Kelley Mary—†	215	houseworker	67	here
	O	Kenealy Frank P	215	clerk	46	Malden
	P	Johnson Josephine—†	215	houseworker	40	here
	R	Josselyn Herbert C	215	paperhanger	42	"
	S	Josselyn Mary E—†	215	houseworker	36	"
	T	Cosgrove Edward J	216	chauffeur	30	"
	U	Cosgrove Helen—†	216	housewife	26	"
	V	Tansey Catherine—†	216	"	52	"
	W	Tansey Patrick	216	laborer	56	"
	X	Tansey William J	216	student	29	"
	Y	Brown William P	217	laborer	48	3 Wellington
	z	Field Joseph	217	"	45	here
	A	Tibbetts Nellie E—†	217	houseworker	42	Cambridge
	B	Tibbetts William L	217	printer	39	"
	c	Dorsey Michael J	219	retired	71	47 Calumet

5

Page.	Letter.	FULL NAME.	Residence, April 1, 1926.	Occupation.	Supposed Age.	Reported Residence, April 1, 1925. Street and Number.

Cabot Street—Continued

	D	Fallon James V	219	clerk	31	here
	E	Fallon John F	219	retired	70	"
	F	Fallon John F, jr	219	clerk	26	"
	G	Downey Annie M—†	219	housekeeper	35	"
	H	Downey Joseph F	219	clerk	41	"
	K	Gorman Mary L—†	219	houseworker	42	"
	L	Collins Margaret—†	221	"	50	"
	M	Boogusch Edward	221	chauffeur	27	"
	N	Boogusch Elizabeth F—†	221	houseworker	25	"
	O	Birkman John	221	janitor	65	"
	P	Birkman Marie J—†	221	housekeeper	60	"
	R	Kenney Daniel	222	laborer	56	"
	S	Kenney Margaret B—†	222	matron	50	"
	T	Clark Helen G—†	222	cashier	20	1196 Tremont
	U	Cusack Edward B	222	loomfixer	32	S Framingham
	V	Cusack James J	222	chauffeur	34	here
	W	McCarthy Catherine E—†	222	housewife	49	"
	X	McCarthy Michael J	222	laborer	50	"
	Y	McCue Thomas	222	"	55	"
	Z	Atkins Frank	223	"	67	36 St Francis de Sales
	A	Atkins Frank A	223	"	32	20 "
	B	Lawlor James E	223	"	32	New York
	C	O'Donnell Mary A—†	223	houseworker	50	here

Church Place

	E	Brinkert Alice—†	1	housewife	22	here
	F	Brinkert Frederick	1	chauffeur	24	"
	G	Berger Rose—†	1	laundress	36	New Orleans
	H	Marmand Margaret—†	1	housekeeper	56	28 Terrace
	K	McGillacuddy James F	2	chauffeur	37	here
	L	White Catherine—†	2	housekeeper	57	"
	M	Page Clara E—†	2	clerk	21	"
	N	Page Martha O—†	2	housekeeper	43	"
	O	Glynn Edward C	3	installer	30	"
	P	Glynn Elinore C—†	3	secretary	23	"
	R	Glynn Mary A—†	3	housewife	59	"
	S	Glynn Mary A—†	3	stenographer	26	"
	T	Glynn Michael J	3	bricklayer	60	"
	U	Glynn William J	3	installer	33	"

6

Page.	Letter.	FULL NAME.	Residence, April 1, 1926.	Occupation.	Supposed Age.	Reported Residence, April 1, 1925. Street and Number.

Church Place—Continued

	v	McKeon Elizabeth G—†	3	clerk	36	here
	w	Webber Aemil	4	carpenter	43	"
	x	Webber Della—†	4	housewife	42	"
	y	Burblies Amil	4	laborer	26	31 E Springfield
	z	Burblies Emma —†	4	housewife	32	31 "
	A	Martin Ellen A—†	5	clerk	37	here
	B	Kennedy Patrick	5	porter	43	"
	C	Moriarty Margaret—†	5	housekeeper	50	"
	D	Moriarty Patrick	5	stonemason	49	"
	E	Walsh Daniel	5	laborer	25	"
	F	Semner Charles	rear 6	junk dealer	54	"
	G	Semner Ida—†	" 6½	housewife	54	"
	H	Christian Paul	7	laborer	45	"
	K	Christian Sarah— †	7	housewife	45	"
	L	Morrow Elizabeth—†	7	"	30	"
	M	Morrow John F	7	laborer	42	"
	N	Jacobs Etta— †	7½	housewife	30	"
	O	Jacobs William	7½	laborer	32	"
	P	Dunn Annie—†	8	housewife	45	"
	R	Dunn William P	8	machinist	44	"
	S	Berg Alphia—†	8	dressmaker	20	"
	T	Berg Christina —†	8	housewife	48	"
	U	Lundgren Charles W	8	manager	44	"
	V	Lundgren Sarah — †	8	housewife	40	"
	X	Blume David W	9	laborer	46	28 Hampshire
	Y	Blume Mary S—†	9	housewife	40	28 "
	Z	Elliott Josephine †	9	housekeeper	42	here
	A	Kelly Annie J—†	10	housewife	47	"
	B	Kelly Thomas H	10	janitor	53	"
	C	Golden Annie E †	10	packer	55	"
	D	Heaney Bridget †	10	housewife	50	"
	E	Heaney Patrick	10	repairer	60	"
	F	MacLaughlin Chester B	12	salesman	25	"
	G	MacLaughlin Mary C—†	12	housewife	24	"
	H	Craven Margaret—†	12	"	63	"
	K	Craven Patrick	12	paver	54	"

Columbus Avenue

	N	Carey James F	930	plumber	26	here
	O	Carey Rose—†	930	housewife	26	"

Page.	Letter.	FULL NAME.	Residence, April 1, 1926.	Occupation.	Supposed Age.	Reported Residence, April 1, 1925. Street and Number.

Columbus Avenue—Continued

	w	Glancy Margaret —†	967	at home	72	149 Forsyth
	x	Brennan Martin	967	chauffeur	35	here
	y	Brennan Mary—†	967	housewife	35	"
	z	Tobin Joseph	967	student	23	"
	A	Tobin Nellie A—†	967	housewife	42	"
	B	Tobin Patrick F	967	teamster	56	"
	c	Fallon Katherine —†	968	housewife	40	281 Eustis
	D	Fallon Michael J	968	courier	45	281 "
	E	Fallon Rose—†	968	clerk	21	281 "
	F	Gray Arthur G	968	painter	29	9 Brighton
	G	Gray Mabel—†	968	housewife	28	9 "
	K	Morgan James A	968	electrician	34	here
	H	Morgan Katherine—†	968	housewife	40	"
	L	Barrett James E	969	finisher	47	"
	M	Barrett Mary—·†	969	housewife	46	"
	N	Airey Katherine—†	969	laundress	58	"
	o	Airey Margaret—†	969	operator	20	"
	P	Malbey Katherine—†	969	packer	29	"
	R	McDonough Agnes—†	969	housewife	44	"
	s	McDonough James J	969	clerk	24	"
	T	McDonough Mary M—†	969	librarian	20	"
	v	McDonough Patrick J	969	laborer	52	"
	w	Nolan Joseph E	971	chauffeur	25	"
	x	Nolan Marie E—†	971	housewife	22	"
	y	Linsky Julia E—†	971	"	40	"
	z	Linsky Thomas A	971	teamster	46	"
	A	Kinahan Ellen—†	971	housewife	22	"
	B	Kinahan James W	971	teamster	27	"
	c	Stemmler Charles D	973	truckman	31	"
	D	Stemmler Mildred—†	973	housewife	28	"
	E	Graham Arthur J	975	truckman	36	"
	F	Graham Katherine—†	975	housewife	29	"
	G	Sims Ethel— †	977	storekeeper	52	29 Grove
	H	Sims Morris	977	tailor	62	29 "
	K	Kast Frank J	979	teamster	39	here
	L	Kast Mary— †	979	housewife	34	"
	M	Luhmenn August M	981	janitor	54	"
	N	Luhmenn Emma—†	981	housewife	45	"
	P	McGuire Helen L—†	984	"	32	1057 Col av
	R	McGuire Thomas F	984	fireman	42	1057 "
	T	Burke Irene M †	985	housewife	30	311 Emerson

8

Page.	Letter.	Full Name	Residence, April 1, 1926.	Occupation	Supposed Age.	Reported Residence, April 1, 1925. Street and Number.

Columbus Avenue—Continued

	U	Burke James M	985	electrician	35	311 Emerson
	V	Johnson Alice—†	985	cook	43	here
	W	Johnson William	985	restaurateur	45	"
	X	Mudge Alfred	985	laborer	54	"
	Y	Mudge Joseph E	985	"	27	"
	Z	Mudge Josephine A—†	985	housewife	48	"
	B	Jones Katherine—†	987	at home	62	"
	C	Geelin Frank T	987	machinist	34	"
	D	Geelin Margaret—†	987	housewife	36	"
	E	Harrington Bessie—†	987	laundress	42	"
	F	Foley John T	988	chauffeur	21	"
	G	Foley Mary E—†	988	housewife	40	"
	H	Foley Peter T	988	clerk	45	"
	K	Murphy Agnes C—†	988	housewife	35	"
	L	Murphy Edward J	988	tailor	38	"
	N	Ryan Francis V	989	shipper	20	"
	O	Ryan John J	989	usher	23	"
	P	Ryan Katherine—†	989	cleaner	35	"
	R	Mulvey Catherine C—†	989	housewife	37	"
	S	Mulvey Frederick J	989	painter	44	"
	U	Waters Mary—†	991	boxmaker	49	"
	V	Grant Mary J—†	991	housewife	36	"
	W	Palmer Mary—†	991	at home	80	"
	X	Doyle Sadie—†	991	packer	21	"
	Y	Doyle Sarah—†	991	housewife	53	"
	Z	Gannan Bernard	992	glazier	33	"
	A	Gannon John	992	shoeworker	20	"
	B	Clark Hugh	992	wool sorter	27	"
	C	Clark Mary—†	992	housewife	25	"
	F	Gibbons Delia—†	999	at home	43	"
	G	Gibbons Myles	999	coal passer	40	"
	K	Zwick Anna—†	1003	housewife	31	"
	L	Zwick Lewis A	1003	coal dealer	36	"
	M	Walsh Agnes—†	1003	shoeworker	27	"
	N	Walsh Francis	1003	"	20	"
	O	Walsh Morris F	1003	laborer	58	"
	P	Walsh Patrick	1003	"	33	"
	R	Walsh Sarah—†	1003	housewife	53	"
	S	Tracy James J	1003	electrician	36	"
	T	Tracy Mary—†	1003	at home	68	"
	V	Brown Frederick B	1017	teamster	47	1 Hammett

Page.	Letter.	Full Name.	Residence, April 1, 1926.	Occupation.	Supposed Age.	Reported Residence, April 1, 1925. Street and Number.

Columbus Avenue—Continued

w	Kelley Annetta—†	1017	at home	49	here
x	Kelley William	1017	plasterer	53	"
y	Totten Esther—†	1017	housewife	26	1 Hammett
z	Schoen Charles	1017	chauffeur	26	here
a	Schoen Margaret—†	1017	housewife	22	"
b	McLaughlin Margaret-†	1017	housekeeper	45	"
c	Ford Clarence	1017	teamster	22	"
d	Ford Ritta—†	1017	housekeeper	50	"

Dallas Place

a	Driscoll Daniel	1	laborer	22	here
b	Driscoll Helen—†	1	housekeeper	60	"
c	Driscoll Jeremiah	1	laborer	52	"
d	Driscoll Nora—†	1	housewife	46	"
f	Costello Patrick	3	retired	59	"
g	Costello Susan—†	3	housewife	59	"
h	Costello Theresa B—†	3	bookkeeper	27	"
k	Costello Timothy	3	clerk	23	"
l	Powell Leo	3	janitor	22	"
m	Berry John	5	bricklayer	44	"
n	Berry Margaret—†	5	housewife	38	"
o	McDonald Margaret—†	6	laundress	50	"
r	Tansevich Earl	7	laborer	40	25 Oak Grove ter
s	Tansevich Elizabeth—†	7	housewife	38	25 "
t	Clark Henry C	9	chauffeur	33	here
u	Clark Mary—†	9	housewife	27	"

Downing Street

v	Wallace Alice—†	9	housewife	20	Cambridge
w	Wallace Joseph E	9	salesman	23	here
x	Warner Mary—†	9	housewife	30	48 Maywood
y	Warner Willard C	9	painter	30	48 "
z	McDonald Angus	9	carpenter	40	here
a	McDonald Jennie—†	9	housewife	25	"
b	Morrison Daniel	9	packer	75	"
c	Wallace Arthur L	9	chauffeur	24	"
d	Wallace Edward F	9	lawyer	28	"

Page.	Letter.	FULL NAME.	Residence, April 1, 1926.	Occupation.	Supposed Age.	Reported Residence, April 1, 1925. Street and Number.

Downing Street—Continued

E	Wallace James J	9	lamplighter	59	here
F	Wallace Mary A—†	9	housewife	54	"
G	McKenzie Angus	10	motorman	53	"
H	McKenzie Annie C—†	10	housewife	52	"
K	McKenzie Edwin M	10	printer	20	"
L	Alward Jennie—†	10	housekeeper	60	"
M	Alward Pearl E—†	10	stitcher	29	"
N	Labonte Alice M—†	16	housewife	37	"
O	Labonte Charles M	16	blacksmith	62	"
P	Pettigrew Muriel—†	16	housewife	20	"
R	Pettigrew Thomas	16	chauffeur	25	"
S	Fitzgerald Mary—†	16	housewife	34	"
T	Fitzgerald Patrick	16	machinist	31	"
U	Ramsdell Arsuthia—†	18	housewife	32	7 Fremont pl
V	Ramsdell William C	18	pipefitter	36	7 "
W	Griffin Delia—†	18	housewife	32	here
X	Griffin John	18	cement finisher	45	"
Y	Kelly Cathelene—†	18	housekeeper	25	"
Z	Kelly George	18	machinist	23	"
A	Kelly Michael	18	laborer	45	"
B	Doherty John	19	janitor	50	"
C	Doherty Mary A—†	19	housewife	40	"
D	Corbett Nellie—†	19	clerk	48	"
E	Hardy Albert J	20	carpenter	55	"
F	Hardy Edith—†	20	housewife	36	"
G	Alvarese Edward	20	shipper	33	"
H	Alvareser Rebecca—†	20	housewife	25	"
K	McDonald Catherine—†	20	housekeeper	53	"
L	McDonald Mary—†	20	tel operator	20	"
M	Sutherland Ellen—†	21	houseworker	29	59 Warwick
N	Sutherland Josefa—†	21	housekeeper	65	59 "
O	McKenzie Charles S	21	salesman	30	8 Lambert
P	McKenzie Helen—†	21	housewife	30	8 "
R	Locke George	23	carpenter	40	New Hampshire
S	Locke Sophie—†	23	housewife	50	"
U	Handrahan Alice—†	23	"	59	here
V	Handrahan Frank	23	carpenter	52	"
W	Handrahan Joseph	23	mechanic	23	"
X	Crowley William J	23	chauffeur	22	"
Y	Walsh Charles J	23	cook	53	"
Z	Walsh Mary—†	23	housewife	39	"

Page	Letter	FULL NAME.	Residence, April 1, 1926.	Occupation.	Supposed Age.	Reported Residence, April 1, 1925. Street and Number.

Downing Street—Continued

	A	Donnelly Ellen V—†	23	housewife	41	here
	B	Donnelly Francis	23	laborer	42	"
	C	Morrissy Marion—†	23	housekeeper	29	"
	D	Otto Mary A—†	23	"	64	"

Hampshire Court

	F	Alvarez Josephine—†	1	at home	43	here
	G	Hall Agnes M—†	1	housekeeper	44	"
	H	Bragg Annie—†	1	"	69	"
	K	Bragg Joseph P	1	teamster	29	"
	L	Kelley Frank	1	laborer	29	"
	M	Kelley Mary—†	1	housewife	34	"
	N	Kelley William E	1	lineman	35	"
	O	Kilduf William	1	factory worker	35	"
	P	Manalio Frank	2	dishwasher	23	"
	R	Manalio Leona—†	2	housewife	34	"
	S	Cummings Anna—†	2	housekeeper	41	Lynn
	T	Meegan John J	2	expressman	24	here

Hampshire Street

	W	West Joseph E	5	laborer	34	here
	X	West Olga—†	5	housewife	30	"
	Y	Bunnell Charlie P	8	laboroer	23	"
	Z	Bunnell George W	8	"	25	"
	A	Bunnell James E	8	brassworker	60	"
	B	Bunnell Mary—†	8	houseworker	28	"
	C	Loonie Anna T—†	8	nurse	21	"
	D	Loonie Barbara A—†	8	stenographer	20	"
	E	Loonie Catherine—†	8	housewife	46	"
	F	Loonie Edward F	8	glassworker	48	"
	G	Bowser Francis B	8	watchman	49	"
	H	Bowser Helen F	8	housewife	43	"
	K	Kelley Anne—†	10	"	50	"
	L	Killion Elizabeth A—†	10	shoeworker	24	"
	N	Bailey Anna V—†	10	housewife	29	"

Page.	Letter.	FULL NAME.	Residence, April 1, 1926.	Occupation.	Supposed Age.	Reported Residence, April 1, 1925. Street and Number.

Hampshire Street—Continued

o	Bailey Peter	10	printer	31	here
p	Coughlin Patrick	12	watchman	75	"
r	Gardner Mary E—†	12	houseworker	55	"
s	Young Harry	12	retired	56	"
t	Fernard Augusta	18	laborer	36	Marshfield
u	Jones Minnie H—†	18	houseworker	45	95 Kendall
v	Grey Elma J—†	18	"	64	here
w	Sorenson Christian	18	retired	75	"
c	Clement Elizabeth—†	22	houseworker	36	"
d	Kimber Christina—†	22	housekeeper	68	"
e	Kimber William A	22	janitor	30	"
h	Ford Anna N—†	28	housewife	22	125 C
k	Ford William	28	conductor	31	10 Leedsville
l	DeVitt Susie J—†	28	houseworker	50	16A E Dedham
m	Gayton Lucy B—†	28	saleswoman	22	16A "
n	Gurney Margaret E—†	28	houseworker	21	22½ Lincoln
o	Gurney Paul W	28	machinist	26	22½ "
r	Norton Margaret A—†	66	housekeeper	59	here
s	Robinson Patrick J	66	laborer	55	"
t	Gass Frank J	66	"	37	15 Alleghany
u	Gass Goldie—†	66	housewife	22	15 "
v	Gallant Columbia—†	66	"	33	here
w	Gallant Joseph C	66	laborer	36	"
a	Jameson Edward R	68	fishcutter	51	"
b	Jameson Josephine—†	68	housewife	47	"
c	Foley Michael	68	clerk	22	Ireland
d	O'Neil Catherine—†	68	housewife	33	here
e	O'Neil John J	68	laborer	39	"
f	Clarke Thomas	68	porter	21	"
g	Clarke Thomas P	68	oiler	51	"
h	Kenney Mary—†	70	housekeeper	41	"
l	Brett Helen C—†	70	packer	21	"
k	Brett Mary E—†	70	candymaker	29	"
m	McManus Bridget A—†	70	housewife	50	"
n	McManus Edward	70	laborer	55	"
o	Hooley Cornelius	70	"	55	"
p	Brett Josephine—†	72	housewife	20	"
r	Brett Thomas	72	clerk	34	"
s	Hooley James P	72	laborer	26	"
t	Hooley Mary E—†	72	housewife	24	"
u	Burke Helen F—†	72	at home	26	"

Hampshire Street—Continued

v	Burke Michael J	72	bricklayer	20	here
w	Gibbons Jennie—†	72	housewife	52	"
x	Gibbons John E	72	bricklayer	53	"

Haskins Street

A	Karlin Hyman	9	storekeeper	41	here
B	Karlin Ida—†	9	housewife	31	"
C	Berinsky Louis	9	tailor	33	"
D	Berinsky Mary—†	9	housewife	29	"
E	Jenkins William	9	messenger	26	15 Ball
F	Johnson Rose—†	9	housekeeper	49	15 "
G	Waterman Blanche—†	9	stitcher	28	15 "
K	Kardonsky Ida—†	11	housewife	40	16 Oak Grove ter
L	Kardonsky Max	11	junk dealer	45	16 "
M	Karlin Dora—†	11	housewife	35	here
N	Karlin Louis	11	newsdealer	35	"
P	Rosen Lena—†	15A	housewife	33	14 Haskins
R	Rosen Morris	15A	junk dealer	33	14 "
S	Sternick Charles	15A	clerk	20	here
T	Sternick Esther—†	15A	housewife	50	"
U	Sternick Joseph	15A	clerk	21	"
V	Sternick Max	15A	junk dealer	54	"
W	Chalmus Joel	15A	plasterer	30	"
X	Chalmus Lucille—†	15A	laundress	24	"
Y	Mills Almena—†	15A	elevatorwoman	26	"
Z	Simons Herbert	15A	letter carrier	30	"
A	Goodman Annie—†	17	housewife	40	"
B	Goodman Morris	17	newsdealer	41	"
C	Cohen Abraham	17	metalworker	32	"
D	Cohen Ethel—†	17	housewife	32	"
E	Reine Lillian—†	17	"	43	111 Ruggles
F	Reine Phillip	17	salesman	23	111 "
G	Heishman Max	19	junk dealer	39	here
H	Heishman Rose—†	19	housewife	33	"
K	Insoft Myer	19	junk dealer	52	"
L	Insoft Sarah—†	19	housewife	49	"
M	Lischinsky Bennie	19	junk dealer	40	95 Ruggles
N	Lischinsky Dora—†	19	housewife	30	95 "

Haskins Street—Continued

O	Bard Benjamin	21	porter	33	here
P	Bard Ruth—†	21	housewife	30	"
R	Watts Thomas	21	mechanic	35	"
S	Nierman Fannie—†	21	housewife	36	"
T	Nierman Harry	21	junk dealer	37	"
U	Griffith Ethel—†	21	housewife	36	"
V	Griffith Nathanel	21	laborer	39	"
W	Bazer Esther —†	23	housekeeper	25	"
X	Bazer Morris	23	storekeeper	26	"
Y	Goldstein Benjiman	23	clerk	25	56 Dudley
Z	Goldstein Issac	23	junk dealer	50	W Boxford
A	Goldstein Jennie—†	23	housewife	48	"
B	Goldstein Myer	23	salesman	22	98 Vernon
C	Ruttenberg Abraham	23	storekeeper	35	37 N Russell
D	Ruttenberg Anna —†	23	husewife	33	37 "
F	Pitraitis John	35	operator	35	49 Haskins
G	Pitraitis Rose—†	35	housewife	33	49 "
H	Sharevich Baley—†	35	"	63	here
K	Sharevich Phillip	35	retired	64	"
L	Michel Ida—†	35	dressmaker	35	"
M	Rosen Benjiman	35	clerk	37	"
N	Rosen Rose—†	35	housewife	38	"
P	Crabtree Julia—†	37	chambermaid	39	"
R	Goldberg Benjiman	37	retired	65	49 Haskins
S	Goldberg Ethel—†	37	at home	65	49 "
T	McDonald Mary —†	37	housewife	43	here
U	McDonald Thomas	37	laborer	43	"
V	Malk John	37	machinist	54	"
W	Negber Otto	37	carpenter	32	"
X	Martinowski Christina—†	37	housewife	43	281 Shawmut av
Y	Martinowski John	37	painter	46	281 "
Z	Lynch Mary—†	37	housekeeper	42	34 E Brookline
A	Scanlan Andrew	37	roofer	39	34 "
B	Nee George B	39	custodian	31	910 E Fourth
C	Nee Margaret V—†	39	housewife	26	910 "
D	Melinesky Jennie —†	39	"	38	here
E	Melinesky Louis	39	laborer	55	"
F	Provst Mary—†	39	laundress	38	24 Rutland
G	Tandin Gertrude—†	39	housewife	28	here
H	Tandin Ralph	39	painter	33	"
K	Tuchem Henry	39	laborer	32	"

Page	Letter	Full Name.	Residence, April 1, 1926.	Occupation.	Supposed Age.	Reported Residence, April 1, 1925. Street and Number.

Haskins Street—Continued

	L	Lipsky Golder—†	39	at home	65	here
	M	Clark Henry	41	painter	37	30 Lenox
	N	Clark Rose—†	41	housewife	20	30 "
	O	Steinberg Esther—†	43	bookkeeper	21	here
	P	Steinberg Sarah—†	43	housekeeper	32	"
	R	Kazansky Anna—†	45	waitress	32	Cambridge
	S	Kanzansky Joe	45	laborer	37	"
	T	Meeney Mary—†	45	domestic	35	here
	V	Bowman Mary—†	49	housewife	37	"
	W	Cusick Charles	49	laborer	45	289 Shawmut av
	X	Singer Solomon B	51	junk dealer	51	here
	Y	Zalikoff Fannie—†	51	housewife	42	"
	Z	Zalikoff Samuel	51	retired	47	"
	A	Gottlieb Lewis	51	student	20	Brooklyn N Y
	B	Karsh Meyer J	51	"	22	"
	C	Milikof David	51	"	26	New York City

Motley Street

	G	Snow Catherine—†	1	housewife	34	here
	H	Snow Frank	1	welder	47	"
	N	Granger Annie—†	3	housewife	26	1104 Tremont
	O	Granger Fred H	3	laborer	36	1104 "
	P	Walnut Etta E—†	3	housewife	44	6 Grinnell
	R	Walnut Frederick P	3	mechanic	49	6 "
	S	Kinahan Mary A—†	3	houseworker	49	here
	T	O'Brien Frank H	4	janitor	29	"
	U	O'Brien Jennie—†	4	housekeeper	68	"
	V	Rickels Charles J	4	boxmaker	54	Medford
	W	Rickels Lucy—†	4	housewife	46	"
	X	Foley Helen—†	4	"	35	161 Vernon
	Y	Foley John	4	chauffeur	34	161 "
	B	Murphy Daniel F	5	laborer	29	here
	C	Murphy James F	5	electrician	34	"
	D	Murphy Mathew F	5	stableman	56	"
	E	Walsh Josephine—†	5	housekeeper	26	"
	F	Marobello Catherine—†	6	housewife	24	"
	G	Marobello Samuel	6	chauffeur	28	Cambridge
	H	Foshey George, jr	6	photographer	26	here
	K	Foshey Marion—†	6	housewife	24	"

Motley Street—Continued

L	Foshey Charles A	6	machinist	22	here
M	Foshey Helen E—†	6	housewife	50	"
N	Burke Mary—†	7	housekeeper	35	"
O	McLaughlin Myrtle—†	7	housewife	28	Winchester
P	McLaughlin Robert	7	machinist	64	Lowell
R	McLaughlin Robert	7	chauffeur	30	Winchester
S	Clark Julia—†	7	housewife	30	156 D
T	Clark Thomas	7	chauffeur	35	156 "
U	Ketch Robert	8	clerk	35	here
V	Ritchie Edgar	8	painter	49	"
W	Ritchie Josephine—†	8	houseworker	47	"
X	Mills Ethel—†	8	housewife	35	"
Y	Mills William A	8	janitor	35	"
Z	Regan Elizabeth—†	9	factory worker	30	"
A	Logan Mary—†	9	housekeeper	52	2 Motley
B	Logan Ruth—†	9	stitcher	24	2 "
C	Agnello Elizabeth—†	9	housewife	22	2 Worcester pl
D	Mahoney Daniel	9	laborer	51	5 Sherwin
E	Mahoney Elizabeth—†	9	housewife	54	5 "

Old Whittier Street

A	McLaughlin Catherine—†	2	storekeeper	66	here
B	Sullivan Catherine A—†	2	houseworker	42	"
C	Sullivan Michael D	2	laborer	48	"
D	Dooley Margaret E—†	2	housekeeper	33	"
E	Dooley William F	2	watchman	37	"
F	McMaster Elizabeth—†	2	housewife	57	"
G	McMaster James	2	laborer	51	"
H	McMaster Mary E—†	2	clerk	21	"
K	Doherty Hannah J—†	4	housewife	42	"
L	Doherty May—†	4	clerk	21	"
M	Doherty Thomas F	4	laborer	45	"
N	Clougher Mary A—†	4	housewife	26	"
O	Clougher Timothy F	4	laborer	28	"
P	Sullivan Jeremiah	4	"	60	"
R	Lynch Catherine—†	4	housekeeper	45	"
S	Lynch Samuel	4	carpenter	46	"
T	Hull Margaret W—†	6	houseworker	50	"
U	Hull William F	6	laborer	48	"

9—11

17

Page.	Letter.	FULL NAME.	Residence, April 1, 1926.	Occupation.	Supposed Age.	Reported Residence, April 1, 1925.
						Street and Number.

Old Whittier Street—Continued

	v	Wiegus John F	6	laborer	32	here
	w	Hannigan John	6	"	50	"
	x	Hannigan Rose—†	6	houseworker	42	"
	y	Sullivan Annie—†	6	housewife	50	"
	z	Sullivan Daniel	6	laborer	52	"
	A	Sullivan John P	6	teacher	23	"
	B	Sullivan Nora M—†	6	clerk	21	"
	c	Cronin John	8	laborer	21	Ireland
	D	Malloy Ellen—†	8	housewife	33	217 Cabot
	E	Malloy William P	8	cement finisher	39	217 "
	F	Clark Peter E K	8	porter	50	here
	G	Hornish Mary E--†	8	stitcher	47	"
	H	Sullivan Margaret—†	8	"	52	"
	K	Coffey John	8	laborer	52	"
	L	Coffey Julia M—†	8	stenographer	20	"
	M	Coffey Nora J—†	8	houseworker	50	"
	N	Heavey John	10	laborer	46	"
	o	Heavey Mary—†	10	housewife	44	"
	R	Henneberry Catherine—†	10	"	36	"
	s	Henneberry Edward F	10	roofer	37	"
	T	Halfkenny Cynthia—†	12	houseworker	21	67 Wheaton av
	U	Halfkenny Peter E	12	painter	24	67 "
	V	Laflin Gladys J—†	12	stitcher	26	16 Ray
	W	Laflin John L	12	laborer	27	16 "
	X	Hall Ambrose	12	cook	56	here
	Y	Hall Margaret B—†	12	houseworker	44	"
	z	Meegan Bridget—†	12	housekeeper	58	"
	A	Meegan Joseph P	12	machinist	25	"
	B	Dwyer Liza—†	14	houseworker	52	"
	c	Dwyer Thomas	14	laborer	62	"
	D	Kelley John J	14	chauffeur	35	"
	E	Kelley Sadie J—†	14	housewife	30	"
	F	Crehan Elizabeth M—†	16	houseworker	38	"
	G	Crehan James J	16	fireman	41	"

Ruggles Street

	X	Blakley Bertha P—†	137	housewife	39	here
	Y	Blakley Ira P	137	carpenter	53	"

18

Page.	Letter.	FULL NAME.	Residence, April 1, 1926.	Occupation.	Supposed Age.	Reported Residence, April 1, 1925. Street and Number.

Ruggles Street—Continued

	Letter	FULL NAME	Res.	Occupation	Age	Reported Residence
	z	Donovan Ellen—†	137	housewife	54	here
	A	Donovan John A	137	real estate	37	"
	B	Donovan John W	137	stableman	60	"
	c	McKernan Mary E—†	137	housewife	33	3 Auburn
	D	McKernan William J	137	fireman	34	3 "
	E	Glynn John J	137	laborer	20	2904 Wash'n
	F	Glynn Joseph P	137	"	47	2904 "
	G	Glynn Mary A—†	137	housewife	44	2904 "
	K	Collins Angela M—†	141	"	39	here
	L	Collins William J	141	hotelworker	34	"
	M	Bogosian Agnes—†	141	housewife	29	"
	N	Bogosian Toros	141	carpenter	35	"
	o	Demorgian Harry	141	machinist	22	"
	P	Malk Catharine—†	141	houseworker	54	"
	R	Malk Mildred J—†	141	stenographer	21	"
	T	Blankenship James A	143	porter	65	"
	U	Blankenship Mary F—†	143	housewife	50	"
	W	Murray Jane F—†	144	"	30	"
	X	Murray Michael L	144	cableworker	34	"
	Y	Parker Eugenie—†	144	housewife	57	"
	z	Parker George N	144	carpenter	59	"
	A	Flanagan Ellen M—†	144	housewife	43	86 W Fifth
	B	Flanagan George P	144	molder	48	86 "
	c	Flanagan William D	144	chauffeur	23	86 "
	R	Lakin Edward	214	clerk	21	Malden
	s	Robinson Elizabeth—†	214	storekeeper	57	"
	T	Walsh Annie M—†	214	houseworker	61	250 Ruggles
	U	Walsh Luke J	214	watchman	62	250 "
	v	Walsh Thomas L	214	creameryman	28	250 "
	w	Hawes Mary—†	214	housewife	71	here
	x	Hawes Nathaniel	214	retired	81	"
	Y	McLean Mary A—†	214	housekeeper	60	"
	z	Devine Helen F—†	216	housewife	54	"
	A	Devine Thomas J	216	operator	75	"
	B	McGreevy Annie E—†	216	housewife	55	"
	c	McGreevy Michael T	216	retired	60	"

Salvisberg Avenue

E	Connelly Elizabeth—†	1	housekeeper	67	here
F	Sweeney Margaret—†	1	"	60	"
G	Norton Elizabeth—†	1	clerk	25	"
H	Norton John W	1	salesman	22	"
K	Denehy Bridget—†	1	houseworker	45	"
L	Reed Mary—†	2	"	38	"
M	Maxwell Julia N—†	2	housewife	40	"
N	Maxwell William L	2	buffer	42	"
O	Harrington Mary—†	2	housekeeper	47	"
P	Harrington William	2	chauffeur	20	"
R	Walsh Mary—†	3	housekeeper	50	"
S	Kenney Ellen—†	3	cleaner	51	"
T	Griffin Catherine—†	3	housekeeper	51	"
U	Robinson Amelia L—†	4	"	54	60 Dudley
V	Killion Margaret—†	4	"	75	here
W	Kelleher Edward J	4	clerk	27	"
X	Garfield Martha—†	5	houseworker	60	"
Y	Earley Frank	5	retired	64	"
Z	Earley Mary—†	5	housewife	64	"
A	O'Connell John J	5	cement finisher	31	36 Vernon
B	O'Connell Josephine—†	5	housekeeper	62	36 "

Sumner Place

C	Coleman Elizabeth—†	1	housewife	69	here
D	Coleman Mary—†	1	housekeeper	29	"
E	Coyne Daniel L	1	chauffeur	28	"
F	Coyne Margaret E—†	1	housewife	27	"
G	Gordon Robert	2	clerk	32	"
H	Gordon Sarah—†	2	housewife	28	"
K	Drury Anna J—†	2	stenographer	22	"
L	Drury Catherine—†	2	housewife	62	"
M	Drury Helen V—†	2	clerk	28	"
N	Drury Thomas E	2	chauffeur	25	"
O	Molasky Catherine A—†	2	housewife	31	"
P	Molasky James H	2	salesman	31	"
R	Foley John A	3	chauffeur	32	"

Page.	Letter	FULL NAME.	Residence, April 1, 1926.	Occupation.	Supposed Age.	Reported Residence, April 1, 1925. Street and Number.

Sumner Place —Continued

s	Foley Mary D—†	3	housewife	32	here
v	Campbell Grace C—†	4	"	33	"
w	Campbell Roy H	4	chauffeur	33	"
y	Gallant Neil	4½	laborer	46	Cambridge
z	Gallant Veronica—†	4½	housewife	43	"
A	Tanner Owen A	4½	packer	28	24 Beach
B	Tanner Violet B—†	4½	housewife	28	24 "
c	Glennon Frank	4½	laborer	30	here
D	Glennon Margaret—†	4½	housewife	28	"
E	Burton Lucius D	5	accountant	49	50 Turner
F	Hunter Helen—†	5	housekeeper	64	here
G	Hunter Jannette G—†	5	"	38	"
H	Hunter Robert M	5	printer	36	"
K	Timilty Charles J	5	clerk	23	"
L	Timilty Francis J	5	"	27	"
M	Timilty James E	5	"	33	"
N	Timilty Joseph F	5	"	31	"
o	Timilty Walter F	5	"	21	"
R	Sullivan James L	6	clerk	41	48A Linden
P	Sullivan Mary G—†	6	housekeeper	21	here
s	McFarland Anna—†	6A	"	52	"
T	McFarland Anna T—†	6A	shoecutter	28	"
U	Ryan Anna F—†	6A	tailoress	43	"
V	Ryan Annie F—†	6A	housekeeper	67	"
w	Ryan Daniel	6A	clerk	38	"
X	Ryan Elizabeth—†	6A	operator	34	"
Y	Ryan Sarah—†	6A	clerk	36	"
z	Ryan Thomas	6A	shoecutter	40	"
A	Murray Margaret J—†	7	at home	76	"
B	Page John M	7	student	24	"
c	Page John V	7	merchant	54	"
D	Page Margaret M—†	7	clerk	20	"
E	Page Susie J—†	7	housewife	50	"
F	Page Susie V—†	7	stenographer	22	"
G	Brooker John	8	chauffeur	46	"
H	Craven Catherine M—†	8	housewife	40	"
K	Craven Patrick J	8	machinist	42	"
L	Moriarty Daniel	8	teacher	37	"
M	Norton John F	8	clerk	37	"
N	Ryan James E	8	machinist	53	"

Page.	Letter.	FULL NAME.	Residence, April 1, 1926.	Occupation.	Supposed Age.	Reported Residence, April 1, 1925. Street and Number.

Sumner Place—Continued

	o	Ryan Margaret—†	8	housewife	40	here
	p	Smith George F	8A	inspector	65	"
	R	Smith Julia—†	8A	housewife	63	"
	s	Schnetzer Benjiman	9	clerk	42	"
	T	Schnetzer Margaret G—†	9	housewife	33	"
	U	Norton Bridget A—†	10	housekeeper	70	"
	V	Norton Elizabeth A—†	10	stenographer	34	"

Terry Street

	W	Byrnes Walter J	1	life guard	51	here
	X	Grainger Harry	1	instructor	48	"
	Y	O'Brien John M	1	custodian	46	"
	Z	Gilmore Agnes—†	2	housekeeper	36	"
	A	Moraski Joseph	2	baker	35	"
	G	Moraski Stella—†	2	housewife	30	"
	C	Sowenski Rose—†	2	clerk	24	"
	D	Flynn Annie—†	2	factory worker	24	"
	E	Flynn Catherine—†	2	housekeeper	53	"
	F	Flynn Catherine—†	2	forewoman	27	"
	G	Flynn Margaret—†	2	factory worker	20	"
	H	Flynn Mary—†	2	operator	32	"
	K	Kelly Ellen C—†	3	housewife	49	"
	L	Kelly James	3	salesman	20	"
	M	Kelly John J	3	chauffeur	31	"
	N	Kelly Richard	3	cleaner	62	"
	O	Kelly Richard, jr	3	plumber	27	"
	P	Kelly Thomas J	3	chauffeur	24	"
	R	Foley Bertha—†	4	housewife	32	"
	s	Foley Jeremiah	4	teamster	35	"
	T	Donegan Helen—†	4	operator	24	"
	U	Donegan Josephine J—†	4	"	23	"
	V	Manning Catherine—†	4	matron	51	"
	W	Manning Catherine V—†	4	stenographer	22	"
	X	Manning Francis E	4	conductor	31	3 S Worthington
	Y	Quinn Arthur H	4	designer	30	here
	Z	Quinn Josephine—†	4	housewife	30	"
	A	Doyle Elizabeth F—†	5	"	29	"
	B	Doyle Joseph F	5	salesman	32	"

22

Page.	Letter.	FULL NAME.	Residence, April 1, 1926.	Occupation.	Supposed Age.	Reported Residence, April 1, 1925. Street and Number.

Terry Street—Continued

c	McGee Annie V—†	6	housewife	35	here
d	McGee Percival G	6	policeman	38	"
e	Brady Catherine—†	6	labeler	40	"
f	Brady John J	6	painter	51	"
g	Brady Mary—†	6	houseworker	50	"
h	Flynn Bridget—†	6	housewife	60	"
k	Flynn John J	6	engineer	59	"
l	Flynn Joseph F	6	bookkeeper	25	"

Tremont Street

k	Tobin Charles W	1165	painter	74	here
l	Tobin Mary E—†	1165	housewife	62	"
w	Devlin Henry	1177A	laborer	45	"
x	McCann Elinor—†	1177A	housewife	42	"
y	McCann Henry	1177A	laborer	20	"
z	McCann Hugh	1177A	"	44	"
a	Downs Catherine—†	1177A	housewife	56	"
b	Downs Frank J	1177A	bookkeeper	29	"
c	Downs John J	1177A	chauffeur	32	"
d	King Frederick H	1177A	"	31	"
e	King Vera M—†	1177A	housewife	28	"
f	Walsh Annie—†	1177A	"	45	"
g	Walsh Matthew	1177A	chauffeur	59	"
h	Hart Mary—†	1177A	housewife	47	"
k	McDermott Catherine-†	1177A	"	26	"
l	McDermott William	1177A	butcher	30	"
m	Anderson Arthur	1177A	laborer	26	"
n	Anderson Carl	1177A	clerk	58	"
o	Anderson Nellie—†	1177A	housewife	49	"
r	O'Brien Richard	1177A	teamster	46	"
p	O'Brien Joseph	1177A	chauffeur	21	"
u	Nott Delia—†	1180	housewife	47	"
v	Nott James	1180	carpenter	52	"
w	May Clarence D	1180	laborer	25	"
x	May Mary—†	1180	housewife	25	1615 Tremont
y	Chappell Ernest	1180	waiter	40	here
z	Durweller Adam H	1180	salesman	50	"
a	Donovan Edward	1180	"	22	149 W Concord
b	Donovan Ida—†	1180	housewife	28	149 "

Tremont Street—Continued

C	Bruce Bettsy—†	1180	housewife	54	here
D	Bruce John H	1180	stonemason	52	"
E	Adams Nellie—†	1180	houseworker	40	Brookline
K	Loupovitz Dabbie—†	1182	housewife	42	here
L	Loupovitz Morris	1182	junk dealer	42	"
M	Kousolian Garabe	1182	shoemaker	35	"
N	Kousolian Mary—†	1182	housewife	32	"
O	Audonian Kachardor	1182	laborer	60	"
P	Audonian Mary—†	1182	housewife	50	"
R	DerMinasian Garabed	1182	carpenter	26	"
S	DerMinasian Sousalzin—†	1182	housewife	23	"
T	Mazmanin Mary—†	1182	houseworker	40	"
W	Cox Madelena A—†	1183	housekeeper	77	"
X	Auchiello Antonetta—†	1183	housewife	31	"
Y	Auchiello Ralph	1183	laborer	31	"
Z	Donahue Catherine—†	1183	housekeeper	55	"
A	O'Brien Catherine—†	1183	housewife	47	"
F	Schacht Alfred	1186½	milkman	37	Everett
G	Schacht Rae—†	1186½	housewife	32	"
H	Hughes Mary—†	1186½	houseworker	76	here
K	Tate Ruth—†	1186½	factory worker	49	"
L	Burns Mary—†	1186½	cashier	36	"
M	Hopwood Catherine T—†	1187	housewife	39	"
N	Hopwood Charles H	1187	painter	42	"
O	Carlson Caroline—†	1187	housewife	83	17 Bromley
P	Carlson Gustace	1187	laborer	73	17 "
R	Corba Guy	1187	boxmaker	39	here
S	Corba Jennie—†	1187	housewife	35	"
T	Pollack Clara—†	1187	housekeeper	58	"
U	Rines Rebecca—†	1187	"	63	"
V	Whitten Martha J—†	1187	matron	60	"
W	Hampson Benjamin	1187	photographer	36	"
X	Hampson Veronica—†	1187	housewife	36	"
C	Oppenheim Bessie—†	1195	houseworker	44	876 Harris'n av
D	Oppenheim Louis	1195	laborer	24	876 "
E	D'Amone Pasquale	1195	brasspolisher	40	here
F	D'Amone Theresa—†	1195	housewife	38	"
G	Geddny Grace—†	1195	"	28	"
H	Geddny Walter	1195	foreman	29	"
K	Kerrigan John	1195	laborer	70	"
L	Kerrigan John	1195	lather	25	"

Tremont Street—Continued

M	Kerrigan Loretta—†	1195	housewife	20	Tiverton R I
N	Permacchio Frances—†	1195	"	28	3 Albert
O	Permacchio Frank	1195	mechanic	33	10 Margaret
P	Brown Catherine—†	1195	housewife	52	here
R	Brown Frank	1195	teamster	53	"
T	Callahan John F	1195	chauffeur	25	"
S	Callahan John J	1195	foreman	54	"
U	Callahan Mary—†	1195	housewife	52	"
V	Callahan Mathew J	1195	carpenter	22	"
W	Callahan Timothy	1195	laborer	20	"
X	Phipps Alice H—†	1196	housewife	54	"
Y	Phipps John H	1196	laborer	48	" .
Z	Halligan Christina—†	1196	housewife	27	"
A	Halligan William	1196	conductor	27	"
B	Brennan Abbie—†	1196	housewife	23	"
C	Brennan Frank	1196	conductor	24	"
D	Reid Samuel	1196	machinist	54	"
E	Poret Anna—†	1196	housewife	24	"
F	Poret Robert	1196	painter	27	"
G	Nestor Eleanor—†	1196	housewife	25	"
H	Nestor James	1196	machinist	27	"
K	Smith Edwin	1196	electrician	46	"
L	Stracthan Isabelle—†	1196	houseworker	45	"
M	Autonvitz Carl	1196	cook	30	"
N	Autonvitz Walter	1196	laborer	28	"
O	Healey Delia—†	1196	housewife	31	"
P	Healey Robert	1196	laborer	28	"
R	Bersen John	1196	carpenter	28	Cambridge
S	Bersen Tiana—†	1196	housewife	24	Brookline
T	Biggins Fred	1196	painter	24	12 Sarsfield
U	Biggins Nellie—†	1196	housewife	24	12 "
V	Riley Alice—†	1196	"	23	12 "
W	Riley Mark	1196	baker	26	12 "
X	Hawly Lillian—†	1196	housewife	38	here
Y	Hawly Robert	1196	chauffeur	38	"
B	Kreponetsky Fannie—†	1198½	storekeeper	39	"
C	Davis Benjamin	1199	"	55	"
D	Davis Bertha—†	1199	housewife	57	"
E	Davis David	1199	storekeeper	23	"
F	Kantrovitz Mary—†	1199	operator	20	73 Ruggles
G	Kennedy Mary—†	1199	housekeeper	52	here

Tremont Street—Continued

H	Kennedy Thomas	1199	inspector	31	here
K	Mason Annie—†	1199	housewife	36	12 Gurney
L	Mason Eugene	1199	bricklayer	63	12 "
M	Quigley Catherine—†	1199	housewife	53	76 Chandler
N	Quigley Joseph	1199	cook	55	76 "
O	Maguire John	1199	laborer	37	here
P	Maguire Mary—†	1199	cashier	27	"
R	Pantelskan Leonidan	1199	laborer	43	"
V	Bishop Samuel P	1203	houseman	50	11 Village
W	Johnston Mary—†	1203	cook	40	11 "
Y	Hanson Ernest	1203	storekeeper	45	here
Z	Hanson Margaret—†	1203	housewife	49	"
A	Fitzpatrick Patrick	1203	machinist	46	"
C	Mendes Annie—†	1204B	housewife	34	"
D	Mendes Peter	1204B	longshoreman	35	"
E	Silva Joseph	1204B	"	28	"
F	Johnson Lucy—†	1204B	housewife	27	1045 Tremont
G	Johnson William	1204B	mechanic	33	1045 "
K	Joseph John	1204B	cook	29	Cambridge
L	Joseph Louise—†	1204B	housewife	26	"
M	McIlvaine Bessie—†	1204B	"	43	74 Hammond
N	McIlvaine William	1204B	porter	54	74 "
O	Cooper Mary F—† •	1204B	housewife	42	here
P	Cooper Samuel B	1204B	retired	66	"
S	McVey Ernest	1204B	laborer	24	"
R	Paine Robert	1204B	janitor	25	"
W	Horgan Daniel	1207	mechanic	42	"
X	Horgan Margaret—†	1207	housewife	32	"
Y	Baldwin Charles	1207	motorman	40	"
Z	Baldwin Eva—†	1207	housewife	36	"
A	Burns Joseph H	1207	motorman	37	"
B	Burns Marion R—†	1207	housewife	30	"
C	Horgan Margaret—†	1207	housekeeper	34	"
O	Campbell Florence—†	1223	"	55	4 Motley
P	Dyotte Alfred	1223	oiler	22	11 Delle av
R	Dyotte Annie—†	1223	housewife	60	11 "
S	Dyotte Louis	1223	janitor	60	11 "
T	Dyotte Margaret—†	1223	housekeeper	25	11 "
U	Larimee Edmund	1223	oiler	20	11 "
V	Locke Emma—†	1223	housewife	50	4 Motley
W	Locke Philip E	1223	painter	39	4 "

Tremont Street—Continued

x	Moriarty James E	1223	weaver	20	772 Col av
y	Moriarty Mabel—†	1223	housewife	48	772 "
z	Moriarty Timothy H	1223	painter	54	772 "
A	Hall Elizabeth M—†	1225	storekeeper	49	here
B	Athridge Katherine H-†	1225	housewife	27	"
C	Athridge Thomas P	1225	accountant	28	"
D	Hooley Daniel F	1225	laborer	30	"
E	Hooley Marie G—†	1225	housewife	29	"
K	Hayes Daniel	1237	laborer	46	1234 Tremont
L	Hayes Hilda L—†	1237	housewife	46	1234 "

Vernon Street

A	Dooley Annie—†	103	housewife	33	here
B	Dooley Leo	103	chauffeur	20	"
C	Dooley Michael H	103	laborer	54	"
D	Robertson Anna E—†	105	housewife	33	"
E	Robertson Lawrence W	105	baker	32	"
F	Hardy Alice—†	105	housewife	68	2495 Wash'n
G	Hardy Ernest D	105	painter	22	2495 "
H	Hardy Frank B	105	"	66	2495 "
K	Hardy Howard B	105	"	43	2495 "
L	Hardy John J	105	operator	24	2495 "
M	Copson Florence G—†	105	housewife	29	here
N	Copson William A, jr	105	paperhanger	28	"
O	Richard Lillian J—†	105	housewife	34	222 Cabot
P	Richard William D	105	clerk	34	222 "
R	Goldsmith Bertha—†	107	housewife	29	12 Haskins
S	Goldsmith Joseph	107	metalworker	29	12 "
T	Krotman Myer	107	retired	64	here
U	Krotman Bessie—†	107	housewife	37	"
V	Krotman Frank	107	storekeeper	47	"
W	Krotman Eli	107	"	38	"
X	Krotman Jennie—†	107	housewife	34	"
Y	Werner Anna—†	109	"	25	"
Z	Werner Harris	109	meatcutter	27	"
A	Cooperstein Esther—†	109	housewife	45	"
B	Cooperstein Eva—†	109	saleswoman	23	"
C	Cooperstein Harry	109	manager	44	"
D	Foley Margaret—†	109	housewife	32	217 Cabot

Page.	Letter.	FULL NAME.	Residence, April 1, 1926.	Occupation.	Supposed Age.	Reported Residence, April 1, 1925. Street and Number.

Vernon Street—Continued

E	Foley Thomas F	109	salesman	32	217 Cabot
F	White Anna E—†	111	housewife	34	here
G	White Walter J	111	chauffeur	36	"
H	Cronin John J	111	mechanic	27	"
K	Cronin Joseph	111	ropemaker	64	"
L	Stone Helen M—†	111	housewife	22	"
M	Stone Samuel	111	meatcutter	22	"
N	Thurston Catherine—†	r 113	housewife	59	746 Shawmut av
O	Thurston William P	" 113	shipper	60	746 "
P	Walker Chester S	" 113	laundryman	35	here
R	Walker Olivia R—†	" 113	housewife	35	"
S	Burford Emily—†	115	"	25	"
T	Cunningham Walter	115	machinist	39	"
U	Douglas Emily—†	115	housewife	56	"
V	Douglas Maud—†	115	housekeeper	21	"
W	Douglas Samuel	115	printer	26	"
X	Kissick James H	115	retired	84	"
Y	Harold James M	119	motorman	39	"
Z	Harold Nora—†	119	housewife	38	"
A	Gilmartin Maria—†	119	cleaner	46	"
B	Killeen Bridget—†	119	housewife	48	"
C	Killeen Joseph	119	clerk	34	"
D	Donovan Agnes L—†	119	stitcher	31	"
E	Donovan Helen M—†	119	"	28	"
F	Donovan Mary—†	119	housewife	60	"
G	Donovan Mary J—†	119	stenographer	34	"
H	Crowley Alice C—†	121	housewife	47	3319 Wash'n
K	Crowley Walter P	121	electrician	40	3319 "
L	McDonough Thomas F	121	pianomaker	60	3319 "
M	McLaughlin Peter J	121	gardener	22	Great Barrington
O	Blair Bertha—†	125	housewife	43	31 St Francis de Sales
P	Killeen Lena—†	127	"	30	here
R	Killeen Thomas	127	welder	31	"
S	Maher Mary—†	127	housewife	45	P E I
T	Maher Vincent J	127	coatmaker	43	5 Burrell
V	Bennett Arthur A	129	machinist	39	Waltham
W	Bennett Catherine—†	129	housewife	30	"
X	Durkin Edward D	129	laborer	44	here
Y	Durkin Winifred—†	129	housewife	45	"
Z	Walsh Mary E—†	131	"	35	262 Cabot
A	Walsh Michael J	131	laborer	42	262 "

23

Page.	Letter.	FULL NAME.	Residence, April 1, 1926.	Occupation.	Supposed Age.	Reported Residence, April 1, 1925. Street and Number.

Vernon Street—Continued

	Letter	FULL NAME	Res.	Occupation	Age	Reported Residence
	B	Sullivan Marion—†	137	housekeeper	79	1115 Harrison av
	C	Virgin Mary A—†	137	"	63	1115 "
	D	Maloney Joseph	137	expressman	35	here
	E	Maloney Marion—†	137	housewife	35	"
	F	Lucy Mary—†	137	"	42	"
	G	Lucy Michael	137	electrician	46	"
	H	Wilson Sarah—†	139	housekeeper	60	"
	K	Reuder Emily S—†	139	"	82	"
	N	Shuley Annie—†	147	housewife	54	"
	O	Shuley James S	147	brassmolder	55	"
	P	Wilfand Abraham	147	storekeeper	42	"
	R	Wilfand Ida—†	147	housewife	38	"
	S	Shea Margaret—†	147	"	37	5 Highland pl
	T	Glennon Thomas	147	tinsmith	27	here
	U	Kelley Nora—†	147	housewife	64	"
	V	Kelley Patrick J	147	teamster	66	"
	Y	Watson Almeda—†	147	housewife	25	Cambridge
	Z	Watson Frederick	147	chauffeur	29	"
	B	Brown Ernest E	161	fireman	23	"
	C	Brown Lillian E—†	161	housewife	23	"
	D	Naugler Florence—†	161	"	23	Nova Scotia
	E	Naugler Morris	161	rubberworker	23	"
	F	Tracy Nora—†	161	housekeeper	45	1118 Tremont
	G	Connor Elizabeth—†	175	housewife	34	here
	H	Connor Joseph	175	clerk	43	"
	K	Glynn Ann—†	175	housekeeper	48	"
	L	Glynn Thomas	175	elevatorman	22	"
	M	Glynn Helen M—†	175	housewife	26	"
	N	Glynn John F	175	paver	28	"
	O	Glynn Joseph P	175	chauffeur	30	"
	P	O'Rourke Patrick F	175	laborer	33	"
	R	Pinkham Lillian—†	177	housekeeper	52	"
	S	Glynn Daniel—†	177	chauffeur	22	"
	T	Glynn John	177	lineman	31	"
	U	Glynn Patrick	177	laborer	62	"
	V	Glynn Thomas H	177	mechanic	25	"
	W	Fallon Daniel J	177	laborer	68	"
	X	Fallon Margaret E—†	177	housewife	58	"
	Y	Hughes Catherine—†	179	housekeeper	57	15 Weston pl
	Z	Kelliher Ellen—†	179	laundress	41	here
	A	Holloran Margaret—†	179	housekeeper	71	"

29

Page.	Letter.	FULL NAME.	Residence, April 1, 1926.	Occupation.	Supposed Age.	Reported Residence, April 1, 1925. Street and Number.

Vernon Street—Continued

	B	Holloran Thomas	179	laborer	51	here
	C	Daley Mary I—†	181	housewife	30	"
	D	Daley Micheal D	181	lamplighter	40	"
	E	Daley William T	181	upholsterer	47	"
	F	Lynch Catherine—†	181	housewife	23	"
	G	Thorpe Anna E—†	181	housekeeper	24	"
	H	Thorpe Catherine—†	181	cleaner	45	"
	M	Chin Yen	193	laundryman	26	New Hampshire
	N	Lei Mein Wey	193	"	41	here
	O	Wong Nen	193	"	50	"
	P	Wong Yet	193	"	25	"
	R	Wong Ying	193	"	48	"
	S	McDonald Byron G	195	salesman	29	107 Ruggles
	T	McDonald Ruth—†	195	housewife	25	107 "
	U	Nash Nellie A—†	195	"	47	8 Plant av
	V	Nash Thomas J	195	foreman	53	8 "
	Z	Bland Iolene—†	197	housewife	25	27 Bay State rd
	A	Bland James	197	chauffeur	25	27 "
	C	Deshon Alfred M	199	collector	54	101 Norfolk av
	D	Deshon Laura—†	199	housewife	43	101 "

Warwick Street

	G	Gibson Amos	115	electrician	29	64 Ruggles
	H	Haywood Ada—†	115	clerk	26	665 Shawmut av
	K	Paris Florence—†	115	housewife	46	Canada
	L	Paris James	115	painter	41	"
	M	Totman Roy	115	laborer	22	Cambridge
	N	Pryor Powell	117	carpenter	64	here
	O	Pryor Sarah—†	117	housewife	54	"
	P	Jenkins Charles	117	laborer	41	"
	R	Jenkins Ruberta—†	117	housewife	37	"
	S	Hunter Lucy—†	119	cook	24	"
	T	Lundy Delia—†	119	maid	50	"
	U	Robinson Phillip	119	porter	35	"
	V	Williamson Carrie—†	119	housekeeper	45	"
	W	Saunders Clara—†	121	housewife	41	"
	X	Saunders Frederick	121	foreman	29	"
	Y	Thomas James L	121	cleaner	57	"

Page	Letter	Full Name.	Residence, April 1, 1926.	Occupation.	Supposed Age.	Reported Residence, April 1, 1925. Street and Number.

Warwick Street—Continued

	z	Thomas Jessie L—†	121	housekeeper	37	here
	A	Latham Hattie—†	121	housewife	31	"
	B	Latham Herbert	121	shipper	31	"
	C	Jones Elizabeth—†	123	maid	29	Cambridge
	D	Peay Belle—†	123	housewife	36	35 Warwick
	E	Peay Hilbert	123	cook	37	35 "
	F	Smith Elmira—†	123	housekeeper	45	here
	G	Thompson Arthur	123	printer	21	"
	H	Hunter Loydie—†	125	housekeeper	64	"
	K	Shearer Charles	125	bellboy	27	"
	L	Shearer Margaret—†	125	housewife	26	"
	N	Duggett Ama—†	127	maid	45	Cambridge
	O	Fountain James M	127	laborer	30	"
	P	Huggins Laura S—†	127	housekeeper	60	"
	R	Phillips Coraine—†	129	domestic	32	31 Eustis
	S	Phillips Julia—†	129	at home	56	31 "
	T	Phillips Grace—†	129	bookkeeper	30	New York City
	U	Bennett Clifton	131	machinist	40	Cambridge
	V	Ritson Bertha M—†	131	student	21	here
	W	Ritson Eugene F	131	chauffeur	52	"
	X	Stewart Lucille J—†	131	domestic	39	"
	Y	Cooper Clifton B	133	student	28	"
	Z	Cooper Fredica L—†	133	housewife	49	"
	A	Cooper Thomas G	133	real estate	53	"
	C	Curley Ellen T—†	135	houseworker	61	"
	D	Curley Rose A—†	135	housekeeper	38	"

Weston Street

	E	Voisin Celina—†	10	housekeeper	74	here
	F	Voisin Lewis J B	10	mechanic	66	"
	G	Kingston Honora—†	10	at home	70	"
	H	Twohig Francis V	10	letter carrier	35	"
	K	Twohig Jerome J	10	waiter	38	"
	L	Cunningham Evylne—†	10	housewife	21	"
	M	Cunningham Harold	10	printer	25	"
	N	Moran Mary E—†	10	housekeeper	50	"
	O	Moran Maurice	10	upholsterer	55	"

Page.	Letter.	FULL NAME.	Residence, April 1, 1926.	Occupation.	Supposed Age.	Reported Residence, April 1, 1925. Street and Number.

Whittier Street

s	Bozzelli Anna—†	3	housekeeper	72	here
T	Bozzelli Mary—†	3	"	43	"
U	Coady Hugh	5	chauffeur	62	"
V	Coady Nellie—†	5	housewife	58	"
W	Doherty Margaret—†	5	"	60	"
X	Doherty Neil	5	laborer	76	"
Y	Vereker Daniel J	5	chauffeur	32	"
Z	Vereker Delia—†	5	housewife	33	"
A	Haley Joseph	15	accountant	21	"
B	Haley Mary V—†	15	tel operator	45	"
C	Cox Thomas J	15	shipper	54	"
D	Haley Nellie C—†	15	housekeeper	42	"
E	Sheehy Ellen—†	17	housewife	48	"
F	Sheehy John	17	laborer	58	"
G	Reitsma Olive—†	17	housekeeper	50	"
H	Horton Edith—†	rear 17	housewife	30	"
K	Horton John	" 17	laborer	25	"
L	Trayers Delia F—†	19	housekeeper	46	"
T	Hoar Abbie—†	56	housewife	50	"
U	Hoar Cornelius	56	laborer	52	214 Ruggles
V	Marshman Margaret—†	56	housekeeper	72	here
W	Marshman Robert H	56	janitor	46	"
X	Horgan Lawrence E	56	clerk	22	"
Y	Horgan Mary—†	56	housewife	21	"
Z	Ferber Ellen—†	56	"	42	"
A	Ferber Micheal	56	steward	39	"
B	Webber Bertha E—†	56	housewife	28	"
C	Webber Edwin L	56	shipper	31	"
D	Webber Robert H	56	chauffeur	49	"
E	Geary Julia—†	56	housekeeper	37	8 Queensberry
F	Lawrence Minnie M—†	56	"	49	136 Vernon
H	Samargarn Henan—†	59	"	45	here
K	Tuteain Egsa—†	59	"	34	"
M	McAteer Nellie—†	61	housewife	52	"
N	Patterson James	61	laborer	25	Lawrence
O	Patterson Mary—†	61	housewife	23	"

Ward 9—Precinct 12

CITY OF BOSTON.

LIST OF RESIDENTS
20 YEARS OF AGE AND OVER

(FEMALES INDICATED BY DAGGER)

AS OF

APRIL 1, 1926

HERBERT A. WILSON, } Listing

JAMES F. EAGAN, } Board.

CITY OF BOSTON—PRINTING DEPARTMENT

Page.	Letter.	FULL NAME.	Residence, April 1, 1926.	Occupation.	Supposed Age.	Reported Residence, April 1, 1925. Street and Number.

Allard Court

	A	Scott Frances—†	1	housewife	35	here
	B	Scott Frank J	1	tester	41	"
	C	Simmons Catherine—†	1	housekeeper	48	70 Circuit
	D	Young Frank D	1	janitor	49	here
	E	Young Mary—†	1	housewife	37	"
	M	Crowley Catherine—†	4	"	41	"
	N	Crowley Jeremiah	4	teamster	48	"

Columbus Avenue

	P	Lessard Armend	1038	operator	24	742 Parker
	R	Lessard Martha—†	1038	housewife	24	742 "
	T	MacLeod Catherine—†	1038	"	21	here
	U	MacLeod Joseph	1038	garageman	22	"
	V	Cohen Frances R—†	1038	housewife	23	"
	W	Cohen Myer	1038	salesman	26	"
	X	Hammond Catherine A-†	1038	housewife	28	129 Smith
	Y	Hammond William A	1038	fireman	30	129 "
	Z	Strauss Dora—†	1038	housewife	50	here
	A	Strauss Theodore	1038	laborer	56	"
	C	Hurley Elizabeth—†	1040	housekeeper	54	"
	D	Hurley Timothy J	1040	wool grader	51	"
	E	Reynolds Bernard J	1040	plumber	23	90 E Newton
	F	Reynolds Julia—†	1040	housewife	22	90 "
	K	Burns Catherine—†	1046	laundress	36	here
	L	Burns James	1046	laborer	38	"
	M	Fallon Thomas	1046	"	44	1267 Tremont
	N	Quinn Martin J	1046	watchman	46	here
	O	Quinn Mary A—†	1046	bookeeper	38	"
	P	Quinn Mary A—†	1046	clerk	27	"
	R	McMackin Isabella—†	1048	housewife	37	1248 Tremont
	S	McMachin William J	1048	salesman	38	1248 "
	T	Wong Samuel K	1048	chauffeur	25	189 Vernon
	U	Comerford Charles A	1048	merchant	50	688½ E Second
	V	Comerford Mary E—†	1048	housewife	48	688½ "
	W	Comerford Thomas J	1048	guard	23	688½ "
	X	Comerford William	1048	painter	21	688½ "
	Y	Cagol George	1048	laborer	40	here
	Z	Hart Caterine S—†	1048	housekeeper	45	"

2

rage.	Letter.	FULL NAME.	Residence, April 1, 1926.	Occupation.	Supposed Age.	Reported Residence, April 1, 1925. Street and Number.

Columbus Avenue—Continued

A	Dobkin Solomon	1048	metalworker	38	1046 Col av
B	Wolf Anna—†	1048	housewife	42	here
C	Wolf Phillip	1048	storekeeper	47	"
D	Sheingold Elizabeth—†	1048	stengrapher	22	"
E	Sheingold Leah—†	1048	housekeeper	43	"
G	Smolinsky Anna—†	1050	housewife	39	"
H	Smolinsky Frank J	1050	agent	39	"
K	Tolson Emma—†	1050	housewife	40	Middleboro
L	Tolson Harry W	1050	steward	47	"
M	Reid Mary—†	1051	housekeeper	45	1014 Tremont
N	Seymour Margaret—†	1051	"	50	1014 "
O	Garabedian Krikor	1051	laborer	53	here
P	Hill Mary—†	1051	housekeeper	52	"
R	Williams Amelia—†	1051	"	49	310 Shawmut av
S	Williams Elmer	1051	brakeman	27	310 "
T	Williams Mary J—†	1051	housewife	22	310 "
V	Dolan Catherine A—†	1055	housekeeper	58	here
W	McLaughlin Anna G—†	1055	forewoman	32	"
X	Charles Etna H—†	1055	housewife	27	New London Ct
Y	Charles Theron	1055	truckman	32	"
Z	Quinn Mary A—†	1055	housekeeper	38	here
B	Lee Rose—†	1057	paperworker	30	25 Station
C	O'Llila Hazel M—†	1057	housekeeper	26	183 D
D	Spinney Louise—†	1057	"	52	1293 Tremont
K	Kerkell Anthony	1067A	student	20	here
L	Novokofsky Annie—†	1067A	housewife	40	"
M	Novokofsky Valitine	1067A	baker	44	"
P	Catarius Cornelius	1073	chauffeur	24	1309 Tremont
R	Catarius Edith A—†	1073	housewife	26	1309 "
S	Scaralato Anna—†	1073	"	21	here
T	Scaralato Joseph	1073	metalworker	27	"
U	VonBrinckert George C	1073	cabinetmaker	43	"
V	VonBrinckert Jennie—†	1073	housewife	41	"
W	VonBrinckert Joanna—†	1073	housekeeper	85	"
X	Stanley Agnes—†	1073	housewife	27	"
Y	Stanley Warren	1073	laborer	28	"
B	O'Shaughnessy Joseph	1077	salesman	50	"
C	O'Shaughnessy Mary A—†	1077	housewife	46	"
D	Long Annie E—†	1077	matron	55	"
E	McCormack Mary E—†	1077	housekeeper	65	"
W	Newton Ellen—†	1100	housewife	36	10 Hampshire

3

Page.	Letter.	FULL NAME.	Residence, April 1, 1926.	Occupation.	Supposed Age.	Reported Residence, April 1, 1925. Street and Number.

Columbus Avenue—Continued

x	Newton James F	1100	laborer	38	10 Hampshire
y	Bennett Rose—†	1100	housekeeper	41	5 King ter
A	Connolly Josephine E–†	1101	housewife	30	71 Wachusett
B	Connolly Patrick H	1101	painter	41	71 "
K	Connolly Agnes C—†	1107A	stenographer	32	here
L	Connolly Anna V—†	1107A	housekeeper	36	"
M	Connelly Patrick	1107A	gatetender	78	"
N	Connelly Martha A—†	1107A	housewife	43	"
O	Connelly Thomas F	1107A	foreman	46	"
P	Regan Martin H	1107A	superintendent	67	"
E	Mullen James J	1129	undertaker	43	1336 Tremont
R	Morris Henry J	1140	painter	55	England
s	Sarkin Margaret—†	1140	housewife	41	1185 Boylston
T	Sarkin Robert A	1140	janitor	45	1185 "
s	Nyhan Harold L	1174	clerk	23	here
T	Nyhan Nora—†	1174	matron	43	"
U	Bettie Isabella R—†	1174	housewife	43	"
v	Bettie William S	1174	fisherman	46	"
Y	Shydecker Martha—†	1184	housewife	43	"
z	Shydecker Otto F	1184	florist	48	"
A	Lewis Eleanor—†	1184	housekeeper	45	"
F	Tobin Louise—†	1190	housewife	37	129 Smith
G	Tobin William	1190	carpenter	53	129 "
H	Tallent Edward	1190	chauffeur	28	Somerville
K	Tallent Frank S	1190	teamster	45	"
L	Tallent Vesta A—†	1190	housewife	44	"
M	Cram Rhea J—†	1190	housekeeper	33	77 Bickford

Conant Place

P	Howe Mary T—†	1	housekeeper	43	130 Norfolk av
R	Magerdishian Anthony	1	laborer	30	here
s	Greene Lillian—†	1	housewife	26	"
T	Pratt Amy—†	2	"	53	"
U	Pratt Fred	2	teamster	54	"
v	Molloy Bridget—†	2	housekeeper	52	2 Motley
w	Martinez Ella L—†	2	housewife	30	Cambridge
x	Martinez John R	2	carpenter	36	"
Y	Gildea Francis M	3	printer	21	here
z	Gildea Nora—†	3	housekeeper	45	"

4

Page	Letter	FULL NAME.	Residence, April 1, 1926.	Occupation.	Supposed Age.	Reported Residence, April 1, 1925. Street and Number.

Crawshaw Place

	B	Russell Minnie —†	1	stitcher	35	here
	C	Saunders Mary —†	1	housekeeper	79	"
	D	Pfeifer Virginia—†	1	nurse	26	"
	F	Norton Arduno	2	laborer	35	"
	G	Norton Beatrice—†	2	housewife	25	"
	H	Cosgrove Sarah —†	2	compositor	53	"

Crossin Place

	L	Mitchell John J	4	storekeeper	64	1466 Wash'n
	M	Lumsden Gertrude M—†	4	housewife	50	980 Harris'n av
	N	Lumsden William	4	electrician	52	980 "
	O	Bartlett Mary —†	4	housewife	48	84 Montgomery
	P	Kenney John T	5	laundryworker	45	37 Worcester
	R	Kenney Martha —†	5	housewife	43	117 Appleton
	S	Keeley Bridget T—†	5	"	47	here
	T	Keeley Patrick J	5	laborer	54	"
	U	Fallon Daniel E	5	expressman	37	11A Elmwood pl
	V	Fallon Helen —†	5	housewife	33	11A "
	W	Logan John	6	laborer	64	here
	X	Logan John T	6	"	37	"
	Y	Logan Katherine —†	6	housekeeper	76	"
	Z	Carey Ellen E—†	6	housewife	47	"
	A	Carey Thomas J	6	machinist	48	"
	B	Grottindeck Arthur V	6	laborer	22	"
	C	Igoe Bridget—†	6	housekeeper	56	"
	D	Igoe Michael	6	laborer	27	"
	E	Rockwell William	7	retired	70	"
	F	Fallon Elizabeth—†	7	housewife	53	"
	G	Fallon Ellen—†	7	housekeeper	67	"

Dunlow Street

	K	Mason Althea—†	8	housekeeper	38	here
	L	Mason David	8	barber	40	"
	M	Schuster Hans	8A	motorman	49	"

5

Page.	Letter.	FULL NAME.	Residence, April 1, 1926.	Occupation.	Supposed Age.	Reported Residence, April 1, 1925. Street and Number.

Dunlow Street— Continued

	N	Schuster Leonard	8A	electrician	25	here
	O	Schuster Martha M—†	8A	housekeeper	47	"
	P	French Annie—†	8A	"	43	"
	R	French Frank	8A	teamster	37	"
	S	French William J	8A	laborer	25	"
	T	Drausehke Ferdinand	10	"	36	"
	U	Drausehke Senma—†	10	housekeeper	29	"
	V	Knadlar Mary—†	36	"	42	"
	W	Knadlar William	36	foreman	42	"
	X	Perkins Edna—†	38	housekeeper	31	"
	Y	Perkins George	38	porter	48	"
	Z	Cavney Michael J	38	retired	76	"
	A	Glennon Edward M	38	mechanic	23	"
	B	Glennon Ellen E—†	38	housekeeper	31	"
	C	Glennon Frank L	38	chauffeur	29	"
	D	Glennon George F	38	"	25	"
	E	Glennon Walter J	38	laborer	20	"
	F	Horan Hannah—†	40	clerk	37	"
	G	McLaughlin Mary—†	40	housekeeper	35	"
	H	Crock John	40	laborer	63	"

Elmwood Court

	L	Corrigan Margaret—†	1	housekeeper	30	here
	M	Corrigan Matthew	1	ironworker	35	"
	N	Peritzian Estelle—†	1	housekeeper	32	"
	O	Dundon Catherine C—†	1	"	38	"
	P	Sullivan James	2	electrician	27	"
	R	Sullivan Julia—†	2	teacher	33	"
	S	Sullivan Louise—†	2	housekeeper	65	"
	U	Duffy William	4	yardman	61	"
	W	Obert Catherine—†	5	housekeeper	69	"
	X	Obert Frank C	5	policeman	38	"
	Y	Obert Kasper	5	retired	74	"
	Z	Schmuck Mary—†	7	housekeeper	66	"
	A	Schmuck Otto	7	cook	72	"
	B	Kitson Ella M—†	9	stenographer	36	"
	C	Kitson Fred	9	collector	54	"
	D	Kitson Sarah J—†	9	housekeeper	42	"

Page	Letter	Full Name.	Residence, April 1, 1926.	Occupation.	Supposed Age.	Reported Residence, April 1, 1925. Street and Number.

Elmwood Place

	Letter	Full Name.	Residence April 1, 1926.	Occupation.	Supposed Age.	Reported Residence, April 1, 1925. Street and Number.
	E	Robertson Christian	1	mechanic	72	here
	F	Robertson Mary—†	1	housewife	71	"
	G	Keaveny Daniel F	1	clerk	24	"
	H	Keaveny Evylen—†	1	housewife	22	"
	K	Keaveny Mary—†	1	houseworker	47	"
	L	O'Day Bridget—†	1	operator	43	"
	M	O'Keefe Alice—†	2	housewife	45	"
	N	O'Keefe John	2	horseshoer	46	"
	O	Plunkett Elizabeth E—†	3	housewife	23	"
	P	Plunkett Richard	3	fireman	26	"
	R	Schilling Arthur F	3	chauffeur	31	"
	S	Schilling Marion—†	3	housewife	24	"
	T	McNulty Mary A—†	3	laundress	65	"
	U	McNulty William	3	chauffeur	25	"
	V	Stevenson George R	4	superintendent	37	"
	W	Stevenson Selma—†	4	housewife	73	"
	X	Stevenson Simeon J	4	retired	73	"
	Y	Leonard Beatrice A—†	5	housewife	31	"
	Z	Leonard Owen J	5	conductor	38	"
	A	Connors John J	5	steamfitter	46	"
	B	Connors Nina—†	5	housewife	40	"
	C	Anderson Charles E	5	mechanic	33	245 Cabot
	D	Anderson Josephine—†	5	housewife	29	245 "
	E	Whelpley David H	7	mechanic	27	here
	F	Whelpley Pearl R—†	7	housewife	33	"
	G	Keegan Bertha—†	7	clerk	38	"
	H	Barry Mary—†	9	housekeeper	77	"
	K	Wise Nora—†	9	"	82	"
	L	Smith Alice E—†	9	secretary	23	"
	M	Smith Elizabeth J—†	9	housewife	54	"
	N	Smith George D	9	clerk	24	"
	O	Smith Mary C—†	9	"	20	"
	P	Bennett Mary J—†	11	housewife	36	170 Cabot
	R	Bennett William H	11	shoemaker	38	170 "
	S	Ridlon Leola M—†	11A	housewife	20	2975 Wash'n
	T	Ridlon Oscar G	11A	expressman	20	2975 "

Page.	Letter.	FULL NAME.	Residence, April 1, 1926.	Occupation.	Supposed Age.	Reported Residence, April 1, 1925. Street and Number.

Elmwood Street

	U	Claus Alfred E	1	metalworker	21	here
	V	Claus Ambrose	1	manufacturer	62	"
	W	Claus Magdelina—†	1	housewife	58	"
	X	King Herman G	2	janitor	46	"
	Y	King Ida W—†	2	housewife	45	"
	Z	Earley William G	7	chauffeur	37	70 Regent
	A	Gately Edward L	7	"	29	here
	B	Gately Helen L—†	7	housewife	24	"
	C	Gately James W	7	chauffeur	32	"
	D	Green Russell	7	lather	56	"
	E	Gurril Frank E	7	clerk	20	"
	F	Goehring Catherine—†	10	housewife	64	"
	G	Goehring John C	10	machinist	58	"
	H	Barry David J	10	clerk	49	"
	K	Goehring John A	10	machinist	31	"
	L	Goehring Minna A—†	10	housewife	32	"
	M	Economos Emanuel	11	cutter	43	890 Hunt'n av
	N	Economos Mary—†	11	housewife	43	890 "
	O	Foley Albert G	11	electrician	23	here
	P	Foley Elizabeth T—†	11	housewife	52	"
	R	Foley Harry A	11	cashier	21	"
	S	Foley Thomas A	11	electrician	54	"
	T	Meade Charles W	11	real estate	67	"
	U	Meade Helen L—†	11	housewife	47	"
	W	McDonald John H	15	brakeman	34	"
	X	McDonald Lucy—†	15	housewife	34	"
	Y	McCormack Effie—†	15	"	52	"
	Z	McCormack Joseph S	15	painter	61	"
	A	McCormack Joseph S	15	chauffeur	28	"
	B	Hill Addie A—†	15	housewife	75	"
	C	Hill George H	15	shipper	34	"
	D	Hill Mary A—†	15	dressmaker	38	"
	E	McCormack Margaret M—†	18	housewife	36	Cambridge
	F	Hill David H	18	machinist	35	here
	G	Hill Helen—†	18	housewife	22	"
	H	Page Florence—†	19	"	24	"
	K	Page John F	19	laborer	27	"
	L	Wilson Edward K	19	mechanic	42	"
	M	Wilson Josephine—†	19	housewife	45	"
	N	Corrigan Abigal M—†	21	"	49	

8

Elmwood Street—Continued

o	Corrigan Edward P	21	fireman	40	here
p	Corrigan James E	21	laster	22	"
r	O'Leary Timothy	21	carpenter	22	"
s	Kelley Mary—†	22	housewife	26	"
t	Kelley William A	22	fireman	32	"
u	Quigley Francis D	22	"	39	"
v	Quigley George J	22	carpenter	37	"
w	Quigley Mary E—†	22	housewife	41	"
x	Donovan Dennis A	22	laborer	56	"
y	Shaw Catherine—†	22	housewife	46	"
z	Shaw James H	22	lineman	48	"
a	Hurney Andrew	23	laborer	43	"
b	Murphy Joseph A	23	student	20	"
c	Murphy Martin J	23	laborer	43	"
d	Murphy Mary C—†	23	housewife	50	"
e	Winterson Katherine—†	23	"	46	"
f	Winterson Patrick J	23	laborer	51	"
g	Gillis Catherine—†	26	housewife	67	"
h	Gillis Isabella—†	26	stitcher	48	"
k	Stewart Arthur H	26	clerk	26	"
l	Stewart Charles A	26	draftsman	21	"
m	Stewart John C	26	storekeeper	64	"
n	Stewart Margaret—†	26	housewife	60	"
o	McGrail Catherine—†	26	operator	25	"
p	McGrail Florence—†	26	stenographer	20	"
r	McGrail John	26	retired	60	"
s	McGrail John F	26	secretary	24	"
t	McGrail Maria—†	26	housewife	53	"
u	McGrail Maria J—†	26	secretary	21	"
v	Brodie Mary—†	26	housewife	45	"
w	Brodie William	26	stonecutter	50	"
x	Tucker Edward	26	clerk	30	"
y	Donnelly Catherine—†	30	housewife	62	"
z	Donnelly James E	30	manager	38	"
a	Walsh Andrew J	30	plasterer	40	1419 Tremont
b	Pickett Helen—†	30	housewife	33	here
c	Pickett William	30	printer	34	"
d	Russell Catherine—†	30	housewife	31	"
e	Carroll Ann—†	32	"	50	"
f	Page Anna V—†	32	clerk	25	"
g	Page Charles A	32	teamster	20	"

9

Page.	Letter.	FULL NAME.	Residence, April 1, 1926.	Occupation.	Supposed Age.	Reported Residence, April 1, 1925. Street and Number.

Elmwood Street—Continued

H	Page Ellen L—†	32	housewife	48	here
K	Page Michael A	32	laborer	52	"
L	Matheson Cassie—†	34	housewife	71	14 Huckins
M	Tremblay Arthur J	34	sorter	42	Chelsea
N	Tremblay Elva—†	34	housewife	28	"
O	Horne Freda—†	36	"	28	5 Carnes pl
P	Hammond Ellen L—†	36	"	50	here
R	Hammond John L	36	chauffeur	20	"
S	Hogan Charles F	36	"	26	1 Greenville
T	Hogan Gertrude—†	36	housewife	26	1 "
U	Mallaney Patrick	38	fireman	52	here
V	McCarthy Isabella M—†	38	housewife	51	"
W	McCarthy John F	38	carpenter	28	"
X	Moran Catherine—†	38	clerk	27	"
Y	Moran Elizabeth—†	38	housewife	52	"
Z	Moran Michael J	38	mechanic	52	"
A	Perkins Enez—†	43	housewife	37	"
B	Perkins William H	43	watchman	34	"
C	Denehy Andrew	43	laborer	79	Worcester
D	Denehy Deliah—†	43	laundress	35	here
E	Goode George H	43	laborer	60	"
F	Goode Thomas	43	clerk	23	"
K	Hamilton Arthur H	45	laborer	26	3379 Wash'n
L	Hamilton Charlotte—†	45	housewife	26	3379 "
M	Hamilton Ellsworth C	45	laborer	24	3379 "
N	Landers Mary—†	45	housewife	50	here
O	Swift John	48	retired	56	"
P	McDonald Flora—†	48	housewife	63	"
R	Dolan Annie—†	48	"	39	"
S	Ball Mary—†	48	stitcher	32	"
T	Ball Peter	48	laborer	21	"
W	McLean Angus	49	carpenter	25	Canada
X	McLean Jane—†	49	housewife	26	"
Y	Daley John F	50	laborer	41	here
Z	Daley Mary E—†	50	housewife	42	"
C	O'Brien Helen—†	52	"	24	"
D	O'Brien Thomas J	52	laborer	29	"
E	Mulcahy Catherine—†	52	shoeworker	29	"
F	Mulcahy Mary—†	52	"	35	"
G	Mullen Thomas	52	laborer	63	5 Fenton
H	O'Brien John	52	"	41	here

Page	Letter	FULL NAME.	Residence, April 1, 1926.	Occupation.	Supposed Age.	Reported Residence, April 1, 1925. Street and Number.

Elmwood Street—Continued

	K	O'Brien Thresa—†	52	housewife	31	here
	M	Linehan Margaret—†	54	"	33	"
	N	Linehan Thomas	54	porter	40	"
	O	Donnelly Caroline—†	54	housewife	32	"

Gurney Street

	B	Dunn Sadie E—†	2	houseworker	48	here
	C	McDonald John W	2	clerk	48	"
	D	D'Andre Angelina—†	2	houseworker	70	"
	E	D'Andre John	2	shoeworker	35	"
	F	Whalen Annie B—†	2	housewife	52	1448 Tremont
	G	Whalen Patrick H	2	machinist	53	1448 "
	H	Boucher Harold E	2	chauffeur	20	here
	K	Boucher Mary—†	2	housewife	42	"
	M	Kelley Ellen—†	12	"	58	45 Terrace
	N	Kelley James	12	laborer	53	45 "
	O	Murray Patrick J	12	"	24	100 Pearl
	P	Sheehan John J	12	"	33	45 Terrace
	R	Barry Catherine M—†	12	houseworker	47	here
	S	Barry James J	12	surveyor	22	"
	T	Barry Patrick J	12	waiter	50	"
	U	Crimmins Dennis J	12	shoeworker	21	"
	V	Crimmins John	12	laborer	49	"
	W	Crimmins Mary—†	12	shoeworker	23	"
	X	Kenney Nellie J—†	14	houseworker	33	668 Parker
	Y	Shaughnessy Mary—†	14	"	37	here
	Z	Shaughnessy Michael J	14	laborer	37	"
	A	Singleton Daniel J	14	"	49	"
	B	Singleton Margaret M—†	14	housewife	38	"
	C	Fox Catherine E—†	20	domestic	48	Brookline
	D	Luther Catherine—†	20	houseworker	39	here
	E	Nagle Catherine—†	20	"	34	"
	F	Nagle Dennis	20	cook	36	"
	G	McQuillan Annie—†	20	houseworker	44	"
	H	McQuillan Joseph A	20	clerk	28	"
	K	McQuillan Mary A—†	20	stenographer	24	"

11

Gurney Street—Continued

L	McQuillan Teresa C—†	20	stenographer	21	here
M	Quinlan Anna G—†	22	houseworker	25	"
N	Quinlan James P	22	shoeworker	34	"
O	Burke Charlotte M—†	22	clerk	21	"
P	Burke John A	22	electrician	32	"
R	Burke John B	22	conductor	57	"
S	Burke Margaret—†	22	houseworker	55	"
T	Burke Rosetta E—†	22	stenographer	23	"
U	Burke William C	22	underwriter	29	"
V	Fitzgerald Evelyn M—†	22	waitress	28	1276 Tremont
W	Shore Agnes—†	22	houseworker	52	1276 "
X	Shore Agnes G—†	22	actress	23	1276 "
Y	Kasper Frederick	28	laborer	55	here
Z	Kasper Johanna G—†	28	houseworker	58	"
A	White Bridget M—†	28	housewife	46	63 Terrace
B	White John F	28	laborer	54	63 "
C	Flynn Catherine—†	28	houseworker	30	here
D	Flynn James	28	laborer	31	"
E	Laydon Daniel J	28	"	39	"
F	Cullen John H	30	plumber	49	"
G	Cullen Mary C—†	30	houseworker	46	"
H	Cullen Rita A—†	30	clerk	20	"
K	Delaney Laurence	30	laborer	41	86 Francis
L	Magoun George T	30	fireman	48	here
M	Magoun Mary J—†	30	housewife	46	"
N	Wagner William	30	laborer	21	"
O	Curran Theresa C—†	30	houseworker	50	"
P	McCarthy Daniel F	36	watchman	65	66 Whitney
R	McCarthy Dennis J	36	foreman	57	66 "
S	McCarthy John F	36	steamfitter	24	66 "
T	McCarthy Margaret—†	36	houseworker	46	here
U	Daily Ellen M—†	36	"	33	"
V	Daily William M	36	roofer	36	"
W	Dolan Catherine E—†	36	houseworker	70	"
X	Dolan Robert W	36	laborer	71	"
Y	Ippilitto Peter	36	plumber	37	"
A	Meade Catherine A—†	54	housewife	47	"
B	Meade Eleanor V—†	54	shoeworker	21	"
C	Meade Patrick E	54	laborer	57	"
D	McShane Anna—†	56	housewife	38	"
E	McShane Michael F	56	meatcutter	40	"

Page.	Letter.	FULL NAME.	Residence, April 1, 1926.	Occupation.	Supposed Age.	Reported Residence, April 1, 1925.
						Street and Number.

Halleck Street

	G	Hennessey Elizabeth G—†	80	clerk	60	here
	H	Hennessey Martin	80	paperhanger	63	"
	K	Kane Delia—†	82	cook	68	"
	L	Schlehuber Lucy—†	82	housekeeper	40	"
	M	Cook Madeline—†	86	"	92	"
	O	Gifford Isaac	132	shoeworker	40	55 Queensberry
	P	Gifford Mary—†	132	housewife	34	55 "
	S	O'Neil James J	132	foreman	35	here
	T	O'Neil Mary—†	132	housewife	36	"
	U	Taylor Mary—†	134	"	25	723 Parker
	V	Taylor Walter	134	shipper	35	723 "
	W	Bansback Hazel M—†	134	housewife	26	here
	X	Bansback Marvin	134	milkman	29	"

Hampshire Street

	A	Sullivan John J	91	teamster	53	here
	B	Brattin Mary—†	91	housewife	27	Brookline
	C	Brattin Thomas	91	teamster	33	Framingham
	D	Jenkins Robert	91	watchman	70	here
	E	Simpkins John	91	fireman	68	"
	G	Langley Catherine T—†	93	housewife	26	39 Prentiss
	H	Langley George A	93	salesman	34	39 "
	K	McDonald John	93	carpenter	55	here
	L	McDonald Margaret—†	93	housewife	45	"
	M	Kenney George D	97	mason	21	"
	N	Kenney John J	97	laborer	56	"
	O	Kenney Marie—†	97	boxmaker	22	"
	P	Kenney Thomas F	97	weaver	25	"
	R	Daley Annie—†	99	housewife	56	"
	S	Daley James	99	machinist	57	"
	T	O'Toole Celia—†	99	housewife	56	"
	U	O'Toole Peter J	99	clerk	30	"
	V	Rockford Joseph T	99	tel installer	22	20 Glenwood
	W	Geogsen Amanda—†	99	laundress	49	here
	X	Keefe Bridget—†	99	housewife	56	"
	Y	Keefe Helen E—†	99	bookbinder	21	"
	Z	Keefe Patrick J	99	laborer	62	"

Page.	Letter.	FULL NAME	Residence, April 1, 1926.	Occupation	Supposed Age.	Reported Residence, April 1, 1925. Street and Number.

Hampshire Street — Continued

	A	Keefe Thomas A	99	chauffeur	27	here
	B	Boos Henry	101	laborer	39	"
	C	Boos Mary—†	101	housewife	28	"
	D	Snyder Edward J	101	painter	49	"
	E	Snyder Margaret J—†	101	clerk	21	"
	F	Snyder Mary E—†	101	housewife	46	"
	G	Daley Lawrence J	101	foreman	33	"
	H	Daley Stella F—†	101	housewife	29	"
	K	Conaty John	103	polisher	52	"
	L	Conaty Rose E—†	103	school teacher	58	"
	M	Conaty Thomas F	103	metal worker	35	"
	N	Duncan Charles E	103	retired	70	"
	O	Reid Catherine—†	107	saleswoman	48	"
	P	Reid Eleanor—†	107	at home	37	"
	R	Reid Henry E	107	sexton	58	"
	S	Reid John	107	laborer	50	"
	T	Palmer Otis L	119	carpenter	34	Waterville Me
	U	Palmer Rilla—†	119	housewife	26	"
	V	McGeever Annie—†	119	"	40	here
	W	McGeever Patrick	119	laborer	55	"
	X	Kelly Mary—†	119	at home	65	"
	Y	McNeil James	119A	roofer	58	"
	Z	McNeil Mary—†	119A	housewife	44	"
	A	McCann Thomas	119A	laborer	61	520 Shawmut av
	B	Crowley Josephine—†	119A	housewife	40	117 Ruggles
	C	Crowley Thomas I	119A	teamster	48	117 "
	E	Arakelyan Joseph G	123	printer	47	here
	F	Arakelyan Lucy—†	123	housewife	36	"
	G	Tracey Harold	123	chauffeur	29	1 S Worthington
	H	Tracey Helen—†	123	housewife	23	42 Whitney

Johns Court

	L	Lavoie Ida—†	2	housekeeper	40	here
	M	Lavou Oscar	2	machinist	39	"
	N	Collier Alice E—†	4	housewife	32	r 15 King
	O	Collier Ernest N	4	chauffeur	35	r 15 "
	R	Daley Frederick M	8	laborer	23	here

14

Page.	Letter	FULL NAME.	Residence, April 1, 1926.	Occupation.	Supposed Age.	Reported Residence, April 1, 1925.
						Street and Number.

Johns Court—Continued

	s	Daley Mary H—†	8	housewife	49	here
	t	Daley Michael J	8	mechanic	54	"
	u	Daley Paul R	8	gasman	25	"

King Street

	v	Sweeney William J	9	lather	45	here
	w	Lynch Frances—†	9	bookkeeper	24	"
	x	Lynch Hannah—†	9	housewife	47	"
	y	Lynch Joseph	9	chauffeur	22	"
	z	Lynch Patrick	9	blacksmith	50	"
	A	Kehoe George	11	laborer	21	90 Terrace
	B	Butler Helena F—†	11	clerk	20	here
	C	Evans Bridget—†	11	car cleaner	43	"
	E	Travers Mary E—†	15	housekeeper	68	"
	F	Hayes Hattie—†	15	"	57	E Freetown
	G	Hayes Leon	15	chauffeur	23	"
	H	Kelley Nellie—†	15	housewife	38	2644 Wash'n
	K	Kelley Thomas	15	shoeworker	39	2644 "
	L	Kelley Thomas H	15	laborer	20	2644 "
	N	Austin Annie—†	18	housekeeper	36	1126 Tremont
	O	Murrey Bridget—†	18	housewife	40	here
	P	Murrey John	18	carpenter	44	"
	R	Carey Joseph	18	trackman	34	"
	s	Carey Theresa—†	18	housewife	31	"
	v	Cluney Henry E	20	fireman	23	132 London
	w	Cluney Margaret—†	20	housewife	22	132 "
	x	Martin Ellen—†	20	"	33	1 Davis pl
	y	Martin Herbert	20	oiler	43	1 "
	z	Dunfey Evelyn—†	24	boxmaker	24	here
	A	Dunfey Grace—†	24	stenographer	21	"
	B	Dunfey James	24	fireman	52	"
	C	Dunfey Sarah—†	24	housekeeper	42	"
	D	Mitchell John J	26	storekeeper	63	1806 Wash'n
	E	O'Connor Ethel—†	28	laundress	33	Phila Pa
	F	Bader Annie—†	28	housekeeper	55	7 Crossin pl
	G	Hartford Helen F—†	28	housewife	30	here
	H	Hartford William T	28	trainman	31	"
	K	Wilson Fred	31	laborer	41	Milton

Page	Letter	Full Name.	Residence, April 1, 1926	Occupation.	Supposed Age.	Reported Residence, April 1, 1925. Street and Number.

King Street — Continued

	L	Daley James P	31	teamster	27	2 Motley
	M	Daley William F	31	chauffeur	28	2 "
	N	Luppold Mary E—†	31	housekeeper	47	here
	P	Morrow Mary M—†	33	"	41	"
	R	Morrow Robert R	33	porter	42	"

King Terrace

	U	Lee Alexander	1	steamfitter	35	Cambridge
	V	Walsh Helen—†	1	housewife	23	here
	W	Walsh Joseph P	1	molder	31	"
	X	Byrne Helen—†	1	housekeeper	52	"
	Y	Byrne James	1	molder	21	"
	Z	Lawrence Margaret—†	3	bookkeeper	21	"
	A	Murrey John J	3	polisher	40	"
	B	Murrey William T	3	machinist	30	"
	C	Gleason Arthur	3	laborer	20	"
	D	Gleason Ethel W—†	3	housekeeper	48	"
	L	Bennet Annie—†	7	"	64	76 Weston
	M	Perrigo Mabel—†	7	clerk	27	7 Elmwood pl
	N	Goldsmith Annie—†	9	shoeworker	45	here
	O	Blaney John	9	teamster	42	"
	P	Blaney Rosetta †	9	housekeeper	38	"
	R	Bagwell Nora—†	9	"	43	"
	S	Bagwell Patrick	9	clerk	55	"

Linden Park Street

	T	Hardiman Catherine—†	121	housewife	52	3238 Wash'n
	U	Hardiman John M	121	laborer	64	3238 "
	V	Hardiman Martin F	121	"	24	3238 "
	W	Corcoran Helen—†	121	housewife	25	here
	X	Corcoran John	121	laborer	28	"
	Y	Manning George E	125	steamfitter	52	"

Leutman Place

z	Hartnett Daniel F	3	retired	76	here
A	Hulbert Josephine A—†	3	housewife	37	"
B	Hulbert Roy J	3	laborer	36	"
c	Purcell Susan M—†	5	clerk	65	"
D	Lamond Catherine M—†	7	secretary	34	"
E	Lamond George	7	shipper	28	"
F	Lamond Jennie—†	7	clerk	29	"

Mindoro Street

G	Hacunda James	16	steamfitter	33	here
H	Hacunda Mary—†	16	housewife	67	"
K	Hacunda Stephen	16	fireman	62	"
L	Hacunda Stephen, jr	16	laborer	38	"
N	Miller Bridget—†	18	housewife	41	"
o	Miller Charles	18	printer	40	"
P	Miller William	18	molder	34	"
R	Huber Frank	21	laborer	34	"
s	Huber George G	21	roofer	28	"
T	Huber John	21	laborer	28	"
U	Huber William	21	chauffeur	32	"
v	Nesbitt Catherine—†	21	housewife	37	"
w	Nesbitt William J	21	laborer	34	"
X	Havey John L	22	"	41	"
Y	Havey Mary E—†	22	housewife	45	"
z	Wolf Rose—†	22	housekeeper	60	"
c	Brehm Joseph	42	shipper	44	"
D	Brehm Mary—†	42	housewife	42	"
E	Comeau Bridget—†	42	housekeeper	41	"

Parker Street

F	Luby Josephine E—†	586	housewife	27	here
G	Luby Walter R	586	expressman	32	"
H	Moore May A—†	586	housewife	49	"
K	Moore Walter E	586	fireman	24	"

9—12

Page.	Letter.	FULL NAME.	Residence, April 1, 1926.	Occupation.	Supposed Age.	Reported Residence, April 1, 1925. Street and Number.

Parker Street—Continued

L	Gould Rose —†	588	laundress	24	here
M	Lenhardt Charles H	588	chauffeur	53	"
N	Lenhardt John	588	laborer	21	"
O	Lenhardt Mary — †	588	housewife	53	"
R	Caldwell Catherine—†	596	"	55	"
S	Caldwell Harry	596	shoeworker	25	"
T	Caldwell Joseph	596	laborer	52	"
U	Caldwell Mary—†	596	housekeeper	22	"
V	O'Connell Bridget—†	596	housewife	43	"
W	O'Connell Catherine—†	596	clerk	20	"
X	O'Connell John J	596	chauffeur	22	"
Y	O'Connell Joseph	596	laborer	50	"
Z	Rice Christopher	596	"	26	"
A	Cleary John	596	shoeworker	22	"
B	Hickey Catherine —†	596	cashier	22	"
C	Manning Nora —†	596	housewife	48	"
D	Hayes Anna—†	598	"	48	"
E	Hayes John	598	chauffeur	49	"
G	O'Rourke Charles	598	laborer	34	"
H	O'Rourke James	598	"	60	"
K	O'Rourke James	598	street cleaner	29	"
L	O'Rourke Margaret —†	598	stitcher	24	"
M	O'Rourke Mary —†	598	housekeeper	36	"
O	Wagner Catherine —†	604	boxmaker	20	"
P	Wagner Frederick W	604	fireman	48	"
R	Wagner Mary E —†	604	housewife	44	"
S	Farrell Helen L —†	604	shoeworker	24	"
T	Farrell John H	604	chauffeur	22	"
U	Farrell Margret T—†	604	housewife	55	"
V	Farrell Mathew	604	clerk	62	"
W	Quinn Mary B—†	604	housewife	25	"
Y	Looney Cornelius J	608	buffer	48	"
Z	Looney John J	608	storekeeper	50	"
A	Looney Mary C—†	608	housekeeper	37	"
C	Apostle Naom	612	pedler	52	"
D	Harris Joan —†	614	housewife	42	"
G	Gill Annie †	650	"	40	"
H	Gill John	650	waiter	34	"
K	McCue Margaret —†	650	housewife	31	5 Salvisberg av
M	Adams John	654	cook	34	here
N	Adams Theodore	654	retired	58	"

Page.	Letter.	FULL NAME.	Residence, April 1, 1926.	Occupation.	Supposed Age.	Reported Residence, April 1, 1925.
						Street and Number.

Parker Street—Continued

o	Dillon Edward F	668	meatcutter	35	here
p	McFarland Edward D	668	car cleaner	40	"
r	Curley Thomas	668	chauffeur	24	"
s	Dillon John J	668	laborer	30	"
t	Dillon Margret M—†	668	tel operator	38	"
u	Dillon William T	668	chauffeur	27	"
v	Jennings Ellen—†	668	housekeeper	53	"
w	Clinton Catherine—†	668	bookkeeper	27	"
x	Clinton John	668	salesman	38	"
y	Clinton Margret—†	668	housewife	65	"
z	Carrigg Catherine—†	670	housekeeper	52	"
a	Carrigg Michael	670	stonecutter	57	"
b	McDonald George J	670	plumber	34	Cambridge
c	McDonald Leo J	670	clerk	27	here
d	McDonald Lulu—†	670	housewife	22	Cambridge
e	McDonald Mary—†	670	"	56	here
f	McDonald Patrick J	670	janitor	58	"
g	Siefert Emma—†	670	housekeeper	57	"
h	Siefert Gustave	670	storekeeper	65	"
k	Leonard Delia A—†	676	clerk	26	"
l	Leonard Martin J	676	"	42	"
m	Gaffney Catherine—†	676	housewife	43	"
n	Gaffney Henry	676	clerk	45	"
o	Gaffney Mary A—†	676	housekeeper	72	"
p	Conlon Ellen—†	680	housewife	60	"
r	Conlon Mary M—†	680	saleswoman	35	"
s	Loescher Adolph	680	mechanic	35	"
t	Loescher Clara—†	680	clerk	31	"
u	Crowe Catherine A—†	680	housekeeper	70	702 Parker
v	Niland Joseph P	680	latherer	49	702 "
w	Niland Marie C—†	680	bookkeeper	22	702 "
x	Niland Mary A—†	680	housewife	45	702 "
y	Green Mary—†	682	housekeeper	43	here
z	Norton Annie L—†	682	housewife	55	"
a	Norton Patrick	682	teamster	54	"
b	Sacco Jennie—†	684	housewife	46	"
c	Sacco John	684	barber	52	"
d	Kelley Mary—†	686	housekeeper	55	"
e	Kelly Mary—†	686	housewife	31	"
f	Kelley Michael	686	foreman	55	"
g	Kelley Michael, jr	686	chauffeur	30	"

19

Page.	Letter.	Full Name.	Residence, April 1, 1926.	Occupation.	Supposed Age.	Reported Residence, April 1, 1925. Street and Number.

Parker Street—Continued

	H	Putnam Eva—†	688	housewife	53	here
	K	Putnam Peter	688	carpetmaker	68	"
	M	Lyons Walter J	692	chauffeur	21	"
	N	Welch Catherine—†	692	housekeeper	41	"

Prentiss Street

	S	Walsh Mary—†	5	housewife	38	here
	T	Walsh William	5	mechanic	40	"
	U	Callan Margaret—†	6	housewife	64	"
	V	Callan Mary—†	6	"	62	36 Columbia rd
	W	McKinnan Catherine B—†	6	houseworker	33	Nova Scotia
	X	Anderson Annie—†	6	housewife	63	here
	Y	Anderson Edward B	6	chauffeur	22	41 Linden Park
	Z	Anderson Herbert A	6	teamster	32	Fitchburg
	A	Vassily Jennie—†	6	housewife	40	41 Linden Park
	B	Vassily William G	6	baker	52	here
	C	O'Malley James	6	laborer	40	Ireland
	D	O'Malley John	6	"	38	here
	E	O'Malley Mary T—†	6	housewife	36	"
	F	Carlitros Bessie—†	6	"	36	8 Motley
	G	Cocola Brandas J	6	retired	36	8 "
	H	Devlin Mary A—†	6	housewife	36	Ayer
	K	Devlin Michael	6	salesman	35	"
	L	Burns Lauvina—†	6	housewife	50	145 Silver
	M	Joaquin Francis	6	chauffeur	35	145 "
	N	Caparell Helen—†	6	housewife	32	here
	O	Caparell Sarados	6	laborer	55	"
	R	Parker Annie—†	6	housewife	48	123 Pembroke
	S	Parker Chester J	6	fireman	38	123 "
	T	Burns John	6	engineer	49	3 Nason pl
	U	Burns Mary A—†	6	housewife	49	3 "
	W	Norton Martha P—†	9	"	50	1344½ Tremont
	X	Carey Carl R	9	chauffeur	29	1344½ "
	Y	Tomberg Emily L—†	9	housewife	31	1326 "
	Z	Tomberg Henry E	9	chauffeur	33	1326 "
	D	Merriam Bruce E	31	"	22	here

Page	Letter	FULL NAME.	Residence, April 1, 1926.	Occupation.	Supposed Age.	Reported Residence, April 1, 1925. Street and Number.

Prentiss Street—Continued

	Letter	FULL NAME.	Res.	Occupation.	Age	Reported Residence
	E	Merriam Mabel J—†	31	housewife	22	here
	F	Tangney Annie E—†	31	"	54	"
	G	Tangney Patrick E	31	retired	64	"
	H	Brodrick Margaret—†	31	factory worker	38	"
	K	Reddish Catherine—†	31	laundry worker	40	"
	L	O'Flaherty Bridget—†	33	housewife	26	"
	M	O'Flaherty Edward	33	laborer	29	"
	N	Kelley Catherine—†	33	housewife	65	"
	O	Kelley James H	33	shoeworker	23	"
	P	Kelley Robert E	33	laborer	38	"
	R	Kelley Catherine L—†	33	housewife	32	"
	S	Kelley Patrick G	33	teamster	36	"
	U	Pherson Albert L	37	clerk	26	Lexington
	V	Pherson Ethel J—†	37	housewife	26	"
	W	Lucke Lewis	37	retired	66	here
	X	Lucke Lewis H	37	laborer	31	"
	Y	Lucke Minnie D—†	37	housewife	65	"
	Z	Murphy Elizabeth—†	37	houseworker	40	"
	A	Hines Daniel D	37	clerk	45	"
	B	Hines Rose E—†	37	housewife	38	"
	C	McGrath Nora L—†	39	"	70	"
	D	Maguire John J	39	laborer	38	1199 Tremont
	E	O'Rourke James P	39	"	48	here
	H	Schroth Anthony J	45	painter	48	"
	K	Schroth George A	45	"	38	"
	L	Schroth Joseph C	45	laborer	43	"
	M	Schroth Josephine—†	45	housewife	75	"
	N	Linderman John F	45	printer	52	"
	O	Linderman Josephine—†	45	housewife	42	"
	P	Wanders Annie E—†	47	"	64	"
	R	Wanders Florence T—†	47	clerk	44	"
	S	Gogan Martha G—†	47	housewife	43	"
	U	Connelly Joseph F	49	bottler	38	"
	V	Connelly Margaret—†	49	housewife	70	"
	W	Connelly Margaret E—†	49	boxmaker	30	"
	B	Rohner Mary M—†	65	housewife	70	"
	C	Stockman Elizabeth—†	65	"	73	"
	D	Kaps Christopher	65	mason	63	"
	E	Kaps Emma—†	65	housewife	50	"
	G	Brooks Bridget J—†	66	"	22	"
	H	Brooks Matthew T	66	laborer	25	"

Page.	Letter.	FULL NAME.	Residence, April 1, 1926.	Occupation.	Supposed Age.	Reported Residence, April 1, 1925. Street and Number.

Prentiss Street—Continued

	K	Edwards Anna G—†	66	housewife	22	5 Millmont
	M	Liebert Bertha—†	71	housekeeper	60	here
	N	Pretigen Anna—†	71	factory worker	26	10 Normandy

Roxbury Street

	A	Barter Edward T	221	painter	34	here
	B	Cummings Dorothy A—†	221	housekeeper	25	"
	C	Schlums George F	223	machinist	22	"
	D	Schlums Ida—†	223	stenographer	26	"
	E	Schlums Ida A—†	223	housekeeper	63	"
	F	Schlums Theodore	223	machinist	28	"
	G	Stewart Corilla E—†	223	tag writer	28	254 Ruggles
	H	Stewart Duncan J	223	meatcutter	30	254 "
	K	Stewart Mary A—†	223	housewife	48	254 "
	L	Stewart Neil A	223	watchman	50	254 "
	M	Wright Duncan M	223	laborer	27	here
	N	Wright Jennie J—†	223	bookkeeper	26	"
	O	Wright Joseph	223	fireman	60	"
	P	Wright Mary A—†	223	housewife	61	"
	R	Wright Robert	223	shoeworker	21	"
	S	Miller Anna M—†	227	housewife	56	"
	T	Miller Anna M—†	227	saleswoman	23	"
	U	Miller Charles	227	butcher	60	"
	V	Miller William A	227	salesman	25	"
	W	Golden Marion A	227	operator	27	20 Williams
	X	Rogers Alice—†	227	houseworker	46	20 "
	Z	Linehan John T	227	mechanic	53	here
	A	Linehan Mary E—†	227	operator	62	"
	B	Linehan Stecia—†	227	"	62	"
	C	Pitman Harriet E—†	227	"	60	"
	D	Ryan George L	227	clerk	45	"
	F	Barrell Margaret—†	227	operator	30	"
	G	Barrell Patrick	227	blacksmith	40	"
	L	Sheehan Catheribe A—†	245	housewife	43	"
	M	Sheehan Grace A—†	245	tel operator	20	"
	N	Sheehan John J	245	laborer	43	"
	O	Murphy Bessie—†	245	housewife	30	1871 Com av
	P	Murphy John D	245	laborer	34	130 Emerald
	R	Briggs Cecelia M—†	245½	housewife	35	here

Roxbury Street—Continued

s	Briggs Fredrick	245½	leatherworker	35	here
t	Marsh Emily W—†	247	housekeeper	75	"
u	Morrison Evelyn—†	247	stenographer	35	"
v	Cripp George H	247	retired	81	"
w	Cripp Joseph F	247	foreman	42	"
x	Donovan Michael	249	retired	82	"
y	Donovan Patrick J	249	machinist	50	"
z	Donovan William F	249	plumber	48	"
a	Duggan Mary E—†	249	housekeeper	43	"
b	Duggan Mary J—†	249	clerk	20	"
c	MacLellan Alfred J	249	foreman	48	"
d	MacLellan Mary E—†	249	housewife	36	"
e	Gerety John J	251	laborer	56	"
f	Keane Mary A—†	251	housekeeper	44	"
g	Magrath Catherine—†	251	houseworker	54	"
h	Clark James H	251	fireman	53	"
k	Clark Mary G—†	251	housewife	40	"
n	Carnes Annie F—†	259	compositor	35	"
o	Carnes Bridget M—†	259	housekeeper	75	"
p	Clougherty Mary A—†	261	housewife	41	"
r	Clougherty Michael	261	laborer	47	"
s	Patten Thomas E	261	"	36	"
t	Melling Joseph P	263	painter	34	"
u	Melling Margaret G—†	263	housekeeper	52	"
v	Marshall Cecelia—†	265	housewife	42	"
w	Marshall Cornelius F	265	optician	22	"
x	Marshall John P	265	machinist	23	"
y	Marshall Thomas F	265	blacksmith	48	"
z	Rasmussen Anna M—†	267	housewife	30	"
a	Rasmussan Arthur B	267	motorman	30	"
b	Power Elizabeth—†	269	housewife	21	"
c	Power Joseph F	269	shoecutter	36	"
d	Power Phillip	269	watchman	41	"
e	Toole Cora J—†	271	seamstress	44	"
f	Toole George H	271	clerk	22	"
h	McInnis John A	275	engineer	44	34 Lambert
k	McInnis Mary—†	275	housewife	24	34 "
l	Gibson Kathleen—†	275	stenographer	25	here
m	Markey Prescilla—†	275	bookkeeper	34	"
n	Price Henry E	275	engineer	37	"
o	Price Mary—†	275	housewife	42	"

23

Roxbury Street—Continued

R	Josselyn George	277	stock clerk	35	here	
S	Keogh Mary H—†	277	housewife	33	"	
T	Keogh William J	277	laborer	38	"	
V	Mosig Adolph E	277	watchman	60	"	
W	Mosig Annie—†	277	housewife	37	"	
X	Mackay Mary C—†	279	"	55	137 Eliot sq	
Y	Mackay Rufus	279	painter	65	137 "	
Z	Parad Gertrude—†	279	housewife	31	here	
A	Parad Maurice	279	storekeeper	38	"	
C	Claus August	285	butcher	35	"	
D	Claus Emma J—†	285	housewife	33	"	
E	Schmid Sophie—†	285	housemaid	67	"	
F	Vey Frida—†	285	at home	65	"	
G	Vey Otto	285	chauffeur	25	"	
K	Heumann Albert J	311	photographer	26	"	
L	Heumann Amelia M—†	311	stenographer	21	"	
M	Heumann Edward F	311	clerk	28	"	
N	Heumann Minnie—†	311	housewife	50	"	
O	Heumann Walter H	311	chauffeur	25	"	
P	Hasselman Dorothy—†	311	clerk	26	"	
R	Hasselman Frederick	311	cigarmaker	66	"	
S	Hasselman Louis	311	teamster	37	"	
T	Hasselman Margaret—†	311	housewife	65	"	
U	Francis Catherine—†	313	"	62	"	
V	Francis Edward	313	shoeworker	31	"	
W	Clark Joseph	313	clerk	52	"	
X	Clark Mary—†	313	housewife	49	"	
Y	Fallon John	313	laborer	45	"	
B	Flanagan Ellen —†	317	housewife	68	"	
C	Flanagan John	317	laborer	68	"	
D	St John Alice—†	317	housewife	45	"	
E	St John Arthur	317	painter	43	"	
F	Filisen Hannah—†	317	housewife	44	23 Anita ter	
F¹	Filisen John F	317	carpenter	41	23 "	

Station Street

N	Trainor Harriet J—†	17	housewife	23	here	
O	Trainor Owen J	17	laborer	25	"	
P	Kunz Lewis J	17	stableman	55	1916 Col av	

Page	Letter	Full Name.	Residence, April 1, 1926.	Occupation.	Supposed Age.	Reported Residence, April 1, 1925. Street and Number.

Station Street—Continued

R	Kunz Mary—†	17	housewife	48	1916 Col av
U	Collins Ellen—†	25	housekeeper	55	here
V	Trainor Helen—†	25	"	55	"
W	Brehm Arthur A	25	porter	53	"
X	Brehm Rose—†	25	housewife	43	"
Y	Cosby Mary—†	25	housekeeper	59	"
A	Daniels Mary M—†	25	housewife	50	"
B	Daniels William J	25	painter	59	"
C	Webber Barbara—†	25	housewife	61	"
D	Webber Mary—†	25	shoeworker	30	"
E	Duffy Agnes—†	25	packer	30	1104 Col av
F	Hanahan Beatrice—†	25	"	45	1104 "
G	Newberger Mary—†	25	"	60	here
K	Newton Ellen—†	27	housewife	61	"
L	Newton John J	27	laborer	65	"
M	Newton William	27	"	36	"
N	Mullen Elizabeth—†	27	housewife	28	"
O	Mullen James L	27	laborer	38	"
P	Frezen Henry	27	"	65	"
R	McLean Andrew	29	gardener	63	20 Terrace
S	McLean Christena—†	29	housewife	55	20 "
U	Howard Sarana—†	29	laundress	63	here
V	Fossman Harold O	29	shoeworker	25	88 Heath
W	McLaughlin Charles	29	cook	55	New York
X	Neas Frederick J	29	retired	78	1241 Col av
Y	Neas Helen—†	29	housekeeper	72	1241 "
E	Gilmore Albert C	70	laborer	22	613 "
F	Gilmore Helen—†	70	housewife	20	278 Bowdoin
G	Cashman Catherine—†	70	"	40	here
H	Taylor Elizabeth—†	70	"	40	Canada
K	Taylor Robert G	70	laborer	53	"
L	Kowl Katherine—†	70	waitress	28	here
M	Ganis Elsie—†	70	housekeeper	28	"
N	Murphy John	70	laborer	68	"
O	Flanagan Clara—†	72	housewife	48	"
P	Flanagan George A	72	laborer	48	"
R	Calapia Leo	72	barber	49	135 Dorr
S	Calapia Mary—†	72	housewife	44	135 "

Texas Street

U	DeCoste Arthur	7	mechanic	27	Nova Scotia
V	DeCoste Gertrude—†	7	housewife	26	"
W	Sutcliffe John	7	barber	64	here
X	Sutcliffe Mary—†	7	clerk	32	"
Y	Corbett Clara—†	7	housewife	36	"
Z	Corbett Levi	7	teamster	59	"
A	O'Brien Bessie—†	7	housewife	52	"
B	O'Brien John	7	steamfitter	28	"
C	O'Brien Micheal	7	teamster	38	"
D	Sexton Mary—†	7	housekeeper	50	"
E	Campbell Margaret—†	7	cook	70	"
F	Carey Bridget—†	7	domestic	55	"
G	Connelly Josephine—†	16	housewife	34	Wakefield
H	Connelly Timothy	16	chauffeur	38	"
K	Lundy Patrick	16	electrician	32	here
L	Lundy Rose—†	16	clerk	23	"
O	Sadowski Catherine A—†	16	housewife	28	4 Nason pl
P	Sadowski Stephen	16	laborer	27	4 "

Tremont Street

U	Lamoretti Clotilde—†	1216	storekeeper	43	here
V	McDonald Mary—†	1216	housekeeper	73	"
W	McDonald Roderick	1216	clerk	40	"
X	Kreamer Frank	1218	laborer	35	"
Y	Kreamer Nellie—†	1218	housekeeper	46	"
Z	Hines Patrick	1218	laborer	50	"
F	Agnew George	1228	glazier	58	"
G	Agnew Jane M—†	1228	housewife	56	"
K	Egan Helen—†	1230	housekeeper	30	"
L	Heinrick Minnie—†	1230	"	68	"
M	Heinrick Peter C	1230	chauffeur	33	"
O	Parker Mary J—† 2d rear	1232	housewife	35	12 Norwich
P	Parker William F "	1232	pianomover	37	12 "
W	Lewis Nellie—†	1238A	housekeeper	49	here
X	Lewis William H	1238A	teamster	26	"
Y	Sherman Grace—†	1238A	stitcher	27	"
Z	Webber Evelyn S—†	1238A	"	28	"
A	Webber Henry E	1238A	painter	35	"

Page.	Letter.	FULL NAME.	Residence, April 1, 1926.	Occupation.	Supposed Age.	Reported Residence, April 1, 1925. Street and Number.

Tremont Street—Continued

	B	Bourget Alfred	1238A	carpenter	40	532 Mass av
	C	Bourget Annie—†	1238A	housewife	36	532 "
	D	Durkin Annie J—†	1240	"	50	here
	E	Durkin James	1240	laborer	51	"
	F	Durkin Winifred—†	1240	shoeworker	21	"
	G	Fishman Henry	1240	storekeeper	36	"
	H	Fishman Mary—†	1240	housekeeper	36	"
	M	Saef Gertrude—†	1242A	housewife	37	"
	N	Saef Leon	1242A	storekeeper	45	"
	P	McCarthy David rear	1246	junk collector	56	"
	R	McCarthy Julia—† "	1246	at home	56	"
	S	Giblin James	1248½	laborer	64	"
	T	Giblin James J	1248½	machinist	21	"
	U	Giblin Mary—†	1248½	housewife	55	"
	V	Giblin Sarah E—†	1248½	accountant	25	"
	W	McGeever Francis H	1248½	policeman	29	"
	X	McGeever Helen L—†	1248½	housewife	26	"
	Y	Feeley Bridget—†	1248½	"	36	84 Conant
	Z	Feeley Charles	1248½	plasterer	34	84 "
	A	Murphy Mary A—†	1250	housekeeper	47	here
	B	Dolan Katherine—†	1250	clerk	24	"
	C	McGuinness Annie—†	1250	"	28	"
	D	McGuinness George W	1250	fireman	27	"
	E	Mahoney Ellen F—†	1250	housekeeper	75	"
	F	Mahoney Michael F	1250	fireman	39	"
	H	Perkins Harold	1252	chauffeur	33	"
	K	Perkins Helena E—†	1252	housewife	22	"
	L	Cullati Frank	1252	laborer	39	"
	M	Cullati Louise—†	1252	housewife	36	"
	N	Cherry John T	1252	laborer	25	38 St Francis de Sales
	O	Cherry Nora—†	1252	housewife	24	38 "
	P	DePrizio John	1252	laborer	40	here
	R	DePrizio Theresa—†	1252	housewife	40	"
	S	Campbell Charles	1252	manager	21	"
	V	Benro Marie—†	1263	housewife	50	"
	W	Carlino Adeline—†	1263	"	61	"
	X	Carlino Angelo	1263	painter	21	"
	Y	Carlino Frank S	1263	laborer	23	"
	Z	Prochillo Michal	1263	"	25	"
	Z¹	West Herbert	1263	painter	23	34 Vine
	B	Cohen Minnie—†	1265	housewife	40	here

27

Tremont Street—Continued

Letter	Full Name	Residence	Occupation	Age	Reported Residence
C	Shamban Ethel—†	1265	housewife	40	here
F	Brundidge Alberta—†	1267	housekeeper	28	Cambridge
G	Camburn Julia—†	1267	waitress	29	"
H	Waldmeyer Charles D	1267	chauffeur	33	27 Sarsfield
K	Waldmeyer Hazel—†	1267	housewife	28	27 "
L	Bernasco Ernesto	1267	laborer	41	here
M	Maffiali Eugene	1267	clerk	29	"
N	Tomsini Mary—†	1267	housewife	26	"
O	Tomsini Vincent A	1267	manufacturer	32	"
P	Gordon Annie—†	1267	housewife	45	"
R	Gordon Esther—†	1267	clerk	42	"
S	Gordon Miriam—†	1267	"	49	"
T	Gordon Raphael	1267	cutter	54	"
U	Gordon Sarah--†	1267	clerk	47	"
X	Ross Abram	1273	teamster	46	"
Y	Ross Ida—†	1273	housewife	44	"
Z	Smith Jessie—†	1273	dressmaker	32	"
A	Gimoukous Arthur	1273	shoemaker	31	"
B	Gimoukous Peter	1273	"	31	"
C	Sales Mary—†	1273	housewife	50	90 E Newton
D	Sales William	1273	laborer	45	90 "
K	Schoen Jacob	1275A	"	56	here
L	Schoen John	1275A	chauffeur	28	"
M	Schoen Mary—†	1275A	housewife	55	"
O	Banos Frank	1275A	laborer	32	"
P	Doolin Anna—†	1275A	housewife	33	52 Whittier
R	Doolin Charles	1275A	teamster	35	52 "
S	Parry Nicholas	1275A	merchant	28	here
T	Harris Annie—†	1276	housekeeper	36	"
X	Dolan Peter F	rear 1280	mechanic	49	"
Y	Gorman Mary A—†	" 1280	housewife	49	"
Z	Gorman Michael	" 1280	paver	57	"
A	Gorman Michael H, jr	" 1280	chauffeur	24	"
B	Gorman Peter F	" 1280	"	22	"
C	Kelley Martin J	" 1280	"	37	"
D	McCusker Mathew	" 1280	teamster	52	"
R	Minsk Arthur	" 1293	clerk	26	"
S	Minsk Harry	" 1293	storekeeper	58	"
T	Minsk Zepara—†	" 1293	housewife	51	"
U	Moriarty Johana-†	" 1293	"	24	Scotland
V	Moriarty Timothy	" 1293	fireman	29	"

Tremont Street—Continued

Letter	FULL NAME	Residence April 1, 1926	Occupation	Supposed Age	Reported Residence April 1, 1925
w	Dixfield Margaret—† rear	1293	housekeeper	70	Scotland
y	McFadden Sadie—† "	1297	housewife	33	here
z	Reddish Edward J "	1297	storekeeper	40	"
a	Reddish Mary E—† "	1297	housewife	35	"
b	Wilbur Vernon "	1297	roofer	26	Canada
c	Simoni Joseph "	1297	barber	35	here
f	Hardy Charles	1301	shoeworker	55	"
g	Hardy Elizabeth—†	1301	housewife	56	"
h	Hardy Theresa—†	1301	housekeeper	29	"
k	Eserin Robert	1301	carpenter	36	"
l	Grubi Betty—†	1301	housewife	32	"
m	Grubi Hans	1301	brewer	39	"
p	McFadden Catherine—†	1309	housekeeper	63	"
r	McFadden John	1309	electrician	34	"
s	Geagen Marion—†	1309	candyworker	24	70 Palmer
t	LeMann Dorothy—†	1309	housekeeper	28	here
u	Dawson George A	1309	porter	31	"
v	Dawson Mary A—†	1309	housewife	43	"
w	O'Neil John M	1309	teamster	41	"
x	Croke Catherine—†	1309	housewife	33	"
y	Croke John F	1309	machinist	39	"
z	Delaney Mary A—†	1309	operator	39	"
a	McLeod Effie—†	1309	housewife	40	Nova Scotia
b	MacLeod John	1309	laborer	51	"
c	MacLeod Kenneth	1309	"	22	Everett
d	Dexter Benjamin T	1309	stockman	42	here
e	Dexter Frances L—†	1309	housewife	38	"
f	Salt Walter A	1309	porter	65	"
g	Fay Nora—†	1309	housewife	52	"
h	Fay Peter F	1309	clerk	61	"
k	White Agnes M—†	1309	"	28	"
l	White Christiana—†	1309	housewife	51	"
m	White Nicholas	1309	cook	71	"
n	Barrett Alice—†	1309	housewife	57	"
o	Barrett William H	1309	conductor	64	"
x	Cook Edith—†	1324	housewife	33	"
y	Cook William	1324	roofer	27	"
z	Glennon Della—†	1324	housekeeper	40	Cambridge
a	Glennon Margaret—†	1324	"	42	"
b	Lowe Eileen—†	1324	housewife	22	23 E Springfield
c	Lowe Emory	1324	clerk	23	23 "

Page.	Letter.	FULL NAME.	Residence, April 1, 1926.	Occupation.	Supposed Age.	Reported Residence, April 1, 1925. Street and Number.

Tremont Street—Continued

G	Goodman Morris	1326	real estate	38	here
H	Goodman Rose—†	1326	housewife	37	"
K	Callahan Dasiy A—†	1326	"	42	23 E Springfield
L	Callahan Danial J	1326	inspector	50	23 "
U	Perrigo Ida—†	1342	housewife	34	here
V	Perrigo Merrill	1342	painter	32	"
X	Brooks Jennie—†	1344½	nurse	56	31 Vernon
Y	Brooks Robert	1344½	laborer	26	31 "
Z	Kelley Hugh L	1344½	teamster	50	134 "
A	Kelley John J	1344½	clerk	23	134 "
B	Kelley Mary—†	1344½	housewife	50	134 "
D	McCarthy Elizabeth—†	1346½	millworker	35	here
Y	LaFreniere Joseph	1429	storekeeper	79	"
Z	Vandolen Corine—†	1429	housewife	45	"
A	Vandolen William	1429	clerk	47	"
B	Turvaud Nicholini—†	1429	housewife	44	"
C	Turvaud Salvatore	1429	woodfinisher	46	"
G	Chin George	1437	laundryman	32	"
K	Estrange Joseph P	1441	clerk	26	"
L	McIntyre James	1441	teamster	59	"
M	McIntyre Margaret—†	1441	bookkeeper	22	"
N	McIntyre Mary J—†	1441	housekeeper	27	"
O	McIsaac Angus	1441	carpenter	54	"
P	McIsaac Flora—†	1441	housewife	52	"
R	McIsaac Sadie—†	1441	housekeeper	22	"
V	Edwards John T	1445	shoeworker	30	"
W	Water Mary—†	1445	housewife	75	"
X	Ledden Catherine—†	1445	cook	40	"
Y	Shew Hannah—†	1445	housekeeper	41	"
Z	Snyder Constance—†	1445	"	65	"
A	Stegmaier Caroline—†	1445	"	74	"

Vernon Street

C	Meyer Dorothy—†	186	housewife	75	here
D	Meyer Henry	186	cigarmaker	74	"
E	McCall Lillian—†	186	housewife	42	"
F	McCall Louis	186	chauffeur	43	"
G	Ostman Andrew	190	painter	62	"
H	Murray Margaret F—†	190	housewife	37	1187 Tremont

30

	Letter.	FULL NAME.	Residence, April 1, 1926.	Occupation.	Supposed Age.	Reported Residence, April 1, 1925. Street and Number.

Vernon · Street—Continued

	K	Murray Peter F	190	laborer	41	1187 Tremont
	L	Donahue Joseph	192	"	50	here
	M	Bernard Grace—†	192	laundress	48	"
	N	Francis Romeo	192	chef	62	"
	O	Grace Patrick	192	shoemaker	35	"
	S	Pistachio Josephine—†	r 196	housewife	29	"
	T	Pistachio Pasquale	" 196	insurance agent	29	"
	U	Brushingham James	" 196	laborer	38	111 Queensberry
	V	Brushingham Mary E-†	" 196	housewife	44	111 "
	W	Caruso Angelo	" 196	barber	64	here
	X	Caruso Domonico—†	" 196	housewife	63	"
	Y	Brushingham Harry	198	superintendent	35	Brookline
	Z	Brushingham Marion—†	198	housewife	26	"
	A	Caruso Angelena—†	198	"	23	here
	B	Caruso Rosario	198	barber	27	"
	C	Haffenden Ivan	200	salesman	35	"
	D	Haffenden Unice—†	200	housewife	33	"
	E	Binns Nilda—†	200	"	25	Baltimore Md
	F	Binns Nurrin	200	cook	27	"
	H	Morrow Joseph	204	weaver	27	here
	K	Morrow Martha—†	204	factory worker	22	"
	L	Morrow Nora—†	204	housewife	60	"
	M	Morrow William	204	teamster	62	"
	N	Buoy Clyde	204	machinist	36	"
	O	Buoy Emma—†	204	housewife	32	"

Ward Street

	P	Barrows Albert E	2	molder	27	133 Roxbury
	R	Barrows Annie F—†	2	housewife	27	133 "
	S	Barrows Mary A—†	2	housekeeper	67	133 "
	T	Kastipis Eva—†	2	housewife	40	Connecticut
	U	Kastipis George	2	laborer	55	"
	V	Doherty Bernard	6	teamster	45	here
	W	Doherty Elizabeth—†	6	housewife	35	"
	X	Culnan Anna—†	6	clerk	28	"
	Y	Culnan Edward	6	chauffeur	25	"
	Z	Schlums Mary—†	6	housekeeper	47	"
	A	Keough Catherine—†	6	"	72	"
	B	Keough Timothy	6	shoeworker	37	"

Page.	Letter.	FULL NAME.	Residence, April 1, 1926.	Occupation.	Supposed Age.	Reported Residence, April 1, 1925. Street and Number.

Ward Street—Continued

c	Nolan Anna T—†	8	housekeeper	25	here
d	Nolan Frank J	8	chauffeur	28	"
e	Ivanic Theresa—†	8	housewife	43	"
f	Gately Bernard F	8	lather	37	"
g	Lynch Annie—†	8	cleaner	41	"
h	Spall George	16	painter	52	91 Hampshire
k	Pupek Alex	16	polisher	37	here
l	Pupek Blanche—†	16	housewife	37	"
m	McDonald Gertrude—†	20	"	21	"
n	McDonald Thomas	20	garage man	26	"
o	Nolan James W	20	mailer	34	"
p	Nolan Margaret E—†	20	housewife	54	"
r	Nolan Mary R—†	20	bookbinder	23	"
s	Allgaier Anna J—†	24	housewife	54	"
t	Allgaier Charles L	24	shipper	50	"
u	Allgaier John J	24	garageman	23	"
v	Hartman John J	24	watchman	64	"
w	Perz Dora—†	24	maid	57	"
x	Woods John	24	stableman	59	"
y	Woods Margaret—†	24	housewife	45	"
z	Traynor Margaret—†	38	housekeeper	75	"
A	Welch Annie—†	38	"	63	24 Ward
c	Schlehuber Delia—†	42	housewife	52	here
d	Schlehuber George	42	laborer	45	"
e	Schlehuber Marie—†	42	clerk	20	"
f	Gray Pauline—†	42	housewife	54	"
g	Gray Ralph E	42	cutter	53	"
h	Bradley Dennis	44	plasterer	59	"
k	Sullivan Catherine—†	44	housewife	43	"
l	Sullivan Helen—†	44	tel operator	23	"
m	Sullivan James	44	teamster	49	"
n	Johnson Mary—†	46	housekeeper	60	"
o	Swierk Catherine—†	46	housewife	39	"
p	Swierk Jacob	46	shoeworker	44	"
r	Callahan Eugene	46	laborer	27	"
s	Callahan Mary E—†	46	housewife	26	"
t	Wilkinson Henry P	46	laborer	25	"
u	Hull Julia T—†	48	housewife	45	"
v	Hull Margaret F—†	48	"	69	"
w	Hull Walter J	48	teamster	42	"
x	Hull William F	48	retired	75	"

Ward 9—Precinct 13

CITY OF BOSTON.

LIST OF RESIDENTS
20 YEARS OF AGE AND OVER

(FEMALES INDICATED BY DAGGER)

AS OF

APRIL 1, 1926

HERBERT A. WILSON, } *Listing*

JAMES F. EAGAN, } *Board.*

CITY OF BOSTON—PRINTING DEPARTMENT

Page.	Letter	FULL NAME	Residence, April 1, 1926.	Occupation.	Supposed Age.	Reported Residence, April 1, 1925. Street and Number.

Alvah Kittredge Park

A	Maguire Maud—†	2	secretary	34	here
B	Murphy Agnes L—†	2	"	39	"
C	Murphy Mary F—†	2	housewife	63	"
D	Murphy Thomas J	2	clerk	33	"
E	Murphy William D	2	real estate	37	"
F	Deans Margaret—†	3	forewoman	40	"
G	Donley John	3	superintendent	51	"
H	Donely Lena A—†	3	housewife	50	"
K	Drea John A	3	bookkeeper	22	"
L	Drea John T	3	barber	54	"
M	King Frank D	3	manager	48	"
N	Schmidt Mortiz	3	metalworker	50	"
O	Thompson Annie E—†	3	shoeworker	35	"
P	Donahoe Alice K—†	4	housekeeper	61	39 Forest
R	Donahoe Annie L	4	saleswoman	30	39 "
S	Donahoe John T	4	civil engineer	29	39 "
T	Balar Harry	4	presser	32	here
U	Balar Minnie—†	4	housewife	32	"
V	Vickers Lillian V—†	5	"	38	"
W	Vickers William D	5	broker	48	"
Y	Murphy Margaret—†	5	housewife	22	18 Greenwich
Z	Murphy Robert H	5	machinist	22	18 "
A	Gardner Joseph E	6	dyer	53	here
B	Gardner Nellie C—†	6	housewife	36	"
C	Duncan Robert	6	repairman	53	"
D	Vega Dante	6	barber	26	19 Linwood
E	Vega Josephine—†	6	housewife	25	19 "
F	Flanders Emily—†	6	"	35	here
G	Flanders Morris	6	pedler	43	"
K	Barnett Blanche—†	8	housewife	24	31 St Germain
L	Barnett Oliver S	8	auto mechanic	28	31 "
M	Donnelly Mary L—†	8	housewife	44	60 Bartlett
N	Donnelly Richard	8	laborer	48	60 "
O	McDonald Agnes—†	8	housewife	75	Cambridge
P	McDonald Hector	8	printer	82	"
R	Williams Henry F	8	real estate	63	here
S	Williams Regina M—†	8	housewife	63	"

2

Page.	Letter.	FULL NAME.	Residence, April 1, 1926.	Occupation.	Supposed Age.	Reported Residence, April 1, 1925. Street and Number.

Bartlett Street

	T	Kilduff Frances B—†	56	housewife	47	here
	U	Kilduff James T	56	superintendent	48	"
	V	Steele Helen E—†	56	housewife	24	638 Tremont
	W	Steele Philip E	56	lineman	28	638 "
	X	Wade Josephine C—†	56	operator	25	23 W Cottage
	Y	Brock Minnie F—†	58	housekeeper	48	here
	Z	Farnsworth Anna—†	58	housewife	24	"
	A	Farnsworth Henry	58	elevatorman	35	"
	B	Hart Rita—†	58	stitcher	23	"
	C	Riley Margaret—†	58	housekeeper	52	179 Vernon
	D	Riley Mary—†	58	laundress	50	179 "
	E	Tarten Richard	58	machinist	46	here
	F	Wood John E	58	waiter	47	"
	G	Donnelly Frances—†	60	stenographer	22	"
	H	Donnelly Margaret—†	60	"	23	"
	K	Donnelly Sarah A—†	60	housewife	46	"
	L	Donnelly Walter J	60	carpenter	51	"
	M	Proctor Jessie—†	60	laundress	47	4 Oakville av
	N	Tarr James	60	painter	69	90 Norfolk
	O	Compton Catherine—†	64	retired	76	here
	P	Coney Katherine—†	64	cook	64	"
	R	Emery Martha I—†	64	attendant	57	9 Crawford
	S	Hall Sarah—†	64	retired	76	Dedham
	T	Morley Sarah E—†	64	matron	73	here
	U	Norton Sarah E—†	64	retired	84	"
	V	Packard Philophrine F—†	64	"	78	"
	W	Payson Clara—†	64	"	78	"
	X	Plumber Ella—†	64	"	78	N Easton
	Y	Randall Belinda—†	64	"	89	here
	Z	Shaw Harriet—†	64	"	87	"
	A	Thayer Caroline—†	64	"	85	"
	B	Whipple Ella—†	64	"	75	"
	C	Donavon Justin	68	carpenter	22	88 Cedar
	D	Dunlap Anna—†	68	teacher	65	here
	E	Killion John	68	storekeeper	35	"
	F	Thompson Charlotte—†	68	housewife	30	"
	G	Thompson Robert L	68	salesman	42	"
	K	Gjoberg Arthur	70	mechanic	40	"
	L	Gjoberg Janette—†	70	housekeeper	52	"

3

Page	Letter	Full Name	Residence, April 1, 1926.	Occupation	Supposed Age	Reported Residence, April 1, 1925. Street and Number.

Bartlett Street—Continued

	Letter	Full Name	Residence	Occupation	Age	Reported Residence
	M	Chase John	70	chauffeur	22	Brookline
	N	Daley John	70	letter carrier	56	here
	O	Dunn Clara C—†	70	teacher	55	"
	P	Dunn Margaret—†	70	housekeeper	60	"
	R	Harrison Benjamin	70	chauffeur	21	Manchester N H
	S	Cloy Jessie—†	70	teacher	23	here
	T	Cloy John	70	superintendent	55	"
	U	Cloy Mary—†	70	housewife	53	"
	V	Cloy Robert	70	singer	30	"
	W	Cloy William	70	machinist	28	"
	X	Harney Annie—†	70	housekeeper	45	"
	Y	Harney Elizabeth—†	70	"	40	"
	Z	Murphy Adeline—†	70	housewife	40	"
	A	Murphy James	70	mechanic	45	"
	B	Ryan Thomas	70	starter	50	"
	C	Walsh Mary —†	70	clerk	55	Brookline
	D	Bullard Carrie J—†	70	housewife	58	here
	E	Bullard George	70	retired	60	"
	F	Hooker Henry L	70	banker	35	"
	G	Hooker Jessie †	70	housewife	33	"
	H	Catarius Margaret—†	70	housekeeper	38	12 Wise
	L	Tenney Margaret—†	70	at home	85	here
	M	Tenney Mary A †	70	teacher	50	"
	O	McDonald Agnes—†	70	housewife	30	"
	P	McDonald Bettie †	70	bookkeeper	27	"
	R	McDonald Neil	70	carpenter	35	"
	S	Armstrong Iva D †	70	housewife	20	"
	V	Armstrong Jennie †	70	"	54	"
	T	Armstrong John †	70	janitor	53	"
	U	Armstrong John J	70	"	30	"
	W	Dadmun George W	70	chauffeur	28	81 Roxbury
	X	Dadmun Helen †	70	housewife	21	81 "
	Y	Stone Marie—†	70	"	24	P E I
	Z	Stone Theadore	70	carpenter	30	Quincy
	A	Everett Amelia †	70	housewife	33	here
	B	Everett Edward	70	clergyman	35	"

4

Letter.	FULL NAME.	Residence, April 1, 1926.	Occupation.	Supposed Age.	Reported Residence, April 1, 1925. Street and Number.

Blanchard Street

c	McCarthy William J	4	salesman	45	here
D	Sullivan Elizabeth—†	4	housekeeper	46	"
E	McLean Bernard J	6	chauffeur	48	"
F	McLean Hattie B—†	6	housekeeper	47	"
G	Manning Alice E—†	8	"	66	"
H	Manning Mary A—†	8	housewife	36	"
K	Manning Thomas M	8	B F D	35	"
L	Tansy John F	10	clerk	26	"
M	Tansy Michael J	10	longshoreman	26	"
N	Tansy Patrick J, jr	10	stenographer	25	"
O	Tansy Patrick J	10	laborer	54	"
P	Tansy Thomas P	10	teamster	27	"

Centre Street

V	Woon Lee	1	laundryman	56	Lynn
X	St George Mary T—†	2	houseworker	50	51 Centre
Y	Baxter Hiram L	2	conductor	55	53 Beech Glen
Z	Fay Alice T—†	2	housekeeper	45	here
A	Lowther Richard W	2	salesman	39	"
B	Caulfield Thomas F	3	laborer	24	"
E	Dion Omer	3	"	38	Nashua N H
F	Doherty Ellen—†	3	housewife	35	here
G	Flaherty Catherine—†	3	at home	70	"
H	Good Marion R—†	3	clerk	29	"
K	Hawkes Leo A	3	laborer	38	Bangor Me
L	Hawkes Nick B	3	"	42	"
M	Hawkes Thomas	3	"	46	here
C	McColgan James	3	"	39	"
D	McColgan Mary—†	3	maid	40	127 Marlboro
N	Perry Raymond E	3	laborer	26	Bangor Me
O	Smith Rodney	3	meatcutter	59	here
P	Winchester Frederick H	3	plasterer	45	Bangor Me
R	Winchester Mary E—†	3	housewife	39	here
S	Halpard Ada—†	4	housekeeper	30	"
T	Sullivan William M	4	engineer	32	"
U	Grant Allen	4	clerk	25	30 Leyland
V	McGrath Jennie—†	4	housekeeper	58	here
W	McGrath Jennie C—†	4	factory worker	36	"

5

Centre Street – Continued

x	Mullen Carrie —†	4	saleswoman	40	here
y	Smythe Charles	4	salesman	68	New York
y¹	Lynch Michael	4	gardener	42	66 Dudley
z	Manning John	4	policeman	27	here
z¹	Manning Thomas	4	"	28	"
A	Manning Wilhemina —†	4	housewife	26	184 Cabot
B	Manning William H	4	chauffeur	24	here
E	McSherry Catherine —†	4½	housekeeper	71	"
F	Shannon Mary L—†	4½	clerk	48	"
G	Johnson Alexis V	4½	storekeeper	28	Cuba
H	Johnson Emil J	4½	manager	54	here
K	Johnson Mary L—†	4½	housewife	54	"
L	Donovan Agnes E —†	4½	"	51	"
M	Donovan John J	4½	watchman	54	"
N	Wright Emma—†	6	housewife	40	"
O	Wright Henry O	6	cleanser	38	"
P	Ackhurst Jack	6	machinist	66	"
R	Cronin Eugene	6	porter	30	5 Whitney pl
S	Cronin Hughie	6	mechanic	30	New York
T	Everle Frederick J	6	operator	62	here
U	Smith Paul	6	porter	30	"
V	Wixon Carrie—†	6	houseworker	37	"
W	Wright Mae—†	6	housekeeper	66	"
X	Arakalian Ropen	6	dishwasher	45	"
Y	Mosier Frank	7	clerk	22	"
Z	Pickett Margaret—†	7	housewife	45	"
A	Pickett William	7	painter	52	"
B	Boyd Catherine R—†	7	housewife	44	2475 Wash'n
C	Reardon Charles J	7	accountant	20	224 Roxbury
D	Reardon Margaret E †	7	housewife	43	224 "
E	Cahill Jmaes J	8	shoemaker	58	here
F	Carey Howard	8	clerk	25	67 Roxbury
G	Carey Jarvice	8	"	22	67 "
H	Goodrich Charles B	8	conductor	45	1 Malbon pl
K	Gosnell Joseph	8	laborer	25	19 Burt
L	Gosnell William	8	"	35	here
M	Hanson John	8	machinist	75	"
N	Harrigan Daniel	8	conductor	38	"
O	Larken Jennie—†	8	laundress	59	"
O¹	Peterson Charles	8	cutter	45	"
P	Peterson Hannah —†	8	housewife	57	"

Centre Street—Continued

R	Peterson Herman	8	factory worker	69	here
T	Randell Harriet—†	8	cashier	56	"
U	Randell William O	8	machinist	60	"
V	Doran Agnes G—†	9	housewife	32	"
W	Doran Charles J	9	chauffeur	30	"
Y	Misiewiezz Felix	9	weaver	32	"
Z	Cenderlund Arthur G	9	clerk	22	"
A	Cenderlund Gustaf	9	mechanic	54	"
B	Gilmore William F	9	B F D	34	2756 Wash'n
C	Delbac John	13	laborer	25	here
D	Hurley Margaret—†	13	housewife	38	"
E	Hurley Michael J	13	plumber	48	"
F	Greene Elsie—†	13	clerk	33	Maine
G	Telly Lettie—†	13	"	28	"
H	Jones Albert H	14	mason	60	here
K	Jones Elizabeth F—†	14	housewife	60	"
L	Jones Evelyn F—†	14	secretary	25	"
M	Hall Elizabeth M—†	15	housewife	31	"
N	MacKenzie Alexander	15	repairman	40	"
O	Corliss Charles P	16	manager	69	"
P	Corliss Emmeline—†	16	housewife	62	"
R	Stamatus George	16	dishwasher	28	67 Dudley
S	Stamalus James	16	chauffeur	35	873 Harris'n av
T	Drouin Louis P	16	wigmaker	51	here
U	Drouin Ruth—†	16	stenographer	21	"
V	Johnson Swen G	16	pianomaker	25	"
W	Klein Anna—†	16	houseworker	54	"
X	Klein John L	16	clerk	55	Lakeville
Y	Hagerty Nora E—†	16	housewife	45	896 Parker
Z	Hagerty Timothy	16	carpenter	53	896 "
B	Sheehan Arthur F	17	laborer	36	here
C	Sheehan Ellen—†	17	housewife	75	"
D	Sheehan John A	17	garmentworker	30	"
E	Sheehan Mary E—†	17	at home	34	"
F	Seeley Ella—†	17	housewife	29	"
G	Seeley George	17	teamster	32	"
H	Fram Mildred—†	18	shoestitcher	25	Haverhill
K	Fram Solomon	18	counterman	25	"
L	Pike Maud—†	18	stitcher	45	"
X	Botsevales Andrew	18	fruit	26	here
O	Letras Peter	18	storekeeper	27	"

7

Page.	Letter.	FULL NAME.	Residence, April 1, 1926.	Occupation.	Supposed Age.	Reported Residence, April 1, 1925. Street and Number.

Centre Street Continued

P	Martin Earl L	18	florist	35	here
R	Martin Helen E—†	18	housekeeper	41	"
S	Sullivan Annie †	18	domestic	90	"
T	Sullivan Annie—†	18	stitcher	40	"
U	Sullivan Charles G	18	blacksmith	45	"
V	Healey George C	19	clerk	21	"
W	Kealey James K	19	guard	57	"
X	Kealey Minnie W—†	19	housewife	52	"
Y	Ducheney Lydia—†	19½	"	46	88 Park
Z	Ducheney Sylvanus S	19½	watchman	41	88 "
A	MacDonald Charlotte —†	19½	housewife	72	here
B	Parker Anna C —†	19½	stenographer	34	"
C	McNulty John	19½	electrician	42	"
D	McNulty Mary —†	19½	housewife	40	"
E	Segar Ira J	rear 20	machinist	43	8 Rockledge
F	Segar Julia E—†	" 20	bookkeeper	35	8 "
G	Segar Sarah J—†	" 20	housewife	72	8 "
H	Dorgan Daniel J	21	janitor	51	here
K	Dorgan Mary— †	21	tel operator	22	"
L	Lamb Ellen—†	21	housewife	48	"
M	Lamb John J	21	paver	58	"
N	Lamb Mary—†	21	clerk	21	"
O	Glover Edward	21	chauffeur	24	75 Centre
P	Glover Lillian —†	21	housewife	20	75 "
R	Rivers Theresa †	23	"	29	883 Albany
S	Cremins Daniel	23	laborer	37	here
T	Cremins Elizabeth —†	23	housewife	37	"
U	Conroy Mary—†	23	laundress	35	12 Highland
V	Dietel John S	26	baker	59	here
W	Dietel Sophie—†	26	housewife	52	"
Y	Hirsch Gabriel	29	cigarmaker	66	31 Manchester
Z	Hirsch Leah—†	29	housewife	63	31 "
A	Marellie Frank	29	cigarmaker	41	31 Adams
B	Dunning John J	29	laborer	37	101 Fairmount av
C	Dunning Patrick	29	shoeworker	30	9 Downing
D	McCormack Hannah—†	29	"	34	9 "
F	Kustawaskey Celia—†	31	housewife	35	here
G	Kustawaskey Joseph	31	insurance agent	36	"
H	Blank Albert	31	clerk	30	30 Savin Hill av
K	Wiggett Catherine—†	31	housewife	30	here

	Letter.	FULL NAME.	Residence, April 1, 1926.	Occupation.	Supposed Age.	Reported Residence, April 1, 1925. Street and Number.

Centre Street—Continued

	Letter.	FULL NAME.	Residence	Occupation	Age	Reported Residence
	L	Wiggett Charles H	31	laundryman	36	here
	M	Atherton James	45	retired	72	"
	N	Davis Hattie C—†	45	matron	56	"
	O	Putnam Emmet P—†	45	nurse	28	"
	P	Taylor Frederick L	45	physician	55	"
	R	Taylor Guenn Q—†	45	at home	39	"
	S	Vasey Catherine—†	45	cook	40	"
	T	White Frances—†	48	storekeeper	21	"
	U	White Joseph	48	"	22	"
	V	White Morris	48	"	49	"
	W	White Rebecca—†	48	"	47	"
	X	Berg Emily—†	48	scrubwoman	36	146 Cedar
	Y	Petersberg Mary—†	48	domestic	48	133 Centre
	Z	Petersberg Peter	48	carpenter	46	133 "
	A	Morash Charles A	64	teamster	40	13 Oakland
	B	Morash Elizabeth—†	64	housewife	42	13 "
	E	McHugh Nellie—†	66	"	48	here
	F	McHugh Thomas H	66	chauffeur	25	"
	G	McHugh Thomas J	66	laborer	50	"
	D	O'Dowd Charles	66	"	48	"
	L	Madden Mary—†	68	housewife	27	22 Clive
	M	Schaffer Janet G—†	68	"	69	here
	N	Schaffer Jessamine M—†	68	"	69	"

Eliot Terrace

	Letter.	FULL NAME.	Residence	Occupation	Age	Reported Residence
	O	Crowley Ethel F—†	1	housewife	36	here
	P	Crowley William J	1	mailer	52	"
	R	Rogers Florence—†	1	saleswoman	42	"
	S	Donovan Catherine J—†	1	housewife	42	"
	T	Donovan Michael F	1	letter carrier	47	"
	U	Hoffman Charles M	2	carpenter	61	"
	V	Hoffman Irene M—†	2	housekeeper	32	"
	W	Higgins Catherine—†	3	clerk	22	"
	X	Higgins Mary—†	3	housekeeper	76	"
	Y	Higgins Mary A—†	3	saleswoman	41	"

Page.	Letter.	FULL NAME.	Residence, April 1, 1926.	Occupation.	Supposed Age.	Reported Residence, April 1, 1925. Street and Number.

Highland Avenue

z	Desmond Frank E	10	candymaker	41	here
A	Desmond Hattie B— †	10	housewife	35	"
B	Bellevau Frederick	10	upholsterer	30	"
C	Nehiley Addie M—†	10	housewife	36	"
D	Nehiley Joseph P	10	painter	41	"
E	Gamash Catherine—†	10	housewife	27	2940 Wash'n
F	Gamash Raymond	10	chauffeur	24	2940 "
G	Connelly Catherine— †	11	clerk	21	here
H	Connolley John J	11	chauffeur	24	"
K	Connelly Loretta—†	11	clerk	24	"
L	Connelly Margaret—†	11	tel operator	28	"
M	Connelly Mary F—†	11	housewife	55	"
N	Connelly Mary F—†	11	tel operator	25	"
O	Connelly Michael	11	laborer	59	"
R	Connor John H A	12	storekeeper	64	"
S	Connor Myra P—†	12	housewife	61	"
T	Seagrave Carrie E—†	12	dressmaker	69	"
U	Stimler Albert G	12	floorman	59	"
V	Stimler Susette—†	12	housewife	59	"
X	Lehr Amelia—†	13	"	34	"
Y	Lehr Eugene	13	painter	34	"
Z	Didion Sophie S— †	14	housekeeper	77	"
A	Cavanagh Elizabeth—†	14	housewife	48	"
B	Cavanagh Elizabeth A—†	14	stenographer	24	"
C	Cavanagh Isaac	14	blacksmith	52	"
D	Monast Augustine—†	14	bookkeeper	21	"
E	Monast Melia—†	14	dressmaker	50	"
F	Monast Victorine—†	14	school teacher	24	"
G	Insoft Charles	15	clerk	26	"
H	Insoft Ida—†	15	housewife	57	"
K	Insoft Morris	15	real estate	59	"
L	Insoft Samuel	15	clerk	33	"
M	McDonnell Duncan	15	laborer	25	482 Mass av
N	Richards Gertrude M—†	15	housewife	20	91 E Brookline
O	Richards Richard R	15	teamster	26	91 "
P	Edwards Anna M—†	15	housewife	30	194 Walnut av
R	Edwards Arthur C	15	clerk	32	194 "
S	Thompson Reduers	17	mechanic	24	15 Highland av
T	Thompson Sadie—†	17	housewife	25	15 "
U	Zirul Anna—†	17	"	47	here

Page.	Letter.	FULL NAME.	Residence, April 1, 1926.	Occupation.	Supposed Age.	Reported Residence, April 1, 1925. Street and Number.

Highland Avenue—Continued

v	Zirul Christopher	17	carpenter	49	here
w	Ayer Augusta—†	17	laundress	42	Framingham
x	Schwolman Theodor J	17	bricklayer	47	Canada
y	Pawel Joseph	17	carpenter	44	here
z	Timerman Minnie—†	17	houseworker	40	"
B	Blake Hattie—†	19	housekeeper	66	"
c	Morrill Charles F	19	real estate	76	"
D	Small Albert	20	shoecutter	30	6 Hammett
E	Small Amy—†	20	housewife	27	6 "
F	Shaw Alfred	20	laborer	34	3 Malbon pl
G	Shaw Fannie—†	20	housewife	32	3 "
H	Cahill James J	21	laborer	32	here
K	Cremms Eugene C	21	clerk	20	"
L	Cremms Julia—†	21	housewife	62	"
M	Cremms Julia L—†	21	bookkeeper	29	"
N	Cremms Mary I—†	21	"	24	"
o	Hamlon Thomas J	21	policeman	31	"
P	Swift Albert E	22	"	30	"
R	Swift Mary A—†	22	housewife	28	"
s	Lynds Arthur	22	blacksmith	34	47 Delle av
T	Lynds Phyllis—†	22	housewife	27	47 "
U	Hall Henry	23	retired	76	here
v	Hall Mary J—†	23	housewife	73	"
w	Marsteller Carrie—†	23	missionary	39	"
x	Marsteller Kate—†	23	housewife	69	"
Y	Shield Mary—†	23	nurse	59	"
z	Weaver Sarah—†	23	houseworker	65	"
A	Christopherson Astrid—†	24	clerk	22	"
B	Christopherson Michael	24	baker	44	"
c	Christopherson Oscar	24	shoeworker	23	"
D	Christopherson Raynhild—†	24	housewife	25	"
E	Carrell Helen B—†	25	at home	34	"
F	Carrell Joanna—†	25	housewife	82	"
G	Carrell Theresa B—†	25	"	39	"
H	Campbell Daniel D	26	cook	57	"
K	Campbell Eleanor—†	26	housewife	53	"
L	Forrester Charles	26	vocal teacher	50	"
M	Forrester Eleanor—†	26	housewife	45	"
N	Marton Mary—†	26	housekeeper	45	"
o	Brady James	27	bricklayer	63	"
P	Finn Mary F—†	27	clerk	25	71 Charles

Page.	Letter.	FULL NAME.	Residence, April 1, 1926.	Occupation.	Supposed Age.	Reported Residence, April 1, 1925. Street and Number.

Highland Avenue—Continued

	R	Phillips Helen T—†	27	tel operator	20	here
	S	Vincent Mary C—†	27	housewife	59	"
	T	Bateo Abby E—†	28	companion	60	"
	U	Camel John A	32	carpenter	35	4 Harris av
	V	Camel Margaret †	32	housewife	32	here
	W	Kevin Elizabeth C—†	32	housekeeper	32	"
	X	Kevin John T	32	salesman	32	"
	Y	Pelky Emmetine—†	32	housewife	27	Lynn
	Z	Pelky Herbert	32	laborer	26	"
	A	Deschane Ellen—†	34	housewife	46	here
	B	Deschane John B	34	painter	34	"
	C	Anderson Charlotte—†	34	housekeeper	59	"
	D	Mosher Corinne D—†	34	housewife	27	"
	E	Mosher Noye F	34	bank guard	27	"
	F	Lettery George	34	barber	33	"
	G	Porter Mary M—†	38	housewife	30	"
	H	Porter Walter F	38	trimmer	31	"
	K	Meagher Joseph	38	inspector	55	"
	L	Porter Alfred J	38	ironworker	54	"
	M	Porter Catherine—†	38	housewife	54	"
	N	Porter Margaret—†	38	"	32	"
	O	Porter Walter F	38	tailor	28	"
	P	Merten Hattie—†	40	music teacher	35	"
	R	Merten Minnie—†	40	bookkeeper	25	"
	S	Merten Rosa—†	40	housewife	72	"
	T	Baker Cora F—†	40	bookbinder	46	4 Millmont
	U	Wallace Corris A—†	40	housewife	46	4 "
	V	Wallace Winfield P	40	policeman	64	4 "
	X	Blanchard Hannah J—†	42	housewife	41	here
	Y	O'Connor Ellen F	42	school teacher	55	"

Highland Place

	A	Hurley Joseph	1	mechanic	25	Newton
	B	Hurley Ruth I—†	1	housewife	22	"
	C	Kissler Alva J—†	1	factory worker	45	153 Highland
	D	Bradley James F	1	painter	67	2632 Wash'n
	E	Bradley Mary A—†	1	housewife	55	2632 "
	F	Gildart George	1	carpenter	43	here

12

Page.	Letter.	FULL NAME.	Residence, April 1, 1926	Occupation.	Supposed Age.	Reported Residence, April 1, 1925.
						Street and Number.

Highland Place—Continued

	G	Gildart Margaret —†	1	housewife	39	here
	H	Nichols Charles	1	shoecutter	32	"
	K	Nichols Josephine —†	1	housewife	32	"
	L	Carney Bernard	2	policeman	34	"
	M	Carney Rose F—†	2	housewife	31	"
	N	MacKay Malcolm	2	painter	33	7 Crossin pl
	O	MacKay Maria —†	2	housewife	30	7 "
	P	Smith Catherine —†	2	"	43	here
	R	Smith George	2	clerk	45	"
	S	Garrity John	2	factory worker	62	"
	T	Garrity Margaret †	2	housewife	62	"
	U	Braun Charles	3	pipefitter	27	Wash'n D C
	V	Braun Josephine— †	3	housewife	24	here
	W	Clusrchuk Peter	3	baker	40	"
	X	Kosey Leontina —†	3	housewife	36	"
	Y	Kosey Stanley	3	painter	38	"
	Z	Maurer Anna—†	3	factory worker	35	"
	A	Maurer Monica—†	3	housekeeper	77	"
	B	Dollmann Hugo R	3	clerk	43	"
	C	Egan Alice— †	4	housewife	42	"
	D	Egan John P	4	cook	42	"
	E	Fay Francis E	4	guard	26	22 Hallet
	F	Fay Myrtle—†	4	housewife	24	22 "
	G	Bowers Helen F—†	4	housekeeper	25	here
	H	Bowers Leslie E	4	chauffeur	25	"
	K	Donald Audrey—†	4	housewife	23	66 Longwood av
	L	Donald Harold	4	lineman	31	here
	M	O'Kucian Corinne—†	5	housewife	30	"
	N	O'Kucian Mesrop	5	electrician	30	"
	O	Clark Mary—†	5	housekeeper	36	111 Cedar
	P	Hooley Timothy	5	milkman	23	9 Delle av
	R	Kennedy Elizabeth—†	5	laundress	45	Cambridge
	S	Lowney Richella—†	5	housewife	32	16 Winslow
	T	Lowney Stanley W	5	lawyer	36	16 "
	U	Ward Edmond	6	chauffeur	50	here
	V	Ward Marie C—†	6	housewife	42	"
	W	McGlone Mary E—†	6	dressmaker	55	"
	X	Thomas Albert J	6	clerk	28	"
	Y	Thomas Helen M—†	6	tel operator	25	"
	Z	Thomas Nora—†	6	housekeeper	51	"

13

Page.	Letter	FULL NAME.	Residence, April 1, 1926.	Occupation.	Supposed Age.	Reported Residence, April 1, 1925. Street and Number.

Highland Place—Continued

A	Lundquist Hilda—†	6	housewife	42	here
B	Lundquist John	6	laborer	52	"
C	Douglas George H	6	salesman	58	"
D	Frazier Victoria—†	6	laundress	50	"

Highland Street

E	Camfield Esther—†	1	housekeeper	37	here
F	Camfield Pierce	1	plumber	41	"
G	Tilt Clara—†	1	housewife	46	"
H	Tilt John W	1	conductor	47	"
K	Tilt Ruth E—†	1	school teacher	21	"
L	Green Mary E—†	1A	housewife	31	7 Centre
M	Green William V	1A	brakeman	35	7 "
O	Dallas Dorothy—†	3	teacher	20	here
P	Dallas Herbert A	3	agent	46	"
R	Dallas Margaret—†	3	housewife	42	"
S	Dallas Marie I—†	3	clerk	37	"
T	Salter Herbert	3	foreman	48	"
U	White Jeremiah	3	custodian	48	"
V	Kittrick Catherine—†	4	housewife	60	"
W	Kittrick Peter	4	carpenter	64	"
X	Lekbelac George	5	shoeworker	49	3 Putnam pl
Y	Paine Emery J	5	engineer	29	here
Z	Paine Mary I—†	5	housewife	28	"
A	Kelleher Helen—†	7	matron	42	"
B	Pettigrew Anna M—†	7	housekeeper	66	"
C	Stenberg Waine	7	oiler	34	"
D	Warren Gowane	7	printer	65	"
E	Wensen John S	7	carpenter	40	"
F	McNeil Annie—†	8	housewife	46	"
G	McNeil Archibald J	8	shipper	29	"
H	McNeil Christine F—†	8	clerk	26	"
K	McNeil Henrietta W—†	8	"	21	"
L	McNeil William H	8	gasfitter	24	"
M	Jones Etta C—†	9	housewife	54	"
N	Jones Harry A	9	barber	55	"
O	Kenney Leroy A	9	salesman	30	"
P	Kenney Rose—†	9	stenographer	26	"
R	Doyle Elizabeth—†	10	housekeeper	44	"

Letter	FULL NAME.	Residence, April 1, 1926	Occupation.	Supposed Age.	Reported Residence, April 1, 1925. Street and Number.

Highland Street—Continued

s	Scott Roy	10	laborer	38	here
T	Martel Frances—†	10	housekeeper	62	s Alvah Kittredge pk
U	Willis Arthur S	10	foreman	47	8 "
V	Duff Mary—†	10	housewife	39	2 Shirley
W	Duff William R	10	painter	49	2 "
X	Peterson Alma—†	10	housewife	29	Brookline
Y	Peterson Oscar J	10	cabinetmaker	28	29 Dever
Z	Bell Catherine S—†	12	housewife	51	here
A	Bell Thomas A	12	brassfinisher	54	"
B	Brooks Benjamin	12	shipper	52	"
C	Duffy William	12	manager	30	"
D	Duguay Henry	12	carpenter	35	"
E	Frost Michael	12	longshoreman	54	"
F	Kane Thomas	12	lineman	32	"
G	Neal Charles	12	marketman	60	8 Malbon pl
H	Netzer Louis	12	baker	51	here
K	O'Connell Patrick	12	laborer	60	31 Delle av
R	Alvin Albin	14	carpenter	36	here
S	Alvin Ellen—†	14	stitcher	46	"
L	Buckingham Caroline—†	14	housekeeper	41	"
M	Buckingham Henry A	14	mechanic	42	"
N	Cronin Agnes—†	14	housewife	24	Hingham
O	Cronin Patrick	14	salesman	26	"
P	Doran Andrew	14	laborer	56	here
T	Kennedy Ellen—†	14	housewife	22	112 W Eighth
U	Kennedy William	14	waiter	24	112 "
V	Olson Adolph	14	carpenter	30	here
W	Olson Signa—†	14	stitcher	28	"
X	Peirson Bede—†	14	"	58	"
Y	Peirson John	14	laborer	51	"
Z	Brown Hiram E	16	chauffeur	42	"
A	Brown Julia—†	16	housewife	38	"
B	Mullen Helen F—†	16	brushmaker	25	"
C	Mullen Henry R	16	laborer	41	"
D	Mullen Lillian E—†	16	brushmaker	34	"
G	McMahan Bessie—†	18	waitress	43	"
H	Conners Lawrence A	18	meatcutter	45	137 Highland
K	Conners Mary T—†	18	housewife	43	137 "
L	O'Conner Catherine—†	18	clerk	32	90 Monument
M	O'Conner Hannah—†	18	housekeeper	45	137 Highland
N	O'Conner Helen—†	18	nurse	38	137 "

15

Page.	Letter.	FULL NAME.	Residence, April 1, 1926.	Occupation.	Supposed Age.	Reported Residence, April 1, 1925. Street and Number.

Highland Street—Continued

o	Misillo John	18	cook	28	Cambridge
p	Misillo Mary —†	18	housewife	25	"
r	Golden Joseph A	19	letter carrier	54	177 Highland
s	Golden Mary L —†	19	housewife	56	177 "
t	Gordon George	19	butcher	35	here
u	Donahue Bridget —†	19	housewife	59	"
v	Donahue Patrick	19	laborer	62	"
w	Baker Elsie —†	20	housekeeper	21	Cambridge
x	Baker William J	20	agent	45	11 Morley
y	Bishop Martha—†	20	housekeeper	40	14 Claremont pk
z	Bishop Sidney	20	porter	56	14 "
A	Richardson Elmira—†	20	student	38	Brookline
B	Kane Edward J	21	machinist	29	here
c	Kane Frank W	21	repairman	33	"
D	Kane Joseph P	21	butcher	31	"
E	Kane Katherine I —†	21	houseworker	27	"
F	Kane Mary— †	21	housekeeper	41	"
G	Famularo Angelo	21A	fruit	50	"
H	Famularo Gaetano	21A	"	24	"
K	Paino Grace —†	21A	housewife	38	"
L	Paino Guisepe	21A	fruit	44	"
M	Swenson John	21A	longshoreman	45	"
N	Connelly Agnes †	22	housewife	33	"
o	Connelly Robert D	22	laborer	35	"
P	Digby Helen F— †	22	clerk	23	Cambridge
R	Flannagan Bernard	22	watchman	45	"
s	Flannagan Bridget—†	22	housewife	46	"
T	Morrison Bridget—†	22	"	35	here
u	Morrison Francis P	22	compositor	35	"
v	Liddy Daniel J	23	teamster	50	"
w	Liddy Nora M †	23	housewife	46	"
x	Moran William	23	florist	36	"
y	Kane Katherine —†	23A	housewife	54	"
z	Kane Lawrence	23A	shipper	24	"
A	Kane Sarah —†	23A	inspector	27	"
B	Alexander Elizabeth—†	25	clerk	60	"
c	Brown John	25	"	42	"
D	Demeritt Mark C	25	pressman	21	"
E	Logan John	25	clerk	23	"
F	Logan Micheal	25	"	25	"
G	Taft Dora D †	25	housewife	56	"

16

Highland Street —Continued

H	Taft William E	25	chauffeur	56	here
K	Walsh Mary—†	25	storekeeper	75	"
L	Ball Ellen—†	28	housewife	54	"
M	Ball Joseph D	28	lineman	27	"
N	Ball Marion C—†	28	nurse	21	"
O	Ball Michael E	28	clerk	20	"
P	Delaney Thomas J	28	tailor	38	57 Dudley
R	Kehone Timothy J	28	meatcutter	30	here
S	McLeod William N	28	baker	45	151 Thornton
T	Pendergast Frederick	28	postal clerk	30	here
U	Woodford Michael J	28	boilermaker	29	66 Blue Hill av
V	Buchanan Edgar W	30	salesman	36	here
W	Buchanan Florence L—†	30	housewife	35	"
X	Sanchuk Margaret A—†	30	housekeeper	37	"
Y	Sanchuk Mitchel	30	carpenter	36	"
Z	Crommey Andrew	33	laborer	56	"
A	Crommey Fred	33	foreman	31	"
B	Crommey Katie—†	33	housekeeper	57	"
C	McGinnis Delia F—†	33	cook	39	"
D	McGinnis Nora—†	33	"	32	"
E	McGinnis Sarah—†	33	housekeeper	28	"
F	Patt Mary—†	33	housewife	60	"
G	Patt Peter	33	clerk	59	"
L	Carroll Mary J—†	42	student	23	"
M	Houghton Mary E—†	42	housekeeper	69	"
N	Mihlenberg Frederick	42	machinist	43	"
O	Mihlenberg Mary—†	42	housewife	43	"
P	Sullivan Charles J	42	shipper	52	"
R	Sullivan Frank T	42	salesman	45	"
S	Sullivan Mary E—†	42	dressmaker	55	92 Marlboro
T	Sullivan Timothy M	42	superintendent	42	here
U	Appel Lena—†	44	saleswoman	24	"
V	Appel Max	44	newsdealer	27	"
W	Appel Sarah—†	44	housewife	22	"

Highland Terrace

X	Marks Manuel G	1	elevatorman	34	here
Y	Marks Marie B—†	1	housewife	34	"

9—13   17

Highland Terrace—Continued

z	McIntyre Hector	1	machinist	52	4 Highland pk
A	McIntyre Margaret—†	1	housewife	44	4 "
B	McIntyre Margaret—†	1	shoeworker	20	4 "
c	Tjaerlis Censtantine	1	cook	35	here
D	Tjaerlis Sophia—†	1	housewife	55	"
F	O'Brien Andrew M	1	painter	24	"
G	O'Brien Theresa V—†	1	housewife	22	"
H	Sariah Mary—†	1	"	25	"
K	Sariah Stephen	1	laborer	26	"
M	Peterson Ernest	3	mason	55	"
N	Peterson Olga—†	3	housewife	49	"

John Eliot Square

s	Bigley Mary E—†	14	neckwear	57	here
T	Boynton Abbie W—†	14	candyworker	30	"
U	Butler Mary E—†	14	clerk	50	"
V	Chamberlin Mary I—†	14	teacher	50	"
W	Crowell Alice M—†	14	"	63	"
X	Dorman Elizabeth J—†	14	tutor	66	"
Y	Gay Clara S—†	14	teacher	35	"
Z	Hodge Mazie—†	14	clerk	26	"
A	Holmes Anna—†	14	"	35	"
B	Libby Gracia D—†	14	matron	35	"
C	Lynch Sophie G—†	14	clerk	59	"
D	Mendum Estelle M—†	14	social worker	40	"
E	Nye Kathleen—†	14	secretary	39	"
F	O'Leary Betty—†	14	stenographer	22	"
G	Powers Helena—†	14	clerk	55	"
H	Rose Peter	14	insurance agent	40	"
K	Sackett Mary L—†	14	demonstrator	40	"
L	Sherman Bertha—†	14	maid	43	"
M	Smith Fanny E—†	14	clerk	75	"
N	Soule Frederick J	14	director	42	"
o	Soule Grace M—†	14	housewife	41	"
P	Wood Harriett M—†	14	proofreader	49	"
U	Ross Philip	24	storekeeper	51	1482 Wash'n
V	Allen Anna—†	26	bookbinder	40	here
W	Hald John J	28	painter	69	"
H	Donovan John R	50	clerk	23	"

18

John Eliot Square—Continued

K	Donovan Margaret J—†	50	housewife	23	here
L	McNary Michael	50	laborer	56	"
M	Wilson James	50	clerk	23	"
N	Wilson Margaret J—†	50	bookkeeper	26	"
O	Wilson Mary—†	50	housewife	46	"
P	McDonnell Annie—†	50	dressmaker	70	"
R	McDonnell Ellen L—†	50	housekeeper	72	"
S	McDonnall John B	50	painter	74	"
T	Tagen Alice G—†	50	clerk	32	"
U	Tagen John H	50	rodman	39	"
V	Tagen Sarah E—†	50	housewife	76	"

Lambert Avenue

Y	Richards Carolina C—†	5	school teacher	47	here
Z	Richards Lorena S—†	5	housekeeper	84	"
A	Tyler Helen M—†	5	housekeeper	66	"
B	Bridgeman Edwin B	5	janitor	70	"
C	Bridgeman Lucy W—†	5	secretary	33	"
D	Bridgeman Mary S—†	5	"	69	"
E	Bridgeman Ruth—†	5	"	39	"
F	Bogan John	17	probat'n officer	43	"
G	Carlson Oscar	17	machinist	41	Cambridge
H	Dysart Frederick N	17	laborer	47	here
K	Laney Emma—†	17	housekeeper	40	"
L	Richardson Einar	17	painter	43	6 Winslow
M	Allard Annie—†	19	housewife	23	2578 Wash'n
N	Allard Frederick	19	chauffeur	26	2578 "
O	Callahan James	19	plasterer	28	49 Delle av
P	Callahan Matthew F	19	boilermaker	21	49 "
R	Connolly Annie B—†	19	housewife	61	2578 Wash'n
S	Connolly John P	19	lawyer	31	2578 "
T	Connolly Mary J—†	19	housekeeper	25	49 Delle av
U	Connolly Patrick H	19	laborer	24	2578 Wash'n
V	Connolly Robert E	19	clerk	21	2578 "
W	Connolly Rose E—†	19	assembler	26	2578 "
X	Connolly Thomas F, jr	19	laborer	28	2578 "
Y	Connolly Thomas F	19	retired	68	2578 "
Z	Steenbruggen John	19	tel installer	31	2578 "
A	Steenbruggen Mary K—†	19	tel operator	29	2578 "

Page	Letter	FULL NAME.	Residence, April 1, 1926.	Occupation.	Supposed Age.	Reported Residence, April 1, 1925. Street and Number.

Lambert Avenue—Continued

	B	Cunniff Elizabeth M—†	21	housewife	29	here
	c	Cunniff Patrick J	21	taxi agent	32	"
	D	O'Leary James	21	laborer	34	"
	E	O'Leary Jessie—†	21	dressmaker	38	"
	F	Pevear Hannah—†	21	housekeeper	31	"
	G	Pevear William	21	sign painter	39	"
	H	Auclair Oscar	21	chef	20	Detroit Mich
	K	Tracy Edward	21	court officer	58	here
	L	Tracy Mabel M—†	21	housewife	59	"
	M	Billotte Adolphe	23	B F D	30	"
	N	Billotte Anna V—†	23	housewife	26	"
	O	Billotte Lena—†	23	housekeeper	47	"
	P	Phelan Gerald	23	brakeman	30	"
	R	Phelan John J	23	clerk	34	New Haven Ct
	S	Phelan Mary F—†	23	housewife	27	here
	T	McKinnon Anna—†	23	housekeeper	50	"
	U	Post Clifford	25	fishcutter	31	7 Melbourne pl
	V	Post Helen—†	25	housewife	30	7 "
	W	Flygare August	25	baker	61	19 Lambert av
	X	Flygare Matilda—†	25	housewife	47	19 "
	Y	Randall Arthur	25	cleaner	41	here
	Z	Randall Christine B—†	25	housewife	58	"
	A	Power John H	27	foreman	41	"
	B	Power Margaret—†	27	housewife	40	"
	C	Dakin Harold P	27	grocer	27	"
	D	Dakin Margaret G—†	27	housewife	28	"
	E	Drew Harry L	27	salesman	33	"
	F	Turner Edward H	27	chauffeur	32	"
	G	Turner Inez C—†	27	bookkeeper	29	"
	H	Turner Margaret G—†	27	housekeeper	66	"

Lambert Street

	K	Scovelle William L	4	lawyer	52	here
	L	Stewart Samuel W	4	painter	50	"
	M	Coyne Catherine—†	8	housekeeper	35	138 George
	N	Coyne Patrick	8	plasterer	33	138 "
	O	Rhine James E	8	painter	67	here
	P	Rhine James E, jr	8	meatcutter	21	"

Lambert Street—Continued

R	Rhine Mary—†	8	housekeeper	51	here
s	McMahon Edward	8	chauffeur	22	"
T	McMahon Louise—†	8	housekeeper	46	"
U	Leonard Marion—†	10	"	29	65 Water
V	Holden Fred H	10	glazier	21	here
W	Holden Fred J	10	electrician	48	"
X	Holden Mary—†	10	housewife	45	"
Y	D'Arcy Mary T—†	10	"	36	"
Z	D'Arcy Thomas	10	ironworker	47	"
A	Anders Delina—†	12	housekeeper	31	"
B	Anders Frederick	12	chauffeur	25	"
C	Penny James	12	"	44	"
D	Penny Robey—†	12	housekeeper	39	"
E	Anders Catherine—†	12	"	57	"
F	Anders Edward	12	salesman	27	"
G	Ebju Erling	13	painter	24	"
H	Ebju Gulborg	13	shoeworker	21	"
K	Ebju John	13	clerk	57	"
L	Ebju Marie—†	13	housekeeper	59	"
M	Hansen Aagot—†	13	housewife	33	"
O	Purslow Amy—†	14	housekeeper	21	"
P	Purslow Caroline—†	14	"	64	"
R	Harris William F	15	retired	75	"
s	Hickey Blanche A—†	15	checker	40	"
T	Durham Charles	16	painter	66	"
U	Durham Sarah—†	16	housekeeper	67	"
V	Durham Thomas	16	clerk	29	"
W	Lamontagne Elsie—†	17	housewife	54	"
X	Lamontagne Eugene	17	leatherworker	53	"
Y	McLaughlin Celia—†	17	cook	27	"
Z	McLaughlin Helen—†	17	domestic	38	"
A	McLaughlin Joseph	17	carpenter	25	"
B	McLaughlin Margaret—†	17	housekeeper	35	"
C	McLaughlin Rose—†	17	envelopemaker	37	"
D	Byrne Frank L	20	retired	70	"
E	Byrne Helen R—†	20	housekeeper	62	"
F	Flint Calvin	21	laborer	48	Revere
G	McDonald Daniel	21	shipper	28	here
H	McDonald Mary F—†	21	elevatorwoman	31	"
K	McDonald Mary L—†	21	housekeeper	64	"
L	Brawley Evelyn M—†	22	school teacher	27	"

21

Lambert Street Continued

M	Brawley James L	22	letter carrier	56	here
N	Brawley James R	22	art editor	26	"
O	Brawley Mary E—†	22	housekeeper	58	"
P	Cooper Agnes—†	23	housewife	49	"
R	Cooper Ebenezer	23	carpenter	49	"
S	Miller James	23	"	43	"
T	Telpner Etta—†	24	housekeeper	45	"
U	Telpner Isidor	24	tailor	47	"
V	Fennessey Bernard	24	laborer	57	Canada
W	Puddister Nellie—†	24	housekeeper	30	Somerville
X	Puddister Steven	24	fisherman	34	"
Y	Rains Elizabeth—†	24	housekeeper	54	15 Norfolk
Z	Letzing Bernadina—†	25	housewife	67	here
A	McDade Elsie F—†	25	shoeworker	36	"
B	Norton Edmund	26	skin cutter	22	9 Linwood sq
C	Norton James G	26	laborer	30	9 "
D	Norton Peter	26	boxer	24	9 "
E	Norton Thomas	26	laborer	29	9 "
F	Kenney John L	26	watchman	60	50 Lambert av
G	Kenney Thomas G	26	teamster	56	50 "
H	Savage Marguerite—†	26	housekeeper	31	here
K	Savage Paul	26	steamfitter	33	"
L	Lehr Anton	27	retired	79	"
M	Lehr Helen—†	27	clerk	38	"
N	Lehr Paulina—†	27	"	35	"
O	Galloway Blanche E—†	28	"	45	"
P	Galloway Carita—†	28	cashier	24	"
R	Dolan Mary E—†	28	housekeeper	36	"
S	Dolan Thomas J	28	chauffeur	36	"
T	Weinfield Coleman	28	grocer	50	16 Highland
U	Weinfield Rose—†	28	housekeeper	50	16 "
V	Muise John	30	clerk	26	here
W	Roche Joseph	30	tinsmith	29	"
X	Roche Mary—†	30	housekeeper	27	"
Y	Crowley Harriet E—†	30	"	42	"
Z	Crowley Harry B	30	chauffeur	45	"
A	Crowley James E	30	clerk	20	"
B	Sullivan Anna—†	30	housekeeper	45	"
C	Sullivan Ethel—†	30	saleswoman	22	"
D	Sullivan William T	30	steamfitter	48	"

rage	Letter	FULL NAME.	Residence, April 1, 1926.	Occupation.	Supposed Age.	Reported Residence, April 1, 1925. Street and Number.

Lambert Street—Continued

	Letter	FULL NAME.	Res.	Occupation.	Age	Reported Residence
	E	Kraft Lillian —†	31	housekeeper	30	9 Cliff
	F	Kraft Western	31	janitor	32	9 "
	G	Abolin Emily —†	31	housewife	42	here
	H	Abolin Fred	31	machinist	42	"
	K	Zelms Anna—†	31	housekeeper	31	"
	L	Zelms Robert	31	clerk	37	"
	M	Dyer Catherine—†	31	housewife	44	"
	N	Dyer William	31	shipper	43	"
	O	Brownfield Jacob	31	machinist	37	29 Beech Glen
	P	Brownfield Olga—†	31	housewife	28	29 "
	R	Dump Anna—†	31	"	30	26 Juniper
	S	Dump Edward	31	pianomaker	38	26 "
	T	Chamberlin Hazel—†	31	clerk	24	here
	U	Cushing Annie E—†	31	housewife	60	"
	V	Cushing George F	31	rubberworker	66	"
	W	Cushing Stephen	31	plumber	29	"
	X	Wilson Alice B—†	31	housekeeper	48	"
	Y	Wilson Elsie B—†	31	bookkeeper	22	"
	Z	Wilson Marjorie M—†	31	"	20	"
	A	Crossen Christine—†	31	waitress	45	"
	B	Kohr Christine—†	31	housekeeper	20	"
	C	Kohr John S	31	accountant	22	Cambridge
	D	Jacobson Alexander	31	bottler	69	here
	E	Jacobson Edgar	31	"	22	"
	F	Jacobson Lena—†	31	housekeeper	59	"
	G	Pernaw Jennie—†	31	"	41	"
	H	Pernaw John	31	machinist	44	"
	K	Starr Walter	31	"	30	"
	L	Madower Annie—†	34	housewife	26	33 Milford
	M	Madower Peter	34	radiators	42	33 "
	O	Ferguson Alice M—†	38	housekeeper	38	here
	P	Ferguson John H	38	retired	57	"
	R	McCarron Barbara—†	40	housewife	41	"
	S	McCarron Edward J	40	letter carrier	50	"
	T	Sullivan James J	40	bricklayer	38	13 Kenney
	U	Sullivan Mary—†	40	housewife	30	13 "
	V	Hardy Andrew	42	floorlayer	30	here
	W	Hardy Nora—†	42	housekeeper	31	"
	X	Kickham Charles	42	student	25	"
	Y	Kickham Joseph M	42	superintendent	58	"

23

Lambert Street Continued

z	Kickham Mary E —†	42	housekeeper	38	here	
A	Leahy Agnes V— †	42	"	32	"	
B	Leahy Dennis	42	retired	38	"	
C	Leahy Thomas J	42	foreman	41	"	

Linwood Square

A	DeSilva Albert	2	retired	73	here	
B	DeSilva Lillian I —†	2	housewife	74	"	
C	Homer Ella S— †	4	"	57	"	
D	Homer Thomas J	4	editor	67	"	
E	Homer Thomas J, jr	4	salesman	27	"	
F	LaBadessa Anna †	5	housewife	49	135 Dover	
G	LaBadessa Carmelo	5	barber	66	135 "	
H	LaBadessa Francis P	5	architect	25	135 "	
K	Davis Martha M—†	6	artist	60	here	
N	Arnett John	7	chauffeur	24	P E I	
O	Arnett Ruby †	7	factory worker	21	"	
P	O'Brien Clara †	7	housewife	40	here	
R	O'Brien William J	7	engineer	41	"	
S	Kaidan Annie —†	8	housewife	42	137 Ruggles	
T	Kaidan Leo	8	factory worker	47	137 "	
U	Mallog Hannah —†	8	housewife	65	69 Smith	
V	Mallog John	8	laborer	39	69 "	
W	Mallog Joseph F	8	"	37	69 "	
X	Hemingway William A	9	"	50	127 Cedar	
Y	Morris Mary —†	9	housekeeper	75	127 "	
Z	Shelton Elizabeth —†	9	housewife	45	127 "	
A	Shelton Joseph P	9	janitor	54	127 "	
B	Redway Emily M †	10	housewife	38	here	
C	Redway Walter E	10	janitor	40	"	
D	Widner Alvina †	10	housewife	28	18 New Heath	
E	Widner John	10	woodworker	35	18 "	
F	Thompson Andrew	10	piano polisher	45	73 Hunt'n av	
G	Thompson Elsie —†	10	housekeeper	34	73 "	
H	Tobias Abraham	12	machinist	40	here	
K	Tobias Jennie †	12	housewife	62	"	
L	Tobias Louis	12	florist	28	"	
M	Tobias Minnie —†	12	saleswoman	22	"	
N	Tobias Nathan	12	tailor	65	"	

Page.	Letter.	FULL NAME.	Residence, April 1, 1926.	Occupation	Supposed Age.	Reported Residence, April 1, 1925. Street and Number.

Linwood Square - Continued

o	Crawford Jacob	12	screenmaker	38	here
p	Crawford Rachael— †	12	housewife	37	"
r	Merrill Addie C—†	13	"	29	Vermont
s	Merrill Frank H	13	bookkeeper	29	"
t	Murphy Agnes—†	13	housewife	22	here
u	Murphy William A	13	machinist	21	"
v	Wisentaner Anna—†	13	housewife	45	"
w	Wisentaner Frank R	13	chauffeur	23	"
x	Wisentaner J Albert	13	auditor	24	"
y	Wisentaner John B	13	machinist	54	"
z	Donovan Nellie—†	14	bookkeeper	50	"
a	Kilday John W	14	inspector	57	"
b	Kilday Margaret—†	14	student	21	"
c	Dosenberg John	16	carpenter	34	Lawrence
d	Gregis Alide—†	16	housewife	31	45 Fort av
e	Gregis John	16	factory worker	34	45 "
f	Seedin Peter	16	carpenter	29	here
g	Stabin John	16	"	27	"
h	Weichel Mary—†	16	housewife	43	"
k	Weichel Victor	16	mechanic	47	"
l	Burns Blanche—†	20	housewife	39	"
m	Burns John M	20	machinist	44	"
n	Shea Thompkins	20	porter	24	"
o	McDonald Burnett	20	chauffeur	25	160 Hillside
p	McDonald Mary—†	20	housewife	22	160 "
r	Norton Amy—†	20	stitcher	40	Maine
s	Finneran Catherine N—†	22	housekeeper	32	here
t	Finneran James J	22	chauffeur	31	"
u	Finneran Patrick	22	retired	78	"
v	Finneran Patrick B	22	policeman	33	"
w	Finneran William	22	laborer	30	"
x	O'Connor Helen—†	22	bookbinder	34	"
y	Kiley Doris—†	24	stitcher	30	"
z	Kiley Simon J	24	salesman	32	"
a	McDade Elizabeth—†	24	clerk	32	"
b	Stuart Elizabeth—†	24	housewife	56	"
c	Stuart James M	24	salesman	28	"
d	Stuart Thomas	24	superintendent	58	"
e	Donnelly Mary A—†	26	housewife	31	81 Centre
f	Donnelly Michael	26	chauffeur	35	81 "

Page.	Letter.	FULL NAME.	Residence, April 1, 1926.	Occupation.	Supposed Age.	Reported Residence, April 1, 1925. Street and Number.

Linwood Street

G	Bennett Charles	1	grocer	35	here
H	Bennett Maude—†	1	housewife	29	"
K	Hairston Elizabeth—†	1	waitress	31	35 Cunard
M	Berry David	19	clerk	29	here
N	Berry Ida—†	19	housewife	23	"
O	Leafer Fannie—†	19	"	52	"
P	Leafer Samuel	19	carpenter	55	"
R	Pederson Hans	19	painter	39	"
S	Pederson Magda—†	19	housewife	33	"
T	Bulkley Bertha V—†	21	teacher	43	"
U	Bulkley Suzan—†	21	housekeeper	84	"
V	Bulkley Walter	21	mechanic	59	"
W	Edwards Ann—†	23	housewife	52	"
X	Edwards William	23	carpenter	50	"
Y	Crowley Charles F	23	painter	29	"
Z	Pike Catherine—†	23	housewife	28	7 Millmont
A	Pike James N	23	laborer	27	7 "
B	Robertson Catherine F—†	25	housewife	58	here
C	Robertson Edward J	25	clerk	23	"
D	Robertson Gladys M—†	25	housewife	27	"
E	Robertson Harry R	25	chauffeur	27	"
F	Robertson William G	25	retired	64	"
G	Shruhan Frank F	25	chauffeur	22	"
H	Shruhan Margaret E—†	25	housewife	22	"
K	Curley Mary A—†	27	housekeeper	69	"
L	Flint Martha E—†	27	"	90	"
M	O'Hare John	39	clerk	30	"
N	O'Hare Mary—†	39	housewife	30	"
O	Carr Winifred—†	39	housekeeper	68	"
P	Greaney James P	39	retired	70	"
R	Emerson George N	39	chauffeur	33	"
S	Emerson Mary E—†	39	housewife	31	"
T	McNamara Mary L—†	39	housekeeper	56	"
U	Paton Louise M—†	39	saleswoman	38	"
V	Murray Celia—†	41	housewife	50	"
W	Murray George	41	carpenter	50	"
X	Miller Alma—†	41	housewife	37	"
Y	Miller Henry F	41	engineer	37	"
Z	Keskula Elizabeth—†	41	housewife	34	37 Walden
A	Keskula John	41	carpenter	41	37 "

26

Page	Letter	FULL NAME.	Residence, April 1, 1926.	Occupation.	Supposed Age.	Reported Residence, April 1, 1925. Street and Number.

Linwood Street—Continued

B	Hash Edward	41	machinist	50	here
C	Hash Jennete—†	41	housewife	50	"
D	Wall Mary—†	43	housekeeper	60	"
E	Boland Mary—†	43	housewife	31	224 Roxbury
F	Boland Nicolas	43	warehouseman	37	224 "
G	Lynch John	43	janitor	70	here
H	Thorson George	43	chauffeur	26	10 Highland av
K	Thorson Viola—†	43	housewife	20	10 "
L	Ginter Ida—†	45	stenographer	21	here
M	Ginter Mary—†	45	housewife	47	"
N	Gust Martin	45	machinist	45	"
O	Gust Mary—†	45	housewife	45	"
P	Higgins Julia—†	45	"	30	1 Johnson av
R	Higgins Thomas J	45	laborer	35	1 "
S	Parfenchook George S	45	machinist	44	here
T	Hannon Daniel P	51	meatcutter	63	"
U	Hannon Mary A—†	51	housewife	54	"
V	Thompson Albert A	51	teacher	29	18 Auburn
W	Thompson Alice E—†	51	housewife	29	216 Ruggles
X	O'Donnell Ann G—†	53	housekeeper	54	here

Millmont Street

Y	Decker Beatrice M—†	4	housewife	44	49 Walnut av
Z	Decker Robert E	4	chauffeur	40	49 "
A	Leitch Mary K—†	4	tel operator	22	49 "
B	Stefaney Anna—†	6	housewife	39	here
C	Stefaney John A	6	floorlayer	42	"
E	Pidgon Joseph	6	laborer	30	Quincy
F	Pidgon May—†	6	housekeeper	31	"
G	Bigi Benjamin	8	clerk	32	24 Lambert av
H	Bigi Marie—†	8	housewife	30	24 "
K	Muise Charles D	8	mechanic	40	23 Centre
L	Muise Virginia A—†	8	housewife	31	23 "
M	Hurvitz Jacob	10	printer	25	here
N	Hurvitz Louis R	10	advertising	35	"
O	Hurvitz Shirley D—†	10	stenographer	23	"
P	Krivitsky Ada G—†	10	housewife	36	"
R	Salemme Elizabeth—†	10	housekeeper	31	"
S	Salemme Joseph W	10	shoeworker	33	"

Page	Letter	Full Name	Residence, April 1, 1926.	Occupation.	Supposed Age.	Reported Residence, April 1, 1925. Street and Number.

Millmont Street—Continued

T	Skinner Otis A B	12	draftsman	36	here
U	Skinner Sarah B—†	12	housewife	67	"
V	Skinner Sarah C V—†	12	elevatorwoman	29	"
W	Whitche Chester	12	cook	43	"
X	Michalson Rachael—†	14	housewife	60	"
Y	Michalson Samuel	14	retired	70	"
Z	Solomon Emanuel	14	chauffeur	33	"
A	Solomon Rose—†	14	housewife	31	"
B	Austan August	14	chauffeur	43	"
C	Austan Matilda—†	14	housewife	40	"
D	Calloway Bertice J—†	16	"	30	"
E	Calloway William A	16	porter	52	"
F	Jackson George M	16	clerk	28	23 Fort av
G	Jackson Marcelena—†	16	housewife	27	23 "
H	Kenney Margaret—†	24	clerk	31	here
K	Kenney Mary—†	24	housekeeper	46	"
L	Freda Felix	26	cigarmaker	35	"
M	Freda Lena—†	26	housewife	26	"
N	Gherardelli Andrew	26	inspector	28	"
O	Gherardelli Frank	26	electrician	25	"
P	Gherardelli John	26	retired	59	"
R	Gherardelli Teresa—†	26	housewife	49	"
S	Paretchanian Esther—†	30	housekeeper	35	"
T	Paretchanian Harry	30	shoeworker	46	"
U	Johns Florence—†	30	bookkeeper	23	"
V	Margosian Almas—†	30	housewife	54	"
W	Margosian Anon	30	shoeworker	56	"
X	Morrill Ernest S	30	milkman	26	232 Bay State rd
Y	Morrill Grace A—†	30	housewife	26	Maine
Z	Harold Edward J	46	custodian	30	here
A	Nugent Mary V—†	46	housewife	39	"
B	Nugent William B	46	janitor	43	"
C	Nugent William B, jr	46	"	21	"

Morley Street

E	Robinson Grace—†	11	housewife	38	here
F	Robinson William A	11	real estate	43	"
G	Dorgan Elizabeth—†	12	housekeeper	46	"
H	Dorgan John J	12	glazier	46	"

28

Page	Letter	FULL NAME.	Residence, April 1, 1926.	Occupation.	Supposed Age.	Reported Residence, April 1, 1925. Street and Number.

Morley Street--Continued

K	Dorgan John J, jr	12	painter	23	here
L	Feeley John	12	laborer	45	"
M	Adler Charles	12	painter	43	"
N	Berson Julius	12	carpenter	44	"
O	Loorks Peter	12	"	37	"
P	Loorks Wilhemina—†	12	housewife	33	"
R	Shenburg Emily—†	12	domestic	40	84 Highland
S	Yurawitz Joseph	12	retired	75	here
T	Yurawitz Lucy—†	12	housekeeper	35	"
U	Lavender Fred	14	boxmaker	40	"
V	Nicholson Minnie—†	14	housekeeper	42	297 Tremont
W	Pinezich Cyprian	14	floorlayer	52	5 Dudley
X	Vlazanzich Marko	14	"	55	5 "
Y	Zec Blez	14	"	55	New York
Z	Kockery Catherine—†	15	housekeeper	40	here
A	Moran Michael	15	wool sorter	41	"
B	Moran Nellie—†	15	housewife	32	"
C	Ryan John	15	metalworker	26	"
D	Ryan Nora—†	15	housekeeper	25	"
E	Frazer Winifred L—†	16	saleswoman	37	"
F	Robinson Flora M—†	16	housekeeper	69	"
G	Holland Fred	17	chauffeur	38	"
H	Holland Margaret—†	17	housewife	30	"
K	Reynolds Edward A	17	contractor	28	"
L	Reynolds Katherine—†	17	housewife	56	"
M	Reynolds Mary M—†	17	stenographer	38	"
N	Crondell Ilene—†	18	copyholder	29	New York
O	Glenn Elizabeth M—†	18	housewife	30	here
P	Glenn John H	18	salesman	35	"
R	Rice James J	18	retired	60	14 Dorr
S	Rice Mary B—†	18	housewife	58	14 "
T	Shinderwolfe Walter O	18	salesman	26	here
U	Burns James	19	draftsman	30	"
V	Burns John	19	carpenter	38	"
W	Elberry John	19	janitor	50	"
X	Quinn Jack J	19	laborer	35	"
Y	Thorna Anna—†	19	housewife	35	"
Z	Thorna John	19	mechanic	40	"
A	Heumuller Catherine—†	20	housewife	47	"
B	Heumuller Emil	20	laborer	54	"
C	Kenney Edward T	20	clerk	46	"

Page	Letter	FULL NAME.	Residence, April 1, 1926.	Occupation	Supposed Age.	Reported Residence, April 1, 1925. Street and Number.

Morley Street —Continued

	D	Kenney Marion G—†	20	housewife	50	here
	E	King Albert E	20	shipper	35	25 Fort av
	F	King Helen—†	20	stitcher	32	25 "
	G	Canty Timothy F	21	clerk	65	here
	H	Ganley Joseph V	21	mechanic	40	"
	K	Kinsley Anna C—†	21	housewife	42	"
	L	Kinsley Charles L	21	carpenter	50	"
	M	Lohne Alfred	21	sandblaster	23	"
	N	Graney James	22	retired	82	"
	O	Graney John	22	tinsmith	52	"
	P	Graney Patrick	22	"	50	"
	R	Herlihy Mary—†	22	housekeeper	49	"

Norfolk Street

	S	Campbell Agnes M—†	5	housewife	41	here
	T	Murphy Anna D—†	5	"	27	"
	U	Murphy Joseph	5	agent	30	"
	V	Desautelle Edith—†	5	housewife	40	"
	W	Desautelle Joseph	5	embalmer	40	"
	X	Harn Michael J	7	fireman	36	317 Roxbury
	Y	Harn Rose A—†	7	housewife	37	317 "
	Z	Barrie Catherine—†	7	"	38	2806 Wash'n
	A	Barrie James	7	laborer	41	2806 "
	B	Yensan Carolina—†	7	housewife	30	31 Fort av
	C	Yensan William	7	laborer	28	31 "
	D	Hannon Frederick T	9	machinist	31	here
	E	Hannon Henry E	9	painter	33	"
	F	Hannon Marion A—†	9	housewife	28	"
	G	Andrews Secilia—†	9	"	24	"
	H	Andrews Walter	9	chauffeur	23	"
	K	Connors Hellen—†	9	housewife	53	"
	L	Connors John	9	chauffeur	23	"
	M	Hanna Albert J	9	laundryman	31	"
	N	Hanna Susie M—†	9	housewife	31	"
	O	Burgess Hattie E—†	10	"	39	37 Linden Park
	P	Burgess William	10	bellboy	22	37 "
	R	Delliro Cormela—†	11	housewife	24	5 Highland pl

30

Page.	Letter.	FULL NAME.	Residence, April 1, 1926.	Occupation.	Supposed Age.	Reported Residence, April 1, 1925. Street and Number.

Norfolk Street—Continued

s	Delliro Vito	11	laborer	33	5 Highland pl
T	Natorp Herman E	11	clerk	31	here
U	Smith Marian—†	11	houseworker	30	"
V	Smith Sarah—†	11	housewife	32	"
W	Merry Mary—†	11	"	44	"
X	Merry Thomas T	11	laborer	43	"
Y	Conroy Annie—†	12	housewife	30	"
Z	Conroy Thomas	12	mechanic	35	"
B	Williams Catherine—†	14	housewife	33	"
C	Williams Francis A	14	metalworker	36	"
D	Goss Joseph	15	painter	34	700 Tremont
E	Goss Mae—†	15	housewife	36	700 "
F	Cunniff Francis	15	steamfitter	32	here
G	Cunniff Hellen—†	15	housewife	29	"
H	Robinson James	15	U S N	40	"
L	McGee Alice T—†	15	housewife	28	"
K	Ward Mary—†	15	laundryworker	36	"
M	McGee William C	15	teamster	25	"
N	Mooney Daniel	17	steamfitter	42	"
O	Mooney Elizabeth—†	17	housewife	38	"
P	Foley Catherine—†	17	"	35	"
R	Foley John	17	laborer	21	"
S	Foley Mary A—†	17	bookkeeper	23	"
T	Murphy Catherine—†	19	housewife	45	"
U	Murphy Daniel J	19	cashier	54	"
W	Gabriel Catherine —†	23	housewife	40	"
X	Gabriel Ernest	23	machinist	51	"
Y	Cadigan Mary—†	23	housewife	39	"
Z	Cadigan Michael	23	laborer	40	"
A	Shaw Florence C—†	23	housewife	32	"
B	Shaw William	23	laborer	34	"
C	Costello Mary—†	25	housewife	45	15 Dudley
D	Carter Elliot—†	25	at home	80	here
E	Fowler Hazel E—†	25	clerk	22	"
F	Furbish Alma M—†	25	chemist	30	"
G	Allingham Alice—†	25	nurse	62	"
H	Temple Lucy—†	25	housewife	61	"
K	Kane Gladys—†	27	"	28	"
L	Kane John E	27	machinist	29	"

Page.	Letter.	FULL NAME.	Residence, April 1, 1926.	Occupation.	Supposed Age.	Reported Residence, April 1, 1925. Street and Number.

Norfolk Street—Continued

	Letter	FULL NAME	Res.	Occupation	Age	Reported Residence
	M	Slater Rose A—†	27	housewife	53	here
	N	Slater William	27	sexton	57	"
	O	Matson Frederick	30	barber	44	"
	P	Matson Olma—†	30	housewife	48	"
	R	Shine Joseph	30	clerk	24	710 Tremont
	S	Shine Margaret—†	30	housewife	24	710 "
	T	Marshall Joseph	30	metalworker	24	here
	U	Marshall Margaret—†	30	housewife	23	"
	V	Archibald Annie—†	31	"	50	"
	W	Archibald Walter	31	chauffeur	30	"
	X	Smith Alexander	31	clerk	28	Weymouth
	Y	Smith Samuel	31	janitor	56	"
	Z	Smith Susanna—†	31	housewife	55	"
	A	Bradbury James H	31	policeman	30	here
	B	Bradbury Winifred D—†	31	housewife	30	"
	C	Hugo George	rear 32	electrician	30	"
	D	Hugo Theresa—†	" 32	housewife	68	"
	E	Coughlin Charles J	38	engineer	51	72 Medford
	F	Coughlin Mary I—†	38	housewife	42	72 "
	G	Redington Margaret—†	38	housekeeper	38	238 Sylvia
	H	Redington Margaret L—†	38	candymaker	36	238 "
	K	Redington Rose G—†	38	saleswoman	26	238 "
	M	Brown Eleanor M—†	49	housewife	28	Medford
	N	Brown William	49	machinist	31	"
	O	Carthy Louise—†	49	housewife	26	here
	P	Carthy Ralph	49	machinist	30	"
	R	Wilson Christina L—†	49	housewife	51	"
	S	Wilson Hugh C	49	electrician	58	"
	T	Gately John P	51	clerk	46	"
	U	Gately Mary—†	51	housewife	43	"
	V	Gately Michael J	51	bricklayer	33	"
	V¹	Mason Jane Y—†	51	housewife	33	"
	Z	Mason Herbert G	51	U S N	36	"
	W	McGee Charles	51	retired	76	"
	X	Moller Jessie—†	51	housewife	38	England
	Y	Moller Reinold O	51	toolmaker	43	S America
	B	Baumpton Isabella T—†	53	housewife	40	here
	C	Baumpton John	53	superintendent	44	"
	D	Powers Charles W	53	clerk	62	"
	E	Powers Gertrude B—†	53	housewife	57	"

Letter.	FULL NAME.	Residence, April 1, 1926.	Occupation.	Supposed Age.	Reported Residence, April 1, 1925. Street and Number.

Roxbury Street

G	Smith John	224	laborer	24	1 Carnes pl
H	Smith Mary R—†	224	housewife	25	1 "
K	Fraser Christopher	224	laborer	45	here
L	Fraser Nellie—†	224	housewife	45	"
L¹	O'Toole Laurence	224	foreman	32	65 Bower
M	O'Toole Rose—†	224	housewife	26	65 "
N	Connors John J	224	chauffeur	27	197 Eustis
O	MacKenzie Helen—†	224	housewife	26	197 "
P	MacKenzie Thomas H	224	steamfitter	27	197 "
R	Shruher Delia—†	230	housekeeper	48	here
S	Shruher Dorothy—†	230	saleswoman	30	"
T	Shruher Parker A	230	car cleaner	38	"
V	Moran Margaret—†	234	laundress	24	27 Prentiss
W	Duffey John	234	laborer	67	here
X	Duffey Norah—†	234	housewife	68	"
Y	Voitusik Paul	234	cook	40	"
Z	McMahon Annie—†	234	housewife	50	"
A	McMahan Martin	234	motorman	49	"
C	Weidenhamer John	244	fireman	30	"
D	Weidenhamer Marie—†	244	housewife	25	"
E	Peterson Sophie—†	244	at home	75	"
F	Ford John	246	laborer	50	"
G	Ford Mary—†	246	housewife	45	"
H	O'Brien Catherine—†	246	"	40	"
K	O'Brien Timothy	246	laborer	47	"

Willoughby Place

N	MacKenzie Lela—†	1	housewife	26	here
O	MacKenzie Stanley J	1	electrician	26	"
P	Stuart Ethel—†	1	housekeeper	35	16 Cliff
R	Littlefield Herbert F	1	shoemaker	41	11½ W Cottage
S	Littlefield Lottie R—†	1	housewife	34	11½ "
U	Carnes Christina—†	2	housekeeper	40	38 Norfolk
V	Carnes Howard	2	carpenter	45	38 "
W	Keaveny Mary—†	2	housewife	27	here
X	Keaveny Michael J	2	clerk	28	"

Page.	Letter.	FULL NAME.	Residence, April 1, 1926	Occupation.	Supposed Age.	Reported Residence, April 1, 1925. Street and Number.

Willoughby Place—Continued

Y	Gately John	3	laborer	68	34 E Dedham
Z	Gill Annie M—†	3	housewife	39	34 "
A	Gill William	3	baker	41	34 "
C	Duggan Margaret—†	4	housekeeper	54	here
D	Duggan Patrick J	4	watchman	55	"
B	Griffin Edward	4	elevatorman	45	"
E	Devett Amos S	5	salesman	45	"
F	Devett Carrie—†	5	housewife	36	"
G	Russell Anna C—†	6	"	35	"
H	Russell James B	6	laborer	37	"

Ward 9—Precinct 14

CITY OF BOSTON.

LIST OF RESIDENTS
20 YEARS OF AGE AND OVER

(FEMALES INDICATED BY DAGGER)

AS OF

APRIL 1, 1926

HERBERT A. WILSON, ⎰ *Listing*

JAMES F. EAGAN, ⎱ *Board.*

CITY OF BOSTON—PRINTING DEPARTMENT

Bartlett Street

	F	Nolan Lillian †	7	housekeeper	38	here
	G	Edmunds Gertrude—†	7	housewife	36	"
	H	Edmunds Walter F	7	chauffeur	31	"
	K	Hull Donald	7	machinist	24	980 Harris'n av
	L	Hull Myrtle †	7	housewife	20	980 "
	M	Mulholland Delia—†	9	"	25	91 Marcella
	N	Mulholland James	9	painter	28	91 "
	O	Thompson John J	9	chauffeur	36	here
	P	Thompson Mary—†	9	housewife	33	"
	R	Corliss Emma—†	9	"	35	"
	S	Corliss Thomas	9	B F D	39	"
	T	Flanagan Lillian—†	11	housewife	37	79 Dudley
	U	Flanagan Michael	11	clerk	38	79 "
	W	McPhee Donald G	11	retired	71	here
	X	McPhee Mary—†	11	housewife	70	"
	Y	Picks Martha K—†	11	cashier	26	"
	Z	Kressler Johanna—†	13	domestic	45	"
	A	Simpson LeBarron	13	checker	35	49 Fulda
	B	Simpson Margaret—†	13	housewife	33	49 "
	C	Blair Marion—†	13	operator	30	here
	D	Leear Jennette—†	13	houseworker	33	"
	E	Webb Mabel †	15	housewife	22	8 Alvah Kittredge pk
	F	Webb Mason	15	chauffeur	24	8 "
	G	Eno Frances—†	15	housewife	69	here
	H	Eno Walter F	15	carpenter	28	"
	K	Eno Wilfred L	15	"	62	"
	L	Casey Marion—†	15	operator	22	"
	M	Casey Mary—†	15	buyer	45	"
	N	Fountain Amelia †	17	housewife	22	56 Bartlett
	O	Fountain Joseph H	17	chauffeur	23	56 "
	P	Driscoll Annie—†	17	housekeeper	47	here
	R	Driscoll Patrick J	17	laborer	57	"
	S	Bean Arthur H	17	carpenter	38	"
	T	Bean Chester E	17	"	39	"
	U	Bean Nellie F—†	17	housewife	37	"
	V	Johnson Mary—†	19	housekeeper	28	4 Malbon pl
	W	Chesley Georgianna G—†	19	houseworker	40	here
	X	Galletly Anna M—†	21	housewife	34	"
	Y	Galletly Ella J—†	21	housekeeper	59	"
	Z	Galletly John R	21	machinist	25	"

Page	Letter	Full Name	Residence, April 1, 1926.	Occupation	Supposed Age	Reported Residence, April 1, 1925. Street and Number.

Bartlett Street—Continued

A	Jaworski Henry	21	mechanic	27	21 Gibson
B	Jaworski Mary—†	21	housewife	50	21 "
C	Jaworski Valentene	21	machinist	51	21 "
D	Cloyd Eugene	23	metalworker	54	here
E	Cloyd Helen—†	23	housewife	46	"
F	Rodd Anna A—†	23	"	48	11 Elmwood pl
G	Rodd Edward L	23	carpenter	50	11 "
H	Luks Anna—†	25	housewife	49	151 Leverett
K	Luks Leopold	25	shoemaker	52	151 "
L	Czeszyk Joseph	25	carpenter	50	here
M	Czeszyk Josephine—†	25	housewife	40	"
O	Davison Eugene L	37	billposter	29	"
P	Davison Lillian—†	37	housewife	22	"
R	Ranney Clara F—†	37	clerk	23	"
S	Ranney Elizabeth L—†	37	housekeeper	52	"
T	Ranney Leander D	37	clerk	25	"
U	Lynch Mary C—†	37	stenographer	22	"
V	Madeno Alfred	37	barber	53	"
W	Madeno Ellen A—†	37	housewife	49	"
X	Blackmer Frances—†	39	domestic	55	"
Y	Kruse Carl M	39	starter	38	11 Rosemont rd
Z	Kruse Hattie M—†	39	housewife	40	11 "
A	McClaren Annie—†	39	domestic	50	here
B	Rankin Irving	39	watchman	60	2398 Wash'n
C	Ross Harry	41	shipper	31	here
D	Ross Theresa—†	41	housewife	35	"
E	Hurstak Georgia—†	41	"	48	"
F	Hurstak Peter F	41	shipper	48	"
G	Seeley Catherine L—†	41	housewife	49	"
H	Seeley Robert J	41	machinist	50	"
K	Reardon Mae T—†	55	housewife	34	"
L	Reardon William F	55	milkman	36	"
M	Gilson Agnes—†	55	stitcher	36	"
N	Gilson Ellen—†	55	housewife	72	"
O	Gilson Hugh	55	retired	74	"
P	Gilson Joseph	55	laborer	35	"
R	Gilson Margaret—†	55	forewoman	44	"
S	Gilson William	55	stonecutter	42	"
T	Albisser Benjamin	57	machinist	41	"
U	Albisser Martha—†	57	housewife	37	"

Page.	Letter.	FULL NAME.	Residence, April 1, 1926.	Occupation.	Supposed Age.	Reported Residence, April 1, 1925. Street and Number.

Bartlett Street —Continued

v	Mullaney Harold T	57	chauffeur	35	here
w	Mullaney Mary—†	57	housewife	35	"
x	Rosenfeld Clara—†	59	housekeeper	49	"
y	Rosenfeld Gustave	59	policeman	63	"
z	Rosenfeld Rosa—†	59	bookbinder	37	"
A	Ramsey Mary—†	59½	dressmaker	47	"
B	Murphy Annie J	59½	domestic	55	"
C	Murphy Mary G—†	59½	saleswoman	26	"
F	Keough John	67	gardener	65	"
G	King Anna—†	67	saleswoman	50	"
H	Laird Martha—†	67	"	35	"
K	MacMillen Duncan E	67	janitor	40	Cambridge
L	MacMillen Louise I—†	67	housewife	36	"
M	Michaelson Richard	67	paperhanger	48	here
N	O'Leary Anna—†	67	clerk	45	"
O	O'Leary Lillian—†	67	"	50	"
P	Reidy Mary—†	67	houseworker	25	1 Newsome pk
R	West Jessie—†	67	saleswoman	21	Lynn
S	Butler Edward	69	laborer	50	Ireland
T	Cahill Delia—†	69	housekeeper	42	here
U	Cahill Frank	69	porter	38	"
V	Cavanaugh Annie—†	69	candymaker	33	"
W	Donlon Peter	69	laborer	25	"
X	Harvey Patrick	69	machinist	47	47 Baldwin
Y	Heslan Bernard	69	electrician	50	here
Z	Mitchell John	69	laborer	27	"
A	Monahon Partick	69	fireman	45	"
B	Nangle Thomas	69	laborer	50	8 Linwood sq
C	Sullivan Patrick	69	"	45	268 Dudley
D	Walsh John	69	"	26	here
E	Walsh Thomas	69	"	28	"
F	Collins Delia—†	71	housekeeper	65	"
G	Cunningham Thomas	71	wireworker	50	"
H	McKenzie George	71	brassmolder	35	"
K	Murphy Alice—†	71	stitcher	22	Canada
L	Murphy Theresa—†	71	"	20	"
M	Richards Harold	71	metalworker	35	New York
N	Richards Mary—†	71	housewife	30	"
O	Rosenlof John	71	photographer	40	here
P	Rosenlof Joseph	71	tailor	74	"

4

Bartlett Terrace

R	Andrews Catherine—†	1	housewife	23	986 Parker
S	Burns Florence—†	1	housekeeper	43	126 Heath
T	Magoon Mary A—†	1	"	45	here
U	Feeley George	1	clerk	23	224 Roxbury
V	Feeley John J	1	printer	20	224 "
W	Feeley Mary—†	1	housekeeper	45	224 "
X	McKenzie John D	3	laborer	30	here
Y	McKenzie Josephine—†	3	housewife	30	"
Z	Harris John L	3	fireman	31	"
A	Broms Anna—†	3	laundress	57	"
B	Newman Segrid—†	3	"	50	"
C	Kampen Mary V—†	4	housekeeper	49	100 Wash'n
D	Weeks James J	4	millwright	59	here
E	Weeks Nellie—†	4	housewife	44	"
F	McKinnon Matilda—†	4	housekeeper	57	"
G	Bodge Emma O—†	5	"	76	1057 Col av
H	Bodge Herbert W	5	teamster	45	1057 "
K	Schmitt Agnes—†	5	housewife	51	1106 Tremont
L	Schmitt Otto A	5	painter	50	1106 "
M	Sambursky Anna—†	5	housekeeper	34	here
N	Sambursky Annie—†	5	"	53	"
O	Sambursky Elsie—†	5	clerk	33	"
P	Adario Joseph	6	laborer	31	"
R	Adario Mary E—†	6	housewife	30	"
S	Garfi John	6	real estate	35	"
T	Garfi Prudence—†	6	housewife	36	"
U	Sullivan Frank D	6	machinist	40	"
V	Sullivan Sadie—†	6	housewife	38	"
X	Saccoache Benjamin F	7	glazier	35	43 Fabin
Y	Saccoache Margaret—†	7	housewife	35	43 "
Z	White Ida—†	7	"	40	here
A	White Thomas	7	shoemaker	45	"
C	Pflegle Roy	8	painter	40	"
D	Harms Edna J—†	8	housewife	47	"
E	Harms Frederick G	8	clerk	54	"
F	Queen Frank H	8	"	49	"
G	Fleming Agnes A—†	10	housewife	28	Cambridge
H	Fleming Harold	10	plumber	29	"
K	Dacey John	10	clerk	37	here
L	Dacey Mary—†	10	housewife	37	"

5

Page	Letter	FULL NAME.	Residence, April 1, 1926.	Occupation	Supposed Age.	Reported Residence, April 1, 1925. Street and Number.

Bartlett Terrace—Continued

	M	Fitzgerald Elizabeth—†	10	housewife	30	711 E Seventh
	N	Fitzgerald Patrick	10	expressman	30	711 "
	O	Tootaker Jennette—†	12	housekeeper	44	here
	P	Toothaker William C	12	carpenter	77	"
	R	Dilegarmi Peter	12	shoeworker	33	Cambridge
	S	Dilegarmi Tessie—†	12	housewife	33	"
	T	Neff Bertha—†	12	"	57	here
	U	Neff Jacob B	12	mechanic	23	"
	V	Neff Minnie—†	12	clerk	28	"

Dudley Place

	W	Rhodes Robert H	3	machinist	54	here
	X	O'Brien Elizabeth—†	3	housekeeper	50	3 Ringgold
	Y	Browne Amelea C—†	4	"	60	here
	Z	Browne Anna S—†	4	clerk	29	"
	A	Browne Cassie M—†	4	"	34	"
	B	Browne Edward R	4	printer	66	"
	C	Browne Edward R, jr	4	clerk	33	"
	D	Browne Millie C—†	4	dressmaker	25	"
	E	Browne William	4	estimator	37	"

Dudley Street

	F	Doyle Julia F—†	1	collector	49	here
	H	Kingsley Etta—†	1	packer	40	"
	K	Kingsley Minnie—†	1	stitcher	45	"
	L	Pauly Alice—†	1	packer	20	"
	M	Pauly Eva—†	1	"	40	"
	N	McInnes Florence †	1	cook	42	"
	T	Dahl Hulda—†	1	houseworker	75	"
	U	Smith Mary L—†	1	stitcher	42	"
	V	McCarthy Hannah—†	1	houseworker	50	"
	W	Fay Margaret—†	1	"	50	"
	X	Bates Arthur	1	manager	47	"
	Y	Interson Nettie—†	1	houseworker	55	"
	A	Flynn Mary—†	1	matron	52	"

6

Page.	Letter.	FULL NAME.	Residence, April 1, 1926.	Occupation.	Supposed Age.	Reported Residence, April 1, 1925. Street and Number.

Dudley Street—Continued

	c	Keogh Charlotte—†	1	houseworker	60	76 Weston
	d	Leahy Margaret—†	1	"	62	here
	e	McDonnell Catherine—†	1	checker	32	"
	f	McDermott Margaret—†	1	packer	45	"
	g	Black Mary—†	1	collector	45	"
	h	Wood Elizabeth—†	1	houseworker	70	35 Chadwick
	k	Black Mary—†	1	collector	50	here
	l	Keogh Edward	1	clerk	40	"
	m	Keogh Mary—†	1	stitcher	35	"
	n	Gardener Julia—†	1	dressmaker	50	"
	o	Felton Amelia—†	3	"	62	Harvard
	p	Lane George	3	mason	54	here
	r	McMullin Jean—†	3	housekeeper	21	79 Centre
	s	McMullin Mary E—†	3	housewife	46	79 "
	t	Toomey Michael T	3	chef	50	11 Corning
	u	Brindley Lawrence	5	porter	56	9 Kent
	v	Bugby George W	5	retired	68	155 Boston
	w	Garritty Joseph	5	messenger	27	here
	x	Leone Antonio	5	shoemaker	45	"
	y	McLennan Catherine—†	5	housewife	47	"
	z	McLennan Donald	5	metalworker	21	"
	a	McManus William	5	laborer	53	216 Highland
	b	McNeil John R	5	carpenter	54	Canada
	c	Pratt Bertha—†	5	operator	28	here
	f	Hooley James J	9	milkman	30	9 Delle av
	g	Hooley John	9	"	26	9 "
	h	Minnehan Bridget—†	9	housewife	60	9 "
	k	Minnehan Patrick	9	car cleaner	55	14 Faxon
	l	Bishop Lena—†	9	housewife	33	Maine
	m	Bishop Willard	9	plasterer	36	"
	n	McDonald Chester	9	cook	28	18 St Germain
	o	McDonald Hubbard	9	plasterer	56	Maine
	p	McDonald Jennie—†	9	housewife	50	"
	r	Fitzgerald Mary—†	11	laundress	48	here
	s	Ingraham Margaret T—†	11	"	50	"
	t	McCluskey Frances—†	11	housewife	60	"
	u	Norton Agnes B—†	11	"	31	"
	v	Norton Bartley	11	artist	33	"
	w	Dolan Edward	11	watchman	30	"
	x	Dolan Mary—†	11	shoeworker	26	"

Page.	Letter.	FULL NAME.	Residence, April 1, 1926.	Occupation.	Supposed Age.	Reported Residence, April 1, 1925. Street and Number.

Dudley Street—Continued

	Y	Doolan Agnes—†	11	milliner	28	here
	z	Doolan Elizabeth—†	11	saleswoman	38	"
	A	Doolan Mary—†	11	housewife	69	"
	B	Kelly John T	11	retired	67	"
	c	Savageau Angelina—†	13	housewife	50	"
	D	Savageau Ida—†	13	stenographer	20	"
	E	Savageau Joseph O	13	shoecutter	44	"
	F	Bentley Alice M—†	13	operator	22	26 Lambert
	G	Gammon Elwood G	13	salesman	47	here
	H	Gammon Margaret G—†	13	housewife	39	"
	K	Mullaney Martha—†	15	storekeeper	64	3 Dudley
	M	Yee Wing	19	laundryman	37	here
	N	Dirkman Margeurite—†	21	clerk	21	"
	o	Palmer Catherine—†	21	housewife	54	"
	P	Palmer William A	21	machinist	56	"
	R	Drydale Peter	21	salesman	57	"
	s	Drysdale Raymond R	21	inspector	28	"
	T	Miner Augustine J	27	engineer	40	59 E Springfield
	U	Miner Bridget—†	27	housewife	44	59 "
	v	Corliss Catherine—†	38	housekeeper	50	here
	w	Flynn Mary—†	38	waitress	24	11 Linden Park
	x	Gately John J	38	painter	50	21 Dale
	y	Knaff Flora—†	38	housewife	50	1 Putnam pl
	z	Knaff Lillian R—†	38	stenographer	25	1 "
	A	Knaff Mary—†	38	housekeeper	22	1 "
	B	Lyons Patrick J	38	rigger	42	1100 Col av
	c	McMahon James	38	laborer	70	34 Juniper
	D	Murphy Christopher	38	"	30	here
	E	Parker Colin	38	iceman	24	50 Dudley
	F	Sullivan Charles F	38	laborer	41	6 Winter
	G	Temple Joseph	38	carpenter	41	here
	H	Temple Rose—†	38	seamstress	36	"
	K	Walsh Mary—†	38	laundress	60	11 Linden Park
	L	Walsh Michael J	38	painter	62	11 "
	N	Davey James	40	porter	48	here
	o	DeYoung Ernest H	40	welder	32	"
	P	DeYoung Irene A—†	40	housewife	32	"
	R	Donovan Daniel	40	car washer	50	40 Norfolk
	s	Gillis Alexander	40	carpenter	34	here
	T	Ginty Joseph	40	custodian	36	"
	U	Menezene Delphine—†	40	storekeeper	45	"

8

Dudley Street—Continued

v	Mitchell Catherine —†	40	domestic	48	Ireland
w	Ward Bessie—†	40	waitress	28	5 Alvah Kittredge pk
x	Ward Helen—†	40	hairdresser	20	5 "
y	Carmichael Martha C—†	46	houseworker	33	here
z	Cushman George T	46	physician	67	"
a	Cushman Sylvia F—†	46	housewife	66	"
c	Carey Bertha V—†	48	"	36	"
d	Carey John J	48	teamster	36	"
e	Mone Catherine E—†	48	operator	30	"
f	Twoomey Hanna—†	48	housekeeper	72	"
g	Bell Elizabeth—†	50	candymaker	30	"
h	Brown Mabel—†	50	waitress	35	Worcester
k	Cummings Ross	50	retired	49	Maine
l	Foisy Emily—†	50	housewife	49	here
m	Foisy Louis G	50	painter	48	"
n	Lewis Stella—†	50	dressmaker	30	Maine
o	McCabe Warren	50	chauffeur	21	52 Joy
p	O'Brien Albert G	50	"	35	here
r	Scott Elijah	50	shoemaker	60	Cochituate
s	Sears Willard	50	machinist	40	here
t	Welch Perley	50	"	20	Canada
u	Finneran Delia —†	52	housewife	43	here
v	Finneran Malachi	52	waiter	46	"
w	Lawton Edward P rear	52	salesman	65	"
x	Lawton Margaret—† "	52	housewife	51	"
y	Coleman James B	53	clerk	37	"
z	Crowley Charlotte—†	53	housewife	36	379 Talbot av
a	Crowley John J	53	electrician	37	379 "
b	Maguire James F	53	manager	27	here
e	McCue Daniel J	53	ironworker	31	"
c	McCusker Margaret A—†	53	housewife	58	"
d	McCusker Mary A—†	53	bookfolder	64	"
f	Murphy Joseph J	53	brickmason	30	146 Hillside
g	O'Neil Bernard J	53	bookkeeper	30	96 Vernon
h	Rose Barney	53	upholsterer	24	here
k	Ward Walter J	53	agent	53	"
l	Wiley Theodore	53	clerk	27	"
m	Ananiades Anania A	54	laborer	36	"
n	Ananiades Mary—†	54	housewife	40	"
o	Beaupre Max	55	lineman	28	"

Page.	Letter.	FULL NAME.	Residence, April 1, 1926.	Occupation.	Supposed Age.	Reported Residence, April 1, 1925. Street and Number.

Dudley Street—Continued

	P	Dolan William	55	laborer	30	5 Eliot sq
	R	Hurney John	55	cobbler	40	37 Childs
	S	Kilduff Luke	55	laborer	35	here
	T	Medwar Simon	55	storekeeper	28	38 Dudley
	U	Ryan John F	55	milkman	46	here
	V	Ryan Minnie A—†	55	housewife	47	"
	W	Sullivan John	55	shoeworker	30	331 Centre
	X	Sullivan Thomas	55	"	32	627 Col av
	Y	White Peter	55	motorman	34	here
	Z	Mellon John	56	retired	68	5 Norfolk
	A	Mellon Margaret—†	56	packer	23	5 "
	B	Murphy Harold	56	expressman	37	5 "
	C	Murphy Helen—†	56	housekeeper	32	5 "
	D	Buckley John J	57	shoeworker	37	here
	E	Griffin Delia J—†	57	housewife	44	"
	F	Griffin Mary A—†	57	houseworker	53	"
	G	Johnson Ida—†	57	laundress	50	"
	H	Murray Patrick	57	laborer	45	"
	K	Shulden Rudolph	57	painter	37	"
	L	Toomey James	57	"	44	24 Worcester
	M	Oliver Joseph	58	designer	58	here
	N	Olivier Richard	58	expressman	26	"
	O	Conway Joseph	59	clerk	26	Ireland
	P	Conway Patrick J	59	policeman	31	here
	S	Glennon John	59	plumber	25	1275 Col av
	R	Glennon Julia—†	59	housewife	24	167 Homestead
	T	Messenger Vose	59	carpenter	41	here
	U	Nicholson Lillian—†	59	shoeworker	23	2792 Wash'n
	V	Pierce Albert	59	salesman	46	1 Willoughby pl
	W	Rice Rose J—†	59	housewife	38	here
	X	Rice Walter L	59	chauffeur	40	"
	Y	Spencer Charles	59	laborer	50	"
	Z	Upton Henry B	59	carpenter	24	"
	A	Walsh Mary E—†	59	housekeeper	75	"
	B	McCallum Zella—†	rear 60	medium	48	"
	C	Sullivan John	" 60	actor	59	"
	D	Donovan Daniel	61	roofer	52	"
	E	Donovan Mary A—†	61	housewife	49	"
	F	Ganter Annie—†	61	attendant	39	"
	G	Cheverie Leo	64	carpenter	33	P E I

10

Page.	Letter.	FULL NAME.	Residence, April 1, 1926.	Occupation.	Supposed Age.	Reported Residence, April 1, 1925. Street and Number.

Dudley Street—Continued

H	Hudson Edward G	64	electrician	29	here
K	Kilroy Anna—†	64	housewife	25	"
L	Kilroy Bernard J	64	student	21	"
M	Kilroy Thomas P	64	finisher	23	"
N	Lyons Jennie—†	64	laundress	50	Chelsea
O	McLellan Roderick	64	watchman	55	P E I
P	Ronan Dennis	64	stonecutter	40	here
R	Ronan Mary A—†	64	housewife	45	"
S	Graham Robert	65	installer	55	"
T	McAlder Annie A—†	65	housewife	48	6 Ellsworth
U	McAlder Daniel E	65	barber	63	6 "
V	Finnegan Peter	rear 66	porter	35	here
W	Kennedy Nora A—†	" 66	housewife	55	"
X	Kennedy Patrick J	" 66	watchman	55	"
Y	Lynch Michael	" 66	laborer	35	"
Z	McMorris Mary—†	" 67	housewife	47	"
A	Weihe Annie—†	67	inspector	45	"
B	Weihe William	67	chauffeur	47	"
C	Bassett William	rear 68	manager	45	"
D	Brackett Wilfred	" 68	retired	65	"
E	Carty Thomas	" 68	bookkeeper	40	"
F	Hayes Thomas	" 68	laborer	40	"
G	Healy Vincent	" 68	chauffeur	23	Pawtucket R I
H	O'Donnell John	" 68	mechanic	23	2 Myrtle pl
K	O'Donnell Mary A—†	" 68	housewife	20	2 "
M	Donahue Annie—†	70	laundress	35	here
N	Donahue Edward J	70	chauffeur	40	"
O	Donahue Ellen—†	70	housewife	64	"
P	Fisher Annie—†	70	rubberworker	23	89 Norfolk av
R	King Joseph	70	clerk	41	108 Cedar
S	King Mary—†	70	housewife	38	108 "
T	Sabkie Richard	70	waiter	42	here
U	Schwartz Joseph	70	electrician	38	"
V	Stanz Lillian—†	70	laundress	53	"
X	Irving Phoebe H—†	72	housewife	26	9 La Fayette pk
Y	Irving William F	72	painter	24	9 "
A	Kanas Peter	76	fruit	49	here
B	Wilson Arthur	76	retired	46	Milton
C	Wilson Helen—†	76	housewife	45	"
D	Watson Margaret—†	79	"	44	here
E	Watson William W	79	laborer	47	"

Dudley Street—Continued

F	Watson William W, jr	79	mechanic	25	here
G	McDonald Helen—†	79	housewife	30	101 Marcella
H	McDonald Patrick	79	mechanic	40	144 "
N	Devereaux Helen—†	85	houseworker	60	here
O	Jackson Bernice—†	85	"	30	Dedham
P	Looney Hannah M—†	85	agent	52	here
R	Sullivan Nora M—†	85	at home	55	17 Centre
S	Cavanaugh Alice J—†	87	clerk	26	here
T	Cunningham Edward P	87	chauffeur	20	"
U	Cunningham Mary E—†	87	housewife	49	"
V	Cunningham Peter F	87	mechanic	50	"
Y	Law Albert C	93	cook	38	"
Z	Law Laura—†	93	housewife	38	"
A	Law William	93	salesman	42	"
C	Matheson Edith—†	95	housewife	38	"
D	Matheson John	95	machinist	57	"
E	Seigler Isadore—†	95	cigarmaker	45	652 Harris'n av
F	Seigler Rebecca—†	95	housewife	44	652 "
A	Lewis John	144	shipper	38	Somerville
B	Lewis Leo	144	roofer	37	here
C	O'Brien Peter C	144	motorman	42	"
D	Walsh John	144	clerk	50	"
E	Walsh Mary E—†	144	housekeeper	48	"
F	LeMoind Anna—†	144	housewife	58	"
G	Wentworth Andrew W	144	laborer	34	Medford
H	Wentworth Lavina A—†	144	housewife	32	"
L	Butler John S	144	laborer	38	Somerville
M	Carpenter Josephine—†	144	houseworker	48	106 Hunt'n av
N	Dowling George	144	laborer	34	106 "
O	Wegeler Adell—†	144	housewife	32	Somerville
P	Wegeler George	144	machinist	30	"
R	Bickerstaff Anna E—†	144	housewife	58	here
S	Bickerstaff Robert P	144	laborer	62	"

Dunlow Place

A	Burns Margaret E—†	41	seamstress	56	here
B	Turner George F	41	lithographer	34	"
C	Turner Harry J	41	machinist	38	"
D	Turner Mary E—†	41	housekeeper	66	"

Page.	Letter.	FULL NAME.	Residence, April 1, 1926.	Occupation.	Supposed Age.	Reported Residence, April 1, 1925.
						Street and Number.

Elmwood Street

	E	Brady Julia—†	87	washwoman	68	here
	F	Travers Dorothy—†	87	housewife	26	"
	G	Travers Edward	87	nurse	35	"
	H	Healy William C	87	machinist	42	"
	K	Luby Annie—†	87	housewife	48	"
	L	Luby Arthur	87	clerk	42	"
	M	Luby Edward E	87	baker	24	"
	N	Luby Evelyn—†	87	accountant	22	"
	O	Luby John P	87	clerk	34	"
	P	Luby William	87	"	21	"
	R	Kelliher Christina V—†	93	housewife	33	"
	S	Kelliher Cornelius A	93	rigger	44	"
	T	Jahn Frank L	93	salesman	57	"
	U	Jahn Mary E—†	93	housewife	57	"

Gay Street

	V	Pyne David J	1	laborer	65	here
	W	Pyne Mary—†	1	housekeeper	65	"
	X	McHatton Helen F—†	1	"	35	"
	Y	McHattan James H	1	laborer	35	"
	Z	Kitson Earnest	3	clerk	57	"
	A	Kitson Jarda F—†	3	housekeeper	52	"
	B	Nelson Charles W	3	machinist	47	"
	C	Nelson Mary E—†	3	housekeeper	49	"
	D	Hughes John L	3A	chauffeur	26	"
	E	Hughes Mary E—†	3A	housekeeper	24	"
	F	Hartigan James A	7	chauffeur	35	11 Lamont
	G	Hartigan Joseph F	7	"	24	11 "
	H	Hartigan Mary—†	7	housekeeper	64	11 "
	K	Hartigan Michael	7	laborer	64	11 "
	K¹	Sullivan Elizabeth S—†	7	housekeeper	47	here
	L	Morrison Charlotte A—†	7	waitress	47	"
	M	Morrison Charlotte A—†	7	housekeeper	21	"
	N	Morrison John J	7	draftsman	20	"

Page.	Letter	FULL NAME	Residence, April 1, 1926.	Occupation.	Supposed Age.	Reported Residence, April 1, 1925. Street and Number.

Hayden Terrace

	F	McMorris Alice—†	1	nurse	55	here
	G	VanKampe Catherine—†	1	housewife	41	"
	H	VanKampe Edward	1	butcher	40	"
	K	McDonald James	1	laborer	33	"
	L	McGillvary James	1	carpenter	22	"
	M	Gillis John A	1	"	48	"
	N	O'Neil John	2	laborer	40	134 Terrace
	O	O'Neil Mary—†	2	housewife	38	134 "
	P	Hobbs William N	2	expressman	46	8 Cedar
	R	Levy Bertha—†	2	housekeeper	23	Dedham
	S	Morrison Gladys—†	2	housewife	28	Ayer
	T	Morrison Grover	2	pressman	28	"
	U	Burpee Lockwood E	3	farmer	21	here
	V	Burpee Lockwood S	3	inspector	59	"
	W	Benjamin Catherine—†	3	housewife	30	"
	X	Benjamin Louis	3	clerk	31	"
	Y	Bresnahan John	3	laborer	70	"
	Z	McEllaney Edward	3	"	35	27 Newland
	A	Lane Edson	4	teamster	23	53 Vernon
	B	Lane Larry	4	laborer	27	53 "
	C	O'Donnell Annie—†	4	housekeeper	42	53 "
	D	Calesa Louis	4	garageman	47	3 Bicknell av
	E	Calesa Mary—†	4	housewife	43	3 "
	F	Palmer Elizabeth—†	4	"	55	86 Warrenton
	G	Palmer Millett, jr	4	chauffeur	23	86 "
	H	Palmer Millett	4	stockman	56	86 "

John Eliot Square

| | Z | Southerland Donald | 3 | carpenter | 30 | here |
| | Z1 | Southerland Ethel—† | 3 | clerk | 28 | " |

Kenilworth Street

| | M | Killen Frank | 1 | mover | 37 | here |
| | N | Killen Martha A—† | 1 | housewife | 36 | " |

14

Page.	Letter.	FULL NAME.	Residence, April 1, 1926.	Occupation.	Supposed Age.	Reported Residence, April 1, 1925. Street and Number.

Kenilworth Street—Continued

	o	VonDell Frank L	1	chauffeur	52	19 Bartlett
	p	VonDell Mary B—†	1	housewife	47	19 "
	r	Lenihan Chester F	1	pianoworker	35	here
	s	Lenihan Mary K—†	1	housewife	35	"
	t	Sundine Anna T—†	1	waitress	38	"
	u	Sundine Emily—†	1	tailoress	51	"
	v	Sundine Robert F	1	bookbinder	54	"
	w	Jensen Charles E	1	salesman	22	"
	x	Jensen Charles M	1	"	45	"
	y	Jensen Mennie B—†	1	housewife	41	"
	z	Hurley John P	1	bricklayer	53	3 Bradford
	a	Hurley Mary—†	1	housewife	43	3 "
	e	Connor Catherine—†	7	housekeeper	58	here
	f	Connor Mary E—†	7	clerk	26	"
	g	Connor Patrick J	7	teamster	29	"
	h	Kelly John	7	laborer	20	"
	k	Brown George H	13	bellman	46	"
	l	Brown Josephine L—†	13	housewife	34	"
	m	Echols Anna G—†	13	"	43	"
	n	Echols William J	13	contractor	54	N Carolina
	o	Jones Fanny—†	15	housewife	65	9 Wellington
	p	Jones William H	15	fireman	65	9 "
	r	Hastings Ada E—†	15	housewife	42	here
	s	Hastings Samuel H	15	waiter	46	"
	t	Teixeira Antonio D	15	merchant	39	"
	u	Teixeira Carrie A—†	15	housewife	31	"
	v	Campbell Ellen—†	17	"	50	"
	w	Campbell William D	17	janitor	61	"
	x	Gatwood Charles	17	postal clerk	29	Cambridge
	y	Freeman Catherine—†	19	housewife	51	Chicago Ill
	z	Freeman Henry	19	porter	64	"
	a	Jackson Cora—†	19	housekeeper	68	60 Vernon
	b	Jackson Rosetta—†	19	elevatorwoman	39	60 "
	c	Jenkins Rachel—†	19	housekeeper	65	60 "
	d	Petkin Florida—†	19	curtainworker	38	60 "
	e	Taylor Edna S—†	19	housewife	37	here
	f	Taylor John D	19	porter	61	"
	g	Beauzard Celeste—†	21	hairdresser	42	"
	h	Lewis Alice W—†	21	housewife	26	"
	k	Lewis Henry C	21	waiter	57	"
	l	Lewis Henry O	21	draftsman	31	"

15

Kenilworth Street---Continued

M	Lewis Lucy E—†	21	housewife	52	here
N	Brown Dorothy—†	22	elevatorwoman	27	"
O	Hughes Fannie U—†	22	housewife	47	"
P	Hughes Joseph B	22	porter	54	"
R	Hughes Robert J	22	laborer	52	"
T	Hanson Lucy A—†	24	housewife	58	"
U	Hanson Miles	24	clergyman	60	"
V	Hanson Miles	24	student	33	"
A	Weeman Anna—†	38	housewife	32	"
B	Weeman Edward	38	chauffeur	33	"
C	Mahoney Catherine—†	38	housewife	55	"
D	Mahoney John E	38	plumber	54	"
E	Clark Hattie—†	38	housekeeper	55	55 Forest
F	Emerson Annie—†	40	"	65	here
G	Donigan Catherine—†	40	"	75	"
H	Qualters Margaret—†	40	housewife	29	"
K	Qualters Thomas M	40	foreman	36	"
L	Huette Eugenie—†	42	housewife	26	"
M	Huette Rodolphe	42	postal clerk	28	"
N	Cherrett Florence—†	42	housewife	32	237 Warren
O	Cherrett William A	42	conductor	33	237 "
P	Curtis Annie M—†	42	housekeeper	40	here
R	Curtis Fred J	42	salesman	28	"
S	Curtis Isabel M—†	42	tel operator	30	"
T	Raines Jane—†	44	housekeeper	69	2 Ballou av
U	Raines Mary—†	44	dressmaker	35	2 "
V	Tucker Hattie—†	44	housewife	45	here
W	Tucker Herman D	44	engineer	46	"
X	Butterfield Henry	44	clerk	50	Dedham

Lambert Avenue

Z	Atkinson Andrew	4	candymaker	43	Marblehead
A	Marsh Eugene	4	conductor	40	12 Wash'n
B	Marsh Matilda—†	4	housewife	37	12 "
C	McMahon Emma—†	4	clerk	60	here
D	Baker Robert H	4	chauffeur	32	"

Linden Park Street

H	Brown Hammond C	8	laborer	53	here
K	Chakarian Rose —†	8	bookkeeper	24	"
L	Chakarian Vahran	8	proprietor	22	"
M	Chakarian Yevng—†	8	at home	43	Armenia
N	Bacon Alice G—†	8	housewife	32	here
O	Bacon James A	8	chauffeur	32	"
P	Lyons Delia —†	8	housewife	58	"
R	Lyons Edward	8	printer	20	"
S	Lyons Marion †	8	clerk	23	"
T	Lyons Michael	8	bricklayer	55	"
U	Dunn George W	10	chauffeur	31	"
V	Dunn Mary A —†	10	housewife	29	"
W	Gallagher Anna E—†	10	boxmaker	28	"
X	Gallagher Irene —†	10	clerk	22	"
Y	Gallagher Margaret M—†	10	housewife	47	"
Z	Gallagher Ruth —†	10	boxmaker	26	"
A	Gallagher William J	10	rubberworker	53	"
B	Cochran Christina —†	10	housewife	66	"
C	McPhee Daniel	10	coatcutter	25	"
D	McPhee Florence —†	10	saleswoman	23	"
E	Muldoon Della A—†	12	"	32	"
F	Muldoon Helen —†	12	clerk	26	"
G	Muldoon Margaret —†	12	housewife	32	"
H	Muldoon Margaret J —†	12	stenographer	24	"
K	Muldoon Thomas A	12	adjuster	30	"
L	Muldoon William	12	laborer	28	"
M	Welsh George T	12	dental mech	35	4 Lambert av
N	Devine Catherine —†	18	saleswoman	42	here
O	Devine Dennis	18	retired	78	"
P	Devine Margaret—†	18	laundress	48	"
S	Mountain Ellen—†	24	at home	64	"
T	Mountain James E	24	inspector	37	"
U	Mountain Michael	24	retired	68	"
V	Flannery John J	24	clerk	61	"
W	Flannery Minnie E—†	24	housewife	60	"
X	Flannery Thomas F	24	stenographer	20	"
Y	Robbins Ethel—†	26	housekeeper	42	"
Z	Robbins Irene G—†	26	tel operator	21	"
A	McAndrew Margaret E-†	26	saleswoman	53	20 Ray
B	McAndrew Sarah C—†	26	operator	57	20 "

Linden Park Street —Continued

c	Larkin Catherine E—†	30	housewife	58	here
d	Larkin James W	30	postal clerk	20	"
e	Larkin John M	30	molder	62	"
f	Larkin Joseph C	30	guard	27	"
g	Larkin Paul V	30	clerk	25	"
h	Mulkern Bernard F	30	"	23	73 Centre
k	Nagle Joseph A	34	watchmaker	34	here
l	Nagle Margaret E—†	34	housewife	24	"
m	O'Donnell Dennis P	34	springmaker	59	"
n	O'Donnell Marie—†	34	saleswoman	21	"
o	O'Donnell Mary J—†	34	housewife	59	"
p	Carey Katherine—†	34	"	62	"
r	Connor Natalie M—†	36	stenographer	21	"
s	Connor Sarah E—†	36	housewife	44	"
t	Connor William F	36	clerk	25	"
u	Connor William J	36	inspector	45	"
v	Sweeney Annie J—†	36	operator	43	"
x	Sweeney Margaret G—†	36	housekeeper	42	"
w	Sweeney Nella A—†	36	forewoman	45	"
y	Minkl Arthur J	36	electrician	31	"
z	Minkl Mary M—†	36	housewife	31	"
a	Kenny Catherine—†	42	"	27	"
b	Kenny John M	42	chauffeur	27	"
c	Pierce Everett C	42A	foreman	43	"
d	Pierce Mary A—†	42A	housewife	42	"
e	Olson Emma—†	42A	"	37	"
f	Olson Patrick	42A	carpenter	46	"
n	Marshall Mary—†	44	housewife	22	"
o	Marshall Samuel	44	postal clerk	29	"
g	Andrews Mary—†	44A	housewife	44	"
h	Andrews Alois—†	44A	cutter	20	"
k	Andrews Stanley B	44A	printer	49	"
l	Barry Agnes—†	44A	housewife	41	"
m	Barry John F	44A	waiter	41	"
p	Manning Ellen—†	46	shoeworker	43	"
r	Manning Margaret—†	46	clerk	21	"
s	McNulty Mary J—†	46	at home	49	"
t	McNulty William J	46	laborer	52	"
u	Behnke Charles W	46A	machinist	38	"
v	Barry Frances—†	46A	clerk	22	"
w	Barry John	46A	electrician	46	"

Linden Park Street—Continued

X	Blaney Katherine—†	48	at home	75	here
Y	Lafreniere Catherine—†	48	housewife	23	"
Z	Lafreniere Joseph R	48	painter	25	"
A	Murphy Nellie M—†	48A	housewife	36	105 Union Pk
B	Murphy Patrick J	48A	wool sorter	38	105 "
C	O'Leary Ella J—†	48A	housewife	42	here
D	O'Leary Jeremiah	48A	shipper	41	"
F	Carter George A	50	machinist	31	"
E	Carter Lloyd G	50	painter	35	"
G	Carter Louise M—†	50	laundryworker	32	"
H	Carter Sadie—†	50	housekeeper	65	"
K	Carter Sarah B—†	50	boxmaker	30	"
L	Fogarty Anna V—†	50A	packer	24	"
M	Fogarty Katherine A—†	50A	stitcher	21	"
N	Fogarty Patrick J	50A	draftsman	58	"
O	Boettcher Elizabeth M—†	50A	housewife	51	Quincy
P	Boettcher Emma A—†	50A	shoeworker	22	"
R	Boettcher Mildred—†	50A	stitcher	20	"
S	Boettcher Robert G	50A	machinist	57	"
X	McCullough Edward F	94	laborer	45	here
Y	McCulloughh Margaret—†	94	candymaker	40	"
Z	Gorman Catherine—†	96	housekeeper	61	"
A	Hynes William	96	barber	29	"
B	Kelley Charles	98	lather	60	"
C	Kelley Hannah—†	98	stitcher	35	"
D	Kelley Julia J—†	98	shoeworker	33	"
E	Thompson Louisa—†	102	housekeeper	64	"
F	Thompson Minnie—†	102	operator	24	"
G	Costello Mary—†	102	domestic	29	"
H	Costello Patrick	102	laborer	37	"
K	Costello Thomas	102	"	38	"
L	Clinton Abigail—†	102	housekeeper	33	"
M	Laughlin Helen—†	102	clerk	34	"
N	Laughlin John H	102	salesman	32	"

Malbon Place

P	Connelly Elizabeth—†	1	housewife	33	6 Malbon pl
R	Connelly Matthew	1	marbleworker	36	6 "

Malbon Place—Continued

s	Carey Bridget —†	1	at home	82	here
T	Donlan Anna †	1	tel operator	20	7 Malbon pl
U	Donlan Bridget —†	1	chambermaid	55	7 "
V	Killerman Freda—†	2	houseworker	63	7 "
X	Harkins Michael J	2	cutter	35	here
Y	Harkins Rose E—†	2	housewife	30	"
Z	Bresnahan Florence C—†	3	"	24	"
A	Bresnahan Maurice J	3	bottle worker	26	"
B	Selig Helen D †	3	housewife	21	Somerville
C	Selig Ross C	3	lather	22	"
D	Gavin Mary V —†	3	housekeeper	29	here
E	Gavin William J	3	laborer	34	"
F	McDonald Margaret—†	4	housekeeper	59	127 Warren
G	McKinnon Anna —†	4	shoeworker	21	127 "
H	McKinnon Daniel	4	teamster	62	127 "
K	Gately Mary A—†	4	housewife	38	here
L	Gately Thomas J	4	laborer	39	"
M	Anthony Annie †	4	housewife	51	"
N	Anthony Walter	4	laborer	67	"
O	Hopkins Alice †	5	laundress	27	"
P	Hopkins Michael	5	laborer	29	"
R	Lynch Martin H	5	gasworker	49	24 Faxon
S	Lynch Mary E —†	5	housewife	36	24 "
T	O'Rourke Clarabell —†	5	"	51	here
U	O'Rourke Michael	5	shoemaker	51	"
V	Gately Margaret —†	6	housewife	29	41 Thorndike
W	Gately Thomas L	6	chauffeur	34	41 "
X	Horner Flora M —†	6	housewife	34	here
Y	Horner Hayden M	6	cigarmaker	39	"
Z	Sullivan John P	6	laborer	50	"
A	Sullivan Julia T †	6	housewife	38	"
B	Sullivan Mortimer	6	foundryworker	38	"
C	Banker Annie M —†	7	inspector	25	1 Heath pl
D	Banker Charles A	7	rubberworker	35	1 "
E	Reilly Charles A	7	clerk	23	here
F	Reilly Charles J	7	foreman	50	"
G	Reilly Sarah †	7	housewife	47	"
H	Reilly Warren T	7	clerk	21	"
K	Gilman Carl W	7	grinder	32	41 Linden Park
L	Gilman Mable G †	7	housewife	33	here

Malbon Place — Continued

M	Allison Alesa — †	8	housewife	21	2530 Wash'n
N	Allison Gedwin	8	manager	25	140 W Concord
O	Athridge Mary — †	8	matron	45	5 Atherton
P	Lamont Annie — †	8	housewife	29	5 "
R	Lamont John	8	teamster	31	5 "
S	Blumerfield Mary †	8	housewife	42	here
T	Blumerfield Max	8	printer	40	"
U	Strauch Alice V — †	9	housewife	26	189 Walk Hill
V	Fitzgerald Della J — †	9	housekeeper	39	here
W	Rooney Mark J	9	machinist	39	37 E Brookline
X	Rooney Nora — †	9	housewife	35	249 River
Y	Kervin Edith F — †	10	"	38	2530 Wash'n
Z	Kervin John J	10	painter	40	2530 "
A	Clarke Elizabeth — †	10	housewife	36	52 Guild
B	Clarke Thomas	10	rubberworker	33	52 "
C	Clarke Charlotte — †	10	attendant	52	here
D	DeEntremont John D	11	window cleaner	27	6 Malbon pl
E	DeEntremont Mary — †	11	housewife	29	6 "
G	Lyons Annie — †	11	"	37	here
H	Lyons John J	11	chauffeur	40	"
K	McNamara Grace †	12	housewife	32	207 W Springfield
L	McNamara John	12	fisherman	30	207 "
M	Gallagher Stephen J	12	painter	46	47 Roxbury
N	Sproules Ellen T — †	12	at home	70	here
O	Sproules Mary C †	12	housekeeper	37	"
P	Brown Carl E	12	painter	40	"
R	Brown Florence †	12	housewife	37	"
S	Manning Alice †	12	stitcher	42	414 Amory

Percy Place

X	Adelman Elizabeth †	1	housewife	65	here
X¹	Adelman Frank	1	laborer	36	"
Y	Adelman Mary — †	1	stitcher	40	"
Z	Adelman Peter	1	laborer	33	"
A	O'Neil John	2	carpenter	46	"
B	O'Neil Marie — †	2	housewife	47	"

Perkins Place

c	Heighe Ernest	1	salesman	30	here
d	Igo Bernard	1	clerk	30	Arlington
e	Lowell Leo	1	shoecutter	26	here
f	Morgan Alberta J	1	housekeeper	41	"
g	Morgan Emmie D—†	1	storekeeper	43	"
h	Shrinert Arthur L	1	painter	48	California
k	Springer Paul	1	"	40	Haverhill
l	Sullivan William	1	laborer	28	Maine
m	MacQuarrie Anna J—†	2	housewife	21	2492 Wash'n
n	MacQuarrie James N	2	chauffeur	25	2492 "
o	McKinnon Susie—†	2	forewoman	31	2492 "
p	Staudigal Charles H	2	plumber	66	2492 "
r	Staudigal Harold A	2	chauffeur	36	2492 "
s	Staudigal James J	2	"	30	2492 "
t	Staudigal Lucy A—†	2	housewife	58	2492 "
u	Staudigal Roger D	2	salesman	28	2492 "
v	Staudigal William R	2	collector	34	2492 "
w	Burr Francis H	3	bookbinder	66	here
x	Burr Margaret J—†	3	housewife	61	"
y	Davis Margaret—†	5	housekeeper	58	"
z	Welsh Alexander	7	student	21	"
a	Welsh James	7	clerk	24	"
b	Welsh Joseph	7	electrician	23	"

Putnam Place

c	Sorensen Alfred	1	mechanic	22	here
d	Sorensen Amanda—†	1	housewife	43	"
e	Sorensen Soren	1	chauffeur	48	"
f	Ingstrup Mary—†	2	housewife	47	"
g	Ingstrup Nelson	2	metalworker	49	"
h	Knowles Christina—†	2	housewife	42	"
k	Knowles George	2	mover	39	"
l	Thompson Lillian—†	2	clerk	21	Springfield
m	Glynn Delia F—†	2	dressmaker	53	here
n	Neugebauer Anna—†	2	stenographer	40	"
o	Neugebauer Bertha—†	2	housekeeper	48	"
p	Neugebauer Julius	2	laborer	50	"
r	O'Brien Daniel	2½	bookkeeper	33	"
s	O'Brien Mary—†	2½	housewife	60	"

22

Putnam Place—Continued

T	Emberg Albino	2½	machinist	42	here	
U	Emberg Ellen—†	2½	housewife	33	"	
V	Emberg Grant S	2½	machinist	46	"	
W	Carlson Arird	rear 2½	painter	44	"	
X	Carlson Sarah—†	" 2½	housewife	35	"	
X¹	Trayers Rita—†	3	"	26	"	
Y	Cook Angus	3	carpenter	53	13 Roxbury ter	
Z	Cook Arthur	3	laborer	21	13 "	
A	Cook Ella—†	3	housewife	46	13 "	
B	Trayers Francis A	3	weigher	38	here	
C	White Bertha—†	3	housewife	21	13 Roxbury ter	
D	White William	3	patternmaker	26	670 Tremont	
E	Curwen Thomas	4	rubber grinder	74	here	
F	Ludington Annie L—†	4	housewife	39	"	
G	Ludington Homer	4	letter carrier	41	"	
H	Sonkis Harry	5	cook	35	"	
K	Sonkis Theresa—†	5	housewife	32	"	
L	Massiglia Sadie—†	5	waitress	30	"	
M	Deming Bertha—†	5	shoeworker	20	2737 Wash'n	
N	Deming Gertrude—†	5	"	40	2737 "	
O	Reed Fred	5	chauffeur	30	2737 "	
P	Reed Isabella—†	5	housekeeper	93	2737 "	
R	Lewerenz Mary A—†	8	"	43	here	
S	Lewerenz Max H	8	baker	43	"	

Putnam Street

C	Smith Harriet A—†	13	housekeeper	70	here	
D	Farrar Anna B—†	15	housewife	57	"	
E	Farrar Carrie A—†	15	housekeeper	79	"	
F	Farrar George M	15	clerk	32	"	
G	Farrar Louise—†	15	housewife	21	21 Sargent	
H	Farrar Mordecai	15	woodworker	59	here	
K	Knight Maybelle E—†	15	teacher	50	"	
L	Leverence Georgiana—†	15	waitress	35	"	
M	Leverence Herman	15	iceman	38	"	
N	Parker Adelaide J—†	15	housekeeper	68	"	
O	Campbell Catherine—†	25	shoeworker	35	"	
P	Conley John J	25	laborer	45	"	
R	Deverux Annie—†	25	housekeeper	38	"	

Putnam Street — Continued

s	Deverux Raymond	25	laborer	38	here	
T	Dunne Helen—†	25	nurse	40	27 Linden Park	
U	Early Anna—†	25	bookbinder	55	here	
V	Green Nellie—†	25	housekeeper	45	15 Bay State rd	
W	Harkness Harold	25	policeman	30	here	
X	Murphy Philip	25	mechanic	40	"	
Y	Ridge Mary—†	25	cook	50	Brookline	
z	Sampson George J	25	foreman	44	here	
A	Sampson Margaret C—†	25	housewife	41	"	
B	Verpehoski Victor	25	tailor	60	"	

Roxbury Street

X	Murphy Anne—†	39	housewife	39	here
Y	Murphy Peter H	39	carpenter	55	"
Z	Coleman Daniel	39	laborer	60	"
A	Cunniffe Michael	39	"	35	1417 Tremont
B	Douglass Phillip	39	"	22	112 Mass av
C	Garrity Martin	39	"	39	here
D	Harrington Patrick	39	painter	55	Cambridge
E	Henry John	39	carpenter	64	here
F	Lyons Morris	39	laborer	40	"
G	Monahan James	39	"	48	21 Highland
H	O'Donnell Owen	39	"	30	31 Worcester
K	Sullivan Michael	39	"	24	21 Vernon
M	Ballow Alice C—†	41	housewife	50	here
N	Ballow John M	41	storekeeper	81	"
O	Berrigan Emma C—†	41	paperworker	53	"
P	Berrigan Frank	41	laborer	50	"
R	Berrigan James F	41	"	50	"
S	Conley Patrick	41	"	40	"
T	Marr Richard	41	"	70	39 Roxbury
U	Thompson Fannie D—†	41	nurse	50	here
W	Addems Dora—†	47	housewife	31	New Jersey
X	Addems William G	47	salesman	31	"
Y	Cangelosi John	47	shoeworker	24	401 Second
Z	Cole Byron C	47	meatcutter	62	12 Wait
A	Cole Byron C	47	chauffeur	36	12 "
B	Cole Cora E—†	47	stenographer	28	12 "
C	Courier Margaret—†	47	housekeeper	27	12 "

24

Roxbury Street—Continued

		FULL NAME	Res.	Occupation	Age	Reported Residence
D		Curran Frank	47	tiremaker	34	364 Dorchester
E		Curran Mary—†	47	housewife	22	364 "
F		Deeb Edna—†	47	shoeworker	26	2558 Wash'n
G		Edwards George	47	"	53	52 Waltham
H		Edwards May—†	47	maid	39	52 "
K		Frank Viola M—†	47	clerk	22	Belmont
L		Warren Matilda E—†	47	hairdresser	33	Lowell
M		Williams Walter H	47	salesman	52	9 Islington
N		Barker Charles	49	teamster	47	here
O		McManus Joseph C	49	embalmer	55	"
P		Mulhern Michael	49	janitor	76	"
S		Murray Mary J—†	54	housewife	49	"
T		Murray Patrick E	54	undertaker	55	"
U		McKeon Anna V—†	54	housekeeper	37	"
V		McKeon Emma G—†	54	bookkeeper	35	"
W		Murray Arthur B	54	student	21	"
X		Murray John J	54	undertaker	22	"
Y		Morton Delia—†	56	housekeeper	65	"
Z		Simonds Albert A	56	clerk	34	2 Perkins pl
A		Simonds Maurice	56	salesman	28	2 "
B		Smith Mary—†	56	housekeeper	45	here
C		Smith Rhea—†	56	shoecutter	22	"
D		Woodford Jane—†	56	housekeeper	55	Nova Scotia
E		Andrews Mary L—†	72	clerk	27	here
G		Andrews Warren L	72	"	30	"
H		Heuitz Charles A	72	sheriff	64	"
K		Heuitz Charles B	72	painter	38	"
L		Heuitz Della A—†	72	housewife	58	"
M		Heuitz Millie T—†	72	clerk	34	"
N		Carey Daniel	74	laborer	21	Canada
O		Davis George	74	"	28	Brookline
P		Poor Mary K—†	74	housewife	35	here
R		Poor William H	74	chauffeur	43	"
S		Smith Irving	74	clerk	28	California
U		Stone Catherine—†	80	housewife	39	58 Hunneman
V		Stone Samuel	80	engineer	40	58 "
W		Ryan Catherine—†	80	housewife	39	here
X		Ryan John H	80	electrician	40	"
Y		Murphy Katherine—†	82	housewife	42	"
Z		Murphy Michael J	82	upholsterer	42	"
A		Fuller Anna—†	rear 82	waitress	38	"

25

Roxbury Street—Continued

c	Lihzis Emily—†	98	laundress	40	35 Walnut av
d	McCaul May—†	98	housewife	29	here
e	Ryan Annie C—†	98	housekeeper	59	"
f	Ryan Theresa—†	98	waitress	24	"
k	Detert Lottie M—†	100	embalmer	54	71 Roxbury
l	Langdon Sarah—†	100	housekeeper	54	56 Roxbury ct
n	Lane Daniel F	104	tinsmith	50	here
o	Lane Julia A—†	104	housewife	56	"
p	Norton John F	104	tinsmith	21	"
r	Norton Mary B—†	104	clerk	27	"
s	Shea Edward F	104	bookbinder	28	16 North av
t	Shea Julia R—†	104	housewife	26	16 "
u	Longo Josephine—†	106	clerk	31	here
v	Re Caesar	106	storekeeper	38	"
w	Re Nancy—†	106	housewife	36	"
z	Buckley Anna S—†	120	housekeeper	58	"
a	Morrissey Mary J—†	120	"	70	"
b	Lundwall Axel	122	carpenter	52	"
c	Lundwall Fanny—†	122	housewife	52	"
d	Ryan Michael G	127	laborer	65	"
e	Ryan Sara A—†	127	housewife	33	"
f	Ellis Helen—†	127	"	29	439 Third
g	Ellis John J	127	machinist	31	439 "
h	O'Connor Michael	127	laborer	58	Canada
k	Carney Mary J—†	127	housewife	50	84 Clarkson
l	Carney Robert F	127	brakeman	53	84 "
m	Hayes Elizabeth A—†	129	housewife	61	here
n	Hayes Walter F	129	salesman	54	"
o	Miller Ethel W—†	129	houseworker	22	"
p	Miller John C	129	salesman	65	"
r	Miller William M	129	helper	32	"
s	Finn Daniel J	129	chauffeur	43	32 Dundee
t	Finn Helen—†	129	housewife	35	32 "
u	Oram William H	130	signalman	24	202 Roxbury
v	Riley Lawrence	130	chauffeur	41	here
w	Riley Ovilla—†	130	housewife	36	"
x	Keenan Julia A—†	131	"	26	"
y	Keenan Patrick J	131	janitor	34	"
z	Murray Anna A—†	131	nurse	32	"
a	Jones Elizabeth E—†	131	housekeeper	63	"
b	Jones Hugh C	131	policeman	28	"

Page.	Letter.	FULL NAME.	Residence, April 1, 1926.	Occupation.	Supposed Age.	Reported Residence, April 1, 1925. Street and Number.

Roxbury Street—Continued

C	Churchward James A	131	salesman	37	here
D	Churchward Mary J —†	131	housewife	36	"
E	Boushell Daniel E	133	counterman	58	1356 Dor av
F	Boushell Mary A —†	133	clerk	44	1356 "
G	Durfee Charlotte S—†	133	housewife	36	here
H	Durfee Harry E	133	laborer	37	"
K	Lucas Ellen H —†	133	housekeeper	50	"
L	Lucas Thomas S	133	packer	56	"
M	Lucas William M	133	roofer	54	"
N	Casey Eleanor E —†	135	housewife	39	"
O	Casey John J	135	railway mail	40	"
P	Keay Eulalie M—†	135	housewife	41	"
R	Keay Winford L	135	printer	54	"
S	Galvin Amy E—†	135	housewife	49	"
T	Galvin Lester J	135	clerk	23	"
U	Galvin Thomas F	135	"	52	"
V	Galvin Thomas F, jr	135	foreman	26	"
W	Eldert Albert H	137	repairman	68	"
X	Eldert Margaret A—†	137	housewife	67	"
Y	Cushing Elizabeth—†	139	"	62	"
Z	Cushing Joseph N	139	clerk	62	"
A	Scott John W	139	machinist	25	"
B	Schnider John J	139	laborer	67	"
B¹	Schnider Georgeianna M—†	139	housewife	47	"
C	Schnider William H	139	grinder	21	"
D	Weener Agnes —†	139	housewife	38	"
E	Weener Horace	139	plumber	40	"
F	Combs Harriet O —†	149	matron	68	"
G	Hatch Grace P—†	149	nurse	31	"
H	Smith James E	157	laborer	67	"
K	Smith John E	157	chauffeur	34	"
L	Smith Mary †	157	housewife	60	"
M	Smith Mary E—†	157	"	31	"
N	McAuley Josephine †	157	saleswoman	27	134 Warren
O	McAuley Malcom D	157	laborer	64	Canada
P	McAuley Margaret —†	157	housewife	63	"
R	Mooney Robert	157	carpenter	24	51 Humboldt av
S	Carty John J	157	fireman	43	here
T	Carty Rebecca M—†	157	housewife	44	"
U	Hughes Margaret E —†	157	"	65	"
V	Adler Catherine †	157	"	41	"

27

Roxbury Street—Continued

w	Adler Eric	157	carpenter	49	here
x	Adler Lila C †	157	bookkeeper	20	"
y	Mann Davina G—†	157	housewife	48	"
z	Mann Helen M †	157	dancer	25	"
a	Mann Louis J	157	clerk	48	"
b	McLeod Colin	157	foreman	60	"
c	McLeod Florence †	157	housewife	58	"
d	Meinhardt Annie C—†	157	"	75	"
e	Meinhardt Wilhimina —†	157	designer	46	"
f	Mahan David J	157	letter carrier	57	"
g	Mahan Margaret O —†	157	housewife	48	"
k	Colton Carrie —†	165	at home	60	"
l	Regan Catherine E —†	167	"	73	"
m	Burnham Annie L †	167	housewife	70	"
n	Burnham Edgar L	167	laborer	68	"
o	Herman Earl L	167	janitor	25	"
p	Herman Maybelle B †	167	nurse	53	"
r	Gore Elizabeth A	169	housewife	60	"
s	Schlchuber Ella L †	169	"	45	"
t	Schlchuber Henry	169	chauffeur	46	"
u	Dobbs John T	169	mechanic	24	58 Highland
v	Dobbs Josephine B †	169	housekeeper	54	58 "
w	Mooney John J	171	carpenter	49	here
x	Mooney Mary A †	171	housewife	46	"
y	O'Brien Harry	171	brakeman	40	Waverley
z	Tillson Erastus	171	floorman	59	here
a	Collins Ellen †	173	housewife	52	1199 Tremont
b	Collins William H	173	mechanic	53	1199 "
c	McDonald Mary B—†	173	housewife	60	24 Greenville
d	Romanos Sina K —†	173	"	40	here
e	Romanos Victor P	173	dealer	49	"
f	Butterfield David W	183	retired	65	"
r	Coutu Ethel † 1st rear	199	housewife	38	"
s	Coutu Isiah J 1st "	199	painter	40	"
t	McLean Daniel 2d "	199	mechanic	63	"
u	McLean Donald J 2d "	199	laborer	27	"
v	McLean Sadie I † "	199	housewife	61	"
c	McInnis Daniel J	209	mechanic	35	Canada
d	McInnis Ethel—†	209	housewife	34	4 Highland pk
e	McInnis John F	209	mechanic	44	9 Dartmouth
f	McInnis Michael A	209	"	40	4 Highland pk

28

Roxbury Street—Continued

G	Morris Catherine E—†	209	housewife	42	here
H	Morris John J	219	clerk	42	"
L	Diblee Emily E—†	219	housewife	21	"
M	Diblee Hattie G—†	219	"	45	"
N	Diblee John C	219	carpenter	52	"
O	Diblee William F	219	chauffeur	24	"
P	Curran Maude L—†	219	presser	55	"
R	Hill Grace R—†	219	housewife	40	"
S	Hill Robert	219	mechanic	55	"

Roxbury Terrace

T	Paterson Margaret—†	1	housekeeper	37	here
U	Paterson Walter	1	laundryman	48	"
V	Kenny George	1	carpenter	30	4 Roxbury ter
W	Kenny Hannah—†	1	housewife	22	4 "
X	Falvey Ellen—†	1	"	67	here
Y	Falvey Ellen E—†	1	saleswoman	26	"
Z	Falvey Joseph B	1	chauffeur	25	"
A	Dunn Alice—†	2	housekeeper	29	"
B	Dunn William	2	laborer	29	"
C	Gibbons Agnes—†	2	domestic	39	"
D	Gibbons James E	2	laborer	46	"
E	Mahoney John	2	"	31	"
F	Mahoney Mabel—†	2	housewife	35	"
G	Morrissey John J	3	molder	46	"
H	Daley Joseph P	3	laborer	41	24 Dover
K	Daley Margaret—†	3	housewife	39	24 "
L	Mulvin Joan—†	3	"	60	here
M	Mulvin William N	3	painter	70	"
N	O'Neil Nora—†	4	housewife	28	10 Bartlett
O	O'Neil Robert	4	bookkeeper	33	10 "
P	Hughes Mary—†	4	housekeeper	36	here
R	Hughes Walter J	4	machinist	39	"
S	Hartford John W	4	shoeworker	51	1324 Tremont
T	Hartford Margurite—†	4	housewife	36	1324 "
V	Belyea Catherine S—†	13	"	43	here
W	Belyea Fredrick R	13	painter	52	"
X	Belyea Walter C	13	wireworker	23	"
Y	O'Neil William	13	welder	30	Quincy

Page	Letter	Full Name.	Residence, April 1, 1926.	Occupation.	Supposed Age	Reported Residence, April 1, 1925. Street and Number.

Shawmut Avenue

	z	Carpenter Benjamin H	806	electrician	32	here
	A	Carpenter Charlotte E-†	806	milliner	35	"
	B	Carpenter Elizabeth M-†	806	housekeeper	65	"
	c	Conlin Walter E	806	printer	41	"
	D	Kelley James	806	teamster	50	"

Vernon Street

	K	Pond Bertha G—†	18	housewife	39	here
	L	Pond Frank E	18	millworker	52	"
	M	Redman Andrew A	18	piano mover	69	"
	N	Magunson Annie—†	18	housewife	66	"
	o	Magunson Annie—†	18	clerk	28	"
	P	Magunson Augusta	18	watchman	69	"
	R	Magunson Christina—†	18	clerk	29	"
	s	Magunson Hilda—†	18	dressmaker	31	"
	T	Magunson Oscar	18	painter	25	"

Warren Street

	K	Markus David	53	physician	50	here
	M	Anderson Charles	53	foreman	39	144 Dudley
	N	Kimball William	53	photographer	50	here
	o	McPherson William	53	carpenter	46	"
	R	Galbraith Christine—†	53	teacher	55	"
	s	Galbraith George	53	bookbinder	61	"
	T	Ribers Charles	53	salesman	60	"
	c	Charest Evon—†	53	housewife	26	746 Shawmut av
	v	Charest Robert C	53	painter	33	746 "
	w	Geary Frederick	53	counterman	22	2161 Wash'n
	x	Geary Violet—†	53	waitress	21	2161 "

Washington Street

	D	Martz Elmer R	2379	manager	31	here
	E	Martz Susan—†	2379	housewife	27	"
	M	Dunham Elizabeth E—†	2397	nurse	32	113 Sheridan

Page.	Letter.	FULL NAME.	Residence, April 1, 1926.	Occupation	Supposed Age.	Reported Residence, April 1, 1925. Street and Number.

Washington Street—Continued

N	Famullaro Angelo	2397	storekeeper	48	21A Highland
O	McElroy Peter	2397	janitor	59	21A "
P	Paino Gaetano	2397	storekeeper	45	21A "
R	Paino Grace—†	2397	housekeeper	39	21A "
S	Brearton John J	2397	roofer	48	here
T	Gilman John S	2397	insurance agent	72	"
U	Manchester Isabel—†	2397	housekeeper	50	"
V	Sears Edgar S	2397	advertising	38	59 Dudley
W	Washington Charles	2397	clerk	53	here
X	Belyea Gertrude—†	2397	cook	54	1939 Wash'n
Y	Grant Richard S	2397	repairman	21	2536 "
Z	King Margaret—†	2397	waitress	33	623 Mass av
A	Porter Joseph R	2397	fireman	28	623 "
B	Simonds Florence—†	2397	seamstress	71	21A Highland
C	Geary Carrie E—† .	2397	housewife	57	here
D	Schackley Catherine—†	2397	stenographer	24	"
E	DeFlurin Frank	2397	chauffeur	50	72 Dudley
F	Harding Perlie	2397	motorman	45	here
G	Davis Ormus C	2397	retired	85	"
H	MacDougall Roderick	2397	brassworker	40	"
K	Webster Annie D—†	2397	housewife	43	"
L	Adams Robert McB	2397	carpenter	45	"
M	Hunton Flora B—†	2397	housewife	56	"
N	Hunton Frank W	2397	carpenter	75	"
N¹	Hunton Harry D	2397	clerk	28	"
O	McPherson Sarah—†	2397	cashier	36	"
P	Power Lawrence J	2397	laborer	38	2161 Wash'n
R	Mulrey Elizabeth—†	2397	housewife	45	12 Highland
S	Fisher Florence—†	2397	"	45	here
T	Jackson John	2397	painter	35	"
U	Jordon William	2397	clerk	62	53 Warren
V	Leary George	2397	salesman	40	here
W	Haley Herman	2397	carpenter	21	"
X	Haley Winifred—†	2397	housewife	20	53 Waverly
Y	Vernot Manson	2397	shipper	50	here
Z	Wilson Nina—†	2397	housewife	48	"
L	Doyle Henrietta—†	2455	"	39	"
M	Hart Eliza A—†	2455	"	53	"
N	Hart Rueben C	2455	finisher	60	"
O	Gogain Carey J	2455	chauffeur	40	"
P	Gogain Marie C—†	2455	housewife	38	"

Washington Street—Continued

T	Fay Ferdinand L	2457	machinist	70	2467 Wash'n
U	Mooney Catherine E—†	2457	housewife	39	here
V	Mooney John J	2457	steamfitter	39	"
Y	O'Mara David C	2457B	machinist	59	"
Z	O'Mara Grace †	2457B	housewife	57	"
A	McCluskey Margaret C-†2457B		"	35	"
B	Sheehan Annie —†	2457B	"	35	"
C	Sheehan James	2457B	laborer	34	"
E	Hardy Helen B †	2457B	at home	41	"
F	Murphy Elizabeth—†	2457B	housewife	53	21 Williams
G	Murphy James W	2457B	laborer	49	21 "
H	Connell Edward	2459B	janitor	65	21 "
L	Cairness Sarah—†	2459B	housewife	65	here
M	Meuise James E	2459B	tinsmith	22	"
N	Henry Viney †	2459B	housewife	30	936 Harris'n av
O	Henry William	2459B	teamster	31	936 "
P	Newmyre Alice †	2459B	housewife	29	here
R	Newmyre Joseph	2459B	machinist	39	"
S	McKeon Catherine —†	2459B	housewife	45	12 Meehan
T	Mettieve Dorothy—†	2463	"	32	here
U	Mettieve Walter	2463	laborer	40	"
V	Nicholson Elizabeth—†	2465	housewife	44	5 Bills ct
W	Nicholson Frank M	2465	compositor	46	5 "
X	Hayes George D	2465	salesman	28	66 Field
Y	Hayes Kathaleen †	2465	housewife	21	66 "
Z	Fallon Bessie †	2467	"	46	here
A	Fallon Helen †	2467	folder	27	"
B	Fallon James	2467	laborer	48	"
F	Ryan Mary †	2493	housewife	32	"
G	Ryan William F	2493	longshoreman	32	"
K	Bottary Jennie †	2493	housewife	30	"
L	Bottary Joseph	2493	barber	35	"

Willis Terrace

T	Galvin Margaret T †	1	milliner	50	here
U	Wilson Alice †	2	housewife	62	"
V	Wilson James	2	laborer	58	"
W	McCloud Mary—†	2	housewife	72	"
X	McCloud William C	2	clerk	74	"

Page.	Letter.	FULL NAME.	Residence, April 1, 1926.	Occupation.	Supposed Age.	Reported Residence, April 1, 1925.
						Street and Number.

Willis Terrace — Continued

Y	Whiting Nellie —†	2	operator	47	here
z	Greenan Annie —†	2	housekeeper	59	21 Kent
A	Davis Edward	2	fireman	31	Cambridge
B	Davis Margaret —†	2	housewife	21	"
c	Dolan Thomas F	3	salesman	57	132 Day
D	McClutchy Herbert S	3	"	33	131 Dale
E	Scott Bridget —†	3	housekeeper	62	here
F	Scott John	3	chauffeur	28	"
G	Scott Joseph F	3	"	24	"
H	Mercey Alfred A	3	watchman	65	"
K	Mercey Inez Y —†	3	housekeeper	60	"
L	Scott Estelle —†	3	housewife	34	"
M	Scott William E	3	chauffeur	32	"
N	Rumrill Jessie —†	4	housewife	29	"
o	Rumrill William	4	salesman	30	"
P	McCloud Mary —†	4	housewife	72	"
R	McCloud William C	4	clerk	74	"
s	Norton Edward M	4	"	53	"
T	Norton Elizabeth A —†	4	housewife	54	"
U	Norton Walter M	4	clerk	50	"
V	Mackay Isabelle —†	4	housewife	49	"
w	Mackay Kenneth	4	undertaker	57	"

Ward 9—Precinct 15

CITY OF BOSTON.

LIST OF RESIDENTS
20 YEARS OF AGE AND OVER

(FEMALES INDICATED BY DAGGER)

AS OF

APRIL 1, 1926

HERBERT A. WILSON, } Listing

JAMES F. EAGAN, } Board.

CITY OF BOSTON—PRINTING DEPARTMENT

Bartlett Street

c	Bursiel Harold M	20	radioworker	22	here
d	Bursiel Mary S—†	20	housewife	67	"
e	Bursiel Willis E	20	laborer	29	"
f	Bursiel Willis H	20	retired	74	"
g	Timmins Mary J—†	20	housekeeper	67	"

Cathedral Street

k	Smith Catherine N—†	4	housewife	33	859 E First
l	Smith Patrick	4	machinist	32	859 "
n	Manton Bridget—†	4	housewife	57	here
o	Manton Michael	4	laborer	58	"
p	Butler Margaret—†	6	housewife	24	"
r	Maguire Mary C—†	6	"	29	"
s	Maguire Owen J	6	engineer	36	"
t	Murphy James P	6	clerk	21	"
u	Murphy Margaret—†	6	forewoman	27	"
v	Murphy Mary—†	6	housewife	50	"
w	Murphy Treasa—†	6	saleswoman	23	"
x	Menton Bridget M—†	8	housewife	35	"
y	Menton Patrick J	8	painter	42	"
z	Corbett Christina A—†	8	housewife	43	"
A	Corbett Elizabeth M—†	8	saleswoman	20	"
B	Corbett James	8	laborer	43	"
c	Wells Julia B—†	8	housewife	41	"
D	Wells Richard A	8	fireman	67	"

Cedar Square

F	Sarno Elmer A	1	clerk	39	here
G	Sarno Theresa—†	1	housewife	33	"

Cedar Street

K	Fox James	1	machinist	54	here
L	Janverin George W	1	painter	71	"
M	Janverin Laura W—†	1	housewife	65	"

2

Cedar Street—Continued

N	Lurson Joseph J	1	painter	61	here
O	McKinson Anna—†	1	dressmaker	41	"
P	Currier Maria L J—†	2	authoress	87	"
R	Gallagher William C	3	laborer	45	"
S	Meyers Henry F J	3	manufacturer	60	"
T	Meyers Nellie G—†	3	housewife	59	"
U	Brady Charles J	4	laborer	41	"
V	Brady Josephine L—†	4	housewife	41	"
A	Broderick John M	4	gardener	54	"
B	Pattee Rena E—†	5	at home	58	"
C	Raymore Charles F	5	laborer	62	"
D	Lilly Mary—†	5	housewife	42	"
E	Lilly Thomas J	5	chauffeur	42	"
F	Goodine Bessie A—†	5	housewife	20	Calais Me
G	Goodine John A	5	laborer	24	"
H	Drinkwater Sadie—†	6	housewife	59	here
K	Drinkwater William J	6	manager	70	"
L	Hennessy Margarett—†	6	at home	55	"
M	Martin Annie—†	6½	housekeeper	63	"
N	Martin Helen—†	6½	clerk	35	"
O	Martin Malcomb	6½	"	30	"
R	Ellinger Carl F W	8	real estate	63	"
V	Fisher Annie A—†	10	housekeeper	65	"
W	Fisher Gertrude C—†	10	clerk	34	"
X	Oddy Ann M—†	10	housewife	81	"
Y	Oddy William P	10	salesman	81	"
Z	Kale Margaret—†	12	housewife	40	"
A	Kale William	12	clerk	36	"
B	Douglass Aubrey A	16	teacher	39	"
C	Douglass Mary E—†	16	housewife	39	"
D	Fitzsimmons Amina L—†	16	teacher	49	"
E	Fitzsimmons Florence A-†	16	"	53	"
F	McGourthy David G	18	sailor	26	"
G	McGourthy Patrick J	18	salesman	57	"
H	Sullivan Jeremiah	20	clerk	59	"
K	Sullivan Mary R—†	20	school teacher	22	"
L	Davis Eveline—†	22	housewife	25	"
M	Davis Henry	22	cook	30	"
N	Fuller James	22	porter	42	"
O	Fuller Willis—†	22	housewife	40	"
S	Smith Fredrick M	24	cook	59	Waltham

3

Cedar Street— Continued

P	Sheehan Madaline L—†	24	housewife	28	here	
R	Sheehan Thomas H	24	grocer	28	"	
T	Joyce Patrick	24	laborer	60	"	
U	Arond Louise—†	26	domestic	46	"	
V	Coleman Julia F—†	26	housewife	56	"	
W	Coleman Robert J	26	printer	66	"	
X	Leech John, jr	26	chauffeur	23	21 Baker pl	
Y	Leech Katherine M—†	26	housewife	24	52 Johnson	
Z	Welmar Charles	29	machinist	35	here	
A	Welmar Lena †	29	housewife	40	"	
B	Rowicks John	29	clerk	40	"	
C	Walkowicz John P	29	salesman	45	"	
D	Adelman Anna †	49	housewife	22	11 Thorndike	
E	Adelman Morris	49	foreman	33	137 Crawford	
F	Chubb George	49	painter	25	here	
G	Chubb Marjorie—†	49	housewife	25	"	
H	Huebner Katherine E—†	49	"	29	"	
K	Huebner William J	49	painter	30	"	
L	Lentendorf Hans	49	cook	28	3155 Wash'n	
M	Lentendorf Martha—†	49	housekeeper	54	3155 "	
N	Lenrendorf Walter	49	cook	24	3155 "	
O	Pozerski Jadwiga †	49	housewife	29	Cambridge	
P	Pozerski Stanislaw	49	foreman	33	"	

Circuit Street

A	Bryden Elizabeth H—†	50	piano teacher	44	here	
B	Bryden Robert H	50	vocal teacher	44	"	
C	Galligan Anna H—†	50	housewife	39	"	
D	Joy Almon E	50	janitor	50	"	
E	Barberian Setrak	62	grocer	35	"	
F	Corigan John	64	machinist	36	22 Fenwick	
G	Corigan Mary—†	64	housewife	33	22 "	
H	MacVicar Angus	64	tailor	31	Nova Scotia	
K	MacVicar John	64	laborer	29	here	
L	MacVicar Margaret—†	64	confectioner	24	"	
M	MacVicar Mary †	64	"	25	"	
N	MacVicar Sarah †	64	housewife	50	"	

Page.	Letter.	Full Name.	Residence, April 1, 1926.	Occupation	Supposed Age.	Reported Residence, April 1, 1925. Street and Number.

Circuit Street—Continued

o	Lawrence John W	66	laundryman	42	1241 Col av
A	Lawrence Lenora E —†	66	housewife	28	1241 "
c	Kemp Mary E—†	66	"	30	586 Ashmont
D	Kemp William R	66	chauffeur	28	586 "
E	Francis Fred C	68	gardener	51	here
F	Kelly Annie M—†	68	housewife	35	"
G	Kelly Edward J	68	laborer	36	"
H	Rogers Delia N—†	68	housewife	45	"
K	Rogers Thomas J	68	shoeworker	50	"
L	Stack Annie M—†	70	housewife	24	3 Regent ct
M	Stack William T	70	laborer	28	3 "
o	Nelson Carl W	70	machinist	28	here
P	Nelson Ethel E—†	70	housewife	25	"
R	Katz Samuel H K	74	upholsterer	28	683 Mass av
s	Katz Sarah—†	74	housewife	27	683 "
T	Cronin Mary E—†	74	"	30	here
U	Cronin Patrick J	74	fireman	29	"
V	Carew Ellen—†	74	housewife	31	82 Roxbury
W	Carew James J	74	manufacturer	32	82 "
X	Goodwin Rose B—†	74A	housewife	45	2614 Wash'n
Y	Mannette Jennie M—†	74A	"	25	Newton
z	Mannette Oliver J	74A	machinist	35	"
A	Burgess Edwin W	74A	plumber	54	here
B	Burgess Ellen V—†	74A	housewife	43	"
c	Dushky George	74A	grocer	25	97 Circuit
D	Curran Patrick F	76	laborer	36	here
E	Curran Rose E—†	76	housewife	34	"
F	Coffey Bridget—†	76	"	38	"
G	Coffey Dennis P	76	fireman	37	"
H	Bishop Catherine M—†	76	housewife	39	"
K	Bishop Charles S	76	chauffeur	49	"
L	Bishop Thomas F	76	laborer	21	"
M	Rafferty Catherine E—†	78	housewife	38	"
N	Rafferty Joseph	78	chauffeur	45	"
o	Toale Alice C—†	80	housewife	56	"
P	Toale James	80	clerk	61	"
R	Duffley Bessie—†	82	saleswoman	30	"
s	Duffley Mary—†	82	housekeeper	39	"
T	Flannigan Catherine—†	82	"	75	"
U	O'Neill Elizabeth—†	82	housewife	40	"
V	O'Neill Patrick	82	laborer	47	"

5

Page	Letter	FULL NAME.	Residence, April 1, 1926.	Occupation.	Supposed Age.	Reported Residence, April 1, 1925. Street and Number.

Dale Street

W	Trainor Catherine V—†	111	housekeeper	50	here
X	Trainor Lawrence	111	retired	80	"
Y	Trainor Michael J	111	policeman	53	"
Z	Connors Harold M	111	manager	34	"
A	Connors Winifred J—†	111	housewife	36	"
B	Power James B	111	lastmaker	42	51 Regent
C	Power Josephine J—†	111	housewife	41	51 "
D	Snow Jesse C	111	salesman	66	26 "
E	Jackson Catherine—†	113	housewife	67	here
F	Jackson Margaret S—†	113	saleswoman	30	"
G	Jackson Winifred—†	113	millhand	28	"
H	Morrissey Maud—†	113	saleswoman	40	"
K	Wermers Joseph B	113	laborer	50	"
L	Wermers Mary V—†	113	housewife	49	"
M	Hines Delia F—†	113	"	65	"
N	O'Neil Mary T—†	113	"	35	"
O	O'Neil Thomas E	113	salesman	35	"
P	Adams Alice J—†	115	housewife	85	7 Hilburn
R	Alexander Alice T—†	115	stenographer	59	7 "
S	Alexander Hannah—†	115	housewife	87	7 "
T	Dexter Lena E—†	115	clerk	57	7 "
U	Zitzow Ada L—†	115	housewife	31	here
V	Zutzow Harris	115	chauffeur	33	"
Y	Knight Evelyn T—†	115	housewife	47	86 Thornton
Z	Knight Fred W	115	salesman	53	86 "
A	Rivers Claire—†	115	housewife	40	2729 Wash'n
B	Rivers Frank	115	carpenter	64	2729 "
C	Martyn Mary A—†	115	housewife	60	here
D	Fallon Delia—†	115	"	65	"
E	Fallon Frances E—†	115	saleswoman	29	"
F	Miller Florence H—†	115	housewife	32	"
G	Miller Trygoe A	115	bookkeeper	38	"
H	Ryan Margaret E—†	115	school teacher	49	"
K	Ryan Mary A—†	115	housewife	67	"
L	Ryan Rose E—†	115	school teacher	55	"
M	Coffin George W	117	salesman	27	"
N	Coffin Mildred A—†	117	bookkeeper	24	"
O	Deighan Mary V—†	117	housewife	25	Canada
P	Deighan Russell	117	carpenter	30	"
R	Lisotte Louis P	117	shoeworker	49	here

6

Page.	Letter.	FULL NAME.	Residence, April 1, 1926.	Occupation.	Supposed Age.	Reported Residence, April 1, 1925. Street and Number.

Dale Street—Continued

	s	Rokus Frank B	117	carpenter	46	403 Warren
	т	Rokus Leora F—†	117	housewife	40	403 "
	u	Waite Raymond S	117	glazier	24	here
	v	Waite Vivian E—†	117	clerk	24	"
	w	McCarthy Denis	119	motorman	35	"
	x	McCarthy Katherine—†	119	housewife	32	"
	y	Burke Daniel	119	shoeworker	50	"
	z	Pitty Annie—†	119	housewife	59	"
	a	Samaras Arrtenes—†	119	"	27	44 E Dedham
	b	Samaras Sevastos	119	manager	34	44 "
	c	Monthorne Margaret—†	121	housewife	72	here
	d	Monthorne Mina M—†	121	"	58	"
	e	Monthorne Theophilus	121	special police	52	"
	f	Coogan Annie L—†	121	bookkeeper	43	"
	g	Coogan James	121	retired	79	"
	h	Coogan Josephine—†	121	housewife	40	"
	k	Coogan Katherine J—†	121	bookkeeper	36	"
	l	Coogan Mary E—†	121	"	46	"
	m	Archibald Hattie S—†	121	housewife	56	"
	n	Archibald John A	121	retired	64	2794 Wash'n
	o	Rossborough James A	131	milkman	30	3 Bainbridge
	p	Rossborough Sarah T—†	131	housewife	26	3 "
	r	Fitzpatrick Patrick	133	laborer	21	21 Valentine
	s	Vena Emilie—†	133	housewife	40	here
	т	Vena Ernesto	133	mason	41	"
	u	Waters Barbara—†	133	housewife	22	21 Valentine
	v	Waters John	133	laborer	24	21 "

Dorr Street

	w	Dooner Helen—†	6	housewife	55	here
	x	Dooner John P	6	baker	60	"
	y	Griffin Mary E—†	6	housekeeper	52	"
	z	Griffin Walter L	6	draftsman	27	"
	a	Deveney Lillian M—†	6	housekeeper	38	"
	b	Deveney Patrick H	6	painter	50	"
	c	Goodwin George F	6	mechanic	34	739 Hunt'n av
	d	Goodwin Thomas J	6	fireman	38	here
	e	Moorhouse Ernest F	6	painter	42	Quincy
	f	Curtis Leola E—†	8	bookkeeper	40	137 Highland

Page.	Letter.	FULL NAME.	Residence, April 1, 1926.	Occupation.	Supposed Age.	Reported Residence, April 1, 1925. Street and Number.

Dorr Street—Continued

G	Harney Sarah E —†	8	dressmaker	56	137 Highland
H	Trueman Catherine—†	8	housewife	38	here
K	Trueman Fredrick	8	clerk	40	"
L	Ruputz Cathrine —†	8	housewife	44	"
M	Ruputz John J	8	tailor	45	"
N	Wahlers Eda C —†	10	milliner	42	"
O	Brown Patrick H	10	retired	77	"
P	Clark Ella C —†	10	housewife	37	"
R	Clark Roswell S	10	salesman	36	"
T	Connors Charles J	12	laborer	42	"
U	Connors Helen F —†	12	housewife	24	"
V	Cronin Diana E —†	12	dressmaker	56	"
W	Cronin John J	12	operator	26	"
X	Grabert Emma C —†	12	housekeeper	70	"
Y	Moriaty Eugene J	14	special police	47	"
Z	Moriaty Nora —†	14	housewife	36	"
A	Holzman Josephine C —†	14	"	44	"
B	Holzman Soloman C	14	conductor	40	
C	Gillis Josephine —†	14	stitcher	32	149 Columbia rd
D	MacArthur Mary A —†	14	"	22	Sydney N S
E	McPhee Catherine L —†	14	housewife	31	Westboro
F	McPhee Joseph N	14	carpenter	30	"
G	O'Brien Michael	14	window washer	24	here
H	Cook Albert G	rear 16	foreman	41	"
K	Cook Mabel —†	" 16	housewife	41	"
L	Larkin Agnes —†	18	housekeeper	50	1584 Tremont
M	Larkin Helen —†	18	clerk	29	1584 "
N	Spellman Anne—†	18	housewife	30	1584 "
O	Spellman Charles R	18	policeman	32	1584 "
P	Carter Marion L —†	18	housewife	32	here
R	Carter William J	18	foreman	32	"
S	Ford Martin J	18	motorman	43	"
T	Bairsto Claude	20	bookkeeper	20	"
U	Bairsto John	20	"	29	Canada
V	Nickerson Anna—†	20	housewife	35	here
W	Nickerson Clifton	20	factory worker	22	"
X	Nickerson Gladstone	20	bookkeeper	37	"
Y	Blanchard Gertrude C —†	20	housewife	34	13A Fountain
Z	Blanchard William S	20	fireman	33	13A "

8

Page.	Letter.	FULL NAME.	Residence, April 1, 1926.	Occupation	Supposed Age.	Reported Residence, April 1, 1925. Street and Number.

Dorr Street— Continued

A	O'Leary Anna M—†	20	housewife	33	here
B	O'Leary John M	20	blacksmith	33	"
C	Sullivan Mary E—†	22	housewife	29	"
D	Sullivan Michael	22	blacksmith	32	"
E	Lindsey Margaret E—†	22	housekeeper	46	"
F	Wellbrock Fred M	22	accountant	42	"
G	Wellbrock Helen M—†	22	housewife	32	"
H	Cook Wallace A	22	clerk	42	1346½ Tremont
K	Ryan Edward F	22	bookkeeper	22	1346½ "
L	Ryan Elizabeth G—†	22	stitcher	45	1346½ "
M	Ryan James W	22	bookkeeper	39	1346½ "
N	Ryan Mary F—†	22	brushmaker	50	1346½ "
O	Ryan Mary G—†	22	clerk	24	1346½ "
P	McGettrich Annie R—†	24	housekeeper	56	here
R	McGettrich Charles E	24	student	23	"
S	McGettrich Francis M	24	"	25	"
T	Gately Esther C—†	26	clerk	20	"
U	Gately Francis W	26	salesman	25	"
V	Gately Frederick J	26	riveter	24	"
W	Gately Winifred J—†	26	bookkeeper	35	"
X	Gately Martin J	26	manager	41	"
Y	Gately Mary J—†	26	packer	37	"
Z	Clark Catherine—†	26	housewife	35	"
A	Clark Raymond	26	grocer	35	"
B	MacClure James	28	retired	74	18 Dorr
C	Ray Alfred W	28	shoeworker	42	18 "
D	Ray Lillian L—†	28	housewife	37	18 "
E	Quinn Delia M—†	28	"	38	here
F	Quinn John E	28	plumber	45	"
G	Rigney John	28	tel inspector	23	"
H	Donnelly Annie F—†	28	housewife	58	"
K	Donnelly Esther L—†	28	stenographer	20	"
L	Donnelly John T	28	printer	58	"
M	Donnelly Walter E	28	clerk	25	"
N	Dunning Katherine I—†	32	"	30	Belmont
O	Monahan Charles S	32	"	57	here
P	Monahan Elizabeth J—†	32	housekeeper	59	"
R	Monahan James E	32	clerk	61	"
S	Monahan John F	32	"	68	"

9

Fenwick Street

T	Hanrahan John P	2	shipper	34	here
U	Hanrahan Mary E—†	2	housewife	35	"
V	Clune Annie F—†	2	"	66	"
W	Clune James	2	carpenter	71	"
X	Murry Josephine—†	2	bookkeeper	33	"
Y	Bartlett Ella M—†	2	housewife	59	"
Z	Bartlett Fred A	2	clerk	60	"
A	Craven Frances—†	4	houseworker	70	"
B	Luby Bridget—†	6	housewife	50	"
C	Burns Annie G—†	6	"	43	"
D	Burns Joseph F	6	steamfitter	59	"
E	Driscoll Mary—†	8	houseworker	72	"
F	Willis Margaret—†	8	"	65	"
G	Willis Mary—†	8	housewife	32	"
H	Willis Richard J	8	roofer	35	"
K	Murphy Bridget—†	10	houseworker	60	"
L	Vaughn Louise—†	10	saleswoman	28	"
M	Vaughn Margaret—†	10	houseworker	62	"
N	Fay John E	10	retired	71	"
O	Killian Richard A	10	"	73	"
P	Ryan Mary—† 1st rear	10	housewife	24	269 Heath
R	Ryan Michael J 1st "	10	foreman	30	269 "
S	Flanagan Mabel—† 2d "	10	housewife	22	Beachmont
T	Flanagan William E 2d "	10	brushmaker	25	"
U	Clark Margret—† 2d "	10	laundress	51	here
V	Shedd Catherine—†	14	housewife	40	"
W	Shedd John J	14	machinist	42	"
X	Moynihan Agnes—†	14	houseworker	28	"
Y	Moynihan Annie—†	14	bookkeeper	32	"
Z	Moynihan Frank	14	pedler	25	"
A	Moynihan Joseph	14	plumber	30	"
B	Moynihan Mary—†	14	houseworker	55	"
C	O'Brien Charles H	14	machinist	29	"
D	O'Brien Mary—†	14	houseworker	22	"
E	Mahoney Dennis	14	coachman	48	"
F	Mahoney Mary A—†	14	houseworker	50	"
G	McDermott Bartholomew J	16	electrician	36	"
H	McDermott Mary E—†	16	housewife	32	"
K	Owen Philip J	16	salesman	25	"
L	Cronin Dennis	16	engineer	35	Somerville

Fenwick Street—Continued

M	Murtagh Annie—†	16	housewife	32	Somerville
N	Murtagh John E	16	teamster	33	"
O	Clark John A	16	mechanic	65	here
P	Clarke Josephine—†	16	housewife	70	"
R	Ryan David	18	painter	45	"
S	Ryan Margaret A—†	18	houseworker	75	"
T	Ryan Mary E—†	18	dressmaker	43	"
U	Longin Johannah—†	18	housewife	36	"
V	Longin John	18	chauffeur	59	"
W	Hoey Rose A—†	18	housewife	35	"
X	Hoey William P	18	carpenter	36	"
Y	Renaud Alfred D	20	chauffeur	32	6 Fort av
Z	Renaud Anna—†	20	housewife	26	6 "
A	Macaulay Eresis—†	20	houseworker	74	California
B	Templeton Catherine—†	20	"	69	15 Kensington
C	Callanan Catherine B—†	20	brushmaker	27	64 Alpine
D	Callanan Gertrude M—†	20	"	34	64 "
E	Callanan Jeremiah	20	clerk	23	64 "
F	Callanan Mary—†	20	houseworker	65	64 "
G	Thompson Mary V—†	22	cook	32	here
H	Kirby Mary—†	22	housewife	26	"
K	Kirby Vincent E	22	machinist	26	"
L	Lecek Anna—†	22	houseworker	50	82 Leverett
M	Lecek Carl	22	salesman	34	82 "
N	Wiles Perley A	24	electrician	32	here
O	Wiles Vida E—†	24	housewife	29	"
P	McDougall Dan	24	laborer	29	"
R	McDougall Duncan	24	carpenter	32	"
S	McDougall Isabella—†	24	houseworker	69	"
T	Wilkinson Annie G—†	24	"	54	"

Guild Street

B	Anthony Frank J	40	salesman	45	here
C	Anthony Sadie—†	40	housewife	40	"
D	McNally Bertha M—†	40	"	40	44 Guild
E	McNally Hugh J	40	shipper	38	44 "
F	Bowditch John	40	merchant	72	here
G	Buckley Annie—†	42	housewife	38	"
H	Buckley John B	42	clerk	32	"

Guild Street—Continued

K	McDonald Mildred—†	42	clerk	22	here
L	Bernard Lester D	42	printer	35	"
M	Hancock Frederick W	42	carpenter	87	"
N	Minard Edith—†	42	housewife	40	"
P	Taylor Frances G—†	44	domestic	57	84 Humboldt av
R	Taylor Ruth C—†	44	"	34	84 "
T	Herbert Egbert	44	laborer	38	70 Williams
U	Herbert Ivy—†	44	housewife	30	70 "
V	Graham Benjamin	46	carpenter	55	49 Elmwood
W	Graham Laura—†	46	housewife	41	49 "
X	Berry Ella L—†	46	"	63	here
Y	Berry William	46	salesman	61	"
Z	Dodge Charles A	46	clerk	38	"
A	Boch Carrie S—†	46	"	55	"
B	Boch Rudolph T	46	laborer	51	"
C	Chandler Christie	48	clerk	28	73 Westland av
D	Payrow Charles	48	operator	63	2971 Wash'n
E	McCarthy John	48	laborer	32	New York
F	McCarthy Nora—†	48	housewife	30	222 Prince
G	Healey Margaret L—†	48	"	51	here
H	Healey Patrick J	48	clerk	55	"
K	Maybin Eva J—†	50	housewife	32	"
L	Maybin Mack R	50	chauffeur	34	"
M	Scott Edward	50	laborer	50	"
N	Bland Albert	50	fireman	38	74 Westminster
O	Bland Ella—†	50	housewife	40	74 "
P	Smallcomb Anna G—†	52	"	36	16 Ray
R	Smallcomb Thomas J	52	operator	39	16 "
S	Peebles Micheal A	52	carpenter	48	48 Guild
T	Peebles Mary R—†	52	housewife	36	48 "
U	Bertino Caroline—†	52	"	34	2530 Wash'n
V	Bertino Frank	52	barber	51	2530 "
W	Laplaca Mary—†	52	domestic	21	2530 "

Highland Street

Y	Smith Fred O	52	salesman	63	here
Z	Smith Mary P—†	52	housekeeper	79	"
A	Smith Percy W	52	salesman	39	"
B	Brooker Catherine—†	52	housewife	56	"

12

Page.	Letter.	FULL NAME.	Residence, April 1, 1926.	Occupation.	Supposed Age.	Reported Residence, April 1, 1925. Street and Number.

Highland Street—Continued

c	Brooker Florence—†	52	operator	22	here
d	Brooker Frank	52	clerk	20	"
e	Brooker John P	52	"	30	"
f	Hadley Elizabeth L—†	54	housewife	31	Everett
g	Hadley Henry C	54	painter	31	"
h	Pendergast Gertrude M–†	54	housewife	35	here
k	Pendergast John W	54	chauffeur	37	"
l	Dakin Bessie A—†	54	houseworker	32	"
m	Donnelly Margaret T—†	56	housewife	32	"
n	Donnelly Thomas L	56	clerk	35	"
o	Gordon Jennie E—†	56	housewife	56	10 Highland
p	Gould Jean M—†	56	stenographer	25	10 "
r	Clark Cecil	56	carpenter	36	here
s	Clark Charlotte—†	56	housewife	37	"
t	Fitzgerald Mary A—†	58	at home	52	"
u	Lynch Catherine J—†	58	housewife	26	"
v	Lynch Joseph P	58	policeman	29	"
w	Baggs Hugh	58	laborer	59	21 Bartlett
x	Baggs Joseph P	58	student	26	21 "
y	Baggs Lydia—†	58	housewife	48	21 "
z	Myers Mark	58	pressman	58	here
a	Myers Pauline L—†	58	housewife	53	"
b	Howell Harriet—†	60	housekeeper	75	"
c	Howell Thaddeus	60	conductor	55	"
d	Rollins Laura A—†	60	collector	61	"
e	Meridith Frank	60	salesman	54	"
f	Meridith Lena—†	60	housewife	55	"
g	Lento Anthony	60	barber	39	"
h	Lento Mary—†	60	housewife	38	"
k	Norton Annie—†	62	"	32	"
l	Norton John J	62	laborer	33	"
m	Murphy Mary B—†	62	houseworker	39	109 Cedar
n	McKenzie Hazel I—†	62	nurse	36	here
o	McKenzie Mabel M—†	62	housewife	34	"
p	McKenzie William H	62	police officer	33	"
r	Tibbo Lyda J—†	64	housewife	35	"
s	Tibbo Thomas H	64	watchman	36	"
t	Donovan Edward F	64	bricklayer	22	"
u	Donovan Michael J	64	fireman	43	"
v	Streebel Evelyn—†	64	housekeeper	33	526 Mass av
w	Lucy George	64	cabinetmaker	44	58 Dunster rd

13

Highland Street—Continued

X	Lucy Rose—†	64	housewife	35	113 Cedar
Y	Slason Daniel F	66	salesman	33	here
Z	Slason Helen F—†	66	housewife	30	"
A	O'Rourke Catherine F—†	66	"	39	"
B	O'Rourke Dennis F	66	machinist	50	"
C	Burnett James P	66	carpenter	48	"
D	Burnett Rhoda B—†	66	housewife	49	"
E	Donovan Anna V—†	68	hairdresser	36	"
F	Milliken Pauline B—†	68	housewife	33	"
G	Milliken Walter S	68	grocer	41	"
H	Huckle Albert V	68	printer	20	"
K	Huckle Anna F—†	68	housekeeper	50	1 Centre St ter
L	Huckle Florence H—†	68	operator	25	here

Hulbert Street

N	Schuler Annie—†	2	proprietor	42	here
O	Isbitsky Ada—†	2	housewife	23	"
P	Isbitsky Nathan	2	grocer	43	"
S	Burke Frederick J	6	motorman	38	22 Ray
T	Burke Irene A—†	6	housewife	28	22 "
W	Murphy Harry	12	carpenter	48	here
X	Murphy Jennie—†	12	housewife	35	"
Y	McElroy Mary A—†	12	housekeeper	43	"
Z	Ayers Dorothy E—†	14	housewife	23	2652 Wash'n
A	Ayers Herbert D	14	sailor	31	Pennsylvania
B	Meehan Myrtle E—†	14	housewife	51	2652 Wash'n
C	Meehan William H	14	piano tuner	45	2652 "
D	McDemott Albert E J	14	cooper	53	here
E	McDermott Sarah E—†	14	housewife	45	"
F	Smith Everly E—†	14	"	22	"
G	Smith Frank H	14	compositor	32	"
H	Ahearn James F	14	laborer	29	"
K	Ahearn Nora M—†	14	housewife	29	"
M	Gendron Herbert W	16	dispatcher	36	"
N	Gendron Rose A—†	16	housewife	34	"
O	Malley Bridget—†	16	at home	96	"
P	Malley Bridget C—†	16	housekeeper	60	"

Page.	Letter.	FULL NAME.	Residence, April 1, 1926.	Occupation.	Supposed Age.	Reported Residence, April 1, 1925. Street and Number.

Hulbert Street—Continued

R	Malley Martha J—†	16	stitcher	62	here
S	Malley Susie A—†	16	"	64	"
T	Doyle Catherine A—†	16	housekeeper	45	"
U	Doyle James E	16	watchman	49	"
V	Doyle Marie A—†	16	stenographer	26	"
W	Oertel Adam	17	baker	46	"
X	Cassidy Margaret G—†	17	housekeeper	55	"
Y	Culhane John W	17	laborer	66	"
Z	Brennan Marion A—†	19	clerk	35	"
A	Brophy Catherine—†	19	housekeeper	50	"
B	Dunn Henry	19	motorman	55	"
C	Fitzmorris Elizabeth C—†	19	secretary	20	"
D	Fitzmorris John	19	motorman	54	"
E	Fitzmorris Margaret M—†	19	bookkeeper	23	"
F	Fitzmorris Winifred A—†	19	housewife	49	"
G	Estes Bertrand F	21	chauffeur	26	"
H	Estes Margaret M—†	21	housewife	27	"
K	Sullivan Margaret M—†	21	housekeeper	57	"
L	Conroy Joseph M	23	musician	35	"
M	Conroy Julia A—†	23	housekeeper	65	"
N	Collins John M	23	laborer	57	"
O	Collins Mary A—†	23	housewife	47	"
P	Daly John F	23	laborer	23	"
R	Daly Joseph M	23	teamster	21	"
S	Daly Mary E—†	23	engraver	22	"
T	Bellottie Rose—†	23	dressmaker	66	"
U	Sullivan Jeremiah J	25	foreman	42	3 Regent sq
V	Sullivan Margaret E—†	25	housekeeper	36	3 "
W	Murray Bridget E—†	25	"	62	here
X	O'Brien Mary E—†	25	clerk	45	"
Y	Carey Anna M—†	25	housekeeper	49	"
Z	Carey William J	25	chauffeur	23	"
A	Downey Catherine A—†	27	at home	65	"
B	Guinan Rose H—†	27	housekeeper	47	"
C	Gately Catherine R—†	27	stenographer	25	"
D	Gately Ellen M—†	27	housekeeper	54	"
E	Gately John H	27	clerk	20	"
F	Gately Margaret P—†	27	stenographer	23	"
G	Gately Mary J—†	27	secretary	28	"
H	MacDonnell John J	27	laborer	46	"
K	MacDonnell Mary A—†	27	housewife	46	"

Juniper Street

L	Searle George M	1	repairman	52	here	
M	Searle Nellie R—†	1	clerk	24	"	
N	Searle Rostella M—†	1	housewife	48	"	
O	Hendell Mather—†	1	waitress	35	"	
P	Weston Mabel—†	1	"	37	"	
R	Victerson Florence—†	1	artist	32	35 Valentine	
U	Davidson Emma—†	5	housekeeper	72	here	
V	Davidson Mary A—†	5	clerk	35	"	
W	Andrews Janie—†	7	housewife	29	"	
X	Andrews Reginald	7	printer	28	"	
Y	Murphy James L	7	steamfitter	27	Rhode Island	
Z	Murphy Louise H—†	7	housewife	28	"	
A	Dale Annie—†	7	"	25	here	
B	Dale Lenord	7	mechanic	30	"	
C	Kane Josephine A—†	9	housekeeper	45	"	
D	Saunders Arthur H	9	mariner	52	"	
E	Saunders Mary F—†	9	housewife	53	"	
F	McDonald Albert	9	carpenter	45	"	
G	Rehm Florence—†	9	housewife	50	"	
H	Rehm Henry	9	repairman	29	"	
K	Simons Nancy—†	11	housewife	48	"	
L	Simons William J	11	garageman	52	"	
M	Andrews Gertrude—†	11	housewife	28	7 Juniper	
N	Andrews Manuel	11	tailor	31	7 "	
O	Beattie Elta—†	11	saleswoman	52	here	
P	Gillespie William E	11	shoeworker	29	"	
R	Kenney Catherine T—†	15	housewife	43	"	
S	Kenney John J	15	painter	50	"	
T	Foye Hellen M—†	15	housewife	30	"	
U	Foye John F	15	repairman	31	"	
V	Giaravinas Annie—†	21	housewife	31	"	
W	Giaravinas Peter	21	pedler	45	"	
Y	Sarno Angiolina—†	22	housewife	40	"	
Z	Sarno Finizio	22	manager	49	"	
A	Jianon Arestalle	23	cook	36	"	
B	Jianon Mary—†	23	housewife	36	"	
C	McDonald Angus	23	chauffeur	50	"	
D	McDonald Dorothy F—†	23	clerk	21	"	
E	McDonald Russell	23	chauffeur	23	"	
G	Davis Madeline E—†	25	housewife	29	38 Thornton	

Juniper Street—Continued

H	Davis Thomas F	25	salesman	32	38 Thornton
K	O'Brien James	25	ironworker	46	here
L	O'Brien Louise—†	25	housewife	33	"
M	Haley Cecilia A—†	26	"	54	"
N	Haley Joseph A	26	reporter	22	"
O	Haley Pierce J	26	clerk	24	"
P	Haley Pierce S	26	inspector	57	"
R	Riley Minnie A—†	26	seamstress	60	"
T	Gumpright Florance	30	radioworker	25	"
U	Gumpright Francis—†	30	housewife	58	"
V	Gumpright Herman	30	piano tuner	60	"
W	Rones Gerard	30	confectioner	32	"
X	Rones Hellen J—†	30	housewife	31	"
Y	Sewell Bertha—†	30	waitress	28	"
Z	Sewell Nora—†	30	housekeeper	60	"
A	McLoughlin Charles H	34	teamster	33	31 Edward
B	McLoughlin Rose M—†	34	housewife	33	31 "
C	Eger Emma T—†	34	"	62	here
E	Eger Lawrence J	34	shipper	23	"
D	Eger Lawrence S	34	finisher	65	"
F	MacKay Ellenor—†	34	housewife	25	"
G	MacKay William	34	printer	25	"
H	Dannenhoffer Marion—†	38	housekeeper	28	"
K	Dannenhoffer Rose—†	38	clerk	25	"
L	Dannenhoffer Rose L—†	38	housewife	59	"
M	Bletzer Conrade	38	engineer	57	"
N	Bletzer Conrade F	38	compositor	24	"
O	Bletzer Lina—†	38	housewife	59	"
P	Bletzer Marion D—†	38	clerk	21	"
R	Campbell Annie—†	42	housewife	54	"
S	Campbell Archie	42	policeman	52	"
T	Gustavson Walter	42	fireman	52	"
U	Overn Carl	42	painter	38	"
V	Overn Olga—†	42	housewife	31	"
W	Reed Julise	42	reporter	66	"
X	Henderson Royster	47	garageman	24	"
Y	Jones Etta—†	47	housekeeper	45	"
Z	Mitchell Bernice L—†	47	at home	24	"
A	Mitchell Henry S	47	repairman	26	"
B	Scully Charles F	48	agent	29	"
C	Scully Eleanor—†	48	housewife	26	"

Page.	Letter.	FULL NAME	Residence, April 1, 1926.	Occupation	Supposed Age.	Reported Residence, April 1, 1925. Street and Number.

Juniper Street—Continued

	D	Lang John	48	broker	21	3231 Wash'n
	E	Weiss Frank X	48	artist	48	here
	F	Weiss Helen—†	48	housewife	49	"
	G	Curley George F	49	chauffeur	21	"
	H	Curley Thomas H	49	florist	26	"
	K	Kelley John W	49	laborer	58	"

Juniper Terrace

	L	Brown Grace—†	2	housewife	40	here
	M	Brown Norman	2	motorman	45	"
	N	Chamberlain Jennie—†	3	houseworker	48	"
	O	Tumulty Catherine—†	4	housewife	28	28 Codman pk
	P	Tumulty Patrick	4	motorman	29	25 "
	R	Nash Arthur F	14	painter	53	here
	S	Nash Caroline—†	14	housewife	52	"
	T	Nash Stewart A	14	salesman	22	"

Lambert Avenue

	U	Harlow Alice M—†	18	housewife	40	here
	V	Harlow Thomas P	18	manager	46	"
	W	Williams Ellen P—†	18	houseworker	72	"
	X	Keenan Alice M	45	dressmaker	33	Barre
	Y	Oches Helen—†	45	stenographer	34	Weymouth
	Z	Reese Mary A—†	45	matron	49	here
	A	Westover Helen—†	45	hairdresser	33	Somerville
	B	Spain Daniel	48	shipper	35	55 Forest Hills
	C	Spain Ethel B—†	48	housewife	27	55 "
	D	Kiersteat Marie—†	48	waitress	46	here
	E	Baker Helena C—†	48	housekeeper	31	"
	F	Wishart James J	48	signalman	69	"
	G	Cauigg Anna—†	50	factory worker	26	131 Highland
	H	Cauigg Edward	50	chauffeur	25	131 "
	K	Silvey Alice—†	50	housewife	49	40 Guild
	L	Silvey Alice M—†	50	factory worker	23	40 "
	M	Silvey John	50	clerk	20	40 "
	N	Silvey John F	50	blacksmith	52	40 "
	O	Silvey Leo F	50	clerk	25	40 "

18

Page	Letter	Full Name.	Residence, April 1, 1926.	Occupation.	Supposed Age.	Reported Residence, April 1, 1925. Street and Number.

Lambert Avenue—Continued

P	Fay Edwin F	50	fireman	36	12 Creighton
R	Scott Catherine M—†	50	housewife	29	here
S	Scott George T	50	fireman	30	"
T	Hughes Anna F—†	52	clerk	24	11 Malbon pl
U	Hughes Catherine A—†	52	saleswoman	26	11 "
V	Hughes Margaret E—†	52	housekeeper	27	11 "
W	Hughes Margaret F—†	52	nurse	52	11 "
Y	Freiberg Anna—†	52	housewife	38	here
A	Freiberg William E	52	carpenter	42	"
A¹	Galvin Emily—†	52	seamstress	40	43 Fort av
B	Farrell Helen J—†	60	housewife	34	here
C	Farrell John	60	ironworker	33	"
D	Galvin Cecilia A—†	60	housewife	42	"
E	Galvin John J	60	laborer	46	"
F	Langdon Elizabeth L—†	60	housewife	26	"
G	Langdon John M	60	conductor	33	"
H	Mathi Elizabeth—†	60	houseworker	60	"
K	Welch Annie M—†	62	housewife	44	"
L	Welch Louis M	62	fireman	52	"
N	Clement Gertrude J—†	62	housewife	32	"
O	Clement Philias O	62	chauffeur	35	"
P	MacLeod Ernest J	64	plumber	47	"
R	MacLeod Ernest J, jr	64	agent	23	"
S	MacLeod Mary J—†	64	housewife	46	"
T	Lawrence Eva R—†	64	"	25	"
U	Lawrence George E	64	clerk	27	"
V	Lawrence Jennie E—†	64	stenographer	30	"
W	Lundy Frederick S	64	clerk	42	"
X	Mulhern Catherine—†	64	houseworker	64	"
Y	Treanor J Albert	64	guard	31	"
Z	Treanor Mary C—†	64	housewife	39	"
A	Madden Anna M—†	80	stenographer	30	"
B	Madden Helen M—†	80	"	24	"
C	Madden John J	80	retired	73	"
D	Madden John J, jr	80	roofer	29	"
E	Madden William J	80	"	21	"
F	O'Connell Mary—†	80	houseworker	40	"
G	McCarron William	88	shoeworker	35	"
H	Nolan James J	88	motorman	50	"
K	Nolan Margaret A—†	88	housewife	47	"

Page	Letter	Full Name	Residence, April 1, 1926.	Occupation.	Supposed Age.	Reported Residence, April 1, 1925. Street and Number.

Logan Street

	L	Black Ester—†	4	houseworker	29	here
	M	Seagren Annie—†	4	housewife	56	"
	N	Seagren Carl	4	painter	62	"
	P	Kenny Andrew F	4	salesman	44	"
	R	Kenny Catherine G—†	4	stenographer	34	"
	S	Kenny George J	4	collector	41	"
	T	Kenny John F	4	shipper	45	"
	U	Kenny Mary—†	4	housekeeper	42	"
	V	Kenny Peter F	4	salesman	46	"
	W	Kenny Sarah J—†	4	at home	77	"
	Y	Gronberge Ewald	6	steamfitter	33	"
	Z	Gronberge Helga—†	6	housewife	33	"
	A	Lavesen Marie O—†	6	housekeeper	68	"

Millmont Street

	C	Hansen Daniel	5	rubberworker	37	here
	D	Hansen Inga—†	5	housewife	40	"
	E	Haukum Thomas	5	factory worker	35	"
	F	Coolidge William L	5	machinist	22	"
	G	Roberts William E	5	chauffeur	35	"
	H	Russo John A	5	engineer	35	"
	K	Russo Lavinia A—†	5	housewife	32	"
	L	Robery Daniel W	5	welder	38	Lynn
	M	Robery Helen—†	5	housewife	36	"
	N	Tierney Joseph F	9	rubberworker	36	here
	O	Tierney Lucy M—†	9	housewife	34	"
	P	Moyston Israel H	9	porter	33	43 Northfield
	R	Moyston Secelia H—†	9	housewife	36	43 "
	S	Dunn Annie T—†	15	"	58	here
	T	Dunn Helen F—†	15	stenographer	35	"
	U	Dunn James	15	motorman	58	"
	V	Dunn Joseph T	15	inspector	24	"
	W	Dunn Mary E—†	15	clerk	33	"
	X	Dunn William G	15	policeman	28	"
	Y	McAuliffe Anna L—†	15	housewife	29	"
	Z	McAuliffe William	15	salesman	29	"
	A	Aigen Joseph B	23	clerk	42	"
	B	Aigen Mary A—†	23	housewife	38	"

Millmont Street — Continued

c	Walleston James L	23	plumber	37	here
d	Walleston Jennie—†	23	vamper	35	"
e	Dwelley Bertha—†	25	clerk	43	Lincoln Me
f	Murphy Grace—†	25	housewife	40	here
g	Murphy James G	25	letter carrier	43	"
h	Smiley Muriel—†	25	housewife	26	84 Highland
k	Smiley Sterling	25	salesman	27	84 "
l	Sweet Cassia—†	25	clerk	40	Maine
m	Lockhart Charles D	29	painter	29	here
n	Lockhart Doris—†	29	housewife	21	"
o	Bermingham Myra—†	29	factory worker	22	19 Dana pl
p	Kelley Charles W	29	printer	40	here
r	Kelley Mary E—†	29	housewife	42	"
s	Lee Ella R—†	31	laundress	44	60 Vernon
t	Nelson Alice R—†	31	domestic	40	60 "
u	Dennis Arthur A	31	laborer	43	37 Sterling
v	Dennis Mary E—†	31	housekeeper	64	37 "
w	Jones Annie L—†	31	housewife	26	637 Shawmut av
x	Jones Phillip J	31	laborer	31	637 "
y	Kushum Emilea—†	39	housewife	30	here
z	Kushum Rigold	39	carpenter	33	"
a	Meshak John	39	machinist	45	Cambridge
b	Polishook Celia—†	39	housewife	40	here
c	Polishook Harry	39	carpenter	42	"
d	Doksir Fanny—†	39	housewife	38	"
e	Doksir William	39	dressmaker	37	"
f	Sherman Benjamin	39	painter	22	"
g	Sherman Isaac	39	"	21	"
h	Sherman Max	39	tailor	45	"
k	Sherman Pearl—†	39	housewife	40	"

Oakland Street

a	Koziewicz Amiela—†	1	housewife	43	here
b	Koziewicz Antonio	1	shoemaker	51	"
c	Koziewicz Felecia—†	1	school teacher	23	"
d	Koziewicz Paul	1	student	21	"
e	Huddsta John	3	laborer	31	"
f	Huddsta Flora—†	3	housewife	23	"
g	Alexander Alice H—†	5	"	48	"

21

Oakland Street—Continued

H	Alexander Andrew J	5	carpenter	83	here
L	Alexander Olive E —†	5	housewife	75	"
M	Alexander William B	5	musician	53	"
N	Alexander William R	5	student	20	"
K	Costa Olive —†	5	musician	23	"
O	Barbara Joseph T	7	millworker	63	Watertown
P	Sanborn Lawrence A	7	woodworker	46	1223 Tremont
R	Sanborn Flora N —†	7	houseworker	76	1223 "
S	Heath Linnie —†	9	housewife	62	here
T	Hosley Benjamin	9	ropemaker	25	"
U	Mubiennan Michael M	9	retired	65	"
V	Parsell Lillian —†	9	houseworker	60	"
W	Timmons Celia —†	11	housewife	43	"
X	Timmons Harry	11	carpenter	43	"
Y	Hatcher Frances —†	13	housewife	33	1223 Tremont
Z	Hatcher Harry	13	chauffeur	34	1223 "
A	Nadeau Joseph	15	laborer	36	17 Oakland
B	Parisse Dominic	15	"	39	here
C	Parisse Mary —†	15	housewife	42	"
D	Bulger Cyril A	17	foreman	26	10 Kingsbury
E	Bulger Lena —†	17	housewife	28	10 "
F	Bulger Raymond	17	teamster	24	10 "
G	Bulger Rita —†	17	stitcher	24	10 "
H	Sullivan Ellen M —†	17	housewife	45	84 Thornton
K	Sullivan Michael	17	carpenter	49	84 "
L	Turner Margaret —†	17	housewife	56	here
M	Turner William B	17	waiter	65	"
N	Lang Frieda R —†	19	housewife	33	"
O	Lang Howard D	19	machinist	35	"
P	Fetter Annie —†	19	housewife	43	"
R	Fetter Peter	19	cabinetmaker	49	"
S	Freffe James B	19	printer	34	"
T	Freffe Nathlyn —†	19	housewife	34	"

Osgood Court

U	Campbell Vincent	2	mechanic	24	18 Ray
V	McPhail Annie —†	2	housewife	36	here
W	McPhail James W	2	leatherworker	47	"

Page.	Letter.	FULL NAME.	Residence, April 1, 1926.	Occupation.	Supposed Age.	Reported Residence, April 1, 1925. Street and Number.

Ray Street

A	Ross Bradford E	8	laborer	21	here
B	Ross Helen —†	8	housewife	45	"
G	Ross Hugh G	8	lineman	22	"
D	Ross Irad J	8	electrician	48	"
E	Davis Manuel F	8	policeman	36	"
F	Davis Sadie J —†	8	housewife	39	"
G	Orpen Mary —†	8	maid	50	20 Greenville
H	Kelley Florence M —†	8	waitress	45	120 Regent
K	Kelley George M	8	proprietor	45	120 "
L	Marsh Charles T	8	clerk	63	120 "
M	Miller Ambrose L	9	ironworker	45	here
N	Miller Jennie —†	9	housewife	45	"
O	Keohane Jerimiah J	9	laborer	38	"
P	Keohane Mary M —†	9	housewife	40	"
R	Lally Bridget —†	9	"	54	"
S	Lally Teresa C —†	9	teacher	20	"
T	Lally Thomas F	9	chauffeur	23	"
U	Lally William	9	fireman	53	"
V	Donovan Edwin L	10	clerk	32	"
W	Donovan Frank A	10	laborer	45	"
X	Donovan Sarah A —†	10	matron	65	"
Y	Craven Catherine A —†	10	housewife	37	"
Z	Craven John	10	clerk	38	"
B	Bowen Alexander H	12	laborer	63	"
C	Bowen Flora —†	12	housewife	43	"
D	Bowen Weston G	12	electrician	22	"
E	Sheehan Daniel B	12	carpenter	46	54 Cliff
F	Sheehan Nellie M —†	12	housewife	36	54 "
G	Sullivan Annie —†	12	"	46	here
H	Sullivan Michael J	12	laborer	46	"
K	Holland Magdalen E —†	14	housewife	27	3 Regent sq
L	Holland Robert F	14	chauffeur	26	3 "
M	Bowes Anna L —†	14	housewife	27	Maine
N	Bowes Arthur T	14	waiter	28	"
O	McNaught Lawrence W	14	laborer	30	86 Eustis
P	McNaught Stella —†	14	housewife	24	86 "
R	Maceuley Charles H	14	teamster	21	18 Highland
S	Maceuley Susan —†	14	housekeeper	36	18 "
T	Morrison Christie B —†	16	housewife	30	3 Goldsmith pl
U	Morrison Roderick P	16	steamfitter	31	3 "

23

Page.	Letter.	FULL NAME.	Residence, April 1, 1926.	Occupation.	Supposed Age.	Reported Residence, April 1, 1925. Street and Number.

Ray Street—Continued

v	Cahoon Jennie—†	16	housewife	31	7 St Francis de Sales
w	Cahoon William	16	policeman	34	7 "
x	Doolan Annie R—†	16	housewife	22	64 Ruthven
y	Doolan Thomas J	16	chauffeur	24	Brookline
z	Blake Henry A	18	inspector	36	2677 Wash'n
A	Blake Julia A—†	18	housewife	37	2677 "
B	Shine Julia J—†	18	housekeeper	36	here
C	Atkinson Thomas W	18	laborer	21	1112 Dor av
D	Bennett Mary K—†	18	housekeeper	40	1112 "
E	Hynes Helen—†	20	housewife	42	here
F	Hynes Michael M	20	laborer	43	"
G	Callahan Elizabeth M—†	20	housekeeper	45	5 Regent ct
K	Zaleski Henry	22	laborer	41	Lawrence
L	Zaleski Mary—†	22	housewife	34	"
M	Cummings Joseph B	22	laborer	41	2277 Wash'n
N	Cummings Verna—†	22	housewife	40	2277 "
O	Condon Jane—†	22	housekeeper	52	464 Shawmut av
P	Hunt John	22	shoemaker	52	464 "
R	Weir James	22	lather	57	New York
S	Cavelius Anna R—†	24	housewife	46	here
T	Cavelius Peter	24	laborer	48	"
U	Seyberlich Marie—†	24	laundress	68	"
V	McCarthy Catherine—†	26	housewife	47	"
W	McCarthy Dennis	26	carpenter	58	"
X	McCarthy Mary F—†	26	stenographer	20	"
Y	Golden Elizabeth F—†	28	"	24	"
Z	Golden Elizabeth V—†	28	housekeeper	75	"
A	Golden Margaret M—†	28	bookkeeper	27	"
B	Dowd James J	28	clerk	38	"
C	Dowd Nora M—†	28	housewife	32	"
D	Splaine James	28	laborer	28	Canada
E	Clancey Joseph F	28	"	29	here
F	Clancey Mary E—†	28	housewife	28	"
G	Heavey John F	28	laborer	24	"
H	Costello Jennie A—†	30	housewife	26	"
K	Costello John J	30	conductor	28	"
L	Costello Thomas M	30	laborer	27	"
M	Long Agnes E—†	30	shoestitcher	31	"
N	Long Alice—†	30	"	29	"
O	Laffoley Mary E—†	30	housewife	47	"
P	Laffoley Reginald S	30	foreman	47	"

Ray Street--Continued

	R	Lapsley John J	35	student	21	here
	S	Lapsley Michael	35	teamster	55	"
	T	Lapsley Sarah H —†	35	housewife	50	"
	U	Fullington Fred V	35	conductor	27	82 Eustis
	V	Fullington Mildred E—†	35	housewife	21	82 "
	W	Burke Mary E—†	35	laundress	45	here
	X	Arnold Catherine E—†	37	housewife	49	"
	Y	Long Michael J	37	motorman	70	"
	Z	Annello Andrew	39	tailor	31	91 Salem
	A	Annello Josephine—†	39	housewife	22	91 "
	B	Pirrello Carmelo	39	chauffeur	20	91 "
	C	Pirrello Mary—†	39	housewife	42	91 "
	D	Pirrello Salvatore	39	laborer	53	91 "

Regent Street

	E	Clark Veronica—†	85	cook	63	here
	F	Condon Garrett J	85	clergyman	39	"
	G	Dolan Anna—†	85	maid	35	"
	H	Phelan John J	85	clergyman	36	"
	K	Splaine Michael J	85	"	51	"
	L	Sullivan Dennis F	85	"	47	"
	M	Buckley Catherine—†	91	teacher	32	"
	N	Finnegan Mary A—†	91	"	28	New Jersey
	O	Glynn Margaret—†	91	"	30	46 Dacia
	P	Hartigan Margaret—†	91	"	35	New Jersey
	R	Henley Margaret A—†	91	"	53	here
	S	McCormack Anna—†	91	"	32	"
	T	McGowen Catherine—†	91	stenographer	22	"
	U	McGowen Rose—†	91	housekeeper	37	"
	V	McHale Mary—†	91	teacher	29	"
	W	McMahon Mary A—†	91	"	29	"
	X	O'Brien Frances—†	91	"	28	"
	Y	Otis Louise—†	91	"	33	"
	Z	Ryan Mary A—†	91	"	30	New Jersey
	A	McKay Benjamin	95	machinist	36	here
	B	McKay Helen G—†	95	housewife	36	"
	C	Duffey Annie—†	95	clerk	22	"
	D	Duffey Ellen—†	95	houseworker	70	"
	E	Archilles Anna R—†	95	"	21	"

Page & Letter		FULL NAME.	Residence, April 1, 1926.	Occupation.	Supposed Age.	Reported Residence, April 1, 1925. Street and Number.

Regent Street—Continued

Letter	Full Name	Residence, April 1, 1926	Occupation	Supposed Age	Reported Residence, April 1, 1925. Street and Number
F	Archilles George H	95	metalworker	37	here
G	Archilles Priscilla—†	95	housewife	66	"
H	Archilles William H	95	laborer	26	"
K	Archilles Winifred—†	95	houseworker	20	"
L	Reid Bessie M—†	95	"	42	"
M	Cameron Flora—†	97	"	25	Canada
N	Fallon John F	97	janitor	58	here
O	Fallon Margaret—†	97	houseworker	62	"
P	Owens Harold J	97	student	21	"
R	Owens Joseph J	97	carpenter	60	"
S	Owens Josephine S—†	97	clerk	28	"
T	Owens Minnie A—†	97	stenographer	25	"
U	Owens Rose A—†	97	houseworker	56	"
V	Hurley David	97	coachman	68	"
W	Hurley Mary—†	97	houseworker	68	"
X	Hurley Mary V—†	97	tel operator	35	"
Y	Foley Catherine—†	99	houseworker	50	"
Z	Shields Bridget—†	99	"	76	"
A	Long Theresa—†	99	school teacher	40	98 Regent
B	Turlay Elizabeth—†	99	houseworker	70	here
C	Turlay Michael	99	plumber	35	"
D	Owen Angus J	103	electrician	48	"
E	Owen Catherine—†	103	houseworker	45	"
F	Owen George H	103	lineman	22	"
G	Hackett Anna J—†	105	houseworker	66	"
H	Hackett Margaret J—†	105	hairdresser	64	"
K	Hackett Mary M—†	105	"	68	"
L	Butler Joseph	113	retired	70	"
M	Carroll Theresa C—†	113	houseworker	37	"
N	Carroll Thomas J	113	boxmaker	43	"
O	Kennedy Agnes M—†	113	housewife	26	"
P	Kennedy Frank H	113	janitor	28	"
R	Finburgh Louis	115	salesman	38	"
S	Finburgh Mary—†	115	housewife	42	"
T	Bishop Harold F	115	fireman	26	"
U	McGonagle Francis	115	clerk	32	"
V	McGonagle Francis J	115	postal clerk	34	"
W	Carey Grace—†	115	houseworker	23	"
X	Sheets Bert R	115	ironworker	45	"
Y	Sheets Marion I—†	115	saleswoman	40	"

Page.	Letter.	FULL NAME.	Residence, April 1, 1926.	Occupation.	Supposed Age.	Reported Residence, April 1, 1925. Street and Number.

Regent Street—Continued

z	Sheets Paul R	115	chauffeur	21	here
A	Cauden Helen M—†	117	houseworker	40	"
B	Cauden John	117	clerk	40	"
c	Carolan James	117	waiter	49	"
D	Carolan Lucy—†	117	houseworker	50	"
E	O'Toole Lucy—†	117	"	67	N Wilmington
F	Donahue Agnes—†	117	"	35	here
G	Donahue Timothy	117	fireman	38	"
H	Curtis Georgina—†	119	houseworker	22	Canada
K	Curtis Lawrence M	119	auto mechanic	22	"
L	Porter Minnie A—†	119	houseworker	43	28 Litchfield
M	Porter Walter J	119	painter	43	28 "
N	Alward Ellen I—†	119	houseworker	30	here
O	Alward Eugene H	119	conductor	31	"

Rockledge Street

w	Flemming Elizabeth—†	2	housewife	33	73 Highland
x	Flemming William	2	tiremaker	38	73 "
y	Davis Lena B—†	2	nurse	39	39 Brattle
A	McDonald Christine—†	2	waitress	25	Brookline
B	Regele Albert L	2	inspector	37	39 Bartlett
c	Regele Catherine A—†	2	housewife	31	39 "
D	O'Connor Barbara F—†	4	"	28	here
E	O'Connor Patrick J	4	fireman	32	"
F	Strudas Adam R	4	baker	46	"
G	Strudas Susana—†	4	housewife	42	"
H	Gilman Charles F	4	salesman	39	"
K	Gilman Horace K	4	retired	67	285 Bunker Hill
L	Gilman Martha E—†	4	housewife	38	here
M	Gilman Mary F—†	4	"	65	285 Bunker Hill
N	Maher Agnes T—†	4A	tel operator	39	here
O	Maher Mary A—†	4A	housewife	69	"
P	Hartigan Margaret A—†	4A	"	38	2 Terry
R	Hartgan Patrick J	4A	chauffeur	46	2 "
S	Hall John	4A	agent	24	here
T	Hall Louise H—†	4A	clerk	24	"
U	Brady Catherine M—†	8	housewife	48	"
V	Brady Patrick J	8	laborer	49	"

Rockledge Street – Continued

w	Velton Agnes G †	8	housewife	34	3215 Wash'n
x	Velton John J	8	metalworker	36	3215 "
y	Beales Ethel J †	8	housewife	24	36 Warren
z	Beales Leon C	8	foreman	26	8 Leon

Thornton Street

A	Hayes Gertrude E †	2	housewife	43	here
B	Hayes John H	2	motorman	45	"
C	Normile John J	4	"	47	"
D	Normile Mary †	4	housewife	43	"
E	Gallagher Lillian †	4	"	31	"
F	Gallagher William W	4	salesman	41	"
G	Hipson Jessie †	4	at home	65	"
H	Fleming John P	6	clerk	47	"
K	Fleming Mary E †	6	housewife	46	"
L	Molloy Walter	6	engineer	45	"
M	Fleming Clara †	6	housewife	40	"
N	Fleming James	6	installer	42	"
O	Fleming Gertrude M †	8	clerk	50	"
P	Fleming Maria J †	8	at home	75	"
R	Roset John	12	painter	33	"
S	Rosit Olga †	12	housewife	40	"
T	Black Mabel †	12	"	27	"
U	Black Nathan L	12	repairman	34	"
V	Sullivan John J	28	motorman	46	"
W	Sullivan Margaret V †	28	housewife	40	"
X	Gramer Albert L	28	stenographer	23	"
Y	Gramer Anna M †	28	housewife	52	"
Z	Gramer Edward	28	piano tuner	66	"
A	Gramer Edward J	28	bookkeeper	25	"
B	Schleicher Annie A †	32	housewife	63	"
C	Schleicher August	32	retired	67	"
D	Schleicher Augusta E †	32	teacher	40	"
E	Norton Alfred	32	motorman	60	4041 Wash'n
F	Norton Elizabeth †	32	housewife	60	4041 "
G	O'Dea Marie †	36	"	31	here
H	O'Dea Thomas	36	guard	31	"
K	Compass Florence †	36	housekeeper	33	"

Page.	Letter.	FULL NAME.	Residence, April 1, 1926.	Occupation.	Supposed Age.	Reported Residence, April 1, 1925.
						Street and Number.

Thornton Street—Continued

	L	Plagemann Clara—†	36	brushmaker	36	here
	M	Plagemann Josephine—†	36	at home	64	"
	N	Plagemann Theresa W—†	36	operator	39	"
	O	Watson James A	38	salesman	45	"
	P	Watson Mary C—†	38	housewife	42	New York
	R	Schaff Alfred B	38	student	23	here
	S	Schaff Edward J	38	repairman	39	"
	U	Schaff John H	38	clerk	41	"
	T	Schaff Louisa—†	38	housekeeper	67	"
	V	Bondous August	45	storekeeper	39	"
	W	Bondous Constien—†	45	housewife	38	"
	X	Dunlop Annie A—†	51	"	49	"
	Y	Dunlop Edward J	51	buyer	25	"
	Z	Dunlop Henry B	51	repairman	21	"
	A	Dunlop Michael J	51	gardener	55	"
	B	Dunlop William F	51	painter	23	"
	C	Quin Hugh P	51	shipper	23	"
	E	Davidson Ida—†	80	housewife	51	"
	F	Davidson John P	80	teamster	63	"
	G	Davidson Harriett—†	80	housewife	24	"
	H	Davidson John P, jr	80	bookkeeper	23	"
	K	Deery Margaret—†	82	cook	57	"
	L	King Ada M—†	82	teacher	21	"
	M	King Clarence F	82	manager	22	"
	N	King Herbert C	82	clerk	25	"
	O	King Herbert H	82	butcher	54	"
	P	King Mary—†	82	housewife	52	"
	R	Johnson Elizabeth—†	84	dressmaker	50	Nova Scotia
	S	Bunker Harold D	86	chauffeur	27	12 Dalrymple
	T	Bunker Hazel—†	86	housewife	32	80 Thornton
	U	Bunker Raymond	86	chauffeur	29	80 "
	V	Bunker Violet E—†	86	housewife	26	12 Dalrymple

Washington Street

	C	Trojack Agnes—†	2595	housewife	29	here
	D	Trojack John	2595	printer	34	"
	O	Dixon Everett	2612	laborer	27	78 Edgewood
	P	Dixon Vera—†	2612	housewife	27	78 "
	R	Clark Christina—†	2612	housekeeper	48	here

Washington Street— Continued

s	Faulkner John A	2612	carpenter	53	here
u	Reid Johannah —†	2614	houseworker	41	10 Nawn
v	Brith Mary —†	2614	"	38	here
w	Brady John H	2616	salesman	39	"
x	Brady Lydia —†	2616	houseworker	38	"
y	Bennett Arthur L	2618	clerk	21	"
z	Bennett Helen —†	2618	houseworker	45	"
a	Boudreault Helen —†	2618	operator	26	"
b	Waters Agnes E —†	2618	housewife	47	"
c	Waters John M	2618	laborer	50	"
f	Flynn Nina —†	2620	housewife	39	"
g	Flynn William	2620	laborer	33	"
h	Flynn Catherine —†	2620	houseworker	59	"
k	Flynn Leo	2620	laborer	23	"
l	Varney Howard	2622	chauffeur	34	Attleboro
m	Figwood Bertrand C	2622	clerk	24	here
n	Figwood Frances C —†	2622	dressmaker	53	"
o	Varney Anita —†	2622	houseworker	22	Attleboro
p	Aylesburg Mary —†	2624	"	61	here
r	Hare Helen —†	2624	"	44	"
s	Hare Ralph	2624	laborer	44	"
t	Bewsher Raymond	2624	clerk	28	"
u	Bewsher Mary —†	2624	housewife	23	"
v	Coer Margaret —†	2626	"	38	918 Albany
w	Coer Peter	2626	carpenter	49	918 "
x	McAllister Joseph E	2626	clerk	54	2530 Wash'n
y	McAllister Margaret E—†	2626	housewife	50	2530 "
z	Mudown Sarah E —†	2626	houseworker	82	2530 "
a	Comingo Bertha —†	2628	forewoman	24	here
b	Fitzgerald Elizabeth—†	2628	bookkeeper	40	918 Harris'n av
c	Small John	2628	laborer	21	Somerville
d	Small Mary —†	2628	houseworker	36	"
e	Corly Catherine —†	2630	housewife	56	here
f	Craddock Catherine —†	2630	"	51	"
k	Craddock Stephen J	2630	teamster	58	"
g	Keating Ellen T —†	2630	housewife	50	12 Groton
h	Keating Michael J	2630	teamster	50	12 "
l	Corby Fredrick	2632	laborer	69	here
m	Corby Katherine —†	2632	housewife	55	"
n	Bradley James F	2632	painter	68	"
o	Bradley Mary A —†	2632	housewife	56	"

Washington Street—Continued

P	Dolan Annie—†	2641	housekeeper	43	here
R	McLean Edward E	2641	laborer	42	1 Dana ct
S	McLean Hilda—†	2641	housewife	36	1 "
T	Dennis Rose—†	2644	houseworker	35	here
U	Ranall Ethal A—†	2644	housewife	52	"
V	Ranall William S	2644	teamster	53	"
W	Ericson Agnes L—†	2644	housewife	45	2652 Wash'n
X	Ericson Eileen A—†	2644	bookkeeper	20	2652 "
Y	Ericson Fritz T	2644	machinist	51	2652 "
Z	Faulkner Anthony	2644	clerk	35	here
A	Faulkner Mary—†	2646	housewife	33	"
B	Hurley Edward	2646	laborer	25	"
C	Hurley Helen—†	2646	houseworker	64	"
D	Moore Daniel T	2646	teamster	54	"
E	Moore Edward J	2646	clerk	22	"
F	Moore Mary—†	2646	housewife	52	"
G	Moore Mary T—†	2646	shoe stitcher	24	"
H	Johnson Annie T—†	2646½	housekeeper	43	29 Cliff
K	Donahue Fred H	2646½	chauffeur	38	8 Tremont av
L	Donahue Pansy—†	2646½	housewife	32	here
M	Thomson Clifford C	2646½	teamster	30	Danvers
N	O'Gara John	2646½	conductor	64	here
O	Willard Margaret—†	2646½	housekeeper	62	"
P	Durken Christine—†	2648	houseworker	51	"
R	Hardiman Micheal S	2648	chauffeur	20	"
S	Riley Marguerite—†	2648	clerk	28	"
T	Riley William	2648	chauffeur	28	"
U	Alexander Agnes—†	2648	housewife	35	"
V	Alexander John D	2648	metal polisher	38	"
W	Roy William	2648	laborer	27	"
X	Ells Amer	2648	fireman	70	2717 Wash'n
Y	Ells Anna—†	2648	housewife	62	2717 "
Z	Purcell John	2652	laborer	25	here
A	Purcell Mary—†	2652	housewife	20	"
B	Copeland Madaline—†	2652	houseworker	27	Cambridge
C	Copeland William	2652	clerk	34	"
D	Cotter Helen E—†	2652	houseworker	64	here
E	Cotter Joseph J	2652	laborer	34	"
F	Cotter Marion G—†	2652	clerk	38	"
G	Cotter Morris J	2652	laborer	36	"
H	Corliss Cecelia—†	2654	housewife	38	"

Washington Street—Continued

K	Corliss Joseph	2654	laborer	46	here
L	Frank Oscar	2654	woodcarver	52	"
M	Mahoney Ida — †	2654	houseworker	52	"
N	Mahoney Mary —†	2654	tel operator	25	"
O	Everson Rose—†	2656	houseworker	70	"
P	Ferdy John J	2656	mattressmaker	61	"
R	Ferdy Mary—†	2656	housewife	70	"
S	Kennelly Helena —†	2656	"	39	"
T	Kennelly John B	2656	clerk	44	"
U	Doyle John rear	2656	laborer	60	"
W	Gormley Mary L—†	2660	houseworker	63	"
X	Gormley William J	2660	undertaker	53	"
Y	McEntee Mary A—†	2664	housewife	41	"
Z	McEntee Philip J	2664	laborer	44	"
A	Murphy Martin	2664	"	55	Somerville
B	Murphy Mary—†	2664	houseworker	50	"
C	Morrissey Adie M—†	2664	housewife	30	here
D	Morrissey John D	2664	clerk	29	"
E	McElheny Mary —†	2664	houseworker	45	"
L	Wasson John E	2671	electrician	39	"
M	Wasson Nettie E—†	2671	housewife	31	"
P	Durgin Horace A	2677	retired	66	"
R	Durgin Frances E—†	2677	housewife	62	"
S	Anderson Blanche E—†	2677	"	44	"
T	Anderson William G	2677	clerk	45	"
U	Blake Harry A	2679	inspector	35	"
V	Blake Juliana A †	2679	housewife	35	"
W	Judge Margaret —†	2679	"	40	"
X	Judge Patrick	2679	fireman	40	"
Y	Barner Henry	2680	laborer	48	"
Z	Barner Rose—†	2680	housewife	41	"
A	Chin Ming	2682	laundryman	48	"
C	Thayer Eugene	2683	physician	49	"
D	Thayer Idella W—†	2683	housewife	48	"
E	Harding Frances J —†	2684	candy packer	32	"
F	Harding Lucy B—†	2684	clerk	41	"
G	Whalan Charles T	2684	warden	74	"
H	Mee George C	2684	teamster	21	"
K	Murray Bertha —†	2684	clerk	36	"
L	Murray James A	2684	laborer	44	"

Lightning Source UK Ltd.
Milton Keynes UK
UKHW051553070720
366156UK00012B/1091

9 789354 031236